LEARNING CONTRACTS

■ ■ ■

by

Jack Graves
Professor of Law
Touro Law Center

Mat #41333836

Learning Series is a trademark registered in the U.S. Patent and Trademark Office.

© 2014 LEG, Inc. d/b/a West Academic
    444 Cedar Street, Suite 700
    St. Paul, MN 55101
    1-877-888-1330

West, West Academic Publishing, and West Academic are trademarks of West Publishing Corporation, used under license.

Printed in the United States of America

ISBN: 978–0–314–28530–0

PREFACE

This book is designed as a primary teaching text for a first-year course in Contracts. Unlike most such texts, this one largely departs from the traditional "case method." Instead, the relevant principles, policies, and rules are presented through explanations, examples, statutes, and summaries. This explanatory material is then followed with a series of problems to which this newly learned material may be applied.

This book is very similar to many current texts in that it seeks to give students ample opportunities to analyze novel fact patterns and apply the legal doctrine they hope to master. However, it is very different in that students are not generally required to "extract" the relevant rules in the first instance by relying largely on decided cases. While case reading and analysis remains an important skill in this course, it ceases to be the primary means of learning the rules. Thus, students are able to learn the basic rule more efficiently in preparing for class—instead of misapprehending a rule, only to spend much of their valuable class time unlearning the original misunderstanding before learning and applying the proper one. This efficiency translates into greater class time to be spent in ways that address many of the existing shortcomings in modern Contracts courses. In effect, this book provides a solid foundation for "flipping the classroom." Students are expected to learn more on their own before class, and class is then used more effectively for collaborative clarification, problem solving, and skills development.

Law school curricular change reflects a strong and continuing trend towards single-semester first-year courses. As such, Contracts is increasingly offered as a single 4 credit hour course. This text is tailored to such a course, as the material is broken down into 50 "lessons," each of which can be reasonably covered in a typical 50 minute class segment. These lessons can of course be broken down and assigned in different ways, and nothing about the structure of the text prevents that. However, the material is presented in a way that it can reasonably be covered, in its entirety, in a 4 credit hour course, and still leave time for a few extended lessons, reviews, or skills building activities. If your school retains the luxury of 5 or 6 credit hours for Contracts, then this text can be easily supplemented with additional problems or, better yet, extensive practical skills building exercises.

The text also gives reasonably comprehensive coverage to the law governing the sale of goods—both Uniform Commercial Code (UCC) Article 2 and the United Nations Convention on Contracts for the International Sale of Goods (CISG). In the modern world of global business, it is no longer acceptable to shortchange the latter, which governs the sale of goods across national borders. Of equal importance, by leaving the traditional "case method" of teaching behind, students should gain a better understanding of how to read and apply a statute. Thus, the successful student should complete the course with a reasonable understanding of both common law methodology and statutory application.

The primary purposes of this text are to provide the means for students to (1) learn and (2) apply the law of Contracts. This text is not intended, primarily, as a "skills" text. However, in fully covering the basic doctrine in 4 credit hours, it is intended to provide ample time and opportunity for a student to use what he or she has "learned" in Contracts while simultaneously developing practical lawyering skills—whether in an extended Contracts course or a separate skills course. A variety of additional materials faculty or students may find useful are available from the author online.

Author Website
www.learningcontracts.com

SUMMARY OF CONTENTS

TABLE OF CONTENTS

TABLE OF CASES

The principal cases are in bold type. Cases cited or discussed in the text are in roman type. References are to pages. Cases cited in principal cases and within other quoted materials are not included.

————

1

Introduction

Key Concepts

- What is a Contract?
- Where Do We Find the Law of Contracts, and How Do We Use it to Solve Problems?
- Common Law, State Statutes, and Federal Statutes

Lesson 1: Contracts, Contract Law, and Course Methodology

Objectives and Expected Learning Outcomes

In this first lesson, you should begin to develop an idea of the basic nature of a "contract." You should also gain an overview of the most common sources of contract law in the United States, along with the methodology used in this course. This lesson is not intended to require a detailed mastery of the concepts introduced at this stage, but should prepare you to begin that process in the lessons that follow.

This lesson begins with an initial attempt to describe the nature of a contract by reference to a variety of examples. The remainder of the lesson is devoted to an overview of the sources of law governing these various contract relationships and the methodology to be employed in this course.

A Contract—the Subject of this Course

We start with a basic question—what is a contract? A contract is often defined as a set of promises the law will enforce. Of course, this only replaces the original question with a second—what sorts of promises will the law enforce? You will discover in Chapter Two that the answer to this latter question involves a variety of rules and exceptions. For now, though, we can say that, as a basic rule, the law generally enforces promised bargains, but not promised gifts. Let's consider a few examples of contracts.

Example 1-1: Tom, a law student, agrees to lease an apartment from Lisa for 3 years. Their lease contract is reflected in a written document, signed by each of them. Under the lease contract, Tom promises to pay $1,500 per month in rent, and Lisa promises to provide the subject apartment for Tom's exclusive and undisturbed use. Each also makes a variety of additional promises relating, among other things, to the general care and condition of the apartment.

Perhaps you too lease an apartment. If so, you have a contract with your landlord. Most leases are written and signed by each of the parties, and we will discover later, in Chapter 4, that the above lease must be supported by a signed writing, or the parties' agreement might not be enforceable. This written lease will typically include significant detail addressing a broad range of issues or questions that might arise during the term of the lease. However, we will also discover that many contracts need not be written or otherwise recorded, and many are quite simple, leaving numerous potentially important details unanswered in the agreement itself. Consider the next example.

Example 1-2: Sam provides yard maintenance services. He meets Beth at a social event in March, and the two verbally agree that Sam will provide weekly lawn and shrubbery maintenance at Beth's home from Memorial Day through Labor Day during the coming summer. In exchange for Sam's services, Beth agrees to pay Sam $40 per week.

Sam and Beth likely have an oral contract. Admittedly, they have left numerous details vague. Precisely what constitutes "weekly lawn and shrubbery maintenance"? When is Beth obligated to pay? We will address the issue of filling such "gaps" in the parties' agreement later in the course. For now, the important point is that many contracts can be very simple and need not be written down, much less formally signed. Today in fact, many of our contracts are formed online, through the click of a mouse or tap of a touch pad.

Example 1-3: Mary wants to purchase a new tablet. After shopping around, she decides to purchase an Acme 123 model tablet from Zenith, an online retailer, at a price of $600. She completes the transaction with a series of mouse "clicks" on Zenith's website, and Zenith ships the tablet. Mary pays for the tablet by providing her credit card information on the website—a credit card that she also applied for online. She pays her credit card online each month from a checking account that she opened online. In each of these transactions—purchasing the tablet, applying for and obtaining a credit card, and opening a checking account— one of the items Mary "clicked" indicated her agreement to "arbitrate" any subsequent disputes.

In the above example, Mary has concluded three different contracts for goods or services—all without ever interacting directly with another person in the traditional sense. She has also concluded agreements to arbitrate any disputes arising under any of these contracts. All of Mary's "digital" interactions with her contracting partners are very likely effective and binding under modern contract law.

Sellers often provide "form" contracts, including extensive "standard" detailed terms. This is particularly true with online contracts, inasmuch as the buyer simply "clicks" his or her acceptance of the seller's terms (or not), with no opportunity to negotiate over the content of those terms. Some such "standard" terms may be merely descriptive of the parties' basic bargain, including their respective continuing obligations. However, some may also significantly limit the buyer's rights in the event of a dispute. One common term is a provision requiring arbitration of all contract disputes, thereby precluding buyer's right to bring a grievance against the seller in court. Typically, the terms of such a "form" contract are fully enforceable. However, there are a few noteworthy exceptions we will address later in Chapter 5.

Thus far, our examples have all included at least some future promises. However, a contract may also arise from a simultaneous exchange.

Example 1-4: Jack agrees to sell to Jill the bicycle he is riding at the moment, "as is," without any representations or promises of any kind as to its condition, for $50, cash on the spot. Jill pays him and takes the bicycle. Jack walks home with his $50.

The exchange between Jack and Jill is a contract, even though neither seemingly has any express continuing obligation to the other. Such an exchange can still raise legal issues, such as the bicycle immediately falling apart and injuring Jill as she rides it home, or the money Jill paid to Jack being counterfeit, or the bike being a stolen one. However, the sorts of issues raised by a simultaneous exchange of this kind tend to be limited, and largely focused on whether the product or service met the expectations of the recipient—an issue we will address further in Chapters 6 and 7. In contrast, contracts involving future promises tend to be the most commercially significant and the most likely to raise interesting legal issues in the event of a dispute.

In theory, the law of contract is wholly unnecessary for a single, simultaneous exchange. We can see this in the interactions of two children bartering for an exchange of toys. Neither is likely willing to part with his or her toy first, inasmuch as there is no assurance the other will complete his or her end of the bargain. The only possible exchange is a simultaneous one in which neither has to "trust" the other to perform later. It is easy to imagine that a modern economy would quickly grind to a screeching halt if we were limited to such simultaneous exchanges, or only exchanges involving individuals we personally "trust." In the absence of personal "trust," contract law provides a substitute. Parties enter into contracts involving the sequential performance of certain promises because they "trust" the legal system to make their contracting partners live up to their promises. Most of us likely just take this for granted in our daily lives. However, a legal system in which certain promises are enforced through the power of the state is by no means a given—and is essential for a modern market economy.

Individuals and businesses generally rely on contracts involving ongoing promises in order to add certainty and predictability to the management of their affairs. An individual buys an airline ticket to insure the ability to travel from one place to another at some future date and time. A business contracts for a supply of a particular raw material over many months to insure the price and availability of the material for its manufacturing process or services.

> **Example 1-5:** Southern Airlines, a Georgia based airline, contracts with Texxo, a Texas oil and refining company, for the purchase of its required jet fuel, at a specified price and quality, for delivery at specified locations within the U.S., for a period of 36 months from the date of contracting.

In the above example, we have a transaction involving the sale of jet fuel that might, perhaps, implicate the contract law of more than one state. In fact, sales of "goods" will often cross state lines, which can raise questions of governing law. This issue of determining governing law is typically referred to in this country as one of a "conflict of laws," while much of the rest of the world characterizes this as a question of "private international law." In any event, the issue has minimal significance in U.S. domestic transactions, because interstate sales of goods are largely governed by uniform law, as explained more fully in this lesson below. However, issues of governing law may become more acute when goods cross national—rather than U.S. state—borders.

> **Example 1-6:** Southern Airlines, a Georgia based airline, contracts with MP, a Mexican oil and refining company, for the purchase of its required jet fuel, at a specified price and quality, for delivery at specified locations within the U.S., for a period of 36 months from the date of contracting.

As an issue of "private international law," or "conflict of laws," we would first have to determine whether the transaction was governed by Mexican law or the law of a U.S. state (in this case, likely Georgia). However, uniform law once again largely avoids the challenge, because both the U.S. and Mexico are Contracting States with respect to the United Nations Convention on Contracts for the International Sale of Goods, which is also explained more fully below.

By now, you've likely just begun to get a sense of the immense variety of transactions governed by the law of contract. Let's look further at the various sources of law applicable to this wide range of contracts.

A Brief Survey of Sources of Contract Law in the United States

Most of our modern rules of contract law are originally rooted in English common law. The **"common law"** is nothing more than the accumulated body of judicial decisions addressing a particular legal issue. The doctrine of *stare decisis* or "precedent" requires courts to maintain consistency when addressing the same legal issues over time. Unlike a legislative enactment, the common law evolves over time, changing in subtle and, occasionally, not so subtle ways in adapting to changing market circumstances or societal mores. Absent legislative intervention, the common law is entirely a product of the courts and the lawyers who argue cases before those courts. In this country, we began with the English common law, and the common law of contracts has evolved from that time to today.

> *"Stare decisis"* is a Latin term requiring a court to stand by its previous decisions, thus largely preserving the pre-existing legal expectations of the contracting parties.

The common law has much to commend it as a system of law allowing for gradual and continuous modernization. It allows for continuous evolution and improvement without the upheaval and disruption often associated with changes in the way we conduct our affairs. However, it also raises challenges. The lawyer's arguments in any given case may not be as clear, or even as correct, as we might have hoped. Or the judge may have graduated law school with a far better understanding of criminal or constitutional law than contract law. Or a case may present particularly challenging facts to which a strict application of existing precedent seems to lead to an unjust result. In short, the development of the common law is sometimes quite messy, imprecise, or even flatly inconsistent with established precedent (without directly admitting as much).

Our law is not, however, limited to the common law. When a state legislature or the U.S. Congress acts within the scope of its authority, the resulting **"statute"** takes priority over the common law. In effect, the common law serves as a backdrop, applicable in the absence of a governing statute. The statute, however, displaces the common law to the extent a legal issue falls within its scope. A former colleague drew an apt analogy to a "sea of common law," within which one could find various statutory "islands." An answer found within a statutory "island" must be applied. However, in the absence of an answer on the island, one is left with the surrounding sea of common law to resolve the issue.

This preeminence of a legislative statutory enactment over contrary common law reflects our basic view as to an appropriate separation of powers between the judicial and legislative branches of government. In a similar vein, our basic notions of federalism dictate that a federal statute, enacted within the scope of constitutional authority assigned to Congress, is the "supreme" law of the land and displaces any contrary state statute or common law. Thus, we can initially establish a top to bottom hierarchy for sources of contract law, as follows:

(1) Federal statutes

(2) State statutes

(3) State common law

This hierarchy might initially suggest that our study of contracts will focus primarily on federal statutes, in view of their preeminence. However, exactly the opposite is true. We will spend the greatest amount of our time and efforts with state common law, followed by state statutes, and, lastly, federal statutes. This is because of the limited range of statutory enactments governing contract law. Most legal issues arising in a typical contract are not addressed by a state statute. Even fewer are addressed by a federal statute. Nevertheless, we will discover that the issues addressed by both state and federal statutes can be very important when they govern the parties' contract.

> At this juncture, you might reasonably ask "what about federal common law?" A complete answer to this question is beyond the scope of this course (though you may encounter the issue in another course), and the modern relevance of federal common law is generally very limited. However, we will briefly examine a bit later a somewhat unique body of federal common law arising from the courts' interpretation of the Federal Arbitration Act, which governs agreements to arbitrate contract disputes.

The Common Law

The common law, itself, is found in the text of actual judicial opinions deciding real cases. One of the roles of a lawyer is reading these cases in order to ascertain the law contained within them. In fact, most traditional Contracts courses focus largely on doing precisely this. A trial or appellate court deciding a legal issue arising in a contract dispute will be bound by prior decisions of any higher court within the relevant jurisdiction. In the case of state common law of contracts, this will be the highest appellate court of the state in question. Even the highest appellate court will typically follow its own precedent, absent a compelling reason to modify it. Thus, a lawyer must be able to read and analyze cases in order to make the most of those that favor a client's case and to distinguish the facts of the client's case from those of less favorable prior cases.

In this or any other Contracts course, it is important to remember that we are working with cases from many different state jurisdictions. Thus, we are not focused on the controlling law of a specific state as much as we are looking at a range of cases that may be controlling in their own jurisdiction (unless they have subsequently been overturned), but are, at best, persuasive outside of that jurisdiction. We are, in effect, working with a broad multi-jurisdictional body of common law in a contracts course, even though such a multi-jurisdictional body of decided cases has no legally binding effect, as such. Our focus in looking at this broad and diverse body of common law is twofold: (1) it provides us with a source of generally applicable rules provided throughout the text; and (2) it provides us with a rich set of practical problems to which we can apply these rules. While the common law of contracts certainly varies from state to state on a number of important issues, most of its fundamental rules are broadly embraced and consistently applied across most individual states.

Lawyers are also provided with a variety of tools intended to make the common law a bit more easily accessible—not as a substitute for the actual cases, but as a compliment to them, especially as an overview or summary of the common law on a particular issue. Likely the most important of these secondary sources of contract law is the Restatement (Second) of Contracts (1980). A restatement is not binding law. It reflects the common law of many different state jurisdictions, so it binds none of them, unless expressly adopted by the courts of any given state. It is not a statute—even though it sometimes reads a bit like one—because it has never been enacted by a state legislature or the United States Congress. It is useful, however, because it reflects a well-reasoned effort to collect and summarize the law from many jurisdictions on a particular contract law issue. The somewhat predictable challenge is that different cases addressing any particular issue are not always consistent.

At this point, a brief discussion of the nature of a judicial opinion may be useful in understanding the difficulty presented by any effort to "restate" the law. Judges generally decide cases based on the arguments made by the lawyers for the parties before them. With a few exceptions, judges (or their law clerks) do not do their own independent research and legal analysis of the factual disputes before them. Instead, they typically evaluate and choose between the individual arguments made by the lawyers. A well written judicial opinion will reflect this process, laying out each party's position and explaining the court's choice between them on any point at issue. In others, however, the court may simply lay out the facts and apply the law, as if it was doing so without any guidance from the parties. In fact, this latter approach rarely, if ever, reflects reality. Instead, the judge almost always relies on the parties' actual arguments—whatever the tone of the opinion. This approach relies on the assumption that each party is well represented by its lawyers, who always make the best available arguments, from which the judge always makes the wisest choice. As you might imagine, it doesn't always work out this way.

Judges are often managing overwhelming caseloads, whether at the trial or appellate level, and may have been appointed based on a reputation for being "tough on crime," as opposed to any expertise in contract law. The range of competency among lawyers varies enormously, both generally and in specific areas of law, and the range of time a lawyer spends on any given case is often driven by the value of the case or the client's ability to pay. While our judicial system arguably works well under the circumstances, the circumstances are such that any given judicial decision is often subject to reasonable debate and, in some cases, quite difficult to justify. In our study of contracts, these challenging cases often provide excellent raw material, as they provide us with the opportunity to take a fresh look at the issues presented and, when warranted, to reach a contrary conclusion. However, the drafters of a restatement attempt to bring consistent coherence to this broad body of cases, to the extent reasonably possible.

Thus, the restatement reflects an attempt to organize and articulate the common law rules of contract in a manner that fairly reflects the broad and diverse body of decided cases, and does so in a manner that makes the rules coherent and internally consistent. Predictably, it succeeds in some instances better than in others. In a few instances, the drafters of the Restatement (Second) of Contracts also included rules they thought likely to evolve going forward. Technically, such rules are not "restatements" of prior case law at all. However, they were based on trends the drafters thought likely to evolve, as well as some of the ideas contained in the Uniform Commercial

Code discussed below. The materials that follow will make liberal use of the Restatement where useful, but it is important to remember that the Restatement is merely one tool for use in understanding and applying the common law, and **it is not a statute**.

We'll talk more about the scope of the application of the common law below, but let's return briefly to a few of our earlier examples. Our apartment lease in example 1-1 would be governed by the common law, as would the yard maintenance contract in example 1-2. The common law, to a large degree, also governs the credit card and checking account contracts addressed in example 1-3, though these two agreements may also be governed, to some extent, by state and federal law. In contrast, the sales of the tablet in example 1-3, the bicycle in example 1-4, and jet fuel in examples 1-5 and 1-6 are largely governed by statute. We now turn to these statutes.

Uniform Commercial Code Articles 1 and 2

The Uniform Commercial Code does not, itself, govern any contract. Instead, it serves as a model for uniform law to be adopted by the legislature of each state. As such, the Code has been largely successful. The Code covers a host of commercial issues, including its general provisions found in Article 1, negotiable instruments (Article 3), banking (Article 4), letters of credit (Article 5), bulk sales (Article 6), documents of title (Article 7), investment securities (Article 8), secured transactions (Article 9), and leases of goods (Article 2A). However, our focus in this course is much narrower. We will explore Article 2, which governs sales of goods, as well as those general provisions of Article 1 that apply to Article 2.

Almost 50 years ago, the original version of UCC Article 2 broadly succeeded in achieving its goal of providing uniform law, as it was largely enacted in every state except Louisiana. While the original version of Article 2 was a resounding success, subsequent efforts to revise or amend it have been considerably more challenging. These challenges largely come down to two basic issues. One involves the scope of Article 2 as it affects (or not) transactions in "digital" property (e.g., is software a good?). The second involves the ability of a seller to bind a buyer to unread terms delivered with the good in question. We will address each of these issues as they arise in the materials that follow. However, the important point here is that these two disagreements have, to-date, prevented a number of other important changes upon which almost all agree.

The effort to revise Article 1 has been considerably more successful than that of Article 2, though it has not yet fully achieved the desired level of uniformity. This course will rely on the revised version of Article 1 (2008).

Examples 1-3 (the sale of the tablet), 1-4 (the sale of the bicycle), and 1-5 (the sale of jet fuel) would all be governed by the enactment of Article 2 of the legislature of the state whose law governed the issue (as supplemented by that state's enactment of Article 1). As you can see, the uniform adoption and application of the Code provisions (with rare exceptions) generally makes the determination of governing contract law much less significant. Before moving on to the federal statute governing international sales, we should initially take note of another source of state statutory law that may often be important.

State Statutes of Frauds

Certain contracts are not enforceable, unless they are in writing and signed by the party against whom they are to be enforced. The state statutes addressing this issue are called "statutes of frauds" in that they are intended to prevent fraudulent assertions regarding unwritten contracts. We will look more closely later at whether such statutes are useful in this respect. One of the types of contracts that typically require a signed writing is a transfer of an interest in real estate, such as the three year lease provided in example 1-1. Another is a sale of goods for a price of $500 or more. Thus, UCC Article 2 would require a signed writing in examples 1-3 and 1-5. You will discover that modern interpretations of a "signed writing" include a broad array of "records," including digital records, and a simple intent to identify the sender will typically suffice as a signature. You will also discover a myriad of "exceptions" to the basic requirement. We will address these and other "statutes of frauds" requirements in far more detail in Chapter 4.

Notably, an international sale of goods is governed by the United Nations Convention on Contracts for the International Sale of Goods (CISG), which typically does not require any sort of writing at all (though a writing or other form of recording is almost always a very good idea to avoid future disputes). Thus, the agreement reflected in example 1-6 would be enforceable even if not in writing, assuming of course a court (or arbitral tribunal) believed that the parties had actually concluded the contract in question.

United Nations Convention on Contracts for the Int'l Sale of Goods (CISG)

The CISG is similar to UCC Article 2 in that it seeks to provide a uniform body of contract law to transactions that might otherwise be governed by very different laws, depending on which country's law governed. However, the CISG accomplishes this differently than the UCC in that the CISG is in fact actual law, as opposed to a mere model for proposed enactment.

The CISG is an international convention, or treaty. It was completed in 1980 by an international group of experts convened by the United Nations Commission on International Trade Law (UNCITRAL), and it came into force in 1988 when ratified by a sufficient number of countries, including the United States. Unlike the UCC, which U.S. states can alter as they choose, nation states are precluded from modifying the CISG, except as allowed by "reservations" within the Convention itself. We will address one such U.S. "reservation" below. The CISG would govern the contract between U.S. and Mexican businesses in example 1-6.

Federal Arbitration Act (FAA)

The FAA governs agreements to arbitrate contract disputes, and generally provides that an arbitration agreement shall be treated like any other contract and fully enforceable. In fact, an arbitration clause within a broader contract (such as the arbitration clause within the contracts reflected in example 1-3) is treated, in most respects, as entirely separate and distinct from the contract within which it is contained. An in-depth discussion of arbitration is beyond the scope of this basic contracts course. However, we will address a number of issues involving arbitration in the materials that follow. A few points are worth noting at here.

First, an arbitration agreement must be in writing. Second, the FAA, as interpreted by the U.S. Supreme Court, is somewhat unique in that it gives full effect to arbitration agreements involving consumers and employees that would not be enforced in many other legal systems. This aspect of the FAA has given rise to a great deal of litigation in which parties attempt to avoid the enforcement of an earlier arbitration agreement on a variety of grounds, which we will discuss more thoroughly in Chapter 5. Lastly, arbitration is often the preferred method of resolving contract disputes between businesses, especially contracts between businesses located in different countries. To a large degree, the substantive contract issues we will address in this course would be subject to the same sort of analysis, whether before a public court or a private arbitral tribunal.

Other State and Federal Statutes Governing Contracts

By now, you are likely thinking "enough already," and you are right. The above referenced common law and statutes are fully sufficient for our basic coverage of contract law in this course. However, it is important to recognize, here at the outset, that there are other state and federal statutes governing specific issues. For example, many states have statutes regulating certain consumer transactions, lending and credit agreements, and franchising and distribution agreements, just to name a few. Federal statutes regulate employment contracts (as do many state statutes), certain advertising and lending practices (as the credit card agreement in example 1-3), banking (as in the checking account in example 1-3), and contracts involving interstate transportation of goods, again just to name a few. These specific statutes are well beyond the scope of this course. However, the principles you learn in this course should make these additional statutes more easily accessible and understandable should you need them later in your legal education or practice of law.

Methodology

The approach used in this textbook is somewhat different than traditional first-year Contracts texts. As such, a brief introduction to course methodology is useful at the outset. It is generally much easier to set out initially on a proper course than to attempt a mid-course correction later.

Each lesson is intended to address a discrete set of legal issues—sometimes building directly on the prior lesson, and sometimes introducing a new topic. At the beginning of each lesson (including this one), the basic learning objectives and expected outcomes are laid out in a text box. You should review and consider its content both before and after completing the lesson.

Traditional casebooks generally require the reader to "extract" the law from the cases themselves. While this is a crucial skill that a lawyer must ultimately master, it is not necessarily the most efficient way for a student to learn and practice the application of basic legal doctrine. This textbook does not generally use the "case method" to convey the basic doctrine. Instead, the doctrine is explained directly within the text, illustrated by a series of examples, and then summarized in an outline form. Each lesson concludes with one or more problems, which you should try to answer as your final class preparation. This format is intended to allow you to grasp the relevant doctrine more fully in preparing for class, so that class time may be used more effectively in clarifying the rules and applying them to various problems—both those in this textbook and, perhaps, additional problems that may be introduced in class.

Examples and Cases

You have already encountered a number of examples earlier in this lesson. Some will raise broad issues for consideration throughout a lesson, while others may raise narrow specific issues or exceptions to a general rule. Many of the "examples" are in fact paraphrased or summarized classic cases. Where an example is based on a case, a citation is provided, and you can read the case itself if you are interested. However, the purpose of the example is to allow you to understand more readily the essential aspects of the case at issue.

You will also find a few traditional actual cases scattered throughout the book. These are provided where they may be particularly useful in understanding the issues involved, and each is followed by a series of questions (all or most of which are answered in the accompanying text). Thus, you should be able to master much of the material in each lesson prior to class. The actual cases will also give you an opportunity to develop your critical case reading skills, and the questions that follow the cases are intended to assist in this development. Many of the examples can also be viewed as "pre-solved" problems, lending guidance to working with the problems provided at the end of each lesson.

Explanations and Cross-References

Each significant element of basic contract doctrine is fully explained in the text. In addition, the text includes extensive cross-references, for context, and comparisons, for a better understanding of the rules in question.

Both prior and future coverage of related issues are often cross-referenced in hopes of helping the reader to fit the various pieces together. It is often said that law is a "seamless web." As such, it is not reasonably possible to lay out the entire body of contract law in a nice, linear sequence. However, the organizational aids provided in the text are intended to help you assemble the pieces of the web in a recognizable and coherent manner.

Summaries of the Applicable Rules

In providing "summaries" of various contract law "rules," the author is treading on admittedly dangerous ground. In fact, the relevant "rules of law" come from either cases or statutes. Any attempt to "summarize" or otherwise paraphrase such rules risks variation from the original—especially in the case of common law, where different jurisdictions (and even courts within the same jurisdiction) will often themselves vary their respective articulations of any given "rule." Moreover, the proper articulation of many important "rules" is subject to genuine disagreement among equally thoughtful, knowledgeable, and well intentioned experts. Finally, most of the common law has already been "summarized" in the Restatement (Second) of Contracts, and the summaries provided in this book might reasonably be deemed a poor alternative to the far more thorough and complete process of producing the restatement.

Under such circumstances, it is very easy to see why traditional "casebooks" rarely attempted to "summarize" most of the basic contract "rules." The problem of course is that a good "summary" helps the student learn the rule, and may even serve as a valuable "point of departure" in the student's efforts to produce his or her own summary. This is one of the issues that drive many students to use external "study aids." By including rule summaries, this text seeks to reduce or eliminate the need for external resources and provide a common point of departure for students' own efforts to articulate the relevant rules—whether in the process of applying the rules to problems, or incorporating them into a student's own course outline.

Thus, the goal of each rule summary is actually quite modest. First, it is intended to help you understand the relevant legal doctrine. Second, it is intended not as a final and authoritative statement, but as a common point of departure from which each student can better develop his or her own articulation of the rule. In some instances, your professor may disagree with the way the rule is stated here—or at the very least may offer an alternative way of phrasing the rule in question. You should of course give priority to your professor's view, as he or she is the one who will be further clarifying the materials in this book and scoring your exam.

In law school courses, confusion all too often ensues when the students buy what are frequently wildly variable external study aids, each of which may explain or characterize a particular rule differently than the professor—and differently from each other. The professor has not likely read many, if any, of these external study aids and, therefore, has no idea where students are getting these crazy rules they mention in class or attempt to apply on an exam. By summarizing the key rules right here in the text, this book attempts to avoid this common problem while making the learning process more efficient and effective. You are much more likely to benefit from any differing perspectives relating to rule summaries within the text, because your professor is fully aware of these summaries and can address them directly, as needed.

A summary will typically take the following outline form:

Summary of Basic Rule: common law "rule"[1]

- The basic rule will be stated,
  - Sometimes including various elements, and
  - Often subject to one or more exceptions,
    - As well as variations or exceptions to the exceptions.
    - Presumably, you get the general idea.

When summarizing a common law rule, the text will sometimes closely track the restatement and sometimes not. In fact, the two have somewhat different purposes. The restatement is intended to pull together a broad body of sometimes disparate case law, and the result can sometimes be quite cumbersome and difficult to dissect. In contrast, the summaries in

---

[1] Where a rule summary relies on or relates to a restatement provision, the provision is cited for ease of reference. However, restatements are not quoted in the primary text. This practice is intended to avoid the common tendency to read restatements as if they are statutes. In contrast, the statutes provided in the text, and their primacy is emphasized.

this textbook serve only to help you learn the relevant doctrine. This brings us to statutes and their related summaries.

Statutes

When we encounter a statutory provision from the UCC or CISG, the full or partial text of the statute will be provided. A statute should be read carefully, recognizing that each word or phrase may be significant. If you attempt to read a statute at the same speed, and with the same level of attention to detail, that you are likely reading this textbook or would typically read a case, you will almost certainly miss something crucial. Thus, throughout this text, you will be asked to: **STOP NOW and READ the statute below.**

UCC § ____ OR CISG ARTICLE ____

The statutory text (or partial excerpted text) will appear in the box below the statutory identifier.

Admittedly, the 30th or 40th time you see this admonition regarding careful statutory reading, you may feel like screaming "okay, I get the point." If so, that's great. U.S. lawyers trained in common law methodology are often notoriously bad at reading statutes. You won't have that shortcoming, and the ability to read a statute will serve you well. Mastering the ability to read, understand, and apply a statute—properly—is one of the primary objectives of this course.

This textbook does not provide every statutory provision of UCC Articles 1 and 2, or the CISG. Instead, it includes the provisions most important to our coverage of basic Contracts principles. The advantage of including the statute here within the instructional text is obvious. You can focus on the actual text while considering its significance, and you can do it all within a single source. However, you should not rely *solely* on the statutory provisions within the text. This textbook is best used in conjunction with a statutory supplement that includes, at a minimum, UCC Articles 1 and 2, and the CISG.

The provisions of a well written statute are often best understood in the context of other related provisions. As such, it is often helpful to locate and consider a statutory provision within the broader statute. When you encounter a statute within this text, it may be helpful to locate and, perhaps, highlight, relevant elements of the statute within your statutory supplement. This way, you can more easily see how this statutory provision relates to another provision covered earlier or subsequently in these course materials.

Sometimes, you will be provided with a summary of the rule expressed in the statute. Other times you will be asked to provide your own summary. The combination of these two approaches is intended to give you the opportunity to read and interpret statutes, frequent assistance in doing so, and, finally, illustrations and opportunities to apply the relevant statutory language in examples and problems.

A Comparative Approach to Learning Contract Law

Some contracts courses may attempt to "simplify" the doctrine by focusing only on the common law, or only on wholly "domestic" transactions. This textbook instead embraces a "comparative" approach, addressing many issues under the common law, UCC Article 2, and the CISG.

There are at least two good reasons to cover basic contract issues under all three primary bodies of U.S. contract law—the common law, the UCC, and the CISG. First, each is important in its own right. Second, our examination of the comparative differences will help to accentuate many of the important details of each. For example, as indicated earlier, UCC Article 2 requires a signed writing to enforce most contracts for the sale of goods. The CISG does not. The various general statutes of frauds require signed writings for some common law contracts, but not for others.

A comparative examination of different approaches to any give legal issue helps to illustrate how a legal system might reasonably take more than one approach to any given rule. This comparative examination will also explore the rationales behind various approaches, all of which may help you in remembering and understanding the actual rule and its application. On one hand, this admittedly takes considerably more work than memorizing one single set of contract rules. On the other, memorized rules are of little, if any, value on their own. Moreover, a working knowledge of the common law is of limited value in a sale of goods transaction, and a working knowledge of UCC Article 2 is of little, if any, value when such a sale of goods transaction crosses national borders. In learning the key differences, you will likely learn each body of law far better than you would in isolation.

Comparing Perspectives on Contract Law and Dispute Resolution

Over time, a variety of different perspectives have influenced the development of contract law, and you will likely note one or more of these different perspectives at various points in this course. The early development of contract law was strongly influenced by a "formalist" approach, favoring clear and predictable rules, applied in a "bright line" manner, wherever that application might lead. Over time, the "realist" movement introduced an approach that often focused more on the "big picture" and doing justice within that big picture than on a dogmatic application of rules. More recently, the law and economics movement has introduced the idea of analyzing contract cases in terms of "economic efficiency" as a fundamental underlying principle of contract law. Today, all three of these perspectives exercise powerful influences over contract law in this country.

UCC Article 2 reflects a strong "realist" tone, as does the Restatement (Second) of Contracts. However, the past couple of decades have also see a resurgence of "neo-formalism" leading to the mix of perspectives we find today. Where differing approaches lead to significantly different rules, the text will point out both approaches. Your professor may also point out various examples in which a formalist, realist, or law and economics influence can be seen.

Working with the Problems

Once you have read the complete lesson text and believe you understand it reasonably well, you should try to address each of the problems. In many respects, each of these is akin to a "mini" exam problem. While most of these involve relatively discrete sets of issues (as opposed to more complex exam problems), they provide excellent practice in spotting and analyzing issues presented by a given set of facts. This first lesson does not include any problems, and it is a bit longer than most. However, it should have prepared you for the lessons that follow.

Having talked a bit about methodology, we will return in the next lesson to our earlier discussion regarding the different bodies of contract law. In doing so, we will look in considerably more detail at a few issues involving governing law.

Lesson 2: Identifying the Governing Law

Objectives and Expected Learning Outcomes

In this lesson, you should learn to identify which body of substantive law governs any particular transaction. You will learn to distinguish between general contracts, governed by the common law, and contracts for the sale of goods, governed by statute. You will further learn to distinguish between interstate sales of goods, governed by UCC Articles 1 and 2, and international sales of goods, generally governed by the CISG. In the process, you will also learn a bit more about each of these statutes governing transactions in goods.

The Common Law Default

Most of the contract law issues we will address in this course are governed by either the common law, UCC Articles 1 and 2, or the CISG. Thus, it is important to be able to determine, at the outset, which will apply to any given legal issue.

Our starting point, or default legal regime, is the common law. We inherited the common law of contract from English law, so its applicability predates either UCC Article 2 or the CISG. If an issue is not governed by UCC Articles 1 or 2, or the CISG, then it is likely governed by the common law. Recall the earlier analogy describing a "sea of common law" surrounding a few "statutory islands." The vast majority of contract issues that do not arise from a sale of goods will be governed by the common law (as indicated above, a few other issues are governed by other state or federal statutes, but these statutes are beyond the scope of this basic course). Thus, our initial task is to determine whether a given case or issue is left to be governed by the common law, or is governed by either UCC Article 2 or the CISG.

UCC Article 2

Basic Scope

UCC Article 2 applies only to sales of goods. **STOP NOW and READ the excerpts from UCC §§ 2-102 and 105(1) below**.

UCC § 2-102

. . . this Article applies to transactions in goods; . . .

UCC § 2-105(1)

(1) "Goods" means all things (including specially manufactured goods) which are movable at the time of identification to the contract for sale other than the money in which the price is to be paid, . . .

A few examples may be useful. The sale of a house that is built of bricks and mortar is not a "good," because it is not "movable" in the usual sense of the word. In contrast, a "mobile home" is a good because it is in fact intended to be "movable." A kitchen sink is a good when purchased from your local home remodeling store, but ceases to be a good when it has been installed in your kitchen and has become part of your immovable house. A contract to build a small custom shed in your back yard is not a sale of goods. A contract to install a new roof on your home is not a sale of goods. Instead, each of the two preceding contracts is a typical construction contract for services. However, a contract to sell you a pre-manufactured shed to be placed in your back yard, or a contract to sell you the shingles you will need for a new roof would each amount to a sale of goods.

Note that nothing in either of the above provisions limits the application of Article 2 to "merchants" or other business people. In fact, Article 2 applies to sales of goods to individual consumers or even between individuals without any business background or expertise. Nor is Article 2 limited to new goods. Recall example 1-4, in which Jack sold his used bicycle to Jill (there is no indication in the example that either is a merchant or in any business related to the purchase or sale of bicycles). This transaction between Jack and Jill is a sale of goods governed by Article 2. Consider the following additional example.

> **Example 2-1:** Amos walks into a bar and orders a Martini. Sara, the bar owner, serves the martini to Amos, who pays for it. As it turns out, the martini glass wasn't washed properly, and Amos becomes ill. Amos may bring a claim for breach of warranty under UCC Article 2.

We will address Article 2 "warranties" in much more detail later, in Chapter 6. However, the example is useful here in illustrating the extraordinarily broad scope of interactions governed by Article 2.

It's worth repeating here—Article 2 is **not** limited to transactions involving merchants. While a party's status as a "merchant" may very well be relevant under certain, specific provisions of Article 2, it is not relevant in determining whether Article 2 applies generally. We will talk more about merchants in Chapter 3, when we reach the first issue in which a party's status as a merchant actually matters.

Mixed Contracts

By now, you are likely getting the idea. It has also perhaps occurred to you that, in some cases, a contract may be mixed. For example, a roofing contract will likely involve shingles, tar, and other materials, along with considerable labor in installing these materials in order to provide a sound roof. Does Article 2 govern the contract and, if so, to what extent? The following example comes from a seminal case addressing the issue.

Example 2-2: *Bonebrake v. Cox*

Frances Bonebrake sought to recover for breach of a contract in which her deceased brother had agreed to sell and install goods for buyer. Bonebrake brought the action in her role as administratrix of the estate of her brother, Woodrow Simek.

The Cox brothers had entered into a written contract with Simek for the purchase of used equipment, including "10 Lane beds complete with one piece gutter, tail planks, kickbacks, etc. 5 Magic circle underlane ball returns 10 Score chairs Fibre glass seating (for 10 lanes) 1 Streamline bubble ball cleaning machine 50 Lockers - 5 Radarays 3 Ball storage racks 50 Pair rental shoes Foundation material." Simek was to install all of this, as well as re-surface the lanes and apply finish coats, for a total price of $20,000. The Cox brothers additionally agreed with Simek to purchase "for $35,000.00, 10 used Brunswick Model A pinspotters delivered and installed in the Tamarack Bowl, with motors and gear boxes carrying a one year guarantee."

Delivery and installation commenced, and part of the purchase price was paid. However, Simek died before completing either the delivery or installation, and the Cox brothers had to seek alternative sources for the undelivered items and completion of the installation and construction work. Bonebrake sought to recover the unpaid portion of the purchase price, and the Cox brothers brought counterclaims for losses arising from Simek's failure to complete the delivery and installation, as agreed. One of the key issues the court had to decide was whether the agreements in question were governed by UCC Article 2.

The trial court had declined to apply Article 2, holding that it did not govern "mixed" contracts involving both goods and services, such as those between Simek and the Cox brothers. The appellate court disagreed, explaining that a "good," as defined in UCC § 2-105 did not lose its identity as such, simply by virtue of being included in a contract that also provided for related services. Instead, a proper inquiry should focus on the "essence" of the contract in question. One must look at the mix of goods and services and determine "whether their predominant factor, their thrust, their purpose, reasonably stated, is the rendition of service, with goods incidentally involved (e.g., contract with artist for painting) or is a transaction of sale, with labor incidentally involved (e.g., installation of a water heater in a bathroom). Applying this test, the appellate court determined that the "predominant purpose" of the contract between Simek and the Cox brothers was a sale of goods. Thus, it applied UCC Article 2 to govern the two contracts in their entirety and reversed the decision of the lower court.[2]

The majority of courts continue to follow the "predominant purpose" test from Bonebrake in "mixed" or "hybrid" contracts involving both goods and services. A minority of courts, however, have applied Article 2 only to the portion of the contract specifically involving goods, while applying the common law to any related services. The viability of this latter approach may depend, to some degree, on whether the services and goods can reasonably be separated.

The Exceptionally Thorny Question of "Information"

A computer is certainly a "good," as defined by UCC § 2-105, and the sale of computer hardware is definitely governed by UCC Article 2. However, the question becomes a bit more challenging when it comes to software. It also turns out that the question is quite political—so much so that it has thus far prevented efforts to revise or amend Article 2.

Most courts have treated computers that include software entirely as goods. When software was still distributed on disks, it often seemed reasonable to treat it as a good as well. While the software industry strongly disagreed, noting that the transaction was a license to use the copyrighted software and not a sale of the code itself, the same could easily be said of books,

---

[2] Bonebrake v. Cox, 499 F.2d 951, 953, 957-960 (8th Cir. 1974)

which have always been treated as goods. In any event, the issue became even more acute as software and other forms of "information" were increasingly distributed online.

The past two decades have seen multiple efforts to amend or revise Article 2, as well as efforts to address "information," first within a separate UCC Article 2B and later within a standalone Uniform Computer Information Transactions Act (UCITA). None of these met with any degree of success, as industry and consumer groups seem unable to find common ground. Thus, today, the extent to which UCC Article 2 governs computer software and other "information" remains largely unresolved.

One approach to addressing "information," as well as other potential applications of Article 2 that do not quite perfectly fit the definition of "goods," is a policy based approach. To what extent would the policies underlying Article 2 achieve analogous objectives as applied to the transaction at issue? To be clear, Article 2 only applies, by its own terms. However, a number of courts have judicially extended it, *by analogy*, to individual cases in which its policies and purpose seemed to fit.

The Role of UCC Article 1

UCC Article 1 supplements all of the other sections of the Code, including, *though not limited to*, Article 2. Article 1 addresses a variety of threshold issues, such as choice of law and common law supplementation. It also addresses a number of concepts that apply, generally, throughout the code, such as the use of conduct in ascertaining the parties' contractual intent. Except as otherwise stated or displaced by a more specific provision in Article 2, itself, each provision of Article 1 should be read as if it was a part of Article 2. **STOP NOW and READ UCC § 1-102 below.**

UCC § 1-102

This article applies to a transaction to the extent that it is governed by another article of [the Uniform Commercial Code].

A few important provisions of Article 1 follow immediately below.

The Importance of Uniformity

The UCC is intended as a "uniform" law, such as to facilitate interstate sales of goods, without concern over questions of governing law. If the law of Missouri and Kansas are the same (each a legislative enactment of UCC Article 2), then it shouldn't make any significant difference whether a Missouri seller's law or a Kansas buyer's law governs the sale.

The problem, of course, is that UCC Article 2 is, like any statute, imperfect. In standing the test of the last 50 years, Article 2 has held up remarkably well. However, it contains its share of gaps and ambiguities, each of which must be filled or interpreted by the courts. If the statute is to serve its purpose as "uniform law," then it is important that courts of different states give it a "uniform" interpretation. **STOP NOW and READ UCC § 1-103(a) below.**

UCC § 1-103(a)

(a) [The Code] must be liberally construed and applied to promote its underlying purposes and policies, which are:

(1) to simplify, clarify, and modernize the law governing commercial transactions;

(2) to permit the continued expansion of commercial practices through custom, usage, and agreement of the parties; and

(3) to make uniform the law among the various jurisdictions.

Thus, a court faced with a novel issue arising under its own state's enactment of the UCC will often look to the decisions of other state courts addressing the same statutory provisions. While the courts of one state are not strictly bound to follow those of other states, the stated statutory policy of uniformity provides a strong motivation to do so, absent some compelling reason to do otherwise. This does not, of course, mean that perfect uniformity has been achieved. However, it remains a worthy aspirational objective.

Common Law Supplementation

A common law statute does not typically purport to answer every conceivable question regarding its subject matter. Instead, it seeks to answer the questions expressly addressed by the statute, along with those that might reasonably be answered by extension or implication of its express language. However, the mere existence of a statute does not preempt or displace other background sources of law. The continuing vitality of the common law—to the extent not displaced by the statute—is expressly noted within the statute. **STOP NOW and READ UCC § 1-103(b) below.**

UCC § 1-103(b)

(b) Unless displaced by the particular provisions of [the Uniform Commercial Code], the principles of law and equity, including the law merchant and the law relative to capacity to contract, principal and agent, estoppel, fraud, misrepresentation, duress, coercion, mistake, bankruptcy, and other validating or invalidating cause supplement its provisions.

Thus, in looking for the law governing a sale of goods, one should first seek an applicable rule in UCC Article 1 or 2. However, issues not addressed and, therefore, "displaced by" the UCC remain subject to the common law. We will see a number of these in the materials that follow.

UCC Official Comments

Only the provisions of the statute, itself, constitute binding law. However, in interpreting and applying the express statutory provisions, the accompanying official "comments" are often quite valuable. For example, one might reasonably question whether the "list" of common law principles in UCC § 1-103(b) is exclusive (i.e., preclusive of any principle not listed). Consider the following excerpt from the official comment to that provision.

OFFICIAL COMMENT 4 (UCC § 1-103)

4. **Listing not exclusive.** The list of sources of supplemental law in subsection (b) is intended to be merely illustrative of the other law that may supplement the Uniform Commercial Code, and is not exclusive. . . .

Thus, the comment clarifies the non-exclusive nature of this list. Again, the comments are not, themselves, binding statutory law. However, they are typically given great weight in a court's interpretation of the actual text of the statute. We will frequently refer to the comments in interpreting various provisions of Articles 1 and 2. In contrast, the CISG, which we will begin to examine immediately below, does not include any official comments.

The CISG

Basic Scope

Under U.S. law, the CISG applies only to contracts for the sale of goods between parties from two different CISG Contracting States. **STOP NOW and READ the excerpts from CISG Article 1 below.**

CISG ARTICLE 1

(1) This Convention applies to contracts of sale of goods between parties whose places of business are in different States:

(a) when the States are Contracting States; or

. . .

Thus, whenever you encounter a sale of goods between parties from different "nation states" (i.e., different countries, as compared to U.S. states within a single federal nation state), you should first determine whether each is a "Contracting State." A Contracting State is merely a nation state that has agreed to be bound by the CISG. As of this writing, there are 79 such Contracting States, including the vast majority of the major industrialized trading countries. The few notable exceptions include India, Ireland, South Africa, and the United Kingdom. A complete list of Contracting States can be found on a freely accessible CISG website at http://www.cisg. law.pace.edu/cisg/countries/cntries.html.

Recall example 1-6, in which a Mexican seller contracted to sell jet fuel—a good—to a Georgia buyer. The seller had its place of business in Mexico, a CISG Contracting State, and the buyer had its place in Georgia, which is within the U.S., a Contracting State. Therefore, the CISG will govern the transaction pursuant to Article 1(1)(a).

In contrast, suppose our Georgia buyer had contracted to buy jet fuel from a United Kingdom seller. In that case, the CISG would not apply under Article 1(1)(a), because the seller does not have its place of business in a Contracting State. Unfortunately, this conclusion raises more questions than it answers. Whose law does apply—that of the seller (the U.K. Sale of Goods Act) or that of the buyer (Georgia's enactment of UCC Article 2)? The answer to this question is sufficiently complex to leave it to a future course covering "conflict of laws," also known as the "rules of private international law." For our purposes here, it's enough to be aware of the question. Fortunately, in transactions between parties who are each from Contracting States, we don't need to answer it, because the answer is the same no matter whose law applies. The CISG applies in either case. This predictability with respect to governing law is one of the major benefits of the CISG.

> CISG Article 1(1)(b) also provides for the application of the CISG when only one of the parties has its place of business in a Contracting State. However, when it ratified the CISG, the United States invoked its right not to be bound by this provision by making a declaration to that effect under CISG Article 95. In this course, we will, therefore, focus solely on the application of the CISG under Article 1(1)(a). However, Article 1(1)(b) may apply to cases that do not involve U.S. parties, or to proceedings held in a forum outside of the U.S.

Limitations on the Application of the CISG

While CISG Article 1 states a broad rule of applicability to transactions in goods, Article 2 includes a number of limitations. **STOP NOW and READ the excerpts from CISG Article 2 below.**

CISG ARTICLE 2

This does not apply to sales:

(a) of goods bought for personal, family or household use, unless the seller, at any time before or at the conclusion of the contract, neither knew nor ought to have known that the goods were bought for any such use;

. . .

(e) of ships, vessels, hovercraft or aircraft;

(f) of electricity.

Unlike UCC Article 2, the CISG does not apply to consumer transactions. In example 1-3, if Mary, an individual U.S. consumer, had purchased her tablet from Acme, a Canadian business, the CISG would not govern the sale. In example 1-4, if Jack, from Texas, had sold his bike to Jill, from Mexico, the CISG would not govern Jill's purchase of the bike for her individual use (the fact that the bike is "used" is not relevant to the application of the CISG, which applies to either new or used goods, if sold to a business instead of a consumer). Many national laws include significant protection for consumers, as distinguished from business buyers. The nature of such protections is of sufficient national importance and varies to such an extent that uniformity is not possible (for example, Continental European laws often provide more consumer protection than U.S. laws).

The CISG also expressly excludes certain sea and air craft, in contrast to UCC Article 2. The exclusion of electricity, however, is fully consistent with judicial interpretations of the scope of UCC Article 2. In contrast, each governs the sale of natural gas.

Opting Out of the CISG

It's worth noting here that the CISG governs solely as a matter of "default." The parties can, instead, choose other law to govern their transaction, including a specific state enactment of UCC Article 2. **STOP NOW and READ the excerpt from CISG Article 6 below.**

CISG ARTICLE 6

The parties may exclude the application of this Convention or, . . . , derogate from or vary the effect of any of its provisions.

Thus, the parties may, in their contract, include a choice of law provision stating that "This contract is governed by the law of the State of New York applicable to wholly domestic transactions, including New York's adoption of UCC Articles 1 and 2, and the parties expressly exclude any application of the CISG." If so, they will effectively "opt out" of the CISG.

The clause above may be somewhat more specific than entirely necessary, but a clause that is not sufficiently clear may be ineffective. Consider the following example.

> **Example 2-3:** In a contract for the sale of gasoline between a Texas seller and an Ecuadorian buyer, the parties' contract included a provision choosing "Ecuadorian law." The court held that the parties' agreement failed to exclude the application of the CISG and applied the CISG, as "Ecuadorian law," to the instant dispute. *BP Oil Int'l, Ltd. v. Empresa Estatal Petroleos de Ecuador*, 332 F.3d 333 (5th Cir. 2003).

In the same vein, a choice of "Texas law," without more, would not succeed in opting out of the CISG. Texas law with respect to a sale of goods between a Texas seller and an Ecuadorian buyer is the CISG. While Texas has enacted UCC Article 2, the CISG is federal law, which is takes priority over state law under the Supremacy Clause of the U.S. Constitution.

The key point here is that, if a party wishes to avoid the application of the CISG, it must do so clearly. Whether "opting out" is a good idea is an entirely different question and one that you should be far better qualified to answer in any given set of circumstances when you have completed this course. A lawyer should never recommend that a client "opt out" of the application of the CISG based on the lawyer's ignorance of the statute.

Mixed Contracts

As in the case of UCC Article 2, "mixed" contracts can raise difficult issues as to the applicability of the statute. However, the CISG addresses the issue within the statute, itself. **STOP NOW and READ CISG Article 3(2) below.**

CISG Article 3(2)

(2) This Convention does not apply to contracts in which the preponderant part of the obligations of the party who furnishes the goods consists in the supply of labour or other services.

Most courts interpreting the statute have focused on the relative "economic value" of the goods and services, applying the CISG, unless the value of the services clearly exceeded that of the goods.

At first glance, CISG Article 3(2) looks similar to the rule of the *Bonebrake* case addressing mixed transactions under Article 2. However, there is at least one potentially significant difference. Do you see it? If a court were to determine that a contract was evenly balanced between goods and services, would the CISG apply? Would you necessarily reach the same answer under the *Bonebrake* test? The CISG applies, <u>unless</u> services provide the preponderant party of the contract. In effect, the CISG governs in the event of a "tie." In contrast, *Bonebrake* does not address the issue, simply asking which predominates.

The above comparison is largely intended to point out that perceived similarities can sometimes mask important differences, unless we consider each statute (e.g., UCC Article 2 and the CISG) on its own terms. This sometimes apparent similarity between certain provisions of UCC Article 2 and the CISG can also present significant problems in the interpretation of the CISG, unless one follows the guidance of each statute, itself.

The Importance of Uniformity

The goal of "uniformity" stands as one of the single most important purposes of the CISG—much like the importance of a uniform interpretation and application of the UCC discussed earlier. In fact, the goal of uniformity is arguably even more crucial in the case of the CISG, because it applies across wholly different legal systems. However, this can also make it somewhat more difficult to achieve this goal. **STOP NOW and READ CISG Article 7 below.**

CISG ARTICLE 7

(1) In the interpretation of this Convention, regard is to be had to its international character and to the need to promote uniformity in its application and the observance of good faith in international trade.

(2) Questions concerning matters governed by this Convention which are not expressly settled in it are to be settled in conformity with the general principles on which it is based or, in the absence of such principles, in conformity with the law applicable by virtue of the rules of private international law.

Article 7(1) clearly articulates the objective of international uniformity, and courts have little difficulty reading and recognizing this principle. However, its application, under Article 7(2) has proven considerably more challenging for U.S. courts. This provision logically breaks down in two clauses, before and after the first comma.

The first clause reflects a typical civil law approach to statutory interpretation, essentially filling any statutory "gaps" by implication based on the "general principles" underlying the statute. One such general principle, good faith, is found in Article 7(1). Other examples include "reasonableness" and the protection of a party's "reliance" interest, each of which are reflected in numerous provisions of the CISG. We will talk more later about these principles, broadly, but here the important point is their use in interpreting the CISG. In the event of a gap or ambiguity, an interpretation that is "reasonable" or comports with "good faith" or protects a party's "reliance" interest would generally be favored over a contrary interpretation. In some cases, however, in the event such principles do not resolve the issue in question, resort to the second clause may be necessary.

If the contract issue in question is governed by the CISG, but cannot be re-solved by reference to its statutory language, or even its general principles, then it is to be resolved by domestic law—not the CISG. The issue in that event is simply which domestic law will govern—that of the seller or buyer. In no event, however, is any domestic law to be used to interpret the CISG.

Unfortunately, U.S. courts tend to skip the first clause and misapply the second. Instead of looking for the general principles upon which the CISG is based, the court looks to analogous provisions of the UCC for guidance. The court is not applying the UCC, as an alternative, but is using it to interpret the CISG. This approach is not consistent with any part of CISG Article 7. Most importantly, it is plainly inconsistent with the uniformity requirement of CISG Article 7(1).

If the courts of each CISG Contracting State look to their own respective domestic law to interpret the CISG, and their respective interpretations and applications of the statute will be anything but uniform—instead reflecting their individually diverse and distinctive domestic laws that the CISG was expressly intended to displace. The problem is analogous to one in which individual U.S. state courts each sought to interpret their respective legisla-tive enactments to UCC Article 2 by reference to their individual state common law. Fortunately, state courts don't generally do this—instead looking to sister state interpretations and applications of UCC Article 2 in the interest of uniformity. Unfortunately, courts in the U.S. have yet to learn the same lesson with respect to the CISG.

In this course, we will often compare and contrast analogous provisions of UCC Article 2 and the CISG, because such a comparative approach is often useful in better understanding each. However, such comparisons are not intended in any way to suggest that either statute should be used to interpret the other. Each must be interpreted and applied autonomously, consistent with the stated objective of the UCC to achieve uniformity across the United States and the CISG to achieve uniformity across inter-national Contracting States.

Issues Not Governed by the CISG

You will recall that UCC Article 1 allows for supplementation by the common law where the statute does not address the issue in question. In effect, the gaps in the UCC to be supplemented by common law are determined by omission. In contrast, the CISG expressly carves out certain issues as not governed by the statute. One of the most significant involves issues of validity. **STOP NOW and READ CISG Article 4(a) below.**

CISG ARTICLE 4(a)

This Convention governs only the formation of the contract of sale and the rights and obligations of the seller and the buyer arising from such a contract. In particular, except as otherwise expressly provided in this Convention, it is not concerned with:

(a) the validity of the contract or of any of its provisions or of any usage;

We will address issues of contract validity later, in Chapter 5. The point here is simply to note their express exclusion from the CISG. As in the case of consumer transactions, a uniform approach to issues validity proved impossible in the drafting of the CISG. For similar reasons, CISG Article 5 also exempts application to actions involving liability for personal injury or death.

To recap briefly, in addressing a purported contract, a court in the U.S. will apply the common law of contracts, unless the contract involves a sale of goods. In the case of a sale of goods, the court will apply UCC Article 2, unless the transaction is between parties from different CISG Contracting States, in which case the CISG will govern, unless expressly excluded by the statute under CISG Articles 2, 3, 4, or 5, or by the parties under Article 6. You should be able to apply this basic framework to the problems that follow below.

APPLYING THE RULES

Problem 1: Delta manufactured snowboards in Colorado. It purchased fiberglass from Alpha, and it outsourced the design and application of the snowboard graphics to Beta, each of which were also Colorado businesses. Delta sold ten snowboards each to Max and Fay. Max was a retail seller of snowboards in Montana, and Fay was a retail seller of snowboards in France. Delta also sold one snowboard each to Inez and Gunter, each of whom intended to use them for snowboarding. Inez lived in Idaho, and Gunter lived in Germany. Inez later decided she did not like snowboarding and sold her used snowboard to Hilda, her neighbor. During a recent storm, Delta's roof was seriously damaged, and Delta contracted with Roy to repair it. Repairing the roof involved replacing over half of the shingles. Roy purchased the shingles locally from SuperShingle. How many contracts can you identify in this fact pattern, and what body of law governs each?

Problem 2: In a contract governed by UCC Article 2, when, if ever, might the common law be relevant in determining the parties' contractual rights and obligations? In a contract governed by the CISG, when, if ever, might the common law or UCC Article 2 be relevant in determining the parties' contractual rights and obligations?

Quick Summary

Here is a very brief summary of the basic principles addressed in Chapter 1. We can say generally that contract promises are legally enforceable. However, we also know that contracts may arise in an amazingly wide variety of contexts, each of which will likely raise some common and some unique issues. Thus, our first inquiry must generally ask which body of contract law governs the issue. Having answered this threshold question, we can move on to analyze the various substantive issues that may arise when one party seeks to enforce the purported promise of another. Our substantive analysis will begin in Chapter 2 by focusing on the question posed at the outset of this introductory material—"what sorts of promises will the law enforce?" We will also attempt to answer what it means to "enforce" a promise or other related legal rights.

2

Enforcement and Consideration

Key Concepts

- When and How is a Promise Enforceable?
- Bargains Versus Gifts
- Alternative Theories of Recovery

Lesson 3: The Nature of "Enforcement"

Objectives and Expected Learning Outcomes

In this lesson, you should learn what it means to enforce a promise. You will discover the basic "expectation" remedy, as well as alternative remedies based "reliance" and "restitution." You will also learn when a remedy is achieved through payment of money and when actual performance may be required. You should be able to apply each of these concepts in a manner that provides for proper "enforcement" of a broken contract promise.

The Expectation Interest

When we talk about "enforcement" of a promise, a variety of possible options arise. Should parties who break, or threaten to break, their promises be punished—either as a manner of retribution or to discourage such a breach? Should a court simply require a party to perform its promise, subject to sanctions for contempt of court in the event of refusal? Should a court, instead, attempt to quantify the economic value of the broken promise and award this to the disappointed promisee, as a substitute? Or should the breaking of one party's promise simply excuse its contracting partner's promise of performance, such that a court will "unwind" the deal, as between the parties, and perhaps even compensate the disappointed promisee for any additional loss arising from his or her reliance on the broken promise? If the promisor makes a profit from breaking a promise, should the promisee be entitled to recover such profit, even if it exceeds the amount the promisee expected to make from performance of the contract?

In fact, the law could reasonably take a variety of possible approaches in "enforcing" promises. As you will see, however, the common law focuses, first and foremost, on the "expectation interest" and typically enforces this interest through a "substitutional" award of money damages.

> A party who breaks a promise made in a contract is said to "breach" the contract. The breaching party is often called the "promisor" of the promise at issue, and the party who is aggrieved or injured by the breach is often called the "promisee." In most contracts, each party is both a promisor and a promisee, inasmuch as each makes promises to the other. Moreover, a contract dispute may involve multiple breaches. Thus, it is important to understand each of these terms by reference to a specific contractual promise.

When a promisor breaches its contractual promise, the aggrieved promisee is normally entitled to be placed in as good a position as if the contract had been fully performed. This legal remedy is called the "expectation interest." As a rule, this remedy is achieved by requiring the breaching promisor to pay to the aggrieved promisee an amount of money equal to the value of this "expectation interest," as damages.

In theory, calculating the interest is very straightforward. One need only determine the value of the contract as promised (A), the value of the contract as actually performed (i.e., as "breached") (B), and subtract the latter from the former to determine damages (C). Thus, A − B = C. In fact, the process often raises a variety of challenges, which we will address in Chapter 8, when we more fully explore remedies. However, this basic rule providing for an "expectation" remedy is applied in the vast majority of contract cases.

Summary of Basic Rule (brief version): enforcement of the "expectation interest"[1]

- An aggrieved promisee is entitled to recover his or her "expectation interest" in the event of breach by the promisor.

  ○ This "expectation" remedy entitles the promisee to be placed in as good a position as if the contract had been fully performed.

  ○ This "expectation" remedy is ordinarily achieved by awarding a sum of money equal to the difference in value between promised performance and actual performance.

---

[1] This basic rule summary is reflected in Restatement (Second) of Contracts §§ 344(a), 345(a), and 347.

The logic of the rule, along with its well-established exceptions or alternatives, is best understood by exploring a few examples. Let's start with a very easy case.

> **Example 3-1:** A contractor agrees to construct a building on a lot owned by a manufacturer, for a price of $5 million. The manufacturer pays $1 million to the contractor in advance, and the contractor builds the building, as promised. However, the manufacturer refuses to pay any more. The manufacturer will be liable for $4 million in damages—the difference between the $5 million amount promised and the $1 million amount actually paid.

This is an easy case, because the breached promise was a promise to pay a fixed amount of money. However, when the breached promise is otherwise, the calculation can be more difficult.

> **Example 3-2:** A contractor agrees to construct a building on a lot owned by a manufacturer, for a price of $5 million. The manufacturer pays $1 million to the contractor in advance, but the contractor fails to perform any work. The manufacturer is entitled to the value of its "expectation interest," but how do we calculate that?

Here, the owner's "expectation" may be a bit more difficult to calculate. However, at least two alternatives present themselves.

Perhaps the manufacturer can simply hire another contractor to do the work. If so, the manufacturer's expectation can be quantified by the difference between the promised performance (a building for an additional $4 million beyond the $1 million paid in advance) and the actual performance (a building at whatever price was paid to the alternate contractor, along with any related costs). If an alternative contractor is not reasonably available, then the manufacturer may be entitled to recover what it expected to earn from the promised building—perhaps its lost manufacturing profits. Again, each of these approaches to calculating expectation will be explored more fully in Chapter 8. However, this example raises a further question. What if we simply cannot calculate the manufacturer's lost expectation interest? Is there any possible alternative?

Common sense would seem to dictate that, at the very least, the manufacturer ought to get its down payment back under these circumstances, along with any money the manufacturer spent in reliance on the contractor's promise. Indeed, that's the same result the law would likely reach. However, one might reasonably ask why this isn't the normal remedy, instead of expectation? After all, if our manufacturer gets its down payment back, along with any reasonable reliance expenses, hasn't it effectively been made whole again? We'll answer this question a little later in this lesson.

Two classic cases are often used to illustrate enforcement of contract promises. They are each atypical in many respects, but are useful in illustrating certain key concepts regarding the enforcement of promises.

Example 3-3: *Hawkins v. McGee*

Dr. McGee agreed to perform skin graft surgery on the right hand of young Mr. Hawkins, promising—in fact "guaranteeing"—"to make the hand a hundred per cent perfect" as a result of the surgical graft. The surgery did not result in a perfect hand. In fact, the hand was worse after the surgery than before, and Hawkins sued for breach of contract (the accompanying tort claim was dismissed).

The court first acknowledged that a doctor's prognosis would rarely be given effect as a contractual promise. However, in this case, Dr. McGee actively sought the opportunity to operate on Hawkins (this was a new process at the time) and made very specific guarantees as to the promised result. Therefore, Dr. McGee's promise of a perfect hand was enforceable as a contract promise. Having addressed the issue of enforceability, the court next moved to damages.

At trial, the jury had been instructed that Hawkins was entitled to damages for (1) the pain and suffering arising from the operation; and (2) the extent to which his hand was made worse by the operation. However, the appellate court held that each of these instructions was wrong. First, Hawkins was not entitled to recover for his pain and suffering, because this was in fact exactly what he had bargained for and been promised—a surgical operation, complete with pain and suffering. Second, while Hawkins was, in fact, entitled to recover for any worsening of his condition, he was also entitled to recover for the lack of the promised improvement in the condition of his hand. In short, Hawkins was entitled to recover the full difference between the promised hand and the actual condition of his hand after surgery. He could also recover for any additional damages that would not have occurred had the Dr. McGee performed as promised. Again, though, he could not recover for the pain and suffering that was part and parcel of the bargain itself.[2]

Thus, the court held that the patient was entitled to the value of the promised perfect hand, as his "expectation interest." Now consider the following similar case decided some years later.

Example 3-4: *Sullivan v. O'Connor*

Dr. O'Connor contracted with Alice Sullivan, a professional entertainer, for plastic surgery "to enhance her beauty and improve her nose." As with the previous case, Dr. O'Connor's promises were sufficiently specific to bring this case into the realm of contract. And much like the previous case, the surgery ultimately resulted not only in a failure to enhance or improve Ms. Sullivan's nose, but also considerably worsened its appearance. However, in this case, Ms. Sullivan was required to undergo one more surgical procedure than contemplated by the parties' agreement. Dr. Connor had promised two operations, but actually performed three, after which it was clear that nothing further could be done to improve Ms. Sullivan's nose.

Dr. O'Connor had argued that Ms. Sullivan's damages should be limited to her "out-of-pocket" expenses—i.e., her payments to him and to the hospital. In contrast, Ms. Sullivan had argued that she should receive "expectation"

---

[2] Hawkins v. McGee, 84 N.H. 114, 146 A. 641 (1929).

damages, just like Hawkins. The court ultimately chose a middle path, purporting to award Ms. Sullivan her "reliance" damages. As a procedural matter, the court never reached the question of her right to expectation, because Ms. Sullivan had waived a right to press this argument on appeal, as long as she was awarded at least reliance.[3]

In the actual case, the court seemed to have miscalculated Ms. Sullivan's reliance damages by compensating her for only her pain and suffering associated with the third surgery. However, we can apply our own analysis to a hypothetical set of numbers approximating those at issue in the actual case. First, however, we should further develop the basic rules for recovery of damages based on a "restitution" or "reliance" interest, as alternatives to damages based on "expectation."

Alternatives to Expectation

As explained at the outset, the common law gives presumptive effect to the expectation measure of damages for breach of contract, absent extraordinary circumstances or a party's choice to pursue an alternative remedy based on a reliance or restitution interest. On rare occasions, an aggrieved contractual promisee may be better off seeking reliance or restitution, as a remedy. However, in the vast majority of cases involving an actual "breach of contract," the "expectation" remedy will be the most generous, and the aggrieved party will be entitled to that remedy. We will, however, discover a variety of circumstances in which a disappointed party may not be entitled to damages for "breach of contract," but may be entitled to damages based on alternative legal theories, based on either reliance or restitution.

Thus, our purpose in exploring all three bases for calculating damages is threefold. First, distinguishing between the three different interests helps to understand each better. Second, in a few circumstances, an aggrieved promisee may actually be better off seeking a reliance or restitution-based remedy. Finally, a party that cannot establish a breach of contract claim may be entitled to reliance or restitution, as an alternative to breach of contract damages.

---

[3] Sullivan v. O'Connor, 363 Mass. 579, 296 N.E.2d 183 (1973).

Reliance

At the most basic level, reliance differs from expectation in that it seeks to return the parties to their "pre-contract" position, as if the contract had never been made. This is exactly the opposite of expectation, which attempts to put the parties in the same position as full performance of the contract. In effect, reliance is backward looking, while expectation is forward looking. Of course, an aggrieved promisee cannot recover both its expectation and reliance interest, inasmuch as this would amount to the proverbial "having one's cake and eating it too."

The remedy of reliance is intended to avoid the injustice that would otherwise arise when one party reasonably and detrimentally relies on the other party's promise and spends money or otherwise incurs losses as a result of that reliance—including transactions with third-parties.

Summary of Basic Rule: enforcement of the "reliance interest"[4]

- An aggrieved promisee may be entitled— as an alternative to expectation—to recover an amount of damages sufficient to compensate for the promisee's reasonable "reliance" and, thereby, to be placed in as good a position as if the contract had never been made.

Restitution

The remedy of restitution is intended to prevent one person from being unjustly enriched at the expense of another. Thus, restitution typically focuses only on two parties—one who is providing a benefit of some sort and the other receiving that same benefit. A party entitled to restitution is entitled to return of the benefit provided or payment for its value. Thus, we can see that, unlike reliance, restitution focuses only on transactions between the two parties to the dispute.

---

[4] This basic rule summary is reflected in Restatement (Second) of Contracts §§ 344(b) and 349.

Summary of Basic Rule: enforcement of the "restitution interest"[5]

• As an alternative to expectation, a party may be entitled to "restitution" for any benefit provided to the party from whom restitution is sought.

You will note that this basic rule of restitution is stated somewhat more broadly than that of reliance. In fact, we will discover later in this chapter that restitution does not even require a promise. Here, however, we will address the restitution interest in the context of a promisee's right to recover from a promisor who failed to deliver as promised.

Applying Expectation, Reliance, and Restitution

Now we can return to the basic facts of *Sullivan v. O'Connor* and attempt to quantify these three interests in the context of those facts. Here are the numbers we will use (these are similar, but not identical, to the actual case):

(1) Sullivan paid a "lump sum" fee to O'Connor, which covered all of the services he was to perform. This fee was $400.

(2) Sullivan paid a $100 fee to the hospital in which the surgeries were performed—for each of the three separate surgeries (i.e., $300 total).

(3) The monetary value of Sullivan's pain and suffering associated with each of the three surgeries was $1,000 (i.e., $3,000 total).

(4) After the three surgeries, the "value" of Sullivan's nose (remember, she was a professional entertainer) was reduced by $12,000.

(5) As promised by Dr. O'Connor, the value of Sullivan's nose would have been increased by $15,000.

First, let's calculate Sullivan's restitution interest. This is the simplest, because all she gets is what she paid to O'Connor--$400. She can't recover anything else, because none of it benefitted O'Connor. As you can see, the restitution interest is quite limited. Nevertheless, we will see later that it can provide a very valuable remedy in an appropriate case.

---

[5] This basic rule summary is reflected in Restatement (Second) of Contracts § 344(c).

Next, let's calculate Sullivan's reliance interest. Here, she is again entitled to the $400 she paid Dr. O'Connor, because she paid it in "reliance" on this promise. However, she also gets the $100 she paid to the hospital for each surgery, as well as the $1,000 worth of pain and suffering she endured in each surgery, because all of these were incurred in "reliance" on Dr. O'Connor's promise. She is also entitled to the $12,000 by which her nose was worsened when she allowed Dr. O'Connor to operate in "reliance" on his promise. Thus, to return Ms. Sullivan to her pre-contract position, Dr. O'Connor must pay her the following, as "reliance" damages:

$$400 + (3 \times 100) + (3 \times 1,000) + 12,000 = \$15,700$$

Finally, we can calculate Sullivan's expectation interest. Now, our focus changes from a backward looking remedy to one that looks forward, as if Dr. O'Connor's promise had been fully performed. In this case, Sullivan is not entitled to recover the fee she paid to O'Connor, because this was part of her "expectation." Nor can she recover either the hospital fee or the pain and suffering associated with the first two operations, because each was part of her expectations. However, she can recover the cost, along with the pain and suffering, associated with the third, because it was not—Dr. O'Connor promised only two surgeries. Sullivan is also entitled to the full difference between the value of her nose, as promised, and the value of her nose as actually "delivered" by Dr. O'Connor. This includes both the amount that the surgery made it worse and the amount the surgery failed to make it better, as promised—just as the court stated in *Hawkins v. McGee*. Thus, Ms. Sullivan's expectation damages are calculated as follows:

$$100 + 1,000 + (12,000 + 15,000) = \$28,100$$

Having more fully explored the basic differences between these three remedies, we can now return to and further examine "expectation," as the presumptive normal remedy for breach of contract.

Expectation—the Presumptive Remedy for Breach of Contract

So why do we award "expectation" rather than reliance or restitution? The following case represents an excellent example of a court weighing the opposing parties' arguments between a forward looking remedy of "expectation" and a backward looking remedy, seeking to return the parties to their original position, as if a contract had never been formed.

FROM THE COURT

Menzel v. List

New York Court of Appeals (1969)
24 N.Y.2d 91, 246 N.E.2d 742

BURKE, J.

In 1932 Mrs. Erna Menzel and her husband purchased a painting by Marc Chagall at an auction in Brussels, Belgium, for 3,800 Belgian francs (then equivalent to about $150). When the Germans invaded Belgium in 1940, the Menzels fled and left their possessions, including the Chagall painting, in their apartment. They returned six years later and found that the painting had been removed by the German authorities and that a receipt for the painting had been left. The location of the painting between the time of its removal by the Germans in 1941 and 1955 is unknown. In 1955 Klaus Perls and his wife, the proprietors of a New York art gallery, purchased the Chagall from a Parisian art gallery for $2,800. The Perls knew nothing of the painting's previous history and made no inquiry concerning it, being content to rely on the reputability of the Paris gallery as to authenticity and title. In October, 1955 the Perls sold the painting to Albert List for $4,000. However, in 1962, Mrs. Menzel noticed a reproduction of the Chagall in an art book accompanied by a statement that the painting was in Albert List's possession. She thereupon demanded the painting from him but he refused to surrender it to her.

Mrs. Menzel then instituted a replevin action against Mr. List and he, in turn, impleaded the Perls, alleging in his third-party complaint that they were liable to him for breach of an implied warranty of title. At the trial, expert testimony was introduced to establish the painting's fair market value at the time of trial. The only evidence of its value at the time it was purchased by List was the price which he paid to the Perls. The trial court charged the jury that, if it found for

> An action for "replevin" seeks to recover personal property—here the painting. A defendant, such as List, may "implead" a "third party," such as the Perls, who may be liable to the defendant, if the defendant is found liable to the plaintiff.

Mrs. Menzel against List, it was also to "assess the value of said painting at such an amount as you believe from the testimony represents its present value." The jury returned a verdict for Mrs. Menzel and she entered a judgment directing the return of the painting to her or, in the alternative, that List pay to her the value of the painting, which the jury found to be $22,500. (List has, in fact, returned the painting to Mrs. Menzel.) In addition, the jury found for List as against the Perls, on his third-party complaint, in the amount of $22,500, the painting's present value, ...

The Perls appealed to the Appellate Division, First Department, from that judgment and the judgment was unanimously modified, on the law, by reducing the amount awarded to List to $4,000 (the purchase price he had paid for the painting), with interest from the date of the purchase. In a memorandum, the Appellate Division held . . . that the "applicable measure of damages was the price List paid for the painting at the time of purchase, together with interest", (citations omitted).

Today, the sale of the painting from the Perls to List would be governed by UCC Article 2, which includes an implied warranty of title. We will address implied warranties later, in Chapter 6. However, you may safely assume that the issue of "breach" in this case would be resolved in the same manner under Article 2. Having concluded that the Perls had breached the implied warranty of title, the court moved on to the key issue of proper damages.

List filed a notice of appeal as of right from the unanimous modification insofar as it reduced the amount of his judgment to $4,000, with interest from the date of purchase. . . .

List's appeal . . . present[s] only questions of law for resolution, the facts having been found by the jury and affirmed by the Appellate Division (its modification was on the law as to the proper measure of damages and the running of interest). The issue on the main appeal is simply what is or should be the proper measure of damages for the breach of an implied warranty of title (or quiet possession) in the sale of personal property. . . .

The Perls contend that the only loss directly and naturally resulting, in the ordinary course of events, from their breach was List's loss of the purchase price. List, however, contends that that loss is the present market value of the painting, the value which he would have been able to obtain if the Perls had conveyed good title. [The argument made by the Perls] has been severely criticized by a leading authority in these terms: "This rule [limiting damages to the purchase price plus interest] virtually confines the buyer to rescission and restitution, a remedy to which the injured buyer is undoubtedly entitled if he so elects, but it is a violation of general principles of contracts to deny him in an action on the contract such damages as will put him in as good a position as he would have occupied had the contract been kept." (11 Williston, Contracts [3d ed.], § 1395A, p. 484.) Clearly, List can only be put in the same position he would have occupied if the contract had been kept by the Perls if he recovers the value of the painting at the time when, by the judgment in the main action, he was required to surrender the painting to Mrs. Menzel or pay her the present value of the painting. Had the warranty been fulfilled, i.e., had title been as warranted by the Perls, List would still have possession of a painting currently worth $22,500 and he could have realized that price at an auction or private sale. If List recovers only the purchase price plus interest, the effect is to put him in the same position he would have occupied if the sale had never been made. Manifestly, an injured buyer is not compensated when he recovers only so much as placed him in status quo ante since such a recovery implicitly denies that he had suffered any damage. . . . Instead, [h]e is entitled to the "benefit of his bargain" (citations omitted). This measure of damages reflects what the buyer has actually lost and it awards to him only the loss which has directly and naturally resulted, in the ordinary course of events, from the seller's breach of warranty.

An objection raised by the Perls to this measure of damages is that it exposes the innocent seller to potentially ruinous liability where the article sold has substantially appreciated in value. However, this "potential ruin" is not beyond the control of the seller since he can take steps to ascertain the status of title so as to satisfy himself that he himself is getting good title. (Mr. Perls testified that to question a reputable dealer as to his title would be an "insult." Perhaps, but the sensitivity of the art dealer cannot serve to deprive the injured buyer of compensation for a breach which could have been avoided had the insult been risked.) Should such an inquiry produce no reasonably reliable information as to the status of title, it is not requiring too much to expect that, as a reasonable businessman, the dealer would himself either refuse to buy or, having bought, inform his vendee of the uncertain status of title.

Furthermore, [a seller can expressly exclude such implied warranties, if done properly]. Had the Perls taken the trouble to inquire as to title, they could have sold to List subject to any existing lawful claims unknown to them at the time of the sale. Accordingly, the "prospects of ruin" forecast as flowing from the rule are not quite as ominous as the argument would indicate. Accordingly, the order of the Appellate Division should be reversed as to the measure of damages and the judgment awarding List the value of the painting at the time of trial of the Menzel action should be reinstated.

On the cross appeal by the Perls, the issue is as to the time from which interest should run on the judgment in favor of List against the Perls. The Appellate Division indicated that interest should be recovered from the date of purchase in October, 1955, but it did so only in conjunction with its determination that the measure of damages should be the purchase price paid by List on that date. Manifestly, the present-value measure of damages has no necessary connection with the date of purchase and is, in fact, inconsistent with the running of interest from the date of purchase since List's possession was not disturbed until the judgment directing delivery of the painting to Mrs. Menzel, or, in the alternative, paying her the present value of the painting. Accordingly, List was not damaged until that time and there is no basis upon which to predicate the inclusion of interest from the date of purchase. Accordingly, on the cross appeal, the order of the Appellate Division, insofar as it directed that interest should run from the date of purchase, should be reversed and interest directed to be included from the date on which Mrs. Menzel's judgment was entered, May 10, 1966.

Order reversed, with costs to third-party plaintiff-appellant-respondent, and case remitted to Supreme Court, New York County, for further proceedings in accordance with the opinion herein.

CASE QUESTIONS

(1) Which party argued for a backward looking remedy, seeking to return the parties to their pre-contractual position? How much would List have received, excluding interest, if that argument prevailed?

(2) Which party argued for a forward looking remedy, based on the "expectation interest"? How much would List have received, excluding interest, if that argument prevailed?

(3) Which argument did the New York Court of Appeals accept, and why?

(4) What did the New York Court of Appeals decide regarding interest, and why? Was this decision consistent with List's "expectation interest"?

You should attempt to answer each of the above questions yourself. While the answers will not be provided directly here in the text, the next section should give you a pretty clear idea of whether or not you are on the right track.

Lost Opportunity Cost

A variety of reasons are offered to support an "expectation" instead of a reliance approach to damages. To the extent that contract law is intended to facilitate the operation of the market, parties are more likely to find contracting desirable if they can count on the enforcement of their "expectation" interest. Moreover, the fact and extent of reasonable and detrimental reliance are often difficult to prove, as compared to the fact of breach and value of expectation. Finally, there is also one crucial shortcoming with respect to a reliance remedy, as applied to many cases of breach. This is the lost opportunity cost.

The goal of reliance is to return the aggrieved promisee to his or her pre-contractual position. In theory, if returned to this position, the promisee has lost nothing on the failed contract. However, the promisee has in fact lost the opportunity to contract with another, instead of the breaching party. This is the "lost opportunity cost." We cannot return the disappointed promisee to that same point in time so that he or she can make a different contract to replace the one that failed. The facts of *Menzel v. List* illustrate this perfectly.

If List had recovered only the amount he had paid Perls, as "reliance," there is no way he could have gone back to October 1955 and invested this amount in an alternative piece of art. In effect, he would not be able to recover for his "lost opportunity cost." To some degree, an award of interest from the time of the purchase to the time compensation is received might seek to provide for this lost opportunity. However, an award of interest cannot really substitute for a lost investment opportunity, inasmuch as most individuals "invest" when they expect that such investments will provide a greater return that mere "interest." Thus, an "expectation" remedy is arguably the only remedy that fully compensates an aggrieved promisee for the unfulfilled bargain.

Willfulness, Penalties, and Disgorgement

What if one of the parties breaches the contract on purpose? Should that make a difference in determining the appropriate remedy?

Example 3-5: *White v. Benkowski*

The Whites and Benkowskis agreed that, for 10 years, the Benkowskis would supply water to the Whites, their neighbors, in exchange for the White's promise to make fixed monthly payments and share repair and maintenance costs. After a couple of years, the relations between the parties turned hostile, and, out of spite, the Benkowskis began maliciously shutting off the White's water from time to time. The Benkowskis had clearly breached their contract with the Whites, as determined by the jury, and the Whites were entitled to actual damages. However, the Whites further sought additional damages to "punish" the Benkowskis for their malicious conduct.

The court refused to allow an award of punitive damages—even though the breach was willful and malicious—because no tort had been pleaded or proven.[6]

---

[6] White v. Benkowski, 37 Wis. 2d 285, 155 N.W. 2d 74 (1967). *See also* Restatement (Second) of Contracts § 355, Comment a., illustration 2., which is based on the foregoing case.

Intentional tort claims will often give rise to punitive damage remedies. However, this court points out that a breach of contract claim will not, itself, give rise to liability for punitive damages. One can find a number of purported "exceptions" to this "rule," but all are arguably based on a related tort or "tort-like" claim.

Most contracts impose only promissory duties, as opposed to a "fiduciary" duty. A "fiduciary" takes on the added, and extraordinary, obligation of not only keeping a promise, but of actually looking out for another's interest— over and above the self-interest of the fiduciary. For example, a "trustee" engaged to manage a trust for the benefit of the trust "beneficiary" has a "fiduciary" obligation to act for the benefit of the "beneficiary" with respect to the trust assets, rather than acting for the trustee's own self-interest. While claims for breach of a fiduciary duty may arise from a variety of circumstances and may be classified, formally, as either tort or contract claims, such claims are far more "tort-like" than a breach of contract claim. As such, it is not surprising that a breach of fiduciary duty claim may give rise to punitive damages.

Another "atypical" example of punitive damages involves a claim for "bad faith" breach of an insurance contract. Normally, there is no distinction between a "bad faith" (whatever that might mean) and a "good faith" (we'll talk more about this later) breach of contract. However, there is a notable exception for insurance contracts. While an insurer is not necessarily deemed a "fiduciary" with respect to the insured, the relationship is sufficiently unique that an insurer is expected to treat its insured in a reasonable manner, and an intentional refusal to pay claims reasonably due may give rise to punitive damages.

A thorough examination of the foregoing "exceptions" to the normal contract "rule" barring punitive damages is beyond the scope of this basic course. However, these exceptions are intended as examples to help understand the nature and limits of the basic rule.

One other distinct, but somewhat related, issue involves the remedy of "disgorgement." If the promisor actually profits from breaching a promise to the promisee, should the promisor be required to disgorge those profits—essentially paying them over to the aggrieved promisee as a form of damages? What if these profits exceed the promisee's expectation, had the contract been fully performed as agreed? Consider the following example.

Example 3-6: Alpha contracts to sell corn to Zoe, who intends to use it to feed livestock. In January, they settle on a price of $3 per bushel of corn, for July 1 delivery. In June, Alpha learns that it can sell the same corn to Beta for use in producing ethanol, at $6 per bushel. Alpha also knows that, because corn is in short supply, Zoe won't likely be able to buy corn and will have to sell off her livestock prematurely, resulting in a total commercial loss equal to $2 per bushel of the promised corn.

Alpha sells the corn to Beta and breaches its contract with Zoe. As a direct result, Alpha receives an extra $3 per bushel for the corn originally promised to Zoe, and Zoe suffers a $2 per bushel loss, as compared to her expectation had the contract been fully performed as agreed.

Zoe's expectation damages are $2 per bushel, but what about the $3 Alpha made in its sale to Beta? Should this amount be added to, or substituted for, Zoe's expectation damages? Adding the two together (resulting in $5) would seem fully punitive and, therefore, inappropriate. However, the extra dollar—the difference between Zoe's expectation damages and Alpha's profit arising from the breach—presents an interesting question. Who should get this extra dollar—Zoe or Alpha?

A remedy of "disgorgement" would allocate the extra dollar to Zoe, requiring Alpha to give up any amount it made from the breach, beyond its obligation to pay expectation damages. In effect, if Alpha was required to pay $2 per bushel as expectation damages, and further required to "disgorge" the additional $1 per bushel in profits, then it would be precluded from "profiting" on its breach. While this theory of disgorgement has received significant support from some contract scholars, it is not consistent with the basic common law rule of "expectation" applied by most courts today, because it would overcompensate the aggrieved promisee by providing more than the party expected from full performance of the contract. As such, any "disgorgement" remedy is generally considered punitive. The issue of disgorgement is closely related to the doctrine of "efficient breach."

Efficient Breach—a Law and Economics Perspective

The breach by Alpha in example 3-6 is an example of what is often referred to as an "efficient breach." This is a breach in which at least one party (the breaching party) is better off as a result of the breach, and neither party is any worse off (the aggrieved promisee having received damages). If neither party is any worse off, and at least one is better off, then society as a whole is better off, and the breach is therefore said to be "efficient." In its simplest form, the theory is reasonably straightforward. However, the reality of contracting is rarely this simple.

Even the "expectation remedy" will sometimes undercompensate an aggrieved party. For example, some damages may not be possible to quantify. There is also a basic question of fairness. The theory of efficient breach addresses only the overall societal gain—not who gets it. Why should the breaching party benefit over the party who keeps its promise?

We will return to the issue of efficient breach in Chapter 8. For now, two basic points are important. First, the theory of efficient breach is often used to justify a number of contract "rules" related to remedies. Second, the soundness of the theory is subject to considerable debate.

Specific Performance

While the normal or ordinary form of "expectation" entails a substitute for actual performance in the form of money, in some cases an aggrieved promisee may be entitled to seek actual performance of the promise at issue. This exceptional or extraordinary remedy is typically called "specific performance." For example, a buyer will generally have a right to specific performance by seller in a contract for the sale of real property.

> **Example 3-7:** Ann promises to convey Greenacre to Ben in exchange for $50,000. If Ann refuses to convey Greenacre, Ben is likely entitled to specific performance by Ann. She will have to convey Greenacre, and Ben will of course have to pay the $50,000.

Any given piece of real property is generally considered "unique." Thus, money is deemed an ineffective substitute for a promised parcel of real property. We will consider a variety of other contexts for specific performance in Chapter 8.

We can now state a more detailed version of the basic rule regarding damages for breach of contract.

Summary of Basic Rule (expanded version): enforcement of the "expectation interest"[7]

- An aggrieved promisee is entitled to recover his or her "expectation interest" in the event of breach by the promisor;

  ○ This "expectation" remedy entitles the promisee to be placed in as good a position as if the contract had been fully performed,

    ▪ But not in a better position than full performance, and

    ▪ The aggrieved party is not entitled to punitive damages in a simple breach of contract case, even if the breach was willful

  ○ This "expectation" remedy is normally achieved by awarding a sum of money equal to the difference in value between promised performance and actual performance

    ▪ However, in exceptional cases, such as a sale of real property, a party may be entitled to specific performance of the promise at issue

---

Expectation under the UCC

The UCC generally applies this same rule enforcing a promisee's expectation interest. **STOP NOW and READ the excerpts from UCC § 1-305(a) below.**

UCC § 1-305(a)

(a) The remedies provided by [the Uniform Commercial Code] must be liberally administered to the end that the aggrieved party may be put in as good a position as if the other party had fully performed, . . .

---

[7] This basic rule is reflected in Restatement (Second) of Contracts §§ 344(a), 345, 347, and 355.

UCC Article 1 clearly states its adherence to the expectation principle and an aggrieved party's right to "be put in as good a position as if the other party had fully performed." In Chapter 8, we will explore the detailed application of this principle found in Part 7 of UCC Article 2.

Expectation under the CISG

The CISG also provides for the enforcement of a promisee's expectation interest. **STOP NOW and READ the excerpts from CISG Article 74 below.**

CISG Article 74

Damages for breach of contract by one party consist of a sum equal to the loss, including loss of profit, suffered by the other party as a consequence of the breach. . . .

CISG Article 74 has been consistently interpreted based on the "expectation interest" and enforcing an aggrieved party's right to a remedy based on what it reasonably expected from full performance of the contract. A more detailed application of this principle is also explored in Chapter 8.

Expectation Damages Do Not—as a Rule—Include Attorney Fees

One final point is worth mentioning here. If one were to take the "expectation interest" to its logical conclusion, it would provide for recovery of attorney fees reasonably expended by a successful promisee. After all, if the agreement had been fully performed, as promised, the attorney fees never would have been spent. However, this is not the "American Rule." Under the normal rule in this country, in the absence of a statute or a contract provision to the contrary, each party is responsible for its own attorney fees. Reasonable people may differ as to the wisdom of including a "fee shifting" provision (requiring the losing party to pay the prevailing party's reasonable attorney fees) in any given contract. However, it is often worth giving serious consideration.

APPLYING THE RULES

Problem 1: A book publisher (N) sold the rights to publish the paperback version of a book to another publisher (B). B was granted the right to publish the paperback "not sooner than October." Prior to October, N expected to continue to sell the hardback version of the book without competition from any less expensive paperback sales. However, B began selling the paperback version in September, in breach of its promise to N. You may assume that B's early sales of the paperback had the following effects, as factually determined by the court:

(1) As a direct result of B's paperback sales in September, N made $8,000 less profit on hardback sales during the same time period;

(2) B's own profit was $35,000 on the September paperback sales that directly displaced September hardback sales by N; and

(3) B also made additional profits on September paperback sales of $690,000. These sales had no effect on N's hardback sales, as they were made to individuals who were waiting, in any event, to buy the paperback version.

How much is N entitled to recover from B for breach of contract?

This problem is based loosely on the facts of *United States Naval Institute v. Charter Communications, Inc.*, 936 F.2d 692 (2d Cir. 1991). The actual case also involved copyright issues, which are omitted here in order to focus solely on the contract damages question.

Problem 2: A manufacturer of "widgets" purchases a machine that is designed to increase the efficiency of the manufacturer's widget making process. The widget maker reasonably expects—based on the representations of the seller—that the use of the machine will result in a 20% net savings on the cost of manufacturing widgets.

> "Widgets" are fictional generic goods that are often used in contract hypotheticals in which the actual nature of the goods is not particularly important to the issues raised. They will be used from time to time in hypotheticals throughout this textbook.

The seller also promised that the machine would be maintenance-free for at least 5 years. In fact, the machine saved the manufacturer only

10% on its manufacturing costs, and the seller incurred additional costs to repair the machine, when it unexpectedly broke down during the first year. Moreover, the manufacturer had reasonably and necessarily spent significant money in preparing its factory for the installation of the machine.

Assuming that the manufacturer retains the machine, but seeks damages for breach, which of the following would be included in awarding damages based on the manufacturer's restitution interest? How about its reliance interest? How about its expectation interest?

1) The purchase price of the machine;

2) The cost of preparing the factory for the machine;

3) The 10% manufacturing costs not saved;

4) Extra unexpected maintenance costs.

Which of the three "interests" reflects the proper measure of damages in this case?

Lesson 4: Enforcing Bargains—Not Gifts

Objectives and Expected Learning Outcomes

In this lesson, you should learn the basic rule of consideration. You will learn to distinguish between bargains and gifts at a fundamental level, and you will learn that only the former are legally enforceable under the basic rule. By the end of this lesson, you should be able to identify the basic issues in a particular fact pattern that will determine whether a promise is supported by consideration so as to make it legally enforceable, and you should be able to analyze these issues by applying the rule to the relevant and material facts.

A "contract" requires (1) a bargain; and (2) agreement to that bargain. This very basic rule of contract law is found in Restatement (Second) of Contracts § 17(1). The rest of the current chapter will address the "bargain" requirement, along with alternative theories of enforcement. Chapter 3 will then address the issue of "agreement"—typically characterized as "offer and acceptance." Our discussion of "bargains" begins with the somewhat arcane concept of "consideration."

A Bargain in Exchange for "Consideration"

"Consideration" is a "term of art" when it comes to contract law. It is that which is given or promised in exchange for that which is sought from the promisor. A promisee that has given or promised something "in consideration of" or "in exchange for" the promise of the promisor can generally enforce that promise.

At the most basic level, the Anglo-American requirement of "consideration" can be stated very simply: "the law enforces promises made as part of a bargain, but does not enforce promises of a gift." As with many "simple" concepts, the devil is in the details. Before moving to those details, however, we might reasonably ask "why does the law distinguish between bargains and gifts?"

Much has been written on contract theory, and a great deal of it has focused on the basis for enforcing promises (or not). However, two broad theoretical bases typically emerge and focus either on facilitation of the market or on the sanctity of a promise. While admittedly an oversimplification, the foundation of Anglo-American common law rests primarily on the former, while continental European civil law rests primarily on the latter.

Presumably, two parties agree to a "bargain" only when each believes he or she will be better off after the exchange. Thus, facilitation of the "bargain" by providing an "enforcement" mechanism will help to make the "market" work and increase the well-being of society, as a whole. Admittedly, this very simple construct assumes true consent on each side of the transaction (we'll see instances later that seriously challenge this assumption) and completely ignores externalized transaction costs (e.g., the environmental costs of our jet fuel transaction in Example 1-5). However, it does help to explain the law's focus on enforcement of bargains. In contrast, when one party makes a gift to another, we have no reason to believe that there is any overall societal gain. We simply assume that the loss to the person making the gift equals the gain to the recipient. While this is not always the case, absent more information, it is our beginning assumption.

Thus, the law generally favors bargains over gifts based on at least a preliminary assumption that bargains lead to overall societal gain through the functioning of the market, while gifts do not. The next few examples all involve "family" promises, and, in this context, the idea of an overall gain may be somewhat more nebulous than in a typical business deal. In fact, you will discover that we don't really focus at all on actual gains or losses—asking instead whether a real "exchange" has been agreed upon. However, this approach is based—at least in part—on the premise that bargains are more valuable than gifts.

The following example provides a useful context to begin our discussion. While "family" promises are not necessarily run-of-the-mill typical contracts, they serve to illustrate the basic concept of consideration quite nicely.

Example 4-1: Jane promised her grandson, Joe, that she would give him $150,000 to attend the law school of his choice. Joe said, "Gee, that sounds great, but it's a lot of money—are you sure?" Jane replied, "Yes, absolutely! You've been a perfect grandson, always doing everything I ever asked of you, always making outstanding grades, and behaving as a model young adult. You have earned this money many times over, and I really want you to have the opportunity to become a lawyer, just like your grandpa." Jane added, "so, all you'll have to do is graduate from law school and pass the bar exam in whichever state you'd like to practice." Joe was very grateful inasmuch as he had already been thinking seriously about going to law school. He promptly took the LSAT, enrolled in law school, and three years later passed the bar. Joe had actually managed to qualify for a number of scholarships along the way, and his entire legal education had cost him only $60,000. He borrowed that $60,000 along the way, confident that he would be able to repay it with the $150,000 promised by his grandmother. He also did very well in law school and landed a job with a prestigious law firm, paying him a starting salary of $160,000 per year.

However, when Joe asked Jane for the promised money, she refused, saying she no longer thought he needed it with his fancy big law firm job (Joe's grandfather had been a small town solo practitioner, and Jane did not think much of "big city" lawyers). Can Joe enforce Jane's promise to pay him $150,000?

Was Jane bargaining for Joe to go to law school and pass the bar exam, or was she simply promising a gift, which he might (or might not) use to do so? Did Joe go to law school and pass the bar solely based on Jane's promise? Should that matter? What about the fact that law school cost less than the amount promised, and what about his fabulous job offer? Should either of these matter? We will come back to this fictional hypothetical after looking at a few actual cases. Watch for similarities and differences between the example above and those that follow.

Example 4-2: *Dougherty v. Salt*

Aunt Tillie gave to her young nephew, Charley, "a promissory note for $3,000 payable at her death or before." The written note included the words "value received." In giving Charley the note, Tillie commented that he was a nice boy, she loved him very much, and she was going to take care of him. As Tillie handed the note to Charley, she said, "You have always done for me, and I have signed this note for you. Now, do not lose it. Some day it will be valuable."

When Aunt Tillie died, her estate refused to pay the note, and Charley sued. The court held that Charley had no right to enforce the note because it lacked any consideration.[8]

Aunt Tillie's promise to her nephew was deemed to be an unenforceable gift. Now consider the next example in which a court enforced Uncle William's promise to pay money to his nephew. What, if anything, justifies the different result in the two cases?

---

[8] Dougherty v. Salt. 227 N.Y. 200, 125 N.E. 94 (1919).

Example 4-3: *Hamer v. Sidway*

Uncle William Story promised his nephew, William, that "if he would refrain from drinking, using tobacco, swearing, and playing cards or billiards for money until he became 21 years of age [all of which he otherwise had a legal right to do], he would pay him the sum of $5,000." The nephew said he would so refrain and, in fact, did so. Upon reaching the age of 21, nephew William wrote to his uncle requesting payment. Uncle William wrote back, agreeing that his nephew was entitled to the money, but he did not pay it immediately, instead holding it "on interest" for later payment to his nephew.

When Uncle William died, his estate refused to pay the note, and a successor to his nephew's right (nephew William had transferred his right to payment) sued. Uncle William's estate argued that the promise lacked consideration because the uncle had received no benefit and the nephew had suffered no detriment—in fact being better off having abstained from the conduct in question. The court nevertheless enforced the promise, holding that the nephew's voluntary abandonment of his legal right to engage in the conduct in question provided consideration given in exchange for the promise.[9]

> **Executory Promises versus Completed Gifts**
> Note that "enforcement" is only an issue when a promise has not yet been performed. If Tillie had handed Charley $3,000 instead of the note, the lack of consideration would have been irrelevant. Having delivered the "gift" to Charley, Aunt Tillie would have no right to its return (under the law of property, the transfer is irrevocable). A promise that has not yet been performed is said to remain "executory," and only "executory" promises are tested for "consideration."

Do you see the evidence of a "bargain" in the latter case that is missing in the former? Tillie said many nice things about her nephew and even suggested he had done some nice things in the past giving rise to her current affection for him. However, she demanded nothing of him "in exchange for" payment of the sum re-

---

[9] Hamer v. Sidway, 124 N.Y. 538, 27 N.E. 256 (1891). *See also* Restatement (Second) of Contracts § 71, Comment d., illustration 9., which is loosely based on this case.

flected in the note. In contrast, William conditioned his nephew's right to payment on the nephew abstaining from activities in which he might have otherwise engaged. In effect, William's nephew did something bargained for by his uncle that he might not have otherwise done—and did so specifically in exchange for his uncle's promise. Do you see the crucial distinction between the two cases now? At this junction, what do you think—is Jane's promise in example 4-1 enforceable? Is it more like example 4-2 or 4-3?

The *Dougherty* and *Hamer* cases above raise a few additional issues. Why can't Charley rely on his past conduct as consideration to make Tillie's promise enforceable? Does the "bargain" offered by Uncle William seem reasonable—$5,000 in exchange for something that actually benefitted his nephew and did nothing for uncle? And if William's nephew's conduct amounted to consideration, then why doesn't Tillie's "recital" that she had made her promise in exchange for "value received" make any difference in the enforceability of her promise? These questions are each addressed in turn below.

Past Consideration

The facts of the following case potentially raise the first issue—the timing of any purported consideration. In reading it, consider the multiple contracts involved. Is the promise at issue part of a bargain for current consideration?

FROM THE COURT

Stonestreet v. Southern Oil Co.

Supreme Court of North Carolina (1946)
226 N.C. 261, 37 S.E.2d 676

Action by C. C. Stonestreet against the Southern Oil Company to recover half the cost of digging a water well on land leased to defendant by plaintiff. Judgment for plaintiff, and defendant appeals.

Reversed.

Civil action to recover one-half cost of digging well on land leased and optioned by plaintiff to defendant, which the defendant later purchased by exercising option.

On October 24, 1934, the plaintiff and his wife leased to the defendant a lot for a filling station on the Kannapolis-Concord Highway for a term of ten years with privilege of buying at any time during the term of the lease at a price of $5,000. The lease contained the following stipulation: 'Said Stonestreet and wife agree to furnish Lessee with water for the station insofar as they are able to do so with their present water supply. In case said Lessor's well fails to supply ample water, they are not to be responsible, and the Lessee will be required to make their own arrangements for securing water.'

In June, 1935, the lessee needed more water; whereupon plaintiff and defendant engaged C.W. Fisher to drill a well on the premises, each agreeing to pay one-half the cost. The Southern Oil Company paid its half amounting to $329 and the plaintiff credited Fisher with a like amount on his grocery bill.

It is alleged that at the time C. W. Fisher was engaged to drill the well, under a written contract signed by all the parties, it was further agreed orally between plaintiff and defendant that if the lessee exercised its option to buy the premises the defendant 'would repay the plaintiff his one-half paid for boring said well, but if the defendant did not exercise the option to buy, then the well would belong to plaintiff and he would not be reimbursed the one-half he had paid.'

The defendant denied the alleged oral agreement, and pleaded . . . no consideration for the alleged oral agreement to reimburse the plaintiff.

On cross-examination, the plaintiff testified as follows: 'While they were digging the well Mr. Brinson (defendant's representative) came down and talked to me and promised me, in the event he took the property under the option in the lease to pay me back whatever I put into it. He promised to pay me back the $329.00 if he exercised the option. I did not give him anything in money, or property or make any promises in return for his promise to pay me back my one-half the cost of digging the well. I did not promise him any money, didn't give him any money, I didn't think I had to. I thought he was an honest man.'

There was a verdict and judgment for plaintiff, from which the defendant appeals, assigning errors.

STACY, Chief Justice, . . . [I]t would seem that under the facts appearing of record . . ., the defendant's plea of no consideration has been made out and constitutes a bar to the plaintiff's case. . . .

It may be stated as a general rule that "consideration" in the sense the term is used in legal parlance, as affecting the enforceability of simple contracts, consists of some benefit or advantage to the promisor, or of some loss or detriment to the promisee. . . . It has been held that "there is a consideration if the promisee, in return for the promise, does anything legal which he is not bound to do, or refrains from doing anything which he has a right to do, whether there is any actual loss or detriment to him or actual benefit to the promisor or not." . . . On the other hand, a mere promise, without more, lacks a consideration and is unenforceable.

It is said that when one receives a naked promise and such promise is not kept, he is no worse off than he was before the promise was made. He gave nothing for it, loses nothing by it, and upon its breach he suffers no recoverable damage. . . . For example, 'A' promises to give 'B' a horse at Christmastime, or to leave him a legacy in his will, and does neither. There being no consideration for the promise, 'B' would have no cause of action against 'A' or his estate. . . . A bare promise, made without consideration, creates no legal rights and imposes no legal obligations. Its fulfillment is a matter of grace or favor on the part of the one making the promise.

In the instant case the promise on the part of the defendant to reimburse the plaintiff "his one-half paid for boring said well" was no more than a gratuity. Plaintiff promised nothing and gave nothing in return for the defendant's promise. . . . The agreement to dig the well was in writing and its terms stated. The defendant, therefore, acquired by the exercise of its option exactly what it would have acquired had the promise of reimbursement not been given. The plaintiff lost nothing by the promise. His rights and obligations were fixed and determined by the written instruments. . . . The promise, if made, was without consideration to enforce it. . . . It seems that plaintiff trusted to the mere gratuitous promise of favor from another.

The motion for judgment of nonsuit was well interposed.

Reversed.

CASE QUESTIONS

(1) How many contracts were potentially concluded by Stonestreet and Southern Oil? Identify them, including the contract claimed by Stonestreet, but denied enforcement by the court.

(2) Where might Stonestreet have found consideration to support the purported promise by Southern Oil to reimburse him for his share of the well if Southern Oil exercised its option to purchase the property? Let's look at each possibility:

    a. The original 1934 lease contract?

    b. The 1935 contract to dig the well?

    c. The conversation between Stonestreet and Brinson while the well was being dug?

(3) Take a look at the court's discussion of benefit/detriment. Is this consistent with the court's decision in Hamer v. Sidway in example 4-3?

You should have found two enforceable contracts and one naked promise—the last one at issue—which lacked consideration. First, Stonestreet and Southern Oil concluded a lease contract in 1934, which included an option for Southern Oil to purchase the land during the term of the lease. Second, Stonestreet and Southern Oil concluded a contract to dig a well on the leased land, for which each would pay half the cost. Each agreed to something it was not required to do under the initial lease contract—Southern Oil had no obligation to drill a well (it could have gone without water or purchased it elsewhere), and Stonestreet had no obligation to share in the cost of the well if Southern Oil chose to dig a new one.

Thus, each side provided consideration with respect to this second agreement that was fully independent of the first. However, Stonestreet provided no new consideration with respect to the final promise by Southern Oil to reimburse him for his half of the drilling costs—if Southern Oil exercised its option (which it already had a right to do under the original lease). In effect, the only consideration provided by Stonestreet was prior to the promise he sought to enforce, and it is often said that "past consideration is no consideration at all."

The simplest explanation of why "past consideration" will not support a bargain is that one cannot "bargain" for something that has already occurred. The basic concept of a "bargain" is "this for that." However, if "this" has already been promised or performed, then "that" is simply a subsequent gift. The original concerns underlying the requirement of consideration under English common law also shed some additional light on the issue.

Consideration was intended to serve two crucial purposes: (1) evidentiary; and (2) cautionary. The presence of consideration given by the promisee provided at least some evidence making more likely the corresponding promise of the promisor. Moreover, the presence of consideration would likely lend a greater sense of seriousness to the circumstances in which the promise was made. Would you think more seriously about making a casual promise without anything expected in return or a promise in which the other person provided you with something you wanted in exchange for your promise? Most would seem to take the latter circumstances more seriously.

In *Stonestreet*, the representative from Southern Oil disputed having made the purported promise. Thus, in the absence of any consideration flowing from Stonestreet to Southern Oil, we are left with a simple case of two conflicting stories. Even if Brinson actually made the promise, do we think he thought about it in the same manner he would have if Stonestreet had proposed something in exchange for the promise? And of course any "past consideration" answers neither of these concerns. Such past consideration is no evidence at all of a new promise, nor does it provide the promisor with any cautionary basis for pausing for thought before making an improvident promise. Thus, the facts of *Stonestreet* seem to support the earliest historical concerns that gave rise to the doctrine of consideration. We can now move on to the second additional issue potentially raised by *Hamer*—the adequacy of consideration.

Adequacy of Consideration

In 1869, Uncle William Story promised his nephew $5,000 in exchange for behaving in a way that was arguably good for his nephew and provided no tangible benefit to Uncle William. That same $5,000 would be conservatively worth $85,000 today (based on the purchasing power of that amount of money). Does this seem like a reasonable bargain? Before we try to answer this question, consider the following example.

Example 4-4: *Batsakis v. Demotsis*

During the Nazi occupation of Greece, in 1942, Eugenia Demotsis borrowed 500,000 drachmae from George Batsakis, promising to repay Batsakis $2,000, along with 8 percent annual interest. At the time of the loan, 500,000 drachmae were worth approximately $25. However, Demotsis had no access to any other financial resources at the time, as her assets were all in the U.S. and unavailable during the wartime occupation.

When Demotsis later refused to pay, Batsakis sued, and Demotsis defended, asserting that the 500,000 drachmae was inadequate consideration to support a promise to repay $2,000. The court enforced the contract, holding that "[m]ere inadequacy of consideration will not void a contract," and Demotsis "got exactly what she contracted for . . ."[10]

As with *Hamer*, the above example seemingly presents a poor bargain. A loan in which the borrower promised to pay back an amount of principal (separate and apart from interest) equal to 80 times the amount of the loan. And yet, if we look at the context, we can see that, in each case, that was the bargain the promisor honestly and genuinely wanted to make. As such, the law generally enforces the resulting bargain—subject only to certain public policy exceptions that we will address in Chapter 5 (we'll come back to the apparent harshness and potential unfairness of the bargain above in those materials). If the parties agreed on a true "bargain," then the law will rarely second guess the wisdom of that bargain. By enforcing bargains, without second guessing their wisdom, the law provides a reasonable degree of certainty as to the likely enforceability of contracts.

If, however, the parties are free to make any bargain—including a bad bargain—then why didn't the court enforce Aunt Tillie's promise in example 4-2, in which she stated in writing that she'd received value (i.e., adequate consideration)? The key to answering this question requires us to distinguish between "real"—albeit seemingly unwise—bargains and "sham" bargains that are not bargains at all.

---

[10] Batsakis v. Demotsis, 226 S.W. 2d 673 (Tex. Civ. App. 1949).

Peppercorn and Sham Bargains

Sometimes a gift promisor, such as Aunt Tillie, will try to turn the unenforceable promise of a gift into an enforceable bargain by reciting purported consideration. For example, many form contracts will include language such as, "for valuable consideration, the receipt of which is hereby acknowledged . . . ," which in times past might have been given legal effect. However, the modern approach to consideration treats this recital as mere peppercorn, which has no effect on the enforceability of the promise. A mere pretense of a bargain or sham recital of consideration is ineffective, as consideration.

The challenge comes in distinguishing between peppercorn or sham consideration on one hand and a questionable, but real, bargain on the other. The answer ultimately depends on the parties' intent, which can generally be determined by the circumstances. If the promisor truly seems to be desirous of that which is bargained for, then it's likely real consideration. On the other hand, it the promisee doesn't seem to care whether or not he or she actually gets the purported consideration, then it's likely peppercorn.

In some respects, it might seem unreasonable to preclude the promisor from using a recital of consideration to make a gift promise enforceable. However, the promisor can always make the gift effective by simply delivering it. Remember, the doctrine of consideration only applies to "executory" promises—those that have not yet been performed. After a gift has been delivered, the lack of consideration is irrelevant. The requirement of "real" consideration simply precludes the promisee from enforcing the promise of a gift through the legal system.

Statutory Exceptions to the Rules on Consideration

The above common law "rules" regarding consideration are of course subject to exception to the extent any given state has enacted a contrary statute. For example, New York General Obligations Law § 5-1105 provides that:

> A promise in writing and signed by the promisor or by his agent
> shall not be denied effect as a valid contractual obligation on the

ground that consideration for the promise is past or executed, if the consideration is expressed in the writing and is proved to have been given or performed and would be a valid consideration but for the time when it was given or performed.

Under this particular statute, a written recital makes what would otherwise be deemed past consideration fully effective. As explained in lesson 1, any full coverage of unique, exceptional statutes of this sort is beyond the scope of this course. However, you should generally be aware of the existence of such statutes.

"Consideration" under UCC Article 2 and the CISG

You may have noticed that we have not yet talked about sales of goods in our treatment of consideration. This is because the doctrine is largely irrelevant in a sale of goods. One might say that consideration is not required under Article 2 or the CISG—indeed, there is no express requirement in either. Or one might simply say that there is no need for such a requirement, because it is inherent in the nature of a "sale" of goods. Either way "consideration" is not generally an issue under either of these statutes.

The Basic Rule of Consideration

We can now state a reasonably detailed version of the basic rule regarding consideration.

Summary of Basic Rule: consideration[11]

- A contract requires consideration;
  - Consideration must be "bargained for" and must take the form of either:
    - A specified performance; or
    - A return promise of specified performance.
  - Consideration is bargained for if it is, in fact, sought by the promisor in exchange for a promise and given by the promisee in exchange for that promise.

---

[11] This basic rule is reflected in Restatement (Second) of Contracts §§ 17, 71 (including comment b), 75 and 79.

> - If bargained for, consideration is not subject to any further test for adequacy; however,
>
> - Consideration must be "real" and not a mere pretense or sham—irrespective of any formal recitations.
>
> ○ Absent consideration, an executory promise is not legally enforceable; however,
>
> - The lack of consideration has no effect after performance or delivery of a gift.

APPLYING THE RULES

Problem 1: Consider again the facts of example 4-1. Can Joe enforce Jane's promise? Consider how each side (Joe arguing in favor of enforcement and Jane arguing against it) would attempt to characterize the transaction and each of the arguments that might support his or her position.

Problem 2: Anna Sacks Feinberg had worked for Pfeiffer Co. for 37 years, attaining the positions of bookkeeper, office manager, and assistant treasurer during that time. She had received a salary, bonuses, and shares of company stock in exchange for her services. At a board meeting of Pfeiffer Co. on December 27, 1947, the President of the company noted the many years of skilled, devoted and faithful service by Ms. Feinberg to the corporation. He further stated that

> although [the board] sincerely hoped and desired that Ms. Feinberg would continue in her present position for as long as she felt able, nevertheless, in view of the length of service which she has contributed provision should be made to afford her retirement privileges and benefits which should become a firm obligation of the corporation to be available to her whenever she should see fit to retire from active duty, however many years in the future such retirement may become effective.

On the basis thereof, Ms. Feinberg's current salary was raised by $50 per month, and the board resolved to pay her $200 per month upon retirement, at whatever time she might elect to retire. This latter promise of $200 per month was made with "the distinct understanding that the retirement plan is merely being adopted at the present time in order to afford Mrs. Feinberg security for the future and in the hope that her active services will continue with the corporation for many years to come." Ms. Feinberg was told of the pension plan the same day, and was told that she could retire and begin taking pension payments that very day, or she could work as long as she wished, after which she would begin receiving the pension.

Ms. Feinberg was delightfully surprised by the gesture and indicated that she would have continued her employment in any event, but very much appreciated the promised pension plan. As it turned out, she worked for an additional year and a half, after which she retired, and the company began paying her $200 per month, as promised. After making such payments for seven years, the company's lawyers and accountants indicated that they were not legally required, and the company stopped making the payments. Ms. Feinberg sued to collect the payments. Is she entitled to enforce the company's promise to continue to pay her $200 per month for life? Explain the likely arguments on each side and the likely outcome. Is there anything Pfeiffer could have done differently to make it easier for Ms. Feinberg to enforce the promise?

This problem is based loosely on the facts of *Feinberg v. Pfeiffer Co.*, 322 S.W. 2d 163 (Ct. App. Mo. 1959). If, however, you choose to read the case at this juncture, it is important to distinguish between two different theories that might have supported recovery by Ms. Feinberg—one based on an actual contract, fully supported by consideration; and another based on Ms. Feinberg's reliance on her employer's promise. This current problem asks only for your analysis of the former. We will, however, return to this case with example 7-2 in lesson 7, at which time we will add additional facts and analysis.

Lesson 5: Further Distinguishing Between Bargains and Gifts

Objectives and Expected Learning Outcomes

In this lesson, you should learn to distinguish bilateral from unilateral contacts, along with a number of corollaries to the basic rule of consideration. These corollaries address additional distinctions between unenforceable gifts and enforceable bargains. They include rules addressing contracts intended to settle disputes; proposals in which it may be difficult to determine whether a contract or gift has been offered; circumstances in which the relationship between an offered bargain and the requested performance is unclear, and attempts to modify an on-going "employment-at-will" relationship. Each of these circumstances will also afford opportunities to develop a deeper understanding of the content and application of the basic rule, while applying these new corollaries to that basic rule.

Unilateral and Bilateral Contracts

Thus far, we have focused on the basic requirement of consideration evidencing a real "bargain." In fact, such consideration comes in two basic forms: (1) performance; or (2) a promise of performance. While seemingly subtle, at first blush, the difference between these two forms can be very important.

In a unilateral contract, only one person makes a promise. The promisee of that promise does not actually commit to doing anything. Of course, the promisee can only enforce the promise if he or she performs the "bargained for" performance. However, a failure to perform by the promisee is not a breach of contract, because the promisee never actually "promised" to perform. *Hamer v. Sidway*, in example 4-3, provides an excellent example of a unilateral contract.

Uncle William promised to pay his nephew for the nephew's "performance" according to a specified standard of conduct (i.e. refraining from certain disfavored conduct). However, the nephew never actually promised such performance, nor was his promise sought by Uncle William. Instead, Uncle William was bargaining for actual performance, and that's exactly what the nephew provided. Had the nephew gone out drinking, smoking, and gambling on his 20th birthday, he would not have been entitled to enforce

Uncle William's promise. However, he would not have been in breach of contract, because he never actually promised anything.

In summary, in a **unilateral contract**, only one party makes a promise, and, through that promise, seeks only the performance of the promisee. Unilateral contracts are more typical in informal or family settings, like *Hamer v. Sidway*. However, we will see a few examples of unilateral contracts in business settings as well.

The more typical contract is one in which each party makes one or more promises—a bilateral contract. In effect, each party is both a promisor and a promisee with respect to at least one promise. Thus, the identity of the promisor and promisee will depend on the promise at issue. We have seen a number of examples of bilateral contracts thus far. In both *Hawkins* and *Sullivan*, a doctor promised a certain surgical result in exchange for the patient's promise to pay a certain amount. When the doctor failed to perform as promised, this did not simply absolve the patient of the obligation to pay the promised amount, this failure also provided the patient with an affirmative legal claim against the doctor for breach of contract.

The key difference between a unilateral and bilateral contract is that both parties are bound to promises in the latter, and each may be liable for a breach of such promise. In summary, each party bargains for at least one promise by the other party in a **bilateral contract**. Each party therefore gains the benefit of knowing the other will do something in the future and further knowing that the other's promise is legally enforceable. This mutually binding nature of a bilateral contract is what makes such contracts particularly valuable in a business setting. However, bilateral contracts can also raise a few uniquely challenging questions, which we will address both later in this chapter and in future materials throughout the course.

As a matter of **consideration**, both a unilateral and a bilateral contract require consideration. However, a return **performance** will serve as consideration to bind the promisor's promise in a unilateral contract, while a return **promise** will serve as consideration to bind a promisor in a bilateral contract. The rule can be summarized as follows.

> **Summary of Basic Rule**: "consideration" as to unilateral versus bilateral contracts[12]
>
> • Both a unilateral and a bilateral contract require consideration.
>   ○ The promisor in a unilateral contract bargains for performance.
>   ○ A promisor in a bilateral contract bargains for a promise.

Settlement Contracts

A settlement contract is unique in that it typically arises out of an earlier dispute. The prior dispute may have been based on contract, tort, or other liability. However, the "settlement" brings the dispute to an end. In some circumstances, such a settlement of a pending action may take the form of a court judgment or arbitration award (either or both of which you may address in a course on procedure). However, our focus here is on a settlement as a contract. As such, a settlement contract is generally enforceable, just like any other contract—and perhaps even more so.

The problem with settlement agreements is that one or more of the parties may subsequently experience what is often called "buyer's remorse." What seemed like a good deal at the time of the agreement, no longer looks so great—often because the party has learned something new since agreeing to the settlement. This phenomenon is particularly prevalent in the context of a settlement in that the basic nature of most settlements is such that neither party is entirely happy with the bargain, because it typically represents a compromise of sorts. If parties to settlements were subsequently able to change their minds, those settlements would have little, if any value, in removing the disputes from the formal justice system, and courts would likely grind to a halt. Thus, it should not be surprising that the law might often tend to favor enforcement of settlement agreements. The application of the doctrine of consideration to settlements is arguably consistent with such a pro-enforcement bias.

Example 5-1: *Fiege v. Boehm*

Hilda Boehm sued Louis Fiege for his alleged breach of a settlement agreement between them. Boehm had originally claimed that Fiege was the father of her unborn child and

---

[12] This basic rule is reflected in Restatement (Second) of Contracts §§ 71(3) and 75.

threatened legal action on that basis. Prior to Boehm instituting that action, the parties settled the claim. In exchange for Boehm dropping the legal action against him, Fiege promised to make certain payments to Boehm relating to the birth and support of the child.

After the birth of the child, Fiege learned, through a blood test, that the child was not his (this fact was not disputed) and stopped making the promised payments. Boehm then brought the contact action, seeking the unpaid promised payments. Fiege defended by asserting that the settlement agreement was not enforceable because it lacked consideration. Fiege argued that Boehm had not given up anything in exchange for Fiege's promise, because she had no right to require him to pay for the child in the first place. Fiege's promised payment was, therefore, nothing more than a gift.

Boehm successfully countered, however, that she had given up her original claim in good faith, without knowing that Fiege was not the father, and the fact that she was wrong should have no effect on the validity of the consideration. In agreeing with Boehm, the court ruled that, as long the original claim is made honestly, based on a good faith belief in its truth, a forbearance to assert such a claim is valid consideration to support a settlement agreement—even if the claim is later discovered to be false. Thus, Boehm was entitled to the remaining payments promised by Fiege in the settlement agreement.[13]

In *Hamer v. Sidway*, in example 4-6, we focused on the fact that the nephew refrained from conduct in which he otherwise had a legal right to engage. In contrast, prior to the settlement agreement, Boehm had no right to demand payment from Fiege, so she technically gave up nothing by foregoing her original claim. However, her forbearance to assert the claim was nevertheless deemed to be valid consideration, because she honestly believed her claim to be valid. This rule may well be influenced by a general policy in favor of enforcement of settlement agreements. As a practical

---

[13] Fiege v. Boehm, 210 Md. 352, 123 A.2d 316 (1956).

matter, settlements are important in bringing disputes to a conclusion, without the need for full court proceedings.

There remains one potentially troubling issue with settlements. To what extent must the original claimant's subject "good faith" belief also be objectively reasonable? In *Fiege v. Boehm*, the court required only that Boehm's claim not be "frivolous, vexatious, or unlawful," seemingly focused almost entirely on her subjective purpose. The court nevertheless separately suggests a minimum requirement of "a reasonable degree of intelligence," and some suggest both a subjective and objective requirement. The restatement of the rule seems to provide for proof of either subjective or objective uncertainty—either of which makes the settlement agreement fully enforceable—and that characterization of the rule is summarized below.

Summary of Basic Rule: "consideration" as to settlement contracts[14]

- Forbearance of a claim or defense constitutes valid consideration—even if the claim or defense is itself later found to be invalid—if:

  o The claim or defense was objectively uncertain based on reasonable doubt as to the facts or applicable law; or

  o The claim or defense was subjectively asserted in good faith.

"If" Promises—Offers of a Conditional Gift or Unilateral Bargain?

In *Fiege v. Boehm*, it would have been very clear that Louis Fiege was offering an actual bargain if he had said to Hilda Boehm, "if you will drop your public claim that I am the child's father, I will pay you for the related costs." In *Hamer v. Sidway*, in example 4-6, it was also reasonably clear that Uncle William was actually bargaining for his nephew to behave in a certain way. "If" the nephew refrained from certain conduct, the uncle promised to pay for this sought after behavior. Under some circumstances, however, it may be less clear that the promisor is in fact bargaining for the referenced performance. Consider the following example.

Example 5-2: *Kirksey v. Kirksey*

Brother Kirksey wrote a letter to the widow of his brother, who was living 60 miles away with her children. He

---

[14] This basic rule is reflected in Restatement (Second) of Contracts § 74 (1). The restatement actually states the rule in the negative, allowing for two exceptions.

proposed to her "If you will come down and see me, I will let you have a place to raise your family, and I have more open land than I can tend; and on the account of your situation, and that of your family, I feel like I want you and the children to do well." Soon after receiving the letter, widow Kirksey abandoned her leasehold and moved her family to her brother-in-laws residence, where she and her children were given a place to live and land to tend. After a period of time, she was required to leave.

Widow Kirksey brought an action for breach of the promise by her brother-in-law. The appellate court ultimately rejected her contract claim because it lacked consideration. Instead, the court characterized the promise as a mere gratuity or gift.[15]

The court reasoned that brother Kirksey was not bargaining for his sister-in-law and her children to come and join him, but was merely stating an obvious "condition" necessary for the making of his intended gift. As such, the promise did not reflect a true "bargain" and was not enforceable. Notably, the court must have characterized the widow's initial presence on brother Kirksey's property as in the nature of a leasehold, which he could decline to continue providing. If the interest had been of a more permanent nature, then it would have been a completed gift instead of an executory promise, and the lack of consideration would have been irrelevant.

In some cases, it may be difficult to distinguish between an offer of a unilateral bargain and a proposal to make a gift—conditioned upon some action by the recipient that is necessary in order to receive the gift. The key is to focus on the "bargain" element of the proposal (or the lack thereof).

Mixed Motives in Performance as Consideration

In order to support a promise, consideration must be given "in exchange for" that promise. However, a promisor may sometimes have mixed motives for making a promise, or a promisee may have mixed motives for providing the requested performance. Consider the following hypothetical example.

---

[15] Kirksey v. Kirksey, 8 Ala. 131 (1845).

Example 5-3: Jane is an art critic and newspaper reporter, and Mark is a new artist, whose work is just beginning to be noticed. Mark would very much like to get Jane to place one of his paintings in her personal art collection, because it would provide excellent promotional exposure for his work. Jane would very much like to get an exclusive interview with Mark, as an "up and coming" artist. Jane promises to pay $5,000 to Mark for one of his paintings. Does the painting serve as consideration to bind Jane to her promise to pay $5,000?

Yes, as long as Jane bargained for the painting and Mark provided it to Jane in exchange for her promised payment, it does not matter that Jane was also hoping to get an exclusive interview or that Mark was also hoping he would gain additional recognition for his art through its inclusion in Jane's collection.

As this example illustrates, mixed motives don't matter. It is unnecessary to determine which motives (if any) predominate, as long as the consideration is bargained for by the promisor and given in exchange for the promise by the promisee. This rule can be summarized as follows.

Summary of Basic Rule: "consideration" and "mixed motives"[16]

- Consideration must have been bargained for by the promisor and given in exchange for the promise by the promisee, and

  ○ Additional or "mixed" motives of the promisor or promisee do not affect the bargain.

Consideration Involving Others Not Party to the Contract

Another important corollary to the basic rule involves the nature of any promise or performance as consideration. We can return to *Batsakis v. Demotsis* in example 4-4 in order to illustrate the issue. In the actual case, the performance by Batsakis in delivering 500,000 drachmae to Demotsis served as consideration such that Batsakis could enforce the promise by Demotsis to pay Batsakis $2,000, plus interest. However, suppose Demotsis had, instead, bargained for Batsakis to give the money to Jones—would this

---

[16] This basic rule is reflected in Restatement (Second) of Contracts §§ 74 and 81.

make any difference in the ability of Batsakis to enforce against Demotsis? No, it ultimately does not matter if the performance of the promisee runs back to the promisor or runs to a third party—as long as the promisor gets what he or she bargained for.

In another variation, what if Batsakis had not been in Greece, but had a brother who was. Instead of bargaining for performance by Batsakis, Demotsis might have said "if your brother will give me 500,000 drachmae now, I will repay you $2,000 later." Again, the promise by Demotsis is fully enforceable—as long as the brother provides the requested 500,000 drachmae pursuant to the bargain sought by Demotsis. Thus, the involvement of third parties, as either performers or beneficiaries, will not typically affect the enforceability of a contract. Third parties can raise other interesting issues. However, we will address those much later in Chapter 10.

Summary of Basic Rule: "consideration" to and from third parties[17]

- Consideration may be given to or provided by either the promisee or a third party or parties.

Bargaining between an Employer and an "at-will" Employee

The default assumption in the United States is that employment is "at-will." Either the employer or the employee may legally terminate their contractual relationship any time, for any reason (even for no reason at all). The employer and employee may change this "at-will" relationship by contract, and any employment relationship is, to some degree limited by state and federal statutes (e.g., statutes precluding termination of employment for certain precluded discriminatory reasons). However, the basic default rule is one of "at-will" employment—present work in exchange for present pay, with no promise of any continuing relationship.

> **Agreements Not to Compete**
> An employee will sometimes be required to sign an agreement not to compete with the employer once the employment relationship has ended. An employer that has done substantial training or conveyed important company secrets to the employee in the course of the relationship may have legitimate interests to protect. However, such agreements also raise a number of public policy issues, which are addressed later in Chapter 5. Here, the basic issue is "consideration."

---

[17] This basic rule is reflected in Restatement (Second) of Contracts § 71(4).

Of course, an employment relationship will often go on for a very long time, because each of the parties is largely content with the relationship. The relationship will also often change over time, such as the employee taking on greater responsibility in exchange for greater pay by the employer. However, an employer may sometimes attempt to change the nature of the bargain without giving anything new in return. In some respects, this is the "flip side" of the issue faced in problem 2, lesson 4, and the case of *Feinberg v. Pfeiffer*. Consider the example below.

Example 5-4: *Lake Land Employment Group v. Columber*

Lee Columber was employed by Lake Land as an "at-will" employee. After a period of time, Columber was approached by his employer and told to sign a "non-competition" agreement. Upon termination of the employment relationship, Columber began competing with his former employer, and the employer sued.

Columber defended by asserting a lack of consideration for his agreement to the agreement not to compete. Nothing about his job had changed before or after his signature of the agreement. He was an at-will employee before signing and remained an "at will" employee afterwards. Thus, the employer had provided no new consideration for his promise, and it was unenforceable. The employer, however, asserted that it had provided consideration by foregoing its legal right to terminate Columber in exchange for his promise not to compete.

A majority of the appellate court ruled in favor of the employer, while the dissent opined that the employer had foregone nothing, because it had retained the right terminate Columber any time thereafter.[18]

The majority finds consideration in the employer's forbearance of its right to fire the employee "at-will." In contrast, the dissent points out that noth-

---

[18] Lake Land Employment Group of Akron, LLC v. Columber, 101 Ohio St.3d 242, 804 N.E.2d 27 (2004).

ing has changed, because the employee remains subject to being fired at the whim of the employer any time after signing the agreement. Some courts have tried to "finesse" the issue in ruling in favor of an employer by only finding consideration where the employment relationship has continued for some substantial period. However, this presents its own sort of challenges with uncertainty and indefiniteness. Arguably, the more fundamental problem here is not about "consideration," but about "consent." Has Columber truly "consented" to anything, or was his signature "coerced"? Should that matter if the employer had a perfectly legal right to engage in such "coercion"? We will return to a series of similar questions in Chapter 5. For our purposes here, the key point is that state courts are split on this issue in the context of at-will employment, as generally reflected by the majority and dissent in the case above.

APPLYING THE RULES

Problem 1: Consider again the facts of example 4-1. Do the materials covered in this lesson add anything to your analysis of whether Joe can enforce Jane's promise? By now, your analysis of the question of consideration under this example should be very complete.

Problem 2: Tom was a devoted paragliding enthusiast, who had been enjoying the sport for years. A few months prior, he had been planning to launch his paraglider from a new and spectacular location. As it turned out, the winds that day were not as favorable as he would have liked. However, Tom decided to launch anyway, figuring that his skills and his paraglider were sufficient to handle the conditions. As it turned out, Tom crashed and was injured. Tom's initial instinct was that it was his own fault, and he had no one to blame but himself. His paraglider had inexplicably dropped precipitously at an inopportune moment, but he thought this was most probably attributable to the unfavorable winds, though of course one could never be certain about this sort of thing.

Tom's friend, Tina, had recently graduated from law school, and had just passed the bar and been admitted to practice. Tina had decided to "hang out a shingle," and practice on her own, so she really needed work. She told Tom that he really ought to bring a claim against PowerGlide, the manufacturer of his paraglider. Tom was not particularly interested in bringing the suit himself, but he wanted to help out his friend, Tina. He also figured that it was at least possible that his paraglider had caused the crash.

Tina contacted PowerGlide and engaged in settlement negotiations on Tom's behalf. After a series of negotiations, PowerGlide sent Tom a letter in which it stated "if you will sign and return the enclosed release, PowerGlide will pay you $10,000 within 30 days of receipt." Tina was thrilled, because she was entitled to one third of the amount, and Tom was happy to sign the release as recommended by Tina, his friend and attorney. Tom signed and returned the release, as requested. The release simply waived and released any and all claims against PowerGlide related to the accident, and said nothing more. Soon thereafter, PowerGlide learned from another friend of Tom's that Tom actually believed his accident was most likely his own fault. As a result, PowerGlide decided not to pay the $10,000.

Can Tom enforce PowerGlide's promise to pay him $10,000? If so, is his contract with PowerGlide a unilateral or bilateral contract?

Problem 3: Sara had been employed by Gamma for two years as an engineer. Her employment was not subject to any other specific terms, other than her compensation, benefits, and basic job responsibilities. During the middle of a major project, on which she was the lead engineer and her specific expertise was crucial to the success of the project, Sara approached her employer, Gamma, with a proposal. Her friend, Sam, was entering his final year in engineering school, and he would need a job upon graduation. Sara explained that she really wanted to work with Sam—one way or another—and she thought he would be a perfect fit for Gamma. She therefore sought a promise from Gamma that it would hire Sam upon graduation, further indicating that she would seek other employment if Gamma was unwilling to make such a promise. Gamma made the requested promise to Sara. However, when Sam graduated, Gamma refused to hire him. Coincidentally, the above described major project had been completed.

Sara seeks your wise counsel. Does she have a claim against Gamma for breach of contract? Does it matter that Gamma's promise to Sara involves Sam, who was not part of the original negotiations? You need not worry about quantifying damages (which would likely be quite difficult). This question solely asks whether Gamma is bound to its promise, as a matter of contract.

Lesson 6: Consideration in a Business Context

Objectives and Expected Learning Outcomes

In this lesson, you should learn more about the basic nature of a "bilateral" contract in a business context. You will learn that, in a bilateral contract, each party must be bound in some manner, or its promise will be deemed "illusory" and, therefore, unenforceable. You will also learn that a necessary promise may often be implied based on the circumstances, thereby providing the necessary consideration to bind the parties. Finally, you will briefly encounter the doctrine of consideration, as applied to contract modification—a subject that is more fully explored later. As with the previous lesson, you should also continue to develop a deeper understanding of the basic rule along the way.

As indicated in the last lesson, bilateral contracts are far more common in a business context than unilateral contracts. Most businesses are bargaining for, among other things, predictability and certainty in order to pursue commercial objectives. In most cases, each party will make one or more reasonably clear promises to the other. While the precise content of a given promise may be open to question (we will deal with this issue in Chapter 6), each party has definitely promised to do or refrain from doing something. However, on in some cases, it may be less clear whether one of the parties has actually promised anything. If the party's purported promise does not bind it to at least "something," the promise is said to be "illusory."

The Issue of "Illusory" Promises

An "illusory" promise is, essentially, a promise that cannot be breached. If your professor says, "I promise that I will either show up for our next class or I will not to show up," the promise is "illusory." If he or she shows up, the promise has been kept. If not, the promise has also been kept. The promise is impossible to breach, because there are no possible outcomes other than those "promised." While this initial example is rather obvious, some are not so clear.

In some contracts, the promisor will want to condition his or her promise upon the occurrence of an event. Such "conditions" are more fully addressed in Chapter 7. However, our focus here is on a specific type of condition and its potential to render a promise illusory. If a home buyer promises to buy the house in question, "subject to" a satisfactory termite report from a pest control expert, it is pretty easy to determine whether or not the report is "objectively" satisfactory. A report indicating the presence of termites would be unsatisfactory, while one indicating the absence of any termites would be satisfactory. If the termite inspection was not satisfactory, the buyer would not be be required to perform the promise to purchase the house. These are considered "objective" standards, because any "reasonable" person would almost certainly agree. However, a "subjective" standard is potentially more problematic because is more personally individualized.

What if a buyer promised to buy the house in question, "subject to" a satisfactory personal inspection by the buyer? Does this provide for an objective standard? Not likely. What will the buyer deem personally satisfactory? The problem here is that the buyer seems to be suggesting a "subjective" standard, which the buyer is entitled to define. In effect, the buyer has a free way out of the deal based on a stated lack of subjective satisfaction, which is quite difficult to disprove (short of perhaps brain surgery or psychoanalysis). Consider how the court dealt with this challenge in the following case.

Example 6-1: *Mattei v. Hopper*

Mattei contracted with Hopper to purchase her land. Mattei planned to build a shopping center on the land, and his obligation to purchase the land from Hopper was "subject to" his realtor obtaining tenant leases that Mattei found "satisfactory." Mattei did not want to go through with the purchase unless he was confident that he could generate sufficient tenant lease revenue to support the shopping center project, and he had 120 days to determine whether the realtor had obtained "satisfactory" leases.

Prior to the expiration of the 120 days, Hopper notified Mattei that she no longer intended to perform her promise to convey the property. Mattei replied that he was, in fact, fully satisfied with the tenant leases already obtained, and he proposed to tender the purchase price, as agreed. However, Hopper refused to tender the deed, and Mattei sued (in this case, for damages, though he likely could have requested specific performance in this real property transaction).

Hopper argued that the contract was unenforceable, because Mattei's promise was "illusory." As such, Hopper's promise was not supported by consideration and, therefore, unenforceable. A purported bilateral contract in which one of the promises is said to be "illusory" may also be characterized as lacking "mutuality" in that only one of the two parties is actually bound to a promise.

> **"Illusory" contracts lacking "mutuality"**
> Remember, this issue of mutuality applies only to bilateral contracts, because bilateral contracts require a promise from both parties. In a unilateral contract, only one of the parties is ever bound to a promise, so the issue of mutuality never arises.

However, the court agreed with Mattei that his right to determine whether the leases were "satisfactory" was limited by his exercise of "good faith" in doing so. Thus, he was fully bound, and his promise—which would have been breached had he failed to exercise good faith—was not illusory.[19]

The express terms of Mattei's conditional promise arguably did not include any limit on Mattei's ability to walk away from the deal, asserting that any leases his broker had obtained were "unsatisfactory." However, the court implied a term requiring Mattei to exercise "good faith" in determining whether any such leases were satisfactory. If Mattei failed to exercise good faith, then he would have breached the implied obligation. Thus, Mattei was fully bound to the contract. He was bound to a promise to exercise good faith, and he was bound to close, unless, he, "in good faith," found the leases unsatisfactory.

As a practical matter, it may of course be difficult to determine in some instances whether a party is exercising good faith. Absent unusual circumstances (e.g., in which Mattei simply says "I am deeming the leases unsatisfactory because I don't like you, Hopper"), the best evidence of "subjective" good faith may be "objective circumstances (e.g., a purported lack of satis-

---

[19] Mattei v. Hopper, 51 Cal.2d 119, 330 P.2d 625 (1958).

faction in the face of a fully leased up shopping center with all financially solid tenants). However, the implied obligation of "good faith" nevertheless provides a legal framework within which to conduct the analysis.

Another potentially illusory promise can be found in a contract in which one party is granted an exclusive right to do something for the other. Consider the following case in which Lucy, Lady Duff-Gordon, an English fashion designer, granted Otis Wood an exclusive right to market her designs and "indorsements" in the U.S.

FROM THE COURT

Wood v. Lucy, Lady Duff-Gordon

Court of Appeals of New York (1917)
222 N.Y. 88, 118 N.E. 214

CARDOZO, J.

The defendant styles herself "a creator of fashions." Her favor helps a sale. Manufacturers of dresses, millinery and like articles are glad to pay for a certificate of her approval. The things which she designs, fabrics, parasols and what not, have a new value in the public mind when issued in her name. She employed the plaintiff to help her to turn this vogue into money. He was to have the exclusive right, subject always to her approval, to place her indorsements on the designs of others. He was also to have the exclusive right to place her own designs on sale, or to license others to market them. In return, she was to have one-half of "all profits and revenues" derived from any contracts he might make. The exclusive right was to last at least one year from April 1, 1915, and thereafter from year to year unless terminated by notice of ninety days. The plaintiff says that he kept the contract on his part, and that the defendant broke it. She placed her indorsement on fabrics, dresses and millinery without his knowledge, and withheld the profits. He sues her for the damages, and the case comes here on demurrer.

> **Court of Appeals of New York**
> In most states, the Supreme Court is the highest appellate court. However, in New York, the Court of Appeals is the highest court, and this particular opinion was authored by one of its greatest luminaries, Benjamin Cardozo.

The agreement of employment is signed by both parties. It has a wealth of recitals. The defendant insists, however, that it lacks the elements of a contract. She says that the plaintiff does not bind himself to anything. It is true that he does not promise in so many words that he will use reasonable efforts to place the defendant's indorsements and market her designs. We think, however, that such a promise is fairly to be implied. The law has outgrown its primitive stage of formalism when the precise word was the sovereign talisman, and every slip was fatal. It takes a broader view today. A promise may be lacking, and yet the whole writing may be "instinct with an obligation," imperfectly expressed [citation omitted]. If that is so, there is a contract.

The implication of a promise here finds support in many circumstances. The defendant gave an exclusive privilege. She was to have no right for at least a year to place her own indorsements or market her own designs except through the agency of the plaintiff. The acceptance of the exclusive agency was an assumption of its duties [citation omitted]. We are not to suppose that one party was to be placed at the mercy of the other [citation omitted]. Many other terms of the agreement point the same way. We are told at the outset by way of recital that "the said Otis F. Wood possesses a business organization adapted to the placing of such indorsements as the said Lucy, Lady Duff-Gordon has approved." The implication is that the plaintiff's business organization will be used for the purpose for which it is adapted. But the terms of the defendant's compensation are even more sinificant. Her sole compensation for the grant of an exclusive agency is to be one-half of all the profits resulting from the plaintiff's efforts. Unless he gave his efforts, she could never get anything. Without an implied promise, the transaction cannot have such business "efficacy as both parties must have intended that at all events it should have" [citation omitted]. But the contract does not stop there. The plaintiff goes on to promise that he will account monthly for all moneys received by him, and that he will take out all such patents and copyrights and trademarks as may in his judgment be necessary to protect the rights and articles affected by the agreement. It is true, of course, as the Appellate Division has said, that if he was under no duty to try to market designs or to place certificates of indorsement, his promise to account for profits or take out copyrights would be valueless. But in determining the intention of the parties, the promise has a value.

It helps to enforce the conclusion that the plaintiff had some duties. His promise to pay the defendant one-half of the profits and revenues resulting from the exclusive agency and to render accounts monthly, was a promise to use reasonable efforts to bring profits and revenues into existence. . . .

The judgment of the Appellate Division should be reversed, and the order of the Special Term affirmed, with costs in the Appellate Division and in this court.

CUDDEBACK, MCLAUGHLIN and ANDREWS, JJ., concur; HISCOCK, Ch. J., CHASE and CRANE, JJ., dissent.

Judgment reversed, etc.

CASE QUESTIONS

(1) Consider what was promised by each party, as well as what was not expressly promised, but was implied by the court.

    a. What did Duff-Gordon expressly promise Wood?

    b. What did Wood expressly promise Duff-Gordon? Why wasn't this express promise sufficient to bind Duff-Gordon?

    c. The court implied that Wood had also made another promise to Duff-Gordon. What was the nature of that promise?

(2) As with many of Judge Cardozo's opinions, the logic at first seems beyond reproach, and yet he barely commanded a majority of the court (the decision was 4-3, as indicated above). Can you find the potential flaws in his analysis?

    a. Judge Cardozo suggests that the written document is "instinct with an obligation," but, in reaching his observation, hasn't he already implied that the purpose of the transaction is for Wood to generate profits? Doesn't this raise a problem of circularity—assuming the conclusion in order to reach it?

b. Can you think of any other intent Otis Wood might have had in mind in seeking an exclusive right to these designs and indorsements? What if he solely sought the rights in order to avoid competition with other designs he marketed, or he solely sought them in order to improve his own business stature? Might such a purpose have been characterized as bad faith?

(3) In any event, the rule arising from this case is fully established today. We will revisit a few additional applications of the rule in Chapter 6. Our purpose here is solely to address the question of potentially "illusory" promises.

The court implies a promise by Wood to use "reasonable efforts" to market the designs and indorsements of Lucy, Lady Duff-Gordon, so as to generate profits to be shared pursuant to the agreement. Thus, each of the parties has made fully binding promises. If Wood had failed to make any efforts to market her designs or indorsements, he would have breached his obligation. An "implied" obligation is every bit as binding as one that is expressly stated in a written document. As a result, Wood's promise to share profits is not "illusory," and the parties are "mutually" bound to the bilateral contract at issue.

Avoiding "Illusory" Promises in a Sale of Goods Transaction

As noted in lesson 4, consideration issues do not typically arise in a sale of goods transaction. However, Article 2 also implies a binding promise in a manner similar to the common law. In a manner similar to that of *Wood v. Lucy*, UCC Article 2 implies a necessary promise in cases of exclusive dealing. **STOP NOW and READ UCC § 2-306(2) below.**

UCC § 2-306(2)

(2) A lawful agreement by either the seller or the buyer for exclusive dealing in the kind of goods concerned imposes unless otherwise agreed an obligation by the seller to use best efforts to supply the goods and by the buyer to use best efforts to promote their sale.

While *Wood v. Lucy* involved designs and indorsements, one could easily imagine a very similar case involving the sale of dresses, themselves.

> **Example 6-2:** DG, a New York maker of dresses, contracted to sell dresses to Wood, a Florida women's clothing distributor. DG granted Wood an exclusive right to purchase and sell DG dresses in Florida. The contract is silent with respect to either DG's obligation to provide dresses to Wood, or Wood's obligations to generate sales (and, thereby, purchases from DG) of DG dresses in Florida.
>
> DG will be deemed to have impliedly promised to use best efforts to supply the necessary dresses to Wood, and Wood will be deemed to have impliedly promised to use best efforts generate sales of such dresses.

Note that this promise of "best efforts" is only implied in the absence of an expression of contrary intent by the parties. As such, this rule is called a "default" rule, in that the parties may agree otherwise. In contrast, the obligation of good faith is a "mandatory" rule, which cannot be changed by the parties.

Article 2 also employs "good faith" in a manner analogous to that employed in Mattei v. Hopper above. Specifically, a contract in which the quantity of goods sold is to be measured by the conduct of one of parties might be thought "illusory," absent some means of limiting the discretion of that party in setting the quantity—especially if the contract might call for no quantity at all.

> **"Default" Rules/Terms**
> The vast majority of contract terms implied under UCC Article 2 are "defaults." This concept of terms implied via default rules is addressed most fully in Chapter 6. However, we will encounter a number of other default rules along the way.

An "output" contract is one in which the seller promises to sell to the buyer all of seller's output. A "requirements" contract is one in which the buyer promises to buy from seller all of buyer's requirements. Do you see the potential problem in determining the "quantity" term in this sort of contract? **STOP NOW and READ UCC § 2-306(1) below.**

UCC § 2-306(1)

(1) A term which measures the quantity by the output of the seller or the requirements of the buyer means such actual output or requirements as may occur in good faith, except that no quantity unreasonably disproportionate to any stated estimate or in the absence of a stated estimate to any normal or otherwise comparable prior output or requirements may be tendered or demanded.

The seller sets the quantity term based on its "output," which must be generated in "good faith." An output contract will often involve scrap or other incidental output generated as a result of some other activity. For example, a meat packing plant, primarily engaged in producing and selling meat products, might also sell its "output" of hides generated as a byproduct of its meat packing business.

> **Example 6-3: *Laredo Hides v. H & H Meat Packing***
>
> H & H Meat Products was a Texas meat processing and packing business. It sold cattle hides as a by-product of this business. Laredo Hides, also a Texas business, purchased cattle hides and sold them to tanneries in Mexico. Laredo Hides agreed to purchase the entire cattle hide production of H & H Meat Products during a ten month period in 1972.
>
> While the contract did not expressly provide for any specific quantity of hides, UCC Article 2-306(1) provides that the parties are obligated, respectively, to sell and purchase the hide "output" of H & H, as may occur in the good faith operation of its meat processing and packing business.[20]

While an "output" contract is measured by the seller's good faith "output," a requirements contract is measured by the buyer's good faith "requirements." For example, an airline might agree to purchase all of the jet fuel required for refueling its aircraft at certain specified airports.

---

[20] Laredo Hides Co., Inc. v. H & H Meat Products Co., Inc., 513 S.W.2d 210 (Tex. Civ. App. 1974).

Example 6-4: *Eastern Air Lines v. Gulf Oil*

Eastern Air Lines contracted with Gulf Oil to purchase all of Eastern's jet fuel requirements at certain specified airports for a period of five years. The agreement also provided a price adjustment mechanism intended to reflect changes over the term of the agreement in the cost of crude oil used to produce jet fuel. Approximately two years into the term of the relationship, Gulf sought to get out of the contract, because its costs had risen beyond those adequately addressed by the price adjustment mechanism. One of Gulf's arguments was that Eastern's promise was illusory and the contract, therefore, lacked mutuality, because Eastern was not obligated to purchase any specific quantity of jet fuel.

The court rejected Gulf's argument, relying on UCC 2-306(1). Gulf was fully obligated to purchase its fuel requirements, as might occur in good faith at the designated locations.[21]

The CISG does not expressly address either of the above issues. However, it would likely reach similar conclusions by reference to the general principle of good faith, as provided in Article 7(1). Thus, if the buyer in example 6-3 was itself located in Mexico (where the hides were ultimately being sold), the contract would be governed by the CISG, but would likely impose the same basic quantity obligation on the parties. The CISG would not, in any event, address either issue as one of "consideration" in view the absence of any mention of consideration in the CISG and the doctrine's distinctly common law roots.

Thus far, our discussion has focused entirely on the initial bargain. However, bargains are often changed or "modified."

---

21 Eastern Air Lines, Inc. v. Gulf Oil Corp. 415 F.Supp. 429 (S.D. Fla. 1975).

Consideration in the Context of Contract Modification

The common law generally requires consideration to support a new or modified promise in much the same manner it requires consideration to support the original promise. This is often called the "pre-existing duty rule," to emphasize that mere performance of a "pre-existing duty" will not serve as consideration to bind the other party to a new or modified promise.

> **Example 6-5:** Nancy agrees to do excavation work in Dan's back yard in for $1,000. As the work progresses, Nancy wishes she had charged more and asks Dan if he will pay her an extra $500 to complete the work. Dan agrees. However, when Nancy completes the work, Dan refuses to pay more than the original $1,000.
>
> While the original contract was fully supported by consideration on each side (excavation work in exchange for money), the additional $500 promised by Dan was not. Thus, Nancy is legally entitled only to the original $1,000.

This corollary to the basic rule of consideration, as applied in the context of contract modification, functions in much the same manner is the basic rule. In effect, the original consideration is "past consideration" with respect to any subsequent modification. As such, the original consideration will not serve to bind or make enforceable any new or modified promise.

Summary of Basic Rule: "consideration" in the context of modification[22]

- Any new promise arising in the modification of a contract must, itself, be supported by new consideration.
  - The original consideration or "pre-existing duty" will not support the new promise.

---

[22] This basic rule is reflected in Restatement (Second) of Contracts § 73.

The above rule does not apply to a sale of goods transaction. UCC Article 2 does not require consideration. A modification requires only the consent of the parties to be binding. **STOP NOW and READ UCC § 2-209(1) below**.

UCC § 2-209(1)

(1) An agreement modifying a contract within this Article needs no consideration to be binding.

The CISG does not require consideration. A modification requires only the consent of the parties to be binding. **STOP NOW and READ CISG Article 29(1) below**.

CISG ARTICLE 29(1)

(1) A contract may be modified or terminated by the mere agreement of the parties.

Contract modification may also raise a variety of other issues, which are addressed more fully in Chapters 4, 5, and 6, along with an exception to the general common law rule stated above. Here, our purpose is simply to introduce the general rule requiring consideration in the context of common law modification, while fully dispensing with any such requirement in a sale of goods transaction governed by either UCC Article 2 or the CISG.

APPLYING THE RULES

Problem 1: Zenith manufactured car parts using metal castings and, in doing so, generated a significant amount of sand, as a byproduct. At some point, this sand was no longer useable in Zenith's manufacturing process (after being used a number of times), but was useful as fill material in road construction. Zenith operated three different plants in Michigan that generated sand as a byproduct—plants A, B, and C. Plant A contracted to sell all of its sand to Wayne, a Wisconsin contractor specializing in road construction. Plant B contracted to Mary, a Minnesota contractor, all of the sand she needed for her road construction projects. Plant C contracted with Mark, Michigan supplier of materials to the construction trade. Zenith granted Mark an exclusive right to sell its sand in Michigan.

Are any of these three contracts (of plants A, B, and C) illusory? If not, describe the nature and legal basis for any implied promise in each contract.

Problem 2: Alpha, an Alabama business, contracted to paint 20 cars for Mega, a Mississippi used car dealership, at a price of $100 per car, with the $2,000 total to be paid upon completion. Prior to Alpha beginning work, Mega contacted Alpha and requested that Alpha paint 25 cars for this same $2,000 total price, suggesting that Mega might, perhaps, contract for more painting of cars in the future if Alpha agreed to paint the extra cars for the same price under this initial contract. In response, Alpha agreed to Mega's request. No other changes were made to the parties' agreement, and Alpha painted the first 20 cars as agreed. Alpha then demanded payment in full, or $2,000, for painting the 20 cars. Can Mega enforce Alpha's promise to paint an additional 5 cars for the original $2,000 price?

How, if at all, would your analysis change if Matt, an individual from Mississippi, had contracted with Alpha to purchase 20 gallons of paint for $10 per gallon, or $200, and had subsequently requested that Alpha agree to deliver 25 gallons of paint at the same price, suggesting that Matt might, perhaps, purchase more paint in the future if Alpha agreed. Again, assume that Alpha agreed to the requested change, but subsequently sought to deliver only 20 gallons for $200. Can Matt enforce Alpha's promise to deliver the 5 additional gallons of paint at the same price? What if the facts were the same as the latter variation, except that the paint was purchased by Miguel, a professional house painter in Mexico?

Lesson 7: Reliance as an Alternative Theory of Liability

Objectives and Expected Learning Outcomes

In this lesson, you will discover "reliance," as an alternative theory upon which a promise may be enforced. You will learn the basic rule providing for such enforcement, as well as its limits. You will then apply it in a variety of contexts designed to highlight differences in the manner in which one may apply the rule. Thus, when you have completed this lesson, you should have a reasonably complete understanding with respect to the enforceability of a promise—under traditional bargain theory, as well as reliance, as an alternative, when no "bargain" is present.

Promissory Estoppel—Reliance in the Absence of Consideration

As a general rule, a promise that is not supported by consideration will not be enforceable. However, the common law provides for a significant exception in certain cases of reliance by the promisee. When a party foreseeably relies on a promise, that promise may be enforced to the extent necessary to avoid injustice—even in the absence of consideration. Consider the following example of a promise of a gift by a grandfather to his granddaughter.

> ### Example 7-1: *Ricketts v. Scothorn*
>
> Andrew Ricketts executed a promissory note in which he promised to pay Katie Scothorn, his granddaughter, $2,000. Upon delivering the note to Katie, her grandfather said, "I have fixed out something that you have not got to work any more. None of my grandchildren work, and you don't have to." Immediately thereafter, Katie notified her employer of her intention to quit her job and then did so. After about 12 months without working, Katie decided that she wished to return to work, and her grandfather Ricketts assisted her in securing a new position.
>
> Ricketts died sometime later, without having paid off the note, and the executor of his estate refused to honor it. Scothorn sued on the note, and the executor defended by asserting that the note reflected nothing more than a promise of a future gift. The promise lacked consideration and was, therefore, unenforceable.

While not suggesting the presence of any actual consideration, the court nevertheless applied the doctrine of "estoppel" to preclude the assertion of any defense by the estate based on a "lack of consideration." Ricketts should have reasonably anticipated that Scothorn would rely on his promise in the manner she did (specifically suggesting such reliance), Scothorn in fact did so rely, and it would be an injustice for her to suffer any detriment based on such reasonable reliance. Thus, the promise was enforced.[23]

> **"Estoppel"**
> The doctrine of "estoppel" generally protects the reasonable and detrimental reliance of one party against the inconsistencies of another. "Equitable" estoppel precludes inconsistent factual assertions, while "promissory" estoppel precludes broken promises. The latter doctrine largely grew out of the former.

The above example is an easy one, inasmuch as Ricketts had clearly invited reliance. In fact, Scothorn argued that Ricketts had even "bargained" for her to quit her job, in which case the promise would have been fully supported by consideration—in much the same manner as the uncle's promise to his nephew in *Hamer v. Sidway*. However, it was difficult to find actual bargaining in the words of Ricketts as he presented the note, and his assistance in helping Scothorn to get another job later would seem to belie any claim that he was originally "bargaining" for her to quit her job. In the end, however, the court ruled in favor of Scothorn by precluding the estate's assertion of the defense and announcing what has come to be known as the doctrine of "promissory estoppel."

A plaintiff seeking to enforce a contractual promise must initially plead that the parties in fact concluded such a contract and the defendant made the promise at issue. The defendant will often challenge the plaintiff on the facts. However, a defendant may also sometimes raise what are called "defenses." We will talk more about a variety of different defenses in Chapters 4, 5, and 9, but the concept is worth noting here, because the issue of "consideration" (i.e., the lack of consideration) is generally raised as a "defense" to a claim based on a purported contractual promise. Thus, if the defense is barred or precluded based on "promissory estoppel," then the promise remains—unless factually contested—and is enforceable.

If we change the facts of example 7-1 slightly, we can easily see some of the contours of the basic rule. If, for example, Katie had done nothing, then

---

[23] Ricketts v. Scothorn, 57 Neb. 51, 77 N.W. 365 (1898).

her grandfather's expectations that she might rely would be irrelevant, because she did not in fact rely. If Katie had instead gone out and purchased a new computer for $2,000 (having modernized our facts a bit as well), then it becomes more difficult to say that her grandfather should have reasonably foreseen this sort of reliance—even though Katie did in fact rely on the promise. Finally, if Katie had indeed quit her job, but the very next day had obtained a new and better job for better pay, then her reliance would not have been detrimental in any way. While she might be unhappy about her grandfather's broken promise, her "reliance" would have nothing to do with any detriment arising from that broken promise. In effect, there would be no "injustice"—arising specifically from Katie's reliance in quitting her job—in declining to enforce the promise. This focus on the promisee's reliance raises another interesting question.

Should a promisee, such as Katie Scothorn, receive the full value of the promise, or should her recovery be limited to the extent of her "reliance"? In other words, should she recover her "expectation" interest or her "reliance" interest? Courts have not always answered this question the same way. Not only is it possible in some cases to get to different outcomes, but the manner in which one approaches the issue may itself affect the outcome. Here, we will refer to the "promissory" approach and the "reliance" approach. To highlight the difference, we can add a few simple facts to example 7-1.

Katie's wages at her original job were $10 per week, and her wages at her subsequent new job were also $10 per week. She incurred no quantifiable costs related to leaving the first or obtaining the second job, and she was out of work exactly 50 weeks. In the actual case, the note involved interest and a partial payment, but we'll leave those out in order to keep things simple. Katie's damages can then be calculated under each approach as follows:

Promissory Approach - $2,000 (promise amount)

Reliance Approach – 50 weeks x $10 per week = $500 (reliance loss)

Which seems fairer to you? If the doctrine of estoppel is applied as an "all or nothing" concept, then clearly the promissory approach provides the "right" answer, because the estate is wholly precluded from asserting the defense. If, however, one focuses on the idea of compensating a party for the extent of its detrimental reliance, then the reliance approach seems far more reasonable. The difference between these two fundamental perspectives is fairly clear. However, another distinction is more subtle.

The Restatement (Second) of Contracts § 90(1) initially articulates the doctrine of promissory estoppel in terms of "enforcement of the promise." It then goes on to say that the remedy "may be limited as justice requires." Thus, the restatement arguably begins from a "promissory" approach, which is then perhaps tempered by the "reliance" perspective. In contrast, some courts seem to begin from a "reliance" perspective, enforcing the "promise" only when reliance is seemingly complete. When facts are clear and complete, the approach one takes should make little, if any, difference. However, when facts are less clear, then one's starting point may significantly affect one's ending point as well.

The terminology can be further confusing, depending on whether one characterizes "promissory estoppel" as enforcing "contracts without consideration" or simply enforcing a naked promise to the extent of reasonable and detrimental reliance. In this text, the author will generally focus on "promissory estoppel" as a theory of recovery grounded in "reliance" and analytically distinct from a fully enforceable "contract" supported by "consideration." The material is presented in this way because the author believes it to be the easiest to understand in relation to other doctrine. However, your professor may approach the issue differently, and courts will often approach the doctrine in differing ways. Hopefully, this initial explanation of some of the differences will be useful in navigating some of the challenges of grappling with the doctrine of promissory estoppel.

In some circumstances, it may be difficult to calculate either the value of the promise or the financial extent of any detrimental reliance, thus suggesting an approach under which a remedy can most easily be calculated.

In example 5-2, sister Kirksey failed to recover on her brother-in-law's promise because it was not supported by consideration. The actual case predated the evolution of promissory estoppel in that state. However, she likely could have recovered based on "promissory estoppel." The problem is that it might have been very difficult to calculate the value of her brother-in-law's promise to give her a place to live and some land to tend. We will later talk about the requirement of a reasonable degree of certainty with respect to both contract terms and contract remedies. Here, one might reasonably ask "exactly what was he promising, and for how long?" In contrast, she left behind a leasehold interest based on a government land patent, which likely had a calculable value. Thus, her "reliance" interest is likely calculable, while her "promissory" interest is probably not.

While in *Kirksey*, the promisee's reliance interest was arguably easier to determine than her promissory interest, the reverse will often be true. We can return now to the factual setting first introduced in problem 2, of lesson 4.

> **Example 7-2: *Feinberg v. Pfeiffer***
>
> Pfeiffer Co. had promised Anna Feinberg $200 per month upon retirement. The promise lacked consideration, but Feinberg nevertheless relied on it in retiring a year and a half later. The company paid her for some time, but eventually ceased the payments. At that time, Feinberg's health and age realistically precluded any return to work.
>
> While holding that the promised retirement payments were not supported by consideration, the court further held that Feinberg was entitled to receive the promised payments based on "promissory estoppel." Pfeiffer Co. should have foreseen that she would rely on the promised retirement payments by retiring, and Feinberg did so rely.[24]

In *Feinberg*, it would have been extraordinarily difficult to quantify the extent of her reliance. How long might she have worked, and at what rate of pay? Perhaps even more importantly, her reliance was complete. Unlike Katie Scothorn, Anna Feinberg could no longer reenter the workforce. Thus, she was entitled to the full amount of the payment promised by Pfeiffer Co.

One of the more challenging applications of promissory estoppel involves a promise in the context of a broader contractual relationship—in which the promise and the nature of the contract relationship are seemingly inconsistent. Normally, a party may only rely on promissory estoppel in the absence of a contract. However, sometimes the "promise" at issue may arguably be "extra-contractual"—in effect, outside of the scope of the parties' contract. This commonly arises in the context of a "promise" of "at-will" employment.

---

[24] Feinberg v. Pfeiffer Co., 322 S.W. 2d 163 (Ct. App. Mo. 1959).

Example 7-3: Mary was initially employed by Acme, in California. However, John approached Mary about a new job with Zenith, in Iowa. After a thorough interview, John offered Mary a job with Zenith, promising twice the salary she had been making with Acme. Both Mary's job at Acme and the job offered by Zenith were "at-will." Mary accepted John's offer of a job with Zenith. She resigned her job at Acme, sold her home in California, and moved to Iowa. When she showed up at Zenith on the first day of work, John said "sorry, but our sales have recently fallen off badly, and we won't be able to hire you after all."

Mary has incurred costs in the sale of her home, as well as her moving expense, and she also gave up an excellent job. Moreover, she was promised twice her old salary by Zenith. She would of course like to recover whatever she can from Zenith based on its breach of the promise made by John (as an "agent" of Acme). The problem, of course, is that she would have been "at most" an "at-will" employee of Zenith, so it could have terminated her anyway. If Mary tries to use "promissory estoppel" to enforce the promise by Zenith to employ her at the new higher salary, she will almost certainly lose, because the wage promised by Zenith is governed by an actual contract, which allowed for termination any time, for any reason. However, Mary will likely focus on what she gave up—in reliance on the promise of a new job—instead of on the promised new job, itself.

The promise to give her a new job is fully distinct from the job itself (work in exchange for pay). John should have expected her to rely on the promised new job in giving up her old one, selling her home, and moving, and she did so. Thus, Mary should be entitled to recover her "reliance" interest in relocating to Iowa based on the promised new job with Zenith. It may be difficult to calculate the value of what she gave up with Acme (being "at-will" employment), and she will not likely recover anything based on her promised pay from Zenith (again, "at-will"), but she should certainly be able to recover the costs associated with selling her home and moving—and perhaps something for the job she left behind.

Example 7-3 shows the importance of, in some cases, focusing on a "reliance" theory rather than a "promissory" approach. If Mary had sought to enforce the terms of Zenith's promised job (i.e., the value of the new higher salaried position), she would have almost certainly lost because of the "at-will" nature of the promised job. However, by focusing, instead, on the backward looking remedy of reliance, she would likely be able to recover something from Zenith.

Promissory Estoppel and Promises of Charitable Gifts

The enforceability of promised gifts is particularly important to charitable organizations, which often rely on such gifts for their continuing viability. Consider the following example based on another classic opinion by Judge Cardozo.

> **Example 7-4:** *Allegheny College v. National Chautauqua County Bank*
>
> Mary Yates Johnston promised to donate $5,000 to Allegheny College. The endowment was to be known as the "Mary Yates Johnston memorial fund," and was to be used to educate students preparing for the ministry. Johnston paid the first $1,000, but attempted to repudiate the remaining obligation. Upon her death, Johnston's estate refused to pay the remainder, asserting that her promise lacked consideration. The College sued to collect on the remainder of the promise.
>
> In addressing the enforceability of the promise, Judge Cardozo began by noting that promises to make charitable gifts are subject to the same basic rule requiring consideration and the same basic exception involving promissory estoppel. However, he also noted that the importance of charitable giving raised certain unique policy considerations. With all of this in mind, the court held that Johnston's promise was fully supported by consideration, thus avoiding any need to consider the doctrine of promissory estoppel.

Consideration was found in the implied promise by the College to establish a separate and distinct "memorial fund" for purposes of administering this gift. The court pointed out that this promise to establish a memorial fund was analogous to a promise to endow a chair. Thus, the court held that the parties had concluded a fully enforceable bilateral contract, with Johnston promising money and the College promising to establish the specified "memorial fund."[25]

Today, of course, many charitable entities provide "naming" opportunities (chairs, rooms, halls, buildings, and endowments) in exchange for promised donations. In such cases, the parties have almost certainly concluded a bilateral contract, just as the court found in *Allegheny College*. However, in cases in which the presence of traditional consideration is perhaps more doubtful, the doctrine of promissory estoppel is more generously applied to charitable institutions as well.

A promise of a charitable donation should always be expected to induce forbearance on the part of the charity, and the charity need not prove the promise actually did so (tying together individual promises with individual acts of reliance would typically be quite difficult). Thus, the only requirement of the promisee is proof of injustice to the extent the promise is not enforced. In the case of most charitable institutions, this should be a relatively low hurdle, thus allowing for relative ease of promise enforcement by charities—even in the absence of consideration.

Summary of Basic Rule: "promissory estoppel"[26]

- A promise may be fully or partially enforceable, notwithstanding any lack of consideration, if:

  ○ the promisor should have reasonably foreseen reliance by the promisor, and

  ○ the promisee did in fact rely on the promise in that foreseeable manner.

---

[25] Allegheny College v. National Chautauqua County Bank, 246 N.Y. 369, 159 N.E. 173 (1927). As in the earlier case of *Wood v. Lucy, Lady Duff-Gordon*, Judge Cardozo's creative analysis was not embraced by all. The Allegheny College decision included two dissenting votes.

[26] This basic rule is reflected in Restatement (Second) of Contracts § 90.

> ○ The extent to which the promise is enforced is determined by reference to the extent and effect of any detrimental reliance in furtherance of avoiding any resulting injustice.
>
> • A promise to make a charitable gift may be enforced to the extent necessary to avoid any injustice resulting from non-enforcement.

In this lesson, we have examined "promissory estoppel" as an alternative "reliance" based remedy in the context of promises that are not supported by traditional consideration. In future chapters, we will again encounter reliance as the basis for an alternative remedy in other contexts. As in this lesson, it is important to remember that the nature of a backward looking reliance based remedy will often be quite different from the nature of the forward looking remedy of "expectation."

APPLYING THE RULES

Problem 1: Return to the facts of example 4-1. Suppose that a court had found that Jane's promise to Joe was not supported by consideration. How much, if anything, might Joe recover based on an alternative theory?

Problem 2: Alaska University School of Law (a purely hypothetical institution) decided to construct a new building and solicited pledges to pay for the building. Elaine, an AU alum, contacted the law school and promised $50,000, in exchange for school's promise to name a seminar room after Elaine's decease mother, who had also practiced law in Alaska and had been Elaine's role model. A very small plaque (3" x 8") inside the room would bear the details of the dedication. The very next day, Elaine again contacted the law school and said she had changed her mind. However, the law school indicated that she was already bound and was fully liable for the promised $50,000.

Is Elaine liable to AU? If so, what is the legal basis for such liability? Whatever the original answer, suppose that a court found that Elaine and AU had not formed a contract supported by consideration. Would AU have any alternative theory upon which it might recover?

Problem 3: General was an Indiana liquor distributor and, during a period of market consolidation, lost two of its major product lines. It faced a very clear choice as a result—either (1) downsize and operate with its remaining two brands, or (2) sell what was left of its business. General was offered $550,000 by National for its business, but General's owners preferred—if possible—to downsize and continue to operate the business. However, the latter approach was only possible if General was able to retain its strongest remaining brand, Bacardi—and General's right to continue to distribute Bacardi products was entirely "at will."

General, therefore, approached Bacardi directly and explained its dilemma, asking if Bacardi would continue to sell its products through General. Bacardi promised General that it had no intention of discontinuing the relationship, and repeated the promise just a few days later. Immediately after the second promise, General rejected National's offer to purchase the business. One week later, Bacardi notified General that it was terminating the distribution relationship.

General immediately contacted National in hopes of reviving the earlier sale offer. However, National, knowing that General now had no other real option (National did not actually care about the Bacardi brand, but was simply taking advantage of the change in the circumstances of the negotiations), reduced its purchase offer to $150,000. With no other reasonable choice, General took the $150,000 offer from National. Does General have a claim against Bacardi? Think carefully about how you would best frame this claim. Can General actually enforce the value of Bacardi's promise of continued distribution?

The facts of this problem are based on the case of *D & G Stout, Inc., v. Bacardi Imports, Inc.*, 923 F.2d 566 (7th Cir. 1991).

Lesson 8: Moral Obligations and Restitution

Objectives and Expected Learning Outcomes

In this lesson, you will encounter a number of "hard cases," in which a strict application of traditional contract rules may seem to lead to an unsatisfactory result. You will learn the basic equitable rule providing for "restitution" in order to avoid "unjust enrichment." You will first encounter this rule in the context of what is often called "moral obligation," after which you will more fully discover the basic elements required in a claim for restitution. You will then apply these rules in a context in which neither traditional bargain theory, nor reliance would provide the aggrieved party with any relief. This lesson then concludes with a cumulative problem, allowing you to apply a cross-section of the material learned in Chapter 2.

Moral Obligation as Consideration (Not)

In lesson 4, we noted that "past consideration" will not support the enforcement of a subsequent promise, because one cannot "bargain" for something that has already happened in the past. However, one might nevertheless argue that when a clear and present "moral obligation" arises directly from a past act or omission, the moral obligation itself should serve to bind the subsequent promise in consideration of that existing moral obligation. Courts have largely rejected this argument with respect to the issue of consideration.

Example 8-1: *Mills v. Wyman*

Levi Wyman, 25, returned ill from a sea voyage. Daniel Mills cared for Wyman, who had no means to care for himself. Upon learning of these events, Seth Wyman, Levi's father, promised Mills that he would pay all expenses incurred in the care of his son. When the father later declined to pay, Mills sued.

The court dismissed the case for lack of consideration, drawing a distinction between the moral and legal obligations arising under such circumstances and pointing out that the former are not enforceable in a court of law. The court further pointed out that, in the absence of a binding contract, a father is under no legal obligation to pay for the obligations of his adult son.[27]

Most courts have declined to find "consideration" in a moral obligation arising from a past act or omission. However, a separate and distinct doctrine has often provided an alternative form of relief—"restitution" to avoid unjust enrichment.

Restitution to Avoid Unjust Enrichment

As originally explained in lesson 3, a restitutionary remedy requires a party to return or disgorge the value of any benefit provided by the other party. The doctrine of "unjust enrichment" requires a party to pay such restitution under circumstances in which it would be "unjust" not to do so. In effect, the court must determine whether or not it is "just" to allow the recipient of a benefit to keep the benefit without paying for it.

A claim for restitution is not dependent on a "promise" of any kind. In this way it is entirely distinct from bargain theory or promissory estoppel, each of which fundamentally relies on the existence of a promise. This theory of providing "restitution" to avoid "unjust enrichment" is therefore often referred to as "quasi-contract" or "implied-in-law" contract. Again though, it is important to remember that it is not really a contract at all, because it does not require any sort of promise by either party. The doctrine requires only that one party has conferred a benefit of value on the other. However, not all benefits must be paid for.

> **Unjust Enrichment, as a distinct sort of Moral Obligation**
>
> The doctrine of "unjust enrichment" might be said to arise from a kind of "moral obligation." A party receiving a benefit may have a "moral obligation" to pay for it, and may also have a legal obligation to do so under the doctrine of "unjust enrichment." However, a moral obligation may also arise in other circumstances, without a corresponding legal remedy. For example, in *Mills*, the father likely had a moral obligation to pay for the care of his adult son, but he, himself, arguably received no personal benefit, as required for recovery under the doctrine of unjust enrichment.

---

[27] Mills v. Wyman, 3 Pick. 207, 20 Mass. 207 (1825).

The recipient is not required to pay for unwanted benefits. For example, a lawn service that went around the neighborhood trimming trees—without ever contacting the owners—would not likely be entitled to restitution (and might well be liable as a matter of tort or property law). The tree trimmer would not be entitled to recover, because the "benefit" was unwanted. Even if, objectively, the tree trimming was quite nice, it would be unreasonable to require the owner of the tree to pay for the unwanted benefit, so it would not "unjustly enrich" the owner if he or she was allowed to keep the benefit without paying for it.

The provision of a benefit that is unwanted is sometimes said to be "officious," and one who provides such benefits may be characterized as an "officious intermeddler." Thus, "officious" benefits are not subject to claims for restitution. The recipient's desire to receive the benefit may be express or implied from the circumstances, based either on the recipient's stated subjective desires or the objective circumstances in which the benefit was provided. Even if the provision of a benefit is not officious, the provider may nevertheless be barred from recovery for a benefit that was provided "gratuitously."

If one person provides a benefit to another who desires it, and does so with an expectation of payment, then the recipient will generally be liable for restitution. However, if the provider was acting "gratuitously," then there is no injustice in allowing the recipient to keep the benefit without paying for it.

In most social circumstances, any conveyance of benefits is presumed "gratuitous." One can easily imagine the potential claims that might arise among friends and family in the face of a contrary presumption. Friends and family can certainly contract, as we have seen in earlier examples, and a claim for restitution may also arise in this same context. However, in making such a claim, one must overcome a reasonably strong presumption that friends and family do things for each other without any expectation of payment.

The proverbial "hero" is also normally presumed to act "gratuitously." The bystander who happens to be skilled in first aid is presumed to act gratuitously when rendering assistance upon the scene of an accident. However, an exception is made when the "heroic" aid is rendered by a professional. Thus, the doctor or EMT who renders medical care at the scene of an accident will likely be entitled to restitution for the value of his or her services. This "exception" for professional services has also sometimes been expanded to include particularly burdensome acts, such that one would, objectively, only be likely to perform such acts with an expectation of compensation. However, the general presumption, consistent with our common understandings, is that most "heroes" act without any expectation of payment. Thus, their acts are presumed to be "gratuitous," unless proven otherwise.

Finally, while the doctrine of restitution may, in some instances provide an alternative to contract theory as a basis for recovery, it may in others be limited or precluded by contract. To the extent that any given claim for restitution would be inconsistent with any applicable contract terms, the contract terms must be given effect. Thus, the seller of a parcel of land at a bargain price cannot later seek further compensation based on restitution for the oil beneath the land that was also unexpectedly conveyed (the seller did not know of the oil) pursuant to the contract. We will address apparent "mistakes" of this sort later in Chapter 9, and we will see a few other potential exceptions to the rule in the context of remedies, in Chapter 8. However, to the extent the issue is governed by contract, a claim for restitution will generally be precluded.

In summary, restitution is generally available to the extent not precluded by contract, as long as the provision of the benefit is neither officious nor gratuitous.

> **Summary of Basic Rule: "restitution," generally[28]**
>
> • The recipient of a benefit is generally liable to make restitution to the provider, unless
>
>   ○ such restitution would be inconsistent with any applicable contract terms; or
>
>   ○ the benefit was "officious" or unwanted; or
>
>   ○ the provider of the benefit did so "gratuitously."
>
>   ▪ "Heroic" acts are generally presumed gratuitous, except:
>
>   • When rendered by a professional; or
>
>   • Otherwise sufficiently burdensome that a presumed intent to be paid is appropriate.

Thus, the doctrine of "restitution" to avoid "unjust enrichment" may serve as an alternative to either traditional bargain theory or promissory estoppel in cases lacking even a promise. The existence of a promise will not, however, necessarily preclude a restitution claim. In fact, the subsequent promise will typically be conclusive in proving the benefit was indeed wanted. In the next section, we will encounter two cases in which the analysis seems to raise issues involving both traditional bargain theory and restitution.

Hard Cases

It is sometimes said that "hard cases make bad law." In the proverbial "hard case," a court may be forced to choose between following what appears to be a rather clear application of the law to reach a seemingly "unjust" result, or doing what is necessary to reach a "just" result, even if it may require a somewhat "tortured" path to arrive at that result.

In *Mills*, the court clearly chose to follow settled law, even though this may have led to a less than satisfactory outcome with respect to our more general sensibilities of right and wrong. Part of the court's rational in *Mills* focused on the separate personages of Levi Wyman, the son who received the care

---

[28] This basic rule is reflected in Restatement (Third) of Restitution §§ 1, 2, 20, 21, and 25. Note that this restatement of the common law governing restitution is entirely distinct from the restatement of the common law governing contracts.

benefits bestowed by Mills, and Seth Wyman, his father who subsequently promised to pay for those benefits. The next two cases are arguably even a bit "harder" than Mills, because it was the actual recipient of the benefit who made the subsequent promise to pay—each under rather compelling circumstances. The first case is presented as example 8-2, while the second follows in relatively full case form.

> **Example 8-2:** *Harrington v. Taylor*
>
> Taylor had assaulted his wife, who took refuge in Harrington's home. The next day, Taylor entered Harrington's home to continue his assault, but his wife got the better of him with the help of an axe. When the wife sought to finish the job, Harrington deflected the axe blow, saving Taylor's life, but badly mutilating her own hand in the process. Taylor subsequently promised to pay Harrington for her injuries, but failed to keep his promise.
>
> Harrington brought suit on Taylor's promise, but her claim was dismissed for lack of present consideration to support the promise. The court stated that "a humanitarian act of this kind, voluntarily performed, is not such consideration as would entitle [Harrington] to recover at law."[29]

In effect, the above court followed the same approach as *Mills* in declining to find consideration in a moral obligation. The court also noted the "humanitarian" or "voluntary" nature of the act. In doing so, it also arguably precluded recovery under any alternative theory of restitution to avoid unjust enrichment. Now, consider and compare the court's approach in the following classic case.

---

[29] Harrington v. Taylor, 225 N.C. 690, 36 S.E.2d 227 (1945).

FROM THE COURT

Webb v. McGowin

Court of Appeals of Alabama (1935)
27 Ala.App. 82, 168 So.196

BRICKEN, Presiding Judge.

[Plaintiff's breach of contract action was dismissed by the court for failure to state a claim because the promise at issue lacked consideration. Plaintiff appealed. The Court stated the facts and then provided the following summary.]

. . . [T]he complaint . . . averred in substance: (1) That on August 3, 1925, appellant saved J. Greeley McGowin, appellee's testator, from death or grievous bodily harm; (2) that in doing so appellant sustained bodily injury crippling him for life; (3) that in consideration of the services rendered and the injuries received by appellant, McGowin agreed to care for him the remainder of appellant's life, the amount to be paid being $15 every two weeks; (4) that McGowin complied with this agreement until he died on January 1, 1934, and the payments were kept up to January 27, 1934, after which they were discontinued.

The action was for the unpaid installments accruing after January 27, 1934, to the time of the suit. . . .

1. The averments of the complaint show that appellant saved McGowin from death or grievous bodily harm. This was a material benefit to him of infinitely more value than any financial aid he could have received. Receiving this benefit, McGowin became morally bound to compensate appellant for the services rendered. Recognizing his moral obligation, he expressly agreed to pay appellant as alleged in the complaint and complied with this agreement up to the time of his death; a period of more than 8 years.

Had McGowin been accidentally poisoned and a physician, without his knowledge or request, had administered an antidote, thus saving his life, a subsequent promise by McGowin to pay the physician would have been valid. Likewise, McGowin's agreement as disclosed by the complaint to compensate appellant for saving him from death or grievous bodily injury is valid and enforceable.

Where the promisee cares for, improves, and preserves the property of the promisor, though done without his request, it is sufficient consideration for the promisor's subsequent agreement to pay for the service, because of the material benefit received. [Citations omitted].

In *Boothe v. Fitzpatrick*, 36 Vt. 681, the court held that a promise by defendant to pay for the past keeping of a bull which had escaped from defendant's premises and been cared for by plaintiff was valid, although there was no previous request, because the subsequent promise obviated that objection; it being equivalent to a previous request. On the same principle, had the promisee saved the promisor's life or his body from grievous harm, his subsequent promise to pay for the services rendered would have been valid. Such service would have been far more material than caring for his bull. Any holding that saving a man from death or grievous bodily harm is not a material benefit sufficient to uphold a subsequent promise to pay for the service, necessarily rests on the assumption that saving life and preservation of the body from harm have only a sentimental value. The converse of this is true. Life and preservation of the body have material, pecuniary values, measurable in dollars and cents. Because of this, physicians practice their profession charging for services rendered in saving life and curing the body of its ills, and surgeons perform operations. The same is true as to the law of negligence, authorizing the assessment of damages in personal injury cases based upon the extent of the injuries, earnings, and life expectancies of those injured.

In the business of life insurance, the value of a man's life is measured in dollars and cents according to his expectancy, the soundness of his body, and his ability to pay premiums. The same is true as to health and accident insurance.

It follows that if, as alleged in the complaint, appellant saved J. Greeley McGowin from death or grievous bodily harm, and McGowin subsequently agreed to pay him for the service rendered, it became a valid and enforceable contract.

2. It is well settled that a moral obligation is a sufficient consideration to support a subsequent promise to pay where the promisor has received a material benefit, although there was no original duty or liability resting on the promisor. [Citations omitted.] . . . [A] moral obligation is a sufficient consideration to support an executory promise where the promisor has received an actual pecuniary or material benefit for which he subsequently expressly promised to pay.

The case at bar is clearly distinguishable from that class of cases where the consideration is a mere moral obligation or conscientious duty unconnected with receipt by promisor of benefits of a material or pecuniary nature. [Citation omitted.] Here the promisor received a material benefit constituting a valid consideration for his promise.

3. Some authorities hold that, for a moral obligation to support a subsequent promise to pay, there must have existed a prior legal or equitable obligation, which for some reason had become unenforceable, but for which the promisor was still morally bound. This rule, however, is subject to qualification in those cases where the promisor, having received a material benefit from the promisee, is morally bound to compensate him for the services rendered and in consideration of this obligation promises to pay. In such cases the subsequent promise to pay is an affirmance or ratification of the services rendered carrying with it the presumption that a previous request for the service was made. [Citations omitted].

Under the decisions above cited, McGowin's express promise to pay appellant for the services rendered was an affirmance or ratification of what appellant had done raising the presumption that the services had been rendered at McGowin's request.

4. The averments of the complaint show that in saving McGowin from death or grievous bodily harm, appellant was crippled for life. This was part of the consideration of the contract declared on. McGowin was benefited. Appellant was injured. Benefit to the promisor or injury to the promisee is a sufficient legal consideration for the promisor's agreement to pay. [Citations omitted.]

5. Under the averments of the complaint the services rendered by appellant were not gratuitous. The agreement of McGowin to pay and the acceptance of payment by appellant conclusively shows the contrary. . . .

From what has been said, we are of the opinion that the court below erred in the ruling complained of; that is to say, in sustaining the demurrer, and for this error the case is reversed and remanded.

Reversed and remanded.

SAMFORD, Judge (concurring).

The questions involved in this case are not free from doubt, and perhaps the strict letter of the rule, as stated by judges, though not always in accord, would bar a recovery by plaintiff, but following the principle announced by Chief Justice Marshall in Hoffman v. Porter, Fed.Cas. No. 6,577, 2 Brock. 156, 159, where he says, "I do not think that law ought to be separated from justice, where it is at most doubtful," I concur in the conclusions reached by the court.

CASE QUESTIONS

(1) Is the majority opinion in *Webb* consistent with the court's opinion in *Harrington*, in example 8-2? If not, which do you find more consistent with the contract rules we have covered thus far? Which case do you believe reached the more "just" outcome?

(2) Is the majority relying on bargain theory in reaching its conclusion, or is it relying on a theory of restitution to avoid unjust enrichment? Arguably, the majority has mixed the two together. Is this appropriate?

> **Common Law versus Civil Law and the effect of Precedent**
> A civil law system draws its law primarily from statutes, and courts decide only the matter before them—without binding precedential effect on future cases. Thus, a case like this would be much easier, as the court need only focus on "justice" between the two parties. However, in a common law system, "justice" in one case may result in an "injustice" or uncertainty in the next.
> One of the great virtues of the common law is its ability to "evolve" and "adapt" gradually. However, this same virtuous malleability can sometimes become an arguable "vice" in the face of particularly challenging facts.

(3) What is the logical significance of the "promise" according to the majority?

    a. Does McGowin's subsequent promise support a logical inference that McGowin wanted the benefit conferred by Webb?

    b. Does McGowin's subsequent promise support a logical inference that Webb expected, at the time he provided the benefit, to be paid for doing so? Do you think Webb had the time or inclination to think about payment at the time he acted?

(1) While quite short, the concurring opinion is notable for its apparent acknowledgement the court's analysis is perhaps legally (and logically) flawed, but reaches a "just" conclusion. This case presents an excellent example of the sort of conflict that can sometimes arise between the letter or the law and the spirit of justice.

Another great lesson provided by this case is the importance of "critical" reading. As a practicing lawyer, you may have to accept the decision of a court, because the decision involves your client and cannot (either legally or practically) be appealed further. However, as a law student, you should be continually asking yourself whether the court's analysis seems logically and legally sound. It is also worth noting that an "unsound" analysis is not necessarily the fault of the judge writing the opinion, because most courts will generally rely on the written and oral submissions of the parties. If a case is poorly argued by one or both of the parties' lawyers, it will often be poorly decided by the court.

The "rule" of *Webb* has been somewhat "recast" in Restatement (Second) of Contracts § 86. This restatement provision essentially addresses the analysis in terms of restitution to avoid unjust enrichment. The subsequent promise clearly shows that the provision of the benefit was not "officious." Thus, the only question is whether the benefit was provided "gratuitously." Here, one would nevertheless have to confront the normal restitutionary presumption that "heroes," like Webb, act gratuitously. The restatement's answer to this dilemma is found in comment d to § 86.

Comment d begins by noting the challenge of establishing a claim like Webb's under the traditional formulation of restitution. It then goes on to note the significance of the promise in establishing that McGowin actually desired the benefit provided by Webb. Finally, the analysis then turns the normal presumption on its head and shifts the burden of proof to the recipient of the benefit, who must pay restitution absent proof that the benefit was provided gratuitously. At bottom, this is simply a policy choice, and is certainly defensible as such. It is also arguably much more consistent with the views expressed by the concurring judge in *Webb* than the analysis provided by the majority.

> **Presumptions and the Burden of Proof**
> The approach found in comment d to § 86 also highlights the potential significance of a "presumption" and its effect on the burden of proof. A civil case need only be proven by a "preponderance," of the evidence—a seemingly modest standard (arguably, anything more than 50/50). However, in some cases, there will be no evidence at all on a particular point (e.g., Webb's state of mind when he acted). In these cases, the "presumption" will likely be dispositive, as the party with the burden of proof must necessarily lose in the absence of any evidence.

Summary of Basic Rule: the special case of "restitution" in the context of a promise[30]

- Where the recipient of a benefit makes a subsequent promise to pay a reasonable amount for that benefit, the promise is enforceable, unless

  ○ the recipient of the benefit establishes that the provider of the benefit did so gratuitously.

The issue raised by a subsequent promise may also be addressed via a statute. You may recall New York General Obligations Law § 5-1105, earlier addressed in lesson 4, which provides for enforcement of a promise based on past consideration, as long as it is written and signed, and the consideration would otherwise be valid, but for the issue of timing.

There are also a number of narrow common law exceptions, generally involving a new promise to pay an old debt or ratification of a "voidable," obligation—a subject we will address further in Chapter 5.

---

[30] This basic rule is reflected in Restatement (Second) of Contracts § 86.

Restitution to Avoid Unjust Enrichment (redux)

While the rule of Restatement (Second) of Contracts § 86 provides a very narrow application of the general rule providing for restitution, the general rule may of course be employed to avoid injustice in a broader set of circumstances—even in the absence of any promise at all. Having initially introduced the idea of restitution as a prelude to *Webb*, we can now return to a more typical application of the general doctrine, as summarized earlier in this lesson.

> ### Example 8-3: *Cotnam v. Wisdom*
>
> Wisdom, a physician, rendered emergency care to Harrison, an unconscious victim of a street car accident. Harrison never regained consciousness and eventually died. As such, there was no basis for any real consensual bargain between Wisdom and Harrison. Cotnam, the administrator of Harrison's estate, therefore refused to pay Wisdom for the services provided to Harrison at the scene of the accident.
>
> While acknowledging the lack of an actual contract, the court nevertheless provided relief to Wisdom based on an "implied" or "quasi" contract (i.e., based on the theory of restitution to avoid unjust enrichment). Even though Harrison ultimately died, Wisdom's efforts to save his life provided value by increasing Harrison's chances of survival, and the court reasonably presumed that Harrison would have wanted such services under the circumstances. Inasmuch as Wisdom offered medical services as a professional physician, he was also presumed to do so in this case with an expectation of payment. Therefore, Wisdom was entitled to restitution for his services.[31]

---

[31] Cotnam v. Wisdom, 83 Ark. 601, 104 S.W. 164 (1907).

A party recovering restitution to avoid unjust enrichment is often said to be entitled to "quantum meruit," or as much as is deserved. Courts typically use one of two measures to determine how much is "deserved." Depending on the circumstances, a party may be entitled to either (1) the reasonable value of the benefit based on its cost to the recipient from someone like the person who actually provided it; or (2) the increase in value of the recipient's property or other interests as a result of the receipt of the benefit.[32] In applying the first alternative, it is important to distinguish between the "going rate" (an objective measure applied in the case of restitution) and any "contract rate" (applied only in the case of an actual contract). This distinction can be illustrated with a variation on the example above.

In example 8-3, Wisdom was entitled to recover restitution based on the "going rate" at which Harrison could have obtained the same services from a physician like Wisdom—irrespective of whether Wisdom's individual contract rate was higher or lower. Suppose, however, that Harrison's wife had been present on the scene, and she had contracted with Wisdom, promising to pay him if he would try to save her husband's life. If so, Wisdom would be entitled to recover in contract based on his actual individual contract rate. However, his recourse would be against Mrs. Harrison, with whom he contracted. Wisdom's actual contract with Mrs. Harrison would generally avoid any need to resort to restitution at all, but what if she did not pay? Could Wisdom then seek restitution, as he did in example 8-3? As suggested earlier in this lesson, the existence of a contract will often preclude restitution. However, this final variation raises the additional challenge of restitution in the context of a multi-party transaction.

Thus far, our discussion of restitution has been limited to two parties. However, the issue can also sometimes arise under circumstances involving more than two parties.

Example 8-4: A landlord leases office space to a tenant. The tenant then contracts with a renovator to do work to improve the space, as the tenant is expressly allowed under its lease. The tenant becomes insolvent before paying the renovator. Assuming that the tenant has no money, should the renovator be allowed to recover restitution from the landlord?

---

[32] Restatement (Second) of Contracts § 371.

The general answer in most cases is "no." The renovator contracted with the tenant—not the landlord—and generally cannot use a theory of restitution to turn the landlord into a guarantor of its tenant's contract obligations. However, in some circumstances, in which the party in the position of the landlord has truly received a benefit, a court may consider a claim for restitution. If so, the analysis generally follows the basic rule. Did the landlord want the "benefit"? Did the renovator expect payment? Was this payment expected from the landlord?

As you might intuit from the last question, a successful claim of restitution from a third-party is typically more difficult. There is a sense that the claimant is seeking to substitute an implied contract for the actual contract it made, and any sense of "unjust enrichment" is lessened when the benefit was not provided directly to the ultimate recipient.

APPLYING THE RULES

Problem 1: Fitzpatrick owned a bull, which escaped from its pasture. Boothe happened upon the bull wandering free, and he captured and kept the bull, pending his discovery of the rightful owner. Two months later, Boothe learned that Fitzpatrick owned the bull, and he promptly notified Fitzpatrick that he could come and collect the bull. When he arrived to fetch the bull, Fitzpatrick promised to pay Boothe for having kept the bull for two months (at the "going rate" for such services). However, Fitzpatrick subsequently refused to pay. Can Boothe enforce Fitzpatrick's promise? Consider each of the materials presented in this lesson.

In the actual case, Fitzpatrick asked Boothe to keep the bull a bit longer and promised to pay for both the prior and any future care. The court split its analysis between the promise to pay for prior care and the promise to pay for future care. Do you agree that this approach is necessarily appropriate? Can you construct an argument that might support Boothe's right to recover for the prior care based on traditional bargain theory?

The facts of this problem are based loosely on the case of *Boothe v. Fitzpatrick*, 36 Vt. 681 (1864). This case was cited in support of the majority's analysis in *Webb v. McGowin*. However, you should of course perform your own analysis of the facts presented here.

Problem 2 (cumulative—Chapter 2): Bill had been working for Acme Computers for the past 5 years and, during that time, had been its top sales person, selling direct from Acme to retail computer stores. Mary, the President of Acme, sent the following e-mail to Bill on July 31, [present year]:

> I have been thinking about outsourcing the sales function at Acme. In consideration of your outstanding sales performance as Acme's best salesperson ever, I will appoint you as Acme's exclusive computer distributor if you will set up a sales and distribution business of your own. Instead of selling direct to retail computer stores, Acme will sell its entire line of computers exclusively to you at 50% off of Acme's published retail price, so that you may sell them in turn to retail computer stores.

Bill replied to Mary with his own e-mail resigning his job at Acme (as an "at will" employee), effective immediately, and promising to start his new business as the exclusive Acme Computer distributor in two weeks. During the first two weeks of June, Bill entered into a 5 year office and warehouse lease, purchased office equipment, and hired a staff.

On August 14, Bill telephoned Mary to say that, just as promised, he had formed his business and was ready to start distributing Acme Computers. Mary told Bill that she had changed her mind about her proposal to Bill and had agreed to sell Acme Computers solely through Computers-R-Us. Mary told Bill she was sorry, but that he had obviously acted at his own risk in starting his business without any agreement with Acme. You may assume that Bill can prove with sufficient certainty that he would have made a net profit (after payment of expenses and overhead) on his distribution business had Mary fulfilled her promise on behalf of Acme.

Bill immediately terminated his staff (they were "at will" employees and had not yet begun work, so he owed them nothing), and resold all of his office equipment at a substantial loss. He was unable to sublease the office space, as the real estate leasing market was very poor, and there was a glut of available space. Bill has come to you for advice. What, if any, claims might he have against Acme; what are the strengths and weaknesses of his potential claims; and what damages might be available to Bill based on these claims? (Describe and explain damages only generally—no calculations are involved. I have intentionally omitted any information on the $ amounts involved.)

Additional Question: If Bill had already spent substantial money on advertising and marketing in the same market Computers-R-Us intended to service, might Bill have an additional alternative theory of recovery (assuming that any above theory might fail)? Briefly explain the nature of the claim and against whom it might be asserted.

Quick Summary

Here is a very brief summary of the basic principles addressed in Chapter 2. From a strict, formal "contract" perspective, only true "bargains" are enforceable, and a "bargain" requires "consideration." However, promises that are not supported by consideration may nevertheless be enforced based on reliance—to the full extent of the promise or as measured by the promisee's reliance, as justice may require. Even in the complete absence of a promise, a party may be liable for restitution for a benefit received from another so as to avoid unjust enrichment of the recipient of the benefit. In such circumstances in which the recipient has, in fact, promised to pay for the benefit, the only issue is one of whether it was provided gratuitously. Having addressed first the basic issue of "bargains" and nature of contract enforcement, we can now move on to analyze in Chapter 3 and the issue of "agreement," whereupon we will focus on the "offer and acceptance" process by which a contract is formed or concluded.

3

Contract Formation

Lesson 9: The Nature of Contractual Agreement

Objectives and Expected Learning Outcomes

In this lesson, you should learn the nature of consensual assent to a contract bargain. You will learn to distinguish between subjective and objective evidence of the parties' intent. You will further discover that the law generally focuses on objective evidence of intent, but that subjective intent may also be important in certain respects. By the end of this lesson, you should be able to apply the relevant legal rules to determine whether a given set of facts provides the requisite mutual intent of the parties to bind them to a contract.

As earlier stated at the outset of lesson 4, a "contract" requires (1) a bargain; and (2) agreement to that bargain. The remainder of Chapter 2 addressed the "bargain" requirement, along with alternative theories of enforcement. Chapter 3 will now address the issue of "agreement," along with alternative theories of enforcement. This question of agreement to a bargain is based on the intent of the parties to engage in a consensual legal relationship, as analyzed through the paradigm of "offer and acceptance." We begin by looking at the nature of consensual assent to a bargain.

Defining Objective versus Subjective Intent

It has often been said that a contract requires a "meeting of the minds." In fact, this is not true. However, this falsehood provides an excellent point of departure for an explanation of what is required in terms of intent to contract. The idea of the classic "meeting of the minds" rested on the idea that parties should only be bound to a contract when they each shared precisely the same actual mental intention to be so bound. This actual mental intent of an individual party is what we call "subjective" intent. Like any individual thought process, subjective intent may be clear and concise, or it may be more muddled and murky. However, each potential party will necessarily have some mental attitude vis-à-vis the purported contract—even if that attitude is one of complete ignorance. The challenges come in (1) ascertaining the content of that actual mental attitude at the time of the purported agreement; and (2) deciding what, if any, effect to give one party's actual intent in binding the other party.

The most obvious evidence of an individual's subjective intent is that individual's own statement of what he or she intended (or, in the case of a business organization, the statement of the person acting on behalf of that organization).

> **Acting on Behalf of Another**
> In contracting and other legal interaction, one party—an "agent"—will often act "on behalf of" another—the "principal." A full exploration of the law of agency is beyond the scope of this introductory course in Contracts. However, it is useful to remember that a business organization must act through an "agent"—usually an individual (though modern contracts can also be agreed upon and performed through digital interaction).

> **Example 9-1:** On June 1, Jack and Jill discussed Jack's bicycle over coffee at Jack's house. On June 10, Jill returned to Jack's house, saying she was there to pick up and pay for the bike, as they had earlier agreed. Jack replied that he had never agreed to any such thing and had merely been talking about the value of his bike—not his willingness to sell it to Jill.
>
> Jack and Jill have, through their statements on June 10, established that each had a different subjective intent at the time of the purported contract, on June 1. As such, they did not subjectively mutually consent to be bound to a contract.

If a contract actually required a proverbial "meeting of the minds," Jack and Jill would not be bound in the above example. One can easily imagine such a rule, binding parties only when each actually intended such a result. However, such a rule would raise difficult questions of proof and could also deprive a party of his or her "objectively reasonable" expectations in the event of a misunderstanding.

Do we simply trust a person's memory as to what he or she intended at a time that may be a relic of the distant past when a dispute later arises? Do we trust that person's honesty when his or her interests may have changed since the time of the purported contract? After all, there is no realistic method to examine the question of subjective intent beyond a person's own statement (brain surgery, polygraphs, and truth serum being examples of "unrealistic" methods). While effective cross-examination may cast doubt on the believability of a witness, it will not, itself, affirmatively establish the actual subjective intent of the witness at the time of contracting. As such, a rule requiring mutual subjective intent—or a "meeting of the minds"—is not a particularly satisfactory one in terms of resolving subsequent disputes over party intent. It also fails to protect the parties' reasonable understandings of each other's respective communications.

While we cannot, with any certainty, determine what either party was actually thinking at any particular time, we can more easily discover the content of their communications or conduct at such time. This evidence of communications or conduct is often characterized as the "outward manifestations" of the parties, reasonably observable and intelligible to others. Such outward manifestations amount to "objective" evidence of a party's "intent"—often shortened to "objective intent." Objective evidence may include verbal communications, recorded communications (whether written or otherwise recorded in any retrievable form), or conduct reasonably understood as communicating the intent of the actor. The reason we characterize such communications as "objective" evidence is that they are viewed from an objectively reasonable perspective of the listener, reader, or observer.

Objective evidence does not rely on the intention of the sender. Nor does it rely entirely on the understanding of the actual listener, reader, or observer. Instead, objective evidence relies on the perspective and understanding of a hypothetical "reasonable person" in the position of the listener, reader, or observer. Thus, a person later seeking to determine the parties' earlier "intent" with respect to a purported contract at issue need not rely on either party's individualized understanding. That person simply places his or herself "in the shoes" of the parties and determines what a reasonable person would have understood the parties to have intended. For example, in resolving Jack and Jill's dispute in example 9-1, one would consider what Jack and Jill actually said and did, as viewed from the perspectives of reasonable people in their shoes.

Admittedly, the decision maker may in some circumstances be required to rely on party testimony with respect to oral communications or conduct (i.e., deciding between what "he said" versus what "she said"). However, the vast majority of claims will involve at least some factually clear objective evidence of the parties' intent. We will also discover in Chapter 4 that the enforcement of some contracts requires an actual authenticated record (i.e., a signed writing or other record), and we will discover in Chapter 6 that some contracts may rely exclusively on written or otherwise "recorded" provisions for their content. In short, an "objective" approach to interpreting party intent avoids at least some of the problems of proof presented by a "subjective" approach and also protects the reasonable understanding of the recipient of the communications of another.

At the height of its prominence, objective theory was sometimes said to be near absolute. In one of the more famous of such characterizations, Judge Learned Hand stated:

> A contract has, strictly speaking, nothing to do with the personal, or individual, intent of the parties. A contract is an obligation attached by the mere force of law to certain acts of the parties, usually words, which ordinarily accompany and represent a known intent. If, however, it were proved by twenty bishops that either party, when he used the words, intended something else than the usual meaning which the law imposes upon them, he would still be held, unless there were some mutual mistake, or something else of the sort.[1]

Hand's point is of course an important one—we give priority to the parties' outward and observable manifestations of intent, rather than their secretly held, unexpressed subjective intentions. However, this classic rule can easily be overstated. In fact, the subjective intent of one or both of the parties may be significant under certain specific circumstances—whether proven by the testimony of "twenty bishops" or otherwise.

---

[1] Hotchkiss v. National City Bank of New York, 200 F. 287, 293 (D.N.Y. 1911).

A General Rule of Objective Intent—Including Limited Elements of Subjective Intent

In thinking about the basic preference for objective evidence of intent, it is useful to step back and recall the purpose of such evidence—to resolve a dispute between the parties to the relevant communications. If both parties agree as to their respective subjective intentions at the time of contracting, then there is no dispute to resolve, and there is no need to resort to objective evidence. Thus, our starting point in ascertaining the parties' intent to contract (or not) will always be their respective subjective intent. If that subjective intent is identical, then it will be enforced—even if an objectively reasonable person would not have understood such intent under the circumstances. If the subjective intent of the parties differs, then the dispute arising from this difference must be resolved—most often (*though not always*) by reference to objective evidence.

In most cases, this dispute will be resolved by giving effect to the intent of the party whose intent most closely comports with that of a reasonable person in the position of the parties.[2] The rule is sometimes simply characterized as giving effect to the understanding an objectively reasonable person would have had under the circumstances. However, the choice of alternatives is, in fact, limited to the purported individual intent of each of the actual parties. Thus, in the typical two-party transaction, we give legal effect to whichever purported intent is most objectively reasonable.

> ### Example 9-2: Lucy v. Zehmer
>
> Two friends, W.O. Lucy and A.H. Zehmer were chatting over a few beers at a local bar and restaurant, also joined by Ida, Zehmer's wife. At some point, the conversation turned to discussion of Zehmer's farm, which Lucy offered to purchase for $50,000. Zehmer responded positively to the offer (though later claimed he was just joking). At Lucy's request, Zehmer then wrote out the following terms on the back of a blank restaurant check:

---

[2] *See* Restatement (Second) of Contracts § 20(2)(b).

"We hereby agree to sell to W.O. Lucy the Ferguson farm complete for $50,000. Title satisfactory to buyer." The document was signed by both A.O. and Ida Zehmer. In fact, Mr. Zehmer had originally begun the recital "I hereby agree . . .," but Lucy asked that it be changed to "we" and that Ida sign it as well. Zehmer then whispered to his wife that it was merely a joke, and she should play along by signing, but intentionally did so in a manner such that Lucy could not hear this private conversation between the two Zehmers.

After both of the Zehmer's had signed it, Lucy picked up the document and put it in his pocket. When Lucy then offered $5 to "bind the bargain," Zehmer refused, for the first time saying that he was only joking and had no intention of selling the farm. However, Lucy insisted the Zehmers had already done so and left the premises insisting he had purchase the farm.

Zehmer asserted that he never intended to sell his farm to Lucy, but had merely been bluffing in an effort to get Lucy to admit he did not have $50,000. Lucy asserted that he was entirely serious in contracting to purchase the farm (the next day, he managed to get half of the money from his brother in exchange for a half interest in the farm). The court ultimately held that Lucy's understanding was more reasonable based on the objective manifestations of the parties, as viewed by a reasonable person.[3]

Which, if any, facts supported Zehmer's purported intent? Which, if any, facts support Lucy's purported intent? In the actual case, the court determined that the parties' objective manifestations established an intent to form a binding contract. Do you agree?

What was Lucy trying to accomplish with his offer of $5 to "bind the bargain"? If Zehmer had accepted the $5, would it have had any legal significance? In answering this, you should on one hand return to our discussion in Chapter 2 of "peppercorn," and its ineffectiveness as consideration.

---

[3] Lucy v. Zehmer, 196 Va. 493, 84 S.E.2d 516 (Va. 1954).

On the other hand, does an exchange of a farm for $50,000 require any further consideration? Finally, might Zehmer's acceptance of the $5 at this point have added further objective evidence supporting Lucy's perception that this was a serious bargain?

Zehmer also initially argued that he was sufficiently intoxicated that he lacked the legal "capacity" to conclude a contract. We will address the question of "capacity" later, in Chapter 5. However, in this case, the court found, as a matter of fact, that Zehmer was not too intoxicated to sell the farm.

Suppose we change the facts slightly. Suppose that, when Zehmer whispered to his wife, Lucy actually heard him, because Lucy had extraordinary hearing—far more sensitive than the typical person. Should this single fact change the outcome? If Lucy knew that Zehmer was just joking, then he knew they did not share a common intent—before any contract was agreed upon. Under this circumstance, what should the law expect of Lucy?

In fact, if Lucy actually knew of Zehmer's contrary intent, then he is bound by that intent, and there is no contract in this case. In effect, if Lucy knew in advance that the parties did not share the same subjective intent, but failed to alert Zehmer to this fact, then Lucy would be precluded from taking advantage of the parties' misunderstanding—even if Lucy's view was the most reasonable. Thus, if the parties assert different subjective intents, the first question we must ask—even before looking to objective manifestations of intent—is whether either party knew, at the time of contracting, of the other party's contrary subjective intent.

Let's return now to the basic rule of objective intent and look at another case in which it is more difficult to establish an objective basis for believing the other party seriously intended to contract.

Example 9-3: *Leonard v. Pepsico*

View the video at www.youtube.com/watch?v=U_n5SN rMaL8. After watching this commercial on television, John Leonard sent in a "Pepsi Points" order form, enclosing 15 Pepsi Points and a check for $700,000. While the order form did not specifically mention the Harrier Jet shown in the commercial as available for 7,000,000 Pepsi Points, it permitted the purchase of additional points at 10 cents each. Thus, the check for $700,000 was equivalent to 7,000,000 points—the amount reflected in the commercial as needed to acquire the jet.

The court ruled that no one objectively viewing the commercial could have reasonably expected to buy this military attack aircraft at the stated price equivalent.[4]

Do you agree with the different outcomes in Examples 9-2 and 9-3? Why or why not?

In Example 9-3, the court focused to some degree on the price as evidence that the offer was not objectively serious—the price of a Harrier Jet being roughly $23 million. Thus, an objectively unreasonable price may affect the question of whether the parties objectively intended to be bound. However, it is important not to confuse this reference to price with the issues of consideration addressed in Chapter 2 (the adequacy of consideration is irrelevant in distinguishing between an enforceable bargain and an unenforceable gift, as long as the consideration is real, as opposed to "peppercorn"). Ultimately, the difference comes down to the parties' intent. If the parties objectively intended a bargain, it will be given effect. If not, then they will not be bound.

Failing to Conclude a Contract, Though Both Parties Intended One

In Examples 9-2 and 9-3, the parties purported subjective intent differed. However, the court was able to determine that their outward manifestations, as viewed objectively by a reasonable person in their positions, favored one party's subjective view over the other. In other words, one party's subjective view was more objectively reasonable than the other's. However, in some circumstances, the parties may have differing subjective understandings without any reasonable basis for choosing one over the other.

Example 9-4: *Raffles v. Wichelhaus*

Raffles agreed to sell Wichelhaus 125 bales of cotton for delivery to Liverpool, to arrive on the ship "Peerless," sailing from Bombay. As it turned out, there were two different ships "Peerless" sailing from Bombay to Liverpool, one arriving in October and the other arriving in December.

---

[4] Leonard v. Pepsico, Inc., 88 F. Supp. 2d 116 (S.D.N.Y. 1999).

When Raffles sought to deliver the bales in December, Wichelhaus asserted that it had been referring to the ship Peerless arriving in October—not December. Thus, the seller and buyer had purportedly referred to cotton on two entirely different ships, and the price of cotton has changed significantly within the 2 month time difference. The opinion is considered a "classic," though hardly a model of clarity. Arguably, the court simply found no basis for giving any objective preference to either purported subjective interpretation and, therefore, found no contract.[5]

With Examples 9-2, 9-3, and 9-4 in mind, along with the hypothetical variation of Example 9-2 in which Lucy actually knew that Zehmer was merely joking, we can now summarize the basic rule.

Summary of Basic Rule: ascertaining intent to contract[6]

- Where the parties share the same subjective intent, that intent shall be given effect.

- Where the subjective intent of the parties differs, the difference shall be resolved by giving effect to the subjective intent of one or the other, as follows:

  o If either party actually knew at the time of contracting the differing subjective intent of the other, then that known intent shall be given effect. Absent such actual knowledge, . . .

  o That subjective intent shall be given effect that is most consistent with the outward manifestations of the parties, viewed from the perspective of an objectively reasonable person in the position of the parties.

- However, if neither party had any objectively reasonable basis for understanding the other's differing subjective intent, then there shall be no contract.

Party Intent under UCC Article 2

UCC Article 2 does not expressly address the aforementioned determinations of intent with respect to formation, but does make clear that such intent may take a broad variety of forms and be derived from a broad range of sources. **STOP NOW and READ the excerpts from UCC § 2-204 below.**

---

[5] 2 H. & C. 906, 159 Eng. Rep. 375 (Ct. of Ex. 1864).
[6] This basic rule is reflected in Restatement (Second) of Contracts §§ 18, 19, and 20.

UCC § 2-204(1) AND (2)

(1) A contract for sale of goods may be made in any manner sufficient to show agreement, including conduct by both parties which recognizes the existence of such a contract.

(2) An agreement sufficient to constitute a contract for sale may be found even though the moment of its making is undetermined.

. . .

The foregoing statutory provision is fully consistent with and is supplemented by the common law rules regarding the use of subjective and objective evidence of the parties' intent with respect to formation.

Party Intent under the CISG

The CISG also employs a very similar rule, giving effect to one party's unilateral subjective intent only under very limited circumstances, and generally looking to objective determinations of the outward manifestations of the parties. **STOP NOW and READ the excerpts from CISG Article 8 below.**

CISG ARTICLE 8(1) AND (2)

(1) For the purposes of this Convention statements made by and other conduct of a party are to be interpreted according to his intent where the other party knew or could not have been unaware what that intent was.

(2) If the preceding paragraph is not applicable, statements made by and other conduct of a party are to be interpreted according to the understanding that a reasonable person of the same kind as the other party would have had in the same circumstances.

. . .

Article 8(1) gives effect to one party's unilateral subjective intent when the other party actually knew of that subjective intent (much like the common law) or when it can be said that the party "could not have been unaware" of that intent. This latter language is unique to the CISG. Like most double-negatives, it can be a bit tricky to apply. A party "could not have been unaware" of "facts that are before the eyes of one who can see."[7] As such, the standard arguably provides an evidentiary means of proving a party's "actual knowledge" by reasonable inference rather than "brain surgery" (which is of course impractical at best).

In most cases, the requirements of Article 8(1) will not be met, and the issue will be resolved by reference to Article 8(2). Much like the common law, Article 8(2) gives effect to the outward manifestations of each party based on the objectively reasonable understanding of the recipient or viewer of the manifestations. The remainder of Article 8, along with Article 9, will be addressed when contract interpretation is explored more fully in Chapter 6.

APPLYING THE RULES

Problem 1: Reconsider Examples 4-1, 4-2, and 4-3. We considered these cases earlier in addressing the question of consideration. However, do you think the defendants in any of these cases might have been able to argue that the purported promisor had no intention to conclude a binding contract? Consider the context of each of these promises.

Problem 2: Jane is casually surfing the internet and suddenly discovers that she needs to download some additional software in order to use the website she is currently trying to access. The software is entirely "free," so she downloads it and, in doing so, also "clicks through" a button that says "I agree," though she does not bother to read it. Is Jane bound by these terms connected to the "I agree" button, as a matter of contract? What if they preclude her from using the downloaded software for "commercial" purposes (as opposed to her own personal use)? What if they require her to pay $100 for the downloaded software?

Problem 3: Dr. Oswald, a professional art dealer from Switzerland, was interested in the collection of Swiss art held by Ms. Allen, a professional art

---

[7] *See* John Honnold and Harry Flechtner, Uniform Law for International Sales under the 1980 United Nations Convention (Kluwer, 4th ed., 2009) (specifically addressing the meaning of the same phrase at issue, albeit under CISG Article 35(3)).

dealer from New York. While in New York, Dr. Oswald arranged to see the Swiss art held by Ms. Allen. At the time, Ms. Allen's Swiss art included two separate collections, each housed in a common location. The first collection was much larger in number, while the second collection was kept separate, as it included only a few rarer, and more valuable, pieces. Ms. Allen always referred to the latter collection specifically as her "rare art collection," and did so in her conversations with Dr. Oswald. After viewing all of the art in both collections, Dr. Oswald thanked Ms. Allen and indicated that he would likely be back in touch soon. A few days later, Ms. Allen received a written offer of $3,000,000 from Dr. Oswald for her "Swiss art collection." Ms. Allen understood the offer to include only the first collection—not the second rare art collection. She promptly communicated her agreement to Dr. Oswald. When it came time for delivery, however, it became clear that Dr. Oswald had intended the offer to include both collections.

Have the parties' concluded a contract? If so, whose intent controls?

Suppose Dr. Oswald had known that the portion of Ms. Allen's total Swiss Art collection made up of the "rare art collection" was, by itself, worth $25,000,000. Would this change your answer? If so, what legal authority most directly answers the question?

The facts of this problem are loosely based on the case of *Oswald v. Allen*, 417 F.2d 43 (2d Cir. 1969) (involving two collections of Swiss coins, instead of Swiss art).

Lesson 10: Offer & Acceptance—the Offer

> ### *Objectives and Expected Learning Outcomes*
>
> In this lesson, you should learn to identify an offer from among various communications between parties negotiating towards a possible contract. In doing so, you will consider the intent of the sender of the communication to be bound, the specificity with which intended recipients are identified, and the definiteness of the proposed terms. By the end of this lesson, you should be able to apply each of these requirements to real or hypothetical facts to determine if and when an offer has been made.

The Basic Offer & Acceptance Paradigm

In the last lesson, we focused on the nature of the parties' intent, as established by their communications in various forms. In the rest of this Chapter we will focus on the content and sequence of these communications in establishing a contract (or not). At its most basic level, the "offer & acceptance" paradigm asks two questions: (1) did one party (the "offeror") make an "offer," and, if so, (2) did the recipient of the offer (the "offeree") "accept" it. If the answer to both of these questions is "yes," and if the accepted offer amounts to a "bargain" supported by "consideration" (as thoroughly discussed in Chapter 2), then the parties have a binding contract. In short, offer plus acceptance plus consideration generally equals a binding contract. Or in a more formulaic presentation:

$$\text{O (offer)} + \text{A (acceptance)} + \text{C (consideration)} = \text{K (contract)}$$

The Offer

An offer is a communication that reasonably invites the recipient to conclude a contract between the parties by nothing more than timely assent.[8] Such an offer may follow from or be a part of a lengthy series of preliminary negotiations, or it may arise from a single, initial, unsolicited communication by the offeror.

---

[8] *See* Restatement (Second) of Contracts § 24 ([a]n offer is the manifestation of willingness to enter into a bargain, so made as to justify another person in understanding that his assent to that bargain is invited and will conclude it).

Example 10-1: Ace Electronics was interested having its plant repainted. Ace sent out invitations to a number of local painting companies to submit proposals. Perfect Painting initially contacted Ace to learn more about the sort of painting project it wanted. Perfect then submitted a proposal (as did others), including process and materials suggestions, a time frame for completion, and a complete price. Ace replied to Perfect that its submission looked interesting, but that Ace would prefer a slightly different process and paint product. Perfect replied that it could certainly accommodate Ace's wishes, and also proposed a new price. Ace then replied that it needed a price that was 10% lower than that proposed by Perfect. Perfect replied that it could lower the price by 8%—not 10%—but would need an additional week to complete the project. Ace replied that Perfect's final proposal was acceptable. The parties were bound to a contract based on their series of exchanges, as reflected by the terms of the latest exchange on each relevant issue.

Example 10-2: Hal walks up to a booth at a flea market in which Meg is selling art prints. When she sees Hal looking at a particular print, she says "it's yours for $10." Hal says "you've got a deal." Meg made an offer, which Hal promptly accepted, and they have concluded a binding contract.

The extent of the negotiations in these two examples is of course very different. However, in each case, one of the parties, at some point in the negotiations, made an offer that was accepted by the other party. In this lesson, we will focus on the questions of if and when such an "offer" has been made. The challenge is in determining whether any given communication is merely one of a number of communications constituting "preliminary negotiations"[9] or, potentially (if accepted), the penultimate communication in conclusion of a contract.

---

[9] *See* Restatement (Second) of Contracts § 26.

As indicated at the outset, the essential characteristic of an offer is that it conveys the power to the recipient—the offeree—to conclude a contract with a simple affirmation of agreement. The question of whether such a power has been granted may raise three potential issues: (1) intent of the offeror to be bound; (2) specificity as to the offeree or offerees empowered to accept; and (3) definiteness as to the terms of the offer. Each is addressed in turn.

Intent to be Bound

An offer must indicate, expressly or impliedly, that the offeror intends to convey to the offeree "the last word" in concluding a contract—assuming of course that the offeree is willing to consent to the offered terms. Such intent is determined objectively, by reference to the outward manifestations of the offeror, as explained in the previous lesson.

An intent to be bound must generally be expressed in an affirmative and positive manner.

> **Example 10-3: *Owen v. Tunison***
>
> Tunison owned a tract of land, and Owen wished to purchase said tract. To that end, Owen wrote a letter to Tunison, asking "[w]ill you sell me your store property which is located on Main St. in Bucksport, Me. running from Montgomery's Drug Store on one corner to a Grocery Store on the other, for the sum of $6,000.00?"
>
> In reply, Tunison wrote back, "[b]ecause of improvements which have been added and an expenditure of several thousand dollars it would not be possible for me to sell it unless I was to receive $16,000.00 cash."
>
> Owen promptly responded "[a]ccept your offer for Bradley block Bucksport Terms sixteen thousand cash send deed to Eastern Trust and Banking Co Bangor Maine Please acknowledge." However, Tunison declined to sell, and Owen sued to enforce.

In holding that no offer had been made by Tunison, the court first referred to a prior case in which the words, "[w]ould not consider less than half" were held "not to be taken as an outright offer to sell for one-half." A positive willingness to sell under one circumstance cannot be reasonably inferred from a negative unwillingness to sell under another. Thus, Owen could not reasonably presume that his willingness to buy the property at $16,000 would conclude the deal.

The court also discussed the issue of "specificity," which is addressed in the next section.[10]

In the above example, the court seemingly determined that the purported offer was neither affirmative nor positive. Do you agree? This was not the court's only concern, as you will see in the next section. Example 10-4 below presents a nice contrast to example 10-3 above.

Example 10-4: *Fairmount Glass Works v. Crunden-Martin Woodenware Co.*

(1) CM wrote a letter to F as follows: "Please advise us the lowest price you can make us on our order for ten car loads of Mason green jars, complete, with caps, packed one dozen in a case, either delivered here, or f. o. b. cars your place, as you prefer. State terms and cash discount. Very truly, Crunden-Martin W. W. Co."

(2) F answered via letter: "Replying to your [recent letter], we quote you Mason fruit jars, complete, in one-dozen boxes, delivered in East St. Louis, Ill.: Pints $4.50, quarts $5.00, half gallons $6.50, per gross, for immediate acceptance, and shipment not later than May 15, 1895; sixty days' acceptance, or 2 off, cash in ten days. Yours, truly, Fairmount Glass Works. . . ."

---

[10] Owen v. Tunison, 131 Me. 42, 158 A. 926 (1932).

(3) CM replied: "Your [recent letter] received. Enter order ten car loads as per your quotation. Specifications mailed. Crunden-Martin W. W. Co."

(4) F then responded: "Impossible to book your order. Output all sold. . . . Fairmount Glass Works."

CM asserted that communication #2 was an offer from F, which CM accepted in #3. F asserted that #2 merely reflected preliminary negotiations, and CM made the first offer in #3, which F rejected in #4.

The court focused on F's expression in communication #2, "for immediate acceptance," which, taken in connection with CM's initial communication (at what price would F sell the goods to CM?), strongly suggested evidence of a present offer. Thus CM closed the contract when it "immediately accepted" that offer in communication #3.[11]

Ultimately, the question of intent to be bound tends to be very fact specific, focusing on the manifestations of the purported offeror, as understood by an objectively reasonable person in the shoes of the purported offeree.

Specificity

An offer must be directed to a specific person or group of persons, who are empowered by the offer to accept it. Unless the purported offeror has in some manner identified an intended audience for the purported offer, one cannot reasonably say that anyone is empowered to accept it by mere assent.

In *Owen v. Tunison* (example 10-3), the court suggested that Tunison's communication was more general than specific, in nature, and was not, therefore, clearly directed to Owen. In contrast, the court found in *Fairmount Glass Works* (example 10-4) the language "we quote you" (emphasis supplied), to be sufficiently specific in indicating that the communication

---

[11] Fairmount Glass Works v. Crunden-Martin Woodenware Co., 106 Ky. 659, 51 S.W. 196 (Ct. App. 1899).

was directed specifically to the recipient—notwithstanding the use of the word "quote" (which might otherwise suggest a more general advertisement). This requirement of "specificity" with respect to the offeree is also reflected in the often referenced "advertising rule."

The purpose of the advertising rule should be obvious. A broad communication offering a limited supply of goods or services cannot generally be accepted by all of the recipients of that general communication. One can, of course, easily think of practical exceptions, such as computer software (the supply of downloads being theoretically unlimited). However, the general rule is based on sound practical considerations in most cases. Consider the following example.

> **The "Advertising Rule"**
> Where a seller communicates through a medium of broad circulation that it has a certain quantity or quality of goods for sale at certain prices and on certain terms, such an "advertisement" is not an offer to be accepted by any person to whose notice it may come. Instead, it is construed as an invitation to make an offer to the seller on the terms stated, which the seller may then accept or reject.

Example 10-5: *Moulton v. Kershaw*

C.J. Kershaw & Son mailed the following letter to a number of potential customers for salt, including J. H. Moulton.

Dear Sir, in consequence of a rupture in the salt trade, we are authorized to offer Michigan fine salt, in full car-load lots of 80 to 95 barrels, delivered at your city, at $0.85 per barrel, to be shipped per C. & N. W. Railroad Co. only. At this price it is a bargain . . . . Shall be pleased to receive your order.

Moulton promptly sought to "accept" Kershaw's purported offer by placing an order for 2000 barrels of salt. However, Kershaw refused to honor the order, and Moulton sought to enforce the contract it believed it had concluded with Kershaw.

The court held that the parties had not concluded a contract, because the communication at issue was in the nature of an advertisement and, therefore, merely invited offers from those to whom it was addressed. Moulton had made such an offer, and Kershaw had rejected it. Thus, no contract was concluded. [12]

While the general rule provides that advertisements are not offers, this rule is subject to exception where the nature of the advertisement suggests otherwise. One of the classic exceptions to the general rule involves advertisements specifying "first come-first served."

Example 10-6: *Lefkowitz v. Great Minneapolis Surplus Store*

The Great Minneapolis Surplus Store ran this newspaper ad:

Saturday 9 A.M.

1 Black Lapin Stole Beautiful, worth $139.50 ... $1.00

First Come First Served

Mr. Lefkowitz appeared on Saturday morning before 9 A.M., was first in line, and tendered $1 for the stole. However, the store refused to sell it to Lefkowitz, asserting that the sale was limited to women. Lefkowitz sued for the difference between $1 and the value of the stole.

The court acknowledge the general rule that advertisements are not offers. However, the court went on to explain that when a promise has been made in positive terms in return for something requested, and the offer is "clear, definite, and explicit"—leaving "nothing open for negotiation," it constitutes an offer, acceptance of which will complete the contract.

---

[12] Moulton v. Kershaw, 59 Wis. 316, 18 N.W. 172 (1884).

> In this case, the offer by the store to sell the Lapin stole was "clear, definite, and explicit," and "left nothing open for negotiation." Lefkowitz appeared first in line at the appointed time and place and tendered the requested $1. He was, therefore, entitled to enforce the store's promise.
>
> The court further found that nothing within the ad suggested that the offer was limited to women.[13]

The Lefkowitz case is often cited for this "exception" to the general "advertising rule," where the offer expressly states or reasonably implies "first come-first served." In effect, the offer was not made specifically to Lefkowitz—it was made to the first person in line at the appointed time and place. However, when Lefkowitz was the first to arrive, he became that specific offeree.

Another way to look at this sort of advertisement is that it is actually an offer of a unilateral contract. The store, as promisor, bargains for one of its customers to perform by being the first in line. When one customer does so, the store is bound by its promise to sell the stated goods to that customer at the stated price.

As you can likely see, this "first come-first served" exception avoids the problem of limited supply that underlies the advertising rule. Only the "first" is empowered to accept (whether this may include the "first one" or "first ten" will depend on the language of the advertisement). Like the issue of "intent to be bound," the issue of specificity is also very fact specific outside of the general application of the advertising rule.

Definiteness

An offer must be sufficiently definite for the parties to know what it is they have agreed upon. Without such definiteness, the parties would lack a clear understanding of their rights and obligations arising from any resulting agreement, and a court would be unable to determine whether either party had complied with or had breached its obligations.

---

[13] Lefkowitz v. Great Minneapolis Surplus Store, 251 Minn. 188, 86 N.W.2d 689 (1957).

In the *Fairmount* case, in example 10-4, the buyer argued that the contract was indefinite, because, among other things, 10 car loads was ambiguous as to quantify. However, the court relied on proof showing that "10 car loads" is an expression used in the trade as equivalent to 1,000 gross, 100 gross being regarded a car load. We will much more fully explore the use of such expressions of the trade in Chapter 6. However, they are generally given effect when the parties know of such usages, or should, and does not expressly disavow them. In *Lefkowitz*, in example 10-6, the court found that the offer was "clear, definite, and explicit, thus fully satisfying the requirement of definiteness.

Under the common law, an effective offer must generally include a price or an effective mechanism for determining the price.

Example 10-7: *Walker v. Keith*

Walker leased a small lot to Keith at $100 per month for a term of 10 years. The lease agreement also granted Keith an additional 10 year renewal option, with the monthly rental price to be determined as follows: "rental will be fixed in such amount as shall actually be agreed upon by the lessors and the lessee with the monthly rental fixed on the comparative basis of rental values as of the date of the renewal with rental values at this time reflected by the comparative business conditions of the two periods."

At the end of the initial 10 year period, Keith gave the proper notice to renew, but the parties were unable to agree upon the rent. Keith sought to enforce the lease option and asked a court to determine the rent, while Walker asserted that the option was not enforceable because the price was not sufficiently definite.

In ruling in favor of Walker, the court first pointed out that "the parties had not agreed upon a rent figure." The rent provision instead included two basic components: (1) an "agreement to agree," and (2) an incomprehensible "comparative" adjustment mechanism. The court then went on to explain that an "agreement to agree" to something in the future was no agreement at all and was, therefore, unenforceable. Finally, any attempt by a court to set the rent based on such an ambiguous adjustment mechanism (or based on some sort of "reasonable" rental amount) would entail the court binding the parties to a bargain of its own making—not theirs. Thus, the court declined to enforce the option because it lacked a sufficiently definite price.[14]

In the above example, the court refused to enforce the purported option based on the lack of a "definite" agreement on price. The same rule would have applied to the original lease term had the parties failed to agree on that price, and it is ultimately the offer that must be sufficiently definite. As we explore the nature of "acceptance" in subsequent lessons, it will become clear that an indefinite offer cannot somehow become a definite contract. While the rule is sometimes framed in terms of a requirement of a "contract," it must be fully satisfied by reference to the offer.

Summary of Basic Rule: the offer[15]

- An offer is a communication that reasonably invites the recipient to conclude a contract between the parties by nothing more than timely assent, as reflected by all three of the following:

  ○ The intent of the offeror to be bound by mere acceptance;

  ○ The designation of the offeree (either expressly or impliedly) as a person specifically empowered to accept;

    ▪ An advertisement is not generally an offer, but merely an invitation to recipients to make an offer to the advertiser;

    ▪ However, an advertisement may be an offer where the content and circumstances suggest that a recipient may accept by mere assent.

  ○ The definiteness of the terms of the contract offered.

- Other communications (not offers) in furtherance of a potential contract are construed as mere "preliminary negotiations"

The following case presents a nice opportunity to apply these rules.

---

[14] Walker v. Keith, 382 S.W.2d 198 (Ky. App. 1964).
[15] This basic rule is reflected in Restatement (Second) of Contracts §§ 24 and 26.

FROM THE COURT

Donovan v. RRL Corporation

Court of Appeals of California (1999)
88 Cal. Rptr. 2d 143

RYLAARSDAM, Judge

A first year law student would not be surprised to be called upon to answer the questions we address here. Does an advertisement for a specific used car at a designated price constitute an offer that may be accepted by tendering the purchase price? Does a statute prohibiting an automobile dealer from refusing to sell a vehicle at the advertised price affect the answer? Finally, does the answer change if the erroneous price inserted in the advertisement was the result of an error? We believe the answers are respectively "possibly," "yes," and "no." However, since such cryptic answers would not entitle our hypothetical law student to a passing grade, we must explain these answers below.

FACTS

Plaintiff Brian J. Donovan, intending to shop for a car, noticed an advertisement by Lexus of Westminster . . . in his Saturday local newspaper, the Daily Pilot. The advertisement presented a number of used cars for sale, one of which was a 1995 Jaguar XJ6 Vanden Plas, VIN 720603, which was listed for $25,995.

The next day plaintiff and his wife drove to defendant's lot and noticed the automobile described in the advertisement displayed in a prominent location. With the permission of one of defendant's representatives, the prospective buyers took the car for a test drive. Plaintiff then told the representative he would take the car for the advertised price. Immediately, the representative told plaintiff "that's a mistake." After an exchange during which plaintiff accused the representative of engaging in bait-and-switch advertising he was referred to the sales manager.

Plaintiff offered to write a check for the full amount of the advertised price. After making some calculations, the manager told plaintiff he would sell the car for $37,016. Plaintiff refused to pay this amount and left. After some correspondence wherein he unsuccessfully attempted to persuade defendant to complete the sale, plaintiff filed suit in municipal court.

During a bench trial, [the court heard evidence that the price published in the newspaper was in fact a mistake and ruled in Defendant's favor on that basis].

Plaintiff appealed . . .

DISCUSSION

Is an Advertisement an Offer?

[The court observed that, while generally scarce, California case law generally recognized that] "advertisements are not typically treated as offers, but merely as invitations to bargain." [Citations omitted]. However, [California courts also recognize] "a fundamental exception to this rule: an advertisement can constitute an offer, and form the basis of a unilateral contract, if it calls for performance of a specific act without further communication and leaves nothing for further negotiation." [Citations omitted]. . . . This principle is also supported by the Restatement: "It is of course possible to make an offer by an advertisement directed to the general public ... but there must ordinarily be some language of commitment or some invitation to take action without further communication." (Rest.2d Contracts, supra, § 26, com. b, at p. 76.)

. . . The general rule is clear. The question is: Does the exception apply here?

Did the advertisement, which offered a specific car at a designated price, qualify as calling "for performance of a specific act without further communication and [leaving] nothing for further negotiation"? [Citation omitted]. Or to put it in the words of the Restatement, did it contain "some language of commitment or some invitation to take action without further communication"? (Rest.2d Contracts, supra, § 26, com. b, at p. 76.)

The advertisement did not merely indicate that a generic lot of 1995 Jaguars were available for sale at $26,000; rather, it offered a specific, unique automobile for that price. There was nothing to indicate in the advertisement that the prospective buyer needed to do anything other than tender the purchase price, . . . As to the suggestion that such a ruling would open the dealer to liability, not only to plaintiff, but to all other persons tendering the purchase price, the Restatement provides an answer: "A publishes an offer of reward to whoever will give him certain information. There is no indication that A intends to pay more than once. Any person learning of the offer has power to accept ... but the giving of the information by one terminates the power of every other person." (Rest.2d Contracts, supra, § 29, com. b, illus.1, at p. 84.) So here, obviously, only one person can accept the offer. Presumably, plaintiff was the first person to do so.

Defendant and amicus Times Mirror Company (Times) argue that the exception to the general rule only applies to offers for unilateral contracts. This may be generally true; . . . However, the Restatement contains no such limitation . . . So here, plaintiff's statement after the test drive that he would take the car at the advertised price may be construed as acceptance of a bilateral contract. On the other hand, the advertisement, on its face, required the performance of a specific act: the tender of the purchase price, an act which plaintiff performed. His failure to actually present the purchase price was excused by defendant's refusal. [Citation omitted]. We do not consider the characterization of the contract as either unilateral or bilateral essential to our decision.

Amici California Motor Car Dealers (CMCD) and Times argue that the Vehicle Code contemplates that a written agreement of sale or lease will be made between dealer and customer before a vehicle is delivered. They contend that therefore something more than a mere tender of the purchase price would be required to complete a contract. Although not expressly establishing such a requirement, they are correct in asserting that the Vehicle Code contemplates such a written contract (see, e.g., section 11713.1, subds. (v) & (x)). However, this does not, in and of itself, preclude the formation of a binding contract prior to completion of the contemplated writing. Here also the Restatement provides the answer: "Manifestations of assent that are in themselves sufficient to conclude a contract will not be prevented from so operating by the fact that the parties also manifest an intention to prepare and adopt a written memorial thereof...." (Rest.2d Contracts, supra, § 27, at p. 78.)

Amicus CMCD also argues that a number of non-price issues, such as the amount of the down payment, financing, warranties, trade-in allowances, insurance, delivery dates, service contracts, title and registration issues, pollution control certificates, taxes, and statutory notices and warnings are normally negotiated in connection with the purchase of an automobile. This may be true in general; it was not true in this case. If plaintiff had sought to negotiate any such matters, he would have been making a counter offer. He did not attempt to negotiate any terms; he merely indicated a willingness to tender the advertised purchase price. If he was willing to buy the car without financing, without a trade-in, without warranties, there is no principle of law requiring him to do otherwise.

Ultimately, this is a close case and neither case law nor the Restatement provides a clear-cut answer. However, as we discuss immediately below, the requirement imposed by section 11713.1, subdivision (e) tips the scale in favor of our construing the advertisement as an offer which could be, and was, accepted by an attempted tender of the purchase price.

The Effect of Section 11713.1, subdivision (e)

Section 11713.1, subdivision (e) makes it unlawful for an automobile dealer to "[f]ail to sell a vehicle to any person at the advertised total price, exclusive of taxes [and certain other specified fees]." . . .

[The court went on to determine that the purpose of the statute further supported its construction of the advertisement as an offer under the circumstances of this case.]

Did the Mistake Vitiate the Offer?

[The court of appeals went on to determine that the dealer's mistake did not relieve it of liability here—a determination that was later reversed by the California Supreme Court (the analysis above was left intact). This issue of mistake is taken up later, in Chapter 9.]

DISPOSITION

The judgment is reversed. The case is remanded to the trial court to determine plaintiff's damages. Plaintiff shall recover his costs on appeal.

CASE QUESTIONS

(1) Did the communication of the car dealer reasonably invite Donovan to conclude a contract by merely assenting to its terms?

    a. Did the car dealer intend to be bound?

    b. Did the car dealer specifically empower Donovan to accept?

        i. Did this "ad" fall short of an "offer" based on the general rule; or

        ii. Did the "ad" rise to the level of an "offer" based on the exception?

    c. Was the dealer's communication sufficiently "definite" to constitute an "offer"?

(2) What was the relevance of the California statute addressing "bait-and-switch" tactics? Most cases will not involve such statutes. However, in this case, it would seem to add to the circumstances that would lead a reasonable buyer to believe that he could accept the offer, unless another buyer had already done so.

(3) The "mistake" issue is left for later coverage in Chapter 9. However, in extreme cases, a "mistake" in price may be so extreme as to lead a reasonable person to expect that the price must be an error. If so, then the buyer cannot reasonably expect that his assent will conclude a contract. In the instant case, however, there was no indication that the mistaken price was so great that Donovan should have known it was wrong.

Offers under UCC Article 2

UCC Article 2 does not expressly define the requirements for an offer, but does make clear that an offer need not address all of the required contract terms. **STOP NOW and READ the excerpts from UCC § 2-204 below.**

UCC § 2-204(3)

. . .

(3) Even though one or more terms are left open a contract for sale does not fail for indefiniteness if the parties have intended to make a contract and there is a reasonably certain basis for giving an appropriate remedy.

The foregoing statutory provision is supplemented by the common law rules regarding the requirement of an offer, and this common law analysis controls all of the sales of goods encountered thus far in this lesson. However, Article 2 will displace the common law to the extent that it may be somewhat more liberal or "relaxed" in finding an offer. One of the most significant examples is the requirement of a price.

As explained by reference to example 10-7, the common law traditionally required that an offer include a price. In contrast, UCC Article 2 does not require a price, as suggested by UCC § 2-204(3) above and further clarified by UCC § 2-305, which provides a mechanism for supplying a price if the parties do not. This process of "gap filling" is addressed more fully later in Chapter 6. For now, the key points are that (1) UCC Article 2 is quite generous in finding an offer, and (2) one of the main reasons is that Article 2 includes "default" terms or "gap fillers" addressing the vast majority of the terms necessary for a sale of goods transaction.

Offers under the CISG

The requirement of an offer under the CISG is somewhat similar to the common law and likely more restrictive in finding an offer than UCC Article 2. **STOP NOW and READ CISG Article 14 below.**

CISG ARTICLE 14

(1) A proposal for concluding a contract addressed to one or more specific persons constitutes an offer if it is sufficiently definite and indicates the intention of the offeror to be bound in case of acceptance. A proposal is sufficiently definite if it indicates the goods and expressly or implicitly fixes or makes provision for determining the quantity and the price.

> **(2)** A proposal other than one addressed to one or more specific persons is to be considered merely as an invitation to make offers, unless the contrary is clearly indicated by the person making the proposal.

Unlike UCC Article 2, the language of CISG Article 14 seemingly requires a price (express or factually implied). While a few courts and commentators have suggested otherwise (and this level of analysis of Article 14 is beyond the scope of this introductory course), parties to a contract governed by the CISG would certainly not want to count on a court supplying a price where the parties had failed to do so.

APPLYING THE RULES

Problem 1: Oliver, an Oregon rancher, owned considerable lands and had decided to reduce the size of his operation and sell some of his property, along with some of his Forest Service grazing permits. He conferred with his accountant and decided how best to structure a transaction for tax purposes. The land that Oliver had decided to sell was adjacent to land owned by Southworth, and he knew that Southworth had always wanted this property.

Oliver stopped by Southworth's ranch, explained that he was interested in selling the land in question and asked if Southworth would be interested in buying it. Southworth said "yes," he would. Oliver also mentioned that Holliday, another neighbor, might be interested in this land or in the grazing permits that Oliver also hoped to sell—separate and apart from the land. Oliver showed Southworth a map and pointed out the specific land he intended to sell. However, there was no discussion at the time of either price or sale terms, as Oliver indicated that he needed additional time and information to work those out. Southworth indicated to Oliver that he needed time arrange his finances so as to be able to purchase the land. There was never any discussion of any connection between the sale of the land and the sale of the grazing permits.

About a month later, Oliver had decided on a price. Oliver also changed his mind and decided that he would prefer to sell the land and grazing permits in a single package deal, though he did not mention this directly to anyone. He mailed an identical letter to Southworth, Holliday, and two other neighbors, all of whom he had promised to send information regarding the sale of the land. The letter stated, in relevant part, as follows:

"Selling 2933 Acres in Grant County in T. 16 S., R. 31 E., W. M. near Seneca, Oregon at the assessed market value of $324,419. Terms available: 29% down, balance over 5 years at 8% interest. Negotiate sale date for December 1, 1976 or January 1, 1977.

Also, selling Little Bear Creek grazing allotment permit – 100 head @ $225.

Also, selling Big Bear Creek grazing allotment permit – 200 head @ $250"

Upon receiving the letter, Southworth immediately responded by letter, "Re the land in Grant County near Seneca, Oregon that you have offered to sell; I accept your offer."

A dispute subsequently arose among the 4 neighbors, and Oliver refused to convey the land to Southworth, asserting: (1) he made no offer at all; and, even if he did, (2) the land was not offered independent of the grazing permits, and Southworth only sought to purchase the land. Did Oliver make an offer to Southworth that empowered Southworth to accept it and conclude a contract?

The facts of this problem are loosely based on the case of *Southworth v. Oliver*, 284 Or. 361, 587 P.2d 994 (1978).

Problem 2: Monticello Ford advertised a 1988 Ford Escort Pony in a local newspaper at $7,826, with advertised monthly payments of $159.29 over 60 months at an 11% APR to those with qualifying credit. Dawn Russell wishes to purchase this vehicle at these stated terms. Has Monticello Ford made her an offer that she can accept without further negotiation? Can she accept by tendering the full cash amount?

The facts of this problem are loosely based on the case of *Ford Motor credit Co. v. Russell*, 519 N.W.2d 460 (Minn. App. 1994).

Problem 3: Remington proposed to sell to Sun 1,000 tons of paper per month for 12 months. The size, quality, payment, and delivery terms were all described in detail, and the first delivery was to take place 60 days after the conclusion of the contract. The price for each installment was to be agreed upon by the parties no later than 15 days prior to delivery of the installment. Sun is located in New York, and Remington is located in Massachusetts. Has Remington made an offer that Sun may accept?

What if Sun is located in Montreal, Quebec, Canada?

The facts of this problem are loosely based on the case of *Sun Printing & Publishing Assoc. v. Remington Paper & Power Co.*, 235 N.Y. 338, 139 N.E. 470 (1923).

Lesson 11: Offer & Acceptance—the Acceptance

Objectives and Expected Learning Outcomes

In this lesson, you will learn what is required for an offeree to accept an offer and, thereby, conclude a binding contract. You will learn the rules for acceptance for both unilateral and bilateral contracts, as well as any notice requirements with respect to either. In the process, you will learn when a bilateral contract may be accepted by performance, as well as the difference between acceptance of a unilateral and bilateral contract through performance.

The Acceptance

An "acceptance" is a communication by the offeree exercising the power conveyed by the offeror to conclude a contract and "close the deal." The question of whether an offeree has made an effective acceptance is often inextricably intertwined with two other questions: (1) has the offeree's power of acceptance previously been terminated; and/or (2) did the nature and circumstances of the offer somehow preclude any such termination? These latter two questions will be addressed in Lessons 12 and 13, respectively. However, you will also note their significance in some of the Examples and Problems below.

In this lesson, we will focus on the nature of an effective acceptance—what is required of the offeree to exercise the power of acceptance and conclude a contract? We will also address the issue of "notice"—to what extent is the offeree required to notify the offeror promptly that the offer has been accepted? We will address each of these questions in the context of both unilateral and bilateral contracts.

As indicated earlier, bilateral contracts are of far greater commercial importance than unilateral contracts, because most parties to a commercial transaction seek the certainty and predictability associated with promises. However, it is useful to begin our discussion of acceptance with offers of unilateral contracts, as the differences between unilateral and bilateral contracts helps to highlight a few of the issues associated with acceptance of an offer.

Unilateral Contracts

As you will recall from our earlier discussions, a unilateral contract is one in which only one party makes a promise. The offeror makes a "promise" in exchange for the desired "performance" by the offeree. In many cases, the offeror makes clear whether a return promise (a bilateral contract) or performance (a unilateral contract) is sought. In others, however, the intent of the promisor may be less clear. In the latter cases, it is often useful to ask yourself, "does the promisor likely care if the promisee makes a promise prior to rendering any required performance?" In a similar vein, you might ask "would the promisor expect to be able to sue for breach if the promisee did not perform?" If the answer to these questions is "no," then you are likely dealing with an offer of a unilateral contract.

Acceptance of a unilateral contract requires the full completion of the requested performance. Until performance is completed, the offeror, as a rule, retains the power to change his or her mind (further addressed in lesson 12), subject to certain exceptions (addressed in lesson 13). While the *beginning* of performance by the offeree may, in certain circumstances, limit the offeror's power to change his or her mind (lesson 13), the offer of a unilateral contract is not "accepted" until that performance is complete.

The following example is based on a classic case addressing this issue.

Example 11-1: *Petterson v. Pattberg*

Petterson owed a parcel of land in Brooklyn, NY, and owed Pattberg $5,450 in repayment of a loan secured by a mortgage on that parcel. The principal amount of the loan was repayable in installments, which, as of April 4, 1924, have 5 years remaining for complete repayment. On this same day, April 4, Pattberg wrote to Petterson that he would reduce the principal by $780 if Petterson would timely pay the regular payment due on April 25 and then pay the rest of the loan balance on or before May 31.

Petterson made the April 25 payment, as agreed, and a few days before the end of May appeared at Pattberg's door with the cash required to pay off the balance. When Pattberg learned the identity of his caller—and before opening his door—he announced that he was no longer willing to accept a reduced payoff, as he had sold the mortgage to a third party. Petterson was ultimately required to pay the full amount of the loan to the new mortgage holder, and sued Pattberg to recover the promised $780 early payment discount.

The New York Court of Appeals ruled that Pattberg had offered a unilateral contract that could only be accepted by complete performance. Until Petterson had paid the full amount of the loan, as requested, Pattberg remained free to change his mind, which he did before payment was made.[16]

The facts of this case provide a stark example of the reason that business parties generally prefer bilateral contracts in which both parties are bound by promises. A unilateral contract is not finally concluded by acceptance until the requested performance is fully complete.

Moreover, performance must be rendered by the offeree in exchange for the offeror's promise—at least final completion of such performance.[17] An offeree who performs the performance in question, but only later learns of the offer, cannot recover on the promise.

---

16 Petterson v. Pattberg, 248 N.Y. 86, 161 N.E. 428 (1928).
17 *See* Restatement (Second) of Contracts § 51.

Assuming that an offeree has, in fact, completed performance as requested in an offer of a unilateral contract, there remains one additional question. Has the offeree promptly given any required "notice" of acceptance to the offeror?

Notice

As a general rule, notice of acceptance of an offer of a unilateral contract is not required.[18] However, such notice may, exceptionally, be required where mandated by the circumstances.[19]

Two classic cases provide excellent examples of the rule and an obvious exception.

> **Example 11-2: *Carlill v. Carbolic Smoke Ball Co.***
>
> Carbolic Smoke Ball Co. promised in an advertisement "£100 reward will be paid by the Carbolic Smoke Ball Company to any person who contracts [influenza] after having used the ball three times daily for two weeks," as directed. Carlill purchased and used a ball as directed, and he nevertheless contracted influenza. However, Carbolic refused to pay, arguing that it was not bound to do so because Carlill had not provided prompt notice that he had accepted the Carbolic offer.
>
> The court ruled that notice was unnecessary. Carbolic had offered a unilateral contract, which Carlill accepted by purchasing and using the smoke ball, as directed. Having accepted Carbolic's offer, the only remaining condition to Carbolic's payment obligation was Carlill contracting influenza. He did so, and Carbolic was obligated to pay. It would make no logical sense to require notice that Carlill had purchased and used the ball, as Carbolic had no liability resulting from (or likely interest in) Carlill's performance, unless he actually got sick.[20]

---

18 *See* Restatement (Second) of Contracts § 54(1).
19 *See* Restatement (Second) of Contracts § 54(2).
20 Carlill v. Carbolic Smoke Ball Co., 1 Q.B. 256 (Court of Appeals 1892).

In this case, Carbolic was offering a unilateral contract, and the court was not concerned with any limitations on the supply of smoke balls. Thus, it construed the advertisement as an offer. Carlill had no obligation to notify Carbolic that he had purchased the smoke ball and used it as directed. Carbolic should have known how many smoke balls had been sold and had purportedly set aside sufficient funds to pay the predictable percentage of those buyers who contracted influenza. While a party seeking to collect on the promise would obviously have to notify Carbolic at that time, there was no requirement of prior notification of the party's "acceptance" of Carbolic's offer by way of completing the requested performance.

In contrast, a person who would not typically be obligated to pay the debt of another would almost certainly want to know if his offer to accept such extraordinary liability had been accepted.

Example 11-3: *Bishop v. Eaton*

Frank Eaton asked a friend, Bishop, to assist Frank's brother, Harry, in getting a loan (Frank being geographically distant from his brother and Bishop). Specifically, Frank wrote to Bishop that, if Bishop would assist Harry in getting the loan, Frank would see that it got paid. Bishop signed Harry's note as surety for the loan (we will address contracts of surety further in Chapter 4), in effect promising to pay if Harry did not. When Harry failed to pay, Bishop was required to do so and sought reimbursement from Frank.

The court ruled that Frank had offered a unilateral contract to Bishop, which Bishop had accepted by providing the requested assistance to Harry. However, under the circumstances of this sort of offer of a unilateral contract, in which Bishop's acceptance would uniquely expose Frank to liability for his brother Harry's debt, Frank would reasonably expect notice of Bishop's acceptance. The court went on to find that such notice had been provided.[21]

---

[21] Bishop v. Eaton, 161 Mass. 496, 37 N.E. 665 (1894).

While the normal rule does not require notice of acceptance of a unilateral contract, the nature of such contracts results in most cases in prompt notice by the performing offeree who wishes to collect from the offeror on the promise.

Bilateral Contracts

It is often said that "the offeror is the master of the offer." Indeed, the offeror generally has the right to define the terms of the offer being made—including the place, time, and manner of acceptance.[22] However, in the event that the offeror is less than crystal clear in limiting such an acceptance to a specifically prescribed method, an offeree may generally accept in any manner reasonable under the circumstances.[23]

> **Example 11-4:** Alpha mails an offer to Mega, a used car dealership, to paint 20 cars at a price of $100 per car (*you may remember them from Problem 2, lesson 6*). The offer states that Mega "may accept by countersigning this offer letter and returning it" to Alpha.
>
> Mega does not counter-sign Alpha's original letter, but does promptly send a letter of its own, referencing Alpha's letter and purporting to accept the offer contained therein.
>
> Mega's acceptance is effective, even though it differed from that proposed by Alpha, because Alpha merely "suggested" one means of acceptance, which did not preclude any other reasonable means, such as that selected by Mega. If Alpha had instead "prescribed" that Mega could only accept by countersigning the original letter, then Mega's own letter would have been ineffective in concluding a contract.

The question of whether an offer merely "suggests" a manner of acceptance or "prescribes" one—and only one—manner of acceptance is generally a question of fact, and the intent of the offeree is determined in the same manner as other questions of intent (as addressed previously in lesson 9).

---

[22] *See* Restatement (Second) of Contracts §§ 30(1) and 60.
[23] *See* Restatement (Second) of Contracts §§ 30(2) and 60.

An offeree may often "accept" an offer of a bilateral contract by beginning the performance sought by the offeror—yes, that's right, a "bilateral" contract. Many are often confused between acceptance of a unilateral contract by completing the sought after performance and acceptance of a bilateral contract by merely beginning or commencing performance. The key to this distinction is, however, quite simple. When an offeree of a bilateral contract accepts by beginning performance, the offeree is then fully bound to complete such performance, just as if an express promise had been made to do so.[24]

When purporting to accept an offer of a bilateral contract, the offeree's initiation of performance serves as a replacement or surrogate for a more traditional form of express promise. While the offeror is bargaining for a promise—and not merely some performance without such a promise to complete it—the promise is provided by the offeree's conduct. Thus, the offeror gets exactly what was bargained for—a promise of complete performance. In contrast, an offeree who begins to perform in response to an offer of a unilateral contract is not in any way bound to complete performance, but simply has not accepted the offer until such performance is complete.

Of course, an offeree of a bilateral contract may only accept by beginning performance when either expressly invited to do so by the offer or otherwise reasonable under the circumstances. The following two cases provide examples in which the offeree sought to accept an offer by beginning performance—one successfully and one not.

Example 11-5: *Ever-Tite Roofing Corp. v. Green*

The Greens sought to have their home re-roofed by Ever-Tite. To that end, they signed a form supplied by Ever-Tite. The form provided that Ever-Tite could accept the Greens' offer by "written acceptance" of an office of Ever-Tite "or upon commencing performance of the work." The Greens fully understood that Ever-Tite, who was doing the work "on credit," would perform a credit check prior to accepting the offer. Just over a week later, after completing a successful credit check, Ever-Tite loaded two trucks and headed for the Green's home. On arrival, however, Ever-

---

[24] *See* Restatement (Second) of Contracts § 62(2).

Tite found that another roofing contractor had begun work two days earlier, and the Greens indicated they were no longer interested in doing business with Ever-Tite.

The court ruled that Ever-Tite had effectively accepted the Greens' offer before learning that the Greens had hired another contractor. When Ever-Tite loaded up its trucks and headed for the Greens' home, Ever-Tite accepted the Greens' offer and was fully bound to complete the roofing job, as agreed. By the time that Ever-Tite learned of any contrary intent of the Greens, the parties were already bound by the Greens' offer and Ever-Tite's acceptance.[25]

The above case provides an example of an offer made on the offeree's form. This will typically happen when a seller solicits an order on its own form. This sort of contracting process raises a variety of issues, one of which we will see in lesson 13, and others of which we will address in Chapter 5 and 6. Here, however, the Green's offer was treated like any other offer—irrespective of the fact that it was made on the Ever-Tite form. This case also provides an example in which an offeror's intent to change his or her mind is manifested indirectly to the offeree—here, when the offeree saw others at work on the same roof. We will address this issue further in lesson 12.

Example 11-6: *White v. Corlies & Tift*

Corlies sought to have certain remodeling work done by White. The parties had been engaged in extended negotiations involving price, the type of wood to be used, and the timing, each of which was important to Corlies. On September 28, White had left Corlies with a final proposal specifying the type of wood and price. The next day, Corlies wrote to White "upon agreement to finish . . . in two weeks from date, you can begin at once." Corlies further indicated it would be back in touch later that day. Upon receipt, White immediately purchased the pine lumber needed for the job and began working on it in this shop (which was geographically distinct from location of the remodeling

---

[25] Ever-Tite Roofing Corp. v. Green, 83 So.2d. 449 (La. App. 1955).

job. The next day, Corlies contacted White, saying it did not want the work done, and White sued for breach of contract.

The court ruled that White had not accepted the offer, therefore, leaving Corlies free to change its mind. The opinion is somewhat less than clear. However, the court seemed to have at least two concerns. First, in view of the fact that the issue of timing had not yet been resolved, and considering the importance of completion in two weeks, coupled with the statement by Corlies that it would be back in touch late that day, the offer might reasonably be understood as requiring an actual express promise prior to beginning performance ("upon agreement" . . . "you can begin"). Second, the court did not view the act of a contractor buying a commonly used lumber and beginning to work in his shop to be sufficiently ambiguous to indicate acceptance of the specific offer by Corlies.[26]

Consider the difference between examples 11-5 and 11-6. In the former, the offer expressly invited acceptance by performance. While such a right to accept by performance will often be implied, such implication is more difficult where the circumstances reasonably indicate that the offeror would want an express promise before performance begins. Moreover, Even-Tite was specifically in route to the Greens' home, thereby having unambiguously begun performance of the Greens' offer. In contrast, White's performance was more ambiguous. It is also worth remembering that, when beginning performance is deemed to be a promise to complete, one should take care in ascertaining the intent of that performance. If White had still been thinking over the offer by Corlies while working on another project in his shop on the 28th, he would not, presumably, have wanted to be prematurely bound to the contract with Corlies as a result.

Acceptance may take an almost infinite variety of forms, depending on the specific circumstances of the offer. However, silence, by itself and without more, cannot be deemed to be acceptance.[27] Suppose that Alpha, in example 11-4 above, had mailed the same offer to Mega, but instead of

---

[26] White v. Corlies & Tift, 46 N.Y. 467 (1871).
[27] *See* Restatement (Second) of Contracts § 69.

requesting a countersignature had simply said "if you do not reply within 10 days, your acceptance of this offer shall be assumed, and we shall have a binding contract." Absent additional facts, Mega would not be bound to a contract, even if it tossed Alpha's letter into the trash and never responded.

While silence, by itself and without more, is not acceptance, an offeree's silence in response to an offer may, in some limited circumstances, amount to an acceptance. Most often, such a passive, silent acceptance relies on such a practice established between the parties over time. For example, if Alpha and Mega had a prior understanding that Mega's failure to respond to such an offer by Alpha indicated Mega's agreement, then Mega's failure to reply might indeed amount to an acceptance, assuming the offer was received.

As with unilateral contracts, we must also consider whether an acceptance requires timely notice in order to be effective. Unlike offers of unilateral contracts, however, we presume that acceptance of an offer of a bilateral contract requires timely notice, absent evidence to the contrary.

Notice

As a general rule, acceptance of a bilateral contract requires reasonable efforts by the offeree to provide timely notice of such acceptance to the offeror.[28] The rule does not require that such notice actually reach the offeror, but simply requires reasonable diligence by the offeree under the circumstances. However, such notice may, exceptionally, be required where mandated by the circumstances. The requirement of notice may also be dispensed with where notice is unnecessary, based on either the terms or circumstances of the offer.

Notice was not an issue in example 11-5, inasmuch as Ever-Tite showed up at the Greens' home soon after beginning performance, thereby providing reasonable notice of its acceptance. Notice in example 11-6 is a bit more problematic, because he was not yet doing any work at Corlies. Even if the court had determined that White could reasonably accept by beginning performance, and even if his purchase of lumber and beginning work on it was sufficient to constitute acceptance, one might have questioned whether he was required to give notice to Corlies the same day.

---

[28] *See* Restatement (Second) of Contracts § 56.

Summary of Basic Rule: the acceptance[29]

- Acceptance of an offer of a unilateral contract requires completion of the performance sought by the offeror in exchange for the offeror's promise;

  - Acceptance of an offer of a unilateral contract does not require notice;

    - Unless the circumstances indicate such notice is appropriate

- Acceptance of an offer of a bilateral contract requires a promise by the offeree to be bound by the terms of the offer

  - Such acceptance may take any form that is reasonable under the circumstances—including the beginning of performance, which operates as a promise to complete performance;

    - Unless the offeror has specifically prescribed one or more forms of acceptance to the exclusion of any other

  - Acceptance of an offer of a bilateral contract requires notice;

    - Unless the offer provides otherwise, or circumstances indicate such notice is unnecessary

---

Acceptance under UCC Article 2

UCC § 2-206 addresses "acceptance" of an offer to purchase or sell goods. **STOP NOW and READ UCC § 2-206 below.**

UCC § 2-206

(1) Unless otherwise unambiguously indicated by the language or circumstances

(a) an offer to make a contract shall be construed as inviting acceptance in any manner and by any medium reasonable in the circumstances;

---

[29] This basic rule is reflected in Restatement (Second) of Contracts §§ 30, 50, 51, 52, 54, 56, 60, 62, and 69.

(b) an order or other offer to buy goods for prompt or current shipment shall be construed as inviting acceptance either by a prompt promise to ship or by the prompt or current shipment of conforming or nonconforming goods, but such a shipment of non-conforming goods does not constitute an acceptance if the seller seasonably notifies the buyer that the shipment is offered only as an accommodation to the buyer.

(2) Where the beginning of a requested performance is a reasonable mode of acceptance an offeror who is not notified of acceptance within a reasonable time may treat the offer as having lapsed before acceptance.

The foregoing statutory provision is quite consistent with the common law, but includes a few specific provisions worth noting. Under Article 2, it is arguably even more difficult to specify one manner of acceptance to the exclusion of others, as the statute requires that such exclusion be "unambiguous." In the absence of such "unambiguous" language to the contrary, the statute further provides that a seller's "performance," by promptly shipping the goods, shall operate as an acceptance of an order by the buyer. However, such an acceptance may be ineffective if the seller fails to provide the buyer with timely notice of said shipment of goods.

The statute addresses one other interesting issue. What happens if a seller ships goods in response to a buyer's order, but the goods do not conform to the order (e.g., buyer orders large widgets and seller ships small widgets)— has seller both accepted and breached the contract in one single act? The answer is, "yes," unless the seller provides timely notice to the buyer that the shipment is merely offered as an "accommodation" to the buyer. In this latter instance, the seller is actually making a "counter-offer" to the buyer, which the buyer can accept or refuse. We'll talk more about counter-offers in the next lesson.

Acceptance under the CISG

CISG Article 18 addresses "acceptance" of an offer to purchase or sell goods across national borders. **STOP NOW and READ CISG Article 18(1) below.**

CISG ARTICLE 18

(1) A statement made by or other conduct of the offeree indicating assent to an offer is an acceptance. Silence or inactivity does not in itself amount to acceptance.

. . .

Much like the common law and article 2, we see that acceptance may take any reasonable form, but that silence, by itself without more, is not acceptance. However, like most provisions of the CISG, Article 18 is merely a default rule, and a requirement of acceptance in a specific form would likely be given effect.

APPLYING THE RULES

Problem 1: Holly Vann, convicted of murder and sentenced to death, escaped jail in Dallas County, Texas, where he was being held pending appeal of his conviction. A. L. Ledbetter, the Dallas County Sheriff, posted a reward of $500 in exchange for Vann's capture and return to the jail. Within one month after the escape, S.H. Broadnax recaptured, restrained, held, and returned Vann to Ledbetter at the jail.

Was the "reward poster" an "offer"?

Assuming the reward poster was effective as an offer, consider the following hypothetical variations. In which is Broadnax entitled to the $500?

At the time Broadnax turned Vann over to Ledbetter, he was not aware of the reward. He first saw a reward poster after he walked out of the jail, having already turned Vann over to Ledbetter. He subsequently walked back in and demanded the reward.

As Broadnax was walking up the street towards the jail with Vann in tow, he first saw a poster and became aware of the reward. He walked in to Ledbetter's office and said, "I've got Vann and I am here to turn him in and collect my reward."

Broadnax knew of the reward before setting out. His primary motivation was to save Vann from an angry lynch mob, believing it better to allow the courts to dispense justice. However, as he walked in to Ledbetter's office he said, "I've got Vann and I am here to turn him in and collect my reward."

The facts of this problem are based loosely on the case of *Broadnax v. Ledbetter*, 100 Tex. 375, 99 S.W. 1111 (1907).

Problem 2: On February 10, a traveling salesman from International Filter Company (IFC) approached Conroe Gin, Ice & Light Company (Conroe) with a proposal to sell Conroe a specified water filter at a price of $1,230. The form proposal, provided by IFC, stated that it would "become a contract when accepted by the purchaser and approved by an executive officer of IFC." It further stated that shipment was to be made by March 10. The proposal was immediately signed by Conroe, and the salesman transmitted it to the IFC home office for final approval, where it arrived on February 13 and was signed by P.N. Engel, the President of IFC, who wrote "OK Feb 13 – P.N. Engel." Then next day, on February 14, IFC mailed a package, including a letter, to Conroe acknowledging receipt of the order and requesting a water sample from Conroe for analysis by IFC prior to shipping the filter. To that end, IFC included in the package a special bottle, tag, and instructions for collecting and returning the water sample. The letter made no specific reference to Engel's signature or approval of the written proposal.

On February 20, Conroe contacted IFC, indicating that it no longer wished to purchase the filter. IFC replied the next day insisting that Conroe was already bound to a contract. Did IFC effectively accept Conroe's offer and conclude a binding contract? In thinking about this question, you might want to consider multiple theories on behalf of IFC, and you should also be prepared to address any issue of notice.

The facts of this problem are based loosely on the case of *International Filter Co. v. Conroe Gin, Ice & Light Co.*, 277 S.W. 631 (Comm. App. Tex. 1925).

Lesson 12: Termination of the Power of Acceptance

Objectives and Expected Learning Outcomes

In this lesson, you will learn that an offeree's power of acceptance may be terminated through certain actions of the offeror or of the offeree, or simply by the passage of time or the death or incapacity of a party. You will further learn how these various events that may terminate the offeree's power of acceptance interact with the offeree's attempts to exercise that power. Finally, you will learn the detailed timing rules employed to decide whether an offer was effectively accepted before it was effectively terminated, thereby resulting in a binding contract.

Termination of the Power of Acceptance and Issues of Timing

As illustrated by examples in the last lesson, the question of whether the parties have concluded a binding contract may often be dependent on a question of timing. Did the offeree possess the power of acceptance at the time that power was purportedly exercised? In exploring this question further, the current lesson focuses on the various means by which an offeree's power of acceptance may be terminated, as well as the basic rules regarding the timing at which certain actions involving acceptance or termination become legally effective.

An offeree's power of acceptance may be terminated under the common law in four different manners: (1) lapse of the offer; (2) revocation of the offer by the offeror; (3) rejection of the offer by the offeree; or (4) death or incapacity of the offeror or offeree. Each is considered in turn.

Lapse

An offer does not remain open forever. The offer is said to "lapse"—in effect, to expire or cease to be effective without further action by the offeror—at any such time specified in the offer. If no time is specified in the offer, then it lapses after a reasonable time for acceptance under the circumstances. Once an offer has lapsed, the offeree's power of acceptance is terminated.

The question of lapse is generally a very fact specific one, depending entirely on the nature and content of the offer and all of the surrounding circumstances. However, at least one rule of thumb has emerged—the "conversation rule." An offer made during a face-to-face or telephone conversation is deemed to lapse at the end of the conversation, absent a contrary intent of the offeror. Perhaps, this same historic rule should apply today to online "chats" and other modern forms of "conversations." However, one might alternatively suggest different treatment, inasmuch as an online "chat" or series of "text messages" will create a digital record of the conversation, which might suggest a different rule. At bottom, the issue falls back on the standard of "reasonability" under the circumstances.

Summary of Basic Rule: lapse[30]

- An offer lapses, thereby terminating the offeree's power of acceptance;

  ○ At the time specified in the offer;

  ○ Or, if no time is specified, after a reasonable time;

    ▪ Absent contrary intent, an offer made during a "conversation" lapses at the end of the conversation

---

In some instances, it may be difficult to distinguish whether a future date specified in connection with an offer is merely a date after which the offer lapses or a date through which the offeror promises to keep the offer open for acceptance by the offeree. If intended as a promise to keep the offer open, this may raise additional issues with respect to the effectiveness of such a promise. These issues are explored in the case below, as well as lesson 13.

An offer that has not yet lapsed remains open for acceptance by the offeree, absent other circumstances that may lead to its premature termination. One of these circumstances is revocation—a power exercised by the offeror.

Revocation by the Offeror

As a basic common law rule, an offeror is free to "revoke" an offer until it has been accepted by the offeree. If effectively "revoked," the offer is no longer subject to acceptance by the offeree. The classic English case that follows provides an excellent example of a basic conflict between the offeror's right to change his mind and the offeree's right to accept the offered bargain.

---

[30] This basic rule is reflected in Restatement (Second) of Contracts § 41(1).

FROM THE COURT

Dickinson v. Dodds

In the Court of Appeal, Chancery Division (1876)
L.R. 2 Ch. D. 463

On Wednesday, the 10th of June, 1874, the Defendant John Dodds signed and delivered to the Plaintiff, George Dickinson, a memorandum, of which the material part was as follows:

> I hereby agree to sell to Mr. George Dickinson the whole of the dwelling-houses, garden ground, stabling, and outbuildings thereto belonging, situate at Croft, belonging to me, for the sum of £800. As witness my hand this tenth day of June, 1874.

> (Signed) John Dodds

> P.S. This offer to be left over [i.e., "open"] until Friday, 9 o'clock, A.M., 12th June, 1874.

[Dickinson's Complaint] alleged that Dodds understood and intended that the [Dickinson] should have until Friday 9 A.M. within which to determine whether he would or would not purchase, and that he should absolutely have until that time [the exclusive right to purchase] the property at the price of £800, and that the [Dickinson] in fact determined to accept the offer on the morning of Thursday, the 11th of June, but did not at once signify his acceptance to Dodds, believing that he had the power to accept it until 9 A.M. on the Friday.

In the afternoon of the Thursday [Dickinson] was informed by a Mr. Berry that Dodds had been offering or agreeing to sell the property to Thomas Allan, the other Defendant. Thereupon the Plaintiff, at about half-past seven in the evening, went to the house of Mrs. Burgess, the mother-in-law of Dodds, where he was then staying, and left with her a formal acceptance in writing of the offer to sell the property. According to the evidence of Mrs. Burgess this document never in fact reached Dodds, she having forgotten to give it to him.

On the following (Friday) morning, at about seven o'clock, Berry, who was acting as agent for Dickinson, found Dodds at the Darlington railway station, and handed to him a duplicate of the acceptance by Dickinson, and explained to Dodds its purport. He replied that it was too late, as he had sold the property. A few minutes later Dickinson himself found Dodds entering a railway carriage, and handed him another duplicate of the notice of acceptance, but Dodds declined to receive it, saying, "You are too late. I have sold the property."

. . . [O]n the day before, Thursday, the 11th of June, Dodds had signed a formal contract for the sale of the property to the Defendant Allan for £800, and had received from him a deposit of £40.

The bill in this suit prayed that the Defendant Dodds might be decreed specifically to perform the contract [based on the offer to Dickinson] of the 10th of June, 1874; that he might be restrained from conveying the property to Allan; that Allan might be restrained from taking any such conveyance; that, if any such conveyance had been or should be made, Allan might be declared a trustee of the property for, and might be directed to convey the property to, the Plaintiff; and for damages.

. . .

JAMES, L.J.

The document, though beginning "I hereby agree to sell," was nothing but an offer, and was only intended to be an offer, for the Plaintiff himself tells us that he required time to consider whether he would enter into an agreement or not. Unless both parties had then agreed there was no concluded agreement then made; it was in effect and substance only an offer to sell. The Plaintiff, being minded not to complete the bargain at that time, added this memorandum—"This offer to be left over until Friday, 9 o'clock A.M., 12th June, 1874." That shows it was only an offer. There was no consideration given for the undertaking or promise, to whatever extent it may be considered binding, to keep the property unsold until 9 o'clock on Friday morning; but apparently Dickinson was of opinion, and probably Dodds was of the same opinion, that he (Dodds) was bound by that promise, and could not in any way withdraw from it, or retract it, until 9 o'clock on Friday morning, and this probably explains a good deal of what afterwards took place.

But it is clear settled law, on one of the clearest principles of law, that this promise, being a mere nudum pactum, was not binding, and that at any moment before a complete acceptance by Dickinson of the offer, Dodds was as free as Dickinson himself. Well, that being the state of things, it is said that the only mode in which Dodds could assert that freedom was by actually and distinctly saying to Dickinson, "Now I withdraw my offer." It appears to me that there is neither principle nor authority for the proposition that there must be an express and actual withdrawal of the offer . . . . It must, to constitute a contract, appear that the two minds were at one, at the same moment of time, that is, that there was an offer continuing up to the time of the acceptance. If there was not such a continuing offer, then the acceptance comes to nothing. Of course it may well be that the one man is bound in some way or other to let the other man know that his mind with regard to the offer has been changed; but in this case, beyond all question, the Plaintiff knew that Dodds was no longer minded to sell the property to him as plainly and clearly as if Dodds had told him in so many words, "I withdraw the offer." This is evident from the Plaintiff's own statements in the bill.

The Plaintiff says in effect that, having heard and knowing that Dodds was no longer minded to sell to him, and that he was selling or had sold to someone else, thinking that he could not in point of law withdraw his offer, meaning to fix him to it, and endeavoring to bind him," I went to the house where he was lodging, and saw his mother-in-law, and left with her an acceptance of the offer, knowing all the while that he had entirely changed his mind. I got an agent to watch for him at 7 o'clock the next morning, and I went to the train just before 9 o'clock, in order that I might catch him and give him my notice of acceptance just before 9 o'clock, and when that occurred he told my agent, and he told me, you are too late, and he then threw back the paper." It is to my mind quite clear that before there was any attempt at acceptance by the Plaintiff, he was perfectly well aware that Dodds had changed his mind, and that he had in fact agreed to sell the property to Allan. It is impossible, therefore, to say there was ever that existence of the same mind between the two parties which is essential in point of law to the making of an agreement. I am of opinion, therefore, that the Plaintiff has failed to prove that there was any binding contract between Dodds and himself.

. . .

CASE QUESTIONS

(1) Based on the above facts, do you believe Dodds intended, on June 10, that Dickinson would have until 9 AM on June 12 to decide whether or not to accept the offer? If so, why wasn't that intent sufficient to allow Dickinson to accept the offer and conclude a binding contract when he sought to do so on June 11 and 12?

    a. While the case uses the term "withdrawal," the common law today uses the term "revocation" (in fact, "withdrawal" has a different and distinct meaning under the CISG, as explained later in this lesson).

    b. Did Dodds directly revoke his offer to Dickinson? Did that matter? Why or why not?

    c. We can also approach the same question from our earlier basic definition of an offer. Could Dickinson still reasonably believe, after his conversation with Berry on June 11, that his mere assent would conclude a contract with Dodds?

(2) Did Dodds promise to keep the offer to Dickenson open until June 12 at 9 AM? Why wasn't he bound by that promise?

To restate the basic common law rule, an offeror is free to revoke an offer until it has been accepted by the offeree. As illustrated by the above case, a revocation may involve a direct communication by the offeror to the offeree,[31] or it may involve information that reaches the offeree indirectly,[32] most often through a third party. To be effective, an indirect revocation must arise from definite action by the offeror that is inconsistent with an intention to contract with the original offeree. Typically, such action involves contracting with another party under circumstances in which only one such contract is possible (e.g., the sale of the Dodds property at Croft). The information received by the offeree must also be reliable. When we combine these two requirements—reliable information that the offeror has taken definite action inconsistent with the intent on his or her part to contract with the original offeree—we can see that, under these circumstances,

---

[31] *See* Restatement (Second) of Contracts § 42.
[32] *See* Restatement (Second) of Contracts § 43.

an objectively reasonable person in the shoes of the offeree can no longer presume that his or her assent will conclude a contract.

Admittedly, the application of this rule in some cases may seem harsh. However, the potential harshness of the rule is, to some degree, mitigated by the application of the common law "mailbox rule."

The "Mailbox Rule"

At the risk of confusing the issue at the outset, it is worth noting that the well-known "mailbox rule" might actually be better characterized as the mailbox "exception." Revocations and rejections, including counter-offers (discussed below), along with acceptances not qualifying for exceptional treatment under the "mailbox rule," are all effective when received. In contrast, a qualifying acceptance, if made in a manner and medium invited by the offer, is effective upon dispatch—irrespective of whether or not it is ever received by the offeror. In effect, the risk of such an acceptance that is delayed or even lost in transmission is born by the offeror, who invited the manner and means of transmission.

> **Example 12-1:** Andy has decided that it is time to have the interior of his home repainted. He has heard from friends that Beth is an excellent painting contractor, so he asks her to give him an estimate to do the work. Beth comes by to inspect and measure the house, they talk about colors and quality, and Beth tells Andy she will get back to him with an estimate in a few days. Andy tells her this is fine, as he is not in any big hurry.
>
> On May 1, Beth mails Andy a proposal to perform the work she and Andy discussed, including paint specifications, price, and a timetable for completion. Andy receives the proposal on May 3, and he immediately writes out a reply letter accepting Beth's proposal, dropping it in the mail the very same day. On May 4, Beth telephones Andy and tells him that she cannot do the work, as she has just been engaged to do a much larger (and more financially lucrative) job, which prevents her from painting Andy's house. Beth receives Andy's acceptance on May 5.

Beth is bound to a contract with Andy, because Andy's acceptance was effective as soon as he "dispatched" it by putting it in the mail, on May 3, even though Beth did not receive it until May 5. Therefore, Beth's attempt to revoke her offer, on May 4, was too late, as a contract had already been concluded. The result would be the same if Andy's letter of acceptance had never arrived because it was lost in the mail (assuming of course the finder of fact believed Andy had actually mailed it). This is because Beth, by making an offer by mail, impliedly invited Andy to accept it in the same manner and by the same medium.

Of course, Andy may decide to let Beth "off the hook," and mutually agree to walk away from the contract. However, once a contract has been concluded, neither party can unilaterally terminate it without the consent of the other—or without breach and a potential claim for damages.

The question of whether or not a particular manner or medium of acceptance is invited, so as to qualify for the application of the "mailbox rule" is a factual one. However, a good "rule of thumb" is that the offeree can generally count on the application of the mailbox rule, as long as the manner and medium of acceptance is (1) at least as rapid and (2) at least as reliable in reaching the offeror as the manner and medium used by the offeror. For example, an acceptance using "overnight" mail would almost certainly be afforded the application of the mailbox rule in response to an offer using "standard" mail, because it is likely equal to or better than standard mail in terms of both speed and reliability.

Summary of Basic Rule: revocation and timing of an effective acceptance[33]

- An offer may generally be revoked by the offeror until it has been accepted by the offeree

  - Revocation may arise from:

    - A direct communication to the offeree by the offeror; or

    - Indirect information received by the offeree, which is:

---

[33] This basic rule is reflected in Restatement (Second) of Contracts §§ 42, 43, and 63.

- - Based on a definite action by the offeror that is inconsistent with an intention to contract with the original offeree; and

    - Received by the offeree from a reliable source

  ○ An acceptance is generally effective, thereby precluding revocation, when dispatched,

    - Provided the acceptance is dispatched in a manner and by a medium reasonably invited by the offer—even if it is never received by the offeror

    - Otherwise, an acceptance is effective only upon receipt by the offeror

In the next lesson, we will see a number of exceptions to the general common law rule of revocability. We will also see some different rules regarding the timing of an acceptance in certain circumstances. However, the above "general rules" help to "set the stage" for that further discussion and still apply in the vast majority of common law cases, as well as many cases involving sales of goods.

Rejection by the Offeree

A "rejection" of an offer by the offeree generally terminates the offeree's power to accept the offer.[34] In effect, the offeree has said "I don't want to enter into a contract, as proposed in the offer." Having rejected it, the offeree cannot later accept the offer, unless the offeror agrees. At this juncture, it is worth restating a fundamental difference between "revocation" and "rejection," which are easily confused:

- An offeror "revokes" his or her own offer

- An offeree "rejects" the offer of the offeror

A rejection is effective when received by the offeror.[35]

---

[34] *See* Restatement (Second) of Contracts § 38.
[35] *See* Restatement (Second) of Contracts § 40.

Example 12-2: We can now return to Andy and Beth, from example 12-1.

On May 1, Beth mails her offer to Andy. Andy receives the offer on May 3, and he immediately writes out a reply letter explaining to Beth that her "price is far too high." He drops it in the mail the same day and Beth receives it on May 5. On May 6, Andy speaks with another contractor and realizes that Beth's offer is actually very competitive. He immediately telephones Beth and says he "accepts her offer" of May 1. However, Beth is no longer interested in doing the work for Andy.

Andy's rejection is effective on May 5. Thus, he no longer has the power to accept Beth's offer, and his attempt to do so on May 6 is not effective.

The above simple application of the general "rule" also includes a few interesting variations, some of which are rather technical, but nevertheless possible.

Example 12-3: Returning to the facts of example 12-2, Andy mails his rejection on May 3, but subsequently learns on May 4 that Beth's offer is a competitive one. He telephones Beth that same day and says "I accept your offer."

Andy's acceptance is effective, because his rejection has not yet reached Beth (and does not until May 5). However, if Andy had simply mailed a subsequent acceptance on May 4 that reached Beth on May 6—after the rejection on May 5—it would merely constitute a new offer, even though it was dispatched prior to receipt of the rejection.

The above hypothetical involves what is sometimes called the "overtaking acceptance." As long as the acceptance is actually received prior to the rejection, the acceptance is effective. If not, then the purported acceptance is merely a new offer—even if "dispatched" prior to the receipt of the rejection. Another issue arises with the "overtaking rejection," which presents another challenge with the application of the mailbox rule.

Example 12-4: This time we return to the facts of example 12-1, in which Andy dispatched his acceptance on May 3. On May 4, Andy learns that Beth's price is much higher than her competition, and he telephones her to tell her he is rejecting her offer. She, of course, does not yet know of his earlier acceptance until it is received the next day, on May 5.

The acceptance on May 3 remains effective—despite Andy's belated attempt to revoke it. However, if Beth relies on Andy's attempted revocation (not yet knowing of the acceptance he dispatched earlier) and takes another job on the 4th, precluding her work for Andy, then Andy is estopped from enforcing the contract. In short, Andy loses either way.

A "Counter-Offer," as a Rejection by the Offeree

When the offeree does not merely "reject" the original offer, but also proposes a different bargain, this different bargain is called a "counter-offer." The making of a "counter-offer" has two fully independent effects. First, it serves as a "rejection" of the original offer. Second, it serves as a new offer, subject to acceptance by the original offeror—now the "offeree" with respect to the "counter-offer."[36] Any counter-offer also serves as a rejection, unless the party making the counter-offer clearly indicates the intent to keep both the old and new offer open for consideration by the parties. One might reasonably ask at this point "to what degree must a purported acceptance differ from the offer to constitute a counter-offer, instead of an acceptance." We will discover in lesson 15 that this question is a challenging one, answered differently under different governing law. For now, however, it is enough to recognize the nature and effect of a counter-offer, as both a new offer and a rejection of the original.

---

[36] *See* Restatement (Second) of Contracts § 39.

Summary of Basic Rule: rejection (including a counter-offer)[37]

- A rejection of an offer by the offeree terminates the offeree's power of acceptance

    o A substituted bargain proposed by the offeree is a counter-offer,

        ▪ Which represents a new offer that the original offeror—now the offeree—may accept; and

        ▪ Which rejects the original offer

            ▪ Absent clear intent to the contrary

    o The rejection (including a counter-offer) is effective when received by the original offeror

---

Death or Incapacity of the Offeror

An offeree's power of acceptance is terminated by the death or incapacity of either the offeror or the offeree.[38] While this rule might seem obvious, it is not without a few interesting "wrinkles." First, a contract is not generally terminated by the death or incapacity of either party (though we'll see an exception in Chapter 9), so we will discover in the next lesson that an "option contract" is not affected by the death or incapacity of either party, and the offeree (or his or her successor in interest) of such a contract retains the power to accept the offer subject to such option contract.

Second, most business organizations do not "die" in the sense that a human does. Thus, death will not typically affect "legal persons" in the various business forms, notwithstanding the death or incapacity of one of their agents involved in the offer and acceptance process.

Termination of the Power of Acceptance under UCC Article 2

You will recall from the last lesson that the offeree's failure to provide notice of acceptance within a reasonable time may cause an offer to "lapse" under UCC § 2-206(2). We will also discover in lesson 15 that Article 2 employs a very different rule than the common law in determining whether a counter offer has been made, and further provides for different effects in some circumstances. However, the initial effect of a counter-offer is the same. The original offer is no longer subject to acceptance and a new offer

---

[37] This basic rule is reflected in Restatement (Second) of Contracts §§ 38, 39, and 40.

[38] *See* Restatement (Second) of Contracts § 48.

from the original offeree takes its place. Finally, in the next lesson, we will see a special rule in Article 2 that, to some degree, modifies the traditional common law rule of Dickinson v. Dodds. However, these new issues are better left for coming lessons.

Termination of the Power of Acceptance under the CISG

The most significant issues under the CISG are also addressed in lessons 13 and 15. However, the CISG provides for one interesting variation from the common law that is worth noting here. **STOP NOW and READ the excerpts from CISG Article 18(2) and (3) below.**

CISG ARTICLE 18

. . .

(2) An acceptance of an offer becomes effective at the moment the indication of assent reaches the offeror. An acceptance is not effective if the indication of assent does not reach the offeror within the time he has fixed or, if no time is fixed, within a reasonable time . . .

(3) However, if, by virtue of the offer or as a result of practices which the parties have established between themselves or of usage, the offeree may indicate assent by performing an act, such as one relating to the dispatch of the goods or payment of the price, without notice to the offeror, the acceptance is effective at the moment the act is performed . . .

Contrary to the common law (and Article 2, as supplemented by common law), the CISG does not give effect to an acceptance until it is actually received by the offeror, and it leaves the risk of delay or failure of transmission on the offeree. While subsection 3 recognizes the parties' right to agree to a contrary approach, such agreement requires a good deal more specificity than the offeror's mere "invitation" under the mailbox rule.

Lest one be too concerned, however, about the plight of the offeree under such a rule, we will see in the next lesson that CISG Article 16 provides a great deal of protection to the offeree. *As a preview pertinent to this lesson and the problems below,* Article 16 provides that "dispatch"—while not effective as acceptance—precludes any subsequent revocation by the offeror, without any apparent limitation as to means and medium (other than good faith). We will see, however, that the other protections provided by Article 16 go even farther beyond the common law mailbox rule.

APPLYING THE RULES

Short Problems

Acme is a Kansas seller of widgets and Zenith, an Iowa business, buys widgets for use in its manufacturing process. Zenith seeks to purchase "500 Acme X-5 widgets, at $20 each, for immediate delivery." *Consider each of the following independent communication exchanges, all based on the above described order by Zenith.* In which have the parties concluded a contract?

(1) On April 1, Zenith mails an order for the widgets. On April 3, Zenith mails a revocation of its offer to Acme. On April 4, Acme mails an acceptance to Zenith. On April 5, Acme receives the revocation from Zenith. On April 6, Zenith receives the acceptance from Acme.

(2) On April 1, Zenith mails an order for the widgets. On April 3, Zenith telephones Acme, saying it is no longer interested in the widgets, and also mails a written revocation of its offer the same day. On April 4, Acme mails an acceptance to Zenith. On April 5, Acme receives the mailed revocation from Zenith. On April 6, Zenith receives the acceptance from Acme.

(3) On April 1, Zenith sends an order for the widgets via fax. On the same day, Acme mails an acceptance to Zenith. On April 2, Zenith faxes and Acme receives a revocation of Zenith's offer. On April 3, Zenith receives the acceptance from Acme.

(4) On April 1, Zenith mails an order for the widgets. On April 3, Zenith mails a revocation of its offer to Acme. On April 4, Acme mails an acceptance to Zenith. On April 5, Acme receives the revocation from Zenith. The acceptance never arrives, as it is lost in the mail (you may assume that this fact is established).

(5) On April 1, Zenith mails an order for the widgets. On April 3, Zenith mails a revocation of its offer to Acme. On April 4, Acme ships the widgets Zenith via "overnight" delivery. On April 5, Acme receives the revocation in the morning and Zenith receives the widgets in the afternoon.

(6) On April 1, Zenith mails an order for the widgets. On April 4, Acme sends an e-mail to Zenith saying it has "just increased price to $21 per widget. Please confirm price change." On April 6, Acme reconsiders its position and sends another e-mail saying it "will honor old price of $20 per widget for your order of April 1, and will ship order promptly." Later that same day, Zenith replies by e-mail that it is no longer interested in purchasing the widgets from Acme.

(7) On April 1, Zenith mails an order for the widgets. On April 3, Acme mails a rejection—saying it is out of stock. On April 4, Acme mails an acceptance, having discovered more stock. On April 5, Zenith receives the rejection from Acme. On April 6, Zenith receives the acceptance from Acme.

Which, if any, of the above answers would change if Acme was located in Germany?

Lesson 13: Protecting the Offeree's Power of Acceptance

Objectives and Expected Learning Outcomes

In this lesson, you will learn how an offeree's power of acceptance may be protected from termination under certain circumstances by contract, statute, or basic principles of reliance and estoppel. You will learn to identify each of the relevant sets of circumstances and to apply the relevant rule or exception to those circumstances.

Protecting an Offeree's Power of Acceptance by Limiting an Offeror's Power to Revoke

The last lesson included the basic rule that an offeror remains free to revoke an offer until and unless an offer is accepted by the offeree. Predictably, this basic rule presents significant uncertainty challenges for the offeree, subject to the minimal protection traditionally provided by the "mailbox rule." *This lesson* explores a variety of means by which an offeror's power to revoke an offer may be further limited by (1) a distinct "option contract," (2) reliance on an offer by beginning performance of a unilateral contract, and (3) by operation of statute under UCC Article 2 and the CISG. Then, in the *next lesson*, we will explore "pre-contractual" liability, generally, as well as two more circumstances in which an offeree's reliance on an offer may give rise to liability under the common law.

The most obvious means of precluding an offeror from revoking an offer is by concluding a separate, preliminary contract under which one party provides consideration (usually money) in exchange for a promise by the other to keep a specified offer open for a definite period of time. In addition, the common law will in some cases protect an offeree's reasonable reliance interest to varying degrees.

Option Contracts

In one respect, an "option contract" is simply a contract, like any other, requiring offer, acceptance, and consideration. However, an option contract is also unique in that it is always associated with at least one other potential contract. We can call this second contract the "main" contract here, because it is this second contract that the parties primarily care about. The "option" is merely a means to guarantee the offeree of the "main" contract a specified period to consider the offer, and perhaps to make associated arrangements for concluding the main contract, such as financing or even resale (the proverbial "middleman" may actually enter into a resale agreement in some cases before concluding the purchase contract).

The offeree of the main contract typically pays money to the offeror of the main contract in exchange for a binding promise to keep the offer of the main contract open on specified terms for a specified period of time. For an example, we can return to the basic facts of Dickinson v. Dodds from the last lesson.

> **Example 13-1:** Let's return to Dickinson and Dodds from the last lesson, but change the facts slightly. Suppose Dickinson had approached Dodds about purchasing Croft, and both had agreed on a sum of £800, as well as any additional necessary details. Dickinson, however, indicated that he would need time to arrange the necessary financing and did not want to invest the time and money to do so, unless he knew that the offer to purchase Croft would still be open to him when he was ready. While Dodds understood

Dickinson's concerns, he was also concerned about having Croft "off the market" for any period and being unable to engaged in potential sales negotiations with others. In hopes of resolving the impasse, Dodds proposed a separate and distinct "bargain" to Dickinson.

Dodds would promise to keep the offer of £800 open for 15 days, exclusively to Dickinson, in exchange for payment by Dickinson of £40, which Dodds would be entitled to keep, irrespective of whether Dickenson ultimately accepted the offer to purchase Croft. While Dickinson would necessarily incur the extra cost of £40, he would have the opportunity to make any necessary financing arrangements and further consider the purchase for the full 15 days without fear of losing the "deal."

If, during that 15 day period, Dodds sold Croft to someone else, he would be in breach of his "option contract" with Dickinson. Dickinson would be entitled to enforce his expectation interest—the right to purchase Croft—against Dodds for that breach (depending on the circumstances, his remedy might take the form of Croft, itself, or money damages, as a substitute).

Inasmuch as an option contract is a contract, like any other, it is impervious to most circumstances that would typically terminate a mere "offer." Most obviously, as indicated in the example above, the power to accept the "main" contract offer cannot be "revoked" by the offeror during the period promised in the option contract.

The offeree's power to accept an offer pursuant to an option contract is also generally unaffected by the offeree's rejection of the main contract offer, or the making of a counter-offer. This power to accept the main contract is also unaffected by the death or incapacity of the offeror or offeree. In effect, the contract rights and obligations under the option contract generally pass to the parties' successors in interest, as in any other contract (succession to the contract interests of another is explored more fully in Chapter 10). The only two ways in which an offeree's rights under an option contract terminate is by (1) expiration of the option period; or (2) mutual agreement of the parties (the parties can of course terminate any contract by mutual agreement).

As a final and very important point, an offeree under an option contract is not protected by the "mailbox rule." An acceptance of an option contract must actually be received by the offeror prior to the expiration of the specified time. The risk of transmission is entirely on the offeree. The logic of this approach should be obvious. The purpose of the mailbox rule is to protect the vulnerable offeree from revocation by the offeror. In the case of an option contract, that vulnerability has been eliminated, and the acceptance is treated exactly the same as other communications that take place in the formation process—it is effective only upon receipt.

Summary of Basic Rule: option contracts[39]

- An option contract is a promise to keep an offer of a separate "main" contract open on specified terms for a specified period of time

  o An offer pursuant to an option contract is not subject to revocation by the offeror for the time specified;

  o An offer pursuant to an option contract is not affected by a rejection or counter-offer by the offeree; and

  o An offer pursuant to an option contract is not generally affected by the death or incapacity of the offeror or offeree

- Acceptance of an offer held open pursuant to an option contract is effective only upon receipt by the offeror prior to the expiration of the period of time specified

- The offeree's power of acceptance of an offer pursuant to an option contract is terminated by the expiration of the time specified in the option contract or by mutual termination of the option contract

---

Reliance on an Offer of a Unilateral Contract—Protecting the Right to Complete Performance

In lesson 11, we learned that acceptance of an offer of a unilateral contract requires completed performance by the offeree. This raises the obvious issue of whether an offeror can revoke the offer while the offeree is in the midst of performance.

---

[39] This basic rule is reflected in Restatement (Second) of Contracts §§ 25, 37 and 63.

An excellent, if unlikely, example is provided by a classic contracts hypothetical attributed to the late Professor Maurice Wormser.

> **Example 13-2:** Amy says to Ben, "I will pay you $100 to walk across the Brooklyn Bridge." Amy is offering a unilateral contract, as she is bargaining for Ben's performance—not a promise. Thus, Ben must walk across the entire bridge to accept Amy's offer. Ben starts across the bridge, but as he reaches the half-way mark, Amy flies by in a helicopter with a megaphone shouting "I revoke." Under the basic rule, Amy's revocation would be effective, and Ben would be out of luck. However, Ben's reliance in beginning performance of a unilateral contract is protected by an exception to the basic rule.
>
> Assuming that Amy did not invite Ben to make a promise—and, thereby bind both parties in advance—but solely invited his performance, and further assuming that Ben begins the invited performance, then his reliance in doing so precludes Amy's revocation of the offer until Ben has had a reasonable time to complete the performance sought by Amy.

The above stated exception does not constitute an "option contract." Instead, the offeree's reliance on the offer merely precludes revocation by the offeror, allowing the offeree a reasonable time to complete the performance already begun, thereby accepting the offer.

Unfortunately, the restatement provision addressing the issue calls this an "option contract" in the title of the provision. This characterization is inaccurate and misleading because this exception would not, in mid-performance, avoid termination of the offer based on a rejection by the offeree ("I have changed my mind and will not walk across the Brooklyn Bridge for any amount of money"); a counter-offer by the offeree ("how about $200?"); or the death or incapacity of the offeror or offeree. In short, Ben did not have a true "option contract" by virtue of beginning performance. Amy was simply precluded from revoking for a reasonable period of time allowing Ben to complete performance and thereby accept her offer.

Summary of Basic Rule: reliance on an offer of a unilateral contract[40]

- When an offeree begins performance of an offer of a unilateral contract, the offeror is precluded from revoking the offer for a reasonable time period allowing the offeree to complete performance, thereby accepting the offer

---

Protecting the Power of Acceptance under UCC Article 2

UCC Article 2 provides for the enforcement of certain (*but not all*) promises to keep an offer open. These are called "firm offers." **STOP NOW and READ UCC § 2-205 below.**

UCC § 2-205

An offer by a merchant to buy or sell goods in a signed writing which by its terms give assurance that it will be held open is not revocable, for lack of consideration, during the time stated or if no time is stated for a reasonable time, but in no event may such period of irrevocability exceed three months; but any such term of assurance on a form supplied by the offeree must be separately signed by the offeror.

This statute provides an excellent opportunity for an exercise in close statutory reading (a great deal is packed into its single sentence). Consider the following questions with respect to an offer to purchase or sell goods. You should be able to answer them solely by reference to the statute, itself.

Does the statute apply to all offerors or only certain types?

What else is required—in terms of the "form" of any promise—beyond the basic requirements of any offer?

What else is required—in terms of the "content" of any promise—beyond the basic requirements of any offer?

"Merchants"
You may recall the first mention of "merchants" earlier in Chapter 1. UCC Article 2 of course applies to all transactions in goods—not just those involving merchants. However, certain provisions apply only to merchants. § 2-205 includes our first encounter with such a provision. A "merchant" is defined in § 2-104(1) as who, under the circumstances, can be reasonably expected to have "knowledge or skill peculiar to the practices or goods involved in the transaction."

---

[40] This basic rule is reflected in Restatement (Second) of Contracts § 45.

Does a promise to keep an offer open require consideration?

Does the statute require a statement of a specific time period?

Is there any limit as to how long an offer will be held open under the statute?

Suppose the form at issue in Lesson 11, Problem 2 had included a promise to keep the offer open, would the statute require anything else in that case?

As a further exercise in statutory analysis, we might compare UCC § 2-205 to a general statute taking a similar approach, but including a few differences. Below is a New York statute applied to contracts, generally.

> **NY General Obligations Law § 5-1109**
> Except as otherwise provided in section 2-205 of the uniform commercial code with respect to an offer by a merchant to buy or sell goods, when an offer to enter into a contract is made in a writing signed by the offeror, or by his agent, which states that the offer is irrevocable during a period set forth or until a time fixed, the offer shall not be revocable during such period or until such time because of the absence of consideration for the assurance of irrevocability.
> When such a writing states that the offer is irrevocable but does not state any period or time of irrevocability, it shall be construed to state that the offer is irrevocable for a reasonable time.

Can you identify the significant differences between UCC § 2-205 and NY § 5-1109? Do these differences seem reasonable when you consider the general range of application of the two statutes? We can evaluate their effect by returning to Example 11-5. Suppose the Greens' offer to Ever-Tite to reroof their home had included a promise to keep the offer open for 6 months—would the promise be enforceable under § 5-1109? What if the offer by the Greens had been an offer to buy shingles (i.e., a sale of goods)—would the promise to keep the offer open be enforceable? Do these seem like reasonable outcomes?

Of course, the New York statute in the sidebar above is merely an example of a general state statute seeking to address the issue. However, it is useful in illustrating the significance of a few of the elements of UCC § 2-205, and is also an excellent reminder that, in this basic Contracts course, we cannot claim to cover all of the unique provisions of the law of every state. In a real case, you would of course want to look in greater detail at any unique aspects of governing state law—whether statutes or cases—before offering legal advice.

UCC § 2-205 does not apply to all offers governed by UCC Article 2. It does, however, govern certain offers by merchants in which the merchant makes a signed, written promise that an offer will be held open. Within its scope of application, it provides a useful means of protecting the offeree's power of acceptance in a sale of goods transaction. A few additional points about UCC § 2-205 are also worthy of note.

On one hand, UCC § 2-205 is a bit like an option contract. An acceptance of a "firm offer" under the statute must be "received" within the time period given effect under the statute. As in the case of an actual option contract, the offeree is already protected from revocation, so there is no need for the further protection of the mailbox rule. The risk of transmission of the acceptance is on the offeree. On the other, a "firm offer" is not a true option contract, as its express language provides only that the offer is "not revocable." In direct contrast to an option contract, the statute has no effect on a rejection or counter-offer by the offeree—either of which will terminate a "firm offer."

Protecting the Power of Acceptance under the CISG

An offeree's power of acceptance receives very broad protection under the CISG—far more than the common law or UCC § 2-205. **STOP NOW and READ CISG Article 16 below.**

CISG ARTICLE 16

(1) Until a contract is concluded an offer may be revoked if the revocation reaches the offeree before he has dispatched an acceptance.

(2) However, an offer cannot be revoked:

(a) if it indicates, whether by stating a fixed time for acceptance or otherwise, that it is irrevocable; or

(b) if it was reasonable for the offeree to rely on the offer as being irrevocable and the offeree has acted in reliance on the offer.

This provision of the CISG is one that is particularly important for U.S. lawyers and their clients, because it is so dramatically different from what most are accustomed to under domestic law. Ignorance of this particular rule can lead to a client being bound to a contract in wholly unexpected circumstances—especially in combination with CISG Article 11, which we will address later in Chapter 4.

Subsection (1) of Article 16 looks a great deal like the common law rule, with the offeree's dispatch precluding revocation (though not yet constituting acceptance under Article 18, as discussed in the last lesson). However, the "exception" provided by subsection (2) might reasonably be characterized as virtually "swallowing the rule."

Under subsection (2)(a), an offeree's revocation of an offer may be precluded by an "indication" in the offer that it is irrevocable, and such "indication" may arise by virtue of "stating a fixed time" or "otherwise" "indicating" "that it is irrevocable." The potential breadth of application of the latter possibility ought to give an offeror pause for thought in carefully making an offer. Moreover, an oral offer is just as likely to be deemed irrevocable as a written one. And, even if an offeror is careful not to "indicate"—in any way—that an offer is irrevocable, revocation may nevertheless be precluded under subsection (2)(b) by an offeree's reasonable reliance.

The ultimate effect of Article 16 is arguably much more like the civil law approach to the issue of irrevocability of offers than the common law approach. The common law approach grants the offeror greater freedom to revoke an offer in most circumstances, while the civil law approach grants far more protection to the offeree. Whatever one's perspective as to the relative pros or cons of either rule, a sound understanding of CISG Article 16 is essential for a modern U.S. business lawyer.

APPLYING THE RULES

Problem 1: For the problem, we return to the basic facts of Lesson 11, Problem 1. Broadnax learns of the $500 reward offered for the return of Vann, and he begins searching. After two weeks, Broadnax has turned up a few leads, but has yet to locate Vann. Ledbetter has just received bad news from the Dallas County Commissioners, who have slashed his budget. Ledbetter has no idea that Broadnax is looking for Vann, but takes down all of the reward posters. Smith asks why the posters are coming down, and Ledbetter explains that he is cancelling the reward offer, because the County has no money. Smith does know Broadnax is out looking, and he tells Broadnax the next day about the cancellation of the reward. Broadnax has just discovered an excellent new lead as to Vann's whereabouts, and he is confident he can find Vann within 48 hours. What are Broadnax's rights at this point with respect to the $500 reward offer?

Problem 2: Humble Oil was interested in exploring a possible purchase of a parcel of land owned by Westside Investment. However, Humble sought time to consider the purchase on an exclusive basis. To that end, on January 1, Westside granted Humble the right to purchase the parcel of land for $33,200 and promised to hold open the offer through July 1 in exchange for Humble's promise to pay $1,800 for this right. Humble agreed.

On May 1, Humble mailed a letter to Westside proposing changes to Westside's original offer to sell the land parcel. Westside declined to make the requested changes and asserted that Humble's May 1 letter effectively terminated Westside's offer to sell the land. Humble disagreed and sought to accept the original offer on June 1. Who is right?

The facts of this problem are loosely based on the case of *Humble Oil & Refining Co. v. Westside Investment Corp.*, 428 S.W. 2d 92 (Tex. 1968).

Problem 3: We initially return to our basic "short problems" hypo from the last lesson. Acme is a Kansas seller of widgets and Zenith, an Iowa business, buys widgets for use in its manufacturing process. Zenith seeks to purchase "500 Acme X-5 widgets, at $20 each, for immediate delivery." *Consider each of the following independent communication exchanges, all based on the above described order by Zenith.* In which have the parties concluded a contract?

(1) On April 1, Zenith mails a signed written offer to Acme to buy 500 Acme X-5 widgets, at $20 each, promising to hold the offer open until June 30. On June 15, Zenith telephones Acme and says "I no longer need the widgets, as I bought them from Beta instead. You should have been quicker." On June 20, Acme mails an acceptance to Zenith, which Zenith receives on June 25.

(2) On April 1, Zenith mails a signed written offer to Acme to buy 500 Acme X-5 widgets, at $20 each, promising to hold the offer open until June 30. On June 10, Acme mails a response to Zenith saying "your price is a bit low—how about $21 per widget?" Having heard no response to its letter of June 10, and seeing the market prices for widgets falling rapidly due to a glut of new suppliers, Acme sends an e-mail on June 29 accepting Zenith's offer of April 1. Zenith receives the e-mail immediately, but ignores it and does not bother to answer.

(3) On April 1, Zenith mails a signed written offer to Acme to buy 500 Acme X-5 widgets, at $20 each, promising to hold the offer open until June 30. On April 10, Acme mails the acceptance. On July 3, Zenith receives the acceptance, which the postal service had inadvertently initially sent to Greenland before it eventually arrived in Iowa.

(4) On April 1, the Zenith telephones the Acme sales manager, explaining that he would like to buy 500 Acme X-5 widgets, at $20 each. The Acme SM says "no problem—when would you like them. I can ship them today if you absolutely need them, but it would be much easier if you could give me a week or so—I am really jammed with orders right now. The Zenith PM says "that's fine—I am in no hurry." Acme does in fact send its existing inventory of widgets on hand to other customers, but would have sent them to Zenith immediately, if requested. On April 8, the Zenith PM calls Acme and cancels his order. On April 9, Acme receives additional inventory and that same day ships the widgets to Zenith.

What if Zenith was located in Vancouver, British Columbia, Canada?

Lesson 14: Pre-Contractual Liability

Objectives and Expected Learning Outcomes

In this lesson, you will learn the general rule that neither party is liable for failed contract negotiations—whatever the reason for the failure. You will also learn of exceptions to, or variations on, this general rule, including circumstances in which the parties may have already concluded a contract, despite their intent to draft a later more detailed writing for signature. In doing so, you will gain a greater understanding of both the sort of circumstances that may give rise to pre-contractual liability and the knowledge of how to avoid such liability if desired.

Pre-Contractual Liability—Can a Party Incur Liability for Failed Contractual Negotiations?

As we have seen in the last few lessons, contract negotiations may be brief, or may be extended, complex, and often quite expensive. When these negotiations result in an agreement, any difficulties in the negotiating process are likely to be seen as merely a necessary predicate to the formation of the desired contract. However, when negotiations fail, the parties are often left with nothing of value for their trouble (other than of course a bit of that special wisdom that comes only from experience). If one of the parties believes the other has caused the failure, the aggrieved party may seek to hold the culpable party liable. We will see that the general rule precludes such liability. However, we will also see a few exceptions to, or variations on, this general rule, as well as more circumstances in which an offeree's reliance on an offer may give rise to liability under the common law. Along the way, we will also discover that it may not always obvious to the casual observer as to whether a contract has been concluded.

The General Rule: No Contract—No Liability

As a general rule, parties incur no obligation to each other when they fail to conclude an agreement. While every contract gives rise to an implied duty of good faith in performing one's contractual obligations, no such duty is implied in the context of negotiations leading up to a potential contract.

Example 14-1: A and B engaged in a series of complex negotiations regarding a substantial construction project. Each invested significant amounts of time, and spends considerable sums of money on work by architects and engineers in hopes of reaching a successful agreement. After 6 months of such negotiations, including very significant progress, but not yet resulting in an agreement, A wakes up one morning, telephones B and says "the deal is off. I am no longer interested." B asks "why—what happened?" A simply responds "because I don't want to do it—and you don't get to know my reasons."

A is not liable—whatever his reasons—for refusing to negotiate further, because he has no obligation to do so.

To be clear, the sort of conduct described above is generally a bad idea from a business perspective, where reputational sanctions may be far more severe than legal ones. However, the law imposes no sanction in these circumstances, absent some pre-existing duty to negotiate in good faith.

An Agreement to Negotiate in Good Faith

As with the "option contract" discussed in the last lesson, parties may also agree in advance to "negotiate in good faith" in hopes of concluding a "main" contract in which they are primarily interested. The obligation of "good faith" might be included in some sort of "framework agreement" that governs their overall relationship within which they seek to contract, or it may related solely to a single contract at issue.

Example 14-2: A commercial real estate developer may sometimes engage in a series of distinct steps in financing and constructing the subject development and negotiating various contracts along the way. We saw this in Example 6-1, where Mattei sought to condition his obligation to acquire the land for a shopping center on his ability to obtain "satisfactory" leases. He might then, of course, have used the projection of such lease income in securing financing to build the center.

Suppose that Mattei now has purchased the land and is seeking to conclude a number of actual tenant leases. He is not ready yet to actually sign them, because he is still seeking to finalize this construction financing. One prospective tenant Computers-R-Us (who you'll remember from Lesson 8, Problem 2) is very interested in leasing space from Mattei, but still has a few concerns about some zoning issues, as well as the makeup of the tenants in the shopping center as a whole.

The parties might simply try to draw up a "conditional" agreement, like the one between Mattei and Hopper in Example 6-1. However, in this case, they believe the open issues to be sufficiently complex that they would prefer not to be bound to a lease at all until they have worked through more of these issues. While they are not yet ready to be bound to a lease, Mattei would like to have something to show his bankers, and Computers-R-Us would like some assurance that its continuing efforts to negotiate a lease will not be wasted. Thus, they agree, in an exchange of letters, to continue negotiations, "in good faith" towards a hoped for lease agreement, while making it very clear that neither is yet bound to a final lease.

Mattei and Computers-R-Us have very likely concluded a fully independent contract bargain to negotiate in good faith.

It is important to distinguish between an "agreement to negotiate in good faith" from an "agreement to agree." The former is enforceable, but the latter is not. Moreover, an agreement to negotiate in good faith does not require successful conclusion of a contract. It merely requires honest, good faith negotiations. If the parties simply cannot bridge an honest impasse, then neither has breached its obligation, despite the failure to conclude a contract.

In one sense, a contract to negotiate in good faith gives rise to "pre-contractual" liability vis-à-vis the "main" contract. In another, this is not an example of "pre-contractual" liability at all. It is merely an example of liability under an already concluded contract, albeit one that is preliminary to the main contract at issue. Significantly, the breach of a contract to negotiate in good faith will not generally give rise to a right to recover "expectation" under the main contract, because neither party had any assurance it would be concluded. Instead, the parties' expectation interest is limited to their expectation that their counter party will act in good faith during further negotiations.

Concluding a Contract before the Writing is Completed and Signed

While not "technically" a case of pre-contractual liability in any sense of the term, negotiating parties may also simply find that they are bound to an actual agreement at a point in time before at least one of them expected to be. Negotiating parties often have a pretty good idea of what the key issues are in reaching agreement. These are often called the "dickered terms." Other terms—often added by their lawyers—may or may not matter much to the business people.

Once the business people have reached agreement on the terms they care about, they will often then turn the "deal" they have just negotiated over to their lawyers to "write it up" for their signature. In some cases, the fact that they have yet to sign anything may provide objective evidence that neither yet intends to be bound. In other cases, however, a binding contract may be reached long before the lawyers finish their work—or even if they do not end up completing a final writing for the parties to sign. In Chapter 4, we will address the fact that some contracts must be in writing to be enforced, but many do not.

Example 14-3: *Texaco, Inc. v. Pennzoil Co.*

Pennzoil was engaged in negotiations to buy Getty Oil and the two parties eventually reached a deal, in principle, each instructing their legal teams to draft the appropriate documents to consummate the deal. When the transaction was announced publicly, Texaco decided it might be interested in competing to purchase Getty. Texaco's view of the Pennzoil-Getty deal at that point was that "there was just a handshake on price with other issues still open."

A Texas jury thought otherwise and awarded over $10 billion (back when $10 billion was still a lot of money) to Pennzoil on its claim that Texaco had tortuously interfered with Pennzoil's contract with Getty. While Pennzoil's claim was based in tort, the jury necessarily had to find that Pennzoil and Getty Oil had already concluded a contract— notwithstanding the fact that their lawyers were still dotting "i"s and crossing "t"s.[41]

Summary of Basic Rule: conclusion of a contract prior to an expected signed writing[42]

- The parties' intent to draft and sign a later writing may provide evidence they do not yet intend to be bound;

  o However, such evidence does not in any way preclude the earlier conclusion of an agreement where the words, conduct, and other manifestations of the parties suggest an intent to do so

---

Reliance on Contract Offers, Generally, Prior to Acceptance—Protecting the Actual Reliance Interest

In the prior lesson, we focused on the reliance interest of an offeree of a unilateral contract. In that case, the offeree's right to complete performance actually protects the offeree's full expectation interest. If performance is ultimately completed, the offer has been accepted, and the offeree is fully entitled to enforce the offeror's promise at issue. In this respect, the offeree's right to full enforcement of the basic underlying promise is somewhat like an option contract. In contrast, an offeree may, in some circumstances, be entitled to enforce a reliance interest that falls short of its full expectation interest pursuant to the main contract the offeree seeks to conclude. In this latter circumstance, our focus is solely on identifying and quantifying the extent of the offeree's detrimental reliance.

---

[41] Texaco, Inc. v. Pennzoil Co., 729 S.W.2d 768 (Tex. App. 1987).
[42] This basic rule is reflected in Restatement (Second) of Contracts § 27.

Example 14-4: *Hoffman v. Red Owl Stores*

Joseph Hoffman sought to obtain and operate a franchised Red Owl supermarket store. Hoffman indicated at the outset of negotiations that he had only $18,000 to invest, and he was assured by the Red Owl representative that this would be sufficient for the franchise. Over a period of about a year—all on the advice of Red Owl—Hoffman: acquired and operated a small grocery store to gain experience; sold that store to his likely financial detriment; sold his pre-existing bakery business at a loss; spent money to move himself and his family; and made a down payment on a prospective Red Owl location. During this entire period, Hoffman was consistently told by Red Owl that $18,000 would be sufficient for the franchise and all was proceeding according to plan. However, negotiations ultimately broke down when Red Owl demanded that Hoffman capitalize the franchise with a minimum contribution of $34,000. Hoffman sued for his losses, and Red Owl defended, asserting that the parties had never concluded a contract, and further asserting that promissory estoppel had no application where the parties we negotiating over a bargain, but simply failed to conclude it.

In analyzing Hoffman's claims, the court noted that promissory estoppel was typically "invoked as a substitute for consideration." However, the court saw no reason to limit the doctrine to such use and noted that "it would be a mistake to regard an action grounded on promissory estoppel as the equivalent of a breach of contract action." Thus, while recognizing that the parties had not concluded a franchise contract, the court ruled that Hoffman was entitled to recover his reliance damages based on his fully predictable reliance on Red Owl's promises that $18,000 would be sufficient to capitalize the desired franchise. It made no difference that the parties had never finalized the details of the intended franchise, because Hoffman was not recovering on franchise contract, itself.[43]

---

[43] Hoffman v. Red Owl Stores, Inc., 26 Wis. 2d 683, 133 N.W. 2d 267 (1965).

Do you see any similarity between the application of promissory estoppel in Lesson 7, Problem 3, and Example 14-4 above? In each case, the application of promissory estoppel required the claimant to show that a promise that was separate and distinct from the related contract (in the earlier case, an "at will" contract—in the above Example, a contract that was never concluded).

In *Hoffman*, the court merely applied the traditional doctrine of promissory estoppel in the context of pre-contractual negotiations. As such, Hoffman was entitled only to his reliance interest—being returned to his original financial position, as if he had never engaged in the protracted negotiations with Red Owl (subsequent to Red Owl's promise that his investment capital would be fully sufficient to obtain the franchise). However, at least one line of "reliance based" common law cases goes even further and awards the relying party with its expectation interest based on the contract it ultimately sought to conclude.

Pre-Contractual Reliance on an Offer of a Bilateral Contract—Protecting the Offeree's Expectation Interest

The circumstances in which the following cases arise is arguably unique. Construction projects—especially public projects—are often put out to "bid" and awarded to the lowest qualifying bidder. A general contractor ("GC" in the discussion that follows) will make a single bid to the government or private entity seeking to have the work done. However, the GC will not perform all of the work (in fact, it may do no actual construction work at all). Instead, the GC will rely on various sub-contractors to perform the actual work. In the same manner that the GC must "bid" for the complete project, each sub-contractor must "bid" (to one of more GCs) for the portion it seeks to perform. Typically, the GC will simply take all of the lowest bids for each component of the job, add its own costs and profit for managing the project, and submit its total bid for the project.

As if the above process wasn't already sufficiently complex, most of this is done in a very tight time frame. For a variety of reasons (including a lack of trust as to whether a bid may be "shared" with competitors), a GC will typically make its bid as close to the deadline as possible, and sub-contractors will typically do the same. As such, a GC may be relying on "low bids" from one or more sub-contractors it knows little about, other than the amount bid.

In this context, it is hardly surprising that: (1) mistakes will sometimes happen; and (2) when a mistake is made on a "low bid" by a sub-contractor, an issue will arise as between the sub-contractor's right to revoke an offer prior to acceptance and the GC's reliance interest, having used the sub-contractor's low bid in calculating its own. This first case was decided by Judge Learned Hand.

Example 14-5: *James Baird Co. v. Gimbel Bros., Inc.*

Gimbel submitted a bid to Baird to perform the linoleum work for a construction project upon which Baird was bidding to be the general contractor ("GC"). As a potential GC, Baird relied on bids of various sub-contractors, like Gimbel, in preparing its own total bid on the project. While Baird did rely on Gimble's bid, it did not actually accept the bid in doing so, and remained free to choose another sub-contractor after the bid was awarded.

After Baird had submitted its own bid, Gimbel contacted Baird to revoke its bid on the linoleum, explaining that it had made a mistake. Baird was awarded the general contract and argued that Gimbel could not revoke, because Baird had relied on Gimbel's bid in making its own. However, Baird's argument was rejected, inasmuch as Gimbel had revoked its offer prior to any acceptance by Baird.

Judge Hand specifically rejected any argument that Baird's reliance should be protected under the doctrine of promissory estoppel, because Gimbel had made no promise to Baird to keep the offer open. The only promises made by Gimbel were contained in the offer to perform the linoleum work, which Baird could have accepted, but did not. Moreover, when Baird chose to use Gimbel's bid, it could have easily accepted the bid, conditioned upon Baird receiving the main contract, as GC.[44]

Judge Hand had little sympathy for the GC, who he believed could have easily protected itself by conditionally accepting the bids it relied upon.

[44] James Baird Co. v. Gimbel Bros., Inc., 64 F.2d 344 (2d Cir. 1933).

Having kept its options open as to choosing sub-contractors, the GC necessarily exposed itself to the risk that a subcontractor might revoke its bid—just as Gimbel did. In contrast, Judge Richard Traynor, writing for the California Supreme Court, reached exactly the opposite result on virtually identical facts.

Example 14-6: *Drennan v. Star Paving Co.*

Star submitted a bid to Drennan to perform the paving work for a construction project upon which Drennan was bidding to be the general contractor ("GC"). As a potential GC, Drennan relied on bids of various sub-contractors, like Star, in preparing its own total bid on the project. While Drennan did rely on Star's bid, it did not actually accept the bid in doing so, and remained free to choose another sub-contractor after the bid was awarded.

Shortly after Drennan was awarded the general contract, Star attempted to revoke its bid based on having made a mistake in calculating it. Drennan successfully argued that Star could no longer revoke, because Drennan had relied on Star's bid in making its own. Thus, Star was bound by its original bid, and Drennan was entitled to its expectation damages based on Star's refusal to perform.

Judge Traynor specifically relied upon the doctrine of promissory estoppel, based on Star's promise contained in its offer to perform the paving work at the price bid. Star should have reasonably expected its bid to induce Drennan's reliance, and Drennan did so rely. Thus Star was bound. Judge Traynor further explained that Drennan had only a reasonable time to accept Star's offer and could not abuse that right by shopping it around or trying to renegotiate it with Star (i.e., a rejection of Star's offer). He analogized Drennan's right to that of an offeree of a unilateral contract, who after beginning performance is afforded a reasonable time to complete that performance.[45]

---

[45] Drennan v. Starr Paving Co., 51 Cal. 2d 409, 333 P.2d 757 (1958).

Which rationale do you find more persuasive? Why? Do you agree with Judge Hand that the sub-contractor made no promise to support the application of promissory estoppel, and the GC could have protected itself? Or do you agree with Judge Traynor that the subcontractor's promise in its bid is sufficient, and the GC should be afforded the same sort of rights as the offeree of a unilateral contract under Restatement (Second) of Contracts § 45?

In thinking about these two approaches, do you see any resemblance between Judge Traynor's approach in *Drennan* and the rule provided by CISG Article 16(2)(b)? Does this change your perspective as to which of the above two cases is most persuasive, confirm it, or neither? To be clear, the CISG has absolutely no application to a domestic construction case, but the similarity of the two rules provides a useful point of reference.

The restatement position on the issue reflects the rule of *Drennan*,[46] rather than the rule of *Baird*. However, the application of this "rule" has been largely cabined within the narrow confines of offers by sub-contractors relied upon by general contractors. It is arguably this context—an often hurried, last-minute process of receiving bids from sub-contractors and using them to assemble the GC's own bid—that provides at least some of the justification for the result. Under such circumstances, it may be unreasonable for a GC to devote sufficient "vetting" to each of the "low bidders" relied upon, thus justifying a reasonable opportunity to do so subsequently if selected as the general contractor.

Summary of Basic Rule: reliance on an offer of a bilateral contract in the context of offers by sub-contractors relied upon by general contractors[47]

- An offer in the form of a bid by a sub-contractor, which a general contractor should reasonably be expected to rely upon in calculating its own bid, is irrevocable by the sub-contractor

  o This period of "irrevocability" extends only for a reasonable time after a general contractor has been awarded the main contract;

  o The offer remains subject to termination based on a rejection, including a counter-offer, by the offeree, just as any other offer

---

[46] Restatement (Second) of Contracts § 87(2).
[47] Restatement (Second) of Contracts § 87(2).

Restitution for Benefits Conferred during the Negotiating Process

During the negotiating process, one or both of the parties may, in some fashion confer benefits on each other, without ever concluding a final agreement. To the extent that either does so, the party conferring the benefit may have a claim for restitution to avoid unjust enrichment (as more fully discussed earlier in Lesson 8). As with any claim based on unjust enrichment, the party seeking restitution must prove that:

- The benefit was not "officious," but was desired by the recipient; and

- The party conferring it expected payment and did not act gratuitously

The easiest case is a "down payment" made before the conclusion of a contract. In that case, the party receiving the payment will likely be required to return it, as a matter of restitution. In contrast, where one party's conduct during the negotiation process has arguably enriched the other, the lack of "officiousness" or "gratuitousness" in the context of the negotiations at issue may be difficult to prove.

APPLYING THE RULES

Problem 1: Delta manufactured motors, and Echo manufactured equipment that used such motors. Echo was interested in producing a new piece of equipment that required a particularly high speed, high wattage, light weight motor not currently available on the market. Echo approached Delta about producing such a motor. During the negotiation process, Delta and Echo engineers worked together to design the special motor, ultimately succeeding at an acceptable price. With Echo fully satisfied with the product and the pricing by Delta, the parties concluded their negotiations and turned the matter over to their lawyers to draw up a final writing to be executed by the parties. However, in finalizing the writing, the lawyers raised the question of whether Echo would be entitled to share any revenues Delta might realize on the sale of the jointly designed motor to others. The parties had not considered the issue previously and were subsequently unable to reach an agreement. As a result, negotiations broke down and Delta declined to discuss the matter further. Delta subsequently began to manufacture the jointly designed motor for sale at a nice profit. However, Delta refused to honor the original price it had negotiated with Echo.

What, if any, claims might Echo have against Delta?

Problem 2: Sun Lumber e-mailed a bid to Jones to supply the lumber for a construction project upon which Jones was bidding to be the general contractor ("GC"). The bid said nothing with respect to any time for acceptance. As a potential GC, Jones relied on bids of various sub-contractors, as well as various materials suppliers like Sun, in preparing its own total bid on the project. Sun submitted the low bid for the lumber, and Jones relied on that bid in preparing its own, but did not actually accept the bid in doing so, thereby remaining free to choose a different supplier of lumber after the bid was awarded

Shortly after Jones was awarded the general contract, Sun attempted to revoke its bid based on having made a mistake in calculating it. Jones asserted that Sun was precluded from revoking and promptly indicated its acceptance of Sun's offer. Is Sun bound?

What if Jones was a Montana GC, and Sun was located in Calgary, Canada?

Problem 3: For this problem, we return to the facts of Example 11-1. Pattberg had promised to reduce Petterson's principal obligation on his debt to Pattberg by $780, if Petterson would do two specific things: (1) timely make the regular payment due on April 25; and (2) pay the rest of the loan balance on or before May 31. Petterson performed the first, but Pattberg sought to revoke the offer just as Petterson was about to perform the second. Do any of the materials in this lesson or lesson 13 provide any basis for reconsidering the outcome of this case in Example 11-1?

You should rely on all of the facts presented in Example 11-1, as well as the following additional facts from the actual case. Subsequent to Pattberg's offer to reduce the loan principal, but prior to his attempted revocation of the offer, Petterson had entered into a contract to sell the property subject to the mortgage held by Pattberg (as in the typical real estate transaction, Petterson promised to sell it "free and clear" of any mortgage). Thus, Petterson had no choice but to pay off the mortgage in full to the third party to whom Pattberg had sold it, lest he breach his own sale contract. You may want to consider more than one possible theory, but you should consider each carefully. Is there anything else you would need to know with respect to quantifying any remedy?

The facts of this problem are loosely based on the case of *Petterson v. Pattberg*, 248 N.Y. 86, 161 N.E. 428 (1928).

Lesson 15: The "Battle of Forms"

Objectives and Expected Learning Outcomes

In this lesson, you will learn how to determine whether an acceptance is effective, even though it varies from the offer. You will also learn how to determine the terms included in a contract when it is concluded by an acceptance that varies from the offer. Finally, you will learn how to determine the basic content of the parties' agreement when they fail to reach agreement through their exchange of communications, but nevertheless begin performance as if they had done so. This is a particularly long and challenging lesson. However, it is presented as a single unit for the sake of clarity and followed by a much shorter lesson, which continues to explore many of the same issues.

Dueling Offer and Acceptance and the "Battle of Forms"

Most of the examples in this Chapter thus far have involved acceptances of an offer's precise terms, without any efforts on the part of the offeree to change or add to the terms of the offer, or they have involved substantial "negotiations" in which the parties typically did not intend to conclude a contract until those negotiations were completed (or, at least, largely so). Sometimes, however, an offeree will communicate what purports to be an acceptance, but changes or adds to the terms of the offer. As first explained in Lesson 12, under the common law, any difference between the offer and a purported acceptance will result, instead, in a rejection of the original offer and a new "counter-offer" based on the terms of the purported acceptance. This result arises from the operation of the common law "mirror image" rule.

Until and unless an acceptance matching or "mirroring" an offer or counter-offer is communicated, the parties will not have concluded a contract through their communications. However, the contracting parties often fail to recognize this and will go ahead with performance of the contract they believe they have already concluded. While their earlier communications were not effective in concluding a contract, their subsequent performance is. In effect, the last open counter-offer, or "last shot" is deemed accepted by the performance of the other party.

These two common law rules—the "mirror image" rule and the "last shot" rule—are explained in further detail below. After analyzing the common law rule, we will next consider the rule of UCC § 2-207, which reflects a dramatic departure from the common law rule. Finally, we will address the rule under CISG Articles 18 and 19, which bears a striking similarity to the common law rule. In the portion of this lesson addressing the sale of goods, we will focus exclusively on business-to-business transactions. In the next lesson, we will consider a few unique issues than arise when the "battle" involving sales of goods is carried over into consumer transactions.

No Contract without a Matching Offer and Acceptance—the "Mirror Image" Rule

A reply to an offer (even one that purports to be an "acceptance") requiring the offeror's assent to added or different terms of any kind is not an acceptance at all. Instead, it is a counter-offer.[48] Unless the offeree is very clear that he or she is accepting the precise terms of the original offer and is merely suggesting a new offer to *modify* the "just concluded" contract, the mere presence in the purported acceptance of such added or different terms will generally result in a counter-offer. This counter-offer also serves as a rejection of the original offer, thereby precluding any later acceptance of the original offer unless renewed.

Let's look at a classic case involving the application of the "mirror image" rule to preclude the formation of a contract.

---

[48] Restatement (Second) of Contracts § 59.

Example 15-1: *Ardente v. Horan*

The Horans had placed their home on the market, and Ardente had made a bid of $250,000. The Horans found the price to be acceptable and had their attorney prepare a purchase and sale agreement, which was forwarded to Ardente. Ardente signed the agreement, returning it to the Horans with a check for $20,000, along with a letter from Ardente's attorney stating:

"My clients are concerned that the following items remain with the real estate: a) dining room set and tapestry wall covering in dining room; b) fireplace fixtures throughout; c) the sun parlor furniture. I would appreciate your confirming that these items are a part of the transaction, as they would be difficult to replace."

The Horans subsequently declined to go forward with the transaction. Ardente sued for specific performance (this being a real estate transaction), asserting that he had accepted the Horans' offer and was merely exploring the possibility of acquiring the additional items. However, the court agreed with the Horans that Ardente's letter was not sufficiently clear in expressing an acceptance of the Horans' offer—irrespective of their willingness to part with the additional items—and was, therefore, merely a counter-offer.[49]

The court explained that Ardente could have clearly and unequivocally accepted the offer, while simultaneously proposing to modify the newly accepted agreement (or perhaps even requesting a gift, absent further consideration). However, Ardente's letter did not do this and was, therefore, a counter-offer, instead of an acceptance. The counter-offer also served as a rejection of the Horans' original offer, so that offer could no longer be accepted by Ardente.

---

[49] Ardente v. Horan, 117 R.I. 254, 366 A.2d 162 (1976).

> **Summary of Basic Rule: "mirror image" rule**[50]
>
> • An acceptance must be a "mirror image" of the offer
>
>   ○ Any attempt to vary the terms of the contract to be concluded through a purported acceptance will result in a counter-offer—not an acceptance

In the above example, the Horans noted the additional terms and rejected the counter-offer by Ardente. However, in many instances the added or different terms in a purported acceptance are contained in one or both of the parties' pre-printed forms. These "forms" are typically drafted by the parties' lawyers, and the business people may pay little, if any, attention to them—focusing instead of the "dickered" terms filled out by the business people in completing the forms. Thus, in a classic "battle of [non-matching] forms," the parties will often believe they have concluded a contract and begin performance.

Performance as Acceptance of the Last Counter-Offer—the "Last Shot" Rule

The use of a "form" by at least one party may give rise to a "battle" resulting in the application of the "mirror image" rule, as explained above. However, in many instances, the parties may each use forms. For example, the buyer may use a purchase order and the seller may use an order acknowledgement or invoice. If each form includes "boilerplate" (drafter by the lawyers, and often found on the back of a pre-printed form), it will almost certainly differ, as lawyers will generally draft very different standard terms for buyers and sellers.

This "battle" may include only one "volley" by each party, or it may involve many. However, none of these non-matching volleys or "form communications" will result in the conclusion of a contract. It is, instead, the performance of the parties (who believe they already have a contract) that actually results in acceptance of the last open counter-offer, upon the terms contained in that party's "form" document. In many instances, the determination of which party's terms were accepted by the other will be completely random or arbitrary.

---

[50] This basic rule is reflected in Restatement (Second) of Contracts § 59.

Example 15-2: A shopping center sought to contract for security services. To that end, the center management and service provider exchanged various orders, acknowledgements, and other form documents, all of which agreed on the basic terms of the arrangement, but each of which contained significant pre-printed language (the same party's documents did not even fully match). Finally, after a detailed pro-forma invoice was sent by the service provider to the center, the services were begun, and the center made the first payment. Thus, the center is deemed to have "accepted" the "last shot" by the service provider when it commenced performance.

It is important to note that it is not necessarily the first party to perform that is bound to the other's terms. It is the first to perform at a time when there is an open counter-offer by the other (remember, each counter-offer rejects and terminates the offer to which it responds). Thus, the "last shot" rule is merely one specific example of acceptance of a bilateral contract by beginning performance, as originally addressed in Lesson 11.

Summary of Basic Rule: the "last shot" rule[51]

- Where an exchange of communications results in a series of counter-offers, and the parties begin performance, a contract will be concluded on the basis of the last open counter-offer

---

While perhaps most common in the context of exchanges of "forms," such "battles" can also arise from individualized communications. While business people are generally careful with the most important terms (e.g., the price and nature of the service to be provided or the real estate to be sold), they may not always be as careful with other minor, less important terms. If these terms differ, these individual exchanges may also amount to a series of dueling counter-offers, accepted—if at all—by the performance of one of the parties.

Before leaving the common law treatment of this issue, one other point is worth noting. In Chapter 6, we will fully address a variety of sources from which we may factually imply the intent of the parties. For example, if the

---

[51] This basic rule is reflected in the combination of Restatement (Second) of Contracts §§ 39 and 62.

two contracting parties have always done business in the past in a particular way, we can reasonably assume they will continue to do so in the future, absent some contrary expression of intent. In a similar vein, if the two parties are members of a particular trade, and that trade always conducts business in a particular manner, we can reasonably assume that these two parties intend to do so as well, absent some contrary expression of intent.

Thus, an express term of one party may in fact "match" or "mirror" one of the parties' past practices or a practice of their common trade—even though not expressly found in the other party's communication. Again, the subject of implied-in-fact contract terms will be addressed more thoroughly in Chapter 6, but is worthy of mention here as one means by which at least a few "battles" may perhaps be avoided.

A Very Different Approach to the "Battle" under UCC Article 2

UCC Article 2 takes a very different approach than the common law, departing from both the "mirror image" rule, and the "last shot" rule. **STOP NOW and READ UCC § 2-207 in its entirety below.**

UCC § 2-207

(1) A definite and seasonable expression of acceptance or a written confirmation which is sent within a reasonable time operates as an acceptance even though it states terms additional to or different from those offered or agreed upon, unless acceptance is expressly made conditional on assent to the additional or different terms.

(2) The additional terms are to be construed as proposals for addition to the contract. Between merchants such terms become part of the contract unless:

(a) the offer expressly limits acceptance to the terms of the offer;

(b) they materially alter it; or

(c) notification of objection to them has already been given or is given within a reasonable time after notice of them is received.

(3) Conduct by both parties which recognizes the existence of a contract is sufficient to establish a contract for sale although the writings of the parties do not otherwise establish a contract. In such case the terms of the particular contract consist of those terms on which the writings of the parties agree, together with any supplementary terms incorporated under any other provisions of this Act.

How does UCC § 2-207(1) differ from the "mirror image" rule? If the answer is not immediately apparent, you may find it helpful to try to break this section down into parts in order to understand it more easily. For example, you might cull out the "basic rule" as "[a] definite and seasonable expression of **acceptance . . . operates** as an acceptance **even though it states terms additional to or different from those offered** . . . ." The "basic exception" can then be isolated as applicable *only if* "acceptance is **expressly made conditional** on assent to the additional or different terms." Finally, you might take note of the treatment of "written confirmations"— whatever those might be—as follows: "a **written confirmation** which is sent within a reasonable time operates as an acceptance even though it states terms additional to or different from those offered or agreed upon." Each of these parts of subsection (1) is addressed in the materials below. However, we should first briefly take note of the content of the other two subsections, as well.

How does UCC § 2-207(3) differ from the "last shot" rule? If the answer is not immediately apparent, read this specific subsection again carefully, thinking about how it compares to the common law "last shot" rule described earlier in this lesson. In thinking about this subsection, you might also consider UCC § 2-204(1) and (2) (also addressed below). UCC § 2-207(2) has no analogy under the common law at all. As you read the materials that follow, see if you can see why.

The Effectiveness of an Acceptance under Subsection (1)

UCC § 2-207(1) fundamentally changes the effect of many acceptances that contain terms not found in the offer. If intended as an acceptance, a communication will be effective as an acceptance in concluding a contract, subject to only two limitations—one in the statutory language and one in the basic nature of an acceptance.

First, the statute contains a clear exception. If an offeree adds or changes terms, as compared to the offer, the offeree may contractually invoke the "mirror image" rule as applicable to any purported acceptance. If the purported "acceptance" is "expressly made conditional on assent to the additional or different terms," then it is not an acceptance at all. It is, instead, a counter-offer, just as it would be under the common law mirror image rule—subject to acceptance, or not, by the original offeror. Thus, the "basic rule," allowing for an effective acceptance that varies from the offer, is a mere "default," and the offeree may invoke the common law "mirror image" rule as a matter of simple choice. That said most courts require very precise use of the statutory language in order to invoke the "exception," as the very purpose of the statute is to depart from the common law outcome in a sale of goods transaction.

> **Example 15-3:** Seller offers to sell 100 widgets at $10 each. Buyer replies "I accept your offer, but only on the express condition that you delivery them by Friday. Because the buyer's acceptance is "expressly conditional" upon "delivery by Friday," the purported acceptance is a counter-offer, which the seller can accept or not.

Second, a communication that changes a basic element of the bargain, such as the description, quantity, or price, is not a "definite . . . expression of acceptance" at all. As a matter of common sense, an offer to sell a car cannot be accepted by saying, "great! I agree to buy your bicycle." An offer to sell a car for $5,000 cannot be accepted by saying "great! I agree to buyer your car for $4,000." This sort of basic change in the nature of the bargain (typically, a change in description, price, or quantity) is simply not an "acceptance" at all, and the application of the statutory rule does not turn it into one. It is, instead, a counter-offer, just as it would be under the common law.

> **Example 15-4:** Seller offers to sell 100 widgets at $10 each. Buyer replies "I agree to purchase 200 widgets at $20 each." There is no contract, as buyer's communication is not an acceptance. It a mere counter-offer, and UCC § 2-207(1) is not applicable.

When viewed together, the rule and its exceptions can be seen to give effect to most communications reasonably intended as acceptances, while treating as counter-offers most communications intended as such. Much of the challenge in understanding and applying subsection (1) is that it more properly belongs in § 2-206, along with other rules of "acceptance." In fact, subsection (1) merely governs a specific subset of acceptances—those in which an intended acceptance varies from the offer.

In contrast, subsections (2) and (3) address related, but distinctly separate issues. When a purported acceptance varies from an offer, but—one way or another—the parties nevertheless conclude a contract, which terms are included in that contract?

If the Acceptance is Effective under Subsection (1), which Terms are Included?

If an acceptance is effective under subsection (1), we must then turn to subsection (2) to determine which terms are included in the agreement just concluded between the parties. Subsection (2) is easiest to understand when taken in small steps, one step at a time.

First, any "additional terms are to be construed as proposals for addition to the contract." This provision applies to any acceptance that includes additional terms—whether or not it involves a merchant. In some respects, it merely states the obvious. Newly added terms are proposals to modify the contract. If accepted by the other party, they become part of the contract. You should recall from Lesson 6 that modifications do not require new consideration under UCC § 2-209(1). If not accepted, however, such "proposals" have no legal effect.

Second—but only if both parties are "merchants"—such additional terms presumptively "become part of the contract." Of course, an "unless" clause follows the "presumption." However, it is important to recognize this presumptive incorporation of these terms into the parties' agreement as our starting point for the analysis under subsections (2) (a), (b), and (c). In effect, the additional terms automatically become part of the contract, unless the offeror can establish

> **"Between merchants"**
> In Lesson 13, we first encountered a "merchant" limitation in the context of UCC § 2-205. In this lesson, we first see the term, "between merchants," which, under § 2-104(3), limits the application of the designated provision to circumstances in which "both parties are chargeable with the knowledge or skill of merchants."

that subsections (2)(a), (b), or (c) preclude that result. In the event the acceptance includes more than one additional term, each must be analyzed independently—at least under subsections (2)(b) and (c).

Subsections (2)(a) and (c) each arise from some sort of direct indication by the offeror that the additional terms are unacceptable—either in advance (generally or specifically) or within a reasonable time after notice of their addition. Do you see each of these forms of objection in subsections (2)(a) and (c)? Many "forms" drafted by the parties' lawyers will include the sort of language provided in subsection (2)(a), thereby effectively avoiding any need to analyze the other provisions of subsection (2). However, not every "battle" will include such form language, and parties will sometimes fail to note the added terms until a dispute arises. In such cases, subsection (2)(b) is often crucial in determining whether a given term will become part of the contract.

Subsection (2)(b) excludes an additional term from the final agreement if that term would "materially alter" the originally offered contract. A "material alteration" is certainly less significant than the "basic" terms discussed earlier (description, quantity, and price), but how much so? Official comment 4 to § 2-207 is useful in this respect.

OFFICIAL COMMENT 4 (UCC § 2-207)

4. Examples of typical clauses which would normally "materially alter" the contract and so result in surprise or hardship if incorporated without express awareness by the other party are . . . .

You can of course look at the Comment itself for the list that follows. However, the broadly applicable standard is likely to be more useful in most cases. The following seminal opinion by Judge Richard Posner is very frequently cited on the issue of "materiality."

> **Example 15-5:** *Union Carbide Corp. v. Oscar Mayer Foods Corp.*
>
> Union Carbide, a seller, sought to impose tax liability on its buyer, Oscar Mayer. In ruling that the contract provision at issue (evaluated as an indemnification clause, for purpose of the instant analysis) would have "materially altered" the parties' contract, the Court explained the standard as follows:

An alteration is material if consent to it cannot be presumed. That is our gloss; the cases more commonly speak
of "unreasonable surprise," . . . . But it comes to the same
thing. What is expectable, hence unsurprising, is okay;
what is unexpected, hence surprising, is not. Not infre-
quently the test is said to be "surprise or hardship," . . . , but
this appears to be a misreading of Official Comment 4 to
UCC § 2-207. The comment offers examples of "typical
clauses which would normally 'materially alter' the contract
and so result in surprise or hardship if incorporated without express awareness by the other party." Hardship is a
consequence, not a criterion.[52]

In short, the Court focused on the sort of unexpected "hardship" arising
from terms that a party would be "unreasonably surprised" to find in a
contract without express assent to those terms. In such a case, the terms are
deemed to "materially alter" the parties agreement under UCC § 2-207(2)(b)
and are, therefore, excluded from the parties' agreement.

What about Different Terms?

The application of subsection (2) to "additional" terms is relatively straightforward, if taken a step at a time. However, the issue of what to do with
"different" terms is somewhat more problematic. Subsection (1) allows for
an effective acceptance, even though it contains "additional" or "different"
terms. However, subsection (2) says nothing about "different" terms—only
"additional" ones.

One possible approach is simply to drop the different terms in the acceptance entirely, giving effect to the offeror's "differing" term over that of
the offeree. This seems to track the precise statutory language, allowing for
an effective acceptance under subsection (1) despite the different term, but
thereafter ignoring it based on its omission from subsection (2). Another
is to review different terms under subsection (2) even though not expressly
included, thereby giving the nod to offeree's non-materially different
terms, but giving priority to the offeror on anything else. Each of these ap-

---

[52] Union Carbide Corp. v. Oscar Mayer Foods Corp., 947 F.2d 1333 (7th Cir. 1991).

proaches is somewhat unsatisfactory because both seem to favor the offeror in a manner a bit reminiscent of the "last shot" doctrine.

An alternative approach is suggested by Official Comment 6.

OFFICIAL COMMENT 6 (UCC § 2-207)

6. . . . Where clauses on confirming forms sent by both parties conflict, each party must be assumed to object to a clause of the other conflicting with the one on the confirmation sent by himself. As a result, the requirement that there be notice of objection which is found in subsection (2) is satisfied and the conflicting terms to not become part of the contract. . . . .

At the outset, it must be noted that this Comment specifically addresses only different terms in "confirmations," which are more fully addressed below. However, the logic also has force in the context of different terms in an "acceptance." The very existence of differing terms addressing the same issue would seem to indicate that each party objects to the other's term. Thus, different terms are all removed from the agreement, and any "gaps" are filled by "default" rules contained in Article 2. This is often called the "knock out" rule, and we will see it again below in our discussion of subsection (3).

> **Example 15-6:** Buyer mails a form purchase order to seller, offering to purchase 100 widgets at $10 each. Seller mails a form acknowledgment accepting buyer's offer. Buyer's form includes a 3 year warranty provision, while seller's form includes a disclaimer of all warranties, express or implied. Seller's acceptance is effective under subsection (1), notwithstanding the "different" warranty provision. However, under the "knock out" rule, both parties' warranty terms will drop out, to be replaced by the default warranty provisions supplied by Article 2, part 3.

The majority of courts apply the "knock out" rule to different terms in an acceptance. As such, a court heeding the mandate of "uniform" application, as provided in UCC § 1-103(a)(3) would likely follow this same rule.

Acceptance by Performance

Having fully addressed acceptance under subsection (1) and the inclusion of additional terms under subsection (2), we can now turn to the "exceptional" provision of subsection (1). We noted above that a purported "acceptance" that is "expressly made conditional on assent to the additional or different terms" is not an acceptance at all. It is a counter-offer. If this counter-offer (along with any others made in reply) is not effectively accepted, then the parties will simply fail to conclude a contract. However, if the parties go ahead and begin to perform under the agreement they believe they have concluded, then they will indeed be mutually bound to a contract based on their conduct. **STOP NOW and READ the excerpts from UCC § 2-204 below.**

UCC § 2-204(1) AND (2)

(1) A contract for sale of goods may be made in any manner sufficient to show agreement, including conduct by both parties which recognizes the existence of such a contract.

(2) An agreement sufficient to constitute a contract for sale may be found even though the moment of its making is undetermined.

. . .

It is at this point in our analysis that subsection (3) fully displaces the "last shot" rule. Subsection (3) first recognizes that a contract may be formed by conduct, even though the parties' writings have failed to do so under subsection (1). However, rather than binding one of the parties to the last open counter-offer of the other, subsection (3) provides for a "knock out" approach, giving effect to the terms upon which the parties' writings agree, supplemented by the "default" rules of Article 2.

> **Example 15-7:** Buyer mails a form purchase order to seller, offering to purchase 100 widgets at $10 each. Seller mails a form acknowledgment accepting buyer's offer. Buyer's form includes a 3 year warranty provision, while seller's form includes a disclaimer of all warranties, express or implied. Each party's form also makes its consent to conclude a contract "expressly conditional" upon the other's agreement

to its warranty provision. Inasmuch as each party's form invokes the "exception" to subsection (1), the parties' exchange of writings (no matter how many are exchanged) will not conclude a contract.

If, however, the seller delivers the goods and the buyer pays, then the parties will be deemed to have concluded a contract through performance. Under subsection (3), the terms agreed upon by the parties will be given effect, while both parties' warranty terms will drop out, to be replaced by the default warranty provisions supplied by Article 2, part 3. The question of which party made the last open counter-offer is completely irrelevant under subsection (3).

Thus, we can see that the combination of UCC §§ 2-207(1) and (3) effectively displace the common law "mirror image" and "last shot" rules with very different alternatives, and subsection (2) deals specifically with the question of what to do with any additional terms contained in an acceptance given effect under subsection (1). One final point is also worthy of note here, as the reader may recognize one remaining loose end—counter-offers based on a change in a basic term, such as description, quantity, or price.

In the case of a change in a basic term, the resulting communication cannot be considered an acceptance at all. It therefore falls entirely outside the ambit of UCC § 2-207. As such, the "last shot" rule would still apply in the event of performance without otherwise reaching agreement. The potential for surprise, however, is minimized, because a party would—and certainly should—be very unlikely to perform in the absence of agreement on a basic contract term.

Having fully addressed "acceptances," we can now move on to "confirmations," a unique communication we have yet to consider in this course. This discussion will also necessarily lead us through a very brief preview of the writing requirement applied to transactions in goods, which will be addressed more fully in Lesson 19.

A Written Confirmation

The term "confirmation" is used in two provisions of UCC Article 2—§§ 2-201 and 2-207. While its significance in § 2-207(1) is not obvious in isolation, its use in § 2-201(2) is quite important. As we will further explore in Lesson 19, many contracts for the sale of goods require a signed writing. However, one way of satisfying the requirement is through the use of a written "confirmation" that follows a prior oral agreement. It is called a "confirmation" because it takes place after a contract has already been concluded. However, it may be crucial in satisfying the writing requirement and, thereby, insuring that the parties' prior oral agreement is fully enforceable.

This use of a writing to confirm a prior oral agreement under § 2-201 leads us back to § 2-207. Official Comment 1 of the latter explains that confirmations may relate to prior oral agreements or other "informal" communications between the parties. Of course, the question then arises as to what happens if the "confirmation" of the prior oral agreement includes additional or different terms. That is the question subsection (1) seeks to answer by including "confirmations."

Additional terms in a "confirmation" are generally treated in exactly the same manner as "additional" terms in an "acceptance." Assuming the "knock out" rule is applied to "different" terms in an acceptance, Official Comment 6 is absolutely clear that this rule applies to a confirmation, so—once again—the two are treated identically. In fact, this makes perfect sense when we consider UCC § 2-204(2), which recognizes that it may often be difficult to determine the precise moment of contract formation.

While it does seem a bit strange to think of a "confirmation" as adding a new term to a previously concluded contract, this will typically happen only when the confirmation follows an oral agreement, the precise contours of which may already be somewhat vague, and such additions are limited by materiality under subsection (2)(b). Thus, the overall approach in dealing with confirmations in the same general manner as acceptances seems reasonable.

There remain a few challenges with the framing of the statutory language with respect to confirmations. Surely a "confirmation" doesn't really "operate as an acceptance" when the parties have already concluded a contract; though it may have a similar effect in adding terms to that existing agreement. And does the subsection (1) "exception" apply only to real acceptances, or does it also apply to confirmations that operate as acceptances? The former interpretation seems more logical, but the language is less clear than it might be.

In summary, UCC § 2-207 reflects an attempt to change the common law rules governing the proverbial "battle of forms" in a positive and meaningful way. The issue is nevertheless sufficiently challenging that the statute is not without its own interpretive challenges. We can now compare the approach of Article 2 to that of the CISG that follows. The latter is certainly simpler, but is it better?

A Different Approach to the "Battle" under the CISG

In stark contrast to UCC Article 2, the CISG takes an approach to these issues that—as actually applied—looks much more like the common law "mirror image" rule and "last shot" rule. **STOP NOW and READ CISG Article 19 below.**

CISG ARTICLE 19

(1) A reply to an offer which purports to be an acceptance but contains additions, limitations or other modifications is a rejection of the offer and constitutes a counter-offer.

(2) However, a reply to an offer which purports to be an acceptance but contains additional or different terms which do not materially alter the terms of the offer constitutes an acceptance, unless the offeror, without undue delay, objects orally to the discrepancy or dispatches a notice to that effect. If he does not so object, the terms of the contract are the terms of the offer with the modifications contained in the acceptance.

(3) Additional or different terms relating, among other things, to the price, payment, quality and quantity of the goods, place and time of delivery, extent of one party's liability to the other or the settlement of disputes are considered to alter the terms of the offer materially.

CISG Article 18 also addresses the "materiality" of any variation in terms. How does the use of "materiality" differ, as between UCC § 2-207 and

CISG Article 19? Let's walk through each provision in sequence to see how the application of this statute plays out.

Subsection (1) provides the "rule" that any variation from the offer is a rejection of the offer and a counter-offer. Subsection (2) then provides an "exception" for "non-material" variations, absent objection. Subsection (3) then provides a list of "material" variations, which includes virtually anything that the parties might care about. Thus, one might reasonably characterize the combination of the three as follows. On any issue that the parties care about, CISG Article 19 provides for a "mirror image" rule, much like the common law.

While the statute uses "materiality," it does so to determine *whether the acceptance is effective*. In contrast, UCC § 2-207 uses "materiality" to determine whether a given term is to be included in the contract, *after a determination has already been made that the acceptance is effective*. In addition, a term is far more likely to be material under CISG Article 19(3) than under UCC § 2-207(2)(b).

Thus, varying communications, whether as a result of battling "forms" or otherwise, will typically leave the parties without a contract, unless of course they begin performance. In that case, Article 18(1) simply provides that an offer may be accepted through conduct, as we discussed earlier in Lesson 11. There is no provision similar to UCC § 2-207(3). Thus, the straightforward application of the statutory language leads to the application of a "last shot" rule, again much like the common law.

Few, if any, courts or commentators believe this combination of a "mirror image" and "last shot" rule to be a sound one, and some have suggested various approaches to "interpreting" the statute to reach a different result. However, the actual language of the statute appears quite clear, whatever our view of this often arbitrary and much maligned combination of rules.

APPLYING THE RULES

Problem 1: Collins & Aikman ("C&A") regularly sold carpet to Carpet Mart, a carpet retailer. When seeking to make a purchase, Carpet Mart would telephone the C&A order desk to place an order, in the process learning from the person on the order desk whether C&A had available stock and could make prompt shipment. The person on the C&A order desk would then get clearance from the credit manager to ship the order, after which C&A would, at about the same time, mail an "acknowledgement" form and ship the carpet, each of which (letter and carpet) typically arrived about the same time at Carpet Mart. A few days later, C&A would mail an invoice for the carpet, which Carpet Mart promptly paid. In addition to the carpet description, quantity, price and delivery terms, as expressly agreed upon by both parties, the C&A acknowledgement form included a clause requiring arbitration of any disputes relating to the transaction. Such a provision was never mentioned in any of the parties' other communications.

When a dispute later arose over the quality of the carpet, Carpet Mart sued C&A in court, and C&A sought to enforce the arbitration agreement (arbitration agreements will be addressed in Lesson 24, but you should assume here that the arbitration clause was enforceable if included in the overall contract). Was it included in the parties' contract for the purchase and sale of carpet? In answering this question, you will first want to think about all of the possible ways in which the parties might reasonably be deemed to have concluded a contract under the above facts. Do you need to know anything else to determine under any of these possibilities whether the arbitration clause is part of the contract?

Suppose C&A's acknowledgement had further stated that, as an acceptance, such acceptance was "expressly conditional upon the buyer's assent to all of the terms included herein." Which, if any, of your above conclusions would change?

Returning to the original facts (not the additional language immediately above), what if C&A was in Mexico, and Carpet Mart was in Texas?

This problem is loosely based (albeit with a few added hypothetical variations) on the case of *Dorton v. Collins & Aikman Corp.*, 453 F.2d 1161 (6th Cir. 1972).

Problem 2: Apex manufactured computers, which included a proprietary operating system and certain application software, also developed by Apex. Xenon regularly purchased computers from Apex. When doing so, the parties communicated through e-mails that included only the basic terms of any given order. Apex would then ship the computers, and Xenon would promptly pay.

Each Apex computer, when initially turned on, would immediately display a long list of "contract terms," which the person operating the computer would be required to acknowledge (by checking a box) having read before using the computer. These displayed "contract terms" included (1) an option to return the computer promptly, unused beyond opening this initial screen, for a full refund of the purchase price; and (2) an exclusion of all warranties, express or implied.

Xenon employees using these Apex computers regularly viewed the opening screens, checked the box, and went on to use the computers. No Xenon employee ever communicated with Apex about the content of these "contract terms" displayed on initial startup of the Apex computers.

A problem later arises with respect to the performance of the Apex Computers. Is the disclaimer of warranties a part of the parties' agreement? You may assume that such a disclaimer would definitely be considered "material" under UCC § 2-207(2)(b), if applicable.

This problem raises issues upon which not all courts have agreed. In addressing the problem, you should consider both *Step-Saver Data Systems, Inc. v. Wyse Technology*, 939 F.2d 91 (3d Cir. 1991) and *ProCD, Inc. v. Zeidenberg*, 86 F.3d 1447 (7th Cir. 1996). These two decisions take very different approaches to the issue presented by this problem. Which do you think most accurately applies the governing statute?

Lesson 16: "Battling" with Consumers and Contracting in a Digital World

Objectives and Expected Learning Outcomes

In this lesson, you will have the opportunity to consider the issues typically raised by the "battle of forms" in a different context—that of a consumer of goods. You will also learn about the continuing contextual evolution of consumer transactions in a digital age. Finally, you will have the opportunity to apply the material from Chapter 3, broadly, to a cumulative Problem at the end of the lesson.

Carrying the "Battle" to Consumer Transactions

Practical issues often arise in communicating to consumers the "details" of a product purchase, such as warranty information or dispute resolution provisions. In many cases, the use of lengthy form contracts is impractical, and the consumer is far more interested in the product than in any detailed terms—most of which the consumer has little interest in, until of course something goes wrong with the purchased item.

A seller may take a variety of approaches to the issue, perhaps putting substantial information on a product package. Or the seller might place basic information on the package, with additional details as to the referenced information inside with the product itself, or available in some other easily accessible manner. In most such transactions, the customer is not likely to be very interested in learning the details of such information, and the manufacturer or seller is not likely to be very interested in emphasizing it any more than required.

Another approach used by some manufacturers is to provide detailed contract terms with the product itself, even though such terms may not have reasonably come to the consumer's attention until he or she has received and opened the product. Typically, the terms provide that the consumer is bound, unless he or she returns the product for a refund within a specified time. Such terms, only communicated to the consumer after payment and receipt of the product, would seem to represent "additional" terms introduced after the parties had concluded an agreement. Indeed, that is the traditional approach under UCC § 2-207.

A Traditional Approach to Terms in the Box

Example 16-1: *Klocek v. Gateway 2000*

Klocek purchased and paid for a Gateway computer. When Klocek received the computer, he received a set of "Standard Terms" in the box with the various accessories and manuals. The initial notice provided that by keeping his computer beyond the stated time after delivery, he was accepting all such terms. These terms included an arbitration clause. Klocek later sought to bring a court action related to the purchase, and Gateway sought to compel arbitration based on the arbitration provision.

The court ruled that the arbitration clause was not part of the parties' contract. Inasmuch as Klocek and Gateway had already concluded a contract prior to receipt of the terms by Klocek, the arbitration clause represented an "additional" term in a "confirmation" under UCC § 2-207(1). Thus, the term was properly construed as a proposal for addition to the contract. The court further explained that, because Klocek was not a merchant, the arbitration term would not become part of the contract unless "expressly" accepted by Klocek. His failure to return the computer beyond the stated period did not constitute such express acceptance.[53]

The above approach simply tracks the statutory language, applying subsections (1) and (2), but without the "merchant" provision of the latter. Inasmuch as additional terms only become part of a merchant contract through silent acquiescence if not material, it would seem obvious that they would not become part of a contract with a consumer based on silence where no such materiality limitation exists. However, it turns out this idea was not so obvious to some.

---

[53] Klocek v. Gateway 2000, Inc., 104 F.Supp.2d 1332 (D. Kan. 2000).

A Departure from the Traditional Approach

Example 16-2: *Hill v. Gateway 2000*

Hill picked up a phone, ordered a computer, and gave his credit card number, which Gateway charged for the price of the computer. A box soon arrived containing the computer, along with a "list of terms, said to govern unless the customer returns the computer within 30 days." One of these terms was an arbitration clause, which was unknown to Hill before opening the box. Hill sued over an issue with the computer, and Gateway sought to compel arbitration.

The court ruled that the arbitration clause was part of the parties' agreement, because it had been accepted by Hill through conduct in keeping the computer beyond the 30 day return period. The court relied on an earlier case it had decided, ProCD, Inc., v. Zeidenberg, 86 F.3d 1447 (7th Cir. 1996), in which it had relied on a variety of *common law precedents* and had further stated that *when there is only one form, UCC § 2-207 "is irrelevant."* Thus, Hill agreed to arbitration when he kept the computer.[54]

While the above case has been followed by a number of courts, its analytical flaws are noteworthy. Of course, UCC § 2-207 is not limited to circumstances involving more than one form. Official Comment 1 expressly notes its application in circumstances much like this series of cases, in which the parties conclude an oral contract, which is followed by a written confirmation. Moreover, in view of the dramatic difference in the way the common law approaches the issue, it seems somewhat bizarre to rely on common law precedent in deciding this issue in a sale of goods transaction. However, the rationale supporting this idea of binding a consumer under these circumstances was perhaps somewhat better articulated in a subsequent case decided by the New York Appellate Division. This case reflects what is sometimes called "rolling contract" theory.

---

[54] Hill v. Gateway 2000, Inc., 105 F.3d 1147 (7th Cir. 1997).

A "Rolling Contract" Theory

Example 16-3: *Brower v. Gateway 2000*

Under the same basic circumstances as the prior examples, Brower purchased a Gateway computer and later attempted to sue Gateway in court, at which point Gateway sought to invoke the arbitration clause. Ultimately, this court refused to enforce the clause based on the specific nature of the arbitration required. However, its analysis of the issue under UCC § 2-207 is worthy of note.

While purporting to follow *Hill*, the court went further in explaining that the formation of a contract need not necessarily be concluded in the initial exchange between the parties. Instead, certain contracts may be formed over an extended series of interactions in which one final event serves to bind the parties to a contract. In this case, the court said that the nature of the contract proposed by Gateway was such that a final binding contract was not concluded until Brower had retained the computer beyond the stated period.

In effect, UCC § 2-207 had no applicability here because the only "form" was Gateway's offer by shipping the computer and including the standard terms, and Brower's acceptance in keeping the computer included neither additional nor different terms. Without an acceptance or confirmation, § 2-207 was not applicable. Moreover, in view of the interactions leading up to the offer, including Brower's ordering of the computer, silence was a reasonable means of acceptance.[55]

It is true that, if the Standard Terms were included in the offer, and Brower simply accepted those terms by keeping the computer, then UCC § 2-207 is entirely inapplicable to the transaction. However, one might still raise the following question to a law student who has recently studied the rules

---

[55] Brower v. Gateway 2000, Inc., 676 N.Y.S.2d 569, 246 A.D.2d 246 (App. Div. 1998).

for offer and acceptance. Would an objectively reasonable person believe after calling and ordering a computer, giving a credit card number and being charged in full for the computer, and receiving the computer from that same manufacture, that a contract had already been concluded?

Navigating the Digital World--Just a "Click" Away from a Binding Contract

To a large degree, the issue raised by the Gateway cases above is quickly becoming something of a relic of the past. Today, we are much more likely to order a computer or other goods online by simply "clicking" a link on a website. We do this only after we have agreed to be bound to a list of Standard Terms that virtually none of us will ever take the time to read.

Whether we read the terms or not, however, the website software prevents us from completing the transaction without clicking "I agree" to the terms in question (sometimes even requiring multiple such "clicks" for specific elements of the terms). This sort of terms presentation is often called a "clickwrap" agreement, as an analogy to the earlier practice of printing terms on the "shrinkwrap" packaging that contained certain products.

It will surprise few readers that a properly presented clickwrap agreement, executed by the consumer in the process or purchasing goods or downloading software (even free software) is fully enforceable as a matter of contract law. However, the effect of other terms digitally presented to consumers in some other manner is often less clear and requires us to return to the basic "objective theory" of contracts presented at the outset of this Chapter.

Example 16-4: *Specht v. Netscape Comm. Corp.*

Specht and others sought to bring a class action against Netscape over a free "SmartDownload" program they had downloaded from the internet. Netscape sought to compel arbitration based on a standard term requiring arbitration of all disputes. The case involved two free Netscape "downloads"—Communicator and SmartDownload—and each included a standard term requiring arbitration that might have included the case at issue. However, our focus here is on the arbitration clause directly tied to the SmartDownload software.

Specht sought to download Netscape "Communicator" and, when he visited the Netscape webpage, encountered the opportunity to download the "SmartDownload" software for use in downloading Communicator, as well as other software. At or near the bottom of the screen promoting the SmartDownload software was a prompt stating "Start Download," and a tinted button that said "Download." By clicking the button, Specht initiated and completed the download without further interaction or information.

Specht was then able to open and use the newly installed SmartDownload software—again without any further interaction or information related to the SmartDownload software—in downloading and installing Communicator. In stark contrast, Specht was only able to download the Communicator software after clicking a "yes" button that he had accepted all of the license terms presented directly to him on the screen in front of him. Thus, Specht admitted that he was bound by the Communicator terms, but argued that he never assented to the SmartDownload terms, including the arbitration clause.

Netscape argued that Specht was bound by the terms, because notice of those terms was easily accessible by simply "scrolling down" just below the initially visible portion of the relevant page view. However, the court rejected the argument, explaining that Specht had not expressly agreed to those terms, and notice of their availability below the available screen was not sufficient to lead an objectively reasonable person to believe he was assenting to them by clicking the "download" button on the visible portion of the screen.[56]

---

[56] Specht v. Netscape Comm. Corp., 306 F.3d 17 (2d Cir. 2002) (the full opinion, written by then Judge Sotomayor, is quite lengthy and fully analyzes the relevant issues in much greater detail than the brief example above—for those interested in e-commerce, it remains one of the seminal decisions in the area and should be considered required reading).

Essentially, Netscape asked the court to apply the same sort of rules to an internet page as a paper document. An individual is generally charged with constructive knowledge (in effect, should know) of the contents of any writings exchanged or executed as a part of contract formation. Thus, Netscape argued, Specht should have known what was on the entire page—initially visible or not—and should have then used the clickable links he found when scrolling down below the download button to access other pages, with additional links, ultimately discovering the relevant terms.

While this might initially sound unreasonable, consider the "paper" analogy. A party is bound by the terms on page 2 or 3, or even 57, even though one must "turn the page" to view those terms. Moreover, a party is often bound by terms "incorporated by reference." The actual communication of executed document does not contain all of the terms, but simply provides a reference to an external document. Thus, Netscape's argument was certainly rational. However, the court explained that the circumstances of digital contracting are not perfectly analogous to paper contracting, as defined by the objectively reasonable expectations of the contracting participants.

To be clear, the same basic contracts principles govern. However, the circumstances giving rise to a party's objectively reasonable understanding of the relevant communications are different. We generally know we are typically bound by all of the terms in a paper document, whether read or not. However, we don't necessarily expect to have to explore the entire viewable area of a web page when downloading software—especially "free" software. If you put yourself in Specht's position, as an objectively reasonable user of the internet, and you saw a web page promoting "free software" with a "download" button at the bottom of the page, would you expect to find notice of additional terms governing your download on a separate part of the page, accessible only by scrolling further downward? This court "clicked" "no."

More on Dispute Resolution and Form Contracts

By now you are likely beginning to realize that one of the major issues in consumer contracting is the question of whether consumers can be required to arbitrate their claims, instead of bringing them in court proceedings. We will address this issue in much greater depth in Lesson 24. However, you will learn there that arbitration agreements are generally enforceable, just like any other contract term—even against consumers (the latter is not the case in many other countries).

It is also worth noting that many of the most significant battles over arbitration agreements involve putative class actions. While an arbitration agreement can provide for class arbitration, most do not. In fact, most bar class arbitration, thereby requiring any given consumer to arbitrate claims individually.

> **Example 16-5:** *AT&T Mobility v. Concepcion*
>
> Concepcion was provided with a "free" phone in connection with an AT&T service contract, but was charged sales tax on the retail value of the phone. Concepcion sought to recover the amount of the sales tax in a putative class action brought in California Federal District Court. AT&T sought dismissal based on a clause in the service contract requiring arbitration, but not permitting classwide arbitration.
>
> California state law precluded such a limit on classwide arbitration, but the United States Supreme Court ruled that California law on this issue was pre-empted by the Federal Arbitration Act, which is given priority over inconsistent state law under the Supremacy Clause of the U.S. Constitution. As a result of the Court's ruling, the only recourse Concepcion had against AT&T was to bring an individual claim against AT&T in arbitration.[57]

Arbitration clauses like the one at issue in the above case will often provide simple and easy avenues for the consumer to pursue in an effort to avoid the cost of full arbitration proceedings, as well as a promise by the seller to pay reasonable costs of any arbitration proceedings. In fact, an arbitration proceeding that functionally deprived a consumer of the financial ability to bring the claim might well be unenforceable. However, it is hard to imagine a consumer like Concepcion going to the trouble of bringing an individual claim for the "sales tax" on a cell phone under any circumstances.

The Court's decision in the case above will undoubtedly bar many class actions. Whether or not that is a desirable result undoubtedly depends on whether your perspective is that of a consumer or a seller of goods

---

[57] AT&T Mobility LLC v. Concepcion, 131 S.Ct. 1740 (2011).

or services. Whatever one's perspective, however, the seller's ability to bar classwide claims raises additional questions about the effectiveness of traditional means of consumer redress in American courts.

Contracting in a Digital World—Do the Traditional Doctrinal Paradigms Still Work?

Is court adjudication the best means to protect consumer rights? Do class actions (when allowed) benefit the class plaintiffs? The lawyers? Society as a whole? To the extent that classwide claims are intended to benefit society broadly, are there other means to that end that might be effective? Might there be other means of individual consumer redress?

In today's online world, one might reasonably suggest that a seller of goods and services is more likely to be responsive to negative online "reviews" than to lawsuits. In times past, it was often said that consumers were powerless against industry, because there was no effective means for collective action in response to irresponsible sellers. That may no longer be true in today's digital world.

Moreover, individual consumers have increasing access to simple and easy to use online dispute resolution mechanisms. While many early "arbitration" providers were notably biased in favor of the business interests hiring them, the process seems to be evolving. Business arguably has a significant interest in providing a viable outlet for individual consumer complaints as an effective and far less expensive means of resolving disputes and minimizing the sort of reputational damage that is far easier for disgruntled consumers to inflict in today's digital world.

These new paradigms may also involve changes in the traditional roles played by lawyers engaged in protecting the rights of consumers. Education and mobilization may replace a significant amount of representation in court litigation. None of this is to suggest any sort of "crystal ball" divulging the precise contours of this evolving digital world. However, it is worth keeping in mind the court's rationale in *Specht* that traditional contracts principles will likely continue to serve us well, but the circumstances of their application going forward may be quite different indeed.

APPLYING THE RULES

Problem 1: Apollo, Inc. ("Apollo") sells fully integrated home entertainment systems. A prospective customer can visit Apollo's website to determine what kind of home entertainment components the customer would like to assemble. The customer is then instructed to call an "800" number where a service person will assist in assembling appropriate components for the customer's specific needs. The following statements can be found in Apollo's ads and on its website:

> "The only real 'showroom' for an Apollo system is your living room. See and hear 'real entertainment' by trying our system in your own home. You will have 21 days to decide on your purchase 'risk free.'"

Neither the ads nor website contain further details about any additional terms. Apollo instructs its customer service representatives to provide customers with complete copies of Apollo's "Standard Terms" upon request, but not to provide them without such a request.

Mary Jones first encountered an Apollo advertisement in a magazine, then visited the Apollo website, and finally called the "800" number to order a system. She described the components she wanted and ultimately agreed on a system priced at $9,950. Mary then provided her credit card number, and Apollo charged the full purchase price to her card that same day. The Apollo system was shipped the next day and arrived at Mary's home a few days later.

The Apollo home entertainment system arrived in nine large brown boxes, each marked only with box handling (fragile – this end up) instructions. There was also one smaller box, labeled "Important: Setup Instructions and Contract Terms Included—read before assembling your Apollo home entertainment system." When Mary opened this smaller box, she found four documents: (1) a quick setup guide; (2) a full instruction manual; (3) a warranty; and (4) a long single sheet with printing on both sides entitled "Standard Terms." Anxious to try out her new system, she began reading the quick setup guide and set the box containing the other documents to one side. Mary had no trouble assembling the system components based on the quick setup guide, and the detailed instructions, warranty, and "Standard Terms" went into a drawer in which Mary kept various important papers.

The "Standard Terms" began with a notice providing for a full refund if a system is returned within 21 days, but binding the buyer to all of the terms if not. The terms included, in paragraph 19, an arbitration clause.

A month after she had assembled it, Mary's new home entertainment system abruptly quit working—completely (that of course being one of the downsides of a "fully integrated" system). She contacted Apollo, but was told it was her own fault. She would like to bring a legal action against Apollo in court.

Is Mary bound by the arbitration provision in paragraph 19?

Suppose that, instead of calling an "800" number, Mary had been directed to a page on the Apollo website, with an interactive digital "agent," that assisted her in assembling her system. At the end of the process, including the entry to her credit card and shipping information, Mary was presented with a button labeled "Purchase." The label above the button explained that, by clicking "Purchase," the buyer agreed to be bound by all of Apollo's Standard Terms and Conditions, which were available on Apollo's website (though it did not say where). In fact, the terms were all provided on the same page, but one had to scroll some distance to the bottom of the page to find them.

Is Mary bound by the arbitration provision in the terms at the bottom of the web page?

Problem 2 (cumulative): Sam, a third-year law student, ran a part-time bicycle repair business out of this home to help pay for school. He also occasionally purchased used bicycles that were in less than ideal condition, fixed them up, and resold them at a profit. Beth, one of Sam's classmates, was looking for a bicycle and, on March 1, sent an e-mail to Sam inquiring if he had anything that might be suitable for her at a price under $400. Sam replied by e-mail the same day that he had a Trak 650W, fully refurbished and just her size, for $350. Sam also stated in his e-mail that "This would be a perfect bike for you. I know you'll love it, but I need to know one way or the other by no later than March 10." Beth did not reply immediately, as she wanted to think about it.

On March 8, Beth heard from Fay, a mutual friend, that Sam had received a very lucrative offer to begin work for a law firm after graduation, and he had sold his entire bicycle repair business—including any used bikes—to Tom. Beth was very unhappy to hear this, as she had just that morning decided that she really wanted the Trak 650W, and she had also discovered that it was worth closer to $750. Fay was one of Sam's closest friends, so Beth was pretty sure that Sam no longer had the bike to sell. However, Beth decided that was Sam's problem to deal with, and she sent him an e-mail on the evening of March 8, in which she said, "I accept your offer of the Trak 650W at a price of $350. However, I need to be sure that you will fully warrant your work in refurbishing the bike for a period of 1 year, as I would not want a used bike without a warranty."

The next morning, March 9, Sam replied by e-mail to Beth, "I am sorry, but the Trak 650W is no longer for sale. As you may have heard, I sold my bicycle business—except for the Trak 650W. I actually kept the Trak 650W because I want to give it to my girlfriend for her birthday next month. Moreover, I would never give you a warranty of any kind on a used bike. In short, you are too late and you are trying to change our deal—the bike is not for sale." A few minutes later, Beth replied to Sam by e-mail that she was accepting his offer, irrespective of whether it included a warranty, and that she fully expected Sam to perform his contractual obligations. Sam immediately replied, "I will certainly perform any contractual obligation I owe you, which is precisely nothing, because we have no contract. You obviously should have paid closer attention in contracts class!"

Do Sam and Beth have a contract? If so, does Beth have a 1 year warranty?

Quick Summary

Here is a very brief summary of the basic principles addressed in Chapter 3.

A contract requires offer and acceptance, as determined by the intent of the parties, which is most often assessed through their objective manifestations. Acceptance of an offer of a unilateral contract requires completed performance, while acceptance of an offer of a bilateral contract requires a promise—in one form or another. Either may require notice, depending on the circumstances.

An offer remains open for acceptance by the offeree, unless it is rejected by the offeree (including any counter-offer), lapses, or is terminated by the death or incapacity of one of the parties. However, an offeror can generally revoke the offer any time prior to acceptance, subject to a variety of limitations, which may differ significantly, depending on governing law. As a general rule, subject of course to a few exceptions, parties are not subject to liability, until and unless they actually conclude a contract.

An acceptance must generally "mirror" an offer to be effective, or else it is a counter-offer and rejection of the original. However, UCC Article 2 provides for a different rule, which raises a variety of challenging questions. Finally, our evolving "digital world" provides many new challenges, but we have thus far continued to approach those challenges using traditional legal rules.

Thus, we have now fully addressed the three fundamental requirements of a basic contract—offer, acceptance, and consideration. In the next two chapters, we will learn, however, that not all contracts are enforceable. Specifically, we will next consider in Chapter 4 variety of statutory requirements that certain contracts must be memorialized in writings, signed by any party against who enforcement is sought.

4

Requiring a Signed Writing

Key Concepts

- Which Contracts Require a Specific Form?
- The Requirement of a Signed (or Authenticated) Writing (or Record)

Lesson 17: Typical Statutes of Frauds

Objectives and Expected Learning Outcomes

In this lesson, you will learn that certain contracts are subject to statutory requirements as to "form," generally requiring a signed writing if they are to be enforceable. You will further learn what is required to satisfy these requirements in today's digital world. The problems at the end of this lesson are intended to stimulate your thought process, as opposed to asking you for answers.

Chapters 2 and 3 addressed the requirements of (1) a bargain; and (2) agreement to that bargain. If both requirements are satisfied, then the parties have formed or concluded a "contract." However, sometimes a contract may not be "enforceable" for a variety of possible reasons. The current chapter addresses requirements of "form" applicable to certain (though not all) contracts. Chapter 5 will then address a variety of other specific doctrines—relating in some way to the bargaining process or the bargain's substance—that may render a contract invalid or otherwise unenforceable.

Typical Statutes of Frauds—Real Property, Contracts Requiring More Than One Year to Perform, and Promises of Surety

A "statute of frauds" is a legislative enactment limiting the enforceability of certain kinds of contract, unless they are evidenced in a writing signed by the parties—or at least the party against whom enforcement is sought. This requirement of a signed writing is fully independent of the basic requirements of a contract—offer, acceptance, and consideration. The statute does not tell us whether the parties have concluded a contract. It merely tells is whether such a contract is enforceable, if they have done so.

States apply a uniform statute of frauds to sales of goods, as reflected in UCC § 2-201, and this statute will be fully addressed in Lesson 19. In the current lesson, however, we will focus on "statutes" addressing contracts otherwise governed by the common law. The content of such statutes varies from state to state, and this course will not attempt to survey all such statutes. Instead, we will focus here on three of the most common types of contracts subject to a "statute of frauds," as reflected in the following "generic" statute.

A GENERIC STATE STATUTE OF FRAUDS

No civil action may be maintained in the following cases unless the parties' agreement is reflected in a writing or record, signed or authenticated by the party to be charged:

(1) a special promise to answer for the debt, default, miscarriage, or obligation of another;

(2) an agreement for the sale or transfer of real property or any interest therein; or

(3) an agreement that is not to be performed within one year from the date of its formation.

These are commonly called (1) contracts of surety; (2) contracts involving real property (sale or lease); and (3) contracts requiring greater than one year to complete. These "generic" provisions are of course merely exemplary, and a lawyer should look to actual applicable state law in addressing the enforceability of an actual contract. However, these reflect the most common examples of statutes affecting common law contracts.

The original rationale behind the broad English rule was that parties were legally incompetent to testify in support of their own claim for defense, because it was simply assumed they would lie, as a matter of self-interest. Without oral testimony as a means of proving a contract, the requirement of a writing was quite logical. Today, we generally assume that most individuals take the "oath" to tell the truth quite seriously, and we also generally trust juries to be able to tell when they do not. Thus, oral contracts, generally, are fully enforceable, as long as the judge, jury, or arbitrator believes they were made, and most remaining statutes of frauds focus on something unique about the specific nature of the contract at issue. The concerns behind these select statutes remain, however, largely evidentiary in nature.

If a contract falls within one of the statutory categories, it is not enforceable, unless the content of the contract is reflected in a writing signed by the party against whom enforcement of the contract is sought.

Contracts of Surety

A contract of surety is one in which one party, the "surety" promises a "creditor" to pay the obligation of the "debtor" if the debtor does not.

> **Example 17-1:** Dan (debtor) seeks to borrow money from Cass (creditor). Cass would like to make the loan, but is unsure about Dan's ability to repay it. Sara offers to act as surety for Dan, promising Cass that Sara will pay Dan's debt if Dan does not. Cass agrees to make the loan to Dan in exchange for Sara's promise and does so.
>
> Sara has concluded a contract of surety with Cass. However, this contract will not be enforceable, unless Cass can point to a writing signed by Sara and evidencing Sara's promise.

You may recall that we first encountered a contract of surety in Example 11-3. In that example, we were addressing the need for a creditor to provide notice of acceptance of a unilateral offer of a party to answer for the debt of another (a promise of surety can also involve a bilateral contract—a promise to make a loan in exchange for the promise of the surety to pay it if the debtor does not). Part of the rationale requiring notice, as an exception to the normal rule regarding unilateral contracts, was the unique nature of a promise of surety. This same uniqueness is at least a part of the reason why a writing signed by the surety is required before a creditor can enforce any promise.

A surety is sometimes said to be a "favorite" of the law, because most sureties are performing a role that facilitates another transaction, with little or no actual benefit to the surety (remember, an actual benefit is not required for consideration). In fact, we will see in the next lesson, an "exception" to this particular statute of frauds when the surety is financially "self-interested" in the transaction at issue.

Contracts Involving Real Property

A contract for the sale, lease, or other transfer of an interest in real property must be signed by the party against whom enforcement is sought.

> **Example 17-2:** Recall Example 9-2, in which the Zehmers agreed to sell to W.O. Lucy the Ferguson farm for $50,000. The contract was enforceable by Lucy only because the Zehmer's had both signed the blank restaurant check on which the terms were scribbled. The informal nature of the writing was irrelevant, as long as its content evidenced the contract at issue.
>
> You may also recall that Lucy did not sign the writing. He simply picked it up and put it in his pocket. This made no difference, however, as Lucy was enforcing the contract against the Zehmers who had refused to perform.

Does it seem unfair that Lucy was able to bind the Zehmers, when Lucy, himself, had signed nothing? Of course, the Zehmers could have demanded that Lucy sign the paper as well, and both parties will almost always sign any writings needed to conclude a real estate transaction. However, we will again encounter this "one-sided-signature" issue in Lesson 19 and discover a novel result in certain cases involving goods under UCC § 2-201(2).

Land has always received unique treatment under the common law, as evidenced by the presumptive right to "specific performance" in the event of breach, as opposed to the normal substitutional remedy of money damages in most other cases. Transactions involving real estate must often be recorded with a governmental authority in order to insure the transaction is effective with respect to third parties who may also claim an interest in the subject property. Thus, there are additional compelling reasons why such a transaction should be evidenced by a signed writing.

Most statutes of frauds involving real property will include sales, leases, and other interest transfers (e.g., a "mortgage" granted as security). However, some statutes limit application to leases based on the duration or amount of the lease. This particular statute governing transactions in real property is generally applied quite strictly, as its underlying rational remains largely unchallenged. The next statute does not always enjoy such uniform support.

Contracts Requiring Greater Than One Year to Perform

A contract requiring more than one year to perform is one that cannot, by its terms, be completed by both parties within one year of its formation. Perhaps this description has already triggered your memory of Jane and Joe from Lesson 4.

> **Example 17-3:** In Example 4-1, Jane promised to pay Joe $150,000 if he completed law school. We have already fully explored the question of whether or not Jane was offering a bargain or promising a gift. However, even if Jane was offering a bargain, the resulting contract is not supported by a writing signed by Jane, because her promise was an oral one. Law school cannot be completed within one year (at least not as of the writing of this text), so Jane's promise is not enforceable.

The result here may seem unfair, as Joe has already fully performed. Indeed, we will discover in the next lesson that full performance on one side is often treated as an exception, avoiding the application this provision.

As indicated earlier, the concerns underlying the statute of frauds requirement are largely evidentiary in nature. Thus, at first blush, it would seem perfectly logical to require a signed writing to a contract that will necessarily stretch out over a longer period of time. The longer the time, the vaguer the remembered details of any unwritten bargain. However, the statute requires a signed writing—irrespective of the timing of enforcement—whether 10 minutes after concluding the agreement or 10 years after concluding it. Consider the following two examples.

> **Example 17-4:** A orally contracts with B to construct a small building on land already owned by A (no transfer of real property is involved) at a price of $10,000. The project will take 18 months to complete (B is doing much of the work, herself). The day after the parties concluded their oral agreement, A disavows having agreed to any contract. When B promptly seeks to enforce, A will raise a statute of frauds defense, which will preclude enforcement, even if the fact finder believes A and B made the contract at issue.

Example 17-5: A orally contracts with B to construct a large building on land already owned by A (no transfer of real property is involved) at a price of $100 million. The project will take 10 months to complete (B is a large construction company). 2 years after the project is completed, a dispute arises over whether the building was constructed as promised. The lack of a signed writing will have no legal effect on the parties' rights under the oral contract they concluded (though a may make it more difficult to prove the precise content of that contract).

In which case do you think the application of the statute is more justified? We will come back to both examples in the next lesson. For now, it is enough simply to note that the rationale behind this statute is generally considered to be somewhat less compelling than the two discussed earlier.

This statute can also lead to some "quirky" results, as often pointed out by law professors (and, perhaps, by bar examiners). A contract of employment for "2 years" would certainly be within the statute of frauds. While the employee might die before the first year is out, or might be terminated in breach of contract before the end of the first year, the contract would not be "completed" in either case, because "completion" required 2 years of employment under the contract's express terms.

In contrast, a contract of employment "for life" does not fall within the same statute of frauds, because it would be "completed" upon the death of the employee, which could certainly happen within less than one year. Thus, the contract, by its terms, does not require more than one year for its "completion." The key to understanding these short vignettes is remembering that a contract only falls within the scope of the statute if it cannot, according to its terms, be "completed as agreed." Any other termination short of a year is irrelevant.

Having identified and introduced the three subjects of our "generic" statute, we can now move on to the requirements for satisfying the statute when a contract falls within its ambit. Before doing so, however, it is worth repeating here that this statutory requirement of a signed writing is "fully independent" of the basic requirements of offer, acceptance, and consideration. Unless the parties have at least arguably formed a contract, there is no need to consider whether they have satisfied the statutory requirement.

In evaluating the satisfaction of the statutory requirement, one should assume *arguendo* that the parties have concluded a contract. Otherwise, one is likely to conflate the two issues, which often results in failing to do justice to either.

The Requirement of a "Writing" or Record

Older articulations of the statute of frauds refer solely to a "writing." However, modern, state, national, and global law today recognizes electronic "records" as equivalent to "writings" for purposes of satisfying any requirement of such. While the parties themselves may agree to use one or another form of communication, electronic forms may not be denied legal effect solely on that basis. The Electronic Signatures in Global and National Commerce Act ("E-Sign") was enacted by Congress in 2000 and provides as follows:

15 U.S.C. § 7001

(a) In general. Notwithstanding any statute, regulation, or other rule of law (other than this subchapter and subchapter II of this chapter), with respect to any transaction in or affecting interstate or foreign commerce—

(1) a signature, contract, or other record relating to such transaction may not be denied legal effect, validity, or enforceability solely because it is in electronic form; and

(2) a contract relating to such transaction may not be denied legal effect, validity, or enforceability solely because an electronic signature or electronic record was used in its formation.

. . .

A "record" is further defined in § 7006(9) to include any "information that is inscribed on a tangible medium or that is stored in an electronic or other medium and retrievable in perceivable form." Thus, a "record" necessary to satisfy a statute of frauds requirement may potentially be found in an e-mail, a chat message, a Facebook posting, a voicemail, a YouTube video, or any number of modern forms of electronic records (and, of course, this list will likely be woefully incomplete by the time you read it).

This requirement of a "writing" or "record" is intended to provide evidence of the "content" of the parties' agreement. Applications of most statutes of frauds (though not all, as we will see in Lesson 19) require proof in the subject "writing" or "record" of at least the essential terms of the agreement, and certainly any terms in dispute. However, such proof may be derived from multiple writings or records—even if not all are signed or authenticated. The following seminal case by the New York Court of Appeals provides a classic example of piecing together multiple writings to satisfy the statute of frauds.

FROM THE COURT

Crabtree v. Elizabeth Arden Sales Corp.

New York Court of Appeals (1953)
305 N.Y. 48, 110 N.E. 2d 551

FULD, J.

In September of 1947, Nate Crabtree entered into preliminary negotiations with Elizabeth Arden Sales Corporation, manufacturers and sellers of cosmetics, looking toward his employment as sales manager. Interviewed on September 26th, by Robert P. Johns, executive vice-president and general manager of the corporation, who had apprised him of the possible opening, Crabtree requested a three-year contract at $25,000 a year. Explaining that he would be giving up a secure well-paying job to take a position in an entirely new field of endeavor—which he believed would take him some years to master—he insisted upon an agreement for a definite term. And he repeated his desire for a contract for three years to Miss Elizabeth Arden, the corporation's president. When Miss Arden finally indicated that she was prepared to offer a two-year contract, based on an annual salary of $20,000 for the first six months, $25,000 for the second six months and $30,000 for the second year, plus expenses of $5,000 a year for each of those years, Crabtree replied that that offer was "interesting." Miss Arden thereupon had her personal secretary make this memorandum on a telephone order blank that happened to be at hand:

EMPLOYMENT AGREEMENT WITH

NATE CRABTREE   Date Sept 26-1947

At 681 -- 5th Ave   6: PM

Begin	20000.
6 months	25000.
6 months	30000.
	5000. -- per year
	Expense money
	[2 years to make good]

Arrangement with Mr. Crabtree

By Miss Arden

Present   Miss Arden

                   Mr. John

                   Mr. Crabtree

                   Miss O'Leary

A few days later, Crabtree phoned Mr. Johns and telegraphed Miss Arden; he accepted the "invitation to join the Arden organization," and Miss Arden wired back her "welcome." When he reported for work, a "pay-roll change" card was made up and initialed by Mr. Johns, and then forwarded to the payroll department. Reciting that it was prepared on September 30, 1947, and was to be effective as of October 22d, it specified the names of the parties, Crabtree's "Job Classification" and, in addition, contained the notation that:

This employee is to be paid as follows:

First six months of employment	$20,000. per annum
Next six months of employment	25,000. per annum
After one year of employment	30,000. per annum

Approved by RPJ [initialed]

After six months of employment, Crabtree received the scheduled increase from $20,000 to $25,000, but the further specified increase at the end of the year was not paid. Both Mr. Johns and the comptroller of the corporation, Mr. Carstens, told Crabtree that they would attempt to straighten out the matter with Miss Arden, and, with that in mind, the comptroller prepared another "pay-roll change" card, to which his signature is appended, noting that there was to be a "Salary increase" from $25,000 to $30,000 a year, "per contractual arrangements with Miss Arden." The latter, however, refused to approve the increase and, after further fruitless discussion, plaintiff left defendant's employ and commenced this action for breach of contract.

. . . [D]efendant denied the existence of any agreement to employ plaintiff for two years, and further contended that, even if one had been made, the statute of frauds barred its enforcement. . . . Since the contract relied upon was not to be performed within a year, the primary question for decision [on this appeal] is whether there was a memorandum of its terms, subscribed by defendant, to satisfy the statute of frauds. . . .

Each of the two payroll cards—the one initialed by defendant's general manager, the other signed by its comptroller—unquestionably constitutes a memorandum under the statute. That they were not prepared or signed with the intention of evidencing the contract, or that they came into existence subsequent to its execution, is of no consequence [citations omitted]; it is enough, to meet the statute's demands, that they were signed with intent to authenticate the information contained therein and that such information does evidence the terms of the contract. [Citations omitted.] Those two writings contain all of the essential terms of the contract—the parties to it, the position that plaintiff was to assume, the salary that he was to receive—except that relating to the duration of plaintiff's employment. Accordingly, we must consider whether that item, the length of the contract, may be supplied by reference to the earlier unsigned office memorandum, and, if so, whether its notation, "2 years to make good," sufficiently designates a period of employment.

The statute of frauds does not require the "memorandum * * * to be in one document. It may be pieced together out of separate writings, connected with one another either expressly or by the internal evidence of subject matter and occasion." [Citations omitted.] Where each of the separate writings has been subscribed by the party to be charged, little if any difficulty is encountered. [Citations omitted.] Where, however, some writings have been signed, and others have not—as in the case before us—there is basic disagreement as to what constitutes a sufficient connection permitting the unsigned papers to be considered as part of the statutory memorandum. The courts of some jurisdictions insist that there be a reference, of varying degrees of specificity, in the signed writing to that unsigned, and, if there is no such reference, they refuse to permit consideration of the latter in determining whether the memorandum satisfies the statute. [Citations omitted] . . . The other position—which has gained increasing support over the years—is that a sufficient connection between the papers is established simply by a reference in them to the same subject matter or transaction. [Citations omitted.] The statute is not pressed "to the extreme of a literal and rigid logic" [citations omitted], and oral testimony is admitted to show the connection between the documents and to establish the acquiescence, of the party to be charged, to the contents of the one unsigned. [Citations omitted.]

The view last expressed impresses us as the more sound . . .

. . . The danger of fraud and perjury . . . is at a minimum in a case such as this. None of the terms of the contract are supplied by [oral evidence]. All of them must be set out in the various writings presented to the court, and at least one writing, the one establishing a contractual relationship between the parties, must bear the signature of the party to be charged, while the unsigned document must on its face refer to the same transaction as that set forth in the one that was signed. . . .

Turning to the writings in the case before us—the unsigned office memo, the payroll change form initialed by the general manager Johns, and the paper signed by the comptroller Carstens—it is apparent, and most patently, that all three refer on their face to the same transaction. The parties, the position to be filled by plaintiff, the salary to be paid him, are all identically set forth; it is hardly possible that such detailed information could refer to another or a different agreement. Even more, the card signed by Carstens notes that it was prepared for the purpose of a "Salary increase per contractual arrangements with Miss Arden." That certainly constitutes a reference of sorts to a more comprehensive "arrangement," . . .

The corroborative evidence of defendant's assent to the contents of the unsigned office memorandum is also convincing. Prepared by defendant's agent, Miss Arden's personal secretary, there is little likelihood that that paper was fraudulently manufactured or that defendant had not assented to its contents. Furthermore, the evidence as to the conduct of the parties at the time it was prepared persuasively demonstrates defendant's assent to its terms. Under such circumstances, the courts below were fully justified in finding that the three papers constituted the "memorandum" of their agreement within the meaning of the statute.

> Nor can there be any doubt that the memorandum contains all of the essential terms of the contract. [Citations omitted.] Only one term, the length of the employment, is in dispute. The September 26th office memorandum contains the notation, "2 years to make good." What purpose, other than to denote the length of the contract term, such a notation could have, is hard to imagine. Without it, the employment would be at will [citations omitted], and its inclusion may not be treated as meaningless or purposeless. Quite obviously . . . the phrase signifies that the parties agreed to a term, a certain and definite term, of two years, after which, if plaintiff did not "make good," he would be subject to discharge. And examination of other parts of the memorandum supports that construction. . . .
>
> . . .

CASE QUESTIONS

(1) Did anyone sign anything on behalf of Elizabeth Arden Sales Corp.?

    a. Note that Crabtree's claim was against the corporation—not Arden, personally. Who signed the writing on behalf of the corporation?

    b. Did the signed writing contain all of the essential contract terms? What was missing?

    c. Where was that term found? What was necessary to connect the writing in which the missing term was found to the signed writing? Was the former directly referenced by the latter?

(2) What if there had been no writing, signed or otherwise, containing the "2 year" term?

The foregoing case focuses on the manner in which writings—both signed and unsigned—can be pieced together so as provide evidentiary sources for each essential contract term. In Lesson 19, we will encounter an even more liberal approach to this issue under UCC § 2-201. However, before leaving the general writing requirement, we should briefly address the issue of contract modification.

In Lesson 6, we addressed the general requirement of consideration in the context of contract modification. A similar issue may arise with respect to the writing requirement. To what extent may a writing or record of the original agreement serve as a basis for enforcing a subsequent oral modification of that agreement? The general rule requires than any modification with respect to an essential term must be reflected in a new writing or record evidencing the modification. In short, essential terms of any modification must be supported by a writing in the same manner as the original agreement. Having now addressed both original agreements and modifications, we can move from our examination of "writings" or "records" to that of the "signature" or "authentication" requirement, itself.

The Requirement of a "Signature" or Authentication

In the last section, we focused on a "writing" or "record," as evidence of "content." In this section, we will shift our focus the requirement of a "signature" or "authentication," as evidence of "consent." As indicated in the statute provided in the last section, electronic forms of "signature" or "authentication" are inherently no less effective than traditional "pen and ink."

Like "writings" or "records," what constitutes a "signature" or "authentication" is also quite broadly defined. A signature is generally deemed to include any mark, symbol, sound, picture, or process logically associated with the contract and executed, used, or adopted with intent to authenticate the record by or on behalf of the signer. Ultimately, the requirement is far more focused on intent than form.

In addition to ascribing one's name to a writing, the requirement may be satisfied by typing one's name or initial at the end of an e-mail; sending a text from an account linked to the sender; using paper with a corporate letterhead (assuming the corporation is the actual party to the contract); the proverbial "x" (though some laws still require notarization of an "x"); or any variety of other means by which a party intends to associate himself or herself with the record at issue.

> **Example 17-6:** Andy posts on his Facebook page a complete description of an oral agreement he made with Jill to sell her a small parcel of land. When Jill later seeks to enforce the agreement, Andy asserts a statute of frauds defense, claiming there is no signed writing. Of course, Andy's Facebook post satisfies the requirement. It is certainly a retrievable digital "record" and it was "authenticated" by Andy when he posted it using a Facebook process designed to identify the posting party.

Of course, Andy could try to establish that someone had "hacked" his Facebook account, and the posting was not his. However, that raises only the same sort of issues traditionally raised by a "forgery" defense. If a person's "signature" or "authentication" is real, then he or she is bound. If not, then he or she is not.

Asserting a Statute of Frauds Defense

As indicated in the examples above, the statute of frauds requirement is in the nature of a "defense." A party asserting a breach of contract claim must generally prove offer, acceptance and consideration, along with a breach of the agreed contract. However, the party claiming breach is not initially required to address any statute of frauds requirement (though a party may do so, it is not generally required). Instead, a failure to comply with the statute must be raised affirmatively, as a defense, by the party resisting enforcement (see, e.g., F.R.C.P. 8(c)(1), listing the statute of frauds as an affirmative defense).

If not timely raised, such an affirmative defense is generally deemed waived and is, thereby, lost. The claimant must still prove the existence of a contract, but the statute of frauds requirement is rendered irrelevant.

While the initial presence of consideration is an element of the claimant's case, a subsequent failure of that consideration is an affirmative defense, as are a number of the issues we will address in Chapter 5.

APPLYING THE RULES

Problem 1: Another party has brought a suit for breach of contract against your client. If your client admits to you that he or she agreed to a contract, but you realize that the client has a possible defense based on the statute of frauds, is it ethical to raise that defense—knowing it will preclude enforcement of an honest bargain?

Alternatively, your client asserts that she never agreed to the purported contract. However, you have looked at the applicable statute of frauds and can see no basis for arguing that it applies to this purported agreement. Your client has also shown you a written offer that she signed with all of the relevant terms, but simply asserts that she orally revoked it before it was accepted. Your "answer" in the case is due—should you include the "statute of frauds" in your affirmative defenses, just to be on the safe side? If you haven't yet encountered it in your Civil Procedure class, you might want to consider F.R.C.P. 11(b)(2) in thinking about this question.

Problem 2: Other than contracts formed in face-to-face conversations or by "phone" (whatever the voice transmission medium, assuming it is not recorded), what sort of contract communications might fail to satisfy the statute of frauds requirement of a "signed" or "authenticated" "writing" or "record"?

Lesson 18: Narrowed Applications and Exceptions

Objectives and Expected Learning Outcomes

In this lesson, you will learn a variety of means by which courts seek to mitigate the potential injustice that might arise from a strict application of the statute of frauds—either by limiting its scope or providing for exceptions to its application. You will also learn which means are suitable for which statutes of frauds and which are specifically not suitable as exceptions to any particular statute. Finally, you will have the opportunity to apply some of these exceptions in a variety of fact settings.

Mitigation of Injustice Arising from Strict Application of the Statute

While intended to protect parties from bargains they never made, a statute of frauds also has the potential to render an honest bargain unenforceable, thereby arguably perpetrating rather than preventing a fraud. As a result, where courts believe an honest bargain has been made, and a technical application of the statute is likely to do injustice, they have over time carved out a series of "limitations" on the scope of application of certain statutes and "exceptions" to the strict application of the rule in others. Whether a "limitation" effectively places the contract in question outside the scope or the applicable statute or treats the statute as satisfied on an "exceptional" basis, the effect is generally the same. The bargain is enforced, even though it might not have been under a literal, technical application of the statute.

While the statutes are legislative enactments, these limitations or exceptions at least initially came from the common law, though many have over time found their way into various statutory formulations. We will see a few such statutory examples in the next lesson. In this lesson, however, each will be addressed in terms of common law, judicially created limits or exceptions to a particular statute of frauds provision.

Contracts Requiring Greater Than One Year to Perform

We can now return to Examples 17-4 and 17-5 from the last lesson. Some of you may have had the sense that the results should have been reversed. In fact, they may very well be reversed, as courts often construe the statute requiring a signed writing for contracts requiring more than one year to perform.

You will recall that a contract is only within this statute if it cannot according to its terms be completed within a year. Courts have often shown a willingness to consider the possibility of performance within a year on a very "liberal" basis.

> **Example 18-1 (formerly 17-4):** A orally contracts with B to construct a small building on land already owned by A (no transfer of real property is involved) at a price of $10,000. The project will very likely take 18 months to complete (B is doing much of the work, herself). The day

after the parties concluded their oral agreement, A disavows having agreed to any contract. When B promptly seeks to enforce, A raises a statute of frauds defense.

While there is no signed writing, the court rules that the contract is not within the ambit of the statute, because nothing in the terms of the contract precludes the possibility of B completing it in one year or less.

In effect, B would not breach the contract by completing it in one year and, having done so, would have no further obligations. While it is unlikely she will do so, there is nothing in the terms that precludes her from hiring additional help or working additional hours on this project, thereby completing it within a year.

Another avenue for enforcement is an exception or limitation on the application of the statute where one side has fully performed. In effect, the parties' performance serves as at least some evidence that a promise was made.

Example 18-2 (formerly 17-3): In Example 4-1, Jane promised to pay Joe $150,000 if he completed law school. Assuming that a court believes Jane was offering a bargain, the resulting contract will be enforceable, even though it is not supported by a writing signed by Jane, because Joe has already fully performed his side of the bargain.

This rule also reflects the fact that, if a court believes Jane offered Joe a bargain, then Joe would seem to be entitled, at the very least, to restitution (Jane wanted the benefit, and Joe was not acting gratuitously). The only difference is that Joe will recover on the contract terms if they are enforceable, whereas, a court will be required to determine the value of the benefit to Jane. Under the circumstance of full performance of a contract that requires more than a year to perform, a court will often enforce the contract terms.

This particular statute of frauds has drawn significant criticism over time, and courts seem quite content to avoid its application when possible. The above two judicially created rules serve to mitigate at least some of the potential negative effects of the statute. In contrast to the above statute, the provision addressing transfers of interests in real property is generally taken quite seriously. While it has also seen exceptions to its strict enforcement, these exceptions generally tend to be applied quite rigorously.

Contracts Involving Real Property

The most typical exception to the statute of frauds governing real property involves certain instances of part performance. The buyer's payment of the purchase price, by itself, is not sufficient. However, partial or complete payment by the buyer, in conjunction with other actions, may be sufficient to allow for enforcement of an oral agreement on an exceptional basis. The key to this exception is that the buyer's actions unequivocally provide evidence of a contract to purchase the real property at issue.

In deciding whether to apply the "part performance" exception, a court will evaluate three indices of a contract:

(1) Payment of the contract price;

(2) Taking possession of the property at issue; and

(3) Making improvements on the property at issue.

These indices obviously involve a strong reliance element as well as evidence of the transaction. However, the primary focus of the exception is on sufficient evidence of the contract that a signed writing is deemed unnecessary to prove its existence.

> **Example 18-3:** Smith owns a large undeveloped parcel of land with a residence on it and leases it to Jones for 24 months. For the first 12 months, Jones pays monthly rent to Smith and lives in the residence, working nearby. After the first year, the payments increase significantly, well beyond the amount called for in the lease. Jones also builds a barn at his own expense and begins clearing some of the land in preparation for farming it. At the end of the 2 years, Jones tenders a final payment, which he asserts is the final amount due under a contract with Smith to purchase the land. Smith, however, asserts that he never agreed to sell the land to Jones and, in any event, he never signed anything promising to do so.

Jones asserts that he need not produce a writing, because his payments during the final year at a rate far in excess of the lease amount, which were accepted without question by Smith, coupled with his improvements to the property, unequivocally establish the existence of a contract to purchase the land. A court might well enforce this contract, as the actions of Jones strongly suggest his understanding that Smith had agreed to sell the land to him, and Smith's actions in accepting the increased payments would seem to indicate a similar understanding.

Again, it must be remembered that the statute of frauds analysis only takes place if the fact finder believes the parties have indeed concluded a binding contract.

While the "part performance" doctrine focuses primarily on the evidentiary quality of the performance, an entirely separate exception focuses on "reliance" and the potential injustice resulting from non-enforcement. In such a case, reliance is said to give rise to an estoppel precluding the assertion of the statute of frauds.

Example 18-4: *Monarco v. Lo Greco*

Natale and Carmela Castiglia owned an interest in a family farm. When he reached 18, Christie Lo Greco, one of Carmela's sons, had decided to leave home and seek his own fortune. However, Natale and Carmela convinced him, instead, to stay and work the family farm in exchange for their promise to keep their own interests in a joint tenancy, which would pass to the surviving spouse, who would then bequest it to Lo Greco. Natale and Carmen performed the first part of the promise, putting the property in joint tenancy and each executing wills leaving the property to Lo Greco. However, Natale later terminated the joint tenancy and changed his will, leaving his property interest to his grandson, Carmen Monarco. Natale died soon thereafter.

In the subsequent legal proceeding, Lo Greco asserted that the interest held by Monarco should be treated as a "constructive trust" for the benefit of Lo Greco, because Natale Castiglia was contractually obligated to make sure that his interest would be transferred to Lo Greco upon the death of his mother, Carmela Castiglia (who died during the pendency of proceedings). Monarco raised a statute of frauds defense, pointing out the lack of any writing signed by Natale.

The California Supreme Court ruled in favor of Lo Greco, imposing the requested "constructive trust." The court ruled that Monarco was estopped from asserting the statute of frauds based on a combination of Lo Greco's reliance and the benefit of Lo Greco's efforts that would be unjustly conferred on Monarco absent enforcement.[1]

The case was a challenging one, as the facts were not sufficient to apply the doctrine of part performance (Lo Greco made no direct "payment" other than perhaps foregoing other opportunities), and any recovery limited to restitution would have been almost impossible to quantify and likely inadequate. Thus, the court seemingly relied on a unique blend of detrimental reliance and concerns over unjust enrichment to estop the assertion of the statute of frauds end enforce the oral promise.

While this original case includes a significant dose of restitutionary concerns, the resulting exception to the application of the statute of frauds is often simply characterized in terms of "reliance."[2] The broader contours of the rule, however, would limit its operation under a variety of circumstances, including those in which restitution alone might be

> **A Constructive Trust**
> A "trust" is a legal arrangement by which a "trustee" manages certain assets (such as real property) for the benefit of the "beneficiary." A "constructive trust" is a fictional version of such an arrangement imposed by a court. In effect, the party who improperly ended up with the asset is deemed to hold it "in trust" for the benefit of the party who should have received it. The constructive "trustee" is then of course expected to convey the asset to the beneficiary as soon as reasonably possible.

---

[1] Monarco v. Lo Greco, 35 Cal.2d 621, 220 P.2d 737 (1950).
[2] *See* Restatement (Second) of Contracts § 139(1).

adequate.[3] The rule is generally accepted as a common law exception to the strict application of the statute of frauds involving real property (even though the actual case was decided under a different California statute), and it would likely apply in a proper case involving a statute of frauds applicable to contracts requiring more than one year to perform. However, its potential application to a sale of goods transaction has been far more controversial, as will be addressed more fully in the next lesson.

Estoppel may also preclude the assertion of the statute of frauds in a few other narrow and specific circumstances. A party asserting to its counter-party that a writing is unnecessary may be precluded from asserting the statute as a matter of equitable estoppel. In a slightly different vein, a party promising to execute a subsequent writing may be precluded from assert-ing the statute of frauds as a matter of promissory estoppel.

Contracts of Surety

When attempting to enforce an oral promise of a third person appearing— at least at first glance—to look like a surety, the first step is to determine whether this person has actually made a promise of surety. A number of promises look somewhat like a promise of surety, but are not.

To begin, a promise of surety must be a "collateral," rather than "primary" obligation. A collateral obligation only comes due if the primary obligor does not pay. In contrast, a "co-obligor" incurs a primary obligation to pay the creditor, along with the other obligor. Because the obligations of both obligors are considered primary, neither is a surety for the other.

An obligation of a party other than the original obligor can also arise in a variety of forms, not all of which are contracts of surety. Consider the following two examples. The first is a variation on the contract of surety in Example 17-1.

---

[3] *See* Restatement (Second) of Contracts § 139(2).

Example 18-5: Dan (debtor) owes money to Cass (creditor) and seeks to extend the payment terms. Cass says he would like to help, but is increasingly unsure about Dan's ability to repay the money over any period. Sara offers to act as surety for Dan, promising Cass that, if she will extend the terms, Sara will pay Dan's debt if Dan does not. Cass agrees to extend the terms of Dan's loan in exchange for Sara's promise and he does so.

Sara has concluded a contract of surety with Cass. This contract will not be enforceable, unless Cass can point to a writing signed by Sara and evidencing Sara's promise.

The foregoing is a true contract of surety, because Dan remains the primary obligor, while Sara is solely obligated to Cass if Dan fails to pay. If, however, the facts are changed just a bit—so that the new promisor serves to "replace" Dan as the obligor instead of paying only if Dan does not—then the new obligor is not a surety at all. Instead, the substitution results in what is called a "novation."

Example 18-6: Dan (debtor) owes money to Cass (creditor) and seeks to extend the payment terms. Cass says he would like to help, but is increasingly unsure about Dan's ability to repay the money over any period. Nate offers to pay Dan's debt, provided that Cass will release Dan from any payment obligation. Cass agrees to Nate's proposal.

Nate has concluded a contract with Cass, which includes a "novation" in which Nate assumes Dan's obligations, and Dan is fully released. This contract will be enforceable without any requirement of a writing, because it does not involve a promise of surety.

The role of Sara in Example 18-5 of course looks similar in many ways to the role of Nate in Example 18-6. However, the key difference is that Dan is fully released from liability in the latter example, and Nate is now the primary obligor.

Another third party promise that looks a bit like a promise of surety is one in which a third party assumes a debt obligation from the original debtor and promises to indemnify the debtor for any payments the debtor might be obligated to make to the creditor. This is not, however, a true promise of surety, because the promise runs from the third party to the debtor, instead of running to the creditor.

> **Example 18-7:** *Langman v. Alumni Assoc. of the Univ. of Virginia*
>
> Langman donated a parcel of real property to the Alumni Association of UVA (AAUVA). The deed contained a provision requiring AAUVA to assume the obligation to pay the mortgage on the property and to hold Langman harmless. Revenues from the property were insufficient to pay the mortgage and Langman (still the obligor on the mortgage) had to pay.
>
> Langman sued AAUVA for indemnification. However, only Langman has signed the deed, so AAUVA asserted that this was a contract of surety and the lack of anything signed by AAUVA precluded enforcement. The court ruled, however, that this was not a contract of surety, but was merely a promise of indemnification by AAUVA to pay Langman if he had to pay the mortgage payments to the mortgage creditor. As such, a signed writing was unnecessary to enforce against AAUVA.[4]

The above promise can be a bit more difficult to recognize than a "novation" because the debtor remains primarily liable, as far as the creditor is concerned. However, the subsequent arrangement (including the promise of "indemnification") is entirely between the third person and the debtor, with no promise of "surety" to the creditor.

The above variations involve contracts that are simply not true contracts of surety. Thus, the statute does not apply. However, most traditional "exceptions" do not apply to the statute applicable to contracts of surety, because the exceptions would swallow the rule. The creditor would always be able to assert reliance on the promise of the surety, as the loan would not have

---

4 Langman v. Alumni Assoc. of the Univ. of Virginia., 247 Va. 491, 442 S.E. 2d 669 (1994).

been made or extended absent the promise. Moreover, the creditor will always fully perform before any attempted enforcement against the surety, because the surety's obligation only arises if the debtor fails to pay.

While the traditional exceptions do not apply, there is one exception that is very specific to contracts of surety—the "main purpose" (or sometimes called "leading object") exception.

Example 18-8: Sigma manufactures and sells computers, and it is currently in the midst of producing a very large order for its most important customer. Unexpectedly, Delta, one of Sigma's most essential component suppliers experiences severe cash flow problems and is faced with potentially shutting down its production of the components it produces for Sigma, thereby delaying Sigma's own production. Delta was unable to borrow additional funds on its own because of its precarious financial position. However, CountyBank agreed to make the necessary loan to Delta, provided that Sigma would guarantee repayment of the loan to CountyBank if Delta failed to make timely payment. The President of Sigma telephoned the bank manager at CountyBank and promised that Sigma would pay the loan if Delta did not (being a small, rural bank, the folks at CountyBank were a bit more relaxed about this sort of thing than big city banks), and the bank made the loan to Delta, thereby allowing Delta to resume production and Sigma to meet is production deadlines.

Predictably, Delta again soon found itself in financial trouble and failed to repay the loan to CountyBank. Sigma then refused to honor its promise, and CountyBank sued. Sigma asserted that the alleged promise of surety was not supported by a signed writing and was not, therefore, enforceable. However, the bank argued that a writing was unnecessary because Sigma's promise fell within the "main purpose" exception. Sigma's "main purpose" in making the promise of surety was Sigma's own financial self-interest in meeting its production schedule. A court would almost certainly agree and enforce the promise by Sigma, assuming of course that the court believed it had been made.

The rationale behind this exception is that the logic of the basic rule, protecting the often selfless acts of a surety, no longer applies when the surety is acting in furtherance of its own financial self-interest.

Multiple Statutes

If multiple statutes are involved, the requirements of each must of course be met. For example, a 5-year real property lease would implicate the three statutes considered here. Often, a single signed writing will satisfy both. However, in the case of certain exceptions, the exception may satisfy or avoid the application of one statute, but not another.

Restitution

The potential for a party to recover restitution has already been discussed above as a possible alternative to a number of the remedies at issue. If the parties have formed a contract, but that contract is rendered unenforceable by the statute of frauds, then the parties each simply walk away without liability if neither has performed any obligation under the contract in question. However, if one or both of the parties has conveyed some benefit on the other pursuant to the contract, then that party will almost certainly be entitled to restitution from the recipient in order to avoid unjust enrichment.

Even if the contract is not enforceable, its existence should conclusively establish than any benefit was desired by the recipient (not officious) and that the party conveying it was doing so in exchange for the bargained for consideration (not officious). Thus, allowing the recipient to retain the benefit without paying for it would very likely amount to unjust enrichment.

APPLYING THE RULES

Problem 1: Johnson agreed to purchase 60 acres of farmland from McEnroe at $10,000 per acre. The land consisted of two parcels of 30 acres each, and the written agreement, signed by both parties, called for Johnson to pay the purchase price by conveying land of appropriate value (the deal was structured in this manner for tax reasons). The parties quickly identified one appropriate property owned by Rychart and worth $400,000. Johnson acquired the property from Rychart and deeded it over to McEnroe, thus leaving the remaining $200,000 to be paid through acquisition of other property. McEnroe immediately deeded one of his 30-acre parcels over to Johnson, reflecting the fact that over half of the consideration had been paid. The parties had difficulty locating another suitable parcel, so they agreed to replace the original agreement with an option contract of sorts.

The new written, signed agreement provided the parties one year to find suitable additional property to complete the sale of the second parcel, with the remaining $100,000 unapplied value of the Rychart property treated as partial payment towards the remaining purchase price. If the parties were unable to locate suitable property, then Johnson had the option of tendering the remaining $200,000 in cash on or before April 1. During the year leading up to April 1, Johnson began development of the first parcel, which McEnroe had already conveyed, but did nothing with respect to the second. As April 1 approached, the parties had not yet found suitable property for the exchange, and they orally agreed to extend the option for another 6 months in hopes of finding property, preserving of course Johnson's right to tender cash if not.

During the period between April 1 and October 1, Johnson continued to develop the first parcel, and also spent $6,500 in platting the second parcel in anticipation of beginning development soon after it was conveyed pursuant to the parties' agreement. As October 1 approached, the parties remained unable to find suitable property and, in late September, Johnson tendered the remaining $200,000 purchase price. However, McEnroe refused to accept it. When Johnson brought an action for specific performance, demanding conveyance of the second 30-acre parcel, McEnroe asserted the statute of frauds as a defense to enforcement.

Is Johnson entitled to purchase the remaining 30-acre parcel for an additional $200,000 in cash? If not, is he entitled to any other relief?

The facts of this problem are loosely based on the case of *Johnson Farms v. McEnroe*, 568 N.W.2d 920 (N.D. 1997).

Problem 2: Which of the following include promises of surety by C, requiring a signed writing as such?

(1) A borrows money from B, promising to pay it back over 6 months. After the first month, A wishes to extend the period of repayment to 12 months. B agrees to do so, but only on the condition that C promise to repay the loan if A does not.

(2) A borrows money from B, collateralized by certain licensing rights owned by A. Later, A wishes to sell the licensing rights to C. As part of the sale, C agrees to pay A's debt to B. C also promises to indemnify A in the event A is required to make any further payments to B on the loan.

(3) A borrows money from B, collateralized by certain licensing rights owned by A. Later, A wishes to sell the licensing rights to C. As part of an agreement between A, B, and C, B releases A, and C agrees to pay A's debt to B.

(4) A wishes to borrow money from B. However, B is unwilling to make the loan, unless C promises to repay B if A does not. C agrees.

Problem 3: Which of the following require a signed writing because they involve contracts that cannot be performed within one year?

(1) Author, A, contracts with publisher, P, to write a series of 15 novels, each of which must be at least 500 pages in length.

(2) Joe, a gardener, contracts to do landscaping for Mary, at $100 per month, for as long as she owns her home.

(3) In exchange for her promise to work in her current job at her current salary for at least 6 more months, P promises to pay F $500 per month for life, upon her retirement as an employee of P.

Lesson 19: Sales of Goods: UCC § 2-201 and CISG Article 11

Objectives and Expected Learning Outcomes

In this lesson, you will learn about the requirement of a signed writing applicable to certain sales of goods. You will also learn a variety of ways in which the requirement can be satisfied, as well as a broad array of exceptions contained in the statute itself. You will then have the opportunity to apply the rule and to explore the relationship between the instant rule and others we have already discussed or will discuss in future lessons. Finally, you will learn that the CISG does not impose any requirement at all as to form, so that oral contracts are fully enforceable.

Sales of Goods under Article 2—the "Rule"

As a general rule, UCC Article 2 requires a signed writing for the vast majority of transactions in goods. **STOP NOW and READ UCC § 2-201(1) below.**

UCC § 2-201(1)

(1) Except as otherwise provided in this section a contract for the sale of goods for the price of $500 or more is not enforceable by way of action or defense unless there is some writing sufficient to indicate that a contract for sale has been made between the parties and signed by the party against whom enforcement is sought or by his authorized agent or broker. A writing is not insufficient because it omits or incorrectly states a term agreed upon but the contract is not enforceable under this paragraph beyond the quantity of goods shown in such writing.

This statute is arguably even more complex than UCC § 2-207, so we will approach each subsection independently, and in turn. Most obviously, the statute applies to a contract for the sale of goods "for the price of *$500 or more.*" Thus, an oral contract to sell a table for $499.99 is fully enforceable without reference to the statutory requirements, while the sale of the same table for $500 would not be enforceable, unless the statute is satisfied—one way or another.

The actual writing requirement is, however, considerably more liberal than the common law. You will likely remember from Lesson 17 that, while multiple writings could be used—even unsigned ones—the writings needed to include all of the basic terms of the agreement at issue. In contrast, subsection (1) requires only "some writing sufficient to indicate that a contract for sale has been made between the parties," as long as it is signed by the party against whom enforcement is sought and indicates the "quantity of goods."

The writing need not include any other terms and may even be effective if it misstates one or more terms (though, at some point, one might question whether the number of errors might suggest that the writing is not addressing the contract at issue). The following example helps to illustrate the truly "minimalist" requirement under subsection (1).

Example 19-1: For this example, let's return to Ms. Allen's Swiss art collection from Lesson 9, Problem 3. In this example, however, Ms. Allen has only one collection, and it is being viewed by Mr. Zeller, a collector from Florida. After viewing all of the art in the collection at Ms. Allen's estate in New York, Mr. Zeller said "Ms. Allen, I would like to offer you $3,000,000 for the entire collection." Ms. Allen replied "Well, Mr. Zeller, you certainly don't waste time. As it happens, however, I believe that your offer is very a fair one, and I accept it." Mr. Zeller then stated "Excellent, I will make arrangements to collect it as soon as possible. Please send me your banking information, and I will wire the funds promptly." Mr. Zeller then left and got into his limousine, where he proceeded to send the following "tweet." "Just leaving Allen home, now the proud owner of her Swiss art collection for bargain price of $2 mil." Of course he had paid more, but he wanted to impress his many followers with his bargaining acumen.

The next morning, Mr. Zeller awoke to some very bad financial news, one of his major investments having just failed. As a result, he immediately contacted Ms. Allen to cancel the purchase. When she said he was already bound, and she fully intended to enforce the agreement, he said "good luck trying to do that without anything in writing." Assuming that a mutual acquaintance has provided Ms.

Allen with a digital copy of the "tweet," she can enforce the bargain in court, as long as the court believes she made it. The tweet is a record recoverable in perceivable form, and Mr. Zeller's act of sending it from his personal Twitter account serves to authenticate the record.

While very liberal as to form, subsection (1) does require some sort of signature or other authentication by the party to be charged, and the record must provide evidence that the parties concluded a contract for the sale of goods. If subsection (1) is clearly satisfied, there is no need to consult the rest of the statute.

Subsection (1) is, however, only our starting point if there is any doubt that it has been satisfied. A party seeking to enforce a contract may, alternatively, satisfy the statute under either subsection (2) or (3).

Sales of Goods under Article 2—the "Merchant Confirmation"

Even if subsection (1) cannot be satisfied with a writing "signed by the party against whom enforcement is sought," between merchants, it can alternatively be satisfied by a "written confirmation" of the parties' earlier oral agreement. **STOP NOW and READ UCC § 2-201(2) below.**

UCC § 2-201(2)

(2) Between merchants if within a reasonable time a writing in confirmation of the contract and sufficient against the sender is received and the party receiving it has reason to know its contents, it satisfies the requirements of subsection (1) against such party unless written notice of objection to its contents is given within 10 days after it is received.

Subsection (2) recognizes a common practice between merchants in which a writing is sent in confirmation of an earlier oral agreement. The sender is of course trying to avoid any later questions as to the prior oral agreement. In such circumstances, when the "confirmation" is sent soon after the oral conversation, the recipient can reasonably be expected to take note of its basic contents. Thus, it is reasonable to infer that, absent a prompt objection, the recipient tacitly acknowledges the parties' earlier oral agreement.

However, it is considerably less reasonable to infer that the recipient has carefully read all of the fine print in such a "confirmation" (which, remember, has been received after the contract has already been concluded). Thus, the confirmation merely confirms the existence of the earlier contract, and the recipient is not deemed to accept all of the terms of the confirmation by mere silence. The issue of contract terms leads us back to UCC § 2-207.

Not surprisingly, a written confirmation of an earlier oral agreement might very well contain more detailed information than the earlier conversation. However, UCC § 2-201 does not address the question of whether such terms are part of the parties' agreement. It merely addresses the enforceability of any agreement, as a matter of "form." When terms in any confirmation add to or differ from the prior oral agreement, the potential inclusion of those terms is addressed in UCC § 2-207(2). Between merchants, they become part of the contract, unless they would materially alter it, or the other party objects in some fashion.

The key to analyzing such a "written confirmation" "between merchants" is to recognize its potential effect on two fully independent and distinct issues—enforceability, under § 2-201(2), and the content of the agreement, under § 2-207(2). A failure to analyze the two issues separately will often lead to trouble, as illustrated in the brief case excerpt below.

FROM THE COURT

Ready Trucking, Inc. v. BP Exploration & Oil Co.

Georgia Court of Appeals (2001)
248 Ga. App. 701

POPE, J.

[BP contracted to sell diesel fuel to Ready Trucking in a series of 150 separate purchases over a little more than 2 years. BP did not charge certain local taxes on those sales in the mistaken belief that it was not supposed to do so. The fact that BP was not charging such taxes was expressly indicated in small print on its invoices, but was never otherwise reflected in any of the parties' other communications. When the Georgia Department of Revenue eventually learned that the taxes had not been paid, it assessed them against Ready, along with penalties. Ready then sought reimbursement from BP based on the understanding between the parties (consistent with that of the general trade) that BP's price to Ready included all applicable taxes. BP refused to pay, pointing to the express representation on its invoices that it was not collecting the taxes at issue (thereby indicating that Ready should address the issue if it was in fact liable for those taxes, contrary to BP's belief that Ready was not). Ready then brought suit.

On appeal, the court's analysis focused on whether the terms on BP's invoice— *indicating that BP was not charging the two taxes at issue*—were part of the parties' contracts in question.]

. . . absent an agreement to the contrary, a simple quote to purchase gasoline at a certain price would include an agreement that the price included all applicable taxes.

. . . BP essentially argues that the parties had an agreement to the contrary [based on the language in each of the BP invoices] . . .

. . . each invoice sent as a confirmation of each order shows beyond dispute that BP did not in fact charge Ready the two forms of sales tax at issue in this case on any of the approximately 150 transactions. Don Dougherty, the president of Ready, while reviewing these invoices during his deposition, readily admitted, "[w]ell, obviously it says that there is no sales tax charged on it, that it's sales tax exempt. . ." Although Dougherty conceded that he had probably seen the invoices before being deposed, he explained he had not realized the exemption appeared on them. He further testified that he . . . was aware at the time that Ready was not entitled to such an exemption and he would have expected Ready's office manager to have inquired why BP exempted Ready from the sales taxes. Ready's office manager, the sole employee responsible for accounts payable, testified that she merely verified the price per gallon and paid no attention to the sales tax information on the invoices. Ready never contacted BP to question the exemption.

Under these circumstances, the Georgia codification of the Uniform Commercial Code resolves this dispute. Article 2 of the UCC governs transactions involving the sale of goods. [Case citation omitted.] Where the sale of goods is "between merchants," the sales invoices constitute written confirmation of their agreement. [Case citation omitted.] As "between merchants," if within a reasonable time a writing in confirmation of the contract and sufficient against the sender is received and the party receiving it has reason to know its contents, it [constitutes a writing enforceable] against such party unless written notice of objection to its contents is given within ten days after it is received.

OCGA § 11-2-201(2). [Case citation omitted.] Further, *that writing then becomes the "final expression of their agreement with respect to such terms as are included therein," . . . Thus, if Ready is a merchant for the purposes of OCGA § 11-2-201(2), the invoices govern* and there has been no breach of contract. [Emphasis supplied.]

[the court went on to find that Ready was a "merchant" and was therefore bound by the terms in BP's confirming invoices.]

CASE QUESTIONS

(1) Did the court properly apply the Georgia codification of UCC § 2-201(2)? If you are at all unsure about the answer, you should read the opinion of the U.S. District Court in Ardus Medical, Inc. v. Emanuel County Hospital Authority, 558 F. Supp. 2d 1301 (S.D. Ga. 2008), criticizing the above decision, but applying it as Georgia law (as is required of a Federal Court hearing a case governed by Georgia law).

   a. How should the Georgia court have addressed the terms at issue in BP's confirming invoices?

   b. Does the testimony of the Ready personnel provide any support for the logic behind the proper statutory treatment?

(2) Does this case help you to understand why it is absolutely essential to a proper analysis that issues of contract formation be addressed fully independently of issues of enforceability under any applicable statute of fraud—as well as the reverse?

(3) Can you explain in your own words how the same "confirmation" may be given effect under both UCC § 2-201(2) and UCC § 2-207(2), while pointing out the difference in the effect of the confirmation under each?

To be absolutely clear, the Ready Trucking case above was unequivocally wrong in applying UCC § 2-201(2) to determine the content of the parties' agreement. The provisions of § 2-201(2) are intended solely to address the satisfaction of the writing requirement under § 2-201(1). The purpose of this excerpted case is to illustrate clearly the peril of failing to distinguish between the proper use of a confirmation under UCC § 2-207 (addressing the content of the parties' agreement) and UCC § 2-201 (addressing the requirement of a signed writing as a matter of form).

Let's return now to the text of subsection (2) and review its basic requirements (you should identify each within the text of the statute itself). If

(1) a written confirmation,

(2) between merchants,

(3) of a contract formed earlier,

(4) sent within a reasonable time,

(5) and sufficient against the sender under subsection (1),

(6) is received by a party with reason to know of its basic contents,

and the recipient fails to object to its contents in writing within 10 days, then the written confirmation not only satisfies subsection (1) against the sender, but also satisfies subsection (1) against the recipient—even though the recipient never signed or otherwise authenticated anything.

The most obvious application of the statute involves silent receipt of such a written confirmation.

> **Example 19-2:** The Ready Trucking case, excerpted above, provides an excellent opportunity for a proper application of subsection (2), assuming that the actual agreement was concluded informally before the transmittal of the "confirming" invoice.

BP sent each written invoice, as a confirmation of a transaction between merchants—BP and Ready—of a contract
they formed earlier. The invoice was sent within a reasonable time and was sufficient against BP (any seller sending
an "invoice" requesting payment would certainly authenticate it in some manner). Ready, as a regular customer of BP,
who just recently placed an order, would certainly have
reason to know of the contents. Indeed the Ready bookkeeper regularly verified the price on each of these.

When Ready failed to object (or even respond) within
10 days, the invoice was deemed to satisfy subsection (1)
against Ready, such that BP could enforce the agreement,
if necessary.

You may recall the earlier discussion with respect to Example 17-2 (and
Lucy v. Zehmer) that one party may be bound by its signature on a writing,
while the other is not. In contrast, UCC § 2-201(2) allows one merchant,
by binding itself, to bind the other merchant, absent an objection.

But what if the recipient does object in writing? We can now move to consider
this issue, which we will see does not always preclude contract enforcement.

Example 19-3: Let's return to the same fact pattern from
the prior example. Suppose, however, that the Ready office
manager believed that the invoice price was in error and
immediately brought it to the attention of the Ready President, Don Dougherty. Further suppose that Dougherty
told her "That's just as well, as I don't want that shipment
anyway. Please let BP know ASAP." The office manager
promptly (in much less than 10 days) sent an e-mail to BP
stating "the price of $3 per gallon on your recent invoice is
wrong. It should be $2.90 per gallon. Please cancel order,
as Ready has no current need for the fuel."

Assuming that BP seeks to enforce the contract, and Ready
raises a statute of frauds defense, BP's written confirmation
will be ineffective, because of Ready's timely "objection."
However, Ready's "objection" will, itself, satisfy subsection
(1), because it is a writing signed by Ready that indicates a

> contract for sale was made (whether the $3 or $2.90 price
> is correct makes no difference in this respect).

As you can see from the above example, written "objection" to the content of the "confirmation" will not necessarily avoid enforcement of the prior contract. To be effective, the objection must clearly state the view of the objecting party that "no contract was ever concluded." In that case, the objection prevents the confirmation from being effective under subsection (1) and is not, itself, effective in satisfying subsection (1).

The beauty of UCC § 2-201(2) is that, properly utilized between merchants, it should bring to a head any dispute over an oral or other informal agreement sooner, rather than later. And most disagreements are easier to resolve sooner, rather than later. It also provides an easy means of enforcement when a party to an oral agreement later changes its mind and seeks to renege on the deal by asserting a statute of frauds defense.

Sales of Goods under Article 2—the Rest of the Exceptions

In addition to the merchant exception discussed above, the rule of § 2-201(1) is also subject to a number of other broadly applicable exceptions. **STOP NOW and READ UCC § 2-201(3) below.**

UCC § 2-201(3)

(3) A contract which does not satisfy the requirements of subsection (1) but which is valid in other respects is enforceable

(a) if the goods are to be specially manufactured for the buyer and are not suitable for sale to others in the ordinary course of the seller's business and the seller, before notice of repudiation is received and under circumstances which reasonably indicate that the goods are for the buyer, has made either a substantial beginning of their manufacture or commitments for their procurement; or

(b) if the party against whom enforcement is sought admits in his pleading, testimony or otherwise in court that a contract for sale was made, but the contract is not enforceable under this provision beyond the quantity of goods admitted; or

(c) with respect to goods for which payment has been made and accepted or which have been received and accepted (Sec. 2-606).

In subsection (3)(a), we can see the basic principle of "reliance" in operation, and the seller's reliance also provides evidence of the contract in question. The seller has begun production of unique goods for buyer, and that unique character both ties them to the buyer and makes them unsalable to others. In that case, a signed writing is unnecessary for enforcement—assuming of course the court, jury, or arbitrator believes a contract was made.

> **Example 19-4:** We can return to Delta and Echo from Lesson 14, Problem 1. However, instead of collaborating on a design, Echo simply asks Delta to build a special motor designed specifically for a piece of equipment produced only by Echo. Echo agrees, but nothing is written to memorialize the deal.
>
> The motor is sufficiently unique that it is not reasonably usable for any other purpose. Delta begins production on the motor, and Echo seeks to cancel. In any ensuing litigation over whether the parties' contract is enforceable, any statute of frauds defense by Echo would fail, because Delta's conduct under the circumstances will satisfy UCC § 2-201(3)(a).

While subsection (3)(a) clearly reflects reliance principles, the broader supplementation of the statute with common law reliance exceptions is far more controversial. This issue is addressed further at the end of the lesson.

In subsection (3)(c), we can see reflections of the "part performance" doctrine, which focus largely on such performance as evidence of the parties' agreement. This provision applies only in two circumstances—buyer has paid and seller has accepted the payment; or seller has shipped the goods (lest buyer could not have received them) and buyer has accepted those goods. In each case, we can see clear evidence of performance of the contract exhibited by each party.

> **Example 19-5:** Now, let's change the facts of Example 19-4, such that Delta has agreed to sell standard motors to Echo, but of course they put nothing in writing. If Delta ships the motors, and Echo receives and accepts them, the parties' conduct eliminates any need for a writing to support enforcement of their contract. The same result ensues if Echo pays for the motors, and Delta accepts payment.

"Acceptance" of goods or payment is analytically distinct from acceptance of an offer. Acceptance of goods will be addressed more fully in Chapter 7.

Finally, subsection (3)(b) has no common law analogy and is unique to UCC § 2-201. It reflects the basic idea that it is simply wrong to allow a party to say in one breath "Sure I agreed to a contract," while saying in the next, "But you can't enforce it because I never signed anything."

> **Example 19-6:** As in Example 19-5, Delta and Echo have orally agreed to a contract. However, their respective performances each remain fully executory. Echo seeks to enforce, while Delta has asserted a statute of fraud defense.
>
> During trial, the sales manager of Delta is called to testify. When asked a direct question about whether he and the Echo purchasing manager concluded the oral agreement in question, he squirms a bit, but eventually answers "Yes, we did." His admission satisfies subsection (3)(b).

The effect of subsection (3)(b) is to eliminate the effectiveness of any statute of frauds defenses left after the application of the other subsections, except where there is a genuine issue over whether the parties agreed to a contract in the first instance, or where a party is prepared to lie under oath (from the author's experience, a relative rarity).

Interaction of UCC § 2-201 with Other Statutes and Common Law

Having fully addressed in turn each of the provisions of UCC § 2-201, we can now briefly address its interaction with other statutes and the common law. We have already addressed above the relationship between merchant confirmations under §§ 2-201 and 2-207, so we can next turn to § 2-209, which governs modification of a contract for the sale of goods.

Earlier, in Lesson 6, we noted that UCC § 2-209(1) dispensed with any requirement of consideration in the context of a contract modification. In that same context, § 2-209(3) addresses the requirement of a writing. **STOP NOW and READ the excerpts from UCC § 2-209 below.**

UCC § 2-209(3), (4), AND (5)

(3) The requirements of the statute of frauds section of this Article (Section 2-201) must be satisfied if the contract as modified is within its provisions.

(4) Although an attempt at modification or rescission does not satisfy the requirements of subsection (2) or (3) it can operate as a waiver.

(5) A party who has made a waiver affecting an executory portion of the contract may retract the waiver by reasonable notification received by the other party that strict performance will be required of any term waived, unless the retraction would be unjust in view of a material change of position in reliance on the waiver.

Subsection (3) provides for the application of the statute of frauds in the context of a contract modification. However, subsections (4) and (5) also provide other means for the potential enforcement of modifications that fail to satisfy § 2-201 (which can of course be satisfied in a variety of ways), which we will address more fully in Chapter 6.

Finally, we come to two questions relating to the supplementation of UCC § 2-201 with the common law. Do other overlapping statutes apply to a contract for the sale of goods? Do other common law exceptions beyond those expressly included in the statute apply to a contract for the sale of goods? The provision of the statute that potentially answers those questions is the opening phrase of subsection (1), "[e]xcept as otherwise provided in this section . . ."

The quoted statutory language might reasonably be read to suggest that UCC § 2-201 fully preempts any and all other form requirements or exceptions. Indeed, all seem to agree that a contract for a sale of goods in installments over a period of two years does not separately invoke the statute of frauds governing contracts that cannot be completed in one year. In effect, if UCC § 2-201 is satisfied, that is enough.

In contrast, a contract of surety made in connection with a buyer's promise to pay for the goods is sufficiently distinct that the statute of frauds applicable to contracts of surety applies to that promise, while UCC § 2-201 applies to the contract between the buyer and seller.

Supplementation of the statute with common law exceptions for reliance has been far more controversial. On one hand, the statutory preamble seems to preempt other sources of exceptions, and subsection (3)(a) certainly addresses at least one aspect of reliance, albeit in a relatively narrow context. On the other hand, notions of enforcing a reliance interest to avoid injustice have become a significant element of our jurisprudence. Courts have split on this particular issue, and either position can reasonably be supported.

Sales of Goods under Article 2—What Is Left of the "Rule"?

Having now considered all of the "exceptions" to the basic "rule," one might reasonably ask what is left of the rule. Do any transactions governed by Article 2 really require a signed writing for enforcement? The answer is, yes, but it is in fact a reasonably narrow range of transactions. You are invited to provide your own explanation in Problem 1.

More often than not, UCC § 2-201 is likely applied in circumstances in which it is simply easier to say that the statutory requirements for enforcement have not been satisfied than to say the parties never formed a contract.

The CISG—No Rule at All

The CISG has no requirement of form, whatsoever. **STOP NOW and READ CISG Article 11 below.**

CISG ARTICLE 11

A contract of sale need not be concluded in or evidenced by writing and is not subject to any other requirement as to form. It may be proved by any means, including witnesses.

While domestic transactions require a signed writing (or other satisfaction of the statute), a sale of goods across national borders requires only that the finder of fact believe that the parties really concluded a contract.

Example 19-7: We can now return to Example 19-1, but bring back from Lesson 9, Problem 3, Dr. Oswald, our Swiss buyer, instead of Mr. Zeller, from Florida. The oral contract for the sale of art is now governed by the CISG, and it is fully enforceable, irrespective of any subsequent "tweet" by the buyer.

Here, it is worth emphasizing again the significance of CISG Article 16(2), in conjunction with CISG Article 11. The combination makes it relatively easy for a party to be bound by an irrevocable oral offer under circumstances in which that would not be the case under domestic law. Whatever one may think of this result, it is certainly worthy of note to a lawyer representing clients who are buying or selling goods across national borders.

APPLYING THE RULES

Problem 1: What kinds of contracts governed by Article 2 actually require for enforcement a writing signed by the party against whom enforcement is sought (as contemplated by UCC § 2-201(1))? In answering this question, you should of course consider all of the various exceptional provisions that do not require such a writing signed by the person against who enforcement is sought. What is left?

Problem 2 (cumulative): Alpha was an established manufacturer of digital "tablets," and Beta was a new software developer and tablet reseller specializing in unique, dedicated tablet applications. Ann (Alpha) and Ben (Beta), the Presidents of the two companies, met at a tradeshow to talk about a potential agreement by which Alpha would manufacture 30,000 tablets for Beta, which Beta would resell, complete with its own proprietary software. These tablets were to be assembled by Alpha from components specifically chosen by Beta to meet its particularized and very unique needs, and they were to be delivered in individual shipments of 2,000 tablets per month, over 15 months. The price was to be $100 per tablet, payable by Beta within 10 days after receipt of each delivery.

After a lengthy and very positive discussion, Ann said "Alpha can definitely do this, but only if you will personally guarantee Beta's payment for the tablets. While I have no doubt that Beta will be a very successful business, it is a new one, and I am sure you can understand my payment concerns."

Ben (Beta's majority shareholder, as well as its President) replied, "I fully understand, and you've got yourself a deal on both the tablet purchase and my personal promise to pay if Beta does not." The two shook hands and went on to their next appointments at the trade show.

The next day, Alpha mailed a written, signed order acknowledgment to Beta, which Beta received 2 days later. The acknowledgment correctly stated most of the terms discussed at the trade show, but incorrectly stated a quantity of 1,000 tablets per month (a total of 15,000) and a price of $90 per tablet (both were simply clerical errors due to the large volume of confirming memoranda sent out after the trade show). The acknowledgment also included a provision requiring Beta to pay a "restocking fee," in addition to other damages, in the event that Beta wrongfully rejected any delivery of computers (you may assume that such a "liquidated damages" provision is enforceable if part of the parties' contract—the issue is more fully addressed in Chapter 8). The acknowledgement said nothing about Ben's personal payment promise. Beta did not reply, and 45 days later, the first delivery of 2,000 tablets arrived. Beta refused to accept them—telling the delivery service to return them to the sender. While acknowledging the tradeshow conversation, Ben asserts that he had absolutely no intention of concluding a contract without signing a formal agreement, which he never did. Thus, he does not believe that Alpha and Beta concluded a contract.

Assuming these facts are established, can Alpha enforce a contract with Beta for the purchase and sale of tablets? If so, is it entitled to the "restocking" fee? What are the enforceable quantity and price terms? If Beta cannot pay, is Ben liable?

Problem 3 (cumulative): Fedrick was a general contractor bidding on a U.S. Bureau of Reclamation Project, and Borg-Warner (BW) was a subcontractor bidding to supply pumps for the project. BW's bid was submitted by telephone to Fedrick (at Fedrick's request) only a few minutes before Fedrick was required to submit its own. BW's bid was the lowest for the pumps and Fedrick used the bid in calculating its own.

After the submission of bids, but before the award, BW indicated to Fedrick that, as specified in its bid, BW's pumps would not meet the project requirements. Thus, BW proposed to make a change in the proposed pumps to meet project specifications, along with an increase in price. Fedrick immediately responded by letter that BW was bound by its original offer to supply conforming pumps at its original bid price. The letter further stated that BW's offer was irrevocable, because Fedrick had relied on it and intended to accept the offer if Fedrick received the bid from the U.S. Government.

Fedrick was awarded the contract and soon thereafter sought to accept BW's offer. However, BW asserted that it had earlier revoked the offer and refused to perform. When Fedrick sued, BW also asserted a statute of frauds defense.

Was Borg-Warner liable to Fedrick for breach of contract in refusing to supply the pumps?

What if the pump supplier was Canadian?

The facts of this problem are loosely based on the issues raised in the case of *C.R. Fedrick, Inc. v. Borg-Warner Corp.*, 552 F.2d 852 (9th Cir. 1977) (note the three different views of the three different appellate judges deciding the case).

An "Additional" "Brain Teaser"

A Tennessee farmer regularly sells soybeans to a Georgia producer of tofu. The buyer calls in orders, which the seller accepts—assuming it has adequate current inventory—and promises to ship promptly. The buyer then promptly sends a confirming purchase order, and the parties perform their respective obligations as agreed. The purchase order includes a choice of Georgia law to govern the contract, as well as an unusually generous warranty term. Neither of these terms is otherwise mentioned by the parties. Seller's office manager regularly checks the purchase orders for price and quantity, but nothing else.

Later, a dispute over the quality of the soybeans arises, and the parties end up litigating the issue in a Tennessee court. Under UCC § 1-301, the court will apply Tennessee law, absent any agreement to the contrary. However, the buyer asserts that the contract is governed by Georgia law (as articulated in *Ready Trucking, Inc. v. BP Exploration & Oil Co.* above) based on the term in its purchase order.

Does the buyer get its warranty term? This issue is uniquely challenging because of the problem of "circularity" (also known as "bootstrapping"). It is particularly acute when a party seeks to employ a body of law other than the "default" law to questions involving contract formation. Do you see why?

5

Contract Validity

Lesson 20: The Capacity to Contract

Objectives and Expected Learning Outcomes

In this lesson, we will begin to explore the range of circumstances in which a concluded bargain that fully satisfies any form requirement will nevertheless be denied enforcement because it is deemed "invalid" or otherwise unenforceable. You will first learn the rules regarding the "capacity" to contract, after which we will explore the extent to which individuals should be protected from improvident contracts. Finally, you will have an opportunity to apply the basic rules regarding capacity.

In Chapters 2, 3, and 4, we learned the requirements for a contract, including the requirement as to "form" for certain contracts. In Chapter 5, we assume, at least for purposes of our current focus, that the parties have concluded an otherwise enforceable contract, and we ask whether there might be other reasons not to enforce the contract. Or framed slightly differently, in Chapter 4, we addressed "formal" validity, while in the current Chapter we will address questions of "substantive" and "procedural" validity.

Thus far, we have simply taken the parties' manifestations at "face value" and given them full effect based on a largely "objective" approach to contracting. However, the context of the contracting process may suggest that these manifestations are in some manner adversely affected by one of more of the circumstances of that process in ways that call into question their legitimacy. Such "procedural" defects may relate to culpable behavior by one of the parties or may arise from a legal or factual "impairment" of a party (often called "capacity" to contract). In either event, they at least to some degree lead one to question the reality of any purported "consent" to the contract in question.

In contrast, issues of "substantive" invalidity are often more controversial. You will likely recall from Lesson 4 that consideration is not subject to any "weighing" in search of a balanced bargain, as long as it is real and not a "sham." Thus, any test for substantive fairness would seem to conflict with this basic rule of consideration. Of course, one might look at substantive unfairness as possible evidence of a procedural defect in the contract formation process—in effect, inferring that "something this unfair must have been the product of a flawed or defective process." At some point, however, we must decide "to what extent are we willing to invalidate a contract solely based on substantive unfairness." As we move through lessons 20 through 23, we will begin with process and gradually introduce potential substantive elements in exploring questions of invalidity.

In this first lesson, we will address the issue of "capacity," as a subset of broader "process" issues. We could easily approach this question from either of two perspectives. We could ask "Who has the capacity to contract?" Or, conversely, we could ask "Who lacks the capacity to contract?" The law is generally framed in the latter manner, as the basic capacity to contract is seen as a fundamental right in most modern societies. Thus, the "rule" might be stated as "everyone can contract" (including fictional corporate "persons"), subject to certain narrow specific exceptions.[1]

This lesson addresses three of the most common exceptions and the means by which they are given effect. The lesson then concludes by pointing to other examples of "unfairness" and beginning to ask how far the law should go in limiting the power of parties to conclude a binding contract.

---

[1] *See* Restatement (Second) of Contracts § 12(2) (stating the basic rule as to natural persons and listing the three exceptions to be addressed, along with guardianship).

Limitations on Contracts by Minors

A minor lacks the capacity to enter into a contract that is fully binding. The minor's obligation is, instead, said to be "voidable," at the option of the minor. However, the contract is voidable *only* at the option of the minor— and not the party who has contracted with the minor. The rule is also generally applied strictly in favor of the minor, even if the minor has misrepresented his or her age. The age of "majority" is defined by state statute and in most states, today, is 18.

While potentially harsh in its application to a party unknowingly contracting with a minor, the intent of the rule is clear. No party should contract with anyone who might be a minor without making absolutely certain of the individual's age. Thus, to the extent that businesses and individuals are diligent in avoiding any contract with a minor, the minor is effectively deprived of any right to contract. As a practical matter, this rarely presents an issue for modest purchases for cash. However, it can lead to serious difficulties with more significant purchases.

> **"Rescission" of a Contract**
> When a contract is "voidable" by either party, that party seeks "rescission" of the contract, such that the contract no longer has any legally binding effect. Rescission is an equitable remedy committed to the sound discretion of the court. Neither party to a rescinded contract has any further rights or obligations, with the exception of receiving or making restitution for any benefit conferred in performance of the contract subject to rescission.

The basic rule contemplates that a minor remains under the care of his or her parents and does not, therefore, require an independent capacity to contract. However, this may not be true in the case of an "emancipated" minor, who is caring for him or herself, but lacks the power to contract. As such, courts have sometimes given effect to an "exception" to the general rule, allowing the minor to conclude a fully binding contract for "necessaries." In other cases, a minor seeking to purchase such necessities may simply be held liable, as a matter of restitution, to pay for the value (which may or may not be the same as the contract price) of the goods or services in question.

Finally, a minor who reaches the age of majority without promptly disaffirming the contract will generally be deemed to have tacitly "ratified" his or her earlier contract. A contract that has been expressly or tacitly "ratified" by an individual who has reached the age of majority is no longer "voidable," even though it was originally concluded by a minor.

Example 20-1: Jane agrees with her neighbor, Kent, who has just turned 17 years old (he looks much older) to sell him her used bicycle for $400. The statutory age of majority is 18. A few weeks later, Kent decides he no longer wants the bicycle, but Jane refuses to give him his money back.

A legal action by Kent against Jane for the return of the $400 would be successful, because the contract between Jane and Kent is voidable by Kent, as a minor. Kent would of course be required to return the bicycle to Jane, as a matter of restitution. However, even if the bicycle had been damaged, Kent would be entitled to a refund of the full $400. If, however, Kent was living on his own and supporting himself, and he needed this bicycle to commute to his job, a court might consider the bicycle to be "necessary" for Kent to support himself and might, therefore, enforce the contract.

The law clearly seeks to protect minors by limiting their capacity to contract. Should the law similarly protect the elderly? While mental incapacity may occur at any age, the elderly are often more vulnerable. The problem of course is one of line drawing. With minors, the rule, at least, is reflected in a bright line statutory age of majority. However, line drawing can be far more difficult in determining whether an adult has lost the mental capacity to contract.

Limitations based on Mental Capacity

Like a minor, a person with a mental illness or defect also lacks the capacity to enter into a contract that is fully binding. The obligation of the mentally infirm person is also "voidable," at the option of that person. However, not all mental infirmities are sufficient to preclude effective contracting.

To render a contract obligation voidable, a mental infirmity must amount to either "cognitive" incapacity or a "volitional" incapacity. While the presence of a "cognitive" incapacity will, by itself, render the contract voidable, a "volitional" incapacity will do so only if the other contracting party had "reason to know" of the incapacity.

A cognitive incapacity is one in which a person is unable to understand the very nature of a transaction and its consequences. To some degree, the person cannot be said to have formed a subjective intent to conclude the subject transaction, as it would be objectively understood by a reasonable person. Moreover, this person is not likely even capable of understanding the perspective of such an objectively reasonable person. Consider the following example.

> **Example 20-2:** Wes walks into an art gallery, believing it to be an art library. Wes has been diagnosed with a mental illness and is normally accompanied by friends or family. However, he has temporarily walked away on his own and can appear quite competent to the casual observer. Wes finds a painting that he absolutely loves and says so to the proprietor of the gallery. The proprietor explains that the painting is for sale at a price of $10,000. Wes misunderstands and believes that the owner of the gallery (a library, from Wes's perspective) is offering to allow Wes to take the painting home for a time on loan, as long is Wes signs some papers allowing him to do so (much like Wes signed up some years ago for a library card, allowing him to check out books). Wes also happens to have a credit card (with a very high limit), which he understands to be required as a matter of security—perfectly understandable with such a fine painting. Wes then signs the necessary sale paperwork, including the credit card receipt for $10,000, and leaves with the painting.

> When Wes's daughter, Kate, discovers the painting, she seeks to return it (Kate has a general durable power of attorney to act on his behalf). However, the gallery owner refuses, explaining that Wes seemed to know exactly what he was doing when he purchased the painting. Assuming that Kate can establish Wes's mental illness, and the court believes that Wes failed to understand the nature and effect of the transaction (genuinely believing he was borrowing the painting), then the contract will be deemed voidable by Wes, and he will be entitled to a return of his purchase price upon return of the painting. The fact that the gallery proprietor reasonably believed that Wes was perfectly mentally competent is irrelevant.

In the above example, the behavior of the proprietor of the art gallery is not in any way culpable. The contract is simply voidable because Wes did not have the requisite mental capacity to contract. He is, therefore, relieved of any contract obligation. Moreover, the painting could be returned. While the art gallery was deprived of its expectation interest, it suffered no further loss or injustice. Where such a loss or injustice would result—if, for example, Wes had lost the painting on the way home—then a court might enforce the contract, assuming it was made on fair terms and the gallery owner had no reason to know of Wes's incapacity.

A volitional incapacity is one in which a person is cognitive of the basic nature and effect of the transaction, but is simply incapable of acting in a reasonable manner with respect to this transaction. Thus, a volitional incapacity involves the ability to exercise reasonable control over one's decision-making process in the face of a particular potential bargain. Such an "incapacity" might be reasonably analogized to an "addiction." For obvious reasons, a volitional incapacity must be more than a simple fetish (e.g., "I simply cannot resist chocolate"), which makes "line drawing" particularly difficult in the case of this rule.

Unlike a "cognitive" incapacity, the effect of a "volitional" incapacity—even if proven—is further limited in that it renders a contract voidable only if the other contracting party had reason to know of the specific incapacity at issue. In effect, the rule governing "volitional" incapacity prevents one contracting party from taking unfair advantage of another's known mental weakness for a particular good or service. Consider the following example.

Example 20-3: Mel suffered from vivid delusions that his home was being invaded by intruders at night. He would often awake, certain that there was an intruder, and have to search the entire house before being able to go back to sleep. His regular treatment with a psychotherapist for his diagnosed "phobia" had provided little relief, so he decided to install a very sophisticated home security system. To that end, he visited Acme Home Security, where he fully explained his circumstances to Lee, a security sales consultant. Lee, recognizing Mel's extraordinary level of fear of intruders, sold Mel far more than he needed in the way of security devices, many of which were largely redundant and likely unnecessary. Lee fully explained that Mel did not necessarily need all of this equipment and would likely be fine with far less (thereby avoiding any allegation of fraud or misrepresentation), but of course knew that Mel's phobic fears would likely make it impossible for him to decline any of the offered devices.

Mel's purchase of the excessive security devices is likely voidable, because his phobic delusional fear of intruders would be deemed a "volitional" incapacity with respect to the devices purchased.

Attempts at line drawing between "cognitive" and "volitional" disabilities, as well as determinations of whether either exists, are often difficult. To some degree, diagnoses by mental health experts may be helpful, but even such experts may disagree as to distinctions and degree of either sort of disability. At bottom, determinations of whether a lack of mental capacity justifies relief from contract obligations will often require an attempt to weigh competing values. On one hand, we seek to protect the objectively reasonable expectations of contracting parties. On the other, we seek to protect those with diminished mental capacity from any hardship arising from an improvident contract.

Limitations based on Intoxication

If drawing fine lines is difficult with mental illness, such determinations are likely even more difficult with "intoxication." The obligation of an intoxicated person is "voidable," at the option of that person. However, any resulting "cognitive" of "volitional" incapacity is treated in the same manner, and either is given legal effect only if the other contracting party has reason to know of such an effect.

One might be tempted to suggest that an "intoxicated" individual created his or her own problem and deserves no protection from an ill-advised contract concluded while intoxicated. However, a party who seeks to conclude a contract with one he or she should know to be intoxicated is arguably even more culpable than the intoxicated party. Thus, the rule seemingly seeks a reasonable balance. When dealing with a party that objectively appears sober, the reasonable expectations of the party doing so are fully protected. When dealing with a party that objectively appears intoxicated, a reasonable person should not expect any resulting contract to be enforceable.

We can return now to the issue of intoxication raised earlier in Example 9-2 and the case of *Lucy v. Zehmer*.

Example 20-4: *Lucy v. Zehmer (redux)*

W.O. Lucy and A.H. Zehmer were chatting over a few beers at a local bar and restaurant. At some point, the conversation turned to a discussion of the Zehmers' farm, which they apparently agreed to sell to Lucy for $50,000. In addition to arguing that he had no intention to sell the farm (asserting that it was all a joke), Zehmer also asserted that he was intoxicated. Thus, any contract was voidable at his option.

Zehmer argued that he "was high as a Georgia pine" and that the purported agreement was nothing more than "bluffing" between "two doggoned drunks" (thus seeming to suggest that Lucy was also intoxicated). However, the court pointed out that Zehmer's assertion was inconsistent with his detailed memory of the events of the evening, as well as his wife's testimony that she suggested Zehmer drive Lucy home, inasmuch as the latter was not sufficiently sober to drive. Thus, the court concluded that Zehmer was not too intoxicated to conclude a valid contract.[2]

Notably, the combined testimony of Mr. and Mrs. Zehmer might have been more effective in establishing that Lucy was too intoxicated to contract. However, intoxication does not render a contract "void"—only "voidable," at the option of the intoxicated person—and Lucy had absolutely no interest in walking away from the contract.

---

[2] Lucy v. Zehmer, 196 Va. 493, 84 S.E.2d 516 (1954).

Summary of Basic Rule: the capacity of natural persons to contract[3]

- A natural person has the capacity to contract, except as follows:

  o Minors lack a full capacity to contract,

    ▪ Except for certain necessaries

  o Mental illness precludes a full capacity to contract,

    ▪ If such illness renders the person "cognitively" unable to understand the nature and consequences of the transaction,

      ▪ Unless the other party is without knowledge, the terms are fair, and non-enforcement would be unjust under the circumstances

    ▪ Or if such illness renders the person "volitionally" unable to act in a reasonable manner with respect to the transaction at issue,

      ▪ And the other party has reason to know

  o Intoxication precludes a full capacity to contract,

    ▪ If such intoxication renders the person cognitively or volitionally incapable,

      ▪ And the other party has reason to know

  o In each of the above exceptional cases, the contract is voidable at option of the person lacking capacity,

    ▪ Unless it is ratified after such capacity has been attained or restored

---

While each of the above rules varies in specific ways, all are based on the same principle. The very nature of a contract—based on the concept of knowing and voluntary consent—requires the capacity to provide such consent.

Unfairness

To the extent that the foregoing limits on capacity are intended to protect those most vulnerable to improvident bargains, why should we limit them? The parties negotiating a potential agreement will often come from very different backgrounds, have very different resources and negotiating skills, and have very different abilities to evaluate the fairness of any contemplated

---

[3] This basic rule is reflected in Restatement (Second) of Contracts §§ 12, 14, 15, and 16.

bargain. Should any of this matter in determining whether to enforce their contracts?

In fact, we have already seen at least a few distinctions in UCC Article 2 between the law applied to merchants and non-merchants. In effect, it is generally easier for a merchant to bind itself to something (e.g., a "firm offer" under § 2-205 or an "additional" term under § 2-207(2)) than for a non-merchant to do so. Should the law take this sort of distinction further, treating sophisticated parties differently than unsophisticated parties? The following case provides an excellent illustration of this dilemma.

FROM THE COURT

McKinnon v. Benedict

Supreme Court of Wisconsin (1968)
38 Wis.2d 607, 157 N.W.2d 665

[McKinnon brought an action to enjoin the Benedicts from operating a trailer park and campsite on property adjoining that owned by McKinnon.]

The Benedict property is approximately an 80-acre tract located on the shores of Mamie Lake . . . It is operated as a resort known as Bent's Camp. The Benedict property is completely surrounded by the McKinnon tract of approximately 1,170 acres. The McKinnons have lived on Mamie Lake since 1925, although at the present time they reside there only during the summer months and during the Christmas holidays. During the remainder of the year, the McKinnons reside in Arizona, where Roderick McKinnon is an investment counselor. He is a member of the Wisconsin State Bar and at various times practiced law with [two prestigious Milwaukee firms]. During World War II, he was in intelligence work for the United States government. He served with the United States State Department and was, at one time, vice president of Cleaver-Brooks Company.

Until 1961, Bent's Camp was operated by a Mr. and Mrs. L. L. Dorsey. This property . . . consists of 14 cabins and a main lodge . . . [on] a small, undeveloped parcel of timberland. [The Dorseys wished to sell the property and] located the Benedicts as prospective buyers. They, however, were in need of financial assistance to make the purchase, and they were referred to Roderick W. McKinnon, who agreed to loan the Benedicts the sum of $5,000 as a partial down payment. This loan was made on the basis of an understanding that the Benedicts would continue to operate Bent's Camp as an American Plan family resort. On August 31, 1960, McKinnon wrote a letter to the Benedicts incorporating the terms on which the advance was made:

Dear Roy:

It is my understanding that in consideration of my advancing you $5000 for use as a down payment on Bent's Camp we agree between one another as follows:

(1) You and Mrs. Benedict will sign a non-interest bearing note for $5000, due January 1, 1961, and a first mortgage on your cottage in Gogebic County, Michigan. . . .

(2) As soon as convenient after your acquisition of Bent's Camp, we will sign a recordable agreement providing that for a period of 25 years no trees will be cut between my land and Bent's Camp, . . .

(4) I will help you try to reach a satisfactory solution concerning the lease held by Mrs. J. Stuart Vair. I will also try to generate business for your camp and to otherwise assist you in getting the operation well organized.

If the foregoing meets with your approval, will you and Mrs. Benedict please sign below and return one copy for my files.

The approval was signed by both of the Benedicts, and the letter was returned to McKinnon. Thereafter, the Benedicts executed a note in the sum of $5,000 and a mortgage on their cottage property in Michigan. The promised $5,000 was shortly thereafter transmitted and used as a down payment. The loan was paid in full in the spring of 1961. The Benedicts thus had the use of the $5,000 from early September, 1960, to April, 1961, a period of about seven months. The Benedicts purchased the property from the Dorseys on a land contract at a price of $60,000. . . .

At the time the land contract was executed, Bent's Camp consisted of 14 cottages, only five of which could be used for resort purposes. Between 1961 and 1964, the Benedicts invested $20,000 in cottages, installing bathrooms and kitchens so that all of the cabins were habitable. Roy Benedict testified that during the period between 1961 and 1964, the income from the operations of the American Plan resort substantially decreased and that it became increasingly difficult to make the land-contract payments.

One of the conditions of the letter of August 31, 1960, was that McKinnon would attempt to reach a satisfactory solution concerning the lease held by Mrs. J. Stuart Vair. The record shows that Mrs. Vair held a fifty-year lease on one of the cabins at an annual rental of $5 per year. The record reveals only one attempt, and that unsuccessful, on the part of McKinnon to 'reach a satisfactory solution.' The agreement also provided that McKinnon would try to generate business for the camp and otherwise assist in getting the operation well organized. The record indicates no attempt whatsoever on the part of McKinnon to get the operation 'well organized.' There was evidence that at least one small group had spent a few days at Bent's Camp at the suggestion of McKinnon, but it is apparent that the amount of business generated by him was almost nil.

Because of financial pressures, the Benedicts, in the fall of 1964, decided to add a trailer park and facilities for a tent camp. . . . Roy Benedict bull-dozed the hills . . . and installed sewer, water, and electric facilities for 18 trailers . . . In the spring of 1965 work was commenced on a campsite on a hill located to the south of the cottages and across the bay from the McKinnon property. . . . When the McKinnons returned to Wisconsin in June of 1965, they became aware of the nature of the work done by Benedict and immediately commenced suit to enjoin defendants 'from the acts done or being done and uses to be made or being made' of the property. . .

Opinion

HEFFERNAN, Justice.

. . . The question posed, then, is whether the agreement was enforceable against the Benedicts. No action at law has been commenced for damages by virtue of the breach of the restrictions; and, in fact, the plaintiffs in their complaint claim that they have no adequate remedy at law. We are thus not confronted with the question of damages that may result from the breach of this contract and confine ourselves solely to the right of the plaintiffs to invoke the equitable remedy of specific performance, in this case the enjoining of the defendants from the breach of the contract.

[General legal authority] points out that:

'Courts of equity exercise discretionary power in the granting or with-holding of their extraordinary remedies, and this is particularly true in a case where injunctive relief is sought * * *. The relief is not given as a matter of course for any and every act done or threatened to the person or property of another; its granting rests in the sound discretion of the court to be exercised in accordance with well-settled equitable principles and in the light of all the facts and circumstances in the case * * *.'

[This court has] stated that an injunction 'should not be granted where the inconveniences and hardships caused outweigh the benefits.' It is frequently stated that an injunction will not be granted where to do so shocks the 'conscience' of the court. . . . '[S]pecific performance will not be decreed where the contract is unfair or unreasonable or is not founded on an adequate consideration.' . . . The facts in this case must be examined in light of these accepted principles of equity.

The bargain between the McKinnons and the Benedicts has proved to be a harsh one indeed. If the terms of the agreement of August 31, 1960, are to be enforced literally, the Benedicts have for a period of twenty-five years stripped themselves of the right to make an optimum and lawful use of their property. The agreement provides that no im-provements can be constructed closer to the McKinnon Property than those buildings and improvements that were in existence in 1960. This limits any possible expansion to the precise lakeshore area occupied by the buildings of Bent's Camp on that date. . . . McKinnon by this agree-ment sought the maintenance of the exact status quo for a period of twenty-five years. . . .

There was clear testimony that Benedict found difficulty in meeting his land-contract obligations, and his efforts to construct a campsite and trailer camp were motivated by the desire to put the resort on a more stable finan-cial basis. While it is understandable that McKinnon may object to the

erection of a trailer park and a campsite on adjacent property, nevertheless, they are legal and proper uses, assuming that they conform with
the ordinances and statutes and do not constitute a nuisance; and any
contract that seeks to prohibit them on a neighbor's property must be
supported by consideration that has some relationship to the detriment
to be sustained by the property owner whose uses are thus curtailed.

The great hardship sought to be imposed upon the Benedicts is apparent. What was the consideration in exchange for this deprivation of use?
The only monetary consideration was the granting of a $5,000 loan,
interest free, for a period of seven months. The value of this money for
that period of time, if taken at the same interest rate as the 5 percent
used on the balance of the land contract, is approximately $145; and it
should be noted that this was not an unsecured loan, since McKinnon
took a mortgage on the cottage property of the Benedicts in Michigan.
In addition, McKinnon stated that he would 'help you try' to reach
a solution of the problem posed by Mrs. Vair's occupancy of one of
the cottages on a fifty-year lease at $5 per year. His one attempt, as
stated above, was a failure; and McKinnon's promise to generate business resulted in an occupancy by only one group for less than a week.
For this pittance and these feeble attempts to help with the operational
problems of the camp, the Benedicts have sacrificed their right to make
lawful and reasonable use of their property.

In oral argument it was pointed out that the value of the $5,000 loan
could not be measured in terms of the interest value of the money, since,
without this advance, Benedict would have been unable to purchase the
camp at all. To our mind, this is evidence of the fact that Benedict was
not able to deal at arm's length with McKinnon, for his need for these
funds was obviously so great that he was willing to enter into a contract that results in gross inequities. Lord Chancellor Northington said
'necessitous men are not, truly speaking, free men.' Vernon v. Bethell
(1762), 2 Eden 110, 113.

We find that the inadequacy of consideration is so gross as to be unconscionable and a bar to the plaintiffs' invocation of the extraordinary
equitable powers of the court.

While there is no doubt that there are benefits from this agreement to McKinnon, they are more than outweighed by the oppressive terms that would be imposed upon the Benedicts. [The aesthetic detriments] of which the McKinnons complain, that would be cognizable in an equity action, [are] minimal, while the damage done to the Benedicts is severe.

Considering all the factors—the inadequacy of the consideration, the small benefit that would be accorded the McKinnons, and the oppressive conditions imposed upon the Benedicts—we conclude that this contract failed to meet the test of reasonableness that is the *sine qua non* of the enforcement of rights in an action in equity.

. . . [A]lthough a contract is harsh, oppressive, and unconscionable, it may nevertheless be enforceable at law; but, in the discretion of the court, equitable remedies will not be enforced against one who suffers from such harshness and oppression.

A fair reading of the transcript indicates no sharp practice, dishonesty, or overreaching on the part of McKinnon. However, there was a wide disparity between the business experience of the parties. McKinnon was a man of stature in the legal field, an investment counselor, a former officer of a major corporation, and had held posts of responsibility with the United States government, while, insofar as the record shows, Benedict was a retail jeweler and a man of limited financial ability. He no doubt overvalued the promises of McKinnon to assist in getting the operation 'well organized' and to solve the lease problem and to 'generate business.' These factors, in view of Benedict's financial inability to enter into an arms-length transaction, may be explanatory of the reason for the agreement, but the agreement viewed even as of the time of its execution was unfair and based upon inadequate consideration. We, therefore, have no hesitancy in denying the plaintiffs the equitable remedy of injunction.

CASE QUESTIONS

(1) In this case, McKinnon sought "equitable" relief in the form of an injunction (or specific performance by the Benedicts of their contract promises). Did the court rule that McKinnon would have been precluded from seeking a "legal" remedy of damages against the Benedicts for breach of contract?

a. What if McKinnon had sought damages and introduced undisputed evidence that the value of his own land had been reduced by $1,000,000 as a result of the Benedicts actions?

b. Why should a court refuse to grant an "equitable" remedy under circumstances in which it would award "legal" damages? Under what circumstances, if any, should the nature of the remedy sought make any difference? We will further explore this difference in Chapter 8. However, the legal/equitable distinction can be an important one in a variety of different contexts.

(2) From the facts of the case, do you believe that McKinnon would have concluded the contract with Benedict if he had known in advance that a court would not have granted the relief requested?

a. Assuming you would agree that at least perhaps the answer is "no," is this a desirable result? If the answer to this question seems easy, think a bit more. It should not be an easy question to answer, whatever you believe to be the "correct" answer.

b. The court quotes Lord Chancellor Northington in saying that "necessitous men are not, truly speaking, free men." Is the court's use of the idea of "necessity" consistent with the treatment of the issue with respect to the capacity of minors?

(3) Do you believe the court's decision was a sound one? If so, how far would you take this reasoning? Should it extend to legal claims as well?

UCC Article 2

UCC Article 2 does not address issues of capacity, thereby leaving the issue to be supplemented by the common law. In fact, most validity issues are left to the common law, with one notable exception, which we will address in Lesson 23.

The CISG

The CISG does not govern issues of validity. In a cross-border transaction, these issues might be governed by the law of either party or by a third body of law. This question is resolved by reference to conflicts or laws principles (also called the rules of private international law), which are beyond the scope of this course. The key, for our purposes in this course, is that the CISG does not govern issues of validity. **STOP NOW and READ CISG Article 4(a) below.**

CISG ARTICLE 4(a)

This Convention governs only the formation of the contract of sale and the rights and obligations of the seller and the buyer arising from such a contract. In particular, except as otherwise expressly provided in this Convention, it is not concerned with:

(a) the validity of the contract or of any of its provisions or of any usage;

No further reference will be made to the CISG with respect to additional issues of validity, as they are raised throughout this chapter.

APPLYING THE RULES

Problem 1: Kiefer was married and raising a child, though he had not yet reached the age of majority. He purchased a car from Fred Howe Motors and, in doing so, signed a contract in which he lied about his age (asserting he had reached the age of majority). Kiefer required the car to drive back and forth to his job and also used it for other family transportation needs. Ultimately, however, he was unhappy with the car and promptly returned it to Fred Howe Motors upon reaching the age of majority and sought to recover the price he had paid.

Is Kiefer entitled to a return of the price of the car? If so, is Fred Howe Motors entitled to receive anything for Kiefer's use of the car?

If Kiefer had waited to return the car until 1 year after reaching the age of majority, would this change the above result?

The facts of this problem are loosely based on the issues raised in the case of *Kiefer v. Fred Howe Motors, Inc.*, 39 Wis. 2d 20, 158 N.W. 2d 288 (1968).

Problem 2: Grace Ortelere took a leave from her teaching position due to a mental disorder (involuntary psychosis, melancholia type, and perhaps cerebral arteriosclerosis). Her psychiatrist testified that she could not think rationally, and it was virtually impossible for her to make decisions of any kind. At the same time Grace took leave, her husband quit his job to stay home and care for her.

Grace had a pension provided by her employer of $70,000, which entitled her to $375 per month, and left any unpaid amount to her husband upon her death. However, soon after taking leave, Grace borrowed the maximum amount allowable, $9,000, and accelerated the monthly payments to the highest amount possible, $450 per month. The cost of Grace's election to borrow, while increasing monthly benefits, was the loss of her husband's rights to any unpaid benefits upon her death. Other than the pension fund, Grace and her husband had few assets or other significant sources of income. Grace's communications with the pension administrators clearly established that she fully understood the nature and effect of the election she was making.

Grace died two months after making the election. Is her agreement electing a change in benefits voidable by her husband, as the successor to her legal rights?

The facts of this problem are loosely based on the issues raised in the case of *Ortelere v. Teachers' Retirement Board*, 25 N.Y. 2d 196, 250 N.E. 2d 460 (1969). *The questions involving pension rights raised in this case are subject to various statutory protections today, but this problem is solely intended to address these questions as a matter of basic contract law.*

Lesson 21: Pre-Existing Duty Rule, Duress, and Undue Influence

Objectives and Expected Learning Outcomes

In this lesson, we will return to the "pre-existing duty rule," first encountered in Lesson 6. You will learn more about the nature of this rule, including an exception to its application. You will further learn that, in certain circumstances, the existence of the sort of "one-sided" bargain addressed by the pre-existing duty rule may also give rise to concerns about the nature of the process by which a bargain was modified or concluded. Finally, you will learn to distinguish between the issue of "consideration" raised by the pre-existing duty rule, and the issue of "consent" raised by the "process" concerns addressed in this lesson.

The Pre-Existing Duty Rule Revisited

As explained in Lesson 6, the common law generally requires consideration to support a new or modified promise, in much the same manner as the original promise. This rule is called the "pre-existing duty rule," to emphasize the rule that mere performance of a "pre-existing duty" will not serve as consideration to bind the other party to a new or modified promise. To be binding as a matter of contract, the modified promise of one party requires new consideration from the other party.

In this lesson, we will further explore the issue of seemingly one-sided modifications. In what circumstances might an absence of new consideration on one side of the modified bargain suggest a less than voluntary bargaining "process"? If the bargaining process has in fact been tainted in some manner, there may be additional reasons—beyond the pre-existing duty rule—for declining to enforce the otherwise apparent bargain. We may also find this same sort of "taint" in an original bargain in some cases.

Under other circumstances, an entirely different question may arise. When might we enforce what appears to be a fairly modified bargain under unique circumstances—notwithstanding a lack of new consideration on one side? If a resulting bargain appears to reflect a fair and equitable adaptation to unexpected circumstances, perhaps an exception to the pre-existing duty rule is appropriate.

We begin with the issue of a one-sided modification in which the modification was "negotiated" in a context that calls into question the voluntariness of any purported consent.

Example 21-1: *Alaska Packers' Association v. Domenico*

Alaska Packers contracted with a group of sailors and fisherman to sail from San Francisco to Pyramid Harbor, Alaska, where they would fish for salmon. Each of the workers was to be paid $50 for the specified work. Upon arrival in Alaska, however, the workers demanded twice the pay ($100) for the same work, refusing to perform any work unless their demands were met. With no other workers available anywhere near Pyramid Harbor, the superintendent of the workers signed an agreement increasing the workers' pay, as demanded.

When the ship workers returned to San Francisco, they were paid only the original $50 amount, and they sued for the other additional $50 agreed to in Alaska. The court ruled against the workers on the basis of the pre-existing duty rule, explaining that the workers had done nothing more for the promised $100 than they had already promised to do for the original $50.[4]

The facts underlying the case were actually quite sympathetic to the workers in view of the harsh working conditions at the time. However, as a matter of contract law, the workers' case was entirely unsympathetic. They threatened to breach their contract, under circumstances in which the result would have caused a serious loss to their employer, who had no option for replacing them and could not realistically expect to recover from them on any claim for breach of contract. In short, the employer had no real choice but to capitulate. This brings us to the doctrine of "duress" as a defense to contract enforcement.

---

[4] Alaska Packers' Association v. Domenico, 117 F. 99 (9th Cir. 1902).

Duress

The *Alaska Packers* case provides one example of circumstances under which "duress" may arise. However, there are a variety of others, as well. As with a contract concluded by one without capacity, a contract that is a product of "duress" is voidable at the option of the victim of the duress.

A contract is said to be procured through duress when a "party's manifestation assent is induced by an improper threat by the other party that leaves the victim no reasonable alternative."[5] A threat is improper in a commercial context when it involves a threat to breach a contract solely in an effort to extract a better bargain from one's contracting partner—in effect, a "bad faith" breach intended to change the deal in one's favor. This is the sort of "duress" that was arguably present in the Alaska Packers case.

Another, perhaps more obvious, form of duress involves a threat of criminal or tortious behavior for the purpose of extracting assent to a purported bargain.

> **Example 21-2:** Jack points a gun at Jill and says, "Sign this contract, or I will shoot." Jill of course signs the contract in order to avoid getting shot. However, no one would suggest that she actually "consented" to anything—other than not getting shot.
>
> The contract is voidable by Jill, as the victim of Jack's threat to shoot her, a criminal act.

Of course, Jack has also likely committed a crime and a tort, but those are issues for your other courses.

Two final forms of duress involve misuse of civil process or a threat of criminal prosecution. You will likely recall in Example 5-1 our earlier discussion of a party's willingness to forego a civil claim as consideration to support enforcement of a settlement agreement. Boehm's agreement to forego her civil claim served as consideration to bind Fiege to his promised payments—even though the claim was later determined to be wrong—because Boehm had a good faith belief in the validity of her claim at the time

---

[5] Restatement (Second) of Contracts § 175(1).

of the bargain. In contrast, any bargain arising from a threat by Boehm of a civil claim in which she did not honestly believe, or a criminal prosecution (which only the state has the power to decide upon) would be voidable at the option of Fiege. Moreover, the misuse of criminal process to extort a bargain may itself be a crime.

One of the more difficult issues addressing a "duress" defense is determining whether the victim had "no reasonable alternative." The proverbial "gun to the head" case of duress is easy. No one would suggest that the victim had any alternative to acquiescence to the gun holder's demands. However, economic duress arising from a bad faith breach of contract can raise more difficult questions.

We can return to the *Alaska Packers* case to look at a few of these. If other workers had been available, then the employer would have presumably had a reasonable alternative available in hiring those workers as substitutes for those who refused to work as agreed (of course, this might raise additional issues in the context of an organized labor strike, but that was not the case here). In this case, however, no such alternative was available.

The employer also might have had the alternative of simply sailing back to San Francisco and suing for damages, thus obtaining the benefit of its bargain through legal enforcement. In this case, there was little, if any, likelihood of collecting such a judgment from its workers, so this option did not constitute a reasonable alternative. However, in some commercial cases of duress, it may. The idea of simply turning around, returning to port, and suing also raises an additional issue.

In Chapter 8, you will learn that a party seeking damages for breach of contract is expected to take all reasonable steps to minimize such damages. In *Alaska Packers*, the best way to minimize any damages was to go ahead and fish in Alaska, promising the workers what they demanded and sorting out the legal issues later. Thus, even if the employer might have thought it realistic to sue and recover from its workers, returning home without fishing was not likely a reasonable alternative.

The most frequent "reasonable alternative" in the case of "economic duress" is to seek a substitute service or good, thereby mitigating or minimizing any loss, and then sue the breaching party for any loss that accrues. When such an option is reasonably available, then it cannot be said that the improper threat left the victim without any reasonable alternative, and the defense of duress will likely fail. Instead, the purported victim will be deemed to have freely (albeit somewhat uncomfortably) consented to a fully enforceable contract.

Summary of Basic Rule: duress[6]

- A contract procured through an improper threat, leaving the victim no reasonable alternative to the coerced assent, is voidable by the victim

    o   A threat is improper if what is threatened is a:

        ▪   Bad faith breach of contract with victim of threat;

        ▪   Crime or tort, or would result in the same; or

        ▪   Criminal prosecution or bad faith civil prosecution

- A victim has no reasonable alternative when the victim cannot reasonably respond to the threat in a manner other than simple capitulation

---

Invalidity based on "duress" and the "pre-existing duty" rule raise fully independent issues, though they are often found together. Sometimes a case will clearly present one, or the other, or both. However, sometimes the question of duress is less clear.

Terminating the "Existing" Contract before Concluding Another

The "pre-existing duty" rule of course becomes irrelevant if the pre-existing duty is extinguished. Two parties to any contract may mutually decide to terminate that contract. If so, then they would seem to be starting fresh, with no existing duties to each other. Why, however, would a party terminate an existing contract, knowing the new contract would be less favorable than the original?

---

[6] This basic rule is reflected in Restatement (Second) of Contracts §§ 175(1) and 176(1).

FROM THE COURT

Schwartzreich v. Bauman-Basch, Inc.

New York Court of Appeals (1921)
231 N.Y. 196

CRANE, J.

[In August, 1917, Bauman-Basch, Inc. entered into a 12-month employment agreement with Schwartzreich, to begin in November. Under the contract, Schwartzreich was to design coats and wraps, and Bauman-Basch was to pay him $90 per week. The written agreement further required that Schwartzreich "shall devote his entire time and attention to the business of the party of the first part, and shall use his best energies and endeavors in the furtherance of its business."]

In October the plaintiff was offered more money by another concern. Mr. Bauman, an officer of the Bauman-Basch, Inc., says that in that month he heard that the plaintiff was going to leave and thereupon had with him the following conversation:

> A. I called him in the office, and I asked him, 'Is that true that you want to leave us?' and he said 'Yes,' and I said, 'Mr. Schwartzreich, how can you do that; you are under contract with us?' He said, 'Somebody offered me more money.' * * * I said, 'How much do they offer you?' He said, 'They offered him $115 a week.' * * * I said, 'I cannot get a designer now, and, in view of the fact that I have to send my sample line out on the road, I will give you a hundred dollars a week rather than to let you go.' He said, 'If you will give me $100, I will stay.'

Thereupon Mr. Bauman dictated to his stenographer a new contract, dated October 17, 1917, in the exact words of the first contract and running for the same period, the salary being $100 a week, which contract was duly executed by the parties and witnessed. Duplicate originals were kept by the plaintiff and defendant.

Simultaneously with the signing of this new contract the plaintiff's copy of the old contract was either given to or left with Mr. Bauman. He testifies that the plaintiff gave him the paper but that he did not take it from him. The signatures to the old contract plaintiff tore off at the time according to Mr. Bauman.

The plaintiff's version as to the execution of the new contract is as follows:

> A. I told Mr. Bauman that I have an offer from Scheer & Mayer of $110 a week, and I said to him: 'Do you advise me as a friendly matter—will you advise me as a friendly matter what to do; you see I have a contract with you, and I should not accept the offer of $110 a week, and I ask you, as a matter of friendship, do you advise me to take it or not.' At the minute he did not say anything, but the day afterwards he came to me in and he said, 'I will give you $100 a week, and I want you to stay with me.' I said: 'All right, I will accept it; it is very nice of you that you do that, and I appreciate it very much.'

The plaintiff says that on the 17th of October, when the new contract was signed, he gave his copy of the old contract back to Mr. Bauman, who said: 'You do not want this contract any more because the new one takes its place.'

The plaintiff remained in the defendant's employ until the following December, when he was discharged. He brought this action under the contract of October 17th for his damages.

The defense, insisted upon through all the courts, is that there was no consideration for the new contract as the plaintiff was already bound under his agreement of August 31, 1917, to do the same work for the same period at $90 a week.

The trial justice submitted to the jury the question whether there was a cancellation of the old contract and charged as follows:

'If you find that the $90 contract was prior to or at the time of the execution of the $100 contract canceled and revoked by the parties by their mutual consent, then it is your duty to find that there was a consideration for the making of the contract in suit, viz., the $100 contract, and, in that event, the plaintiff would be entitled to your verdict for such damages as you may find resulted proximately, naturally, and necessarily in consequence of the plaintiff's discharge prior to the termination of the contract period of which I shall speak later on.'

Defendant's counsel thereupon excepted to that portion of the charge in which the court permitted the jury to find that the prior contract may have been canceled simultaneously with the execution of the other agreement. Again the court said:

'The test question is whether by word or by act, either prior to or at the time of the signing of the $100 contract, these parties mutually agreed that the old contract from that instant should be null and void.' . . .

Can a contract of employment be set aside or terminated by the parties to it and a new one made or substituted in its place? If so, is it competent to end the one and make the other at the same time?

It has been repeatedly held that a promise made to induce a party to do that which he is already bound by contract to perform is without consideration. But the cases . . . also recognize that a contract may be canceled by mutual consent and a new one made. . . .

If this which we are now holding were not the rule, parties having once made a contract would be prevented from changing it no matter how willing and desirous they might be to do so, unless the terms conferred an additional benefit to the promisee.

All concede that an agreement may be rescinded by mutual consent and a new agreement made thereafter on any terms to which the parties may assent. . . .

The same effect follows in our judgment from a new contract entered into at the same time the old one is destroyed and rescinded by mutual consent. The determining factor is the rescission by consent. Provided this is the expressed and acted upon intention, the time of the rescission, whether a moment before or at the same time as the making of the new contract, is unimportant.

The decisions are numerous and divergent where one of the parties to a contract refuses to perform unless paid an additional amount. . . . In none of these cases, however, was there a full and complete rescission of the old contract and it is this with which we are dealing in this case. Rescission is not presumed; it is expressed; the old contract is not continued with modifications; it is ended and a new one made.

[In contrast,] [t]he almost universal rule is that without any express rescission of the old contract the promise is made simply for additional compensation, making the new promise a mere nudum pactum.'

As before stated, in this case we have an express rescission and a new contract.

There is no reason that we can see why the parties to a contract may not come together and agree to cancel and rescind an existing contract, making a new one in its place. We are also of the opinion that reason and authority support the conclusion that both transactions can take place at the same time.

For the reasons here stated, the charge of the trial court was correct, and the judgments of the Appellate Division and the Appellate Term should be affirmed, with costs.

CASE QUESTIONS

(1) Upon what legal issue did the court focus its analysis? Was this the proper focus?

  a. Consider first the court's discussion of the pre-existing duty rule in the context of a mutual agreement to terminate the original contract. Do you agree with the court's statement of the legal rules applicable to this specific question?

  b. Now, consider the question of "duress." Does this raise a question about the nature of any mutual "consent" to terminate the original agreement?

  c. Consider the testimony of both Bauman and Schwartzreich. Which, if either, might support a finding of "duress"? Under the facts most favorable to Bauman-Basch, did Bauman put up sufficient resistance to the threatened breach to claim "duress"? To what degree should he be required to resist under the circumstances? To what extent should it matter who initiated the conversation about a potential modification of the agreement?

(2) Judge Chase dissented from the decision of the court, but his reasons for doing so are not included in the decision. Put yourself in the position of Judge Chase. How might you frame such a dissent?

The court's foregoing explanation of the effect of mutual termination is of course absolutely accurate. This discussion, however, begs the question of whether Bauman's consent was in fact voluntary. This is the question raised by the issue of "duress."

The foregoing case is useful in helping to highlight the distinction between the pre-existing duty rule and the defense of duress. The application of the former to a one-sided modification may, in some circumstances, suggest the possibility of the latter. However, one may also find a one-sided bargain without any indication of duress, thus raising the question of whether an exception to the pre-existing duty rule might perhaps be warranted.

An Exception to the Pre-Existing Duty Rule in the Absence of Duress

In the absence of any process concerns, one might reasonably question whether certain one-sided modifications might be enforced. For example, the parties to an existing contract may discover unanticipated circumstances that change the nature of the bargain, making one party's performance considerably more challenging than anticipated. We will discover, in Chapter 9, that some such circumstances may even fully excuse performance. However, the parties may avoid any such question by simply agreeing to modify the original bargain to reflect these newly discovered circumstances. If the resulting change is fair and equitable, then there seems little reason to decline to enforce the parties' bargain.

Example 21-3: *Watkins & Son v. Carrig*

Watkins & Son contracted to excavate a cellar for Carrig at a fixed price. However, Watkins unexpectedly encountered solid rock. Watkins and Carrig spoke about the difficulty presented by the removal of the solid rock and agreed upon a price for that portion of the work to be nine times the original pay rate. When Watkins completed the work, Carrig refused to pay the higher price earlier agreed upon.

There was no indication that the parties had mutually terminated their prior agreement before concluding the subsequent one. However, there was no indication either of duress. Carrig simply acknowledged the unanticipated difficulty and agreed to pay the higher rate. The court found the modified bargain fair and equitable under the circumstances and, therefore, enforced the modified bargain, notwithstanding the lack of consideration to support the increased price for the rock excavation.[7]

Summary of Basic Rule: enforceable modification without consideration[8]

- A modified promise in exchange for a pre-existing executory duty is binding, notwithstanding any lack of new consideration, if:

  o The modification arises from circumstances not reasonably anticipated at the time the contract was concluded; and

  o The modification is fair and equitable under the circumstances

---

Other Issues Involving a Pre-Existing Duty

As earlier explained in Lesson 4, the requirement of consideration applies only to executory promises. Once a promise has been fully performed, a court will not reverse the effects of such performance based on a lack of consideration. This limit applies equally to any test for consideration under the pre-existing duty rule. Once a modified promise has been fully performed, any lack of consideration is no longer an issue. This result also highlights another distinction between the pre-existing duty rule and duress.

We can return to the *Alaska Packers* case, but change one fact. Suppose the workers were actually paid the modified $100 amount in Alaska and the employer sought to recover the extra $50 upon their return to San Francisco. Under the pre-existing duty rule, the employer would have absolutely no case, because its modified promise no longer remained executory.

---

[7] Watkins & Son v. Carrig, 91 N.H. 459, 21 A.2d 591 (1941).
[8] This basic rule is reflected in Restatement (Second) of Contracts § 89(a).

The additional $50 at issue would have already been paid. In contrast, the employer would have retained the right to seek "rescission" of the modified promise and return of the extra $50 by asserting that the modified promise was extracted through duress and was therefore voidable at the option of the employer. The fact that a promise has already been performed has no effect on a claim of duress.

The executory limitation on the application of the pre-existing duty rule raises another interesting issue with respect to partial payment of an amount due and owing. You will recall, from Example 11-1, an offer by Pattberg to reduce Petterson's debt obligation in exchange for early payment of that debt. As such, Pattberg's offered discount contemplated modified performance by Petterson as well (early payment). Suppose, however, that a creditor offered to accept a lesser amount in payment of a debt, without demanding anything more from the debtor than already promised?

Example 21-4: *Foakes v. Beer*

Foakes owed a debt to Beer, who agreed to forego interest if Foakes paid the principal debt as agreed. After Foakes had done so, Beer demanded the interest as well. In a very technical and quite controversial application of the pre-existing duty rule, the House of Lords ruled that Beer was entitled to the interest. There was no question that Foakes had done nothing more than that which he was already legally obligated to do. However, it was less clear whether Beer's promise remained executory.

Foakes had fully performed to extinguish the debt, so it would seem that no part of the modified contract remained executory. However, the House of Lords viewed Beer as having promised "if you will pay the principal as agreed, I will then forego my right to interest." Thus, there was a brief moment in time, after which Foakes had paid, but before Beer had forgiven the interest. During this time, Beer's promise remained fully executory, thus entitling her to assert that her promise to forego the interest was not supported by consideration.[9]

9 Foakes v. Beer, 9 App.Cas. 605 (House of Lords 1884).

Of far more practical significance, the decision in Foakes v. Beer seems to ignore the very real difference between a debt paid and a debt owed. A legal right to receive money is, as a practical matter, often less valuable than the actual receipt of that money—especially when the financial ability of the debtor to pay may be in doubt. It is hard to imagine a court today deciding this issue in the same manner as the case above. Moreover, a party seeking a payment discount will almost always vary the required payment in some meaningful way, thereby providing consideration to support the promised reduction.

A similar, though slightly different, question is clearly answered by statute. It is called "accord and satisfaction." This issue requires a very brief detour into UCC Article 3 (governing negotiable instruments, generally). **STOP NOW and READ UCC §§ 3-311(a) and (b) below.**

UCC § 3-311

(a) If a person against whom a claim is asserted proves that (i) that person in good faith tendered an instrument to the claimant as full satisfaction of the claim, (ii) the amount of the claim was unliquidated or subject to a bona fide dispute, and (iii) the claimant obtained payment of the instrument, the following subsections apply.

(b) Unless subsection (c) [certain exceptions] applies, the claim is discharged if the person against whom the claim is asserted proves that the instrument or an accompanying written communication contained a conspicuous statement to the effect that the instrument was tendered as full satisfaction of the claim.

This statute only addresses a debt or claim that is unliquidated (in effect, not precisely determined as to amount) and/or subject to a bona fide dispute over whether it is owed. If so, the debtor can tender an amount in full satisfaction, or settlement, of the debt or claim. As long as the tender conspicuously notes that it is being offered in full satisfaction of the debt or claim, the recipients' acceptance of the tender (e.g., cashing or depositing a check) amounts to an acceptance of an offer of settlement and extinguishes a debt.

Finally, it should be noted that the pre-existing duty rule also applies with respect to duties to third parties. An existing duty to a third party cannot serve as consideration to bind the promise of another for the same duty.

This rule is merely an extension of the basic rule that consideration must consist of an act not already legally required or forbearance of a right not legally barred (i.e., a legal detriment).

We now return to a slightly different "process" concern. Some circumstances may not justify a finding of duress, but may nevertheless raise questions as to the voluntariness of consent. These circumstances rarely, if ever, arise in relation to contract modification, and instead relate to the broader circumstances surrounding any purported "consent."

Undue Influence

In some circumstances, the free will of a purported contracting party may be overcome, even though the requirements of duress are not met. "Undue influence" involves persuasion that overcomes a person's subjective free will, without convincing the person's objective judgment. When one party effectively "dominates" the will of another by virtue of the relationship between the parties and the circumstances of the interaction, any resulting contract is said to be the product of "undue influence" and, therefore, voidable by the victim.[10]

Example 21-5: Pam is a career high school teacher at Gamma High School. A student has gone to the school administration asserting sexually inappropriate conduct by Pam. On a Friday afternoon after a week of classes, and unexpected by Pam, the school Principal, District Superintendent, and outside counsel to the school district all arrive at Pam's house. Pam is exhausted and entirely unaware of the student's accusations. When Pam answers her door and invites her guests in, they immediately confront her over the accusations and demand that she sign an agreement resigning her position with Gamma High (and mutually terminating her long-term contract with the school district). She is told that she must sign the agreement then and there, or the school district will go public with the accusations on Saturday. She denies the accusations and says she would like to consult with someone before deciding

---

[10] *See* Restatement (Second) of Contracts § 177.

what to do, but is told that there is no time, and she must make a decision—now or never. Counsel for the school district also points out that, under her contract, inappropriate sexual conduct is grounds for termination of the agreement. Overwhelmed by the circumstances, Pam signs the agreement. The next morning, however, she has a different view and wishes to fight the charges.

The actions of the school administrators and counsel do not likely amount to duress, because they merely threatened to enforce a termination right within the contract and to speak publicly about a matter of importance, based on an apparent good faith belief in the accusations by the student. However, the contract is nevertheless likely voidable by Pam based on the undue influence exercised by those confronting her under the specific circumstances of that confrontation.

One might reasonably analogize the rationale of the rule regarding "undue influence" to that limiting the capacity of one who is mentally infirm or intoxicated. In effect, a party subject to "undue influence" lacks the volitional capacity to make an objective decision.

UCC Article 2

You should recall, from Lesson 6, that modification of a contract governed by Article 2 does not require any new consideration, as provided in UCC § 2-209(1). However, the common law doctrine of duress may apply equally to a transaction otherwise governed by Article 2. The application of duress, within the context of a transaction governed by Article 2, helps to highlight the difference between the two distinctly separate issues—consideration (and the "pre-existing duty" rule) and duress.

The common law and UCC Article 2 apply different rules with respect to consideration. The common law generally requires consideration to support a contract modification, while Article 2 does not. The common law rule regarding duress, however, applies with equal force to all transactions, whether otherwise governed by the common law or Article 2.

One might reasonably compare the approaches of the common law and UCC Article 2 as giving rise to differing presumptions. When one considers the pre-existing duty rule, along with its exception reflected in Restatement (Second) of Contracts § 89, it would seem that the common law presumes some sort of process irregularity—subject to contrary proof—when a purported consideration is not supported by consideration. In contrast, UCC § 2-209(1) seems to presume actual consent, subject to contrary proof of some sort of process irregularity.

The CISG

Like UCC § 2-209(1), CISG Article 29(1) was addressed earlier in Lesson 6. CISG Article 29(1) does not require consideration. In this respect, it is much like UCC § 2-209(1). However, the CISG does not address issues of validity, as explained in the last lesson by reference to Article 4(a). Thus, any question of duress is left to otherwise applicable law.

APPLYING THE RULES

Problem 1: Loral Corporation had a contract in 1965 to sell radar sets to the U.S. Navy, an important customer. Loral sought suppliers for certain component parts and contracted with Austin Instruments for some, but not all, of those parts. Loral then obtained a second contract with the Navy in 1966 for more radar sets and again sought suppliers. Austin indicated its desire to supply all of the component parts for the 1966 contract, but was told by Loral that it would be limited to those parts on which it provided the lowest bid of parts meeting the specifications.

The next day, an Austin representative told Loral that it would cease ongoing deliveries under the existing 1965 contract, until and unless Loral agreed to pay a price increase under the 1965 contract and further agreed to contract with Austin for all of the parts required for the 1966 contract. Austin then ceased deliveries under the 1965 contract while awaiting an answer from Loral.

Loral immediately began to inquire as to whether any other supplier could provide the parts needed for the 1965 contract. Numerous alternative parts suppliers were available. However, Loral contacted only those with which it had prior business experience as suppliers. A number of these suppliers could have provided the parts in question, but none were able to perform in time to allow Loral to meet its own delivery deadlines to the Navy, and Loral's contract with the Navy included penalties for late delivery. Following this inquiry, Loral agreed to Austin's demands.

Austin resumed performance of the 1965 contract and was fully paid by Loral at the increased price. After Austin completed all of its deliveries under the 1966 contract, Loral ceased any remaining payments to Austin. In the ensuing litigation, Loral made no claim for damages under the 1966 contract, but sought to recover the amount of the price increase demanded by and paid to Austin under the 1965 contract. Is Loral entitled to recover this amount?

The facts of this problem are loosely based on the issues raised in the case of *Austin Instrument, Inc. v. Loral Corp.*, 29 N.Y.2d 124, 324 N.Y.S.2d 22, 272 N.E.2d 533 (1971).

Problem 2: Fay contracted to design and build a house for Hal on a steep mountainside parcel of land owned by Hal. When Fay began excavating in preparation to pour the foundation, she realized that the design would have to be modified significantly to insure the stability of the house on the hillside. The soil conditions were not sufficiently firm to support the house at this steep gradient, and the changes in the design would add $200,000 to the cost of building the house (originally, $800,000).

Fay contacted Hal and explained the problem, providing him with a set of revised plans reflecting the proposed changes. She said "I will cover the cost of changing the plans, along with my architect, but I can't cover the additional $200,000 in construction costs. It will put me out of business." Hal said "I don't know. It seems to me that you assumed the risk when you agreed to a 'design-build' contract, and you obviously knew my lot was on a mountain side." Fay replied "Yes, I knew you were on a mountainside, but I did not realize how sandy the soil was. That was completely unexpected. And there is simply no possible way I can do this at the original price—you don't seem to understand that." Hal said he would get back to her in a few days. Hal then immediately faxed the revised plans provided by Fay to Gary, another builder Hal knew, and asked for a bid. A few days later, Gary provided Hal with a bid of $1.1 million. Hal then called Fay and said "I agree to pay the additional $200,000."

Fay promptly completed the house according to the revised plans. If Hal refuses to pay more than the original $800,000, can Fay recover the additional $200,000? Suppose that Hal, instead, mailed a check to Fay for $900,000, along with a letter conspicuously stating: "The enclosed check represents payment in full for the house you built for me and fully satisfies any and all payment obligations I may have to you in any way connected to the design and construction of the house. If you accept this offer of settlement, you may cash the check." If Fay cashes the check, can she sue Hal for the remaining $100,000?

Suppose, instead, Hal had accepted Gary's bid and sued Fay for the difference? Should he be able to recover the $300,000? Assuming he is entitled to recover something from Fay, can you think of any basis for reducing that amount? There may be more than one.

Lesson 22: Misrepresentation

Objectives and Expected Learning Outcomes

In this lesson, you will learn about various forms in which a party's assent to a contract may be voidable based on a misrepresentation by the other party. You will further learn that a misrepresentation may take a variety of forms and will explore the extent to which a bare failure of one party to disclose a fact unknown to the other party may constitute a misrepresentation. Finally, you will learn and apply the additional elements required to render a contract voidable based on a misrepresentation.

No General Duty to Disclose

As a general rule, parties negotiating an agreement have no duty to each other to disclose facts one may know and the other may not. You will likely recall from Lesson 14 the general rule that no duty of good faith arises until after the parties have concluded a contract, and these two general rules are fully consistent. A classic application of the general rule declining to require disclosure can be found in the following case.

Example 22-1: *Laidlaw v. Organ*

Organ was engaged in negotiating a purchase of tobacco from Laidlaw & Co. (through its agent, Girault). At the time, the price of tobacco was depressed by 30-50% because of a blockade of the port of New Orleans by the British Fleet during the War of 1812. Organ met with Girault shortly after learning from an associate that a treaty had been signed, ending the war and blockade, and thus dramatically increasing the value of the tobacco at issue. Organ sought to act on this new information—unknown to Girault—and conclude the contract at the lower price, Girault asked if there was any news that might affect the price of the tobacco, but Organ simply remained silent. The parties then concluded the agreement.

When Girault soon thereafter learned of the treaty and end of the blockade (and the resulting sharp rise in tobacco prices), Laidlaw & Co. asserted that its contract was voidable based on Organ's failure to share the information he had just received, inasmuch as it involved a basic assumption related to the price of the transaction. In adopting the basic rule of *caveat emptor*, Justice Marshall explained:

"The question in this case is, whether the intelligence of extrinsic circumstances, which might influence the price of the commodity, and which was exclusively within the knowledge of the vendee, ought to have been communicated by him to the vendor? The court is of opinion that he was not bound to communicate it. *It would be difficult to circumscribe the contrary doctrine within proper limits, where the means of intelligence are equally accessible to both parties.* But at the same time, each party must take care not to say or do any thing tending to impose upon the other (emphasis added)."[11]

---

[11] Laidlaw v. Organ, 15 U.S. 178 (1817).

Justice Marshall's opinion nicely sets out the parameters for the discussion that follows. Each party must take care not to say or do anything to mislead the other. However, any further affirmative requirement of disclosure will necessarily present challenges in line drawing.

On one hand, virtually all would agree that two sophisticated parties negotiating over a piece of property, each having done their own research and analysis as to value, should not be required to divulge the entire content of such research and analysis—no matter how important to the value of the property. On the other, a trustee engaged in a transaction with a trust beneficiary would be held by all to the highest standards of disclosure, lest the transaction be voidable by the beneficiary. The difficulties arise of course in a variety of contexts of "non-disclosure," which lie between these two extremes.

Misrepresentation—In Five Varieties

In this lesson, we will break "misrepresentations" into five categories. While not all articulations of the doctrine do so in exactly the same matter, these five categories are largely consistent with most articulations. The first category—an explicit, affirmative misrepresentation—is relatively easy to define and apply. The other four, however, seek to answer the more difficult question—"When does a non-disclosure become an implicit misrepresentation?" Each of these is addressed in turn.

We will begin with the explicit misrepresentation, a false statement. We then address the proverbial "half-truth." To what extent might a true conveyance of half of the information impliedly misrepresent the half of the information withheld? We next turn to circumstances in which the information is not only withheld, but the discovery of that information is actually inhibited or prevented. We also examine certain exceptionally unique circumstances, in which disclosure may be mandated. These include contracts involving fiduciaries (mentioned at the end of the previous section) or other persons in special positions of trust. Finally, we conclude this analysis with the most difficult question. Under what circumstances should bare non-disclosure—in the absence of any traditional special relationship between the parties—constitute misrepresentation?

Misrepresentation—A False Statement

A false statement or other assertion is easily deemed a misrepresentation. For purposes of contract law, the false statement need not be intentional or even knowing. While the tort of misrepresentation requires proof of *scienter* (either knowledge that the statement is false or reckless disregard of its truth), an innocent mistake may render a contract voidable.

The focus is less on the culpability of the party making the representation and more on the effect on the "consent" of the victim. When a party is misinformed as to a crucial aspect of the bargain, the reality of that party's consent is called into serious question. Moreover, the doctrine of estoppel will generally preclude a party who has misled another from benefitting from that misinformation—whether intentional or not. We can see an example of a misrepresentation based on a false statement by slightly changing the facts of Example 22-1.

Example 22-2: *Laidlaw v. Organ (hypothetical variation)*

When Girault asked Organ if there was any news that might affect the price of the tobacco, suppose that Organ has answered "No, the British are continuing to press the blockade, and there is no end in sight to this war."

In contrast to Organ's silence in the actual case, the foregoing variation clearly constitutes a misrepresentation based on a false statement. It makes no difference whether Organ intended to deceive Laidlaw or was simply mistaken in his understanding of the facts.

In order to render the contract voidable, Laidlaw will further have to establish that the misrepresentation was material, that Laidlaw justifiably relied on it, and that it was a representation of fact—not opinion. These latter elements are addressed more fully after the last of the five varieties of misrepresentation.

Misrepresentation—A Half-Truth

A "half-truth" is a statement that is technically true, but is likely to suggest a false conclusion with respect to another issue on which it is silent. For example, if I were to tell you "the day dawned bright and clear this morning," you would likely assume—absent further information—that the day was fine and sunny. Thus, if the weather had instead taken a rather dramatic turn for the worse immediately after sunrise, and rain was now pouring from a dark, overcast sky, my statement might fairly be deemed a half-truth.

A half-truth requires more than a simple lack of completeness. The part of the statement that is true must reasonably imply a fact that is false, *and* that is not expressly addressed because the statement is incomplete. Again, we can look to another variation on Example 22-1 for an example.

> ### Example 22-3: *Laidlaw v. Organ (hypothetical variation)*
>
> When Girault asked Organ if there was any news that might affect the price of the tobacco, suppose that Organ has answered "Unfortunately, the British are continuing to press the blockade." Further suppose that Organ knew that the treaty ending the war had been signed, but that hostilities were not to end for another two days.
>
> While Organ's statement is technically true, and will remain so for two more days, it implies that no treaty has yet been concluded, which is false. Thus, Organ's statement constitutes a misrepresentation based on a half-truth.

As with a false statement, the knowledge or intent of the person communicating the half-truth should not matter. However, one might reasonably question whether a person has truly stated a "half-truth" if honestly ignorant of the "other half" inadvertently omitted.

At this juncture, we might also return to the original facts of Laidlaw v. Organ. Might one reasonably characterize Organ's silence in the face of Girault's question as something akin to a "half-truth," leading Girault to imply that the answer was "no"? Or should Organ's silence have instead put

Girault on notice that the current circumstances affecting the value of the tobacco might very well be changing? If you had been in Girault's shoes, what would you have inferred from Organ's silence?

Misrepresentation—Prevention or Concealment of Truth

One of the reasons that a "half-truth" operates as a misrepresentation is that the half of the statement that is true will often provide the listener with a false sense of security as to the unspoken, but implicit portion, thereby undermining any motivation to investigate further. In this sense, a half-truth may actually inhibit the discovery of the facts at issue. A party may, however, go beyond a simple half-truth in inhibiting such discovery. If so, the conduct concealing or preventing the discovery of the truth will operate as a misrepresentation. Again, we will return to a variation on the first example in this lesson.

Example 22-4: *Laidlaw v. Organ (hypothetical variation)*

In the actual case, the information was brought from the British fleet by Messrs. Livingston, White, and Shepherd. Shepherd's brother was an associate of Organ, with an interest in the tobacco transaction at issue, and had provided the information to Organ before it was generally available to the public. Soon thereafter, White posted a handbill announcing the treaty and lifting of the blockade.

Suppose that Organ had convinced White to wait an extra hour to post the handbill or had surreptitiously followed White and removed the handbill immediately after it was posted. In either event, proof of such conduct by Organ would constitute a misrepresentation based on Organ's prevention of Laidlaw discovering the treaty and lifting of the blockade.

In the actual case, counsel for Laidlaw argued—at least by implication—that Organ may have in fact caused a delay in the public dissemination of the news. Apparently, Justice Marshall thought enough of the possibility that he remanded the case for a retrial on the question of whether

> Organ had in some way made it more difficult for Laidlaw
> to discover the news.[12]

As with other forms of misrepresentation, concealment or prevention of
a party from learning the true circumstances of the transaction will raise
questions about the nature of any consent, as well as issues of estoppel.

Misrepresentation—Non-Disclosure Involving a Special Relationship or Position of Trust

The general rule of *caveat emptor* is based to at least some degree on the
assumption of a proverbial "level playing field." In fact, Justice Marshall
qualified his justification for the rule in *Laidlaw v. Organ* as applying
"where the means of intelligence are equally accessible to both parties."
This sort of level playing field is often called an "arms-length" relationship, as one in which each party reasonably understands that it must act
to protect its own interests, because the other party is not likely to do so.
However, in circumstances in which one of the parties has reason to place
a unusually high degree of trust in the other by virtue of the unique nature
of their relationship, a duty to disclose may arise based solely on the nature
of that relationship.

A fiduciary relationship is one such special relationship. In fact, a contract
between a fiduciary and beneficiary is subject to even greater restriction
than a mere requirement of disclosure, as any resulting agreement is also
voidable by the beneficiary, unless the fiduciary proves its terms are fair to
the beneficiary.[13] However, a special relationship or special position of trust
may also arise in other contexts. For example, a family relationship, or a
relationship between a mentor and mentee, may rise to the level of one
requiring disclosure.

One might also reasonably suggest that a government official charged with
serving the public interest—or one individually receiving information
from such a person prior to the general public—might be characterized
as a person in a special position of trust, thereby mandating a duty of
disclosure to a contracting partner lacking that same information.

---

[12] Laidlaw v. Organ, 15 U.S. 178 (1817).

[13] *See* Restatement (Second) of Contracts § 173.

Example 22-5: *Laidlaw v. Organ (further analysis)*

A subsequent historical analysis of the events surrounding the case suggests that the three individuals returning from the British Fleet with the information about the treaty and the lifting of the blockade were functioning in governmental or at least quasi-governmental roles. As such Organ's receipt of this information from an official source ahead of the general public might, itself, suggest that he be treated as a person in a special position of trust when contracting with a member of the public who has not yet been afforded a reasonable opportunity to learn the information at issue. If so, Organ's failure to disclose the information would likely be treated as a misrepresentation.[14]

As you may have already surmised, the sort of circumstances presented by the foregoing example are often addressed by statutes, today, which limit the use of certain "inside information" for financial advantage. For example, "insider trading" by corporate management and others with special information is significantly limited by state and federal statutes. Government employees are also often very limited in taking commercial advantage of information they may have as a result of their position of public trust. While such regulation was far less prevalent in the early 1800s, the example suggests that similar results might obtain in at least some cases from the application of the common law.

Misrepresentation—Non-Disclosure without Special Relationship or Position of Trust

We now address the exception to the general rule that Justice Marshall seemingly sought to avoid. Under what circumstances should disclosure be affirmatively required, absent some special relationship or position of trust? Over time, a number of courts have attempted to craft such a rule, which now appears in the Restatement (Second) of Contracts § 161(b). The rule generally provides that the non-disclosure of a fact is equivalent to a false assertion where a party knows that disclosure would correct a basic mistake

---

[14] *See* Kaye, Joshua, *Disclosure, Information, The Law of Contracts, and the Mistaken Use of* Laidlaw v. Organ, 79 Miss. L. J. 577 (2010).

of the other party as to a basic assumption on which that party is making the contract.

Example 22-6: *Two Cases—Two Perspectives*

The seller of a house knows—or at least should know—that the house is infested with termites. The buyer does not ask and is unaware of the termites (termites generally being un-detectable except by a professional). The buyer later asserts that the contract is voidable because the seller's failure to disclose the termite infestation constitutes a misrepresenta-tion. While seller made no express false statement, buyer asserts that seller's failure to correct buyer's basic mistake as to what was obviously a basic assumption of the contract (a termite-free house) turns seller's non-disclosure into the equivalent of a false statement and, therefore, a misrepre-sentation. Courts have split on this sort of issue, including cases specifically involving termites.[15]

The rule seemingly relies on standards of good faith and fair dealing in this particular context—even before the parties are bound to a contract. In effect, the circumstances give rise to this pre-contractual duty where it would not otherwise exist. As indicated in the example above, courts have split on the extent to which they have embraced the rule reflected in § 161(b). While this restatement provision has undoubtedly influenced the continuing development of the rule, not all courts have fully embraced its approach. We can apply § 161(b) to the facts of *Laidlaw v. Organ* and easily see that it reflects a different rule than the one applied by Justice Marshall in that case.

Example 22-7: *Laidlaw v. Organ (applying § 161(b))*

Laidlaw labored under a *basic mistake*, believing that the war and resulting British naval blockade were ongoing, *as*

---

[15] *Compare* Swinton v. Whitinsville Savings Bank, 311 Mass. 677, 42 N.E.2d 808 (1942) (declining to impose a duty to disclose the existence of termites) *with* Hill v. Jones, 151 Ariz. 81, 725 P.2d 1115 (Ct App. 1986) (relying on Restatement (Second) of Contracts § 161, including subsection (b), to impose a duty on the seller of a house known to have termites to convey this information to the buyer).

to a basic assumption, the inability to export the tobacco, thereby artificially reducing its value, with respect to the pricing of the tobacco contract at issue.

Organ knew or should have known that Laidlaw so labored and, therefore, should have disclosed the information to Laidlaw. His failure to do so amounts to a false statement under the instant circumstances. Thus, the undisputed facts of the case would have almost certainly mandated an entry of judgment in favor of Laidlaw if the court had applied the rule reflected in Restatement (Second) of Contracts § 161(b).

When a Misrepresentation Renders a Contract Voidable

Not all misrepresentations will render a contract voidable. For example, a minor misrepresentation may have no effect on the decision of the victim of that misrepresentation to conclude the contract. Or a party may ignore the other's misrepresentation (perhaps recognizing it as such) in deciding whether to conclude the contract. In short, the victim of the misrepresentation must establish a causal connection between the earlier misrepresentation and the victim's current unhappiness with the contract it concluded.

This causal connection requires the victim to establish three elements, in addition to the misrepresentation, itself:

- The misrepresentation is material;

- The victim of the misrepresentation justifiably relied on it;

- The misrepresentation involved a fact or facts—not opinion.

Example 22-8: *Laidlaw v. Organ (applying § 161(b) continued)*

Assuming that a court had found Organ's non-disclosure to be a misrepresentation equivalent to a false statement, the court would next consider the additional elements required to render the contract voidable.

The representation involved the price of the tobacco, which, under the circumstances of a 30 to 50% impact on the market value, was certainly material to a contract for the sale of tobacco.

The question of reliance under the actual facts of the case is somewhat more interesting. On one hand, it would seem that Laidlaw's agent, Girault, believed Organ may have known more than others, as evidenced by Girault's question as to whether Organ knew of anything that might affect the price. On the other, Organ's silence might suggest to a reasonable person that Organ should not be relied upon for such information (or the lack thereof). A court applying the heightened disclosure requirement of § 161(b) would likely find reliance reasonable here, but the issue is not without doubt.

Finally, the false statement by non-disclosure—that nothing had changed with respect to the ongoing war and block-ade—was certainly one of fact, not opinion. As such, the contract for tobacco would likely be voidable by Laidlaw.

In theory, the rule seeks to strike a balance between the relative obligations of a party to disclose relevant information it may already possess and the obligation of its counter-party to exercise reasonable diligence in discovering relevant information. Many such issues are resolved by the use of third parties. For example, every home purchase will include a professional termite inspection, an expense traditionally paid for by the buyer.

Having not fully addressed the range of possible misrepresentations, as well as the additional requirements to render a contract voidable as a result of such misrepresentations, we can now address a crucial distinction between two types of misrepresentation or fraud.

Fraud in the Inducement versus Fraud in the Factum

Misrepresentation, as described above, is often called "fraud in the inducement," in that the misrepresentation causes a party to enter into a contract under terms it would not, absent the misrepresentation. Such a contract is voidable, as the option of the victim. This sort of "fraud in the inducement" can be distinguished from "fraud in the factum," in which the victim is being misled as to the very nature of the transaction.

> **Example 22-9:** A and B have been exchanging and editing draft written agreements in the process of negotiating an agreement. Upon final agreement to a common draft, A volunteers to print the final version and bring it to a meeting at which A and B will both execute this final version, and A will tender an initial payment to B due upon execution. However, A in fact changes a number of key terms, which dramatically change the very nature of the agreement. The agreement is a lengthy one, and the changes would be difficult to notice absent a very close examination of the entire agreement. A and B execute the agreement, B relying on A's representation that the document in question represents their final draft.
>
> A's fraud goes to the very nature of the document executed by B. Unless a court found B's reliance on A's representation to be unreasonable under the circumstances, A's conduct would amount to fraud in the factum, and B's consent in signing the document would be wholly ineffective.

An agreement procured by fraud in the fact is not merely voidable. It is "void," *ab initio*. In effect, it never comes into existence in the first instance.

> **Summary of Basic Rule: traditional rule on misrepresentation**[8]
>
> - A contract is voidable at the option of a victim of misrepresentation if:
>   - The misrepresentation, based on:
>   - A false statement;
>   - A half-truth amounting to a false statement;
>   - Concealment or prevention of the victim discovering the truth; or
>   - A failure to disclose in circumstances involving a special relationship or other special position of trust; or perhaps
>   - Where a party knows that disclosure would correct a basic mistake of the other party as to a basic assumption with respect to the contract
>   - Is material;
>   - Is justifiably relied upon by the victim; and
>   - Amounts to a fact—not an opinion
> - A contract is "void," *ab initio*, if one of the contracting parties has made a misrepresentation as to the very nature of the agreement

APPLYING THE RULES

Problem 1: Annino converted a single-family house into multi-family apartments, in direct violation of a zoning ordinance prohibiting such multi-family units in the neighborhood. Annino then put the building up for sale, advertising it as multi-unit income property. Kannavos purchased the building from Annino for the specific purpose of operating it as a multi-family income generating property. Annino knew how Kannavos intended to use the property, but Kannavos did not know about the zoning ordinance or violation. Kannavos neither asked Annino about the issue, nor inquired by searching available public records and information, which would have disclosed the applicability of the zoning ordinance to these units.

---

[16] This basic rule is reflected in Restatement (Second) of Contracts §§ 159, 160, 161, 163, 164, and 169.

When he learns about the ordinance precluding his intended use as multi-family income property, Kannavos asserts that the contract is avoidance based on misrepresentation. Is Kannavos correct?

The facts of this problem are loosely based on the issues raised in the case of *Kannavos v. Annino*, 356 Mass. 42, 247 N.E.2d 708 (1969).

Problem 2: Return to the basic question presented by Problem 2 in the last lesson. After Fay explained the problem with the sandy soil and Hal investigated other options, Hal then called Fay and said "I agree to pay the additional $200,000." Fay promptly completed the house according to the revised plans. Hal refused to pay more than the original $800,000, and Fay seeks to recover the additional $200,000. How, if at all, would it affect your answer if Hal had previously discussed the possibility of building on his mountainside property with a geologist, and the geologist had stated that it would be very expensive, because the soil was unusually sandy? Hal never mentioned this information to Fay.

Problem 3: Sue was selling her 10-year-old car, and Tom was interested in perhaps buying it. He stopped by Sue's house after work to take it for a test drive. Sue had encouraged him to do so and emphasized that she was selling the car "as is." When Tom returned, he thought it seemed fine. He thought he detected a slight burning smell, but could not be sure. He asked Sue, "How does it run? Any problems you know of?" Sue replied, "I'm no car mechanic, but I absolutely love this car." In fact, Sue had just learned a few days earlier from a mechanic that the engine block was cracked, leaking oil, and would have to be replaced. Sue had asked the mechanic to attach a makeshift oil pan to catch the any leaking oil, explaining that she didn't want oil all over her driveway.

Tom thought about it briefly, considered what Sue had said, and told Sue "Great. I'll take it." After paying Sue and taking the car, Tom quickly discovered the problem. Is the transaction voidable by Tom?

Lesson 23: Contracts of Adhesion and Unconscionability

Objectives and Expected Learning Outcomes

In this lesson, you will learn the nature of a contract of "adhesion" and the circumstances in which such a contract is not enforceable, as inconsistent with "public policy." You will also learn when a court may decline to enforce all or part of an agreement based on the doctrine of "unconscionability," as well as the differing approaches a court may take in considering the question.

Contracts of Adhesion

We begin with a theme carried over from the past two lessons, focusing on a purported flaw in the bargain process that calls into question any consent to the bargain in question. A seller of goods, service provider, or landlord will often propose terms for the buyer or lessee to "take or leave" in a pre-printed form document. In Example 11-5, Ever-Tite Roofing offered the Greens a "form" contract to sign, as an offer for Ever-Tite's acceptance upon credit approval. It is of course very doubtful that the representative of Ever-Tite would have agreed to change any of the pre-printed language in the standard Ever-Tite contract. The contract was very likely offered to the Greens on a "take it or leave it" basis.

Assuming that other roofers were available and willing to negotiate the specific terms of any roofing contract with the Greens, Ever-Tite's form agreement does not present any particular problem. Presumably, Ever-Tite drafted (or had its lawyers draft) a form agreement because it was more cost effective than drafting multiple, individual, custom agreements. If so, Ever-Tite's prices ought to be lower, reflective of its lower transaction costs, and the Greens retain a choice as to roofers, remaining free to negotiate an individual agreement with another roofer if they choose to do so. However, this perspective begins to break down where (1) all sellers seek to impose the same standard terms; and (2) the goods or services are deemed "essential."

For example, all lessors in a given residential real estate rental market might employ exactly the same form lease terms, or all automobile manufacturers might employ exactly the same automobile purchase terms. Most would agree that a residential living space and a car (unless, perhaps, one lives in

a densely populated city with effective mass transit) are reasonably characterized as "essentials." Such standardized form contracts for essentials are
called contracts of "adhesion," because they leave one contracting party
with no real choice. The following classic case provides a perfect example.

Example 23-1: *Henningson v. Bloomfield Motors*

Henningson sued car dealer, Bloomfield motors, and
Chrysler Corporation for personal injuries caused by an alleged defect in the new car purchased by Henningson. Defendants sought dismissal based on a disclaimer of liability
in the contract of sale. This same disclaimer was used at the
time by all of the "big three" auto makers that dominated
the U.S. market at that time, and no manufacturer or
dealer would negotiate any of its terms. Thus, Henningson
had no real choice (he had to have a car) but to agree to the
disclaimer. The disclaimer therefore reflected a contract (or
portion thereof) of "adhesion."[17]

Today, many of the circumstances underlying the above example have
changed. Automobile manufacturers offer a variety of different purchase
options and warranties. UCC Article 2 limits certain disclaimers of liability
(we will explore this issue further in Chapter 8), and federal (and some
other state) legislation also provides additional protection to consumers.
However, the potential for contracts of "adhesion" remains today. Even if
standard terms are not precisely identical for all products and services of a
given type, they may, as a practical matter, limit choice in a way that makes
them "adhesive."

When is a Contract of Adhesion Unenforceable?

The "adhesive" nature of a contract does not, by itself, make the contract
unenforceable. The "adhesive" nature of a given contract makes it unenforceable only if enforcement of the contract or one of its terms is also
"contrary to public policy." Unfortunately, the term "public policy" is used
in enough different contexts that it can be confusing. For example, in lesson 25, we will look at "illegal" contracts (e.g., a "contract" murder for

---

[17] Henningsen v. Bloomfield Motors, Inc., 32 N.J. 358, 161 A.2d 69 (1960).

hire), which are unsurprisingly deemed unenforceable, as contrary to public policy—irrespective of whether they arise out of an "adhesive" contract provision. Thus, "public policy" takes on a somewhat unique meaning in the context of an adhesion contract. With that in mind, we can develop that contextual meaning further.

Enforcement of a term in a contract of adhesion is generally deemed "contrary to public policy" if:

- The term is not reasonably expected,

    o Except where there is notice and actual assent (not mere "tacit" assent via silence)

  OR

- The term is "unconscionable"

Again, we encounter another term that is used in multiple contexts, often with a different meaning. For example, we will discover later in this lesson that "unconscionability," by itself, may render a contract unenforceable. In the current context, however, we are looking at unconscionability solely in the context of an "adhesive" contract.

A classic example of the first manner in which a contract may be deemed contrary to public policy is found in a common coat check claim stub.

> **Example 23-2:** You drop your coat at a coat check while attending the ballet, paying the attendant a small fee and receiving a claim stub with a number on it allowing you to recover your coat at the end of the evening. On the back of the claim stub, in remarkably small print, is a disclaimer of any liability for loss or damage to your checked article, in excess of $10.
>
> Absent further facts, this disclaimer would not likely be enforceable. The stub likely reflects a contract of adhesion, as its terms are not negotiable, and you have no other option for checking your coat. You can also make a good

argument that you did not reasonably expect such a term on a coat check claim stub, and you lacked reasonable notice and certainly did not expressly assent.

This example is not to suggest that such small print under similar circumstances is never enforceable. First, it may be expected. For example, most skiers would not be surprised to discover a disclaimer of liability printed on a lift ticket or otherwise associated with its purchase. Second, it may be statutorily enforceable. Using the same example, a state may choose to protect its ski industry by legislating that such disclaimers are fully enforceable. Absent legislation, however, the inquiry is largely fact based.

The second, alternative, manner of proving unconscionability is much more difficult to define in the specific context of an adhesion contract. The process might be reasonably analogized to Justice Potter Stewart's description of the challenge in identifying pornography, in which he ultimately concluded "I know it when I see it."[18] The following is a classic example of unconscionability in the context of an adhesion contract, and is often cited as a sort of "benchmark," or at least an example, in cases addressing the issue.

Example 23-3: *Graham v. Scissor-Tail, Inc.*

Bill Graham, an experienced concert promoter and producer, contracted with Scissor-Tail, which represented recording artist Leon Russell, for Graham to promote and produce and Russell to perform a concert tour. The parties used a standard form contract provided by the "American Federation of Musicians," which provided that any disputes would be arbitrated by the musician's union International Executive Board. After the union board resolved a dispute in favor of Scissor-Tail (and Russell, a "musician" member of the union), Graham sought to have the decision set aside, asserting that the arbitration agreement was an unenforceable contract of adhesion.

---

[18] Jacobellis v. Ohio, 378 U.S. 184 (1964).

The contract was deemed "adhesive," because it was impossible for Graham to promote and produce concerts, unless he agreed to the standard form agreement. In addressing the "public policy" prong of the inquiry, Graham had no argument that the term was unexpected, because he used the form regularly and was fully aware of its contents. However, the term providing for arbitration of a dispute between Graham and a union member by the union executive board was deemed unconscionable based on the inherently biased nature of any such arbitration process. A biased tribunal would likely deprive Graham of his basic right to a fair dispute resolution process (i.e., "due process"), which would certainly be contrary to "public policy."[19]

It is important to note that the court did not find arbitration, generally, to be unconscionable. Instead, the court focused on the inherent unfairness of subjecting a party to arbitration before a body that, by its nature, appeared to be biased in favor of the other party (like a judge, an arbitrator, under most modern arbitration regimes, must remain independent and impartial—even an appearance of partiality will generally disqualify such an arbitrator). The issue of unconscionability, as specifically applied to arbitration agreements, is more fully addressed in the next lesson.

The above case involved a contract of adhesion. However, one might reasonably question whether the arbitration clause at issue would have been enforceable in any context. While the adhesive nature of an agreement will likely factor into the analysis in some manner, there seemingly exist no clear boundaries between unconscionability in the context of an adhesion contract and unconscionability, more generally. We now move on to consider the latter.

Unconscionability—With or Without Adhesion

In drafting UCC Article 2, Llewellyn had two specific concerns related to unconscionable contract terms. On one hand, he abhorred "sharp practice," whereby a party would seek to draft an agreement right to the edge,

---

[19] Graham v. Scissor-Tail, Inc., 28 Cal.3d 807, 623 P.2d 165, 171 Cal. Rptr. 604 (1981).

or even beyond the bounds of reasonableness. On the other, he was also concerned with the intellectual dishonesty sometimes required for a court to reach a "just" and "fair" result in refusing to enforce the product of such "sharp practice." In hopes of addressing each of these concerns, Llewellyn drafted UCC § 2-302, providing a direct and explicit tool for a court to refuse enforcement of a contract or term it finds "unconscionable."

In the case of unconscionability, the restatement[20] largely tracks § 2-302, so our analysis will focus primarily on the statute. **STOP NOW and READ UCC § 2-302(1) below**.

UCC § 2-302(1)

(1) If the court as a matter of law finds the contract or any clause of the contract to have been unconscionable at the time it was made the court may refuse to enforce the contract, or it may enforce the remainder of the contract without the unconscionable clause, or it may so limit the application of any unconscionable clause as to avoid any unconscionable result.

The rule provided by § 2-302 is both elegantly simple and devilishly ambiguous. It may be used as a scalpel, declining enforcement of only the most overbearing of terms in the most unreasonable of circumstances, or it may be used more broadly to pick and choose which terms to enforce based on nothing more than one's individual perspective on what is "unconscionable." Llewellyn undoubtedly intended the ambiguity, at least to some extent, as it certainly inhibits the sort of "sharp practice" he disdained. Presumably, one is less likely to venture towards an "edge" that remains uncertain. However, the need for some sort of guidance is also obvious.

The Comment associated with § 2-302 provides significant guidance—albeit in two somewhat inconsistent provisions. Read the Comment closely, focusing on both the "basic test" and the "principle." Do you think they are consistent?

---

[20] *See* Restatement (Second) of Contracts § 208.

OFFICIAL COMMENT 1 (UCC § 2-302)

1. . . . The **basic test** is whether, in the light of the general commercial background and the commercial needs of the particular trade or case, the clauses involved are so one-sided as to be unconscionable under the circumstances existing at the time of the making of the contract. . . . The **principle** is one of the prevention of oppression and unfair surprise [citing Campbell Soup Co. v. Wentz] and not of disturbance of allocation of risks because of superior bargaining power (emphasis supplied). . . .

When drafted, § 2-302 was predictably quite controversial, and there is some indication that these two provisions were intended to give each side of the debate something to hang its hat on—the formalists being somewhat mollified by the "principle," and the realists delighted by the "basic test." The case cited by the "principle" is useful in understanding its limits.

Example 23-4: *Campbell Soup Co. v. Wentz*

The Wentz brothers contracted with Campbell Soup to sell their entire crop of special Chantenay carrots to Campbell at $30 per ton. When the time came to deliver, these carrots had become exceptionally scarce, and their market price had risen to $90 per ton. The Wentzes breached their contract with Campbell, selling the "contract" carrots to Lojeski, who subsequently sought to sell them to Campbell at a higher price. Campbell sought equitable relief in the form of an order requiring specific performance by the Wentz brothers of their contract with Campbell.

The court agreed that Campbell's request met the general requirements for specific performance, having determined that the Chantenay carrots constituted unique goods that were not reasonably available elsewhere and were crucial to Campbell's soup production. However, the court nevertheless declined the request for specific performance, finding the bargain too sharp for equity.

Specifically, the court found that the form contract drafted by Campbell contained numerous provisions not only favoring Campbell, but operating in a manner going well beyond that which a reasonable person would expect—e.g., limiting the quantity of carrots Campbell is required to take, or even excusing Campbell from taking any carrots in some circumstances, while simultaneously barring the Wentz brothers from selling their carrots to anyone else (thus, apparently leaving them with unsalable carrots). While declining to grant specific performance, the court made clear that it would have reached a different result on a legal claim for damages.[21]

The court's decision above is in some ways similar to the one in McKinnon v. Benedict in Lesson 20, in that it solely involved a court's refusal to grant equitable relief. It is also easy to see that the combined effect of the contract provisions favoring Campbell would unfairly surprise all but the most astute reader, and these provisions were found in what was arguably a contract of adhesion. While UCC § 2-302 is by no means limited to claims for equitable relief or contracts of adhesion, this case provides a level of guidance in determining what constitutes "oppression and unfair surprise" and what is meant by refraining from "disturbance of allocation of risks because of superior bargaining power."

In contrast, the "basic test" makes no reference to "unfair surprise" and in no way suggests any hesitance in allowing a court to reform a bargain that is deemed too "one-sided." Instead, the test seems to focus primarily on the circumstances in which the specific contract was concluded.

The following case was an early one, decided before § 2-302 had been enacted, but relying on its rationale. It would not be governed by UCC Article 2 today, as it involves a lease, rather a sale, of goods. Thus, it would be governed by Article 2A, which now governs leases. However, § 2A-108 is sufficiently similar to § 2-302 that the reasoning of the case remains as useful as ever in understanding the latter.

---

[21] Campbell's Soup Co. v. Wentz, 172 F.2d 80 (3d Cir. 1948).

FROM THE COURT

Williams v. Walker-Thomas Furniture Co.

U.S. Court of Appeals, D.C. Circuit (1965)
350 F.2d 445

Skelly Wright, Circuit Judge:

[Walker-Thomas Furniture Company operates a retail furniture store in the District of Columbia. Williams] purchased a number of household items from Walker-Thomas, for which payment was to be made in installments. The terms of each purchase were contained in a printed form contract which set forth the value of the purchased item and purported to lease the item to appellant for a stipulated monthly rent payment. The contract then provided, in substance, that title would remain in Walker-Thomas until the total of all the monthly payments made equaled the stated value of the item, at which time [Williams] could take title. In the event of a default in the payment of any monthly installment, Walker-Thomas could repossess the item.

The contract further provided that 'the amount of each periodical installment payment to be made by (purchaser) to the Company under this present lease shall be inclusive of and not in addition to the amount of each installment payment to be made by (purchaser) under such prior leases, bills or accounts; and all payments now and hereafter made by (purchaser) shall be credited pro rata on all outstanding leases, bills and accounts due the Company by (purchaser) at the time each such payment is made.' The effect of this rather obscure provision was to keep a balance due on every item purchased until the balance due on all items, whenever purchased, was liquidated. As a result, the debt incurred at the time of purchase of each item was secured by the right to repossess all the items previously purchased by the same purchaser, and each new item purchased automatically became subject to a security interest arising out of the previous dealings.

[On April 17, 1962, Williams bought a stereo for $514.95. She defaulted shortly thereafter, and Walker-Thomas sought to repossess all the $1,800 worth of items purchased in the past 5 years. Before Walker purchased the stereo, she had reduced the balance in her account to $164. The stereo purchase raised the balance due to $678.]

. . . [A]t the time of this and the preceding purchases, [Walker-Thomas] was aware of Williams's financial position. The reverse side of the stereo contract listed the name of [her] social worker and her $218 monthly stipend from the government. Nevertheless, with full knowledge that [Williams] had to feed, clothe and support both herself and seven children on this amount, [Walker-Thomas] sold her a $514 stereo set. [Williams contended that her lease contracts with Walker-Thomas were unconscionable and, hence, not enforceable.]

. . .

Unconscionability has generally been recognized to include an absence of meaningful choice on the part of one of the parties together with contract terms which are unreasonably favorable to the other party. Whether a meaningful choice is present in a particular case can only be determined by consideration of all the circumstances surrounding the transaction. In many cases the meaningfulness of the choice is negated by a gross inequality of bargaining power. The manner in which the contract was entered is also relevant to this consideration. Did each party to the contract, considering his obvious education or lack of it, have a reasonable opportunity to understand the terms of the contract, or were the important terms hidden in a maze of fine print and minimized by deceptive sales practices? Ordinarily, one who signs an agreement without full knowledge of its terms might be held to assume the risk that he has entered a one-sided bargain. But when a party of little bargaining power, and hence little real choice, signs a commercially unreasonable contract with little or no knowledge of its terms, it is hardly likely that his consent, or even an objective manifestation of his consent, was ever given to all the terms. In such a case the usual rule that the terms of the agreement are not to be questioned should be abandoned and the court should consider whether the terms of the contract are so unfair that enforcement should be withheld.

In determining reasonableness or fairness, the primary concern must be with the terms of the contract considered in light of the circumstances existing when the contract was made. The test is not simple, nor can it be mechanically applied. The terms are to be considered 'in the light of the general commercial background and the commercial needs of the particular trade or case.' Corbin suggests the test as being whether the terms are 'so extreme as to appear unconscionable according to the mores and business practices of the time and place.' [Citation omitted.] We think this formulation correctly states the test to be applied in those cases where no meaningful choice was exercised upon entering the contract.

[The case was remanded for further proceedings consistent with this opinion, which did not resolve the issue of unconscionability, instead leaving it to the trial court to do so.]

DANAHER, Circuit Judge (dissenting):

. . . My view is thus summed up by an able court which made no finding that there had actually been sharp practice. Rather [Williams] seems to have known precisely where she stood.

There are many aspects of public policy here involved. What is a luxury to some may seem an outright necessity to others. Is public oversight to be required of the expenditures of relief funds? A washing machine, e.g., in the hands of a relief client might become a fruitful source of income. Many relief clients may well need credit, and certain business establishments will take long chances on the sale of items, expecting their pricing policies will afford a degree of protection commensurate with the risk. . . .

I mention such matters only to emphasize the desirability of a cautious approach to any such problem, particularly since the law for so long has allowed parties such great latitude in making their own contracts. I dare say there must annually be thousands upon thousands of installment credit transactions in this jurisdiction, and one can only speculate as to the effect the decision in these cases will have.

. . .

CASE QUESTIONS

(1) What were the alleged unconscionable terms at issue?

    a. In this context, what is the effect of leasing goods to Williams instead of selling them?

    b. The Walker-Thomas contract included what is sometimes called a "cross-collateralization" provision. Do you know what that is? Do you fully understand its effect?

    c. What is the combined effect of these terms? If you are at all uncertain of any of these answers, this might bear on at least a part of your analysis of the next question.

(2) Is the court's articulation of the appropriate test of the terms more consistent with the "basic test" or "principle," as described in the Comment to § 2-302? Any determination under § 2-302 must be made by the court—not a jury. Put yourself in the position of the judge.

    a. Consider the terms at issue under the "basic test."

    b. Consider the terms at issue under the "principle."

Compare the previous case with the following example.

> **Example 23-5:** *Jones v. Star Credit*
>
> Jones, described by the court as a "welfare recipient," contracted to purchase a home freezer unit on credit for $900 plus interest and various credit charges of almost $300. When Jones sought to challenge the enforceability of the contract, the court assigned a maximum retail value to the freezer of $300, ruled the contract unconscionable under § 2-302, and reformed the parties' agreement to provide for a total payment by Jones of the $600 already paid.[22]

---

[22] Jones v. Star Credit Corp., 298 N.Y.S.2d 264 (Sup. Ct. 1969).

This example represents one of a number of cases in which a court relies solely on the price of a credit sales contract to find the agreement unconscionable under UCC § 2-302. Is this consistent with the statute? If so, is the court likely relying on the approach reflected in the "basic test" or the "principle"? How does Example 23-5 compare with the case that precedes it?

As should now be obvious, the application of § 2-302 is, to a large degree, dependent on the manner in which it is applied. Should the application of the statute be limited to true "unfair surprise," or should a court in fact be willing to reorder or reform the parties' assignment of risks and rewards based on relative bargaining power where the bargain is simply too "one-sided"? Should a court focus on the "process" of contract formation or the "substance" of the resulting contract? To what extent should a court consider the latter in deciding on the former? There are no easy answers to these questions, and they are by no means answered in the same way by all courts or legal scholars.

As a final point, we should note that, unlike the issues addressed earlier in this chapter, unconscionability does not make the contract "voidable," thereby leading to "rescission" of the entire contract. While a court may decline to enforce an unconscionable contract in its entirety, more often than not, a party raising an unconscionability defense seeks to enforce the contract, as a whole, but merely seeks relief from a specific term at issue.

APPLYING THE RULES

Problem 1: For this problem, we return to the basic facts of Problem 1 in Lesson 21. Austin has "persuaded" Loral to contract with Austin for all of the component parts required by Loral in order to build radar sets for the Navy under the 1966 contract (the second contract between Loral and the Navy). The pricing charged by Austin is quite high (not surprising under the circumstances of its "negotiation")—about double what a reasonable price would be in a competitive market. The Navy has made clear that Loral's timely completion of this contract is absolutely crucial, or the Navy may lose funding from Congress for the entire development project.

Austin suddenly finds itself the subject of a Justice Department investigation and closes up shop virtually overnight (the principals taking the company's funds and heading to a small country where extradition is difficult). Loral immediately begins looking for other potential suppliers, but only Delta can provide the necessary components within the required time frame. Fully aware that it is Loral's sole option, Delta proposes to provide the component parts at three times the price charged by Austin. With no other choice, Loral agrees, and Delta produces and timely delivers the component parts—all at a very nice profit for Delta and its shareholders.

Loral then seeks to recover a portion of the price charged by Delta, arguing that the price is unconscionable. Should Loral be able to recover? How much?

Problem 2: For this problem, we return to Example 4-4 (addressing this same fact pattern as an issue of consideration). During the Nazi occupation of Greece, in 1942, Eugenia Demotsis borrowed 500,000 drachmae from George Batsakis, promising to repay Batsakis $2,000, along with 8 percent annual interest. At the time of the loan, 500,000 drachmae were worth approximately $25. However, Demotsis had no access to any other financial resources at the time, as her assets were all in the U.S. and unavailable during the wartime occupation. Demotsis later refuses to pay any more than $25, plus interest, asserting that any additional amount is unconscionable. What do you think?

The facts of this problem are loosely based on the issues raised in the case of *Batsakis v. Demotsis*, 226 S.W. 2d 673 (Tex. Civ. App. 1949).

Problem 3: A lawyer fee agreement charges one-third of any amount recovered. The day after the client signs the fee agreement, the lawyer telephones counsel for the party that plaintiff seeks to hold liable and negotiates a settlement of $9,000,000, which the client agrees is an acceptable amount in settlement of his claim. However, the client asserts that the lawyer's $3,000,000 fee is "unconscionable" and refuses to pay any more than a reasonable rate for the number of hours actually worked by the lawyer. What do you think?

Problem 4: The Shutes decided to purchase a 7-day vacation cruise with Carnival Cruise Lines. They were issued tickets for the cruise that included all of the relevant information relating to their cruise itinerary and the price of the ticket. The tickets were printed on multi-part forms and included in the lower left hand corner of the front page a note indicating the inclusion of standard terms and conditions on the last page. These standard terms and conditions, in small print, included a "forum selection" clause, requiring that any claim related to travel covered by the ticket must be brought in a Florida court—and nowhere else. The standard terms also indicated that the tickets were non-refundable. The Shutes lived in Washington State.

During the cruise, Ms. Shute was injured, and she sought to bring suit in a Washington court. Carnival sought to dismiss the case based on the forum selection clause. Is the clause enforceable by Carnival against Shute? The facts of this problem are loosely based on the issues raised in the case of *Carnival Cruise Lines, Inc. v. Shute*, 499 U.S. 585, 111 S.Ct. 1522 (1991).

Lesson 24: Arbitration—Just Like Any Other Contract, or a Special Case?

Objectives and Expected Learning Outcomes

In this lesson, you will learn about arbitration agreements, as a distinct form of contract—in some ways like any other contract and in others quite unique. You will discover the basic law applicable to arbitration agreements, and we will more closely examine the issue of unconscionability, as applied to arbitration agreements.

The Arbitration Contract

You will almost certainly encounter arbitration as a form of "alternative dispute resolution" in other first year and/or elective courses. In that context, you will likely focus on arbitration as a "process" for resolving disputes, comparing it to other processes for resolving disputes. In contrast, this lesson will, after a very brief description of the process, focus on the contractual aspects of arbitration as an enforceable bargain, including an exchange of promises, like any other contract.

Arbitration is a process whereby a private tribunal (1 or 3 arbitrators) decides any dispute within the scope of the parties' arbitration agreement, fully and finally, with no right of appeal. The tribunal's award is enforceable in a court of law, subject only to a very narrow range of potential challenges, most of which focus on the failure of the tribunal to follow in good faith the agreed upon arbitral process. The traditional roles of both judge and jury are fulfilled by the arbitral tribunal. The process generally resolves the dispute more quickly than litigation and, in doing so, often employs a decision maker with specialized expertise. However, the process generally does so with less opportunity for discovery and other procedural options typically available in court proceedings.

The speed and efficiency of the process will often make it more cost effective for businesses. However, the parties must pay the cost of the tribunal, unlike court proceedings in which the judge is paid from public taxes. An arbitration agreement will also often designate an arbitral "institution" along with its "rules," providing a framework for the arbitral process. The institution will of course help the process run more smoothly and efficiently, as will a clear set of procedural rules, but the institution also comes at an additional cost to the parties—above and beyond the cost of the arbitrator or arbitrators, who will actually decide the parties' dispute. Ultimately, the financial desirability of arbitration will often involve balancing the additional "out-of-pocket" costs on one hand with the value of a quick and efficient resolution of the dispute on the other.

Under the United States Federal Arbitration Act (FAA), an agreement to arbitrate is fully enforceable, just like any other contract. **STOP NOW and READ 9 U.S.C. § 2 below.**

9 U.S.C. § 2

A written provision in . . . a contract evidencing a transaction involving commerce to settle by arbitration a controversy . . . shall be valid, irrevocable, and enforceable, save upon such grounds as exist at law or in equity for the revocation of any contract.

You will note that an arbitration agreement must be in writing, though there is no requirement that it be signed or otherwise authenticated, as with a typical "statute of frauds" requirement. An arbitration agreement may stand alone, sometimes governing dispute resolution under a broad range of other agreements between the parties. However, arbitration agreements are more typically found as mere "clauses" within a broader "main" or "container" agreement. In either event, the contract for arbitration is treated as a fully separate and autonomous agreement. In fact, it is one of the most common contracts most of us will encounter.

One of the reasons that arbitration agreements have been particularly con- troversial in the United States is that the Supreme Court has interpreted FAA § 2 as applying to contracts involving consumers and employees in exactly the same manner it applies to contracts between merchant busi- nesses. The drafting history of the FAA suggests that it was largely intended to provide for enforcement of business-to-business arbitration agreements, especially in trades in which arbitration was already commonplace. In fact, arbitration remains a preferred mechanism for resolution of contract disputes among many businesses. However, the Supreme Court's interpre- tation has unquestionably broadened the scope of the FAA far beyond its original legislative intent.[23]

In many countries, an arbitration agreement involving a consumer or employee is binding only if agreed upon after the dispute has arisen (i.e., an *ex post* agreement to arbitrate, after the specific nature of the dispute is known—and not in an *ex ante* form contract of adhesion). However, the Supreme Court has interpreted FAA § 2 to provide for enforcement of any arbitration agreement—irrespective of when it was concluded (i.e., including an *ex ante* agreement to arbitrate). As a result, there has been a great deal of litigation by consumers and employees seeking to avoid arbitration agreements barring traditional access to courts and—perhaps most importantly—to juries and class actions.

FAA § 2 provides that such a written arbitration agreement shall be en- forceable, except upon such grounds that would render any other contract invalid. Thus, many parties seeking to avoid enforcement of an arbitration agreement have argued that the agreement was "unconscionable." However, the Supreme Court has further interpreted the language of § 2 to preclude a finding of invalidity, generally, and unconscionability, in particular, based on any ground applied uniquely to arbitration. In other words, the doctrine of unconscionability cannot be applied in any manner that disfavors an arbitration agreement, as compared to other contracts. An arbitration agree- ment can only be deemed unconscionable on grounds that would render any other comparable contract unconscionable as well. A few brief excerpts from a recent case encountered earlier in Example 16-5 are instructive. Cita- tions are omitted without notation purely for ease of reading.

---

[23] Over time, the United States Supreme Court "abandoned all pretense of ascertaining congressional intent with respect to the [FAA], building instead, case by case, an edifice of its own creation." Allied-Bruce Terminix Co. v Dobson, 513 U.S. 265, 283 (1995) (O'Connor, J., concurring).

FROM THE COURT

AT&T Mobility, LLC v. Concepcion

United States Supreme Court (2011)
131 S.Ct. 1740

Scalia, J.

. . .

The FAA was enacted in 1925 in response to widespread judicial hostility to arbitration agreements. . . . Section 2 . . . provides, in relevant part, as follows:

"A written provision in any maritime transaction or a contract evidencing a transaction involving commerce to settle by arbitration a controversy thereafter arising out of such contract or transaction ... shall be valid, irrevocable, and enforceable, save upon such grounds as exist at law or in equity for the revocation of any contract."

We have described this provision as reflecting both a "liberal federal policy favoring arbitration," and the "fundamental principle that arbitration is a matter of contract." In line with these principles, courts must place arbitration agreements on an equal footing with other contracts and enforce them according to their terms.

The final phrase of § 2, however, permits arbitration agreements to be declared unenforceable "upon such grounds as exist at law or in equity for the revocation of any contract." This saving clause permits agreements to arbitrate to be invalidated by "generally applicable contract defenses, such as fraud, duress, or unconscionability," but not by defenses that apply only to arbitration or that derive their meaning from the fact that an agreement to arbitrate is at issue. . . .

. . .

The "principal purpose" of the FAA is to "ensure that private arbitration agreements are enforced according to their terms." This purpose is readily apparent from the FAA's text. Section 2 makes arbitration agreements "valid, irrevocable, and enforceable" as written (subject, of course, to the saving clause); § 3 requires courts to stay litigation of arbitral claims pending arbitration of those claims "in accordance with the terms of the agreement"; and § 4 requires courts to compel arbitration "in accordance with the terms of the agreement" upon the motion of either party to the agreement (assuming that the "making of the arbitration agreement or the failure ... to perform the same" is not at issue).

. . .

CASE QUESTIONS

(1) Does the Court's treatment of an arbitration agreement under FAA § 2 make it equal with other contracts or superior to other contracts?

(2) You will recall from the treatment of this case in Example 16-5 that the Court held that the FAA precluded, as a matter of federal pre-emption, a California law invalidating waivers of class arbitration rights.

   a. Is the State of California precluded from limiting any other contract rights?

   b. Can the State of California make it illegal to sell certain motor vehicles that can be sold in other states?

   c. Could California law limit agreements not to compete?

   d. Could California law limit the terms of a residential lease?

   e. Why can't California limit the nature of arbitration agreements its courts are willing to enforce?

(3) Is there anything unique about an arbitration agreement that suggests a need for a unified national approach to enforcement?

A complete analysis of unconscionability in the context of arbitration agreements is well beyond our scope in this basic contracts course. However, the following three case examples may be useful in setting out a few of its general contours. We first return to Example 23-3 from the last lesson.

> **Example 24-1:** *Graham v. Scissor-Tail, Inc. (redux)*
>
> The court declined to enforce the arbitration agreement between Graham and Scissor-Tail because the agreed upon arbitration process was inherently biased in favor of Scissor-Tail. The resulting unfairness arose not from arbitration, generally, but from the nature of the specific arbitration agreement at issue.
>
> Quoting, in part, prior precedent (citations omitted), the court explained that "'[t]he common law requirement of a fair procedure does not compel formal proceedings with all the embellishments of a court trial, nor adherence to a single mode of process. It may be satisfied by any one of a variety of procedures which afford a fair opportunity for (a disputant) to present his position. As such, this court should not attempt to fix a rigid procedure that must invariably be observed.' When it can be demonstrated, however, that the clear effect of the established procedure of the arbitrator will be to deny the resisting party a fair opportunity to present his position, the court should refuse to compel arbitration."
>
> Finding that the instant arbitration agreement failed to meet these "minimum levels of integrity," the court declined to enforce it as written. Notably, however, the court remanded the matter for the lower court to give effect to the basic agreement to arbitrate—albeit before an unbiased arbitrator.[24]

---

[24] Graham v. Scissor-Tail, Inc., 28 Cal.3d 807, 623 P.2d 165, 171 Cal. Rptr. 604 (1981).

The California court's decision in the foregoing case is almost certainly consistent with the Supreme Court's interpretation of FAA § 2, inasmuch as the application of the contract doctrine of unconscionability did not operate in a way that disfavored arbitration, generally, but merely targeted the specific clause at issue. The same logic invaliding the arbitration agreement, as written, would arguably apply with equal force to any contractual forum selection provision that resulted in the deprivation of a party's basic right to a fair dispute resolution process. For example, one can easily imagine a U.S. court refusing to enforce a forum selection clause in a contract of adhesion providing that all disputes would be resolved in the national courts of a country where such courts were known to be biased against foreigners.

While a clause selecting a biased national court is undoubtedly rare (as are biased national courts, today—though not unheard of), forum selection clauses, generally, are quite common. We will next consider the Supreme Court's analysis of the forum selection clause upon which Problem 4 in the last lesson was based.

Example 24-2: *Carnival Cruise Lines, Inc. v. Shute*

While acknowledging the essentially "adhesive" nature (though not using the word) of the provision requiring any litigation to take place in Florida courts, the Court pointed out that this fact, alone, did not render the provision unenforceable. Instead, the Court explained that such "forum-selection clauses contained in form passage contracts are subject to judicial scrutiny for fundamental fairness."

In this case, the Court found that the Florida forum was chosen in good faith and was in no way unfair to the Shutes. The Court acknowledged that "serious inconvenience of the contractual forum to one or both of the parties" might preclude enforcement, but noted the "heavy burden of proof" associated with such a claim of inconvenience and found the factual record lacking such proof. As such, the Court enforced the forum selection clause.[25]

---

[25] Carnival Cruise Lines, Inc. v. Shute, 499 U.S. 585, 111 S.Ct. 1522 (1991).

While the Court enforced the clause at issue, its analysis made clear that a forum selection provision was subject to "scrutiny for fundamental fairness"—much like the arbitration agreement in *Graham v. Scissor-Tail*. The Court also left open the possibility that a contract provision selecting a judicial forum might be unenforceable to the extent that the financial cost of using the forum essentially precluded access by one of the parties. We now turn to this issue of cost in the context of arbitration.

For this analysis, we return to Example 16-3, addressed earlier in our discussion of "rolling contracts" under UCC § 2-207. After deciding that the arbitration clause was included as a term in the parties' contract, the court next addressed the question of whether that term was unconscionable.

Example 24-3: *Brower v. Gateway 2000 (redux)*

The arbitration clause at issue provided for arbitration in Chicago "in accordance with the Rules of Conciliation and Arbitration of the International Chamber of Commerce" (the "ICC"). The ICC is well known as one of the premier global institutions providing for arbitration of business disputes. Not surprisingly, it is also one of the more expensive institutions.

In this case, the court noted allegations by Brower that "a claim of less than $50,000 required advance fees of $4,000 (more than the cost of most Gateway products), of which the $2,000 registration fee was nonrefundable even if the consumer prevailed at the arbitration. Consumers would also incur travel expenses disproportionate to the damages sought . . ., as well as bear the cost of Gateway's legal fees if the consumer did not prevail at the arbitration . . ."

Relying in large part on the foregoing allegations, the court explained "we do not find that the possible inconvenience of the chosen site (Chicago) alone rises to the level of unconscionability. We do find, however, that the excessive cost factor that is necessarily entailed in arbitrating before the ICC is unreasonable and surely serves to deter the individual consumer from invoking the process . . . . Barred from resorting to the courts by the arbitration clause in the first instance, the designation of a financially prohibitive forum effectively bars consumers from this forum as well; consumers are thus left with no forum at all in which to resolve a dispute. . . ." The court therefore held the clause, as written, to be unconscionable, but remanded the case for enforcement of the arbitration agreement in a more cost-effective forum.[26]

Notably, and fully consistent with the Supreme Court's decision in *Concepcion*, the *Brower* court left undisturbed a lower court holding explaining "that while a class-action lawsuit, such as the one herein, may be a less costly alternative to the arbitration (which is generally less costly than litigation), that does not alter the binding effect of the valid arbitration clause contained in the agreement." The appellate decision in *Brower* focused solely on the extraordinarily prohibitive cost of arbitrating the claims of an individual claimant in arbitration proceedings administered by the chosen institution—costs that very likely would have met even the "high burden of proof" required by the Supreme Court in *Carnival Cruise Lines*.

In this light, it is worth noting the details of the arbitration provision at issue in *Concepcion*. The agreement provided:

> that AT&T must pay all costs for nonfrivolous claims; that arbitration must take place in the county in which the customer is billed; that, for claims of $10,000 or less, the customer may choose whether the arbitration proceeds in person, by telephone, or based only on submissions; that either party may bring a claim in small claims court in lieu of arbitration; and that the arbitrator may award any form of individual relief, including injunctions and presumably punitive damages. The agreement, moreover, denies AT&T any ability to seek reimbursement of its attorney's fees, and, in the event that a customer receives an arbitration award greater than AT&T's last written settlement offer, requires AT&T to pay a $7,500 minimum recovery and twice the amount of the claimant's attorney's fees.[27]

---

[26] Brower v. Gateway 2000, Inc., 676 N.Y.S.2d 565, 246 A.D.2d 246 (App. Div. 1998).
[27] AT&T Mobility, LLC v. Concepcion, 131 S.Ct. 1740 (2011).

The primary battle in *Concepcion* was of course over the class action waiver. However, the details of the specific arbitration agreement—seemingly drafted to make individual arbitration appear as cost-effective as possible— avoided the sort of issue presented by the *Brower* case.

Thus, we can see some common themes here that might suggest at least a few of the contours of "unconscionability" in the context of an arbitration agreement. Arbitration agreements are generally enforceable, and are not unconscionable merely because they are contained in a contract of adhesion requiring arbitration by a consumer or employee—even when such a requirement effectively precludes class action. However, an arbitration agreement may be unconscionable where the nature of the arbitration agreement effectively precludes any basic redress of rights—either because the cost is extraordinarily excessive; or because the proposed decision maker is inherently biased. Other terms precluding such basic redress may also render an arbitration agreement unconscionable, but a bar precluding class arbitration does not.

In fact, a number of cost-effective arbitration forums have emerged in recent years (including online arbitration), and at least one major provider of consumer arbitration has ceased providing such services after allegations of favoring business over consumers. Thus, the few limits that do exist may be having at least some effect on the nature of arbitration agreements. However, a defense of "unconscionability" is also subject to another frequent hurdle in that it must often be brought before the arbitral tribunal—and not in court proceedings.

An Additional Challenge in Raising the Issue of Unconscionability in the Context of Arbitration

In most instances, a party seeking to avoid arbitration is trying to get into court (and often times, in particular, before a jury)—instead of proceedings of any kind before an arbitral tribunal. However, a well-drafted arbitration clause may effectively preclude a court from ever hearing an unconscionability challenge to the arbitration clause itself.

Example 24-4: *Rent-A-Center, West, Inc. v. Jackson*

Jackson executed an arbitration agreement with his employer, Rent-A-Center, which also included a provision "delegating" exclusively to the arbitrator any decision as to whether the parties had agreed to arbitrate the employment dispute in question. Thus, any question of the validity of the arbitration agreement, including any allegation that it was unconscionable, was to be decided by the arbitrator—and not by a court.

When Jackson brought an employment discrimination claim against Rent-A-Center, he sought a court determination that the arbitration agreement was unconscionable. However, the Supreme Court held that a court had no jurisdiction to consider the issue, because it had been "delegated" exclusively to the arbitrators. In effect, the Court treated the "delegation" agreement just like any other dispute submitted to an arbitrator, thus precluding any court review of the decision delegated to the arbitrator beyond the very narrow statutory range of exceptions to which any arbitration award is subject. Jackson could still raise an unconscionability challenge with respect to the arbitration agreement, but could only do so before the same arbitrator charged with resolving his employment discrimination claim on the merits.[28]

As one might reasonably intuit, these sorts of "delegation" agreements are now commonplace—contained either in the arbitration clause, itself, or incorporated into the clause by reference to a set of institutional rules containing such a provision. In either case, a "delegation" agreement is fully enforceable under FAA § 2, just like any other arbitration agreement.

As indicated at the outset, agreements requiring arbitration of consumer or employee claims—at least those agreed upon through the execution of a contract of adhesion before the actual dispute arose—are quite controversial. Businesses argue that they are necessary to control costs and

---

[28] Rent-A-Center, West, Inc. v. Jackson, 130 S.Ct. 2772 (2010).

provide reasonable prices to consumers and reasonable wages to employees. Consumer and employee rights organizations argue that they seriously undermine the enforcement of the substantive rights of those groups. The purpose of this lesson is not to resolve those differences (if such resolution is even possible), but is merely to provide an introduction to the basic nature of arbitration, along with the basic application of unconscionability doctrine to arbitration, as a matter of contract law.

Commercial Business-to-Business Arbitration

We have now seen a few examples of the application of the FAA to contracts involving consumers, but what about business-to-business transactions? Empirical data on arbitration, generally, is of questionable value, because the desirability of arbitration is often very context specific. In many trades, arbitration is the normative means of dispute resolution, with few disputes ever going to court. In contrast, many businesses will rarely commit the sort of agreements often called "bet the company" contracts to arbitration, for fear of losing any potential "second bite at the apple" through a right of appeal. An arbitration clause is merely one arrow in the quiver of the business lawyer drafting an effective contract. It is, however, an important one with which every business lawyer should be thoroughly familiar.

APPLYING THE RULES

Problem 1: Armendariz, an employee of Foundation Health Services, signed an arbitration agreement as part of an overall employment agreement. The agreement required the employee to arbitrate any claim of wrongful termination. The agreement also limited any award by the arbitral tribunal to the amount of wages the employee would have earned from the date of any wrongful termination to the date of the award (fully precluding any award of additional damages, reinstatement, injunctive relief, or any other equitable relief). In contrast, the employer retained the right to bring any claim against the employee in a court of law. The employment agreement also included other obligations of each party not relevant here, but did not include a "delegation" clause.

A year later, Armendariz was terminated and sought to bring a claim for employment discrimination in court, notwithstanding the arbitration agreement. Is the arbitration agreement unconscionable?

The facts of this problem are loosely based on the issues raised in the case of *Armendariz v. Foundation Health Psychcare Services, Inc.*, 24 Cal. 4th 83, 6 P.3d 669 (2000).

Problem 2: A seller's form sales agreement includes an arbitration clause, which provides for arbitration administered by an institution known to be relatively inexpensive, but very slow, as arbitration goes, generally taking from 3 to 5 years (and occasionally more) for final resolution of the dispute. The institutional rules also provide that each party shall pay its own attorney fees and shall share the costs of the arbitration proceedings equally, and the institution shall appoint the arbitrator—not the parties. In concluding their contract, the buyer signs the seller's form agreement.

When a dispute arises, the buyer seeks to bring a claim in court, asserting that the arbitration agreement is unconscionable. What do you think?

Problem 3: You have been asked to draft an arbitration provision for a business client who wishes to include the provision in a contract for the construction of an office building. The client is interested in providing for efficient and effective resolution of any disputes arising under the construction contract. What kinds of issues might you want to consider in doing so?

Suppose your client includes such a provision, and the other party knowingly and voluntarily agrees to it. If one of the parties later breaches the arbitration agreement and seeks to bring a claim in court, should the aggrieved party be able to bring a claim for damages for breach of the arbitration agreement?

Lesson 25: Public Policy

Objectives and Expected Learning Outcomes

In this lesson, you will learn about certain circumstances in which "public policy," by itself, will render a contract unenforceable based on the interests of the public at large. You will learn how courts seek to balance the interests of the parties in enforcement of their freely negotiated contract with the interests of society, as a whole, which might be adversely affected in some way by such enforcement.

Our final consideration of contract validity focuses on issues of public policy. Thus far, we have largely focused on concerns over the process or substance of the bargain, as it affected the parties to that bargain. In contrast, this lesson will focus on concerns for the interest of the public at large, to the extent the contract at issue may implicate or affect these broader interests.

As a general rule, contracts or contract terms contrary to public policy are deemed "void," as compared to other invalid contracts, which are deemed "voidable" by one of the parties. The court, acting in the public interest, typically holds the contract or term invalid, and the right technically belongs to neither party, but to the public at large. However, in many circumstances, the public policy issue will be raised by a party seeking to avoid enforcement (even if the "public policy" issue potentially precluding enforcement is purely fortuitous in its application in this party's favor), and, in a few circumstances, the right to challenge enforceability may be available to one of the parties, but not the other.

In some instances, a legislative enactment may expressly provide that certain contract provisions are void or otherwise unenforceable based on public policy. We will encounter two such statutory provisions in UCC Article 2 at the end of this lesson. However, in absence of such a statute, a court will be required to weigh the interest in enforcement against the interests raised by the public policy at issue.[29] In doing so, a court will generally favor the former, absent clear and compelling evidence of the latter.

---

[29] *See* Restatement (Second) of Contracts § 178(1).

In weighing the interest in favor of enforcement,[30] a court will take account of:

- the general interest in enforcing the parties' agreement;

- any special public interest in enforcing the specific term or contract at issue; and

- any unreasonable forfeiture that might result from refusing enforcement.

In considering the last issue, a court may also consider the possibility of mitigating such forfeiture through restitution. In weighing the interest against enforcement,[31] a court will take account of:

- the importance of the policy at issue;

- the likelihood that non-enforcement will further that policy;

- the seriousness and culpability of any misconduct by either party; and

- the directness of the connection between any misconduct and the term or contract at issue.

Illegal Contracts, Generally

A contract requiring the performance of an act expressly prohibited by law is generally "void"—at least when the law involves a serious crime. For example, a contract for a proverbial "hit"—a murder-for-hire contract—is void, as contrary to public policy. One can easily understand that a court will not entertain an action by the person contracting for the "hit" for specific performance or for damages for a failure to perform. Nor would a court entertain an action to "collect" on the contract after it was performed.

There are two reasons a court will generally decline to enforce a contract expressly requiring an illegal act. First, the court wishes to discourage the illegal conduct contemplated by the contract. Presumably, a refusal to

---

[30] *See* Restatement (Second) of Contracts § 178(2).
[31] *See* Restatement (Second) of Contracts § 178(3).

enforce this sort of contract may make at least some small contribution to discouraging the conduct (or at least not encouraging it). Second, it would be unseemly or inappropriate to sully the hands of the judicial system with enforcement of a contract in furtherance of illegal conduct.

Of course, many cases are more challenging in that they may implicate illegal conduct, while not expressly requiring it. Moreover, there are differing levels of "illegality" and sometimes differing levels of "culpability," as applied to the parties to an illegal contract. We should begin, however, by noting that one may sometimes have to think a bit to distinguish illegal conduct from legal conduct. Consider the following examples.

> **Example 25-1:** Sue agrees in January to sell wheat to Ben in July, at a price of $10 per bushel, which happens to be the market price in January. By contracting for wheat to be delivered 6 months later at a price determined in advance, Sue is "betting" that the price of wheat will be less than or equal to $10 in August. In contrast, Ben is "betting" that the price will be greater than or equal to $10 in August. Of course, this sort of commercial "bet" is not illegal anywhere, inasmuch as this is not the sort of "gambling" that is considered illegal in many jurisdictions. Thus, either Sue or Ben will be able to enforce their contract if the other refuses to perform in August.

> **Example 25-2:** Sue acquires chips on credit to place a "bet" at a roulette wheel in a duly licensed Nevada casino owned and operated by Ben. While this sort of "gambling" is illegal in many jurisdictions, it is legal in Nevada. Thus, Ben will be able to enforce Sue's promise to pay for the chips, because their contract is legal, even though it involves "gambling."

> **Example 25-3:** Sue acquires some chips for cash and others on credit to place "bets" at a roulette wheel in a casino owned and operated by Ben in a jurisdiction in which such gambling is illegal. The statute makes gambling a crime

subject to moderate penalties, but does not address the enforceability of contract terms.

Under the general rule, the court will leave the parties where it found them. Ben will be unable to enforce Sue's promise to pay for additional chips, and Sue will not be entitled to recover restitution for her loses at the roulette wheel.

As a general rule, the parties to a contract unenforceable as a matter of public policy will also be precluded from recovering restitution to avoid unjust enrichment.[32] The court simply leaves the parties as it finds them. However, in certain circumstances, in which the parties are not equally culpable or one party seeks to withdraw from the illegal enterprise before its improper objective is achieved, limited recovery based on restitution may be available.[33] When one party is more culpable than the other, the parties are said not to be *in pari delicto*, or equally culpable.

Example 25-4: If, in example 25-3 above, Ben had been running a "crooked" roulette wheel in which he controlled the outcome to ensure that Sue lost, Ben would likely be deemed more culpable than Sue, and she might be entitled to recover restitution for the cash she lost at Ben's crooked wheel.

In other instances of illegal contracts, a court may actually enforce the agreement if doing so is more likely to deter the illegal conduct at issue than refusing to enforce the agreement. Consider the following example.

Example 25-5: Eli, a Mexican national who is illegally in Arizona, is hired by Frank, who needs workers to ship and receive goods in his produce distribution warehouse. Both federal and state laws make such employment illegal. After working for a month, Eli asks to be paid, and Frank refuses.

---

[32] See Restatement (Second) Contracts § 197.
[33] See Restatement (Second) Contracts §§ 198 and 199.

Which will better advance a public policy seeking to prevent U.S. businesses from hiring illegal aliens—enforcing the contract or refusing to do so? You may assume that, in any event, Eli will be deported and Frank will be fined.

Courts have in fact split on this issue. What do you think? Consider each of the factors both for and against enforcement at the beginning of this lesson.

Finally, we can consider an example in which the legality of the conduct is less clear and the connection between the contract and any illegal conduct is more attenuated.

Example 25-6: Ben purchases roulette wheels (wheels that work properly, unlike Example 25-4) from Sara for use in each of Ben's casinos—one in Nevada, a jurisdiction where gambling is legal, and one for use in another jurisdiction, where gambling is illegal. However, both are shipped by Sara to Ben's warehouse in Nevada. Ben receives a delivery of roulette wheels destined for ultimate use in his "illegal" casino, and he refuses to pay for them. Sara brings a legal action to enforce Ben's promise to pay.

The contract between Ben and Sara for delivery of roulette wheels in Nevada is perfectly legal. However, the ultimate use of the wheels is, in this instance, illegal. In deciding whether to enforce the contract, a court will take note of both the general interest in enforcement, as well as the forfeiture Sara will suffer if Ben does not pay for the wheels. A court will also take note of the significance of the policy against gambling in the jurisdiction in which it is illegal. However, the questionable likelihood that non-enforcement will further the policy, the innocuousness of selling roulette wheels legally in many places today, and the lack of a direct connection between a legal delivery of the goods in Nevada and their subsequent illegal use, would likely leave the court with a balance in favor of enforcement.

In weighing the public interest against enforcement in the foregoing example, a court might also consider Sara's knowledge. If she knew that many of these wheels shipped to Nevada were ultimately destined for illegal use, then the balance might very well tip towards non-enforcement.

Thus far, we have focused on statutory prohibitions. However, public policy may also be implicated where a party fails to comply with a licensing or regulatory requirement. These issues are addressed in the next section.

Licensing and Other Regulatory Rules

A failure to comply with a licensing requirement or other regulatory rule will rarely, if ever, preclude enforcement of a related contract where the primary purpose of the licensing or regulatory scheme is revenue generation. Thus, a failure to pay a tax on a particular enterprise will not generally render the contracts of that enterprise unenforceable as a matter of public policy.

> **Example 25-7:** A contractor is required to obtain a license before providing construction services in a particular jurisdiction. The licensing process includes steps to insure the basic "competency" of the contractor before a license is issued. After the initial license is issued, the contractor must renew the license annually for a fee, but need not submit any additional information in connection with renewal. The fee is used to fund the overall licensing program.
>
> If a contractor is licensed, but fails to pay the annual renewal fee, such failure may be subject to regulatory fines or penalties, but should not affect the contractor's ability to enforce any building contracts.

In contrast, the same sort of failure may preclude enforcement where the primary purpose of the licensing or regulatory scheme is to protect the public.

Where the primary purpose is protection of the public welfare, a failure to comply with a licensing requirement or regulatory rule will render a contract unenforceable based on public policy if the interest in protecting the public clearly outweighs the interest in enforcement.[34]

---

[34] *See* Restatement (Second) of Contracts § 181.

Example 25-8: Under the same licensing regime in Example 25-7, a contractor who failed to obtain a license in the first instance might be precluded from enforcing a building contract. The licensing regime includes an assessment of the contractor's competency and therefore serves to protect public welfare. As such, the contractor's failure to comply with the licensing requirement may preclude contract enforcement, at the option of the person dealing with the unlicensed contractor.

In effect, where the purpose is protection of the public welfare, the analysis is very much like that of a statute prohibiting illegal conduct, as addressed in the prior section. Thus far, our consideration has focused on public policy related to express statutory or regulatory prohibitions or requirements. However, some public policy issues related to contract enforcement are derived more broadly, as largely judicially created public policy.

Restraint of Trade

One of the paramount policies in a capitalist economy is support for a free market, unconstrained by monopolistic behavior or other restraints on open competition. This policy is largely addressed through federal and state statutes. However, the regulation of one area—covenants not to compete—has largely developed as judicially created public policy (though some state statutes also address the issue, today).

Under certain circumstances, an employer may have a legitimate interest in preventing an employee from competing with the employer after leaving its employment—at least within certain reasonable limits. The employer may have invested significant time and money to train the employee as to its means and methods, and may have also given the employee unique access to its customer base and other proprietary information. If the employer was fully precluded from protecting this sort of "investment" in the employee, then it might be less inclined to make such an investment. However, the employer's efforts to protect its investment may collide with a broader public interest.

If a former employee is prevented from competing with his or her prior employer, then the public will lose out on the right to do business with that former employee, as well as the potential benefit of better value that may be derived from a more competitive market. Thus, the public interest in a free and competitive marketplace militates against enforcement of covenants in any way limiting or barring competition.

The law seeks to balance these competing concerns, barring unreasonable restraints of trade, while giving effect to reasonable restraints "ancillary" to a valid relationship or business transaction. Such ancillary restraints might include, for example, a promise by an employee or other agent not to compete with his or her employer, or a promise by a seller of a business not to compete with the business being sold.[35] Consider the following examples.

> **Example 25-9:** Kay hires Len to work in her business with the understanding that Kay will have to spend significant time and money to train Len and the further understanding that Len will require access to substantial confidential information regarding Kay's customers and business operation in order to perform his job. As part of his employment agreement, Len promises, within specified limits, not to compete with Kay's business after his employment with Kay ceases. This covenant by Len not to compete with Kay after the cessation of their employment relationship is "ancillary" to Kay's employment of Len and is, therefore, enforceable, as long as the scope and duration of the covenant are reasonable.

> **Example 25-10:** Len sells his business to Kay, and both understand that Len's knowledge of the business would give him a unique advantage in competing with that business after the sale, thus significantly undermining the value of the business to Kay. In order to encourage Kay to invest in the business, secure in the knowledge that she will have a reasonable opportunity to realize the value of that investment, Len promises, within specified limits, not to compete with the business after it is sold to Kay. This covenant by Len not to compete with Kay is "ancillary" to the sale of the

---

[35] See Restatement (Second) of Contracts §§ 186, 187, 188.

business to Kay and is, therefore, enforceable, as long as the scope and duration of the covenant are reasonable.

Thus, a restraint ancillary to a valid business relationship or transaction is generally enforceable, while any other restraint is not. Even such an ancillary restraint is, however, subject to additional limits. Each aspect of a restraint, including:

- the scope of the goods or services subject to the covenant;

- the geographic scope of the covenant; and

- the duration of the covenant

must be limited such that:

- the restraint is no greater than necessary to protect the legitimate business interests of the promisee; and

- such interests of the promisee are neither outweighed by

  o the hardship on the promisor, nor

  o likely injury to the interests of the public at large.

To the extent a court determines that an ancillary restraint goes beyond such limits, the court may strike the entire provision at issue or may alter the term in such a manner as to provide for reasonable limits on the operation of the restraint.

Wrongful Employment Termination

As indicated earlier, the common law default rule provides for "employment at will" such that the employment relationship is terminable by either employer or employee at any time and for any reason. This common law default is subject to numerous federal and state laws limiting an employer's right to terminate an employee for certain statutorily prohibited reasons (many of which are intended to prevent employment discrimination based on gender, race, ethnicity, age, disability, and other personal attributes). However, other judicially created limits have also evolved. In particular, an employer is generally precluded from certain "retaliatory" terminations of an employee.

The operation of a business is subject to a variety of laws and regulations intended to protect the public interest. In some circumstances, an employee may be in the best position to discover a violation of such a law or regulation. For an "at will" employee, this presents a classic dilemma. Should the employee simply keep quiet, protecting his or her interest in employment? Or should the employee report the apparent violation in protection of the broader public interest? The public policy exception to at will employment seeks to avoid this dilemma by protecting the "whistle blower" employee from any retaliatory employment action. Today, this sort of protection is also provided in many statutes, along with the judicially created common law doctrine.

Contracts Affecting the Family

Contracts affecting the family often touch upon issues raising significant public policy concerns. Two classic areas in which the contract rights may collide with the public interest include contracts between spouses and contracts involving children.

A couple, either prior to marriage or in contemplation or recognition of a co-habitation relationship, may agree in advance as to how their earnings or property will be shared in the event that they later decide to go their separate ways. In the context of an intimate relationship, the nature of the "bargaining" process is often questionable, at best. The very nature of such agreements may negatively impact public interest in the health and stability of existing family relationships. Moreover, a result leaving one spouse indigent may further affect the public interest. As a result, such spousal agreements, while generally enforceable, are often subject to judicial scrutiny to the extent they may be contrary to the broader public interest.[36]

Contracts involving children raise even greater concerns, inasmuch as the children are not even parties to the agreement at issue, nor would they have

---

[36] Restatement (Second) of Contracts § 190.

the capacity to be parties to an enforceable contract. While parents are obviously afforded substantial discretion in raising their children, they have little, if any, power to conclude binding contractual agreements affecting the general welfare of those children in the future.

For example, an agreement between parents determining in advance which will be awarded custody of their child will not be enforceable, unless the court agrees that enforcement is in the best interest of the child.[37] In effect, the public interest in the best interests of the child unequivocally takes priority over the parents' interest in their contract. Courts have also generally scrutinized the increasingly common "surrogacy" agreement on similar grounds. Ultimately, the best interests of the child are consistent given priority to the extent that they may conflict with the interests of the contracting parties.

UCC Article 2

UCC Article 2 contains two examples of statutory provisions precluding enforcement of a contract term based on public policy. In the first instance, the term is deemed "void," while in the second it is deemed "unconscionable," and therefore subject the court's discretion to refuse enforcement under UCC § 2-302. **STOP NOW and READ UCC § 2-718(1) below.**

UCC § 2-718(1)

(1) Damages for breach by either party may be liquidated [determined in advance, as to the amount] in the agreement . . . [However, a] term fixing unreasonably large liquidated damages is **void** as a penalty (emphasis added).

We will explore this provision more fully in Chapter 8 on remedies. However, the general remedial policy barring punitive damages for breach of contract (addressed earlier in Lesson 2) also precludes the parties from contractually agreeing to a penalty in the event of a breach.

---

[37] Restatement (Second) of Contracts § 191.

While not necessarily obvious at first blush, the public policy at issue here is economic efficiency. If a party cannot perform all of its obligations, society as a whole is best off if this party breaches the contract or contracts resulting in the lowest actual quantum of damages, thereby minimizing the total loss to the economy as a whole. However, a penalty may cause inefficient behavior, encouraging a party to perform a contract in which damages caused by a breach would be minimal, but penalties high, while breaching a contract resulting in higher actual damages and a greater overall systemic loss. To be clear, the validity of the above public policy justification for the statutory rule is subject to significant debate. However, there is little question that the provision is grounded in the basic idea of "efficient breach," whatever one may think of the theory.

We will also discover in Chapter 8 that parties may contractually agree to modify or limit many of the remedies typically available to an aggrieved party. However, one such limitation is expressly precluded. **STOP NOW and READ UCC § 2-719(3) below.**

UCC § 2-719(3)

(3) . . . Limitation of consequential damages for injury to the person in the case of consumer goods is prima facie **unconscionable** . . . (emphasis added).

Consider the interests being protected by each. Do you see now why one is "void," in the public interest, while the other is deemed unconscionable and therefore subject to a challenge by one of the parties? Is there a "public" interest in the latter as well? If an individual suffers injury and goes uncompensated for those injuries, society as a whole may very well bear the loss in many cases.

Again, each of these rules related to remedies will be addressed more fully in Chapter 8. However, they provide useful examples at this juncture of statutory rules expressly rendering a contract term unenforceable as a matter of public policy.

APPLYING THE RULES

Problem 1: The Fourteenth Street Store contracted to buy certain clothing items from Sirkin. The contract was concluded on behalf of buyer by McGuiness, its purchasing agent, as a direct result of an illegal bribe paid by Sirkin to McGuiness. The price of the goods was fully consistent with normal market pricing for such goods, and the bribe was 5% of the total price amount. The Fourteenth Street Store received and retained the goods. However, the buyer refused to pay Sirkin for the goods (or return them) upon subsequently learning of the bribe. Sirkin sued to enforce the buyer's promise to pay the price of the goods.

Should a court enforce the contract? If so, at what price should the contract be enforced? How many contracts are involved here?

The facts of this problem are loosely based on the issues raised in the case of *Sirkin v. Fourteenth St. Store*, 124 A.D. 384 (N.Y. App. Div. 1908).

Problem 2: Johnson hired Hopper, a recent veterinary school graduate, to work in his veterinary clinic (All Pet Animal Clinic) in Laramie, Wyoming. Hopper executed an agreement with the All Pet Animal Clinic providing that either party could terminate upon 30 days written notice, and further providing as follows.

> This agreement may be terminated by either party upon 30 days' notice to the other party. Upon termination, Dr. Hopper agrees that she will not practice small animal medicine for a period of three years from the date of termination within 5 miles of the corporate limits of the City of Laramie, Wyoming. Dr. Hopper agrees that the duration and geographic scope of that limitation is reasonable.

All Pet specialized in the care of small animals maintained as household pets, and Dr. Hopper worked under the guidance and supervision of Dr. Johnson for 3 years, at the end of which the employment relationship was terminated consistent with the agreement.

Shortly thereafter, Dr. Hopper purchased Gem City Veterinary Clinic, a veterinary practice including both small and large animals, located within the City of Laramie. Under Hopper's guidance, Gem City's client list grew from 368 at the time she purchased the practice to approximately 950, of which 187 had been clients of All Pet Animal Clinic. At Gem City, slightly more than half of Hopper's work involved small animals. Laramie is a relatively small college town, surrounded by sparsely populated rural areas and ranchlands.

All Pets Animal Clinic sues Hopper for breach of contract. Is Hopper liable for breach?

The facts of this problem are loosely based on the issues raised in the case of *Hopper v. All Pet Animal Clinic*, 861 P.2d 531 (Wyo. 1993).

6

The Content of the Parties' Agreement

Key Concepts

- What are the Parties' Rights and Obligations?
- Contract Interpretation, Parol Evidence, Past and Present Conduct, and Default Rules

Lesson 26: Deciding between Competing Versions of Intent

Objectives and Expected Learning Outcomes

In this lesson, you will learn the basic means and methods of contract interpretation. You will revisit the proper use of evidence of the parties' subjective and objective intent, and you will discover the basic principles, resources, and rules employed in contract interpretation. You will then consider a classic contract interpretation case in preparation for further exploration of contract interpretation in the coming lessons.

You should now have a pretty solid idea of what it takes to form an enforceable agreement. Thus, we can next move on to examine more closely the "content" of such an agreement, assuming—at least for the analysis that follows—that the parties have indeed concluded an enforceable agreement. We briefly looked at the question of "content" earlier, in addressing the question of whether "additional" terms should be deemed included in the parties' agreement under UCC § 2-207. We now begin a much more detailed examination of "content," generally, including the determination and interpretation of the express and implied agreement-in-fact of the parties, as well as the supplementation of that agreement, as necessary, with default terms implied by the governing law absent contrary agreement by the parties. This total contract "content" will ultimately provide the detailed rights and obligations of each party to the agreement.

Our analysis begins with a return to the basic rules for ascertaining party intent, first encountered in Lesson 9. We will then consider a variety of rules relating to the parties' ability to narrow or limit the content of their agreement through the use of formal written instruments. Next, we will examine the actual means and methods by which the parties' words are given meaning and ambiguities are resolved, including the roles of judge and jury. We will also consider the significance of certain circumstances surrounding formation and performance of the contract. Finally, we will examine a variety of default legal rules (along with a "mandatory" rule requiring good faith), which are used to supplement or fill "gaps" in the parties' agreement to the extent that the agreement does not, in fact, expressly or impliedly answer the question at issue.

Interpretation—Ascertaining the Parties' Intent-in-Fact

We have all had the experience of reaching what we believed to be a mutual understanding with another person, only later to discover that we had something quite different in mind from the understanding of the other person. Often, this will happen in the context of oral or other informal means of communications, such as notes, e-mails, texts or other expressions in which we are not always as careful with our words as we might be in a more formal setting. In such a setting, it is easy to see how misunderstandings might arise. However, misunderstandings also commonly arise in the context of far more formal agreements, even those drafted by proverbial armies of lawyers.

At bottom, words are rarely as precise as we might intend—especially in the absence of context. Many words have multiple meanings, and even individual meanings may have a range of possible nuanced variations. Sometimes parties may use a word of phrase with different meanings in mind in circumstances in which they easily could have resolved the issue if they had recognized the misunderstanding at the time. Other times, the parties' differing understanding may reflect a fundamental difference as to the issue in question—one which might have prevented conclusion of the contract if the parties had known. In each instance, the parties' differing views will not affect the enforceability of their contract, as long as there is an objective basis for choosing between them. The process of doing so is called contract "interpretation."

At the outset, it is useful to distinguish between contract "interpretation" and contract "construction." Courts are not always good about properly maintaining or applying this distinction, so it may or may not be helpful in reading a given judicial opinion. However, the distinction is helpful in understanding the distinct nature of two different inquiries into the "content" of the parties' agreement, as explored throughout this Chapter.

Contract "interpretation" is a factual search for what the parties intended. This is not to suggest that it is limited to subjective intent, as their mutual or joint intent will most often be derived from the perspective of an objectively reasonable person. However, the focus of "interpretation" is on the parties' actual, factual agreement, as derived from the specific communications and circumstances surrounding their agreement. This intent-in-fact includes both "express" communications of intent, as well as intent reasonably "implied" from the factual circumstances of the agreement.

In contrast, contract "construction" involves a legal determination of the effect given to the parties' intent-in-fact by the applicable governing law. One of the most obvious examples of contract "construction" is the application of default legal rules to address issues the parties did not. However, we will also encounter other examples in which the court's "construction" of the parties' intent-in-fact may have a significant effect on the rights and obligations of the parties (i.e., the "content" of the contract) arising from the contract provision at issue. In this current lesson, however, we are primarily focused on "interpretation" (though one issue of "construction" will be raised and specifically identified as such later in the lesson).

It is also helpful to distinguish between at least two different sorts of misunderstandings or disagreements as to meaning—those related to the "vagueness" of a word or phrase and those related to "ambiguity." Vagueness often arises from variations within a single given meaning, as a matter of degree. For example, what is meant by the color "blue"? Is that sky blue, sea blue, or one of the many other shades of blue one might encounter? How heavy is "heavy," or how light is "light" as measures of weight? At the end of this lesson, we will encounter the vagueness of the word "chicken," as applied to a range of different food products each constituting "chicken." In contrast, ambiguity will often involve two or more dramatically different meanings.

376 • Learning Contracts •

Ambiguity may arise from missing information, syntax, inconsistent use, or other sources of confusion as to an otherwise clear term. For example, a term in a contract between U.S. and French parties providing for goods to be transported at 15 degrees might require a rather warm or rather cold temperature absent a clear specification of either Fahrenheit or Celsius as a measure of temperature. Syntax will often lead to ambiguity, arising from improper punctuation, word choice, or word sequence. For example, a non-ferrous metal is a metal without iron. However, if one is speaking about a broad range of substances, including metals, plastics, and other compounds, what is meant by non-ferrous-metal substances? Does this include only metal substances without iron, or does it, instead, include any substance that is not a ferrous-metal substance (i.e., not an iron substance)? These are of course very different meanings.

Perhaps least excusable, but all too frequent in lengthy agreements, is the inconsistent use of the same word or phrase in different parts of the agreement. A Definition section is often used in a longer agreement in an effort to avoid such inconsistencies or other misunderstandings. However, even express "definitions" are no guarantee of avoiding ambiguity, unless carefully followed and applied.

Ultimately, a matter of contract "interpretation" involves a choice between too competing versions of intent proffered by the parties' to the contract. The next section provides the basic methodology for making this choice.

Choosing Between the Parties' Proffered Meanings

In Lesson 9, we first encountered the use of subjective and objective intent to choose between the parties' differing assertions as to whether they had concluded a contract. We can return to the same basic rule summary (albeit by reference to a different restatement provision) as a starting point for our analysis in the current lesson. Earlier, we sought to answer whether the parties intended to conclude a contract. In the current lesson, we begin with an assumption that they have concluded a contract, but seek to ascertain the meaning of one or more of its terms. The basic principles for doing so are exactly the same.

Summary of Basic Rule: ascertaining intent as to contract meaning[1]

- Where the parties share the same subjective intent, that intent shall be given effect.

- Where the subjective intent of the parties differs, the difference shall be resolved by giving effect to the subjective intent of one or the other, as follows:

  ○ If either party actually knew at the time of contracting the differing subjective intent of the other, then that known intent shall be given effect. Absent such actual knowledge,

  ○ That subjective intent shall be given effect that is most consistent with the outward manifestations of the parties, viewed from the perspective of an objectively reasonable person in the position of the parties.

- However, if neither party had any objectively reasonable basis for understanding the other's differing subjective intent as to the meaning of a basic term of the contract, then there shall be no contract.

While a common or shared intent will of course be given effect, there is no "choice" to be made, so our first example addresses circumstances in which one party actually knows of the other party's differing understanding at the time of contact formation.

Example 26-1: Ted is negotiating an agreement with Rita to pave her business parking lot. Ted understands that their agreement includes only "paving," and does not include "sealing." Rita understands that the price quoted by Ted also includes "sealing." Just before going to Rita's place of business, Ted encounters Sue, who just happens to mention that she recently heard from Rita that Ted would be paving and sealing Rita's parking lot.

Assuming that Ted and Rita concluded their contract, without further discussion of the "sealing" issue, Ted's actual awareness, through Sue, of Rita's subjective understanding means that Ted will be bound by Rita's understanding. Ted will be required to "seal" the newly paved parking lot at the agreed upon price, as Rita's proffered meaning will be given

---

[1] This basic rule is reflected in Restatement (Second) of Contracts § 201.

effect, irrespective of which party's intent is more objectively reasonable.

Example 26-2: We can now consider the same facts as Example 26-1, but without the serendipitous conversation between Ted and Sue. Assuming that Ted and Rita concluded their contract, without further discussion of the "sealing" issue, their disagreement as to what is meant by "paving"—either paving alone or paving and sealing—will be resolved by determining which meaning is more objectively reasonable.

If, however, neither party has any objectively reasonably basis for understanding the subjective intent of the other over its own, then there is no basis for ascertaining the parties' intent with respect to the contract term at issue. Where that term is basic to the agreement, then there is simply no contract.

Example 26-3: *Raffles v. Wichelhaus (redux)*

Raffles agreed to sell Wichelhaus 125 bales of cotton for delivery to Liverpool, to arrive on the ship "Peerless," sailing from Bombay." As it turned out, there were two different ships "Peerless" sailing from Bombay to Liverpool, one arriving in October and the other arriving in December.

When Raffles sought to deliver the bales in December, Wichelhaus asserted that it had been referring to the ship Peerless arriving in October—not December. Thus, the seller and buyer had purportedly referred to cotton on two entirely different ships, and neither had any objectively reasonable basis for understanding the meaning attached by the other. As a result, there was no contract at all.[2]

In this case, the search for meaning as to a contract term leads instead to a conclusion that the parties never agreed to a contract at all.

---

[2] 2 H. & C. 906, 159 Eng. Rep. 375 (Ct. of Ex. 1864).

UCC Article 2

As earlier explained in Lesson 9, UCC Article 2 does not expressly address determinations of intent, generally, and instead looks to the foregoing common law concepts, as supplementing Article 2. UCC Article 2 does, however, address a number of specific issues raised in the rest of the lessons in this chapter, and each will be addressed in turn.

The CISG

The CISG addresses party intent in a single statutory provision—whether addressing contract formation or the meaning of contract terms. These basic provisions addressing the use of subjective and objective intent were first presented in Lesson 9 and are included again here for ease of reference. **STOP NOW and review the excerpts from CISG Article 8 below.**

CISG Article 8 (1) and (2)

(1) For the purposes of this Convention statements made by and other conduct of a party are to be interpreted according to his intent where the other party knew or could not have been unaware what that intent was.

(2) If the preceding paragraph is not applicable, statements made by and other conduct of a party are to be interpreted according to the understanding that a reasonable person of the same kind as the other party would have had in the same circumstances.

(3) In determining the intent of a party or the understanding a reasonable person would have had, due consideration is to be given to all relevant circumstances of the case including the negotiations, any practices which the parties have established between themselves, usages and any subsequent conduct of the parties.

The remaining CISG provisions addressing contract interpretation are presented in lessons that follow, each of which addresses in much greater detail specific issues in determining the content of the parties' agreement. Having fully reviewed the basic methodology for giving effect to subjective and objective understandings of intent, we now turn to various interpretive principles, resources for employing these principles, and rules in aid of contract interpretation.

Basic Principles, Resources, and Rules in Aid of Interpretation

We begin the interpretive process with the common meaning of any given word or phrase.[3] While a dictionary will by no means end most interpretive inquiries, it is often the best place to start. A given term must also be given effect within the context of the provision or contract within which it is contained.[4] The specific "part" at issue must be interpreted in light of the "whole." This is of course most obviously true when a written contract includes a "definitions" section, but is no means limited to such cases. A term should also be interpreted in a manner consistent with the purpose of the contract at issue—as derived either from contract "recitals" or from the content of the overall agreement.[5]

Thus, we can begin to summarize the process of interpretation looking almost exclusively at the contents of the agreement itself (especially in the case of a written agreement) by reference to:

- the common meaning of words or phrases;

- the provision or contract as a whole; and

- the purpose of the contract.

While the content of the agreement itself is always relevant to the interpretation of its terms, we will discover in the next two lessons that the use of certain resources outside of a written agreement (when one exists) may sometimes be subject to challenge.

As an initial matter:

- all of the circumstances surrounding the negotiation and conclusion of a contract are relevant for purposes of its interpretation.

---

[3] Restatement (Second) of Contracts § 202(3)(a).
[4] Restatement (Second) of Contracts § 202(2).
[5] Restatement (Second) of Contracts § 202(1).

However, a court may, in certain circumstances addressed in the next lesson, decline to consider such evidence for purposes of interpretation. In contrast, a court will always consider technical meanings or terms of art:

- as established in prior transactions between parties; or

- as regularly used within their trade, or

- the conduct of the parties in performing the transaction at issue.[6]

These three latter sources of interpretive guidance are discussed more thoroughly in Lesson 29.

The process of contract interpretation also employs a variety of specific rules. In the event of conflicting terms, specific terms control over general terms.[7] Individually negotiated terms (sometimes called "dickered terms") control over standardized terms or terms incorporated by reference to an external document or resource.[8] Each of the terms of the agreement should be interpreted, to the extent reasonably possible, to give effect and validity to each term. Ideally, no term should be rendered irrelevant or invalidated.[9]

You will also frequently encounter two Latin maxims, employed as rules for contract interpretation. The first is *"expressio unius est exclusio alterius,"* or the expression of one thing impliedly suggests the exclusion of others. The most common example of this involves "lists." A provision addressing "colors, including red, green, and blue" might reasonably be read as excluding yellow based on the express inclusion of the other three without mentioning yellow. In contrast, a provision addressing "colors, including, but not limited to, red, green, and blue" would not impliedly exclude yellow or any other color, because the list was clearly exemplary—not exclusive.

A second common Latin maxim is *"contra proferentem,"* which provides that an ambiguous term should be construed against the drafter. The logic behind the rule is that the drafter was in the best position to avoid the ambiguity and should, therefore, suffer the consequences of any misun-

---

[6] Restatement (Second) of Contracts § 202(3)(b), (4), and (5).
[7] Restatement (Second) of Contracts § 203(c).
[8] Restatement (Second) of Contracts § 203(d).
[9] Restatement (Second) of Contracts § 203(a).

derstanding. Note that this particular rule has nothing to do with the parties' actual intent-in-fact! This is actually a rule of "construction"—not interpretation. In the cases of all of the other foregoing "rules," the focus is on discerning the actual intent of the parties by implication (go back and review each to see if you can see this). However, the rule of *contra proferentem* is solely based on a policy decision to encourage parties to be clear and penalize them when they are not. This rule has significant force in the context of form contracts—especially insurance contracts. In contrast, it has minimal effect in negotiated business-to-business contracts in which either party could have reasonably noted and resolved the ambiguity.

Thus, we can summarize the foregoing basic rules of interpretation (there are others, but these are most common) as mandating that:

- specific terms control over general terms;

- negotiated terms control over standard terms or terms incorporated by reference;

- each term should be interpreted to give effect and validity to all;

- *expressio unius est exclusio alterius*;

- *contra proferentem.*

The following analysis provides an excellent example of many of the principles, resources, and rules discussed thus far, as well as a preview of more detailed coverage to come.

This entirely fictitious arbitration award is based on *Frigaliment Importing Co., Ltd. v. B.N.S. International Sales Corp.*, 190 F. Supp. 116 (S.D.N.Y. 1960), a classic contract interpretation case. After a trial to the court, Judge Friendly wrote an opinion considered by many as a Contracts "classic." This 1960 opinion pre-dated the CISG (as well as UCC Article 2) and was actually decided on common law grounds. However, Judge Friendly's factual account and legal analysis seem equally at home under UCC Article 2 or the CISG—the latter being the law that would govern this same case if it arose today. Interestingly, the parties' contract also provided for arbitration by the New York Produce Exchange. However, neither of the parties raised the issue, and the court deemed their failure a waiver of their right to arbitration. Thus, it seems fitting in this fictional decision not only to add 50 years to the dates in order to bring the case within the purview of the CISG, but also to shift the forum to arbitration under a popular set of modern institutional rules (the caption reflects the practice of protecting the confidential nature of arbitration when publishing an award, though other names and details are left intact here for ease of reading). While the dates, forum, and applicable law have been changed, Judge Friendly's classic prose is, to the greatest extent possible, left as originally written.[10]

FROM AN ARBITRAL TRIBUNAL

Claimant "F" v. Respondent "B"

Final Award
Issued, 31 October, 2010, in New York, NY, USA, by a purely fictional tribunal duly constituted under the Rules of Arbitration of the International Chamber of Commerce

---

The issue is: "what is chicken?" Claimant says "chicken" means a young chicken, suitable for broiling and frying. Respondent says "chicken" means any bird of that genus that meets contract specifications on weight and quality, including what it calls "stewing chicken" and Claimant pejoratively terms "fowl." Dictionaries give both meanings, as well as some others not relevant here. To support its assertion, Claimant sends a number of volleys over the net; Respondent essays to return them and adds a few serves of its own. Assuming that neither party can show that the other knew—or could not have been unaware of—the first party's own subjective intent, the case nicely illustrates the need to focus on the parties' externally manifested signals as viewed through the lens of a reasonable person, rather than any secret or unexpressed intent.

---

[10] My sincere thanks to Professor Joseph F. Morrissey for allowing me to "borrow" this re-write of Judge Friendly's opinion from our jointly authored casebook on International Sales Law & Arbitration.

In this matter, Claimant, a Swiss corporation, has brought claims against, Respondent, a New York corporation, arising out of two contracts between the parties. Each of the contracts included a written, signed provision calling for arbitration. An arbitral panel has been duly constituted and has provided each of the parties with a full and equal opportunity to present its case. Having considered the submissions of each of the parties, the panel of arbitrators has concluded that Claimant has not sustained its burden of persuasion that the contract used "chicken" in the narrower sense and therefore takes nothing from Respondent. Our reasoning in reaching this decision and our ultimate disposition of the matter are provided below.

The two parties have their places of business in different contracting states, each of which is a contracting state with respect to the United Nations Convention on the International Sale of Goods (the "CISG"). The contracts in question do not contain any choice of law provisions. The parties' contracts are, therefore, governed by the CISG, as provided in Art. 1(1)(a).

The action is for breach of the promise that goods sold shall conform to the description. CISG Art. 35(1). Two contracts are in suit. In the first, dated May 2, 2007, Respondent confirmed the sale to Claimant of US Fresh Frozen Chicken, Grade A, Government Inspected, Eviscerated 2 1/2-3 lbs. and 1 1/2-2 lbs. each, with all chicken individually wrapped in cryovac, packed in secured fiber cartons or wooden boxes, suitable for export:

> 75,000 lbs. 2 ½ – 3 lbs . . . @ $33.00
> 25,000 lbs. 1 ½ – 2 lbs . . . @ $36.50
> Per 100 lbs. FAS New York

scheduled May 10, 2007 pursuant to instructions from Penson & Co., New York.

The second contract, also dated May 2, 2007, was identical save that only 50,000 lbs. of the heavier "chicken" were called for, the price of the smaller birds was $37 per 100 lbs., and shipment was scheduled for May 30. When the initial shipment arrived in Switzerland, Claimant found that the 2 ½ – 3 lbs. birds were not young chicken suitable for broiling and frying but stewing chicken or "fowl"; indeed, many of the cartons and bags plainly so indicated. Protests ensued. Nevertheless, shipment under the second contract was made on May 29, the 2 ½ – 3 lbs. birds again being stewing chicken. Respondent stopped the transportation of these at Rotterdam.

Our inquiry into the parties' intent would normally begin with CISG Article 8(1). If either party knew (or could not have been unaware of) the other's intent, then the knowing party's intent controls, and the understanding of a reasonable person under Article 8(2) becomes irrelevant. While there is some evidence that might support a contention that Claimant "could not have been unaware of" Respondent's intended meaning of "chicken," the evidence is sufficiently thin that we believe the case is better resolved by reference to Article 8(2). We do, however, make reference to this evidence at the end of our analysis, after which the necessary factual context has been more fully developed.

CISG Article 8(2) requires us to interpret the parties' intent, and in particular, the word "chicken," according to the understanding that a reasonable person similarly situated as these parties would have had in the same circumstances. In searching for this reasonable understanding, Article 8(3) requires us to give due consideration to all of the relevant circumstances, including negotiations, past practices, usages, and subsequent conduct of the parties. The present case includes a plethora of such potentially relevant circumstances. We now turn to our application of these legal standards in interpreting the parties' agreement.

Since the word "chicken" standing alone is ambiguous, we turn first to see whether the contract itself offers any aid to its interpretation. Claimant says the 1 1/2-2 lbs. birds necessarily had to be young chicken since the older birds do not come in that size, hence the 2 1/2-3 lbs. birds must likewise be young. This is unpersuasive—a contract for "apples" of two different sizes could be filled with different kinds of apples even though only one species came in both sizes. Respondent notes that the contract called not simply for chicken but for "US Fresh Frozen Chicken, Grade A, Government Inspected." It says the contract thereby incorporated by reference the Department of Agriculture's regulations, which favor its interpretation; we shall return to this after reviewing Claimant's other contentions.

The first hinges on an exchange of cablegrams which preceded execution of the formal contracts. The negotiations leading up to the contracts were conducted in New York between Respondent's secretary, Bauer, and a Mr. Stovicek, who was in New York for the Czechoslovak government at the World Trade Fair. A few days after meeting Bauer at the fair, Stovicek telephoned and inquired whether Respondent would be interested in exporting poultry to Switzerland. Bauer then met with Stovicek, who showed him a cable from Claimant dated April 26, 2007, announcing that they "are buyer" of 25,000 lbs. of chicken 2 1/2-3 lbs. weight, Cryovac packed, Grade A Government inspected, at a price up to 33¢ per pound, for shipment on May 10, to be confirmed by the following morning, and were interested in further offerings. After testing the market for price, Bauer accepted, and Stovicek sent a confirmation that evening. Claimant stresses that, although these and subsequent cables between Claimant and Respondent, which laid the basis for the additional quantities under the first and for all of the second contract, were predominantly in German, they used the English word "chicken"; it claims this was done because it understood 'chicken' meant young chicken whereas the German word, "Huhn," included both "Brathuhn" (broilers) and "Suppenhuhn" (stewing chicken), and that Respondent, whose officers were thoroughly conversant with German, should have realized this. Whatever force this argument might otherwise have is largely drained away by Bauer's testimony that he asked Stovicek what kind of chickens were wanted, received the answer "any kind of chickens," and then, in German, asked whether the cable meant "Huhn" and received an affirmative response. Claimant attacks this as contrary to what Bauer testified on his deposition in March, 2009, and also on the ground that Stovicek had no authority to interpret the meaning of the cable. The first contention would be persuasive if sustained by the record, since Bauer was free at the hearing from the threat of contradiction by Stovicek as he was not at the time of the deposition; however, review of the deposition does not convince us of the claimed inconsistency. As to the second contention, it may well be that Stovicek lacked authority to commit Claimant for prices or delivery dates other than those specified in the cable; but Claimant cannot at the same time rely on its cable to Stovicek as its dictionary to the meaning of the contract and repudiate the interpretation given the dictionary by the man in whose hands it was put.

Claimant's next contention is that there was a definite trade usage that 'chicken' meant 'young chicken.' Respondent showed that it was only beginning in the poultry trade in 2007, thereby bringing itself within the principle that his acceptance of the standard must be made to appear by proving either that he had actual knowledge of the usage or that the usage is so generally known and observed within the international community that his actual individual knowledge of it may be inferred—i.e., that he ought to have known. See CISG Article 9(2). Here there was no proof of actual knowledge of the alleged usage; indeed, it is quite plain that Respondent's belief was to the contrary. In order to meet the alternative requirement, CISG Article 9 demands a showing that the usage is of so long continuance, so well established, so notorious, so universal and so reasonable in itself, as that the presumption is violent that the parties contracted with reference to it, and made it a part of their agreement. Article 9 demands that, if the party did not know, it surely ought to have known.

Claimant endeavored to establish such a usage by the testimony of three witnesses and certain other evidence. Strasser, resident buyer in New York for a large chain of Swiss cooperatives, testified that "on chicken I would definitely understand a broiler." However, the force of this testimony was considerably weakened by the fact that in his own transactions the witness, a careful businessman, protected himself by using "broiler" when that was what he wanted and "fowl" when he wished older birds. Niesielowski, an officer of one of the companies that had furnished the stewing chicken to Respondent, testified that "chicken" meant "the male species of the poultry industry. That could be a broiler, a fryer or a roaster," but not a stewing chicken; however, he also testified that upon receiving Respondent's inquiry for "chickens," he asked whether the desire was for "fowl or frying chickens" and, in fact, supplied fowl, although taking the precaution of asking Respondent, a day or two after Claimant's acceptance of the contracts in suit, to change its confirmation of its order from "chickens," as Respondent had originally prepared it, to "stewing chickens." Dates, an employee of Urner-Barry Company, which publishes a daily market report on the poultry trade, gave it as his view that the trade meaning of "chicken" was "broilers and fryers." In addition to this opinion testimony, Claimant relied on the fact that the Urner-Barry service, the Journal of Commerce, and Weinberg Bros. & Co. of Chicago, a large supplier of poultry, published quotations in a manner which, in one way or another, distinguish between "chicken," comprising broilers, fryers and certain other categories, and "fowl," which, Bauer acknowledged, included stewing chickens. This material would be impressive if there were nothing to the contrary. However, there was, as will now be seen.

Respondent's witness Weininger, who operates a chicken eviscerating plant in New Jersey, testified "Chicken is everything except a goose, a duck, and a turkey. Everything is a chicken, but then you have to say, you have to specify which category you want or that you are talking about." Its witness Fox said that in the trade "chicken" would encompass all the various classifications. Sadina, who conducts a food inspection service, testified that he would consider any bird coming within the classes of "chicken" in the Department of Agriculture's regulations to be a chicken. The specifications approved by the General Services Administration include fowl as well as broilers and fryers under the classification "chickens." Statistics of the Institute of American Poultry Industries use the phrases "Young chickens" and "Mature chickens," under the general heading "Total chickens." and the Department of Agriculture's daily and weekly price reports avoid use of the word "chicken" without specification.

Respondent advances several other points which it claims affirmatively support its construction. Primary among these is the regulation of the United States Department of Agriculture, 7 C.F.R. § 70.300-70.370, entitled, 'Grading and Inspection of Poultry and Edible Products Thereof.' and in particular 70.301 which recited:

> Chickens. The following are the various classes of chickens:
> (a) Broiler or fryer . . . ; (b) Roaster . . . ; (c) Capon . . . ;
> (d) Stag . . . ; (e) Hen or stewing chicken or fowl . . . ; (f) Cock
> or old rooster . . .

Respondent argues, as previously noted, that the contract incorporated these regulations by reference. While such a definitional usage based on U.S. governmental regulations would not rise to the level of an international usage, as required under CISG Article 9(2), the usage may nonetheless be expressly adopted by the parties under Article 9(1). Claimant answers that the contract provision related simply to Grade and Government inspection and did not incorporate the Government definition of 'chicken,' and also that the definition in the Regulations is ignored in the trade. However, the latter contention was contradicted by Weininger and Sadina; and there is force in Respondent's argument that the contract made the regulations a dictionary, particularly since the reference to Government grading was already in Claimant's initial cable to Stovicek.

Respondent makes a further argument based on the impossibility of its obtaining broilers and fryers at the 33¢ price offered by Claimant for the 2 1/2-3 lbs. birds. There is no substantial dispute that, in late April, 2007, the price for 2 1/2-3 lbs. broilers was between 35 and 37¢ per pound, and that when Respondent entered into the contracts, it was well aware of this and intended to fill them by supplying fowl in these weights. It claims that Claimant must likewise have known the market since Claimant had reserved shipping space on April 23, three days before Claimant's cable to Stovicek, or, at least, that Stovicek was chargeable with such knowledge. It is scarcely an answer to say, as Claimant does in its brief, that the 33¢ price offered for the 2 1/2-3 lbs. 'chickens' was closer to the prevailing 35¢ price for broilers than to the 30¢ at which Respondent procured fowl. Claimant must have expected Respondent to make some profit—certainly it could not have expected Respondent deliberately to incur a loss.

Finally, Respondent relies on conduct by the Claimant after the first shipment had been received. On May 28 Claimant sent two cables complaining that the larger birds in the first shipment constituted "fowl." Respondent answered with a cable refusing to recognize Claimant's objection and announcing "We have today ready for shipment 50,000 lbs. chicken 2 1/2-3 lbs. 25,000 lbs. broilers 1 1/2-2 lbs.," these being the goods procured for shipment under the second contract, and asked immediate answer "whether we are to ship this merchandise to you and whether you will accept the merchandise." After several other cable exchanges, Claimant replied on May 29 "Confirm again that merchandise is to be shipped since resold by us if not enough pursuant to contract chickens are shipped the missing quantity is to be shipped within ten days stop we resold to our customers pursuant to your contract chickens grade A you have to deliver us said merchandise we again state that we shall make you fully responsible for all resulting costs." Respondent argues that if Claimant was sincere in thinking it was entitled to young chickens, Claimant would not have allowed the shipment under the second contract to go forward, since the distinction between broilers and chickens drawn in Respondent's cablegram must have made it clear that the larger birds would not be broilers. However, Claimant answers that the cables show Claimant was insisting on delivery of young chickens and that Respondent shipped old ones at its peril. Respondent's point would be highly relevant on another disputed issue—whether if liability were established, the measure of damages should be the difference in market value of broilers and stewing chicken in New York or the larger difference in Europe, but we cannot give it weight on the issue of interpretation. Respondent points out also that Claimant proceeded to deliver some of the larger birds in Europe, describing them as "poulets"; Respondent argues that it was only when Claimant's customers complained about this that Claimant developed the idea that "chicken" meant "young chicken." There is little force in this in view of Claimant's immediate and consistent protests.

When all the evidence is reviewed, it is clear that Respondent believed it could comply with the contracts by delivering stewing chicken in the 2 ½ – 3 lbs. size. Respondent's subjective intent would not be significant if this did not coincide with an objective meaning of "chicken." Here it did coincide with one of the dictionary meanings, with the definition in the Department of Agriculture Regulations to which the contract made at least oblique reference, with at least some usage in the trade, with the realities of the market, and with what Claimant's spokesman had said. Claimant asserts it to be equally plain that Claimant's own subjective intent was to obtain broilers and fryers; the only evidence against this is the material as to market prices, and this may not have been sufficiently brought home. See CISG Article 8(1) (if the market prices made Respondent's intent so obvious that Claimant "could not have been unaware what that intent was," then Claimant would have been bound to Respondent's interpretation without reference to the understanding of a reasonable person).

In any event it is unnecessary to determine that issue. For Claimant has the burden of showing under CISG Article 8(2) that a reasonable person in the position of Respondent would have understood that "chicken" was used in the narrower rather than in the broader sense, and this it has not sustained. Claimant's claims against Respondent are therefore denied.

CASE QUESTIONS

(1) In seeking to determine the meaning of "chicken," where does the tribunal begin its search?

    a. What principles or resources does the tribunal employ in seeking to interpret the term by reference to sources within the contract?

    b. To what extent does the tribunal look to the content of and circumstances surrounding the negotiation of the contract?

(2) The tribunal discusses a variety of additional avenues for establishing intent. One of these involves trade usages, which are impliedly deemed to be part of the parties' contract where the parties should have objectively expected this to be the case.

    a. What types of evidence were offered here by Claimant to prove that "chicken" meant young chicken, as a trade usage?

    b. What evidence did Respondent offer in response?

(3) Additionally, the tribunal discussed conduct after the contract had been concluded as a way to discern party intent. This is explicitly allowed by Article 8(3), which provides for due consideration of all circumstances in determining the intent of the parties. Was the evidence persuasive here?

(4) Did you find any reference to any of the rules in aid of interpretation discussed above? The reference is somewhat oblique, but it is there.

(5) Did the tribunal decide the meaning of chicken under Article 8(1) or 8(2)? Might it have decided the issue under the other statutory provision? Why do you think the court made the choice it did?

This entire process of interpretation will be explored more fully in the next three lessons. However, the foregoing case provides a good introduction to the process, along with the following problems.

APPLYING THE RULES

Problem 1: Pam contracts with Ace Interiors to paint the interior of her home. Ace uses a standard printed form contract, with certain terms specific to each painting job inserted into the otherwise standard language. In addition to Pam's name, home address, and the job dates, the specific terms inserted into Pam's contract with Ace stated:

Price: $10,000, complete home interior.

Ace Pro Paint throughout, flat or semi-gloss, as appropriate to nature of surface to be painted—colors as specified in Appendix A.

Paragraph 16 of the pre-printed form read, as follows:

(a) "Flat" finish paint used on all surfaces, except as expressly provided in paragraph 16(b) below.

(b) "Semi-gloss" finish provided on all surfaces requiring easy cleaning and moisture resistance, including baseboard and doors.

Ace has begun painting and uses "flat" finish paint on the bathroom walls and ceilings. Pam insists that Ace is required to use "semi-gloss" finish paint. Who is right?

Problem 2: MCC-Marble Ceramic, Inc. (MCC), a Florida corporation, contracted with Ceramica Nuova d'Agostino S.p.A. (CNA), an Italian ceramic tile maker, to purchase tile. Juan Carlos Monzon, the President of MCC, met Gianni Silingardi, the Commercial Director of CNA, at a trade show in Milan, where they negotiated and concluded the transaction. Having come to an oral agreement on the crucial terms of price, quality, quantity, delivery, and payment, Monzon and Silingardi then recorded these agreed upon terms on one of CNA's standard pre-printed order forms. Monzon then signed the completed form on behalf of MCC.

The standard pre-printed form included a provision requiring notice by the buyer of any product defects by way of a certified letter within 10 days of receipt. MCC later brought legal action alleging that CNA had delivered defective products, and CNA sought dismissal of the action based on MCC's failure to provide the specified notice within 10 days of receipt. Both Monzon and Silingardi (by then, a "former" employee) provided sworn affidavits that they had merely used the standard forms to record the basic dickered terms, and neither had subjectively intended the parties to be bound by any of the pre-printed terms on the CNA form. CNA argued that MCC was nevertheless bound to the 10 day notice provision because any objectively reasonable business person would expect to be bound by all of the terms of the written document signed by Monzon, whether actually read or not.

Was MCC bound by the 10 day notice provision? What if the seller had been located in Alabama instead of Italy?

The facts of this problem are very loosely based on the issues raised in the case of *MCC-Marble Ceramic Center, Inc. v. Ceramica Nuovo D'Agostino SpA*, 144 F.3d 1384 (11th Cir. 1998).

Problem 3: Consider each of the following.

(1) A contract for the purchase and sale of "horse meat scraps" required a "minimum of 50 percent protein." The product delivered contained only 49.53 to 49.96 percent protein. Does the delivered product conform to the contract terms?

(2) A contract for the purchase and sale of asphalt required payment by buyer of seller's "Posted Price at time of delivery." Is the buyer entitled to an earlier, lower price if the buyer had used that price in calculating a paving bid?

(3) A contract provided for the purchase and sale of specified quantities of phosphate at specified prices over three years. The buyer seeks to offer evidence that these specified quantities and prices were mere estimates, subject to "adjustment," depending on the circumstances at the time. Should a court consider such evidence?

As the thoughtful reader may guess, there is more to all of the above "stories," and we will return to each of them, in turn, in the next three lessons.

Lesson 27: The "Parol Evidence" Rule, Merger Clauses & "No Oral Modification" Clauses

Objectives and Expected Learning Outcomes

In this lesson, you will learn the basic application of the parol evidence rule in limiting the scope of extrinsic evidence of the content of the parties' agreement when they have executed a comprehensive of "integrated" writing. You will also learn how a "merger clause" may be useful in clarifying any the intent of the parties to limit or preclude such extrinsic evidence, as well as the role of a "no oral modification" clause in preventing any subsequent modification of a written agreement, except by a further writing.

In the prior lesson, the mythical arbitrator (in fact, Judge Friendly, in a "bench trial" to the court) simply evaluated all of the available evidence in seeking to determine the parties' actual intent-in-fact. However, in some cases, the parties make seek to limit the fact-finder's later consideration of the full range of evidence by giving priority to a single, final, written expression of their intent.

The "Parol Evidence" Rule

It is often noted that the parol evidence rule is neither limited to "parol" (oral) communications, nor is it a rule of "evidence" (a procedural rule limiting admissibility in judicial proceedings). In fact, the parol evidence rule is a substantive contract rule governing the effect of certain writings in discharging any other existing oral or written expressions of the parties' intent.

The parties to any binding agreement can always, of course, mutually agree to terminate that agreement. Moreover, they can also mutually agree to discharge any potential liability arising from any prior negotiations that did not lead to a contract. Thus, the parol evidence rule simply gives effect to an apparent mutual intent, through the execution of a single signed writing, to terminate or otherwise discharge any and all other legal obligations between the parties within the scope of the signed writing. The challenge is in determining whether the parties in fact intended such a discharge and, if so, the scope of the discharge. You should consider each of these questions as you read the following classic "parol evidence" case.

FROM THE COURT

Gianni v. R. Russell & Co.

Supreme Court of Pennsylvania (1924)
281 Pa. 320, 126 A. 791

Schafer, J.

Plaintiff had been a tenant of a room in an office building in Pittsburgh wherein he conducted a store, selling tobacco, fruit, candy and soft drinks. Defendant acquired the entire property in which the storeroom was located, and its agent negotiated with plaintiff for a further leasing of the room. A lease for three years was signed. It contained a provision that the lessee should "use the premises only for the sale of fruit, candy, soda water," etc., with the further stipulation that "it is expressly understood that the tenant is not allowed to sell tobacco in any form, under penalty of instant forfeiture of this lease." The document was prepared following a discussion about renting the room between the parties and after an agreement to lease had been reached. It was signed after it had been left in plaintiff's hands and admittedly had been read over to him by two persons, one of whom was his daughter.

Plaintiff sets up that in the course of his dealings with defendant's agent it was agreed that, in consideration of his promises not to sell tobacco and to pay an increased rent, and for entering into the agreement as a whole, he should have the exclusive right to sell soft drinks in the building. No such stipulation is contained in the written lease. Shortly after it was signed defendant demised the adjoining room in the building to a drug company without restricting the latter's right to sell soda water and soft drinks. Alleging that this was in violation of the contract which defendant had made with him, and that the sale of these beverages by the drug company had greatly reduced his receipts and profits, plaintiff brought this action for damages for breach of the alleged oral contract, and was permitted to recover. Defendant has appealed.

Plaintiff's evidence was to the effect that the oral agreement had been made at least two days, possibly longer, before the signing of the instrument, and that it was repeated at the time he signed; that, relying upon it, he executed the lease. Plaintiff called one witness who said he heard defendant's agent say to plaintiff at a time admittedly several days before the execution of the lease that he would have the exclusive right to sell soda water and soft drinks, to which the latter replied if that was the case he accepted the tenancy. Plaintiff produced no witness who was present when the contract was executed to corroborate his statement as to what then occurred. Defendant's agent denied that any such agreement was made, either preliminary to or at the time of the execution of the lease.

Appellee's counsel argues this is not a case in which an endeavor is being made to reform a written instrument because of something omitted as a result of fraud, accident, or mistake, but is one involving the breach of an independent oral agreement which does not belong in the writing at all and is not germane to its provisions. We are unable to reach this conclusion.

"Where parties, without any fraud or mistake, have deliberately put their engagements in writing, the law declares the writing to be not only the best, but the only evidence of their agreement." [Citations omitted.]

"All preliminary negotiations, conversations and verbal agreements are merged in and superseded by the subsequent written contract, * * * and 'unless fraud, accident, or mistake be averred, the writing constitutes the agreement between the parties, and its terms cannot be added to nor subtracted from by parol evidence.'" [Citations omitted.]

The writing must be the entire contract between the parties if parol evidence is to be excluded, and to determine whether it is or not the writing will be looked at, and if it appears to be a contract complete within itself, "couched in such terms as import a complete legal obligation without any uncertainty as to the object or extent of the engagement, it is conclusively presumed that the whole engagement of the parties, and the extent and manner of their undertaking, were reduced to writing." [Citations omitted.]

When does the oral agreement come within the field embraced by the written one? This can be answered by comparing the two, and determining whether parties, situated as were the ones to the contract, would naturally and normally include the one in the other if it were made. If they relate to the same subject-matter, and are so interrelated that both would be executed at the same time and in the same contract, the scope of the subsidiary agreement must be taken to be covered by the writing. This question must be determined by the court.

In the case at bar the written contract stipulated for the very sort of thing which plaintiff claims has no place in it. It covers the use to which the storeroom was to be put by plaintiff and what he was and what he was not to sell therein. He was "to use the premises only for the sale of fruit, candy, soda water," etc., and was not "allowed to sell tobacco in any form." Plaintiff claims his agreement not to sell tobacco was part of the consideration for the exclusive right to sell soft drinks. Since his promise to refrain was included in the writing, it would be the natural thing to have included the promise of exclusive rights. Nothing can be imagined more pertinent to these provisions which were included than the one appellee avers.

In cases of this kind, where the cause of action rests entirely on an alleged oral understanding concerning a subject which is dealt with in a written contract it is presumed that the writing was intended to set forth the entire agreement as to that particular subject.

"In deciding upon this intent [as to whether a certain subject was intended to be embodied by the writing], the chief and most satisfactory index * * * is found in the circumstance whether or not the particular element of the alleged extrinsic negotiation is dealt with at all in the writing. If it is mentioned, covered, or dealt with in the writing, then presumably the writing was meant to represent all of the transaction on that element, if it is not, then probably the writing was not intended to embody that element of the negotiation." [Citations omitted.]

As the written lease is the complete contract of the parties, and since it embraces the field of the alleged oral contract, evidence of the latter is inadmissible under the parol evidence rule.

"The [parol evidence] rule also denies validity to a subsidiary agreement within [the] scope [of the written contract] if sued on as a separate contract, although except for [that rule], the agreement fulfills all the requisites of valid contract." [Citations omitted.]

There are, of course, certain exceptions to the parol evidence rule, but this case does not fall within any of them. Plaintiff expressly rejects any idea of fraud, accident, or mistake, and they are the foundation upon which any basis for admitting parol evidence to set up an entirely separate agreement within the scope of a written contract must be built. The evidence must be such as would cause a chancellor to reform the instrument, and that would be done only for these reasons [citations omitted] and this holds true where this essentially equitable relief is being given, in our Pennsylvania fashion, through common law forms.

We have stated on several occasions recently that we propose to stand for the integrity of written contracts. [Citations omitted.] We reiterate our position in this regard.

The judgment of the court below is reversed, and is here entered for defendant.

CASE QUESTIONS

(1) What was the "parol evidence" at issue, and why did it matter?

    a. Was the evidence factually disputed?

    b. Did the court resolve the factual dispute as to what was said?

(2) On what basis did the court hold that the writing precluded consideration of any other evidence of the parties' agreement within its scope?

    a. How did the court propose to determine whether the evidence Russell sought to introduce was within the scope of that precluded by the writing?

    b. Russell argued that the promise of exclusivity was part of an independent oral agreement, separate and apart from the lease. Where did Russell purport to find consideration to support this separate oral agreement?

c. If the court had agreed on the presence of an otherwise viable independent agreement, would that have changed the outcome?

"Parol" evidence is often called "extrinsic" evidence in that it is found outside of the "four corners" of the integrated writing. Whether written or oral, this "extrinsic" (parol) evidence can be distinguished from the "intrinsic" words and phrases found within the writing, itself. The application of the parol evidence rule requires a number of determinations, which are generally best addressed in the following sequence.

The first question is whether there is a writing reflecting the parties' agreement. If not, the parol evidence rule is inapplicable. Moreover, this writing must be "integrated" if it is to operate so as to discharge other potential expressions of the parties' intent. The question of integration is one of fact. Its resolution generally looks to the completeness of the agreement as reflective of its status as a final expression of the parties' agreement on at least some range of contract issues. Typically, an integrated writing is a single document or series of documents signed by both parties.

Assuming the parties have executed an integrated writing, the next question is whether the extrinsic evidence falls within its scope. Courts sometimes distinguish between complete and partial integration in an abstract sense. However, the essential question is whether the writing is completely integrated *relative to* the extrinsic evidence at issue. Rarely will a single agreement be completely integrated with respect to the entire array of contractual relationships two parties might have potentially concluded at any given time, so the appropriate inquiry specifically compares the scope of the integrated writing and the extrinsic evidence at issue.

In *Gianni*, the court sought to determine whether Gianni and Russell— had they intended to provide Gianni with an exclusive right to sell soft drinks—would have "naturally and normally" done so in the written, integrated lease. Other courts have used the words "ordinarily" or "naturally" in deciding common law cases. If the term in question is one that would have naturally been included in the writing, then its absence from the writing bars extrinsic evidence of the term under the parol evidence rule. If, in contrast, one **cannot** say that the term would have naturally been included in the writing—in effect, suggesting it might reasonably have been omitted and addressed separately, outside of the writing—then the writing is deemed "partially integrated" with respect to the extrinsic term in question.

This determination of whether the writing is integrated with respect to the term (i.e., whether the term is within the scope of the integrated writing) is typically the most challenging part of the application of the parol evidence rule. In applying the rule, it may be helpful to step back from a mechanical application and ask a simple question. Does the integrated writing establish the signers' intent to create a single, final, definitive statement on the issue in question and to render irrelevant anything else they had written or signed, to date, with respect to that issue? If so, then the writing is likely completely integrated with respect to the term at issue.

> **Example 27-1:** Over a period of two weeks, Meg and Ned negotiate an agreement for Meg to remodel Ned's offices. They have talked about a large range of possible finishes, colors, and designs over that period. When they believe they have finally reached an agreement on the project, they put all of the project specs, pricing, work schedules, and payment schedules into a single written document. Their intent in doing so is to be sure there are no misunderstandings based on anything else they have said or written up to that point (an intent that may be presumed where the document appears complete on its face). They each then sign the document.
>
> The final document signed by Meg and Ned will operate, as intended, to discharge any prior or contemporaneous written or oral evidence of their agreement for the remodeling of Ned's offices. The use of any such evidence to define the content of their agreement will be barred by the parol evidence rule.

Thus, a completely integrated writing will bar any extrinsic evidence with respect to the content of the writing. In contrast, a partially integrated writing will leave the door open to such evidence—but only if the parol or extrinsic evidences does not "contradict" the integrated writing.

A partially integrated writing may be supplemented by evidence consistent with the writing, but may not be contracted by inconsistent evidence. While the distinction makes conceptual sense, its implementation in practice is quite difficult and subject to problems of circularity. Two terms that, in isolation, look inconsistent may, in context, appear fully consistent—assuming of course one accepts the context leading to the interpretation suggested.

Questions involving the extent of integration and consistency are often challenging ones—assuming a court reaches the second. The example that follows raises both issues.

Example 27-2: *Masterson v. Sine*

Dallas and Rebecca Masterson conveyed their ranch to family members Medora and Lu Sine. In the deed used to convey the property, the Mastersons reserved a 10-year option to repurchase the ranch for the selling price. Under governing law, rights such as this option were deemed freely assignable, absent agreement to the contrary. Nothing in the deed providing for the option restricted the assignment of the option.

Dallas later filed bankruptcy, and the bankruptcy trustee sought to exercise Dallas's right to the option on behalf of his creditors (the value of the property at the time was considerably more than the option exercise price). However, the Mastersons asserted that the option was not assignable outside of the family (and could not, therefore, be exercised by the trustee) and sought to offer extrinsic evidence of an agreement between the Mastersons and the Sines to that effect.

The court acknowledge that the deed of conveyance appeared complete on its face, but nevertheless held the deed to be only partially integrated, based on all of the surrounding facts and circumstances, including the fact that the original conveyance took place between family members. Therefore, the written deed left open the door for this collateral agreement barring assignment of the lease. The court further acknowledged that a limit on assignability was in no way inconsistent with the statutory presumption of assignability and, therefore, allowed the Mastersons to introduced evidence of the collateral agreement.[11]

The foregoing decision included a vigorous dissent—first pointing out the obvious convenience of the purported assignment in preventing Dallas's creditors from realizing the value of the property. The dissent went on to point out the lack or any hint of any restriction on assignability in the deed itself (thereby suggesting that any such term should be precluded by the parol evidence rule), as well as the inherent inconsistency of such a restriction with the legal presumption of assignability.

> **"Bankruptcy" Proceedings**
> The following Example involves a bankruptcy "trustee" asserting creditors' rights in an action related to bankruptcy proceedings. When an insolvent party seeks bankruptcy protection, the role of the trustee is to maximize the value of the insolvent's assets so that there is more money available to distribute to those creditors.

In *Masterson*, Judge Traynor, writing for the majority, applied the same test as the court in *Gianni*, asking whether a restriction on assignability might "naturally" be found in the deed granting the option. However, he declined to limit his inquiry to the writing, itself, in determining whether the writing was completely integrated. Instead, he considered all the circumstances, including the nature of the family relationship, as a basis for concluding that the parties might reasonably have chosen to restrict the assignability of the purchase option in a separate, collateral agreement.

In fact, different courts take different approaches on this issue. Some follow a more "formalist" approach, focusing solely on the writing itself in deciding the issue of integration (sometimes called a "four corners" approach). Others follow a more "realist" approach, looking broadly at all of the circumstances, including the evidence at issue, in deciding the issue of integration.

---

[11] Masterson v. Sine, 68 Cal. 2d 222, 436 P.2d 561 (1968).

As indicated in the *Gianni* case, the parol evidence rule includes exceptions for fraud or mistake. Defenses such as fraud or duress (or "mistake," addressed in Chapter 9) seek rescission of the agreement and do not address its "content" (the focus of the parol evidence rule), so the rule has no application. In a similar vein, the parol evidence would not preclude evidence that the parties never concluded an agreement at all. These and other "exceptions" (addressed later, as they arise) are reflected in the summary of the basic "rule" that follows.

Summary of Basic Rule: parol evidence rule[12]

- An integrated writing intended as a final expression / of all or a part of the parties' agreement / fully precludes any extrinsic written or oral evidence / of prior or contemporaneous promises / within its scope / to establish the content of the parties' obligations under the contract, and

  - In any event, precludes any extrinsic written or oral evidence of prior or contemporaneous promises that contradict the writing,

- Except to the extent that the evidence is offered for the purpose of:

  - Establishing that no agreement was ever concluded,

  - Establishing a contract defense to enforcement, such as duress, misrepresentation, or mistake,

  - Establishing an entirely distinct, or collateral, agreement,

  - Resolving an "ambiguity" in the writing,

  - Establishing the right to a particular remedy for breach,

  - Establishing a course of performance, course of dealing, or usage of trade.

The issue of what constitutes an "ambiguity" is addressed in Lesson 28, and the use a course of performance, course of dealing, or usage of trade is addressed in Lesson 29. Remedies are addressed in Chapter 8.

Thus far, we have largely relied on an implication that a comprehensive signed writing suggests the parties' intent to discharge any and all other promises within its scope. However, some writing may make this intent much clearer with an express provision typically called a "merger clause."

---

[12] This basic rule is reflected in Restatement (Second) of Contracts §§ 209, 210, 213, 214, 215, 216.

"Merger" Clauses

A "merger" clause seeks to clarify that the parties' prior or contemporaneous negotiations or discussions are deemed "merged" into the written agreement, thereby discharging or otherwise rendering ineffective anything not found in the writing. Such a clause is also sometimes called an "entire agreement" clause, suggesting that the "entire agreement" is found within the writing containing the clause, and anything missing is not part of the agreement. Of course, to some degree, the use of a merger clause suffers from the same questions of its "scope" as the more general application of the parol evidence rule.

What is the scope of the merger clause? If the parties have one—and only one—agreement, it may be easy to give broad effect to the clause as reaching any and all agreements between the parties. However, if the parties have multiple agreements, then the parties would not want one merger clause to reach a fully independent agreement. Thus, a clause will often focus on the agreement at issue, rather than the entire relationship between the parties. In doing so, however, it may open the door to an argument that any "extrinsic" evidence reflects an entirely distinct "collateral" agreement.

In short, a well drafted merger clause can be very useful in avoiding any dispute over the completely integrated nature of a writing, as precluding any and all other prior or contemporaneous evidence of content. However, drafting such a clause is not always as easy as it might at first appear. The following Example reflects a reasonably comprehensive merger clause.

> **Example 27-3:** "This writing represents the entire agreement between the parties. It fully discharges and supersedes all prior or contemporaneous promises, representations, or other manifestations of any kind regarding or relating in any way to the transaction, including all of its elements, reflected by this writing."
>
> This clause should preclude the use of extrinsic evidence to prove the content of the transaction at issue. It would not, however, have any effect on a wholly unrelated independent transaction between these same two parties.

While a "generic" merger clause may provide a good "starting point" in drafting a specific contract, this is one "standard term" that often should be examined in the context of the transaction at issue before finalizing the agreement. Having fully examined the common law "parol evidence" rule, we can now move to the analogous provision addressing transactions in goods.

UCC Article 2

Article 2 largely follows the basic common law approach. However, it also includes important differences, and it generally tracks the "realist" approach to integration. **STOP NOW and READ UCC § 2-202 below.**

UCC § 2-202

Terms with respect to which the confirmatory memoranda of the parties agree or which are otherwise set forth in a writing intended by the parties as a final expression of their agreement with respect to such terms as are included therein may not be contradicted by evidence of any prior agreement or of a contemporaneous oral agreement but may be explained or supplemented

(a) by course of performance, course of dealing, or usage of trade (Section 1-303); and

(b) by evidence of consistent additional terms unless the court finds the writing to have been intended also as a complete and exclusive statement of the terms of the agreement.

As with the common law, terms contradicting the writing are fully precluded. Unlike the common law, however, § 2-202 does not apply to a contemporaneous written agreement—essentially leaving each writing to stand on its own. The general approach of § 2-202 is also different than the common law, essentially assuming partial integration, unless otherwise established in subsection (b). Comment 1 further clarifies that § 2-202 rejects any assumption of complete integration on all matters, merely because the writing appears to be complete on some matters.

UCC § 2-202 also provides its own unique standard for deciding whether a contract is completely integrated. Whereas, the common law asks whether an extrinsic term would have "naturally" been included in the writing had it been a part of the agreement, Comment 3 explains that § 2-202 asks whether such a term would have "certainly" been included in the writing. The latter standard clearly establishes a higher hurdle for preclusion of the extrinsic evidence, thereby allowing a greater range of extrinsic evidence to "explain or supplement" an integrated writing.

Moreover, subsection (a) makes clear that certain extrinsic evidence—a course of performance, course of dealing, or usage of trade is always admissible to explain or supplement an integrated writing, irrespective of whether the writing such integration is complete. Note that the limitation based on complete integration is included only in subsection (b)—not in subsection (a). The only way to bar evidence of a course of dealing or usage of trade is through express and very specific exclusion. It is not clear that there is any way to exclude a course of performance. All of this will be addressed more fully in Lesson 29.

Finally, a merger clause remains generally effective in rendering a writing completely integrated under subsection (b). However, the need for careful drafting is arguably even greater in a contract for the sale of goods, in view of the more "inclusionary" bias of UCC Article 2.

Thus far, we have solely focused on the use of an integrated writing to preclude resort of extrinsic evidence of oral or written communications prior to or contemporaneous with the conclusion of the contract. However, parties may also wish to preclude any resort to oral communications after the conclusion of the contract that might inadvertently serve to modify their carefully crafted integrated writing.

"No Oral Modification" Clauses

A contract precluding oral modification is called a "no oral modification" or "NOM" clause. Historically, such clauses were not enforced under the common law, as courts would typically point out that any contract—including the NOM clause—can be modified by mere mutual consent. A few states have statutorily changed the common law rule, generally (for example, New York General Obligations Law § 15-301 generally provides for enforcement of NOM clauses). However the most broadly applied statutory recognition of the effectiveness of a NOM clause is found in UCC Article 2. **STOP NOW and READ UCC § 2-209(2), (4), and (5) below.**

UCC § 2-209(2), (4), AND (5)

(2) A signed agreement which excludes modification or rescission except by a signed writing cannot be otherwise modified or rescinded, but except as between merchants such a requirement on a form supplied by the merchant must be separately signed by the other party.

. . .

(4) Although an attempt at modification or rescission does not satisfy the requirements of subsection (2) or (3) it can operate as a waiver.

(5) A party who has made a waiver affecting an executory portion of the contract may retract the waiver by reasonable notification received by the other party that strict performance will be required of any term waived, unless the retraction would be unjust in view of a material change of position in reliance on the waiver.

Subsection (2) makes a NOM clause fully enforceable, subject to the special signature requirement by a non-merchant on a form supplied by a merchant. In many written agreements, the parties will include both a "merger clause" and a "no oral modification" clause—the two of which, in combination, are often called a "zipper" clause (in effect, seeking to "zip up" the past, present, and future into a single writing). An example follows.

> **Example 27-4:** "This writing represents the entire agreement between the parties. It fully discharges and supersedes all prior or contemporaneous promises, representations, or other manifestations of any kind regarding or relating in any way to the transaction, including all of its elements, reflected by this writing. This written agreement may be modified only by another written agreement signed by both parties."

> The parties' agreement now precludes any evidence of its content other than the original writing or a subsequent writing signed by both parties.

While a NOM clause is effective in precluding an oral modification, this is not the end of the story.

Even though a subsequent attempted oral modification is not effective—as a modification—in the face of a NOM clause, it can nevertheless operate as a "waiver," as provided in subsection (4). In one sense, a waiver of a right to a promised performance is no different than a modification of the same right, in that either will preclude enforcement of the original obligation. However, there is one crucial difference.

Once "modified," a contract may only be further modified (including a modification returning to the original contract terms) by the "mutual" consent of both parties. In contrast, a "waiver" remains subject to "unilateral" "retraction," which will return the parties to the original agreement prior to the waiver. Thus, a party "waiving" a right will generally retain full rights to enforce the original agreement, by way of a simple, unilateral retraction of the waiver. However, the right to retract a waiver is subject to its own limits under subsection (5).

A waiver always requires reasonable notice and will be precluded in cases in which the other party has detrimentally relied on the waiver. Consider the following example.

> **Example 27-5:** Al and Zoe concluded an agreement for the purchase and sale of widgets, including the clause contained in Example 27-4. Al was to deliver the widgets to Zoe's warehouse on June 5.
>
> On June 2, Al telephoned Zoe and explained "I am really in a bind, as I don't have enough widgets to deliver to fill all of my orders. However, I have more arriving on June 8. Is there any way that you can wait until the 9th for delivery?" Zoe said "Sure, the 9th will be fine." On June 3, Al delivered his entire widget inventory to other customers. On June 4,

> Zoe called and said "I changed my mind—you'll have to deliver on June 5."
>
> When Zoe originally orally agreed to a later delivery date, her agreement was ineffective as a modification due to the NOM clause. However, it nevertheless operated as a waiver of her right to require delivery before the 9th. On the 4th, she sought to retract the waiver by providing notice to Al that she was reinstating her original right to require delivery on the 5th. Even assuming that the one-day notice was sufficient, her retraction is precluded by Al's reliance on her waiver in delivering his existing inventory to other customers.

The issue of waiver will again be taken up in Chapter 7, along with a further discussion of retraction, reliance, and election (a waiver that is never subject to retraction).

The CISG

The CISG has no parol evidence rule. Instead, the statute clearly provides for consideration of the all of the relevant circumstances of the case. **STOP NOW and review CISG Article 8(3) below.**

CISG ARTICLE 8(3)

. . . .

(3) In determining the intent of a party or the understanding a reasonable person would have had, due consideration is to be given to all relevant circumstances of the case including the negotiations, any practices which the parties have established between themselves, usages and any subsequent conduct of the parties.

As with Article 11, the CISG exhibits no general legal preference for written evidence of a contract over other evidence. However, such written evidence may nevertheless be more factually compelling to a court, jury, or arbitral tribunal deciding a dispute between the parties.

Moreover, a well drafted "merger clause," intended by the parties to operate as such, is fully effective under the CISG. Article 8(3) requires only "due consideration" of extrinsic evidence, and an effective merger clause would suggest that no consideration of extrinsic evidence is due. Alternatively, Article 6 allows the party to derogate from any of the provisions of the CISG, except Article 12, so a clearly drafted merger clause could be seen to "derogate from" Article 8(3) to the extent inconsistent with its language.

The CISG also gives effect to a NOM clause under Article 29(2), but a party may be precluded from asserting the NOM clause where the other party has justifiably relied on conduct other than a written modification. While the formulation is somewhat different than UCC § 2-209, the CISG approach to the issue also seeks to balance strict enforcement of the NOM clause with the parties' reliance on each other's conduct during performance of the contract.

APPLYING THE RULES

Problem 1: The Laths wished to sell their farm. Across the road from the farm, the Laths had an icehouse. Mrs. Mitchill was interested in purchasing the farm, but found the icehouse objectionable. The Laths therefore orally promised, in consideration of the Mitchill agreeing to the purchase of their farm, to remove the icehouse. Relying upon this promise, Mitchill executed a written contract to buy the farm for $8,400. The contract for the purchase and sale of the farm appeared fully complete on its face, addressing any and all terms one might reasonable expect in a contract for the purchase and sale of a farm. The contract was silent, however, on the question of the ice house. The sale was completed, and Mitchill took possession of the property. However, the Laths never removed the ice house. Mitchill sought specific performance of the Laths' promise. Is she entitled to offer proof that the promise was made in furtherance of her claim?
The facts of this problem are loosely based on the issues raised in the case of *Mitchill v. Lath*, 247 N.Y. 377, 160 N.E. 646 (1928).

Problem 2: Shell contracted in 1969 to sell to Nanakuli all of the asphalt Nanakuli required for its paving contracting work, over an extended number of years. The contract specified that all asphalt deliveries would be priced at "Shell's posted price at time of delivery." The contract also included a "zipper" clause. Nanakuli was typically required to commit to a price for its paving contracts well in advance of the delivery of the asphalt. Thus, Nanakuli was particularly vulnerable to unexpected price increases.

In 1971, Shell raised its price. However, the representatives of Shell and Nanakuli orally discussed the matter, and Shell did not require Nanakuli to pay the higher price on all outstanding orders at the time of the increase (as Shell was entitled to do based on the express pricing provision of the agreement). Instead, Shell continued to deliver asphalt at the old, pre-increase, price for an additional 4 months in order to give Nanakuli time to adjust to the new price in bidding its asphalt paving contracts.

In 1972, Shell again plans to raise its price. This time, Shell would prefer to impose the price increase on all outstanding Nanakuli orders, effective immediately. Whatever the wisdom of doing so, as a business matter, can Shell do as, as a legal matter?

The facts of this problem are loosely based on a subset of the issues raised in the case of *Nanakuli Paving & Rock Co. v. Shell Oil Co.*, 664 F.2d 772 (9th Cir. 1981), which we will later return to in another problem in Lesson 29.

Problem 3: We can now return to Problem 2 from the prior lesson. Does any of the material covered in the current lesson change either of your earlier answers? Is the Florida buyer bound to the notice provision with the Italian seller? What if the seller had been located in Alabama?

The facts of this problem are very loosely based on the issues raised in the case of *MCC-Marble Ceramic Center, Inc. v. Ceramica Nuova d'Agostino SpA*, 144 F.3d 1384 (11th Cir. 1998).

Lesson 28: The "Plain Meaning" Rule, "Ambiguity" & the Roles of Judge and Jury

Objectives and Expected Learning Outcomes

In this lesson, you will learn when a court will consider extrinsic evidence of the parties' intent based on the "ambiguity" of the term in question—even in the case of a completely integrated agreement. You will also discover two very different approaches to determining whether a term is "ambiguous," as well as the significance of that determination. As always, you will have an opportunity to apply this knowledge to a few problems.

In the last lesson, we addressed the parol evidence rule and the effect of an integrated writing in precluding extrinsic evidence of additional terms supplementing or further explaining that writing. We also addressed a variety of "exceptions" to the parol evidence rule, including one in which the parol, or extrinsic, evidence is offered to resolve an "ambiguity" in the writing. This "exception" for "ambiguity" is more fully explored in the current lesson.

The "Plain Meaning" Rule

A completely integrated writing that is clear and unambiguous on its face will be enforced according to its "plain meaning," without resort to extrinsic evidence. The rule is often referred to as the plain meaning rule. The traditional application of the rule limits its determination of whether the term at issue has a single "plain meaning" to the document, itself. This is often called a "four corners" approach in that the inquiry is limited to what may be found within the four corners of the document.

Example 28-1: *Steuart v. McChesney*

Steuart granted to McChesney a "right of first refusal" to purchase Steuart's farm in the event that Steuart received a bona fide offer from another buyer. The exercise price was specified to be the "market value of the premises according to the [county and state] assessment rolls" at the time of any bona fide offer. The specified assessed market value was $7,820 at the same time Steuart received a bona fide offer for $35,000.

Steuart sought to introduce extrinsic evidence that the assessed market price was merely a "floor" and that any bona fide offer above that floor controlled the exercise price available to McChesney. However, court declined to consider the extrinsic evidence, ruling that the price provision was clear and unambiguous on its face. McChesney was entitled to purchase the property for $7,820 based on the plain meaning of the price term in the parties' agreement.[13]

In the foregoing case, the court decline to look outside of the writing to interpret the agreement. The interpretive inquiry is not, however, limited solely to the term or provision at issue, as a variety of interpretive principles rely on other provisions of the document in question. A quick reference back to Lesson 26 should serve as a reminder that, within the four corners of a writing, one may find a broader linguistic or purpose context that may be very useful in ascertaining any plain meaning of the term at issue or the lack thereof. The use of such "intrinsic" context is part and parcel of any application of the "plain meaning" rule.

"Ambiguity"

While a single "plain meaning" is simply enforced as written, an "ambiguity" within the writing requires interpretation by reference to evidence "extrinsic" to that writing. A term is said to be "ambiguous" when it is "reasonably susceptible" to more than one meaning. The significance of a determination of ambiguity cannot be overstated.

A completely integrated writing—even one with an extraordinarily well drafted merger clause—is nevertheless subject to further examination based on extrinsic evidence of intent if the term at issue is deemed ambiguous.

---

[13] Steuart v. McChesney, 498 Pa. 45, 444 A.2d 659 (1982).

Example 28-2: Under a written commercial lease agreement, including a merger clause, the tenant is obligated to pay to the landlord a monthly rental amount equal to a certain percentage of its "sales." The tenant's business includes both the sale of goods from the leased premises and service income generated at another location, but often purchased at the instant leased premises.

Two other provisions within the written agreement address tenant's "sales" volume. One clearly uses the term to mean only sales of goods, while the other clearly includes sales of both goods and services.

Absent any further evidence within the agreement, the term "sales," as used to define the tenant's monthly rental payment, is almost certainly "ambiguous." Thus, a court would consider extrinsic evidence offered by the parties to resolve the ambiguity—notwithstanding the merger clause.

We began the Chapter with an example of this process of resolving an ambiguity by reference to extrinsic evidence in the mythical arbitration award based on *Frigaliment*, addressed in Lesson 26.

Of course the lawyers who drafted an agreement in which a key term is deemed "ambiguous" are rarely happy to be greeted by this news. However, the use of extrinsic evidence in this context is clearly essential to resolve the dispute over the ambiguity. What is far more controversial is the use of extrinsic evidence not only to resolve an ambiguity, but to create the ambiguity in the first place. The case that follows is praised by some and scorned by others. However, almost all would agree that it is likely one of the most significant contract law decisions of the last 50 years.

FROM THE COURT

Pacific Gas & Electric v. G.W. Thomas Drayage & Rigging Co.

Supreme Court of California (1968)
69 Cal.2d 33, 442 P.2d 641

Traynor, J.

Defendant appeals from a judgment for plaintiff in an action for damages for injury to property under an indemnity clause of a contract.

In 1960 defendant entered into a contract with plaintiff to furnish the labor and equipment necessary to remove and replace the upper metal cover of plaintiff's steam turbine. Defendant agreed to perform the work 'at (its) own risk and expense'

> **"Indemnification" Agreements**
> An indemnification agreement typically requires "A" to indemnify "B" for any claims by third parties against B, arising from A's use of B's property or from A's activities on B's premises. The significance of the indemnification agreement is that B need not prove A was negligent in order to shift any liability to A.

and to 'indemnify' plaintiff 'against all loss, damage, expense and liability resulting from * * * injury to property, arising out of or in any way connected with the performance of this contract.' Defendant also agreed to procure not less than $50,000 insurance to cover liability for injury to property. Plaintiff was to be an additional named insured, but the policy was to contain a cross-liability clause extending the coverage to plaintiff's property.

During the work the cover fell and injured the exposed rotor of the turbine. Plaintiff brought this action to recover $25,144.51, the amount it subsequently spent on repairs. During the trial it dismissed a count based on negligence and thereafter secured judgment on the theory that the indemnity provision covered injury to all property regardless of ownership.

Defendant offered to prove by admissions of plaintiff's agents, by defendant's conduct under similar contracts entered into with plaintiff, and by other proof that in the indemnity clause the parties meant to cover injury to property of third parties only and not to plaintiff's property.

Although the trial court observed that the language used was 'the classic language for a third party indemnity provision' and that 'one could very easily conclude that * * * its whole intendment is to indemnify third parties,' it nevertheless held that the 'plain language' of the agreement also required defendant to indemnify plaintiff for injuries to plaintiff's property. Having determined that the contract had a plain meaning, the court refused to admit any extrinsic evidence that would contradict its interpretation.

When a court interprets a contract on this basis, it determines the meaning of the instrument in accordance with the '* * * extrinsic evidence of the judge's own linguistic education and experience.' [Citations omitted.] The exclusion of testimony that might contradict the linguistic background of the judge reflects a judicial belief in the possibility of perfect verbal expression. [Citations omitted.] This belief is a remnant of a primitive faith in the inherent potency and inherent meaning of words.

The test of admissibility of extrinsic evidence to explain the meaning of a written instrument is not whether it appears to the court to be plain and unambiguous on its face, but whether the offered evidence is relevant to prove a meaning to which the language of the instrument is reasonably susceptible. [Citations omitted.]

A rule that would limit the determination of the meaning of a written instrument to its four-corners merely because it seems to the court to be clear and unambiguous, would either deny the relevance of the intention of the parties or presuppose a degree of verbal precision and stability our language has not attained.

Some courts have expressed the opinion that contractual obligations are created by the mere use of certain words, whether or not there was any intention to incur such obligations.[1] Under this view, contractual obligations flow, not from the intention of the parties but from the fact that they used certain magic words. Evidence of the parties' intention therefore becomes irrelevant.

---

[1] In footnote 3 of the original opinion, the court here referenced Judge Hand's opinion in *Hotchkiss v. National City Bank of New York*, earlier addressed in Lesson 9. As indicated earlier in both Lessons 9 and 26, the law does indeed give priority to the parties' outward and observable manifestations of intent. However, their respective subjective intent may also be significant in many circumstances. The instant question is whether such intent is admissible in the face of a completely integrated writing so as to create an ambiguity in that writing.

In this state, however, the intention of the parties as expressed in the contract is the source of contractual rights and duties. A court must ascertain and give effect to this intention by determining what the parties meant by the words they used. Accordingly, the exclusion of relevant, extrinsic evidence to explain the meaning of a written instrument could be justified only if it were feasible to determine the meaning the parties gave to the words from the instrument alone.

If words had absolute and constant referents, it might be possible to discover contractual intention in the words themselves and in the manner in which they were arranged. Words, however, do not have absolute and constant referents. 'A word is a symbol of thought but has no arbitrary and fixed meaning like a symbol of algebra or chemistry, * * * [citations omitted]. The meaning of particular words or groups of words varies with the '* * * verbal context and surrounding circumstances and purposes in view of the linguistic education and experience of their users and their hearers or readers (not excluding judges). * * * A word has no meaning apart from these factors; much less does it have an objective meaning, one true meaning.' [Citations omitted.] Accordingly, the meaning of a writing '* * * can only be found by interpretation in the light of all the circumstances that reveal the sense in which the writer used the words. The exclusion of parol evidence regarding such circumstances merely because the words do not appear ambiguous to the reader can easily lead to the attribution to a written instrument of a meaning that was never intended. [Citations omitted.]

Although extrinsic evidence is not admissible to add to, detract from, or vary the terms of a written contract, these terms must first be determined before it can be decided whether or not extrinsic evidence is being offered for a prohibited purpose. The fact that the terms of an instrument appear clear to a judge does not preclude the possibility that the parties chose the language of the instrument to express different terms. That possibility is not limited to contracts whose terms have acquired a particular meaning by trade usage, but exists whenever the parties' understanding of the words used may have differed from the judge's understanding.

Accordingly, rational interpretation requires at least a preliminary consideration of all credible evidence offered to prove the intention of the parties. [Citations omitted]. Such evidence includes testimony as to the 'circumstances surrounding the making of the agreement * * * including the object, nature and subject matter of the writing * * *' so that the court can 'place itself in the same situation in which the parties found themselves at the time of contracting.' [Citations omitted]. If the court decides, after considering this evidence, that the language of a contract, in the light of all the circumstances, is 'fairly susceptible of either one of the two interpretations contended for * * *,' [citations omitted], extrinsic evidence relevant to prove either of such meanings is admissible.

In the present case the court erroneously refused to consider extrinsic evidence offered to show that the indemnity clause in the contract was not intended to cover injuries to plaintiff's property. Although that evidence was not necessary to show that the indemnity clause was reasonably susceptible of the meaning contended for by defendant, it was nevertheless relevant and admissible on that issue. Moreover, since that clause was reasonably susceptible of that meaning, the offered evidence was also admissible to prove that the clause had that meaning and did not cover injuries to plaintiff's property. Accordingly, the judgment must be reversed.

. . .

CASE QUESTIONS

(1) The court's decision in the foregoing case was itself unremarkable and could have been reached with little effect on existing contract doctrine. However, the logic and language of the opinion have profoundly affected contract doctrine—for better or worse, depending on one's perspective. Consider the final paragraph, along with the fourth. Did the court need to look to extrinsic evidence to determine that the "indemnity" provision to be ambiguous?

   a. Footnote 6 of the original opinion points out that the trial court's refusal to consider the extrinsic evidence would have been wrong, in any event, even if the court had confined its analysis of "ambiguity" to the four corners of the writing.

b. Presumably, the inclusion of footnote 6, showing the result could also be reached on traditional grounds, was essential to commanding a majority of the court for what would ultimately be a much more far reaching decision.

(2) A number of the court's observations are quite traditional. Under the traditional doctrine at the time, could a court look to an extrinsic "trade usage" to create an ambiguity in the agreement? What about prior dealings between these parties under other contracts?

a. As noted under UCC § 2-202 in the last lesson, and further explained in the next lesson, each of these extrinsic sources is always admissible—irrespective of integration or ambiguity.

(3) As indicated in Lessons 9 and 26, the question of intent is not limited to objective evidence. In fact, a dispute will almost always involve an assertion between each party as to what it intended and a choice between these two assertions.

a. What sort of evidence did the defendant want to offer as to the plaintiff's subjective intent?

b. Should this be precluded if it is inconsistent (as it likely was) with the position plaintiff took at trial?

(4) Based on the language and logic of this opinion, if a term is absolutely clear on its face to the reader of a completely integrated written agreement, what sort of extrinsic evidence may be used to introduce ambiguity where previously there was none?

a. Based on the language and logic of this opinion, is it possible—even in theory—to interpret any contract without resorting to extrinsic evidence?

Presumably, you found few, if any, limits on the nature of extrinsic evidence the court was willing to consider, and you also noted that all of us rely on our own extrinsic experiences in some manner when we give meaning to words. The court explained that one should not rely solely on one's own understanding, but should look to "all the circumstances" surrounding the contract in deciding whether the provision at issue was "reasonably susceptible" to more than one meaning. In fact, this test is the same as that applied under the more traditional "four corners" approach to the "plain meaning" rule. The key difference is the lens through which the test is applied.

In both the "four corners" and "all the circumstances" approach one asks if the provision at issue is subject only to a single "plain meaning" or, conversely, is "reasonably susceptible" to more than one meaning. Under the "four corners" approach, the search is limited to "patent" ambiguities, arising from the integrated writing, itself. Under the "all the circumstances" approach, the search is broadened to include "latent" ambiguities.

The stark contrast between the "four corners" and "all the circumstances" approaches to the question of ambiguity is nicely illustrated by the following example involving two different agreements subject to New York and California law, respectively.

> **Example 28-3: *Greenfield v. Philles Records, Inc.***
>
> A singer contracted with a music producer, granting the producer all rights in her recordings subject to specified royalty payments, and later married the producer. When the couple subsequently divorced, they executed a general mutual release. Still later, litigation ensured over the use of the recordings in new media.
>
> In deciding the case, the court was required to give meaning to both the original recording contract and the subsequent release. The first was governed by New York law ("four corners"), while the second was governed by California law ("all the circumstances"). The singer sought to offer extrinsic evidence intended to show that each was ambiguous and should ultimately be interpreted in her favor. The court found each to be clear and unambiguous on its face. Applying the appropriate law to each, the court precluded the extrinsic evidence with respect to the recording contract governed by New York law. In contrast, the court relied on

the evidence as creating an ambiguity and then ruled in favor of the interpretation urged by the singer with respect to the release governed by California law.[14]

While a court employing a "four corners" approach to the "plain meaning" rule will not look to a "latent ambiguity" as a matter of contract interpretation, that same court would almost certainly consider a latent ambiguity going to the question of contract formation. For an example, we can again return to the two ships "Peerless."

Example 28-4: *Raffles v. Wichelhaus (redux)*

The parties agreed to purchase and sell cotton to arrive on the ship "Peerless," sailing from Bombay." On its face, the term "Peerless," seems clear and unambiguous—until of course we discover there were two (at least) ships "Peerless" carrying cotton from Bombay. However, neither "Peerless" was any more objectively reasonable than the other, so the court found that the parties had failed to conclude a contract. The court did not look to extrinsic evidence to interpret and enforce the contract.[15]

The thoughtful reader may, at this stage, be wondering if perhaps this whole distinction between patent and latent ambiguities is effectively "much ado about nothing," as a judge deciding that extrinsic evidence might give rise to an ambiguity can simply reject the evidence, if appropriate, when resolving the ambiguity. However, it is not so simple, as "issues of fact"—especially those involving credibility—generally go to a jury (assuming that either party has requested a jury trial).

The Roles of Judge and Jury

The question of whether a provision in a completely integrated agreement has a single plain meaning or is reasonably susceptible to more than one meaning is decided by the judge. If the judge determines that the agreement

---

[14] Greenfield v. Philles Records, Inc., 98 N.Y.2d 562, 780 N.E.2d 166, 750 N.Y.S.2d 565 (2002).
[15] 2 H. & C. 906, 159 Eng. Rep. 375 (Ct. of Ex. 1864).

has a single plain meaning, then the jury must give the term that meaning in deciding any other factual issues before it. If, however, the judge decides that the provision at issue is "ambiguous"—reasonably susceptible to more than one meaning—then the resolution of that ambiguity will typically go to the jury as a question of factual intent.

In choosing between the different meanings proffered by the parties, the jury will consider any and all otherwise admissible (under the applicable procedural rules governing presentation of evidence) extrinsic evidence of the parties' intent-in-fact. The pros and cons of civil jury trials are far beyond the scope of this course, but suffice to say that some parties generally prefer to avoid juries. As such, the court's determination with respect to "ambiguity" takes on added significance.

Not all extrinsic evidence is treated the say way. In noting certain differences in treatment, we turn briefly to UCC Article 2.

UCC Article 2

While the two different approaches to the issue of ambiguity differ dramatically with respect to a specific range of extrinsic evidence, the scope of that range is relatively narrow. All courts agree that certain forms of extrinsic evidence are always admissible, unless expressly negated. **STOP NOW and review the excerpt from UCC § 2-202 below.**

UCC § 2-202

Terms with respect to which the confirmatory memoranda of the parties agree or which are otherwise set forth in a writing intended by the parties as a final expression of their agreement with respect to such terms as are included therein may not be contradicted . . . , but may be explained or supplemented

(a) by course of performance, course of dealing, or usage of trade (Section 1-303);

. . .

The rule is most clearly stated above in UCC § 2-202. However, it has also been followed to a large extent by courts interpreting agreements governed by the common law as well.[16] Thus, the difference between the "four-corners" and "all the circumstances" approach is most likely to arise when specifically addressing extrinsic evidence of the circumstances of contract negotiation and formation.

APPLYING THE RULES

Problem 1: Two sophisticated commercial parties concluded an agreement for a large loan. The agreement stated that the borrower "shall not have the right to prepay the principal amount hereof in whole or in part" for the first 12 years of the loan agreement. In later years, the loan was subject to prepayment, based on a sliding prepayment fee. A few years later, the borrower sought to prepay the loan. While acknowledging the language of the agreement, the borrower asserted that it did not reflect the actual agreement of the parties and sought to introduce extrinsic evidence to that effect. Should the borrower's extrinsic evidence be considered in determining whether the pre-payment provision is ambiguous?

The facts of this problem are loosely based on the issues raised in the case of *Trident Center v. Connecticut General Life Ins. Co.*, 847 F.2d 564 (9th Cir. 1988).

Problem 2: We can again return to Problem 2 from Lesson 26. Does any of the material covered in the current lesson affect your analysis of the variation in which the seller had been located in Alabama?

The facts of this problem are very loosely based on the issues raised in the case of *MCC-Marble Ceramic Center, Inc. v. Ceramica Nuova d'Agostino SpA*, 144 F.3d 1384 (11th Cir. 1998).

Problem 3: Return now to Example 28-1 above. Can you construct one or more arguments in support of a decision in favor of Steuart?

---

[16] Restatement (Second) of Contracts § 202(3)(b), (4), and (5).

Lesson 29: Past Practices, Trade Usages, and Performance as Evidence of Intent

Objectives and Expected Learning Outcomes

In this lesson, you will learn about three unique sources of evidence of the parties' intent—each admissible to explain or supplement the express terms of the parties' agreement, irrespective of ambiguity or the presence of a merger clause. You will also learn how to distinguish these sources from each other and to apply them in a factual context—including circumstances in which they may, themselves, be inconsistent.

In the last three lessons, we have been focused on determining the content of the parties' agreement by searching for their intent-in-fact. We have considered various principles and rules for evaluating the available evidence of intent, as well as certain rules for determining what sort of evidence a court or jury may consider in doing so. Along the way, we have frequently encountered three specific types of evidence, which are almost always relevant in determining the parties' intent-in-fact. These are (1) evidence of the manner in which these same parties have conducted themselves in past agreements governed by similar terms; (2) evidence of the manner in which members of a trade of which both parties are members usually conduct themselves under similar agreements; and (3) evidence of the manner in which the parties have conducted themselves under the actual agreement for which the content is disputed.

All of these three forms of evidence are relevant in determining the intent of the parties, unless expressly and specifically negated in a manner appropriate to the form of evidence at issue. **STOP NOW and review the excerpted language of UCC § 2-202 below.**

UCC § 2-202

[Written t]erms . . . may not be contradicted . . . , but may be explained or supplemented

(a) by course of performance, course of dealing, or usage of trade (Section 1-303); . . .

In the current lesson, each of these specific forms of evidence of the parties' intent-in-fact is addressed in turn. While this lesson is focused entirely on Article 2, the common law follows a very similar tack, to a large degree influenced by the articulation of these principles in UCC Article 2.

The Past Practices of the Contracting Parties

When the same parties have, in past contracts, treated particular expressions or conduct as having a particular meaning, that same meaning is assumed to apply to a current contract, absent an objectively unambiguous reason to believe otherwise. **STOP NOW and READ the excerpts from UCC § 1-303 below.**

> # UCC § 1-303
>
> . . .
>
> **(b)** A "course of dealing" is a sequence of conduct concerning previous transactions between the parties to a particular transaction that is fairly to be regarded as establishing a common basis of understanding for interpreting their expressions and other conduct.
>
> **(d)** A . . . course of dealing between the parties . . . is relevant in ascertaining the meaning of the parties' agreement, may give particular meaning to specific terms of the agreement, and may supplement or qualify the terms of the agreement. . . .

If two parties concluding a contract have, in past contracts between them, given a unique meaning to a particular word or phrase, an objectively reasonable person in the position of these parties would expect this same word or phrase to carry the same unique meaning in the newly concluded contract—absent a very clear indication to the contrary.

> **Example 29-1:** Seller contracted to supply buyer's requirement of "high grade" widgets for one year. Within the "widget trade," product quality was graded on a 0 through 10 scale, with 10 being the highest. During the first year of the contract, all widgets delivered by seller under the contract were of grade 8 or above, with only two exceptions. Seller once delivered grade 6 widgets and once delivered

grade 7 widgets. On each of these two occasions, buyer rejected the delivering, and seller promptly provided a substitute delivery of grade 8 widgets or better, which was accepted by buyer. This same pattern was also followed under a new contract between the parties in year 2.

In year 3, the parties executed a new contract calling for "high grade" widgets, just like the first two. Seller immediately began delivering grade 7 widgets, and buyer refused to accept them. Litigation ensued, with each party asserting that the other had breached. Seller would likely argue that "high grade" should be interpreted based on its common meaning as requiring any grade widget above average or normal (grade 5, in this case). However, buyer will prevail by pointing out that the parties themselves, by their conduct under the two prior contracts, treated "high grade" as requiring grade 8 widgets or better. Thus, the same "high grade" term in their third contract will be interpreted in the same manner, and seller's delivery of grade 7 widgets is a breach.

The key to analyzing a course of dealing comes in determining whether the prior conduct can reasonably be said to establish a common understanding. In the above example, this seems reasonably clear. The facts include regular deliveries of grade 8 or better, coupled with multiple occasions in which the conduct of both parties appears to recognize that grade 7 does not comply with the quality term, and this conduct spans to prior contracts—each with an identical quality term. Moreover, the requirement of a specific numeric quality threshold in no way appears inconsistent with a requirement of "high grade" widgets.

In many instances, however, the analysis may be less "clear cut." Consider the following actual use of "course of dealing" evidence.

Example 29-2: *Columbia Nitrogen Corp. v. Royster Co.*

Columbia sold nitrogen for use in fertilizer, and Royster had on many occasions purchased nitrogen from Columbia. In 1966, for the first time, Royster contracted to sell phosphate to Columbia. Under this contract Columbia promised to purchase a specified minimum of 31,000 tons of phosphate per year, at a specified price, for three years. The contract included a merger clause.

When phosphate prices fell dramatically, Columbia sought an adjustment of the quantity or price, refusing to take the specified quantity at the specified price. Royster sued for breach, but Columbia proffered evidence that, within the relevant trade, quantity and price specifications were "mere projections to be adjusted according to market forces." Columbia also offered evidence that in prior contracts in which Columbia sold nitrogen to Royster, price and quantity adjustments we often made in response to market condition. The court ruled that Columbia had established both a course of dealing and a trade usage in support of its argued interpretation. The court further ruled that these practices of treating specified quantities and prices as "mere projections" was in no way inconsistent with the express specifies terms, themselves. Unless "carefully negated," the course of dealing and trade usage simply gave meaning to the express terms.[17]

Trade usage is addressed in the next section. The course of dealing evidence, however, was somewhat unique in that it involved a reversal of the roles of buyer and seller, as well as different products. Would the sale of nitrogen by one party necessarily establish "a common basis of understanding" with respect to the sale of phosphate by the other?

In theory, express terms control over a contradictory course of dealing or trade usage, but the court found no contradiction between a specific price and quantity and "mere estimates." Seemingly, "contradiction" required "careful" negation of the specific trade usage or course of dealing at issue. This requirement of a clear contrary indication shows the strength of the assumption based on conduct between these specific parties. We next move to consider more fully usages established within the parties' trade.

---

[17] Columbia Nitrogen Corp. v. Royster, Co. 451 F.2d 3 (4th Cir. 1971).

Usages of a Particular Trade

A "usage of trade," as employed to give meaning to the parties' agreement, will typically raise two basic questions. First, the proponent must establish sufficient regularity of observance. Second, the proponent must establish that the transaction at issue falls within the scope of the established usage. Finally, the proponent must establish that its contracting partner knew or should have known of the usage at issue. **STOP NOW and READ the excerpts from UCC § 1-303 below.**

UCC § 1-303

. . .

(c) A "usage of trade" is any practice or method of dealing having such regularity of observance in a place, vocation, or trade as to justify an expectation that it will be observed with respect to the transaction in question. The existence and scope of such a usage must be proved as facts. If it is established that such a usage is embodied in a trade code or similar record, the interpretation of the record is a question of law.

(d) A . . . usage of trade in the vocation or trade in which they are engaged or of which they are or should be aware is relevant in ascertaining the meaning of the parties' agreement, may give particular meaning to specific terms of the agreement, and may supplement or qualify the terms of the agreement. A usage of trade applicable in the place in which part of the performance under the agreement is to occur may be so utilized as to that part of the performance. . . .

As with a course of dealing, any sufficiently regularized conduct within the parties' trade would be an integral part of the understanding a reasonable member of the trade would attribute to the contract term at issue. Thus, the use of both course of dealing and trade usage evidence, to a large extent, merely entails a more specialized application of the general rule focusing on the perspective of an objectively reasonable person in the position of the parties. Consider the following exemplary case, which also includes additional examples of usages.

Example 29-3: *Hurst v. Lake & Co.*

Seller contracted to deliver horse meat scraps containing a minimum of 50% protein, and buyer was to pay for the product delivered at a rate of $50 per ton. The parties' agreement further provided that buyer was entitled to a $5 per ton price reduction for any product containing less than 50% protein content. 140 tons of scraps delivered by seller ranged from 49.53% to 49.96% protein. Buyer paid only the discounted price. Seller asserted that the scraps fully complied with the 50% requirement, thereby entitling seller to the full price.

The court noted that both seller and buyer were in the business of buying and selling horse meat scraps; that such trade regularly observed a practice well known to both parties in which protein content of 49.5% or more was treated as meeting a requirement of 50% protein. Inasmuch as this was a regularly observed and well known practice of the parties' trade, it was reasonably to assume its applicability to the instant agreement, absent an express provision to the contrary. Thus, the court ruled that the product at issue fully conformed to the contract, and the seller was entitled to the full price.

The court also provided other examples of trade usage. In the "bricklaying trade a contract which fixes the bricklayer's compensation at '$5.25 a thousand' does not contemplate that he need lay actually 1,000 bricks in order to earn $5.25, but that he should build a wall of a certain size." In the "lumber industry a contract requiring the delivery of 4,000 shingles will be fulfilled by the delivery of only 2,500 when it appears that by trade custom two packs of a certain size are regarded as 1,000 shingles, and that hence the delivery of eight packs fulfills the contract, even though they contain only 2,500 shingles by actual count."[18]

---

[18] Hurst v. W.J. Lake & Co., 141 Or. 306, 16 P.2d 627 (1932).

As with Example 29-2, we see that trade usage that might seem, at first blush, to contradict an express term may, in fact, give meaning to that term. While it might initially seem obvious that 49.6 is less than 50, the usage of trade provided, essentially, for the "rounding" of all percentages. If one rounds to the closest full percentage point, then 49.6% is, of course, expressed as 50%, thereby satisfying the agreed requirement, as understood and applied within the parties' trade.

Again, both a course of dealing and a usage of trade rely upon a specialized version of the general rule generally giving effect to the objectively reasonable expectations of the parties at the time of conclusion of the contract (both forms of evidence pre-existing that time). In contrast, a "course of performance" arises after the conclusion of the contract. As such, its use rests on an entirely different logical foundation.

The Parties' Performance of the Contract at Issue

It is often said that "it is not what we say, but what we do," or that one should "walk the talk" (in effect, act in a manner consistent with one's statements). Thus, the law looks to a party's actual conduct under the contract at issue as evidence of what that party must have been thinking "subjectively," at the time the contract was concluded.

Any post-formation conduct cannot purport to explain the perspective of an objectively reasonable person at the time of contract formation, because that conduct have not yet "manifested." However, when a party asserts one subjective intent at the time a dispute arises, but has in fact acted in a matter suggesting otherwise, then those actions in performance of the contract may be relevant in evaluating the purported subjective intent.

To be clear, courts rarely, if ever, delve into this distinction between a "course of performance" as evidence of a party's subjective intent and a "course of dealing" or "usage of trade" as informing the objective expectations of a reasonable person. However, the distinction may be useful in understanding the basic differences between the two, as well as some unique challenges presented by "course of performance" evidence. **STOP NOW and READ UCC § 1-303 below.**

UCC § 1-303

(a) A "course of performance" is a sequence of conduct between the parties to a particular transaction that exists if:

> **(1)** the agreement of the parties with respect to the transaction involves repeated occasions for performance by a party; and

> **(2)** the other party, with knowledge of the nature of the performance and opportunity for objection to it, accepts the performance or acquiesces in it without objection.

. . .

(d) A course of performance . . . is relevant in ascertaining the meaning of the parties' agreement, may give particular meaning to specific terms of the agreement, and may supplement or qualify the terms of the agreement. . . .

. . .

(f) Subject to Section 2-209, a course of performance is relevant to show a waiver or modification of any term inconsistent with the course of performance. . . .

Consider subsections (d) and (f). How should one determine whether a given course of performance should be used as evidence of the "meaning" of a contract term or evidence of a waiver of the strict application of that same contract term? In theory, the former applies only to a course of performance consistent with an express term, while the latter applies to a course of performance inconsistent with the express term. However, we have already seen that the idea of "consistency" is particularly malleable in this context. Thus, we are presented with a classic "chicken or egg" dilemma.

In the original Uniform Commercial Code, "course of dealing" and "trade usage" evidence were addressed in Article 1, while "course of performance" evidence was addressed in § 2-208 (thus limiting its application to Article 2). Comment 3 to former § 2-208 directly addressed the inherent ambiguity in determining whether performance might be indicative of a party's understanding of what was required by the contract or mere acquiescence in non-conforming performance by its contracting partner on the occasion in question. Comment 3 provided as follows:

Where it is difficult to determine whether a particular act merely sheds light on the meaning of the agreement or represents a waiver of a term of the agreement, the preference is in favor of "waiver" whenever such construction, plus the application of the provisions on the reinstatement of rights waived (see Section 2-209), is needed to preserve the flexible character of commercial contracts and to prevent surprise or other hardship.

The text of comment 3 to § 2-208 was not carried over to § 1-303, when the treatment of "course of performance" evidence was moved to Article 1 alongside "course of dealing" and "trade usage" evidence. Thus, courts are left with little guidance in addressing the issue.

Of course one party may simultaneously note the other party's performance as falling short of that called for by the contract, while accepting such performance on the occasion in question. Under this circumstance, it is clear that the conduct of the recipient of the performance is a "waiver"—and not evidence that the recipient believes the performance to be in compliance. However, parties are not always careful to note such non-performance, especially where a party chooses not to raise a potential dispute at the time. In the latter circumstance, the statutory treatment of waiver under § 2-209(4) and (5) seems to strike an appropriate balance.

The difference between the use of a course of performance as evidence of meaning or waiver is significant. A term given "meaning" based on conduct cannot be modified, except by mutual agreement of the parties. In contrast, a "waiver" is subject to unilateral retraction by the waiving party, absent retraction, and assuming proper notice. The following example illustrates the difference.

Example 29-4: Seller contracted to sell wheat to buyer. The parties' agreement provided that seller's obligation to "deliver" the wheat was complete when seller loaded the wheat into rail cars destined ultimately to reach buyer (usually, about 7 days later). The agreement further stated that buyer was obligated to pay for the wheat 15 days after "delivery."

After the first two deliveries of wheat, the buyer paid exactly 15 days after receiving the wheat (and 22 days after "delivery," as specified in the contract). Seller accepted each payment without comment. When buyer pays in the same manner after the third delivery, seller objects, asserting its right to be paid within 15 days after seller has "delivered" the goods to the carrier—not 15 days after receipt of the goods by the buyer.

How should a court construe seller's conduct? If seller had noted the lateness each time, without formally asserting a breach or seeking any sort of late payment fee, then seller's conduct would almost certainly be deemed a waiver. If not, then the conduct is inherently more ambiguous. Did seller believe the payment was timely, or was seller simply choosing not to raise the issue the first two times?

If this "course of performance" by seller is used to give meaning to the payment term, then seller cannot in the future demand payment prior to 15 days after buyer's "receipt" of the goods. In contrast, if this "course of performance" by seller is construed as a waiver, then the seller may retract the waiver, with appropriate notice, likely allowing seller to require strict compliance beginning with the fourth delivery.

The definition and effect of "delivery" is further addressed in Chapter 9. However, the above definition is quite typical. While one might reasonably argue that payment upon "receipt" of goods is fundamentally inconsistent with payment upon "delivery," when the latter takes place prior to the former. However, one could easily envision a court explaining that the parties' course of performance merely gives meaning to the word "delivery" in the context of its relation to a payment date, as distinct from the other legal effects of delivery.

Of course, a "course of performance" may also constitute a "modification" under § 1-303(f). However, it is typically somewhat easier to identify a "modification," as it requires mutual consent. Thus, the more challenging inquiry involves distinguishing between a course of performance as evidence of meaning or waiver.

Course of performance evidence raises one additional challenge. As noted earlier, the parties may only avoid the application of a prior course of dealing or trade usage by clearly negating it. Ideally, the parties would note and then expressly reject the application of the course of dealing or usage of trade to the contract to be concluded. In contrast, one might reasonably question how, if at all, the parties could anticipate, identify, and reject the use of a future course of performance as evidence or either intent or waiver.

Dealing with Multiple Sources of Intent

As explained earlier, any express terms of the parties' agreement control to the extent inconsistent with any other evidence of intent (understanding, of course, that "consistency" is a rather malleable concept). Thus, the statute expressly places express terms as the top of the hierarchy and then goes on to give relatively priority to the other forms of evidence addressed in this lesson. **STOP NOW and READ UCC § 1-303 below.**

UCC § 1-303

. . .

(e) Except as otherwise provided in subsection (f), the express terms of an agreement and any applicable course of performance, course of dealing, or usage of trade must be construed whenever reasonable as consistent with each other. If such a construction is unreasonable:

(1) express terms prevail over course of performance, course of dealing, and usage of trade;

(2) course of performance prevails over course of dealing and usage of trade; and

(3) course of dealing prevails over usage of trade. . . .

As indicated earlier, at times an apparent conflict may be reconciled by construction of each of the relevant sources in a manner fully consistent with each other. Indeed, such construction is preferred to the extent reasonably possible. However, to the extent such construction is unreasonable, a clear hierarchy is provided.

We can return to the first example in this lesson to see how this hierarchy might be given effect. This first variation addresses a conflict between a course of dealing and a usage of trade.

> **Example 29-5:** In Example 29-1, seller contracted to supply buyer's requirement of "high grade" widgets for one year. During two success prior contracts, the parties conduct indicated that "high grade" meant grade 8 widgets or higher.
>
> In year 3, the parties executed a new contract calling for "high grade" widgets, just like the first two. Seller immediately began delivering grade 7 widgets, and buyer refused to accept them. Litigation ensued, with each party asserting that the other had breached. In this instance, seller not only argues that a reasonable person would understand "high grade" widgets to include grade 7 widgets, but in fact the widget trade defines "high grade" widgets to include grade 7 widgets. Nevertheless, buyer will again prevail, because a course of dealing takes priority over a trade usage to the extent the two are inconsistent.

The application of this hierarch is reasonably straightforward, as between two inconsistent sources of evidence of objective intent. The statute provides that the course of dealing is given priority, which is also fully consistent with our general rule that the specific (the conduct between these specific parties) controls over the general (the conduct of the broader trade). While the statute alone answers the question, an understanding of the underlying logic may be useful in more easily remembering the hierarchy.

We can next add a course of performance to this same example.

> **Example 29-6:** Let's return to the facts of the last example, but add a few additional facts. During year 3, seller first delivers grade 9 widgets. The next two deliveries are grade 7 widgets, and the fourth is grade 8 widgets Buyer accepts and pays for all four deliveries without comment. When seller again delivers grade 7 widgets in the fifth delivery, buyer refuses to accept them—asserting they do not conform to the requirement of "high grade" widgets.

Litigation again ensues, and the court is required to interpret the term "high grade" in the parties' agreement. If buyer's conduct in accepting two deliveries under the year 3 contract is construed as a "course of performance" used to give meaning to "high grade," then it takes priority over the parties' course of dealing, and seller wins. If, however, buyer's conduct is construed as a waiver, then buyer would likely be entitled to retract the waiver—at least as to future deliveries.

While buyer might not have provided sufficient notice of the retraction to avoid the application of the waiver to the fifth delivery, all future deliveries would likely be governed by the interpretation relying on the parties' earlier course of dealings. Thus, buyer's interpretation of the term would ultimately prevail.

The statute is clear. As a theoretical matter, it is somewhat less obvious—at least initially—how to prioritize "course of performance" evidence of subjective intent, as compared to "course of dealing" evidence (or a trade usage) of objective intent. However, the statutory hierarchy is fully consistent with the general hierarchy applied to evidence of subjective and objective intent.

In the above example, seller asserts that it subjectively intended "high grade" to include grade 7 widgets, while buyer asserts that it subjectively intended the same term to require a grade of at least 8. If, however, buyer's conduct in accepting grade 7 widgets is accepted by a court as evidence of buyer's true subjective intent (notwithstanding buyer's later assertions to the contrary), then the parties' subjective intent matches, and there is no need to examine any objective evidence of intent. Again, the challenge comes in determining whether to construe the course of performance as evidence of subjective intent of the meaning of the term, or merely an intent to waive strict application of the term in the instance at issue.

The CISG

The use of conduct to interpret the parties' agreement is also addressed by the CISG. **STOP NOW and review CISG Article 8(3) below.**

CISG ARTICLE 8(3)

. . . .

(3) In determining the intent of a party or the understanding a reasonable person would have had, due consideration is to be given to all relevant circumstances of the case including the negotiations, any practices which the parties have established between themselves, usages and any subsequent conduct of the parties.

Article 8(3) broadly addresses various sources of extrinsic evidence, including (along with "negotiations," absent a clear merger clause) practices, usages, and subsequent conduct. The proper use of "subsequent conduct" is never clarified elsewhere, but would presumably include any use relevant to determining intent under Article 8, as well as waiver or modification under Article 29. Practices and usages are, however, further clarified in the next provision. **STOP NOW and READ CISG Article 9 below.**

CISG ARTICLE 9

(1) The parties are bound by any usage to which they have agreed and by any practices which they have established between themselves.

(2) The parties are considered, unless otherwise agreed, to have impliedly made applicable to their contract or its formation a usage of which the parties knew or ought to have known and which in international trade is widely known to, and regularly observed by, parties to contracts of the type involved in the particular trade concerned.

Subsection (1) focuses on communications and conduct between the parties themselves. They are bound by any usage to which they have actually agreed, as well as any practice, which they have established between themselves. The former is simply a matter of contract, while the latter is somewhat analogous to "course of dealing" evidence under UCC § 1-303 (though CISG Article 9(1) should of course be interpreted and applied entirely independently of this or any other analogous UCC provision).

Subsection (2) focuses more broadly on usages of the international trade (not uniquely regional trade) of which the parties knew or should have known. This provision also begins by clarifying that any trade usage is subject to any contrary agreement, thus strongly suggesting the priority of subsection (1) over subsection (2). Such a priority is also consistent with the general rule of interpretation addressed in Lesson 26 that the specific (the parties' communications and conduct) controls over the general (the conduct of the broader trade).

While not as clearly expressed as in UCC § 1-303, CISG Article 9 likely establishes a similar hierarchy with respect to the parties' practices under prior agreements and usages of trade. However, the CISG does not directly establish any hierarchy with respect to "subsequent conduct" and other forms of evidence used to give meaning to the parties' agreement.

APPLYING THE RULES

Problem 1: In 1969, Shell and Nanakuli entered into a long term contract under which Shell would supply all of the asphalt Nanakuli required for paving contracts in Hawaii. The price of all asphalt was to be "Shell's posted price at the time of delivery." Nanakuli typically bid its paving contracts using Shell's existing pricing, even though the actual delivery of the asphalt would take place somewhat later. Of course, this timing exposed Nanakuli to a potential risk of any increase in the price of asphalt between the acceptance of its paving bid and the actual delivery of the asphalt.

On January 1, 1974, in response to sharply rising oil prices, Shell raised its price from $44 to $76 per ton. Nanakuli asserted that it was entitled to "price protection," such that it was entitled to purchase sufficient asphalt at the old price to complete existing paving contracts, as of the date of the increase. Shell, however, argued that the pricing term meant exactly what it said—the "posted price at the time of delivery," without any obligation that Shell provide price protection. In support of its position that the asphalt supply agreement required "price protection," Nanakuli offered the following evidence:

(1) Chevron, the only other supplier of asphalt in Hawaii provided price protection to its buyer.

(2) All suppliers of "aggregate" for use in the Hawaiian paving trade provided price protection. Along with asphalt, aggregate (rock and sand) was the second major component used in paving. However, aggregate contained no petroleum products (during the relevant time frame, the price of crude oil often fluctuated dramatically).

(3) On two occasions, in the early 1970s, Shell had increased its price and had contacted Nanakuli suggesting the "need to bargain over price protection." In each of these two instances, Shell provided a level of price protection acceptable to Nanakuli.

Is Shell entitled to the increased price, effective with January 1 deliveries, or is Nanakuli entitled to price protection?

What if Shell had provided notice to Nanakuli 90 days prior to January 1 that it would in all future cases strictly enforce its price term? How would that notice affect the application of the pricing term in the case of the instant price increase? How would it affect future price increases?

How, if at all, would any of the above analysis differ if the seller had been a Canadian business?

The facts of this problem are loosely based on the issues raised in the case of *Nanakuli Paving & Rock Co. v. Shell Oil Co.*, 664 F.2d 772 (9th Cir. 1981).

Problem 2: In 1955, KN Energy (KN) entered into a long term written contract to supply Great Western Sugar (GW) with the natural gas it required to operate certain sugar processing plants in northeastern Colorado. KN's obligation to supply gas to GW was deemed "interruptible," as follows:

> KN, in its absolute discretion and without liability to Buyer for damages or otherwise, shall have the right to, and at any time with or without notice may, interrupt in whole or in part delivery of natural gas to Buyer, as and whenever from time to time KN, in its

sole judgment, may deem necessary or expedient for conservation of gas for users having a higher priority of service.

This 1955 contract included a "zipper clause" (merger and NOM) and remained in force until November 1973. During the period between 1955 and November 1973, KN consistently applied the above provision as follows. Using a 24 to 36 hour anticipated demand window, KN would cut off gas to GW whenever it appeared that, within that demand window, KN would not be able to meet all demands for gas, including that of its "interruptible" customers, like GW.

In November 1973, KN proposed to terminate the 1955 contract and replace it with a new one. The only provisions that were changed involved pricing. GW agreed, and the parties executed the new agreement in place of the old one. At the time the agreement was concluded, the KN representative explained to the GW representative that KN was instituting a new policy for determining when to cut off interruptible customers. KN maintained gas storage reserves for use in times of shortage, and KN's new policy was to cut off interruptible customers any time it had to withdraw gas from storage, irrespective of whether it would have been able to meet the anticipated demands of all customers over the next 24 to 36 hour period.

KN applied this new "interruption" policy for five years, resulting in multiple additional interruptions and GW having to use a greater amount of alternative energy sources (which were all more expensive than natural gas). In November 1978, GW sued KN for breach of contract based on KN's use of the new "interruption" policy under the 1973 agreement. Has KN breached the 1973 agreement?

The facts of this problem are loosely based on the issues raised in the case of *KN Energy, Inc. v. Great Western Sugar Co.*, 698 P.2d 769 (Colo. 1985).

Lesson 30: Gap Filling—Implied Promises Regarding the Nature and Quality of Goods

Objectives and Expected Learning Outcomes

In this lesson, you will move beyond the parties' actual intent-in-fact to begin consideration of certain "default" terms, or "gap filler," implied under governing law, absent a contrary factual intent expressed by the parties. You will learn how the quality of the goods to be delivered by the seller are generally governed by a mix of actual intent-in-fact terms and terms implied under governing law, as well as the requirements for a seller to avoid the application of such "default" requirements as to the quality of the goods.

Gap Filling with Default Rules

Thus far, we have focused almost entirely on the parties' actual intent-in-fact. However, the parties to a contract do not always address every possible issue that may arise in the context of performing their agreement. If is often said that every contract is "incomplete"—the extent to which is merely a matter of degree. Certainly, some contracts attempt to address every possible contingency (including many that seem quite unlikely). But even these may fail to address some unexpected question that arises. Moreover, many contracts are quite simple, addressing only the bare essentials.

> **Example 30-1:** Seller contracts in a signed writing with buyer to supply all of the corn that buyer will need to feed buyer's livestock.
>
> While the foregoing agreement might be ill-advised in terms of its brevity, it is likely enforceable under UCC Article 2.

We have earlier noted that UCC Article 2 does not require a price (which may be supplied by § 2-305) or a specific quantity with respect to a "requirements" contract (as addressed by § 2-306(1)). UCC Article 2, part 3, also addresses common issues such as seller's delivery obligation and buyer's payment obligation (to be addressed later in Chapter 7). All of these provisions are intended to fill "gaps" in the parties' agreement-in-fact, supplying terms where the parties failed to do so. Such provisions are often called "default rules."

A complete discussion of default rules is beyond the scope of this basic course in contracts. However, the most typical approach to default rules—and that generally employed in UCC Article 2 and the CISG—is to provide the parties with the rule that most similarly situated persons in the position of these parties would have chosen, had they taken the time and effort to consider the issue. This is often called a "majoritarian" approach to default rules, as it seeks to provide the rule that the majority of similarly situated parties would likely choose.

Again, however, these "default rules" apply only if the parties have not in fact (expressly or impliedly) agreed to a contrary term. While the vast majority of contract rules provided by UCC Article 2 and the CISG are "default" rules, subject to contrary agreement of the parties, a select few are "mandatory" rules, which the parties cannot change by agreement. Perhaps the most notable "mandatory" rule of UCC Article 2 is the requirement of "good faith," which is addressed more fully in the next lesson.

In addressing Example 30-1 above, we noted default rules filling a number of gaps in the very brief agreement provided. However, one might further ask "what about the quality of the corn?" Surely, not just any corn would suffice. In fact, UCC Article 2 has an extensive set of provisions addressing the nature and quality of the goods to be delivered by the seller by reference to certain specified "warranties." These "warranty" provisions give effect to the parties' actual bargain-in-fact and also include a number of "default" "warranty" provisions, absent an effective agreement by the parties to the contrary. These warranty provisions provide an excellent opportunity to explore the interaction between the actual bargain of the parties and default rules provided by the governing law.

Express Terms

The seller's obligation begins with express terms of the parties' agreement. **STOP NOW and READ UCC § 2-313 below.**

UCC § 2-313

(1) Express warranties by the seller are created as follows:

    (a) Any affirmation of fact or promise made by the seller to the buyer which relates to the goods and becomes part of the basis of the bargain creates an express warranty that the goods shall conform to the affirmation or promise.

    (b) Any description of the goods which is made part of the basis of the bargain creates an express warranty that the goods shall conform to the description.

    (c) Any sample or model which is made part of the basis of the bargain creates an express warranty that the whole of the goods shall conform to the sample or model.

(2) It is not necessary to the creation of an express warranty that the seller use formal words such as "warrant" or "guarantee" or that he have a specific intention to make a warranty, but an affirmation merely of the value of the goods or a statement purporting to be merely the seller's opinion or commendation of the goods does not create a warranty.

As indicated in the statute, a seller may create an express warranty in a variety of different ways, through promise, affirmation, description, or provision of a sample or model—provided such manifestation "is made a basis of the bargain." A full examination of the "basis of the bargain" requirement of each is left to a course in Sales. However, each of the enumerated manifestations of the seller will generally be presumed to be a part of the basis of the bargain, absent evidence suggesting the contrary (e.g., evidence that statement was a mere stray remark to which neither party attached any significance at the time, or evidence of a particular attribute of a sample that reasonably appeared at the time to be irrelevant to the purpose for which it was provided). Subsection (2) further limits the effect of mere opinions or what is sometimes called "puffery."

Consider the effect of the addition of a few additional facts to our original example.

> **Example 30-2:** Seller contracts in a signed writing with buyer to supply all of the corn that buyer will need to feed buyer's livestock. The written agreement provides for "U.S. No. 3 Grade Corn, or better," and seller provided a "sample" of the corn to be delivered consisting entirely of "yellow" corn.
>
> Seller has likely created warranties under § 2-313 that it will deliver yellow corn of U.S. No. 3 Grade, or better.

Any failure of seller to deliver corn, as expressly warranted, will be a breach of contract. However, express warranties may not be the only warranties with which a seller must comply.

Merchantability

Absent an agreement to the contrary, a "merchant" seller—with respect to the goods in question—must deliver goods that are deemed "merchantable." **STOP NOW and READ UCC § 2-314 below.**

UCC § 2-314

(1) Unless excluded or modified (Section 2-316), a warranty that the goods shall be merchantable is implied in a contract for their sale if the seller is a merchant with respect to goods of that kind. Under this section the serving for value of food or drink to be consumed either on the premises or elsewhere is a sale.

(2) Goods to be merchantable must be at least such as

    (a) pass without objection in the trade under the contract description; and

    (b) in the case of fungible goods, are of fair average quality within the description; and

    (c) are fit for the ordinary purposes for which such goods are used; and

> **(d)** run, within the variations permitted by the agreement, of even kind, quality and quantity within each unit and among all units involved; and
>
> **(e)** are adequately contained, packaged, and labeled as the agreement may require; and
>
> **(f)** conform to the promises or affirmations of fact made on the container or label if any.
>
> **(3)** Unless excluded or modified (Section 2-316) other implied warranties may arise from course of dealing or usage of trade.

Compare the merchant limitation in the above statute to the general definition of "merchants" in § 2-104(1). Does § 2-314 apply to all sales involving merchants, as defined in § 2-104(1)? What sort of merchant sale of goods would not give rise to an implied warranty of merchantability? Of course, not all merchant sellers are "merchant[s] with respect to goods of that kind." Thus, the applicability of § 2-314 does not arise with all sales by merchants.

If the seller is a merchant in goods of that kind, then the goods must be "merchantable," which requires that they meet each of the requirements of subsections (a) through (f). This requirement of merchantability applies in any sale by a qualifying merchant seller—irrespective of the status of the buyer.

As with the "basis of the bargain" requirement under § 2-313, a detailed examination of "merchantability" under § 2-314 is left for a course in Sales. However, the concept might reasonably be summarized here as requiring that the goods are of reasonable quality and are reasonably packaged and labeled, as required for ordinary purposes for which such described goods are used. Notably, this provision does not require "top" quality goods. Nor does it require goods that are necessarily satisfactory for every use.

Example 30-3: Seller contracts in a signed writing with buyer to supply all of the corn that buyer will need to feed buyer's livestock. The writing says nothing more about quality. Corn quality is described as U.S. Grades 1 through 5 (1 being the highest) or "Sample Grade" (failing to meet any of Grades 1 through 5), and corn may be yellow, white, or mixed. Within the livestock feed trade of buyer and seller, corn of any color, and of any of U.S. Grade Nos. 1 through 5, is considered "merchantable."

Seller delivers mixed color corn of U.S. Grade No. 5. Notwithstanding the fact that there exist four superior Grades of corn, the corn delivered by seller is likely merchantable under these facts.

The requirement of merchantability focuses on general perceptions quality of largely generic goods, as required for ordinary purposes. However, some buyers will purchase goods with very specific purposes in mind—some of which will be anything but "ordinary."

Fitness for Particular Purpose

A buyer will more often than not have a very particular and specific purpose in mind for the good or goods being purchased (most buyers do not purchase goods just for the sake of doing so). If this purpose is merely an ordinary purpose for which the goods are generally used, then the warranty of merchantability under § 2-314 ought to be perfectly sufficient. However, if buyer's particular purpose is unique or otherwise out of the ordinary, the "merchantable" goods may nevertheless fail to serve buyer's intended purpose. A buyer with a unique extraordinary purpose instead needs a warranty that the goods are fit for that particular purpose. **STOP NOW and READ UCC § 2-315 below.**

UCC § 2-315

Where the seller at the time of contracting has reason to know any particular purpose for which the goods are required and that the buyer is relying on the seller's skill or judgment to select or furnish suitable goods, there is unless excluded or modified under the next section an implied warranty that the goods shall be fit for such purpose.

Of course, a buyer cannot expect clairvoyance from the seller. The seller is expected to anticipate the reasonable requirements of buyers for ordinary uses, but cannot possibly anticipate every potential extraordinary particularized purpose to which a buyer might put the goods. Thus, the statute requires that the buyer establish two things before it is entitled to a warranty of fitness for the buyer's particular purpose. What are those two requirements?

Is it enough that seller merely know of buyer's intended purpose? Why should the statute further require that the seller know that buyer is relying on seller to select goods suitable to buyer's intended particular purpose? The answers to these questions reflect a basic shift in presumed responsibility, as between §§ 2-314 and 2-315. The seller is presumed to be liable when a product fails to meet generally recognized expectations regarding ordinary uses. However, a buyer is presumed to assume responsibility for any extraordinary uses, unless seller is aware of both buyer's use and buyer's reliance on seller to select goods appropriate for that particularized use.

> **Example 30-4:** Seller contracts in a signed writing with buyer to supply a specified quantity of corn. The writing says nothing more about corn quality. Corn may be yellow, white, or mixed, all of which are perfectly useable for ordinary purposes involving the use of corn, as food.
>
> Seller delivers white corn of U.S. Grade No. 1. Buyer intends to use the corn to make methanol, which requires yellow corn. If seller has reason to be aware of buyer's particular purpose for the corn AND has reason to know that buyer is relying on seller to select appropriate corn, then seller's delivery of white corn will be a breach of § 2-315, because the corn is not fit for buyer's particular purpose of making ethanol—even though the corn is otherwise perfectly merchantable for ordinary purposes.

Implied warranties under §§ 2-314 and 2-315 are fully independent of each other, as goods may comply or fail to comply with either, neither, or both. Implied warranties may, however, be excluded or modified, as provided by the parties' actual agreement-in-fact.

Disclaimers

Thus far, we have focused on warranties arising in the absence of any agreement to the contrary. Implied warranties can in fact be excluded or modified by the seller. However, once given, an express warranty may not be disclaimed. **STOP NOW and READ UCC § 2-316 (1) below.**

UCC § 2-316 (1)

(1) Words or conduct relevant to the creation of an express warranty and words or conduct tending to negate or limit warranty shall be construed wherever reasonable as consistent with each other; but subject to the provisions of this Article on parol or extrinsic evidence (Section 2-202) negation or limitation is inoperative to the extent that such construction is unreasonable.

. . .

The statute reminds us that § 2-202 may bar consideration of certain extrinsic evidence of the parties' agreement. However, to the extent that any admissible evidence is contradictory, the grant of an express warranty controls over an attempt to limit or disclaim such a warranty. In effect, the seller is precluded from giving an express warranty with one hand and taking it away with the other.

In contrast to express warranties granted under § 2-313, warranties implied in law under §§ 2-314 or 2-315 are fully subject to disclaimer by the seller, as long as such disclaimer meets certain minimum standards. **STOP NOW and READ UCC § 2-316 (2) and (3) below.**

UCC § 2-316 (2) AND (3)

. . .

(2) Subject to subsection (3), to exclude or modify the implied warranty of merchantability or any part of it the language must mention merchantability and in case of a writing must be conspicuous, and to exclude or modify any implied warranty of fitness the exclusion must be by a writing and conspicuous. Language to exclude all implied warranties of fitness is sufficient if it states, for example, that "There are no warranties which extend beyond the description on the face hereof."

(3) Notwithstanding subsection (2)

(a) unless the circumstances indicate otherwise, all implied warranties are excluded by expressions like "as is", "with all faults" or other language which in common understanding calls the buyer's attention to the exclusion of warranties and makes plain that there is no implied warranty; and

(b) when the buyer before entering into the contract has examined the goods or the sample or model as fully as he desired or has refused to examine the goods there is no implied warranty with regard to defects which an examination ought in the circumstances to have revealed to him; and

(c) an implied warranty can also be excluded or modified by course of dealing or course of performance or usage of trade.

. . .

Subsection (3) provides for three different sets of factual circumstances in which implied warranties may be excluded or modified. Each involves a fact intensive determination under the specific circumstances of the parties' agreement. In contrast, subsection (2) provides for a kind of "bright line" rule or "safe harbor," provided certain requirements are met.

Consider the specific requirements under subsection (2) for excluding or modifying implied warranties arising under §§ 2-314 and 2-315, respectively. While, if either, requires a "writing"? Which, if either, must be "conspicuous"? What is required in terms of the "content" of a disclaimer of each? The following examples highlight some of these answers, as well as the interaction between subjections (2) and (3).

Example 30-5: A merchant seller (with respect to the goods sold) and merchant buyer conclude a contract over the phone, which seller subsequently confirms by e-mail. During the phone call seller states that he is selling the goods "'as is' and there is definitely no warranty of merchantability, nor is there any warranty for any particular purpose." Buyer is later unhappy with the goods and asserts claims for breach of §§ 2-314 and 2-315.

Seller has effectively disclaimed any implied warranty arising under § 2-314 by using the word "merchantability,"
and thus satisfying § 2-316(2). In contrast, the attempted
disclaimer of § 2-315 is not effective under § 2-316(2),
because that provision requires a disclaimer of the implied
warranty of particular purpose to be in writing. However,
the disclaimer of the implied warranty of fitness for particular purpose may nevertheless be effective under
§ 2-316(3)(a) based on the use of the "as is" language, absent facts (not present here) suggesting otherwise.

Example 30-6: A merchant seller (with respect to the
goods sold) and merchant buyer conclude a written contract, executed by each. Prior to executing the agreement,
the seller made the goods available to the buyer and urged
the buyer to examine them. However, the buyer declined.
The written agreement expressly provided, in exactly the
same style and font as the rest of the contract, that seller
provided no warranty or merchantability or fitness for
particular purpose. Buyer is later unhappy with the goods
and asserts claims for breach of §§ 2-314 and 2-315.

Seller has not effectively disclaimed either implied warranty
under § 2-316(2), because the writing was not conspicuous. However, buyer will be precluded under § 2-316(3)
(b) from asserting any claim under either implied warranty
that an examination of the goods ought to have revealed to
the buyer.

Of course, the surest way for a seller to exclude or modify any implied
warranties is to satisfy the requirement of subsection (2). However, the
seller who fails to do so will often find support under subsection (3), albeit
often subject to a somewhat more intensive factual inquiry.

Cumulation or Conflict of Warranties

As with any terms addressing the content of the parties' agreement, those involving warranties may include multiple provisions addressing the same issue. If so, the following provision addresses the manner in which any conflicts shall be resolved. **STOP NOW and READ UCC § 2-317 below.**

UCC § 2-317

Warranties whether express or implied shall be construed as consistent with each other and as cumulative, but if such construction is unreasonable the intention of the parties shall determine which warranty is dominant. In ascertaining that intention the following rules apply:

(a) Exact or technical specifications displace an inconsistent sample or model or general language of description.

(b) A sample from an existing bulk displaces inconsistent general language of description.

(c) Express warranties displace inconsistent implied warranties other than an implied warranty of fitness for a particular purpose.

You will likely note that these rules for resolving conflicts involving warranty provisions are quite similar to general principles of interpretation discussed earlier.

The CISG

UCC Article 2 requires the seller to deliver goods of a certain quality by reference to "warranties." However, the term "warranty" has different connotations in different legal systems, so the CISG uses a more universally understood term, requiring the seller to deliver "conforming" goods. While the terminology is different (as are many of the actual requirements), an astute reader will note a number of familiar concepts, in some ways analogous to those found in UCC Article 2. **STOP NOW and READ CISG Article 35 below.**

CISG Article 35

(1) The seller must deliver goods which are of the quantity, quality and description required by the contract and which are contained or packaged in the manner required by the contract.

(2) Except where the parties have agreed otherwise, the goods do not conform with the contract unless they:

(a) are fit for the purposes for which goods of the same description would ordinarily be used;

(b) are fit for any particular purpose expressly or impliedly made known to the seller at the time of the conclusion of the contract, except where the circumstances show that the buyer did not rely, or that it was unreasonable for him to rely, on the seller's skill and judgment;

(c) possess the qualities of goods which the seller has held out to the buyer as a sample or model;

(d) are contained or packaged in the manner usual for such goods or, where there is no such manner, in a manner adequate to preserve and protect the goods.

(3) The seller is not liable under subparagraphs (a) to (d) of the preceding paragraph for any lack of conformity of the goods if at the time of the conclusion of the contract the buyer knew or could not have been unaware of such lack of conformity.

As a purely "comparative" exercise, consider how CISG Article 35 addresses the following analogous provisions contained in UCC Article 2.

(1) Which provision(s) of CISG Article 35 might reasonably be analogized to each of the following provisions of UCC Article 2?

    a. UCC § 2-313

    b. UCC § 2-314

    c. UCC § 2-315

(2) Does CISG Article 35 allow for the disclaimer of implied obligations regarding the quality of the goods, analogous to that found in UCC § 2-316(2) and (3)(a)?

    a.   Which provision addresses the issue in more detail? Which provision is simpler?

    b.   Is this difference generally consistent with your observations with respect to other provisions of the two statutes?

(3) Does CISG Article 35 limit the seller's liability regarding implied quality requirements in a manner analogous to UCC § 316(3)(b)?

As always, the two statutes should each be interpreted autonomously, without reference to the other. However, a comparison of analogous provisions may help to understand each better.

APPLYING THE RULES

Problem 1

(1) Ace, a manufacturer and seller of boats, purchases boat engines for use in its manufacturing process. In doing so, Ace relies entirely on the expertise of Zip, the seller from whom it purchases engines. Ace provides Zip with the physical specifications of the boat (weight, size, etc.) for which the motor is to be used, as well as the boat's intended use and purpose. Zip then chooses an appropriate motor from its preprinted catalog (including model specifications) and delivers it to Ace at an agreed upon price. The only description on the invoice is Zip's model number (e.g., "A99 inboard motor"). Absent further applicable contract provisions, what, if any, warranties has Zip provided to Ace?

(2) When Ace discovers it has purchased too many of a particular boat engine from Zip, it sells the excess engines to Best, another boat manufacturer. The sales invoice includes only the Zip model number. Absent further applicable contract provisions, what, if any, warranties has Ace provided to Best?

(3) In addition to the facts of question 2, Ace is aware that Best intends to use the engines in boats to be sold in a specific market requiring low carbon emissions. Absent additional facts, has Ace provided any additional warranty beyond those of question 2? What else might you want to know that could change your answer?

Problem 2

Sea Products (SP) sold fish and other seafood for both human consumption and use as commercial fishing bait. Commercial Fisheries (CF) was engaged in the business of commercial off-shore fishing. CF inquired of SP whether SP might be interested in supplying "squid" for use as bait on CF's "longline" fishing boats. SP replied that it was indeed interested and provided a price per 1,000 kilograms of frozen squid for delivery at CF's premises. CF indicated that the price was agreeable, but that CF was specifically concerned about the quality of the "freezing" process (done onboard the boat when the squid is caught), as CF had in the past encountered poor quality (i.e. "spoiled") squid when defrosting the product for use on its fishing boats. SP agreed to provide a sample 5 kilo package from its existing stock of frozen squid for CF to inspect.

When CF received the sample, it defrosted, examined, and weighed each piece. With few exceptions, the squid ranged from 100-150 grams each. The best size range for squid to be used as bait for longline fishing was 100-150 grams per piece, though some minor variation was acceptable, and the foregoing was well known within the off-shore longline fishing trade. Thus, CF found the size range perfect for its purpose. CF also found the quality of the defrosted squid to be excellent and notified SP that it would like to purchase frozen squid "based on its satisfaction with the sample provided."

The parties concluded a signed, written agreement for the sale by SP of 20,000 kilos of frozen squid to CF. The writing provided that all squid would satisfy all applicable U.S. government regulations (largely related to fitness for human consumption and in no way related to squid size) and further stated as follows:

> All squid to be flash frozen in 5 kilo packages, including broad variations in individual squid sizes (dependent on variations in catch at time of freezing). Seller makes no representations or warranties of any kind as to product quality, other than those expressly provided herein.

When SP delivered the squid, CF discovered that most of it ranged in size from 50-100 grams. While perfectly good in all other respects, the squid was too small for use in off-shore longline fishing, as CF had intended.

Assuming SP is located in Massachusetts, and CF is located in Maine, has SP breached their agreement? How, if at all, would your analysis change if SP was located in Nova Scotia, Canada?

The facts of this problem are very loosely based on the issues raised by the competition Problem in the 18th Annual Willem C. Vis International Commercial Arbitration Moot.

Lesson 31: Gap Filling—Good Faith, Best Efforts, and Termination Rights

Objectives and Expected Learning Outcomes

In this lesson, you will learn of more "default" terms implied in law, including some arising in common law contracts. You will also learn more about the obligation of "good faith," implied in every contract. You will discover that, unlike mere "default" terms, the obligation of good faith is "mandatory" and applicable in all contracts, irrespective of any contrary agreement by the parties.

Thus far, our exploration of "gap filling" has focused on the law governing the sale of goods. Perhaps not surprisingly, a narrowly focused body of law—like that governing sales of goods—is more likely to have a more fully developed set of "default rules." The universe of possible contract issues and the range of reasonable resolutions of such issues is far more limited and, therefore, easier to address prospectively (which a "default" rule must do).

This idea of default contract terms, supplied by governing law, goes all the way back to Roman law, which distinguished between "nominate" and "innominate" contracts. The former, including a nominate contract of "sale," included very specific pre-determined provisions governing the parties' rights and obligations pursuant to the specific type of contract at issue. In contrast, the latter included all other contracts and relied entirely upon the parties' actual agreement to define their rights and obligations. In a similar vein, the modern common law of contracts imposes very few default rules, generally. However, we do find a few default rules applicable in certain circumstances involving common law contracts. Examples of a few of these are addressed in this lesson.

In rare circumstances, the law may also fill gaps with "mandatory" terms. While a "default" term is always subject to a contrary agreement by the parties, a "mandatory" term will always apply—even if both parties attempt to agree otherwise. The most important "mandatory" contract law term is likely "good faith." We have already encountered this term in earlier lessons, and we will begin this lesson by exploring its precise contours a bit more.

Good Faith

Every contract includes an obligation of good faith and fair dealing in the performance and enforcement of its terms.[19] As explained earlier in Chapter 3, this obligation does not arise until after a contract has been concluded. However, once the parties are bound to a contract, they are also bound to the obligation of good faith. This obligation is mandatory and is not subject to contrary agreement by the parties. While easy to articulate in a generic sense, good faith is often more difficult to define in practice.

One of the most common misconceptions is that an "intentional" breach is necessarily "bad faith." As explored very early in this course, contracting parties breach contracts for a whole host of reasons, including inadvertence, ignorance, inability, and even intent to do so in some circumstances. A party may simply determine that it is more financially rational to breach and pay expectation damages than to perform the contract, as agreed. This is not, in itself, "bad faith." It is merely an example of what is often called "efficient breach," as discussed earlier in Lesson 3.

It is also important to remember that a breach of contract is generally just a breach of contract (thereby giving rise to expectation damages), even if the breaching party has also acted in "bad faith." A "bad faith" breach of an insurance contract provides for a notable exception. However, in that particular case, the claim against the insurer for "bad faith" is actually grounded in "tort"—not contract. In short, allegations of "bad faith" generally add little to the analysis in most breach of contract actions.

The obligation of "good faith" is most significant in cases in which a party has arguably breached no other obligation, except that of good faith. For

---

[19] Restatement (Second) of Contracts § 205.

example, suppose A and B enter into a simple transaction in which A agrees to perform a service, and B agrees to pay for the service.

> **Example 31-1:** "A" contracts to perform services for "B" for such compensation "as you, [B], in your sole judgement, may decide is reasonable." After A has performed the services, B refuses to make any determination of the value of the services."
>
> B has not "expressly" promised to set the price. However, B's refusal to make a determination "in good faith" of the value of the services is a breach of contract. In this case, a court will, therefore, determine such value and award a remedy to A for B's breach based on that value.[20]

This same sort of "good faith" determination was addressed earlier in Lesson 6, Example 6-1, and the case of *Mattei v. Hopper*, in the context of "illusory" promises (the obligation of "good faith" avoided any assertion that the promise was illusory). "Good faith" served as a limit on Mattei's ability to assert that he had not obtained sufficiently "satisfactory" leases to require him to proceed with the purchase of the real estate at issue. In Lesson 6, we also encountered "good faith" in the context of "output" or "requirements" contracts, addressed by UCC § 2-306(1). In each of these cases, good faith served as a limit on the buyer's ability to define its "requirements" and the seller's ability to define its "output." Such requirements or output are those occurring in "good faith" operation of the buyer's or seller's business.

As each of these examples illustrate, the obligation of "good faith" does not arise in the abstract, fully independent of other obligations. Instead, the obligation of good faith generally attaches to another right or obligation, without which, a purely technical approach to enforcing the right or issue would likely defeat the purpose of the parties' agreement. One might fairly characterize "bad faith" in this context as conduct consistent with the "letter" of the parties' bargain, but inconsistent with the "spirit" of that same bargain. Here is a perhaps extreme, but hopefully illustrative, example.

---

[20] Restatement (Second) of Contracts § 205, illustration 6.

Example 31-2: "A" contracts to pay $1 million to "B" for certain services. B performs as agreed. A pays by delivering (in many trucks) $1 million to B, in assorted pennies, nickels, dimes, and quarters. These coins are of course legal "tender," so A has technically complied with the express terms of the contract. However, A's method of payment appears to be designed to deprive B of a substantial part of the benefit of the parties' bargain. As such, A has breached the implied obligation of "good faith" attached to A's express obligation to pay for the services.

In this case, B's "expectation" loss resulting from A's breach would likely amount to the "cost" of handling all of these coins so as to deposit them into B's account so as to allow B to realize its expected $1 million payment for the services performed.

As should be somewhat obvious by now, defining good faith is quite difficult. Under the common law, good faith is generally defined by reference to examples, such as those addressed thus far. However, UCC Article 2 seeks to define good faith more precisely in the statute. We begin, however, with the statutory requirement, itself. **STOP NOW and READ UCC § 1-304 below.**

UCC § 1-304

Every contract or duty within [the Uniform Commercial Code] imposes an obligation of good faith in its performance and enforcement.

Moreover, this implied obligation may not be disclaimed or excluded by the parties. **STOP NOW and READ the excerpt from UCC § 1-302 below.**

UCC § 1-302

. . .

(b) The obligations of good faith, diligence, reasonableness, and care prescribed by [the Uniform Commercial Code] may not be disclaimed by agreement. . . .

The statutory requirement of good faith is quite straightforward. However, its definition, isolated from context, is considerably more challenging. The definition of "good faith" under the Uniform Commercial Code has also recently become somewhat controversial.

Traditionally, the general obligation of good faith expressly required only "honesty in fact" in the conduct or transaction at issue, while merchants were also obligated under Article 2 to "observance of reasonable commercial standards of fair dealing in the trade." The obligation to observe reasonable commercial standards has now been moved to revised Article 1, in § 1-201(20). However a number of states adopting revised Article 1 have declined to extend this expanded version of good faith to non-merchants.

Should "commercial standards of fair dealing in the trade" serve to define good faith, as applied to non-merchants? What does it mean that good faith requires "honesty in fact"? Is "good faith" just about "honesty," or is something more required? Again, the challenge is in defining "good faith" apart from any specific context. For example, it is much easier to understand the meaning of "good faith" in the context of an output or requirements contract under § 2-306(1) than by reference to an abstract definition isolated from context. **STOP NOW and review UCC § 2-306(1) below.**

UCC § 2-306(1)

(1) A term which measures the quantity by the output of the seller or the requirements of the buyer means such actual output or requirements as may occur in good faith, except that no quantity unreasonably disproportionate to any stated estimate or in the absence of a stated estimate to any normal or otherwise comparable prior output or requirements may be tendered or demanded.

. . .

Under the statute, "good faith" is not required in the abstract, but is employed as a means by with to measure compliance with seller's promise to sell its output or buyer's promise to buy its requirements.

The CISG also provides support for "good faith," albeit in a somewhat less direct manner than other U.S. law. In Lesson 2, at the outset of this course, we noted the requirement of uniform interpretation under CISG

Article 7(1), and further noted the general principle of "good faith" to be employed in its interpretation. Thus, the CISG does not necessarily directly imply a contractual obligation of good faith, but may nevertheless reach a similar result by interpreting any statutory provision governing the parties' agreement in a manner most likely to achieve a result consistent with good faith.

Best Efforts

In the most basic sense, "best efforts" may be distinguished from "good faith" in that the former always requires some sort of affirmatively positive conduct, while the latter more generally serves as a bar to certain negative conduct. A party required to exercise "best efforts" must affirmatively perform an implied obligation in fulfillment of the purpose of the contract. In contrast, a party required to exercise "good faith" is precluded from performing obligations or exercising rights in a manner likely to deprive its contracting partner of the benefit of the parties' bargain. In some circumstances, a party may be required by good faith to perform an act, but such performance is usually mandated to avoid a negative effect on a right held by the other party (such as the right to receive payment in Example 31-1). While it is often difficult to draw clear distinctions between the two, an obligation of "best efforts" will always require something more of a party than will an obligation of only "good faith."

The second major difference between the two is that "good faith" is implied in all contracts, while "best efforts" are only implied under limited circumstances. "Good faith" is also mandatory, while "best efforts" are merely a "default" implied where the parties' agreement is silent. We first encountered the basic principle underlying the implication of "best efforts" in the case of *Wood v. Lucy, Lady Duff-Gordon*, in Lesson 6.

You will recall that the court implied an obligation requiring Wood to use "reasonable efforts" to generate profits from the "exclusive rights" expressly promised to him by Lucy, Lady Duff-Gordon. Today, these "reasonable efforts" are generally characterized as "best efforts" under both the common law and UCC Article 2 (below). Another common law context in which "best efforts" are frequently implied is that of a "percentage lease." In a percentage lease, the lessee's rental payment obligation is determined—in whole or in part—by the revenue generated by the lessee in using the leased premises.

Example 31-3: Lessor leases a retail storefront on Main Street to Lessee, for the express purpose of selling clothing. The lease requires Lessee to pay a monthly rental amount equal to 10% of Lessee's monthly sales volume.

Inasmuch as Lessee essentially has an "exclusive right" to the use of the storefront, and is, therefore, Lessor's sole source of rental income for that storefront, a court will imply a requirement that Lessee exercise "best efforts" to generate sales revenue from the storefront.

The lessee's obligation of best (or at least reasonable) efforts to generate sales volume and, therefore, a lease payment obligation is analogous to Wood's obligations to generate revenue from the rights granted him by Lucy, Lady Duff-Gordon and, therefore, profits to be shared with her. Of course, such an "implication" will not be necessary in every contract.

For example, Wood's obligations might have been expressly spelled out in specific terms. If so, there would be no need to imply any sort of "efforts," as such efforts would be addressed by the express terms. In a similar vein, a lease with a substantial base payment would not likely require "best efforts" of the lessee, even if the lease also included some percentage of sales. While the lessee would still have an exclusive right to the premises, the percentage element of the lease payment would not be lessor's sole source of lease income (assuming, of course, that the "base" portion was substantial). While a court would not likely require "best efforts" of the lessee in this latter case, the lessee might nevertheless be precluded from conduct completely depriving the lessor of additional income based on the obligation of "good faith."

As first encountered in Lesson 6, "best efforts" is also implied in an exclusive dealings contract involving goods. **STOP NOW and review UCC § 2-306(2) below.**

UCC § 2-306(2)

. . .

(2) A lawful agreement by either the seller or the buyer for exclusive dealing in the kind of goods concerned imposes unless otherwise agreed an obligation by the seller to use best efforts to supply the goods and by the buyer to use best efforts to promote their sale.

One of the most frequent examples of such an "exclusive dealings" agreement is an agreement between a manufacturer and distributer of goods.

> **Example 31-4:** Marx manufactures a variety of goods, including motors, while Dix distributes a variety of goods, including motors. Marx enters into a contract with Dix in which Marx grants Dix an exclusive right to distribute Marx motors within Texas, and Dix promises to distribute only Marx motors within Texas.
>
> Marx must exercise best efforts to supply Dix with motors, because Dix cannot sell any other kind of motor within Texas. Dix must exercise best efforts to promote the sale of Marx motors in Texas, because Marx cannot sell them in Texas in any other manner.

The above example involves exclusive dealings on the part of both buyer and seller. However, such exclusive dealings will often involve only one party, in which case "best efforts" are imposed only upon the party with the exclusive right at issue.

As in the case of the common law, a clear definition of the obligations of buyer or seller will generally avoid the implication of "best efforts," as indicated by the statutory language, "unless otherwise agreed." However, even where best efforts may not be implied, the obligation of good faith may nevertheless require a certain level of performance of an otherwise specified obligation, as in the case of an output or requirements contract.

Termination Rights

Another area in which the law will sometimes imply a term involves a party's right to terminate a contract. Of course, any contract is terminable by mutual consent of the parties, and many contracts will provide one or both parties with additional rights to terminate the contract under certain conditions or after a certain period of time. A contract may also terminate automatically after its completion, or upon certain conditions or expiration of a period of time. However, some contracts of indefinite duration will simply fail to address the issue of termination.

In some cases, such as contracts of employment, a contract of indefinite duration will be deemed terminable at the will of either party. It is assumed in such cases that each party is at least impliedly satisfied with the contractual exchange at issue for whatever period it may last. While a party may prefer a longer term contract to a shorter one, it presumably prefers a shorter term contract to no contract at all. In some contracts, however, this will not be the case. When one party necessarily makes a significant investment in the rights provided by the contract, that party will often require a certain period within which to recoup its investment, as well as reasonable notice in advance of termination in order to wind down or otherwise adapt the operation in which it has invested.

Where a contract necessarily requires a party to make a substantial investment in order to perform its obligations under a contract and thereby benefit from the rights granted under the contract, and the contract is silent with respect to duration or termination, the following terms will often be implied.

Summary of Basic Rule: termination rights in the absence of an agreed term

- The contract may be terminated only after the party necessarily making a substantial investment in the contract has had a reasonable time to recoup that investment; and

- The contract may be terminated only with reasonable notice allowing a party making a substantial investment in the contract a reasonable time to wind down or adapt the product of that investment.

As with the issue of exclusive dealings above, the above issue of termination will often arise in the context of a distribution agreement.

> **Example 31-5:** Marx manufactures a variety of goods motors contracts with Dix to distribute its motors in Texas. When the parties conclude the contract, Dix has no existing motor distribution network, and Marx motors have never been sold in Texas. The distribution agreement is silent with respect to termination. Dix makes a significant investment in both building a distribution network for the motors (hiring and training sales reps, etc.) and developing the market for the motors in Texas (advertising, promotion, etc.).

A court would likely preclude any termination by Marx until such time had passed to allow Dix to recoup its investment in the distribution agreement. A court would also likely require sufficient notice by Marx so as to allow Dix to make reasonable adjustments to its distribution network in planning for the cessation of its distribution of Marx motors.

Of course any party entering into an agreement like the foregoing one would be very well advised to include express provisions addressing duration and termination—especially if making a significant investment in the rights granted under the contract. A court may or may not "imply" a term adequate to protect the investing party under any particular set of circumstances. Another common example of an agreement under which one party may make a significant investment is a franchise agreement (an illustration of which we encountered in Example 14-4). In fact, both franchisees and distributors often receive additional protections under various specialized state statutes.

UCC Article 2 also expressly addresses the issue of notice of termination. **STOP NOW and READ UCC § 2-309(3) below.**

UCC § 2-309(3)

. . .

(3) Termination of a contract by one party except on the happening of an agreed event requires that reasonable notification be received by the other party and an agreement dispensing with notification is invalid if its operation would be unconscionable.

The foregoing statutory provision implies a requirement of reasonable notice of termination of a contract for the sale of goods. Is this a "default" or "mandatory" implied provision? Arguably, it's a bit of a hybrid, depending on whether termination without notice would be unconscionable under the circumstances.

APPLYING THE RULES

Problem 1: J.C. Penney contracted with G.E. Pension Trust to finance a number of retail store properties. The financing was accomplished through what is called a "sale and leaseback" agreement, under which Penney sold a property to the Trust, and then leased it back from the Trust for 25 years (this is a common financing mechanism, often providing certain tax and securitization benefits, as compared to a more traditional loan secured by a mortgage).

Paragraph 34 of each lease further entitled the lessee, Penney, to request the lessor, Trust, to finance the costs of additional property improvements, limited to a minimum request of $250,000. Upon receipt of such request, the lessor was obligated to give reasonable consideration to the financing request. If such a request was rejected by the lessor, then the lessee was entitled to repurchase the property from the lessor at a price that amounted to far less than its market value.

One of these leases, in Milwaukee, Wisconsin, was later conveyed to Market Street Associates (MSA), which sought to sublease a part of the property to a drugstore chain. As is common, the new tenant expected MSA to make substantial improvements. MSA initially sought to finance the improvements by borrowing from a local bank, but the bank would only make a loan secured by a mortgage on the property, which MSA could not, as the lessee, provide. MSA's general partner, Orenstein, then approached Erb, a new Trust employee responsible for the lease, about purchasing the property. Erb was initially unresponsive, but ultimately offered to sell the property for $3 million. Orenstein reasonably believed that the market value of the property was closer to $2 to 2.5 million and was, therefore, unwilling to pay Erb's asking price. Erb, however, was unwilling to discuss a lower sale price.

Two weeks after the parties' last communication regarding a possible sale of the property, Orenstein mailed a certified letter to Erb requesting financing of planned property improvements in the amount of $2 million. The letter did not mention Paragraph 34. Erb immediately replied that the Trust had no interest in making any loans for requests below a $7 million minimum. Soon thereafter, Orenstein mailed a second certified letter to Erb stating that MSA was exercising its right to purchase the property pursuant to Paragraph 34—at a price of $ 1 million (the proper calculation under Paragraph 34).

At this point, has either party breached any contract obligation? If you were a judge hearing a request by MSA seeking specific performance of Paragraph 34 and a defense by the Trust asserting it was not required to convey the property at all, what else would you like to know in deciding the case? Assuming you found that one of the parties had breached an obligation, how would you propose to remedy that breach?

The facts of this problem are loosely based on the issues raised in the case of *Market Street Associates v. Frey*, 941 F.2d 588 (7th Cir. 1991).

Problem 2: In 1972, Falstaff Brewing purchased from Ballantine Brewing the Ballantine beer line. The price was $4 million plus a royalty on the amount of Ballantine beer sold. The contract expressly provided as follows:

> Falstaff Brewing will use its best efforts to promote and maintain a high volume of sales of Ballantine beer.
>
> Falstaff Brewing will pay a royalty of $.50 per barrel for a period of 6 years, provided, however, that if during the Royalty Period Falstaff substantially discontinues the distribution of Ballantine beer (except as the result of a restraining order in effect for 30 days issued by a court of competent jurisdiction at the request of a governmental authority), it will pay to Ballantine a cash sum equal to the years and fraction thereof remaining in the Royalty Period times $1,100,000.

Falstaff initially continued Ballantine's own prior practices of seeking high sales volume at low profit margins in a shrinking market. In doing so, Falstaff generated significant net losses and found itself on the brink of insolvency. After three years, Falstaff was acquired by new ownership, which invested additional capital, while dramatically changing management strategies. Essentially, Falstaff sacrificed sales volume on all of its lines, selling less beer, but at higher margins, so as to turn the business around and make it profitable. The volume of other brewers also fell during this same time period. However, the volume of Ballantine's beer, as sold by Falstaff, fell by an even greater percentage than Falstaff's own original beer brand or that of other brewers. As part of its turnaround efforts, Falstaff had continued to make Ballantine beer available to sell it to anyone requested it, but had ceased to spend any significant amount of money on further marketing or promotion of Ballantine beer.

At the end of year four of the Royalty Period, Bloor, the bankruptcy trustee administering the Ballantine insolvency proceedings, brought an action against Falstaff for breach of contract. If you were in Bloor's position, how would you frame your potential claims for breach (there are a variety of possible claims)? We will more fully explore performance and breach in the next chapter, but this problem provides a good bridge in requiring a comparison of the content of the contract terms with the parties' actual conduct under that contract.

If the contract had not expressly provided for "best efforts," would a court have implied such a term?

The facts of this problem are loosely based on the issues raised in the case of *Bloor v. Falstaff Brewing Corp.*, 601 F.2d 609 (2d Cir. 1979).

Quick Summary

Having addressed a variety of possible sources of the content of the parties' rights and obligations, it may be useful to summarize them here in a hierarchical form.

(1) Mandatory terms supplied by governing law (e.g., "good faith")

(2) The terms of the parties' agreement-in-fact

    a. Express terms

        i. "Dickered" or negotiated terms

        ii. Standard terms or terms incorporated by reference

    b. Implied-in-fact terms based on

        i. Course of performance

        ii. Course of dealing

        iii. Usage of trade

    c. Implied-in-fact terms based on other circumstances surrounding the negotiation and conclusion of the contract (unless precluded by the operation of the parol evidence rule)

(3) "Default" terms supplied by governing law to the extent not addressed by the parties' agreement in fact

7

Conditions, Performance, and Breach

Key Concepts

- When is Performance of a Promise "Conditional"?
- What Happens When a Party Breaches the Contract? When is Performance Excused Based on a Breach?
- Express Conditions, Constructive Conditions, Performance and Breach of Contract Obligations

Lesson 32: Expressly Agreed Conditions as Pre-Conditions to Performance

Objectives and Expected Learning Outcomes

In this lesson, you will learn of "conditions," as potential limits on the obligations of one or both of the parties under the contract at issue. You will learn how such conditions are given effect, as well as the circumstances under which their non-occurrence may be waived or otherwise excused. Most importantly, you will learn to determine if and when a given performance obligation is due in the context of a conditional contract.

In the first six chapters, we have addressed the basic requirements for a binding and enforceable contract, as well as the means by which the content of the parties' rights and obligations is determined. Thus, we can now move to the performance of the contract. In this chapter, we will address two general issues: (1) express conditions to performance by one or both parties; and (2) constructive conditions to performance arising from one party's breach of its contract obligations. In addressing the latter, we will further explore a variety of additional issues involving breach, including the nature of a breach, the sequence of the parties' obligations, a breaching party's right to cure any breach, an aggrieved party's obligation to provide notice of any breach, and other doctrines sometimes employed to mitigate the potentially harsh effects of excusing contract performance obligations. Finally, we will explore in the final two lessons the issue of anticipatory non-performance—what happens when performance appears unlikely, or worse, at a time before such performance is actually due?

Conditions

Most contracts involve an exchange of promises by each party (a bilateral contract), and all contracts include at least one promise (even a unilateral contract). In many cases, a promise will be unconditional. Once the contract has been concluded, the promisor is bound, without more, to perform his or her promised obligation or obligations. In other cases, however, a promise may be "conditional," upon something more, before the promisee is entitled to performance. We first encountered a "conditional" promise in Example 6-1, based on the case of *Mattei v. Hopper*, in which Mattei's obligation to purchase the subject property was conditioned upon obtaining satisfactory leases.

A "condition" is an uncertain event, the occurrence of which is a pre-requisite to performance of one or more contract obligations. A performance obligation subject to a "condition" simply does not come due—and is not, therefore, enforceable—until and unless the condition is either satisfied or excused.[1] In the typical contract context, a "condition" is a "condition precedent" to the obligation at issue. Simply put, the condition must happen first, or the obligation never comes due. In contrast, a condition or event may also have the effect of extinguishing, discharging, or otherwise terminating an obligation after it has already arisen. This is called a "condition subsequent." In the materials that follow, we shall focus solely on conditions precedent.

Conditions are often called "express conditions" (as in the opening paragraph above) which is technically inaccurate in that a condition may also be implied-in-fact based on the parties' intent-in-fact even if not clearly "expressed." For example, a "condition" might be implied based on a course of dealing even though it is not directly "expressed" in written or spoken words. With that caveat, however, the term "express condition" is a useful one in distinguishing a true condition from a "constructive condition," the discussion of which will begin in the next lesson.

---

[1] Restatement (Second) or Contracts § 224.

We begin with a relatively simple example.

Example 32-1: *Luttinger v. Rosen*

Buyer contracted to purchase Seller's home for $85,000, "subject to and conditional upon the buyers obtaining first mortgage financing on said premises from a bank or other lending institution in an amount of $45,000 for a term of not less than twenty (20) years and at an interest rate which does not exceed 8 ½ percent per annum." Buyer sought to obtain such financing, but was not able to obtain a rate below 8 ¾ percent. Buyer therefore notified Seller that it would not perform due to the failure of the condition and requested a return of Buyer's deposit. When Seller refused, Buyer brought suit, thereby raising the issue of whether or not Buyer's conditional performance had come due.

The court strictly applied the condition requiring an 8 ½ percent mortgage, finding that an 8 ¾ percent mortgage did not satisfy the condition—even where Seller's attorney had offered to make up the difference to Buyer. Thus, the condition of Buyer's obligation to purchase Seller's home had not been satisfied, and Buyer was entitled to a return of the deposit.[2]

The foregoing case provides a classic case of the general rule of "strict compliance" applied to express conditions. As a general rule, "close" is not sufficient in complying with an express condition. In *Luttinger*, even an offer by the seller's attorney to make up the difference was deemed insufficient. An offer of reimbursement for an additional expense incurred is simply not the same as avoiding the expense in the first instance—even where the increased expense is quite minimal.

The rule of strict compliance has much to commend it in terms of "bright lines" upon which parties can seemingly rely in ordering their affairs. Moreover, the very nature of a "conditional" obligation suggests that any

---

[2] Luttinger v. Rosen, 164 Conn. 45, 316 A.2d 757 (1972).

condition on promisor's consent to be bound by the promised obligation ought to be strictly respected. Any other approach might have the effect of binding a party to a contract to which the party never in fact consented. As with most rules, however, certain circumstances may arise in which "strict compliance" may appear to work an injustice on the promisee. As a result, courts have developed a number of approaches or exceptions designed to mitigate or avoid some of the harshest effects of the rule.

Condition, Duty, or Both?

It is often essential to distinguish between a condition and a duty. A given contract term may provide for one, or the other, or both, and the difference between the effect of a condition or duty may determine whether a given obligation must be performed or is excused.

When a "condition" fails to occur, and the time for its occurrence has passed, then any obligation subject to the condition is discharged, and the promisor of such obligation is no longer bound to perform.[3] Subject to "excuse," addressed later in this lesson, the effect of a failure of a "condition" is generally automatic, absolute, and sometimes harsh. This effect of the failure of a "condition" can be contrasted with the breach of a "duty."

A "duty" is an obligation of one party to render a promised performance. If the duty is not performed, as promised, then the promisor will be liable for breach, including damages if proven (to be addressed in the next Chapter). However, one party's breach of a "duty" will not necessarily excuse the other party's performance. Unlike the rule of "strict compliance" applied to "express conditions," the rules determining whether a breach of a "duty" will excuse performance are far more complex (and are the subject of most of the remaining lessons in this Chapter). The key point here is to note that the breach of a "duty" is significantly less likely to excuse performance than the failure of a "condition." As such, the breach of a "duty" will often be less likely to result in forfeiture than the failure of a "condition."

An example is useful in illustrating the distinction and its effect.

---

[3] Restatement (Second) of Contracts § 225.

Example 32-2: Contractor agrees to build a home for Landowner for a price of $1 million. Landowner knows that Contractor has many other projects and wants Contractor to focus sufficient resources on Landowner's home to complete the job by October 1. In fact, Landowner is willing to pay an extra 10 percent, for a total of $1.1 million, to get the job completed by October 1, and communicates this information to Contractor. In response, Contractor immediately begins working diligently to complete the job and does so by noon on October 2. Landowner suffers no actual loss as a result of the fact that completion is 12 hours late.

Contractor demands $1.1 million in payment for the home. Landowner offers only $1 million, explaining that contractor failed to complete the job by October 1. What do you think?

Was completion by October 1 a "condition" of Landowner's obligation to pay the additional $100,000? Was completion by October 1 a "duty" of Contractor? Was it both? If October 1 completion was a "condition," which party likely prevails? What if October 1 completion was solely a "duty"?

Of course, the Landowner will prevail if compliance with the deadline is deemed a "condition," and "strict compliance" is required. In contrast, if compliance with the deadline is deemed a "duty," then Contractor's failure to do so is merely a breach. We will discover in the next lesson that a *de minimis* breach of this sort will not likely excuse Landowner's obligation to pay the additional promised amount. Thus, it often makes a significant difference whether a term is characterized as a "condition" or a "duty."

In resolving doubts as to whether an obligation is "conditional" upon an event, a court will generally favor a construction of the term at issue that will minimize the obligee's risk of forfeiture, unless the event is within the obligee's control, or the circumstances otherwise indicate that the obligee has assumed the risk.[4] However, even if the event is within the obligee's control—as in Example 32-2—any doubt as to the nature of the term is resolved in favor of construing the term as a "duty" rather than a "condi-

---

[4] Restatement (Second) of Contracts § 227(1).

tion" or both.[5] While this process is often described as "interpretation," the application of the foregoing "preferences" is perhaps more accurately described as judicial "construction" in a manner intended to minimize the risk of forfeiture.

Based on these stated preferences, a court would likely construe the deadline in Example 32-2 as a mere "duty," instead of a "condition" or both, absent additional facts more clearly establishing a "condition." In Example 32-2, the nature of Landowner's intent is sufficiently uncertain to justify such a construction in an effort to avoid forfeiture by the Contractor, who seemingly make the requested effort towards timely completion and only missed the deadline by a matter of a few hours.

Where an event is not within the control of the obligee, and there is no indication that the obligee has assumed the risk of its nonoccurrence, a court may exercise even greater latitude in construing an uncertain provision to avoid forfeiture.

> **Example 32-3:** Apex, a mining company, hires Ben, and engineer, to help reopen one of its mines. Ben is to be paid $10,000 for the job (a reasonable sum for the work) "as soon as the mine is in successful operation." Ben performs his work flawlessly, but the attempt to reopen the mine fails for reasons unrelated to Ben's work and is abandoned by Apex. Ben demands payment for services, while Apex asserts that payment for those services was "conditional" upon the mine resuming "successful operation," which did not happen.
>
> A court would likely construe the agreement as requiring payment by Apex to Ben within a reasonable time after Ben had completed the promised services, thereby avoiding forfeiture by Ben for services fully performed as agreed. Successful reopening of the mine was beyond Ben's control, and there was no indication that he had assumed the risk of failure.[6]

---

[5] Restatement (Second) of Contracts § 227(2).
[6] Based on Restatement (Second) of Contracts § 227, illustration 2.

In the foregoing example, the court did not characterize the "successful operation" provision as either a "duty" of Ben or a "condition" of the Apex's obligation to pay him. Instead, the court merely treated it as a "timing" mechanism for determining when Ben was to be paid, and which was simply replaced by a default term requiring payment within a "reasonable" time when the event did not occur.

In Example 32-3, the court's construction of the term at issue to avoid forfeiture may indeed involve a bit of judicial magic, but nevertheless seems true to the parties' actual bargain, if not its precise terms. But what should a court do in the case of a clear "express condition"—with no other reasonable construction—in which its "strict application" would work a substantial forfeiture? Should a court ignore the condition purely as a matter of equity?

We earlier encountered one context in which a failure of a condition may preclude a party from exercising a right—that of an option contract. As a general rule, an offer pursuant to an option contract must be exercised within the expressly granted option period, and no later. All risks are generally placed on the option holder, who must insure that the promisor actually receives notice of intent to exercise the option within the time period provided by the option. In effect, the right to exercise the option is "conditional" upon "strict compliance" with any timing requirement.

In the case of a "typical" option, there is no "forfeiture" when a party fails to meet a strict deadline, because the party holding the option has no actual rights in the subject of the option until the option is exercised. However, the issue becomes somewhat more difficult in the context of an option to renew an existing property right.

Example 32-4: *J.N.A. Realty Corp. v. Cross Bay Chelsea, Inc.*

CBC leased premises from JNA on which CBC operated a restaurant. CBC was an assignee of the original lease with the consent of JNA, which had modified the original lease to provide for an option to renew the lease at the end of the initial term (5 years remained at the time of the assignment to CBC) for an additional 24 years. Paragraph 58 of the lease required a 6 month written notice of lessee's intent to exercise the renewal option. As the end of the initial lease

476 • Learning Contracts •

period approached, CBC inadvertently failed to provide timely notice pursuant to paragraph 58 and only discovered the oversight 45 days prior to the expiration of the lease. CBC nevertheless sought to exercise the renewal, while JNA asserted that any renewal was "conditional" upon compliance with the notice requirement, which CBC had failed to do. Litigation ensued.

The court noted the normal rule of "strict compliance," as generally applied in the context of an option contract, but further noted the increased potential for forfeiture in the context of an option to renew a lease. CBC had made significant financial investments in improving the property, including investments made since the passage of the 6 month notice requirement. As such, a strict application of the notice requirement would result in CBC's forfeiture of its improvements, as well as the "good will" value of the restaurant it was operating on the property.

While acknowledging that JNA's position was fully supported by the letter of the law, a majority of the court ruled in favor of CBC's position, as a matter of equity, subject to a determination of whether JNA had been in any way prejudiced by the late notice.[7]

In effect, the court balanced the equities—even though CBC's own inadvertence had led to the failure to give proper notice. CBC was entitled to enforce the renewal option, as a matter of equity so as to avoid extraordinary forfeiture in a relative unique context, but only if JNA suffered no material detriment as a result of the late notice. The court's decision was 4-3, reflecting the controversial nature of its reliance solely on the issue of forfeiture in the face of lessee's negligence in failing to satisfy the notice requirement as a condition to renewal of the lease.

Thus, our consideration of examples thus far provides an illustration of the range of possible approaches to conditions, from the general "rule" of "strict compliance" on one end, to a decision based purely on the equities

---

[7] J.N.A. Realty Corp. v. Cross Bay Chelsea, Inc., 42 N.Y.2d 392, 366 N.E.2d 1313, 397 N.Y.S.2d 958 (1977).

on the other. While the application of the general rule is certainly far more common, courts are often willing to consider the equities—especially in the case of substantial forfeiture—in interpreting or construing a condition, or even, in an extraordinary case, simply declining to give it effect.

"Satisfaction"

In some cases, one party's obligation to perform may be conditional upon the "satisfaction" of the other party or a third party. Most often, a buyer's obligation to complete the purchase at issue is conditional upon "satisfaction" with the product, property, or service in question. We saw this in Example 6-1, based on the case of *Mattei v. Hopper*. As in that case, conditions involving purely subjective satisfaction are often the most challenging. The obligation of good faith provides at least some limit on the ability of the promisor to avoid an obligation by merely expressing arbitrary or disingenuous "dissatisfaction" with the product, property, or service, though practical application (i.e., proof of "bad faith") can sometimes be difficult. Where reasonable, however, a court will generally apply an objective standard to a condition requiring "satisfaction," especially one that requires the satisfaction of a third party professional.

A building or other construction project will often involve various progress payments along the way, as well as a final payment upon completion of the overall project. At any given stage, the project owner's obligation to pay the contractor may be "conditioned" upon approval by an independent engineer or architect that the work up to that point is "satisfactory." In many cases, the satisfaction of this engineer or architect is deemed "final and absolute." While courts will often give considerable deference to such a determination, one that is objectively irrational will rarely be given dispositive effect.

> **Example 32-5:** Contractor agrees to build a home for Landowner for a price of $1 million, with progress payments to be made by Landowner over time and a final payment of $100,000, upon final approval that the project has been completed to the satisfaction of the architect, whose "decision shall be final, binding, and non-reviewable." Upon completion, the architect refuses to give final approval, asserting that the roofing material is inferior to that specified.

In a subsequent action by Contractor to collect the final payment, multiple expert witnesses testify that the roofing materials in all cases equal or exceed the project specifications. Landowner produces no objective evidence in support of its architect, who simply remains adamant that the roofing is unsatisfactory. A court would likely rule that the Contractor is entitled to collect the final payment because there is no "objective" basis for the architect's dissatisfaction.

In summary, a "condition" may depend upon either the fully subjective satisfaction of the recipient of the performance or upon the objective satisfaction of the recipient or a third party. To the extent reasonable under the circumstances, however, a court will generally give preference to an "objective" measure of satisfaction, which is more susceptible to subsequent review.

Prevention, Waiver, Estoppel, and Election

At the outset of this lesson, we noted that a conditional obligation will not come due until and unless the condition is satisfied "or excused." We now address "excuse" of a condition based on the conduct or the parties. Perhaps the simplest basis for "excuse" is "prevention."

Where a party's conduct actually prevents the condition from occurring, that party may not assert the failure of the condition as a basis for non-performance. In effect, this is merely a straightforward application of the principle of estoppel. The party who prevents the condition from occurring is estopped by his or her conduct from asserting the failure of the condition as a basis for non-performance of the conditional obligation.

Example 32-6: Sue engages Ron, a realtor, to sell her home. Ron is to receive a 5% commission, conditioned upon successful closing of the sale. Ron successfully locates Beth, a buyer for the home, who signs a contract to purchase the home from Sue. However, the day before closing, Sue inexplicably backs out without any stated reason for doing so. Beth is unhappy, but decides not to pursue the matter when Sue returns her deposit. Ron demands payment from Sue, but she refuses, asserting that payment was conditioned upon "closing," which did not take place.

A court would likely rule that Ron is entitled to payment because Sue "prevented" closing from occurring by her conduct. She is, therefore, estopped from asserting the failure of the condition, and the condition is excused.

Implicit in the above analysis is that the condition was included in the real estate brokerage contract between Sue and Ron for the benefit of Sue. She obviously did not wish to pay a commission to Ron, unless the sale of her home was completed. The application of the rule involving "prevention" would make no sense in this context as applied to any conduct by Ron preventing closing, as the condition is not for his benefit. Instead, any such conduct by Ron would almost certainly be a breach of his brokerage contract with Sue, subject to a claim for damages. In addressing the next set of issues involving "excuse," it is often important first to identify for whose benefit a condition is included.

A party for whose benefit a condition is included in the contract may "waive" the operation of that condition. Typically, this is the party whose obligation is dependent upon the occurrence of the condition at issue. However, a condition may also be included in some contracts for the benefit of both parties, in which case neither party can unilaterally waive the condition (leaving the other party without its protection). This issue is one of party intent and will often be obvious from the context. In some cases, however, the issue may be less clear and must be resolved before determining whether a waiver is effective.

A "waiver" is merely a voluntary current relinquishment of a known right—in this context, a right to withhold performance until and unless the specified condition has occurred. We earlier encountered waiver in the context of UCC § 2-209(4) and (5). As in that case, a "waiver" of a "condition" generally remains subject to retraction, absent detrimental reliance by the other party. However, the waiver of a "condition" includes an additional unique element—the deadline for occurrence of the condition. An example is useful here.

Example 32-7: A contracts to manufacture a machine at a specified price for B, based upon technical specifications provided by B. The technical specifications called for the use of "Rarium," a rare metal with unique characteristics desired by B. A is concerned that it may not be able to acquire Rarium, but B assures A that B can do so at a specified price. Thus, the parties include in their contract the following provision: "A's obligation to produce the specified machine is expressly conditional upon B providing 20 kg of Rarium to A at $100 per kg, by no later than July 1." A has promised to deliver the machine on or before December 1.

On April 1, A contacts B and states that B will not need to procure the Rarium, as A has found an alternative source at a lower price. The legal effect of this communication by A is likely a "waiver" of the condition requiring that B provide Rarium. A will, therefore, be required to deliver the machine even though B does not provide the Rarium.

In the foregoing example, A is concerned about its ability to obtain an essential material and, therefore, conditions its performance obligation upon B providing the material. Inasmuch as this condition was provided for A's benefit, it is subject to "waiver" by A. Having waived the condition, A's performance obligation is now absolute. But what if A should change its mind?

A is entitled to "retract" its "waiver" prior to the deadline for occurrence of the condition, subject to two important limits. First, A must provide B with sufficient notice of the retraction to allow for its satisfaction. This is a factual determination and, in the foregoing example, would likely depend on the time reasonably required by B to obtain and provide the material. Second, A's retraction will be precluded to the extent B has detrimentally relied upon it. For example, if B was planning to provide the material from stock and had sold that stock to another when notified of A's waiver, A would be estopped from retracting its waiver by B's reliance, assuming that B could not reasonably obtain more stock elsewhere. These basic rules are of course quite similar to those found in UCC § 2-209(5). However, the doctrine of estoppel also precludes retraction of a waiver of an express provision after the time has passed for the satisfaction of the condition—in Example 32-7, July 1.

This leads to the obvious question of what happens when the non-occurrence of a condition is waived after the time for its satisfaction has already passed.

Example 32-8: Returning to Example 32-7, and the condition at issue: "A's obligation to produce the specified machine is expressly conditional upon B providing 20 kg of Rarium to A at $100 per kg, by no later than July 1." On July 5, B has not yet provided A with the Rarium. However, A contacts B and states that B will not need to procure the Rarium, as A has found an alternative source at a lower price.

A has "waived" the condition after the time for its occurrence has passed. Thus, the condition is excused, and A is estopped from retracting the waiver. This is called an "election" inasmuch as it is an irreversible choice, once made.

It bears repeating that, in all of the examples in this section, the condition was "excused" solely be reference to the conduct of the party for whose benefit it was initially provided. Thus, we might reasonably summarize "conditions" as a means of strictly limiting one's performance obligation to certain expressly specified circumstances, unless excused by one's own conduct, or avoided by a court's construction of the agreement in a manner to avoid unreasonable forfeiture by the obligee of the promised conditional performance.

APPLYING THE RULES

Problem 1: Consider Example 32-2. In the actual example, the nature of the Landowner's promise of an additional bonus is somewhat unclear. Can you make it clearer?

First, assume that you represent the Landowner and have been asked to draft the additional payment obligation as clearly "conditional" upon meeting the deadline.

Second, assume that you represent the Contractor and have been asked to draft the provision solely as a "duty."

Finally, draft the provision so that it is both a duty and a condition. What is the effect of such a provision if Contractor does not complete the work by the deadline?

Problem 2: Peacock Construction (as general contractor) contracted with Owner to build a condominium project. Peacock further subcontracted the heating and air conditioning work to Modern Air Conditioning (MAC). The comprehensive written subcontract between Peacock and MAC provided that Peacock would make final payment to MAC,

> within 30 days after completion of the work included in this subcontract, written acceptance by the Architect, and full payment therefor by the Owner.

MAC performed the work as agreed, and it was approved and accepted in writing by the project Architect. However, the Owner had become insolvent and failed to pay Peacock for the work. Peacock, thus, declined to pay MAC. Is MAC entitled to payment? In analyzing this issue, are you engaged in "interpretation" or "construction" of the parties' agreement?

The facts of this problem are loosely based on the issues raised in the case of *Peacock Construction Co. v. Modern Air Conditioning, Inc.*, 353 So.2d 840 (Fla. 1977).

Problem 3: River Brand Rice Mills (Seller) contracted to sell 50,000 rice pockets to Internatio-Rotterdam (Buyer) at "$8.25 per pocket, F.A.S. [to be delivered alongside the ship designated by Buyer at the Port of] Houston, Texas. Seller was obligated to deliver the rice in "December 1952, with two weeks call from buyer," and Buyer was obligated to pay by "irrevocable letter of credit," payable against documents indicating delivery in December. The parties agreed that "with two weeks call from buyer" meant that Buyer was to give Seller delivery instructions (i.e., designating the ship to which the rice should be delivered and the precise timing and instructions for delivery) at least two weeks prior to the time of delivery. The notice period was particularly important for shipments in December, which was an unusually busy time for rice and cotton shipments from Texas and Louisiana resulting in unusually congested ports. A "letter of credit" is a mechanism by which a bank guarantees payment to the seller, provided that the seller delivers conforming documents (in this case indicating December delivery by Seller) to the bank. Banks (and courts) "strictly enforce" specific requirements for payment pursuant to a letter of credit. Without the letter of credit, Seller remains entitled to payment, but must seek to collect directly from Buyer.

By December, the market price of rice had risen to $9.25 per pocket. By the end of the day on December 17, Seller had not yet received shipping instructions from Buyer. The next morning, Seller promptly notified Buyer that it would not be delivering the promised rice to Buyer. Seller instead sold the rice elsewhere at the higher market price. Buyer brought an action for breach of contract.

Was Seller obligated to deliver the rice to Buyer, or was it entitled to walk away from its obligation on December 18? Does it matter whether Seller was motivated to do so based on the change in price?

The facts of this problem are loosely based on the issues raised in the case of *Internatio-Rotterdam, Inc. v. River Brand Rice Mills, Inc.*, 259 F.2d 137 (2d Cir. 1958).

Lesson 33: Constructive Conditions and Common Law Termination for Material Breach

Objectives and Expected Learning Outcomes

In this lesson, you will begin to learn when one party's breach of a "duty" under a common law contract may excuse the other party's obligation to perform one or more of its own duties. You will specifically learn about "dependent" promises and the timing and sequence of such dependent promises. Finally, you will learn to that, while all breaches will give rise to a claim for damages, if proven, only certain breaches are sufficiently "material" to perhaps excuse the other party's performance obligations under the contact.

Constructive Conditions of Exchange

When parties include an express condition as a prerequisite to a particular performance obligation, there is generally little question of their actual intent that the obligation is conditioned upon the occurrence of the event in question. However, to what extent might a "bargained for" exchange of mutual "promises" impliedly or "constructively" condition the performance of each party upon the performance of the other? Consider the following simple example.

Example 33-1: Tara owns a business and promises to sell the business to Seth in exchange for Seth's promise to pay her an agreed amount of money for the business. This is a simple bargain of one promise—conveyance of the business—in exchange for another—payment for the business conveyed. Tara has given her promise in exchange for Seth's and Seth has given his promise in exchange for Tara's. There is no reason to presume, absent other facts to the contrary, that either would have made his or her promise without that of the other.

The foregoing example provides an obvious and simple illustration of the basic rule of "dependent" promises made, in whole or in part, in exchange for the other.[8] The inherent interdependency of any such an "exchange" of promises is presumed, absent a clear indication to the contrary.[9] The first example is particularly clear, because each party has made only one promise. Thus, the only other factual possibility would be mutual gifts. However, when one or both of the parties makes multiple promises, the analysis is somewhat more interesting.

Example 33-2: *Kingston v. Preston*

The Owner of a business promised to convey the business to his Apprentice in exchange for two promises by the Apprentice: (1) the Apprentice would pay for the business over time; and (2) the Apprentice would deliver "security" (i.e., some sort of collateral Owner could rely upon if Apprentice later failed to pay as agreed) to the Owner at closing, at the same time the Owner conveyed the business. At closing, the Apprentice failed to provide the promised security, and Owner, therefore, declined to convey the business.

The Apprentice brought an action to require the Owner to perform his promise, arguing that the Owner's promise to convey the business was "independent" of Apprentice's promise to provide "security." However, the court ruled

---

[8] *See* Restatement (Second) of Contracts § 231.
[9] *See* Restatement (Second) of Contracts § 232.

otherwise, explaining that the essence of the agreement was that the Owner would not have to trust the mere promise of the Apprentice, but would also be able to rely on the promised security, without which he could not reasonably be expected to be required to convey the business.[10]

In the foregoing example, the promises at issue—conveying the business and the provision of security—were to be performed simultaneously. In such circumstances involving simultaneous dependent promises, each party is expected to be ready, willing, and able to perform at the appointed place and time. One of the more common examples of simultaneous dependent promises is a real estate closing, where buyer and seller are each generally expected to show up at "closing" ready, willing, and able to perform their respective promises.

Other contracts may not, however, involve simultaneous performance. In that case, the timing or sequence of performance may be important in determining the effect of any failure of either party to perform.

Example 33-3: Kim promises to build a shed for Len for $500. Their agreement describes the shed to be constructed and its location on Len's property, but says nothing else. A week later, Kim shows up at Len's house to start work and demands payment before she starts work. Len says "no way—I will pay you when you are finished."

If the parties' actual agreement had expressly provided for the timing of payment, that agreement would control. However, in the absence of any actual agreement, the law presumes, as a default rule, that where one party's performance requires a period of time and the other's does not, that performance requiring a period of time must be performed first. Thus, Kim must build the shed—which requires a period of time—and then Len must pay—which does not.

---

[10] Kingston v. Preston, Lofft 194, 2 Doug. 689, 99 Eng. Rep. 437 (K.B. 1773).

As is generally the case, the parties' agreement will control the timing or sequence of performance to the extent the issue is addressed. If not, however, the law presumes, as a default rule, that promises that can be rendered simultaneously must be rendered simultaneously. If not, then that promise requiring time to complete (thereby precluding simultaneous performance) must be performed first.[11]

With an understanding of the basic concept of "dependent" promises, along with a framework for addressing the timing or sequence of performance of such dependent promises, we can now turn to the more important issue. Under what circumstances will the breach of a "duty" by one party excuse performance by the other?

The rule of "constructive conditions" generally provides that each party's obligations to perform dependent promises are conditioned upon there being no "uncured" "material" breach by the other party of a corresponding dependent obligation due earlier or at the same time.[12] In other words, the uncured material breach of a dependent obligation will excuse the performance of any subsequent or simultaneous obligation upon which it is dependent.

The issue of "cure" is addressed in Lesson 35. The question of "material breach" is addressed immediately below. At the outset, however, it is very important to keep two basic points in mind: (1) all breaches give rise to a claim for damages, if proven; however, (2) only some breaches will excuse performance by the other party.

Material Breach

Not all "breaches" are "material." A "material breach" will excuse performance, while "substantial performance"—notwithstanding the existence of a breach—will not. Of course, the challenge comes in determining whether any given breach is "material." The following case is a classic on the issue.

---

[11] Restatement (Second) of Contracts § 234.

[12] Restatement (Second) of Contracts § 237.

FROM THE COURT

Jacob & Youngs v. Kent

New York Court of Appeals (1921)
230 N.Y. 239, 129 N.E. 889

Cardozo, J.

The plaintiff built a country residence for the defendant at a cost of upwards of $77,000, and now sues to recover a balance of $3,483.46, remaining unpaid. . . . One of the specifications for the plumbing work provides that "all wrought iron pipe must be well galvanized, lap welded pipe of the grade known as 'standard pipe' of Reading manufacture." The defendant learned . . . that some of the pipe, instead of being made in Reading, was the product of other factories. The plaintiff was accordingly directed by the architect to do the work anew. The plumbing was then encased within the walls except in a few places where it had to be exposed. Obedience to the order meant more than the substitution of other pipe. It meant the demolition at great expense of substantial parts of the completed structure. The plaintiff left the work untouched, and asked for a certificate that the final payment was due. Refusal of the certificate was followed by this suit.

The evidence sustains a finding that the omission of the prescribed brand of pipe was neither fraudulent nor willful. It was the result of the oversight and inattention of the plaintiff's subcontractor. Reading pipe is distinguished from Cohoes pipe and other brands only by the name of the manufacturer stamped upon it at intervals of between six and seven feet. . . .

We think [certain evidence, omitted by the trial judge] would have supplied some basis for the inference that the defect was insignificant in its relation to the project. The courts never say that one who makes a contract fills the measure of his duty by less than full performance. They do say, however, that an omission, both trivial and innocent, will sometimes be atoned for by allowance of the resulting damage, and will not always be the breach of a condition to be followed by a forfeiture [citations omitted].

The distinction is akin to that between dependent and independent promises, or between promises and conditions [citations omitted]. Some promises are so plainly independent that they can never by fair construction be conditions of one another. [Citations omitted.] Others are so plainly dependent that they must always be conditions. Others, though dependent and thus conditions when there is departure in point of substance, will be viewed as independent and collateral when the departure is insignificant [citations omitted]. Considerations partly of justice and partly of presumable intention are to tell us whether this or that promise shall be placed in one class or in another. The simple and the uniform will call for different remedies from the multifarious and the intricate. The margin of departure within the range of normal expectation upon a sale of common chattels will vary from the margin to be expected upon a contract for the construction of a mansion or a "skyscraper." There will be harshness sometimes and oppression in the implication of a condition when the thing upon which labor has been expended is incapable of surrender because united to the land, and equity and reason in the implication of a like condition when the subject-matter, if defective, is in shape to be returned. From the conclusion that promises may not be treated as dependent to the extent of their uttermost minutia without a sacrifice of justice, the progress is a short one to the conclusion that they may not be so treated without a perversion of intention. Intention not otherwise revealed may be presumed to hold in contemplation the reasonable and probable. If something else is in view, it must not be left to implication. There will be no assumption of a purpose to visit venial faults with oppressive retribution.

Those who think more of symmetry and logic in the development of legal rules than of practical adaptation to the attainment of a just result will be troubled by a classification where the lines of division are so wavering and blurred. Something, doubtless, may be said on the score of consistency and certainty in favor of a stricter standard. The courts have balanced such considerations against those of equity and fairness, and found the latter to be the weightier. The decisions in this state commit us to the liberal view, which is making its way, nowadays, in jurisdictions slow to welcome it [citations omitted]. Where the line is to be drawn between the important and the trivial cannot be settled by a formula. "In the nature of the case precise boundaries are impossible" [citations omitted].

The same omission may take on one aspect or another according to its setting. Substitution of equivalents may not have the same significance in fields of art on the one side and in those of mere utility on the other. Nowhere will change be tolerated, however, if it is so dominant or pervasive as in any real or substantial measure to frustrate the purpose of the contract [citations omitted]. There is no general license to install whatever, in the builder's judgment, may be regarded as "just as good" [citations omitted]. The question is one of degree, to be answered, if there is doubt, by the triers of the facts [citations omitted], and, if the inferences are certain, by the judges of the law [citations omitted]. We must weigh the purpose to be served, the desire to be gratified, the excuse for deviation from the letter, the cruelty of enforced adherence. Then only can we tell whether literal fulfilment is to be implied by law as a condition. This is not to say that the parties are not free by apt and certain words to effectuate a purpose that performance of every term shall be a condition of recovery. That question is not here. This is merely to say that the law will be slow to impute the purpose, in the silence of the parties, where the significance of the default is grievously out of proportion to the oppression of the forfeiture. The willful transgressor must accept the penalty of his transgression [citations omitted]. For him there is no occasion to mitigate the rigor of implied conditions. The transgressor whose default is unintentional and trivial may hope for mercy if he will offer atonement for his wrong [citations omitted].

. . . [The court then ruled in favor of the builder on its right to recover the final payment based on the builder's substantial performance of the contract.]

MCLAUGHLIN, J. (dissenting).

I dissent. The plaintiff did not perform its contract. . . .

Under its contract it obligated itself to use in the plumbing only pipe (between 2,000 and 2,500 feet) made by the Reading Manufacturing Company. The first pipe delivered was about 1,000 feet and the plaintiff's superintendent then called the attention of the foreman of the subcontractor, who was doing the plumbing, to the fact that the specifications annexed to the contract required all pipe used in the plumbing to be of the Reading Manufacturing Company. They then examined it for the purpose of ascertaining whether this delivery was of that manufacture and found it was. Thereafter, as pipe was required in the progress of the work, the foreman of the sub-contractor would leave word at its shop that he wanted a specified number of feet of pipe, without in any way indicating of what manufacture. Pipe would thereafter be delivered and installed in the building, without any examination whatever. Indeed, no examination, so far as appears, was made by the plaintiff, the subcontractor, defendant's architect, or anyone else, of any of the pipe except the first delivery, until after the building had been completed. Plaintiff's architect then refused to give the certificate of completion, upon which the final payment depended, because all of the pipe used in the plumbing was not of the kind called for by the contract. After such refusal, the subcontractor removed the covering or insulation from about 900 feet of pipe which was exposed in the basement, cellar and attic, and all but 70 feet was found to have been manufactured, not by the Reading Company, but by other manufacturers, some by the Cohoes Rolling Mill Company, some by the National Steel Works, some by the South Chester Tubing Company, and some which bore no manufacturer's mark at all. . . .

. . . The defendant had a right to contract for what he wanted. He had a right before making payment to get what the contract called for. It is no answer to this suggestion to say that the pipe put in was just as good as that made by the Reading Manufacturing Company, or that the difference in value between such pipe and the pipe made by the Reading Manufacturing Company would be either "nominal or nothing." Defendant contracted for pipe made by the Reading Manufacturing Company. What his reason was for requiring this kind of pipe is of no importance. He wanted that and was entitled to it. It may have been a mere whim on his part, but even so, he had a right to this kind of pipe, regardless of whether some other kind, according to the opinion of the contractor or experts, would have been "just as good, better, or done just as well." He agreed to pay only upon condition that the pipe installed were made by that company and he ought not to be compelled to pay unless that condition be performed. [Citations omitted]. . . .

. . .

CASE QUESTIONS

(1) The court's decision reflected a 4-3 split on the question of whether Jacob & Youngs was entitled to the final progress payment of $3,483.46. The issue of damages in this case will be addressed later, in Chapter 8. However, there was no indication that the change in pipe had any effect at all on the quality of the plumbing system or value of the home.

    a. Final payment was dependent on the issuance of a certificate of completion by the architect. What is the effect of such a requirement? The contract provided that the architect's decision on this issue was final and absolute. Did that preclude the court from reviewing the objective reasonableness of the decision?

    b. How did the dissent characterize the effect of the requirement of Reading Pipe?

    c. How did the majority characterize that same requirement?

    d. Recall the discussion in the last lesson about terms as duties, conditions, or both. With which approach do you agree in this case—the majority or dissent?

(2) Did majority opinion say that there was no breach? If not, what was the significance of its characterization of the breach? Do you see now more clearly the significance of the characterization of a contract provision as a solely a "duty," as compared to a "condition" or both?

(3) The majority seems to suggest at the end of its opinion that the outcome might have been different if the breach had been willful (e.g., if the builder had simply been trying to save money because it found other pipe that was cheaper than Reading Pipe). Should this matter?

"Material breach" and "substantial performance" are of course "two sides of the same coin." Substantial performance is never a material breach, and a material breach is never substantial performance. The question of "material breach" is almost entirely factual, and is generally very much dependent on the individual circumstances, including one or more of the following:[13]

(1) the extent to which the aggrieved party will be deprived of what it reasonably expected under the contract;

(2) the extent to which the aggrieved party's loss can be adequately remedied by an award of damages;

(3) the extent of any forfeiture by the breaching party;

(4) the likelihood of cure by the breaching party; and

(5) the extent to which the breaching party has conducted itself in good faith.

The factors focus primarily on the extent to which the aggrieved party is deprived of its reasonable expectations, but also consider the issue of "forfeiture," as affecting the breaching party—particularly where that party has acted in good faith. As we will see in Lesson 35, cure is also a significant factor. While the "cure" of a prior "breach" will not fully negate the breach (damages remain available, if proven), it will often result minimize the loss to the aggrieved party, resulting in "substantial performance" instead of material breach.

Consider the application of these factors to the following simple example.

> **Example 33-4:** We return to Example 33-3. Kim promises to build a shed for Len for $500. Their agreement describes the shed to be constructed and its location. When Kim finishes, Len points out that the shed is 5% smaller than agreed. Kim is surprised and apologetic, having misread the specifications, but cannot at this point reasonably fix the problem. Based solely on these facts, we can analyze the nature of Kim's breach as follows.

---

[13] Restatement (Second) of Contracts § 241.

While the shed varies from the precise specifications, Len appears to have received the basic shed expected and seemingly can be compensated by damages for the reduced size. In contrast, Kim would suffer significant forfeiture if paid nothing, as it appears cure or removal would be quite burdensome, and there is no indication of "bad faith" on Kim's part. Kim clearly "breached" the agreement by failing to follow the agreed specifications, but nevertheless would likely be deemed to have "substantially performed."

Assuming "substantial performance," Kim's breach would not be deemed "material," so Len's obligation to pay the promised $500 would not be excused. However, Len would be entitled to damages (perhaps $25 here if calculated solely on the reduced space), so his "net" obligation would be $475—or the promise "price," less damages.

The foregoing example helps to illustrate one of the reasons for the rules addressing "substantial performance" and "material breach." If any breach excused Len's promise to pay, the Len would be left with a shed on his property that, unless returned, would likely give rise to a claim for unjust enrichment (not to mention the issue of Kim's suffered "forfeiture"), unless he had no use for it. The rule of "substantial performance" exhibits a preference for enforcing the contract, with an adjustment for damages, in lieu of abandoning the contract altogether, while either awarding restitution or ignoring the breaching party's likely forfeiture.

If, however, the defective performance leaves the obligee with something largely unusable, the calculus will likely change—even in the face of forfeiture on the part of the breaching party.

Example 33-5: In Example 33-4, we might change the facts so that Len was having the shed built to store his riding lawnmower, and the lawnmower will not fit in the shed due to the reduced size as a result of Kim's breach. Under this circumstance, Len will very likely be deprived of his most basic expectation under the contract. As such, Len's deprivation will likely prevail over Kim's forfeiture, and the breach will be deemed "material."

> Because Kim materially breached her obligation in build-ing the shed, which was due before Len's obligation to pay for the shed, Len will be excused from paying Kim under the contact.

You might be wondering at this point whether it makes any difference whether Kim knew of Len's intended use for the shed. Generally, this should not matter under the common law, as we will learn later in Chapter 8 that Len will generally have a right to recover damages for breach based on his own individualized loss in value. In the next lesson, however, we will note by way of comparison a very clearly different rule under the CISG.

We can now begin to lay out a basic framework to be used in trying to de-termine whether a party has a right to withhold performance or walk away from its own contract obligations based on a breach by the other party.

Summary of Basic Rule (in part): the decision to terminate or otherwise withhold performance for material breach of a contract governed by common law

- Has the other party breached a duty?

- If so, does the breach involve a dependent promise?

- If so, was the breached duty due at an earlier time or simultaneous to the performance to be withheld or excused?

- If so, is the breach "material"?

This summary will be developed further in lessons 35 and 36.

APPLYING THE RULES

Problem 1: Plante contracted with Jacobs to build a house based on a stan-dard set of architectural plans, at a price of $26,765. During the construc-tion of the house, Jacobs paid $20,000 in "progress payments" to Plante, as provided by their contract. When the project was near completion, a dispute arose and both parties ceased performing. Plante ceased working, and Jacobs ceased any further payments. At that time, the facts were as follows:

(1) Poor workmanship, which could be repaired at a price of $2,000;

(2) Missing cabinets, countertops, and other items in kitchen, which could be completed at a price of $1,600; and

(3) The living room wall (separating the living room from the kitchen) was misplaced by 14" (reducing the living room size and increasing the kitchen size). The misplacement presented no structural risk, and it could not reasonably be moved.

Is Jacobs obligated to pay the remaining $6,765, subject to any claim for damages? What if Jacobs had a large sectional couch that could not be used as planned in the living room due to the misplaced wall? If Plante was not entitled to payment under the contract, might he have any alternative remedy?

We will return to this problem in Chapter 8 to address an appropriate determination of damages.

The facts of this problem are loosely based on the issues raised in the case of *Plante v. Jacobs*, 10 Wis.2d 567, 103 N.W.2d 296 (1960).

Problem 2: Which, if any, of the following breaches are likely to be deemed material? What, if anything, else would you want to know?

(1) A contract provided for construction of a "boiler" to have a heating capacity of 150% of the existing boiler to be replaced. The boiler provided had only 82% of the capacity of the original existing boiler.

(2) A contract provided for construction of a "boat house" parallel to and in line with a boat owner's dock. However, the boat house was not in line with the dock, such that the owner could not exit the boat onto the dock after placing the boat in the boat house.

(3) A contract provided for the painting of a house, including the removal of old paint, as necessary. The painting of the house was completed, but old paint underneath was not removed and blistered under the new paint, leaving a rough and unsightly surface.

(4) A contract to install a heating and ventilation system in a school, which failed to accomplish either.

Lesson 34: Breach as Excusing Performance in a Sale of Goods under UCC Article 2 and the CISG

Objectives and Expected Learning Outcomes

In this lesson, you will learn when one party's breach of a "duty" in a contract for the sale of goods may excuse the other party's obligation to perform one or more of its own duties. You will encounter a variety of uniquely different approaches to this question under UCC Article 2 and the CISG.

UCC Article 2

In the last lesson, we began by addressing the question of "dependent" versus "independent" promises. Under UCC Article 2, the seller's duty to deliver the goods and the buyer's duty to pay for those goods are statutorily defined as dependent. UCC § 2-507(1) provides that buyer's duty to take delivery of the goods, as well as buyer's duty to pay for the goods (unless the latter is otherwise agreed) is conditioned upon seller's tender of delivery of the goods. UCC § 2-511(1) provides that seller's duty to deliver the goods (unless otherwise agreed) is conditioned upon buyer's tender of payment.

The issue of timing or sequence of performance will generally depend on the circumstances. Where a seller and buyer encounter each other at the same time and place, a simultaneous exchange is presumed. However, when seller delivers by shipping the goods with a third-party carrier, performance will often be sequential, with buyer's obligation arising only after a reasonable opportunity for inspection upon arrival. Article 2 provides a number of detailed rules for addressing these issues, which are left to a later course in Sales.

Cases of buyer's breach by refusing goods or failing to pay are typically pretty straightforward. A failure to pay will generally excuse seller's performance—at least temporarily—in the event that payment is due before delivery. The issue is largely addressed in the context of remedies, which we will more fully encounter in Chapter 8. The more challenging issues typically arise in the context of a breach by the seller to deliver the goods, as agreed. Thus, we will focus, in this lesson, on seller's breach of the obligation to deliver goods.

Seller's Breach of the Obligation to Deliver the Goods

We begin with a "single delivery" contract, in which the agreement contemplates only a single delivery of one item or group of items. Such a "single delivery" contract can be contrasted with an "installment" contract providing for delivery of multiple separate "lots," which will be addressed later in this lesson. As indicated above, the buyer's duty to take delivery is conditioned upon seller's tender of delivery of the goods. The following statutory provision governs the buyer's specific options when the seller breaches this duty. **STOP NOW and READ UCC § 2-601 below.**

UCC § 2-601

Subject to the provisions of this Article on breach in installment contracts (Section 2-612) and unless otherwise agreed under the sections on contractual limitations of remedy (Sections 2-718 and 2-719), if the goods or the tender of delivery fail in any respect to conform to the contract, the buyer may

(a) reject the whole; or

(b) accept the whole; or

(c) accept any commercial unit or units and reject the rest.

How does this rule differ from the common law rule of "material breach"? If the seller in any way breaches the obligation to deliver the agreed goods, does the nature of the breach matter? UCC § 2-601 is often called the "perfect tender rule." Do you see why? Consider the following examples.

> **Example 34-1:** Acme contracts to sell 10,000 blue widgets to Zenith at $5 per widget, deliverable on or before March 1, at Zenith's warehouse. Acme actually delivers 10,000 widgets on March 1, but they are red widgets. The red widgets are generally interchangeable with blue, but Zenith does not want red widgets (and expressly ordered blue) and rejects them all.

Assuming that Zenith is acting in good faith, it is fully within its rights to reject the red widgets, because they fail to conform to the parties' contract for blue widgets. The materiality of the non-conformity is irrelevant, because UCC § 2-601 requires "perfect tender."

Of course, Zenith is not required to reject the goods. It can alternatively accept them all or accept some and reject others. The application of the perfect tender rule is of course not limited to the goods, themselves.

Example 34-2: In Example 34-1, suppose the widgets were blue, as agreed, but were delivered on March 2. Again, Zenith can reject all of the widgets—in this case because the tender of the widgets is a day later than promised.

Close cases like this highlight the potentially harsh effect of the rule when the goods are fully useable by the buyer, but do not perfectly conform to the contract. The positive aspect of the rule is that it will generally provide a relatively "bright line" for the buyer's decision to accept or reject the goods, and the seller will often be able to resale goods that are promptly rejected. It is important to remember that UCC § 2-601 is merely a "default" rule, which the parties can contract around. As a practical matter, however, a buyer may be hesitant to agree in advance to accept and pay for goods that don't conform to the contract or are delivered late.

In theory, the buyer's ability to reject the goods for minor details is limited by "good faith." This would seem to preclude a buyer from asserting that it was rejecting the goods for a minor breach, when in fact the buyer was rejecting the goods because it simply no longer wanted them, even if perfect. The problem is that it will often be very difficult to prove bad faith when a party rejects goods under the perfect tender rule. In fact, the "perfect tender rule" is far more of an "exception" than a general rule, inasmuch as it is limited to the buyer's decision to accept or reject goods delivered in a single delivery contract.

In some instances, the buyer will wish to return non-conforming goods after having initially accepted them. Assuming that the delay in discovering or acting upon the non-conformity was reasonable, the buyer may be entitled to "revoke its acceptance" of the goods. **STOP NOW and READ UCC § 2-608 below.**

UCC § 2-608

(1) The buyer may revoke his acceptance of a lot or commercial unit whose non-conformity substantially impairs its value to him if he has accepted it

(a) on the reasonable assumption that its non-conformity would be cured and it has not been seasonably cured; or

(b) without discovery of such non-conformity if his acceptance was reasonably induced either by the difficulty of discovery before acceptance or by the seller's assurances.

(2) Revocation of acceptance must occur within a reasonable time after the buyer discovers or should have discovered the ground for it and before any substantial change in condition of the goods which is not caused by their own defects. It is not effective until the buyer notifies the seller of it.

(3) A buyer who so revokes has the same rights and duties with regard to the goods involved as if he had rejected them.

What are the key differences between "rejection" of the goods and "revocation of acceptance" of the goods? How does the timing of each differ? How does the "standard" for refusing to retain the goods differ? Is there anything else that buyer must prove to establish a right to "revoke" an earlier acceptance? How does the ultimate effect of a "revocation of acceptance" compare with an initial "rejection" of the goods?

The differences between revocation of acceptance and rejection can be quite important, because a buyer who simply fails to make an effective and timely "rejection" of the goods is generally deemed to have "accepted" them. **STOP NOW and READ the excerpt from UCC § 2-606(1) below.**

UCC § 2-606(1)

(1) Acceptance of goods occurs when the buyer

(a) after a reasonable opportunity to inspect the goods signifies to the seller that the goods are conforming or that he will take or retain them in spite of their non-conformity; or

(b) fails to make an effective rejection . . . , but such acceptance does not occur until the buyer has had a reasonable opportunity to inspect them; or

(c) does any act inconsistent with the seller's ownership; . . .

Thus, a buyer may overtly signify acceptance, or may accept goods by simply failing to reject them after a reasonable opportunity for inspection or exercising control over them (such as readying them for delivery to buyer's customers).

Unlike the perfect tender rule under § 2-601, revocation of acceptance under § 2-608 requires a "substantial impairment," which is more analogous to a "material breach" under the common law. The buyer's earlier acceptance may be revoked only if the "non-conformity substantially impairs its value to him." Comment 2 to § 2-608 confirms that this issue of substantial impairment focuses on the impairment of the value of the goods to this individual buyer, and seller's lack of any objective basis for expecting such a result is irrelevant.

In Examples 34-1 or 34-2, a buyer who initially accepted the goods would likely be precluded from later revoking that acceptance, because the buyer should certainly have noted at the time the non-conforming color or late delivery. However, in circumstances in which the non-conformity is reasonably discovered somewhat later, the right to revoke acceptance may be important.

> **Example 34-3:** In Example 32-7, A and B contracted for a machine made, in part, of a special metal called "rarium." After completing this first contract, B agreed to purchase additional such machines from A. The percentage of rarium in the metal alloy from which the machine parts were made could only be determined by a burdensome and expensive process, which B therefore only employed when it suspected a problem. A also regularly assured B that A was verifying that the proper percentage of rarium was being used in making the metal alloy.
>
> Pursuant to a single purchase order, A delivered 5 machines to B that appeared to conform to their agreement. B promptly accepted and began using the machines, which immediately began malfunctioning in use. B suspected a problem with the metal alloy, performed the necessary testing, and discovered that the percentage of rarium in the metal alloy was far below specifications.

Of course, it is too late for B to "reject" the machines, because it has already accepted them. However, B can likely "revoke its acceptance" based on the non-conforming metal alloy that "substantially impairs" the value of the machines. B can also likely establish under § 2-608(1)(b) that its acceptance was reasonably induced by the difficulty of discovering the issue before acceptance, as well as A's assurances.

Thus, Article 2 provides for two distinct scenarios in which a buyer can refuse to retain goods tendered by the seller—in one case "rejecting" the goods prior to any acceptance, and in the other "revoking" an earlier acceptance. While both ultimately lead to the same result, the standards for refusal are dramatically different based on "perfect tender," as compared to "substantial impairment."

Of course, the buyer who rejects or revokes acceptance of goods will not expect to pay for such goods, and statute indeed provides that the buyer is not obligated to do so. The buyer is entitled to "cancel" the contract. **STOP NOW and READ the excerpt from UCC § 2-711(1) below.**

UCC § 2-711(1)

(1) Where the . . . buyer rightfully rejects or justifiably revokes acceptance then with respect to any goods involved, . . . the buyer may cancel . . .

UCC Article 2 uses the term "cancellation," in contrast to the term "termination," which is more broadly used under the common law to indicate that the parties are excused from further obligations under the contract. However, the two terms have distinctly different meanings under UCC Article 2. **STOP NOW and READ UCC § 2-106(3) and (4) below.**

UCC § 2-106

. . .

(3) "Termination" occurs when either party pursuant to a power created by agreement or law puts an end to the contract otherwise than for its breach. On "termination" all obligations which are still executory on both sides are discharged but any right based on prior breach or performance survives.

(4) "Cancellation" occurs when either party puts an end to the contract for breach by the other and its effect is the same as that of "termination" except that the cancelling party also retains any remedy for breach of the whole contract or any unperformed balance.

Thus, the use of the term "cancellation" may be particularly important in a case governed by Article 2 and involving a breach of obligations that have not yet come due. In any event, "cancel" or "cancellation" is used to indicate that the buyer has no further obligation to pay for goods properly refused—whether by way of rejection or revocation of acceptance.

At this risk of repetition, it is important to remember that, in this lesson, our focus is on the buyer's right to refuse the goods. If the buyer must retain previously accepted goods because any non-conformity does not substantially impair their value that does **not** mean there has been no breach. It simply means the buyer must pay for the goods, subject to any claim for damages arising from the breach. Remember, any breach of a duty will give rise to a claim for damages, if proven. However, only certain breaches will give the buyer the right to refuse to keep and pay for the goods.

Seller's Breach of an Installment Contract

Thus far, we have focused on "single delivery" contracts. We will now consider "installment" contracts providing for delivery of multiple separate "lots." **STOP NOW and READ UCC § 2-612(1) and (2) below.**

UCC § 2-612(1) and (2)

(1) An "installment contract" is one which requires or authorizes the delivery of goods in separate lots to be separately accepted, even though the contract contains a clause "each delivery is a separate contract" or its equivalent.

(2) The buyer may reject any installment which is non-conforming if the non-conformity substantially impairs the value of that installment and cannot be cured . . .

. . .

Thus, a buyer of goods pursuant to a contract requiring or authorizing delivery of the goods in separate lots loses the benefit of the "perfect tender rule." The buyer's right to refuse goods in such an "installment contract" is subject to a "substantial impairment" standard—irrespective of whether the issue arises in the context of "rejection" under § 2-612(2) or "revocation of acceptance" under § 2-608. At this stage, our focus is on each installment, individually. We will address the potential effect of a breach of one installment on the contract as a whole later in this chapter.

This statutory provision also introduces the idea of "cure," which we will explore more fully in the next lesson. As indicated briefly in the last lesson, cure does not fully negate any breach, but simply reduces its effect—sometimes almost entirely and sometimes somewhat less so. However, a breach that can largely be cured should not result in a "substantial impairment," assuming such cure is reasonably completed.

Finally, we can examine this same issue under the CISG. You should consider how the CISG is in some ways similar to the approach of UCC Article 2 and how it is very different in others. Which do you prefer?

The CISG

When an aggrieved party seeks to exit a common law contract based on the other party's material breach, the party is said to "terminate" the contract. When an aggrieved party seeks to exit a sale of goods contract governed by Article 2 based on the other party's qualifying breach (whichever standard may apply), the party is said to "cancel" the contract. When an aggrieved party seeks to exit a sale of goods contract governed by the CISG, the party is said to "avoid" the contract. While some of the nuances differ, the general effects are the same. The terminating, canceling, or avoiding party is largely relieved of any remaining contract obligations, while retaining the right to sue for damages arising from the breach at issue.

Unlike UCC Article 2, the CISG provides for comparable rights of the seller to avoid the contract that are very similar in many ways to those of the buyer. However, our focus in these materials will remain on the buyer's right to avoid the contract based on the seller's breach. **STOP NOW and READ CISG Article 49(1) below.**

CISG ARTICLE 49(1)

(1) The buyer may declare the contract avoided:

    (a) if the failure by the seller to perform any of his obligations under the contract or this Convention amounts to a fundamental breach of contract; or

    (b) in case of non-delivery, if the seller does not deliver the goods within the additional period of time fixed by the buyer in accordance with paragraph (1) of article 47 or declares that he will not deliver within the period so fixed.

. . .

Under Article 49(1)(a), a buyer can avoid the contract if the seller's breach is "fundamental." This of course sounds somewhat similar to a common law "material breach" or a "substantial impairment" under UCC Article 2. However, the CISG expressly defines a "fundamental breach." **STOP NOW and READ CISG Article 25 below.**

CISG ARTICLE 25

A breach of contract committed by one of the parties is fundamental if it results in such detriment to the other party as substantially to deprive him of what he is entitled to expect under the contract, unless the party in breach did not foresee and a reasonable person of the same kind in the same circumstances would not have foreseen such a result.

The test for fundamental breach might reasonably be broken into two parts. The first—a substantial deprivation of that the buyer was entitled to expect under the contract—sounds very much like a "substantial impairment" under UCC Article 2. However, the second, requiring objective "foreseeability" of such a result is quite different from the UCC test, as applied in § 2-608. Can you think of any reason why the drafters of the CISG might have thought that objective foreseeability was important in the context of an international sale of goods? In which case is a seller more likely to be surprised to find that a given breach renders the goods unusable to the buyer—a domestic transaction or one that crosses national borders?

Consistent with other issues involving goods, the treatment of avoidance under CISG Article 49 is limited here to the most basic issues. However, a brief discussion of the novel treatment of late delivery under Articles 49(1)(b) and 47 is useful in understanding one of the basic difficulties in employing any rule requiring a determination of the "extent" of a breach—whether framed as "material breach," "substantial impairment," or "fundamental breach."

You will note that Article 49(1)(b) expressly addresses cases in which the goods have not yet been delivered, without using the term "fundamental breach." In cases in which the goods are not yet delivered, the question will often arise as to whether late delivery is a "fundamental breach." Unless time is expressly "of the essence," this determination would be quite difficult. The CISG resolves this difficulty by borrowing a concept called "Nachfrist" (extension of the original time for performance) from German law. **STOP NOW and READ CISG Article 47 below.**

CISG Article 47

(1) The buyer may fix an additional period of time of reasonable length for performance by the seller of his obligations.

(2) Unless the buyer has received notice from the seller that he will not perform within the period so fixed, the buyer may not, during that period, resort to any remedy for breach of contract. However, the buyer is not deprived thereby of any right he may have to claim damages for delay in performance.

Article 47, in combination with Article 49(1)(b), seeks to strike a balance, precluding avoidance by the buyer for mere late delivery, absent a clear indication that strict compliance with the delivery date is essential, while also providing the buyer with a means of resolving the issue through a reasonable extension of time for delivery. If seller fails to deliver within the time extended under Article 47, then the buyer may avoid the contract under Article 49(1)(b), without any requirement that buyer prove the breach is "fundamental." In effect, buyer's extension of time under Article 47, coupled with seller's continuing non-delivery, converts seller's "late delivery," which is not likely fundamental, into "non-delivery," which is always fundamental.

The combined use of Articles 49, 25, and 47 provide a reasonably effective and balanced framework for addressing the buyer's right to avoid a contract governed by the CISG. However, they also highlight some of the challenges in providing a set of rules that is both fair and practical in deciding when one party's breach will excuse the other party from completing its obligations under the contract. Much like questions of "material breach" and "substantial impairment," the issue of whether a breach is "fundamental" may be subject to significant uncertainty at the moment a party is trying to decide whether to "terminate" or "cancel" or "avoid" the contract at issue. In contrast, the application of the "perfect tender rule" is usually relatively clear—whatever its sometimes harsh effects.

A Final Note on the Perfect Tender Rule

Earlier in this lesson, it was noted that "[i]n fact, the 'perfect tender rule' is far more of an 'exception' than a general rule, inasmuch as it is limited to the buyer's decision to accept or reject goods delivered in a single delivery contract." Having now considered the range and application of all of the rules addressing the issue, do you agree? You will have an opportunity to consider this question further in Problem 2 below.

APPLYING THE RULES

Problem 1: Jacob & Youngs (J&Y) contracted to build a house for Kent, who had specified the use of "Reading" pipe for all of the plumbing in the house. J&Y contracted with Delta Supply to provide the pipe, also specifying "Reading" pipe in its contract with Delta. You may rely on the case in the previous lesson for any additional facts that might be relevant to the analysis.

(1) When Delta delivered the required pipe (all at once), the J&Y job foreman noted that it was Cohoes pipe. Can he refuse the pipe?

(2) What if the J&Y foreman simply told the delivery person to place the pipe in an enclosed area and did not look at it for a week? When he did, he realized it was Cohoes pipe. Can he return and refuse to pay for the pipe?

(3) What if Delta was required to make three separate deliveries over 30 days, and the first delivery was entirely Cohoes pipe? Can the foreman refuse it if he immediately notes that it is not Reading pipe?

(4) Suppose the pipe had all been delivered at once, and the foreman had noted that it was Cohoes pipe. He nevertheless accepted it, because he needed it to begin the plumbing work the next day. The next day, when workers started installing the pipe, they noticed that the metal was not responding properly when heated. Upon further examination, J&Y discovered that Cohoes had used defective metal in making the pipe. Can J&Y return and refuse to pay for the pipe?

(5) Reconsider each of questions 1 through 4 if J&Y was located in far up-state New York, and Delta was located in Montreal, Quebec, Canada.

Do the above distinctions make any logical sense to you? What considerations might motivate each?

Problem 2: Your Kansas client is contracting to sell wheat to a French buyer, for delivery in single shipment by sea, 6 months later (the market price of wheat can vary significantly in 6 months). The French buyer has suggested a choice of the Kansas enactment of UCC Article 2—and not the CISG—to govern the transaction. What, if anything, might you suggest that your client should consider in deciding on the buyer's proposed choice of law?

Lesson 35: Notice of Breach and the Right to Cure

Objectives and Expected Learning Outcomes

In this lesson, you will learn about circumstances in which a breaching party may have the opportunity to "cure" its breach, thereby, limiting or even perhaps eliminating any injurious effect on the other party. You will also learn when, and to what extent, an aggrieved party must provide notice of any breach. Finally, you will learn how and why many "notice" requirements relate, at least in part, to efforts to preserve any possibility of "cure."

Notice of Breach and Right to Cure

When a party breaches an obligation, it will often wish to try to "cure" the breach, essentially minimizing any injurious effect of the breach on the aggrieved party and maximizing the value of the performance ultimately rendered so as to make it as close to that originally promised as possible. An effective cure may of course have a significant effect on the question of whether a breach is "material" or "substantially impairs" the value of goods or is "fundamental." As such, cure arguably serves two purposes—minimizing any losses arising out of the breach and increasing the likelihood that the contract will remain in force. Under UCC Article 2, we will see that cure might even be effective in keeping a deal together in limited circumstances under the "perfect tender rule."

Of course, a breaching party cannot "cure" until and unless it receives "notice" of any breach sufficient to consider whether cure is reasonably achievable. In the materials that follow, consider the relationship between the breaching party's right to cure, the aggrieved party's right to exit the contract, and the aggrieved party's obligation to provide notice of breach.

Cure under the Common Law

Earlier in Lesson 33, we observed that the potential likelihood of "cure" was one factor in determining whether a common law breach is "material." Moreover, only an "uncured" material breach will excuse performance based on the rule of "constructive conditions."[14] A breach that would otherwise excuse performance by virtue of its materiality loses that character if cured. Thus, it is often important to be able to determine whether a cure is effective or when a breaching party may be afforded an opportunity to cure.

The question of whether "cure" has been successfully achieved will generally depend on many of the other factors informing any analysis of the "materiality" of a breach. However, in circumstances in which the breaching party has been provided with an opportunity to cure, the analysis will focus even more acutely on whether the aggrieved obligee has been deprived of reasonable expectations under the contract.

Whether cure by the breaching party is reasonable, or even possible, will generally depend on the circumstances, one of which is timing. If time is "of the essence," effective cure will be far less likely. Where the timing of a given performance is essential to the value of the performance to the obligee, cure will rarely, if ever, be possible after that time for performance. Timing may also be important where it affects the ability of the aggrieved obligee to make alternative arrangements for performance. The breaching party's right to cure will generally give way to the aggrieved party's right to make such alternative arrangements.[15]

> **Example 35-1:** The subcontractor on a building project has failed to complete the foundation by the agreed date. If the foundation is not completed within the next 15 days, the next stages of the project will be delayed, and the general contractor will, itself, be in breach of its contract with the owner. The foundation can still be completed in time by another subcontractor, but only if the general contractor acts immediately in contracting with the alternative subcontractor. The original subcontractor has requested additional time to complete its work, thereby "curing" its incomplete performance.
>
> In this instance, the right to the general contractor to secure alternative performance will likely prevail over the right of the breaching subcontractor to cure its original breach. The

---

[14] Restatement (Second) of Contracts § 237.
[15] Restatement (Second) of Contracts § 242(b) and (c).

inquiry is of course fact specific, but if the general contractor is literally faced with a choice of one or the other—a replacement or the original—and only one will have time to complete the work, the general should not typically be required to give the original breaching subcontractor another chance.

Another issue is whether cure is even possible. In some circumstances, it may not be possible or practical to cure defective performance at all. In the foregoing example, if the foundation had been improperly constructed—instead of simply being late—cure might be impossible, absent tearing the foundation out and starting over, which might scuttle the entire project, leaving behind a host of lawsuits.

Of course, any possibility of cure will require "notice" of the breach at issue. The common law does not provide the sort of strict notice requires we will see in the statutory provisions below. However, the lack of notice may affect an aggrieved party's right to terminate the contract for fundamental breach. Under some circumstances, an aggrieved party's acceptance and retention of non-conforming performance may preclude a later attempt to rely on the same breach to justify termination. This issue is typically addressed by reference to the same principles of waiver, estoppel, and election[16] addressed earlier in Lesson 32.

The issue of notice, as affecting cure, becomes more acute, however, when an aggrieved party seeks to terminate for material breach, but fails to articulate one of more of the reasons that might support a determination that the uncured breach at issue is "material." Consider the following example.

Example 35-2: *New England Structures, Inc. v. Loranger*

General contractor, Loranger, sub-contracted with New England Structures (NES) to install a roof deck on a school. NES began work on November 24. On December 18, Loranger notified NES that Loranger was terminating the contract, effective December 26, based on the failure of NES to provide sufficient skilled workers to maintain satisfactory progress, as expressly required under the contract.

---

[16] Restatement (Second) of Contracts §§ 246 and 247.

At trial, there was conflicting evidence as to Loranger's stated basis for terminating the contract, and Loranger sought to introduce additional evidence further justifying the termination based on poor quality work by NES. The trial court barred the evidence, limiting Loranger to its reasons stated on December 18. However, the appellate court reversed, explaining that Loranger should be allowed to support its termination decision with any evidence—irrespective of whether stated at the time of termination—unless NES had relied on the omission.[17]

Such "reliance" generally takes the form of a failure to cure, as a direct result of the lack of notice of the breach at issue. As a general rule, an aggrieved party may rely upon any breach in justifying its termination for failure of a constructive condition—irrespective of whether the breaching party had received notice of the breach at the time of termination. Exceptionally, however, the aggrieved party may not rely on any breach:

(1) of which the aggrieved party knew or should have known at the time of its decision to terminate the contract; and

(2) that could reasonably have been cured by the breaching party if it had received reasonable notice.[18]

Having addressed the issue of cure, we can now further expand our earlier summary of the basic rules applied to common law constructive conditions first provided in Lesson 33.

---

[17] New England Structures, Inc. v. Loranger, 354 Mass. 62, 234 N.E.2d 888 (1968).
[18] Restatement (Second) of Contracts § 248.

> **Summary of Basic Rule (in part):** the decision to terminate or otherwise withhold performance for material breach of a contract governed by common law
>
> • Has the other party breached a duty?
>
> • If so, does the breach involve a dependent promise?
>
> • If so, was the breached duty due at an earlier time or simultaneous to the performance to be withheld or excused?
>
> • If so, is the breach "material"?
>
> • If so, to what extent is "cure" reasonably possible?
>
>   ○ If so, appropriate notice is particularly important, as omitted reasons may be unavailable in supporting termination right

This common law summary will be completed in lesson 36, and we can now move on to the analogous provision addressing transactions in goods.

Notice and Cure under UCC Article 2

Article 2 directly provides for cure by the seller in two distinct circumstances—when performance is not yet due and when seller reasonably believed the original tender would have been acceptable to the buyer. **STOP NOW and READ UCC § 2-508 below.**

UCC § 2-508

(1) Where any tender or delivery by the seller is rejected because non-conforming and the time for performance has not yet expired, the seller may seasonably notify the buyer of his intention to cure and may then within the contract time make a conforming delivery.

(2) Where the buyer rejects a non-conforming tender which the seller had reasonable grounds to believe would be acceptable with or without money allowance the seller may if he seasonably notifies the buyer have a further reasonable time to substitute a conforming tender.

Subsection (1) provides for a clear, "bright line" rule. As long as seller can make a conforming delivery on or before the required date for performance and gives notice of its intent to do so, the seller has a right to cure the earlier breach—even in circumstances in which the perfect tender rule applies. In effect, under § 2-508(1), a seller may get more than one chance at "perfect tender." However, this rule has no application when the seller delivers on or after the date for performance.

In contrast, subsection (2) requires a more "fact intensive" determination of whether seller had reasonable grounds to believe the original tender would have been acceptable, notwithstanding any non-conformity. The most obvious such circumstances would include a communication between the seller and buyer regarding the non-conformity before delivery. However, such reasonable grounds could also arise from other circumstances surrounding the transaction at issue and the parties' broader commercial relationship. If seller is able to establish such "reasonable grounds," then seller will be allowed additional reasonable time to cure by way of an additional conforming tender.

Consider the following example of the two distinct settings for cure.

> **Example 35-3:** Seller contracted to deliver yellow corn to buyer on or before June 1 for use in feeding livestock. On May 20, seller tendered "mixed" (yellow and white) corn, which buyer rejected. Seller has a right to "cure" the initial non-conforming tender under § 2-508(1) by delivering yellow corn on or before June 1. Of course, "cure" will not entirely absolve seller of any damages arising from the breach (e.g., buyer's cost of inspecting and rejecting the original delivery).
>
> If, instead, seller had tendered the same "mixed" corn at the end of the day on June 1, any right to cure under § 2-508(2) would depend on whether seller had reasonable grounds for believing that buyer would accept the non-conforming mixed corn (e.g., if most buyer's for livestock feed would accept mixed corn when yellow was not reasonably available). If so, then seller would have an additional reasonable time to cure by making a conforming delivery.

Thus, seller's right to cure a non-conforming tender in a single delivery contract is relatively limited. The seller may only cure if such cure can be completed by the time performance is due under the contract or if the seller had reasonable grounds for believing the buyer would accept the non-conforming tender.

In contrast, a relatively broad right to cure is effectively integrated into the provision allowing for rejection of goods delivered under installment contracts. **STOP NOW and READ the excerpt from UCC § 2-612(2) below.**

UCC § 2-612(2)

(2) . . . if the non-conformity does not fall within subsection (3) [addressing a breach of an installment substantially impairing the value of the whole contract] and the seller gives adequate assurance of its cure the buyer must accept that installment.

. . .

As with the buyer's right to reject non-conforming goods, we again see a significant difference in the treatment of single delivery and installment contracts. If Example 35-3 had involved delivery of corn in installments, and the seller had delivered "mixed corn" even a few days late, seller would almost certainly have a reasonable opportunity to cure, unless time was of the essence (irrespective of whether seller had reasonable grounds to believe buyer would accept mixed corn). Which rule do you think is a better one? Do the differences in the nature of the two types of contracts justify differing treatment?

As in the case of any cure, a seller of goods will require notice of the breach in order to cure it. Under UCC Article 2, this notice takes a variety of forms. To begin with, a buyer exercising the right to reject goods must provide notice to the seller that the buyer is rejecting the goods, lest the buyer be deemed to have tacitly accepted them. **STOP NOW and READ UCC § 2-602(1) below.**

UCC § 2-602(1)

(1) Rejection of goods must be within a reasonable time after their delivery or tender. It is ineffective unless the buyer seasonably notifies the seller.

. . .

The buyer's notice of rejection of goods must further indicate all of the reasons for the rejection, lest the buyer may, in certain circumstances, be precluded from relying on such unstated reasons to justify the rejection or even establish breach. **STOP NOW and READ UCC § 2-605(1) below.**

UCC § 2-605(1)

(1) The buyer's failure to state in connection with rejection a particular defect which is ascertainable by reasonable inspection precludes him from relying on the unstated defect to justify rejection or to establish breach

    (a) where the seller could have cured it if stated seasonably; or

    (b) between merchants when the seller has after rejection made a request in writing for a full and final written statement of all defects on which the buyer proposes to rely.

. . .

Subsection (1)(a) is quite similar to the common law rule in that it precludes the buyer from relying on unstated defects where the buyer knew or should have known of the defect, and the seller could have cured had it received timely notice. However, subsection (1)(b) adds an additional basis for preclusion between merchants where seller has made an appropriate written request. Note that his latter preclusion is also limited to defects of which the buyer knows or ought to know, but applies irrespective of whether the seller could have cured.

As in the case of "rejection," a buyer that is "revoking" its earlier "acceptance" of goods must also provide notice thereof. **STOP NOW and review UCC § 2-608(2) below.**

UCC § 2-608(2)

. . .

(2) Revocation of acceptance must occur within a reasonable time after the buyer discovers or should have discovered the ground for it and before any substantial change in condition of the goods which is not caused by their own defects. It is not effective until the buyer notifies the seller of it.

. . .

While the basic notice requirement for "revocation of acceptance" is essentially the same as that required for "rejection" of the goods, the statute provides no direct guidance as to the content of such notice.

§ 2-605(1), addressed above, applies by its terms only to "rejection" of goods. Moreover, comment 5 to § 2-608 clarifies that this same provision does not apply to "revocation of acceptance." Instead, comment 5 explains that the adequacy of any notice should be guided by "good faith, prevention of surprise, and reasonable adjustment." The comment also confirms that any notice of "revocation of acceptance" requires more than the general requirement of notice of breach addressed in the next statutory section below. As a final observation, the content of any notice of a "revocation of acceptance" may be driven, to a large degree, by the need to establish that any breach "substantially impairs" the value of the goods to the buyer, which will generally require reasonable detail as to the nature and extent of any breach.

In the event that the buyer accepts and retains non-conforming goods (either as a matter of choice or because the non-conformity is discovered after acceptance and does not substantially impair the value of the goods), the buyer must nevertheless provide basic notice of any breach. **STOP NOW and READ UCC § 2-607(3)(a) below.**

UCC § 2-607(3)(a)

. . .

(3) Where a tender has been accepted

    (a) the buyer must within a reasonable time after he discovers or should have discovered any breach notify the seller of breach or be barred from any remedy; . . .

Comment 4 to § 2-607 clarifies that this requirement is solely intended to put seller on notice that there is a potential problem with the transaction. Buyer's failure to particularize any defects at issue will not limit the buyer's ability to rely on such defects in bringing any subsequent action for damages arising from seller's breach.

Notice and Cure under the CISG

The CISG provides a more general requirement that a buyer promptly examine the goods and provide notice of any non-conformity to the seller within a reasonable time of discovery. This general requirement arises from two separate statutory provisions. **STOP NOW and READ CISG Article 38(1) below.**

CISG ARTICLE 38(1)

(1) The buyer must examine the goods, or cause them to be examined, within as short a period as is practicable in the circumstances.

. . .

Article 38(1) requires a very prompt inspection, but imposes no direct sanctions on buyer for any failure to do so. However, the time requirement under Article 38 will often determine when a buyer "ought to have discovered" any non-conformity for purposes of the notice requirement under Article 39. **STOP NOW and READ CISG Article 39(1) below.**

CISG ARTICLE 39(1)

(1) The buyer loses the right to rely on a lack of conformity of the goods if he does not give notice to the seller specifying the nature of the lack of conformity within a reasonable time after he has discovered it or ought to have discovered it.

. . .

Essentially, any non-conformity that ought to have been discovered by a prompt examination (in effect, one reasonably discoverable through such a reasonable examination) must be brought to the seller's attention within a reasonable time, or the buyer loses the right to assert such a lack of conformity for any purpose—avoidance, damages, or any other remedy available under the CISG.

Note that CISG Article 39(1) provides a more broadly applicable rule than UCC Article 2 in that the buyer who fails to provide timely and effective notice is precluded from asserting the non-conformity as a breach—irrespective of the seller's ability to cure. While one of the underlying purposes of this rule is to protect seller's right to cure, the rule also protects the seller's right to examine goods promptly (especially perishable goods) when buyer is asserting that such goods do not conform. It also provides for a clear and unequivocal application in cases in which the buyer fails meet its requirements.

The combined effect of Articles 38 and 39 can be quite harsh on a buyer that is insufficiently diligent. Article 40 provides for a complete exception based on the seller's knowledge of the non-conformity (the buyer need not tell the seller what the seller already knows), and Article 44 provides for a partial exception in cases in which buyer's failure to meet the requirements of Article 39 is reasonably excusable. However, the latter exception limits buyer to recovery of certain damages and does not allow buyer to rely upon the breach to avoid the contract. Thus, proper notice of breach is absolutely essential to buyer's right to avoid the contract, absent seller knowing in advance of the non-conformity.

Assuming that the buyer has provided proper notice of any non-conformity to the seller, the buyer will preserve its right to rely on the non-conformity in asserting a breach of contract, including the buyer's right to avoid the contract for fundamental breach. However, the seller may have a right to cure. First, the seller has a broad right to cure, assuming such cure can be completed by the time performance comes due. **STOP NOW and READ CISG Article 35 below.**

CISG ARTICLE 37

If the seller has delivered goods before the date for delivery, he may, up to that date, deliver any missing part or make up any deficiency in the quantity of the goods delivered, or deliver goods in replacement of any non-conforming goods delivered or remedy any lack of conformity in the goods delivered, provided that the exercise of this right does not cause the buyer unreasonable inconvenience or unreasonable expense. However, the buyer retains any right to claim damages as provided for in this Convention.

Compare the foregoing CISG provision to UCC § 2-508(1). Both address similar circumstances in which the seller seeks to cure by making or completing a conforming delivery on or before the deadline for performance.

While CISG Article 37 limits the right to the extent buyer would suffer unreasonable inconvenience or expense, either seems unlikely under the circumstances of prompt cure addressed here. Article 37 also provides an excellent reminder that cure does not preclude a claim for damages (which is also of course true under UCC Article 2 and the common law).

The seller may also be entitled to cure under certain circumstances in which the cure cannot be completed by the time performance was originally due. **STOP NOW and READ CISG Article 48 below.**

CISG Article 48

(1) Subject to article 49, the seller may, even after the date for delivery, remedy at his own expense any failure to perform his obligations, if he can do so without unreasonable delay and without causing the buyer unreasonable inconvenience or uncertainty of reimbursement by the seller of expenses advanced by the buyer. However, the buyer retains any right to claim damages as provided for in this Convention.

(2) If the seller requests the buyer to make known whether he will accept performance and the buyer does not comply with the request within a reasonable time, the seller may perform within the time indicated in his request. The buyer may not, during that period of time, resort to any remedy which is inconsistent with performance by the seller.

(3) A notice by the seller that he will perform within a specified period of time is assumed to include a request, under the preceding paragraph, that the buyer make known his decision.

(4) A request or notice by the seller under paragraph (2) or (3) of this article is not effective unless received by the buyer.

In Article 48, we can see the obvious tension between the seller's right to cure and the buyer's right to avoid the contract. While the statutory language of subsection (1) appears to defer to the buyer's avoidance right, a breach that is reasonably curable is not likely to be "fundamental," and is not, therefore, subject to avoidance. Assuming that a breach is indeed curable, the seller may effect such cure, absent unreasonable delay, inconvenience, or financial uncertainty to the buyer.

In many circumstances, it will be unclear at the time whether the seller is entitled to cure. Subsection (2) may in such cases be helpful to the seller. If the seller proposes cure, and the buyer either agrees or simply fails to object within a reasonable time, then the seller is assured the opportunity to complete the proposed cure. If, however, the buyer objects, then the parties may be left with the seller wishing to cure, the buyer asserting its right to avoidance, and a court or arbitral tribunal ultimately deciding whether the buyer's avoidance was proper or seller should have been allowed the opportunity to cure.

APPLYING THE RULES

Problem 1: A general contractor is concerned that a roofing subcontractor is running behind schedule and will almost certainly miss a deadline for partial completion, which is 10 days away. The general contractor has come to you for advice. The general would like to fire the subcontractor, but does not want to breach its own obligations. How should the general contractor handle the issue, and what, if anything, should it do during the upcoming10 day period? What else do you want to know from your client?

Problem 2: Seller contracted to deliver 100 desktop computers to buyer on or before June 1. Each computer was to include pre-installed anti-virus software and a video camera built into the monitor. Consider each of the following variations under both UCC Article 2 and the CISG.

(1) On May 15, seller delivered 100 desktop computers that did not include either the anti-virus software or the video camera. The buyer promptly refused the delivery, notifying seller that the monitors did not include video cameras. The buyer never turned on any of the computers at that time. On June 1, seller redelivered the same computers, but with conforming monitors. However, the buyer again refused to accept the computers—this time noting the lack of anti-virus software. Is the buyer entitled to refuse the computers?

(2) Assume the same facts as (1) for the original non-conforming delivery on May 15. The buyer took delivery of the computers without comment, set them aside in its warehouse receiving area, and did not inspect them until June 5. Upon inspection, the buyer noted both the lack of monitor cameras and the lack of anti-virus software and immediately notified seller of both. Is the buyer entitled to refuse to retain and pay for the computers—demanding that seller take them back?

(3) Assume the same facts as (2), except that the promised June 1 delivery was one of three monthly deliveries of 100 computers each. Is the buyer entitled to refuse to retain and pay for the computers—demanding that seller take them back?

Problem 3: Your Ohio client is negotiating to sell 100 electric motors to a German buyer, for delivery to the buyer, in Frankfurt, on April 15. The German buyer is a new customer for your client, and your client would like to maximize its opportunity to cure any perceived defects in the goods, as asserted by the buyer. Your client would like to know whether the CISG or UCC Article 2 is preferable with respect to this issue. Explain all of the reasons for your answer.

Lesson 36: Other Mitigating Doctrines & the Decision to Refuse Further Performance Based on the Breach of a Duty

Objectives and Expected Learning Outcomes

In this lesson, you will learn of additional doctrines intended to limit the circumstances in which performance is excused or mitigating unfair effects when it is excused. The lesson will then pull together the materials from Lessons 33 through the current one in addressing the often challenging decision of whether an aggrieved party is entitled to refuse further performance based on the other party's breach of a duty. You will learn how to weigh and consider the key issues in making this determination based on an existing breach of a contract governed by the common law, UCC Article 2, or the CISG.

Mitigating the Harsh Effects of Excusing Performance

We have already fully addressed the common law doctrine of "substantial performance" and similar doctrines under UCC Article 2 and the CISG that may often avoid or "mitigate" the potentially harsh effect of excusing promised performance based on the breach of a duty (also noting the "perfect tender rule," which operates more strictly, when applicable). We further noted the potential for keeping the parties' agreement together through cure. In the current lesson, we will address three additional doctrines that serve, in various ways, to mitigate the effect of a breach that might otherwise fully excuse performance and, thereby lead potentially to forfeiture. These doctrines include (1) divisibility; (2) hindrance or prevention; and (3) restitution.

Divisibility

We earlier encountered the idea of "divisibility" in the context of installment contracts, first addressed in Lesson 34. In that instance, we were primarily focused on the "substantial impairment" standard, as contrasted with the "perfect tender rule" for rejection of a non-conforming tender of goods. However, we also noted that each installment was treated independently for purposes of the analysis. **STOP NOW and READ the excerpts from UCC § 2-612 below.**

> # UCC § 2-612(2) and (3)
>
> **(1)** An "installment contract" is one which requires or authorizes the delivery of goods in separate lots . . .
>
> **(2)** The buyer may reject any installment which is non-conforming if the non-conformity substantially impairs the value of that installment and cannot be cured . . .
>
> **(3)** Whenever non-conformity or default with respect to one or more installments substantially impairs the value of the whole contract there is a breach of the whole. . . .

A breach of one installment is generally treated as "divisible" from other installments. Thus, even a breach resulting in a "substantial impairment" of the value of that installment will only excuse performance of that specific installment. The rest of the contract remains unaffected, unless the breach of the installment substantially impairs the value of the "whole contract"—not just the individual installment at issue. In effect, a contract is not "divisible" with respect to a breach affecting the contract, as a whole. Consider the following examples.

> **Example 36-1:** Able, a manufacturer of air conditioners, contracts to buy 1,200 compressors from Baker, to be delivered in monthly installments of 100 compressors per delivery. Each air conditioner requires one compressor, and Able can sell any number of air conditioners, up to 1,200 within the relevant time frame.

Baker makes the first delivery, as agreed. However, the compressors delivered in the second installment do not conform to the parties' agreement and are fully unusable by Able. The nonconformity cannot reasonably be cured by Baker.

Able will likely be able to reject the second installment and will be excused from its obligation to pay for that installment of 100 compressors, because the nonconformity "substantially impairs" the value of the installment to Able and cannot be cured. However, Baker's breach of the second installment obligation will not likely have any effect on the obligations of each party to perform each of the other eleven installments. Absent additional facts, there is no indication of any interdependency between the installments. Able will only be able to manufacture 1,100 air conditioners (unless it can obtain compressors elsewhere), instead of 1,200. However, there is no indication that it would not wish to do so, as opposed to cancelling the entire project.

Able will also of course have a claim for damages arising from the breach of the second installment obligation by Baker, which will be addressed in Chapter 8. However, in the foregoing example, the analysis solely focuses on the single breached installment, because the usability of each installment is fully independent of the others. This is not, however, always the case.

Example 36-2: Able again wishes to manufacture 1,200 air conditioners. It contracts with Baker to supply three different components—compressors, thermostats, and power supplies. Each of the components (1,200 units of each) is to be delivered in a separate installment.

Baker delivers the thermostats and power supplies, as agreed. However, the compressors delivered do not conform to the parties' agreement and are fully unusable by Able. The nonconformity cannot reasonably be cured by Baker.

Able will likely be able to reject all of the component parts in all three installments (or revoke any prior acceptance of the thermostats or power supplies) and cancel the entire contract. Without compressors, Able cannot manufacture the intended air conditioners and therefore has no use for the thermostats or power supplies. Thus, the nonconforming compressors "substantially impair" the value of the entire contract—compressors, thermostats, and power supplies. Absent additional facts, there is no indication that Able has any reasonable use for the thermostats and power supplies without the compressors.

Able would also have a claim for damages based on Baker's breach of the entire contract—not just the nonconforming air conditioners.

Thus, we can see from the two foregoing examples the difference between a breach of a "divisible" installment, which has value independent of other installments, and the breach of an installment upon which the usability of other installments is dependent. CISG Article 73 similarly addresses the concept of divisibility in the context of avoidance for fundamental breach, focusing in subsection (1) on the individual installment breached and in subsection (3) on the effect of a breach of one installment or other dependent installments.

The common law also recognizes the doctrine of divisibility in circumstances in which a failure of one portion of the exchange would not reasonably affect other portions of the exchange. A contract is divisible if, and only if, (1) the respective performance of the parties can be apportioned into corresponding pairs; and (2) such corresponding pairs can fairly be regarded as agreed equivalents such that reasonable value of each pair is independent of the contract as a whole.[19] Consider the following example of a divisible contract.

19   Restatement (Second) of Contracts § 240.

Example 36-3: *Gill v. Johnstown Lumber Co.*

Gill agreed to "drive" four million feet of logs down a river (a reasonable means of "transporting" harvested timber to the mill) to the Johnstown Lumber Company (JLC). Gill was to be paid a specified price "per thousand feet" of logs delivered. Soon after Gill began performing the contract, an upstream dam broke, and many of the logs were washed out to sea—undelivered.

JLC sought to be excused from performance of its entire contract obligation, asserting that the number of lost logs amounted to a material breach of the parties' contract. If the contract had not been divisible, JLC's argument would have likely prevailed. However, the court ruled that the contract was divisible, because the price of delivery per thousand feet of logs had been expressly apportioned by the parties into corresponding pairs. Moreover, these corresponding pairs could fairly be regarded as agreed equivalents, because there was no indication that the usability by JLC or some portion of the logs was in any way dependent on receiving all of them.

The court, however, rejected any claim by Gill for having driven some logs a part of the distance to JLC. The parties' agreement did not apportion the distance and price of logs driven into corresponding pairs, and, even if it had, a log driven half way and then washed out to sea would have been of no value to JLC.[20]

In contrast to the foregoing example, a contract will not be divisible—even if apportioned into corresponding pairs—where such pairs cannot reasonably be regarded as agreed equivalents.

---

[20] Gill v. Johnstown Lumber, Co., 151 Pa. 534, 25 A. 120 (1892).

Example 36-4: *Pennsylvania Exchange Bank v. United States*

Seller contracted with the U.S. Government to perform a series of three specified "steps" in preparing to stand ready to produce certain microwave communication agreement—as requested by the U.S. Government—for a period of 6 years. The ultimate purpose of the contract, step IV, was simply to be prepared to produce the specified equipment in the event of a national emergency in which it might be required. Steps I, II, and III were necessary prerequisites to such preparedness, and a specific price was to be paid by the U.S. Government in exchange for each. The pricing associated with step IV was also expressly specified by the contract.

The seller ultimately performed steps I, II, and III, but failed to perform step IV. When the seller brought a legal action to be paid for the three steps performed, the court ruled that the contract was not divisible. While the four different steps unquestionably apportioned performance and price into corresponding pairs, there was no indication that steps I, II, and III had any value to the U.S. Government absent performance of step IV, the ultimate basis of the Government's bargain. As such, the Government was excused from paying for any of the non-divisible steps, because the seller's failure to perform step IV was a material breach of the contract as a whole.[21]

As you have likely noted, the common law rule of divisibility functions in a manner quite similar to the manner in which "installment" sales of goods are treated under UCC Article 2 and the CISG. In each case, the treatment of a breached obligation as "divisible" will depend on whether the value of non-breached obligations is specified by the parties' agreement and sufficiently independent of that breached to remain useful despite the breach.

---

[21] Pennsylvania Exchange Bank v. United States, 170 F.Supp. 629 (Ct. of Cl. 1959).

Hindrance or Prevention

The issue of "prevention" was first addressed earlier, in Lesson 32, in the context of "express conditions." Where a party has "prevented" a condition from occurring, the party is precluded from asserting the failure of the condition as excusing performance. A similar rule is applied to "constructive conditions."

Where a party has prevented or substantially hindered its contracting partner's performance, thereby causing the breach of a duty, the party engaging in such prevention or hindrance may not rely on the breach to excuse its own performance—whatever the extent or effect of such breach. In this doctrine, we see a specific application of the broader principle of estoppel, which is captured quite well in CISG Article 80. **STOP NOW and review CISG Article 80 below.**

CISG ARTICLE 80

A party may not rely on a failure of the other party to perform, to the extent that such failure was caused by the first party's act or omission.

Note the broad effect of Article 80 in barring resort of the failure for any purpose, which would preclude its use as either a basis for avoidance or damages. Of course, CISG Article 80 only applies to transactions within its scope, but it provides an excellent example of a statute reflecting the specific idea of prevention or hindrance, based on the general principle of estoppel.

The issues of prevention or hindrance are also addressed by the common law (and supplement UCC Article 2 to the extent not directly addressed by a specific statutory provision). The following United States Supreme Court case provides an excellent example.

Example 36-5: *United States v. Peck*

Peck contracted to deliver hay to the U.S. government. The contract specified hay only reasonably available in a specific location of the Yellowstone valley. Concerned that Peck might fail to deliver, the government paid others to cut and deliver the same hay, thereby precluding Peck from performing.

The Court ruled that the government had in fact hindered and prevented Peck from performing his contract, thereby precluding any liability on the part of Peck under the contract.[22]

While prevention will almost certainly preclude reliance on the resulting breach, the question of "hindrance" may be a more difficult one. For example, if a buyer is actively in the market seeking to buy goods from multiple sellers, its purchases from one seller may affect the ability of another seller to perform (e.g., if both sellers are acquiring goods from the same source). Typically, the issue will turn on the reasonable expectations of the parties in the transaction at issue.

Restitution

When the breach of a duty excuses further performance by the parties, one or both may be left with benefits provided earlier by the other pursuant to the contract. Where the benefit has been provided by the aggrieved party, the issue will, in most instances, be easily addressed by traditional principles of restitution to avoid unjust enrichment. However, one might reasonably ask whether a breaching party should be entitled to recover restitution. The traditional answer[23] is "yes," as illustrated by the following example.

Example 36-6: Builder contracts to construct a home for owner at a specified price, but substantially fails to complete the home as agreed. The breach is fundamental, so the owner's obligation to pay under the contract is excused.

---

[22] United States v. Peck, 102 U.S. 64 (1880).
[23] *See* Restatement (Second) of Contracts § 374(1).

Moreover, the agreed performance and payment are not divisible. Thus, the builder has no right to recover under the contract. However, to the extent that the builder's partial performance has conferred a benefit on the owner, the builder will likely be entitled to restitution to avoid unjustly enriching the owner.

Some courts have suggested that restitution is not available to the breaching party if the breach is intentional. While the intentional (or not) nature of a breach is generally irrelevant in determining legal damages arising from a breach of contract, it is important to remember that restitution is an equitable remedy. Thus, a court may choose to exercise its equitable discretion to deny restitution in certain circumstances involving an intentional breach.

Any claim for restitution by a breaching party will of course be reduced by any damages to the aggrieved party arising from the breach. In some cases—especially those involving a modest "down payment," the breaching party may be deemed to forfeit the down payment as a matter of agreed or "liquidated" damages.[24] The subject of liquidated damages is more fully explored in Chapter 8. However, the following example may be useful in understanding the basic idea.

Example 36-7: Seller contracts to sell a home to buyer for $300,000. Buyer pays $15,000 to seller as a "down payment," with the remainder of the purchase price due at closing. However, Buyer refuses to perform and does not complete the transaction.

While Buyer may seek to assert a right to restitution of the $15,000 down payment price paid, a court may deem this amount to be agreed upon or "liquidated" damages for Buyer's breach (i.e., reflecting the cost and inconvenience to Seller of having to put the house back on the market and having missed other selling opportunities while off the market). As such, any right of Buyer to restitution is fully offset by Seller's damages, and Buyer is entitled to nothing.

---

[24] *See* Restatement (Second) of Contracts § 374(2).

Thus, we can see that restitution is generally available to a breaching party, subject to possible equitable concerns relating to any intentional breach and subject to any claim by the aggrieved party for damages.

The principle of restitution is also operative in the context of a breach of a contract for the sale of goods. When either party is entitled to avoid a contract governed by the CISG, the statute generally provides for restitution of any benefit previously conferred upon the other party pursuant to the contract. **STOP NOW and review CISG Article 81 below.**

CISG ARTICLE 81

(1) Avoidance of the contract releases both parties from their obligations under it, subject to any damages which may be due. . . . .

(2) A party who has performed the contract either wholly or in part may claim restitution from the other party of whatever the first party has supplied or paid under the contract. If both parties are bound to make restitution, they must do so concurrently.

Thus, an effective avoidance relieves the parties of most of their contract obligations (though not provisions addressing dispute resolution), but leaves the parties with restitutionary remedies in most circumstances (subject to other specific limitations addressed by subsequent statutory provisions).

While UCC Article 2 does not include the same sort of broad provision addressing restitution, the buyer's right to restitution of any price paid in advance is addressed in § 2-718. Thus, when seller is excused from delivering goods, the buyer will generally be entitled to restitution of any price previously paid, less any amount owed by buyer to seller, including any liability for damages.

The Basic Decision—Whether to Continue Performance in the Face of an Apparent Breach

At this point, it should be increasingly clear that an aggrieved party will often face a series of difficult questions when considering an early exit from a contract based on the other's breach of a duty. Any uncertainty as to a party's right to terminate, cancel, or avoid a contract is of course amplified by the effect of being wrong. If an aggrieved party believes it is entitled to walk away from its own obligations based on the other party's breach—but is later deemed to be wrong—then the act of refusing to perform the aggrieved party's own obligations will, itself, almost certainly be a material breach. In this section, we will pull together and summarize the various elements of the common law analysis and then apply these summarize elements to an example.

In Lesson 33, we began with the question of whether one party had breached a dependent promise due at an earlier time or simultaneous to the performance to be withheld or excused. If so, we then asked whether the breach was "material" or, conversely, whether the breaching party had nevertheless "substantially performed." In Lesson 35, we focused on cure, along with any necessary notice of breach. Finally, earlier in this lesson, we addressed the doctrines of divisibility, prevention, and restitution. We can now summarize these elements of the analysis, including the key decisional options, as follows.

Summary of Basic Rule: Contract Termination for Material Breach[25]

- Has the other party breached a duty?

- If so, does the breach involve a dependent promise?

- If so, was the breached duty due at an earlier time or simultaneous to the performance to be withheld or excused?

- If so, is the breach "material"?

- If so, to what extent is "cure" reasonably possible?

  - If so, appropriate notice is particularly important, as omitted reasons may be unavailable in supporting termination right

  - Pending cure, an aggrieved party may reasonably suspend performance

  - If the material breach remains uncured, the aggrieved party may:

    - terminate the contract and sue for total breach; or

    - continue with performance of the contract, retaining the right to sue for any actual breach or breaches (in effect, making an "election" not to "terminate" the contract)

---

[25] This basic rule is largely reflected in Restatement (Second) of Contracts §§ 231, 232, 234, 236, 237, 240, 241, 242, and 248.

> • Additional issues:
>
>   ○ Is the contract divisible?
>
>   ▪ If so, the termination issue is addressed solely as to portion breached; and
>
>   ▪ Other portions unaffected
>
>   ○ Is the aggrieved party estopped from asserting breach as a basis for termination because it prevented or substantially hindered the performance of the breaching party?
>
>   ○ Is either party entitled to restitution for any benefit provided pursuant to the contract prior to its termination?

We can walk through much of this analysis using the following example.

Example 36-8: *Walker & Co. v. Harrison*

Walker entered into a lease contract with Harrison to construct and install a large and ornate neon sign for Harrison's dry cleaning business. As lessor, Walker was also obligated to maintain, repair, and service the sign regularly, including cleaning and repainting the sign as often as necessary to keep the sign in "first class advertising condition." In exchange, Walker was obligated to pay $150 per month over the term of the 36 month lease.

Walker constructed and installed the sign, and Harrison made the first monthly payment—each as agreed. Shortly thereafter, someone hit the sign with a tomato, leaving an unsightly stain. In addition, Harrison first noticed some rust on some of the chrome on the sign, as well as dust and cobwebs in its corners. Over the better part of a month, Harrison called Walker numerous times, explaining each of the problems with the sign and demanding that Walker take care of them. By the time the second payment was due, Walker had not responded, and the problems remained (*to be continued*).[26]

---

[26] Walker & Co. v. Harrison, 347 Mich. 630, 81 N.W.2d 352 (1957).

This juncture in our story provides an excellent place to begin our analysis. Harrison is predictably unhappy at this point in time, and he does not want to pay if Walker is not keeping up his end of their agreement. Let us see where the analysis leads.

Has Walker breached the parties' contract? If so, was Harrison's promise to pay the monthly charge dependent on Walker's promise to maintain and clean the sign? If so, was Walker's obligation to maintain and clean the sign due before the current payment obligation? It would certainly appear that each of these questions can reasonably be answered affirmatively. Of course, the more difficult question here is that of "materiality."

The monthly payment presumably reflects both the value of the original sign and Walker's continuing maintenance obligation, and Walker had in fact constructed and installed the sign. While the rust and cobwebs were also, to some degree, an issue, Harrison seemed to be most unhappy about the "tomato." The stain was of course easily "curable," and Harrison had repeatedly asked Walker to take care of it, but to no avail at this point.

What do you think? Does a tomato stain on a sign advertising "dry cleaning" services amount to a fundamental breach of a sign leasing contract that includes a promise to keep the sign in "first class advertising condition"? Has Harrison given Walker sufficient time and opportunity to cure at this point? Assuming that Harrison wishes to withhold the current monthly payment, should he merely suspect performance, pending cure, or should he terminate the contract entirely, asserting a right to do so based on Walker's breach? We can now return to our example to see how the facts actually played out.

Example 36-8 (continued): *Walker & Co. v. Harrison*

Harrison sent a telegraph to Walker purporting to terminate the contract based on Walker's continuing failure to maintain the sign as agreed, and further stating that Harrison would make no further payments as a result. Walker replied by letter, asserting that Harrison had no right to cancel the contract. Walker also fully cleaned the sign a week later.

Walker also noted in his letter a provision in the contract stating that Harrison's failure to pay any payment was a "default," and further expressly providing Walker with an immediate right to repossess the sign and collect the entire balance of monthly payments upon such an event of default. Nevertheless, Walker offered to allow Harrison to cure this "default" by making the past due payment within a specified time. Harrison declined to do so, and Walker sued for the full amount.

Thus, the court was ultimately faced with the question of whether Harrison was justified in terminating the contract. If so, then Harrison did not breach at all. If not, then Harrison's refusal to pay was, itself, a material breach (as expressly provided in the contract) providing Walker with a right to sue for total breach. Of course, it all came down to the tomato. The court found that the tomato stain did not amount to a material breach, and Walker prevailed.[27]

The case provides an excellent example of both the stakes at issue when deciding whether an aggrieved party has a right to exit a contract. Suppose the court had determined that Walker's failure to clean the tomato stain off the sign for a month was material, might Walker have raised any further arguments?

Walker might argue that the contract was divisible, as the respective performance of the parties could be apportioned into corresponding pairs (monthly service for a monthly fee). However, Harrison might respond that these corresponding pairs cannot be fairly regarded as agreed equivalents, because his sign must always be in first class condition if it is to be effective in advertising his dry cleaning business.

Walker might, nevertheless, have argued that, at the very least, he was entitled to recover the sign or its value from Harrison as a matter of restitution. Harrison would be unjustly enriched if allowed to keep the sign—even in the absence of any further monthly maintenance.

Finally, we could change the facts a bit such that Harrison had actually barred Walker from coming on his property at some point, thereby "preventing" Walker from performing his obligation (or curing his earlier failure to do so). As such, Harrison would likely be estopped from relying on Walker's uncured breach as a basis for terminating the agreement.

---

[27] Walker & Co. v. Harrison, 347 Mich. 630, 81 N.W.2d 352 (1957).

Of course, this same foregoing "decision fraught with peril" often plays out as well in a transaction involving goods—most often in the context of seller's breach of its obligation to deliver conforming goods.

Rejection or Revocation of Acceptance under UCC Article 2

You will recall from Lesson 34 that UCC Article 2 employs a variety of different rules governing a buyer's right to walk away from the contract based on seller's breach. In a single delivery contract, the buyer's right to "reject" goods prior to any acceptance is governed by the "perfect tender" rule of § 2-601. Do you see any virtue in this "bright line" rule? Do you see any potential for unfairness?

In contrast, Article 2 applies a "substantial impairment" to in determining whether a buyer has a right to "revoke" an earlier "acceptance" of the goods under § 2-608. Article 2 also applies a "substantial impairment" test to a buyer's right to refuse goods in either manner—rejection or revocation of acceptance—in the case of an installment contract. UCC § 2-612 governing installment contracts also generally provides the seller with an opportunity for reasonable cure.

Avoidance under the CISG

You will also recall from Lesson 34 that the CISG employs a uniform rule of "fundamental breach" to the question of whether a buyer can refuse to take and pay for goods delivered by seller—whatever the timing of the decision or nature of the contract. The buyer's right to do so is characterized as a right of "avoidance" under CISG Article 49(1)(a), and "fundamental breach" is defined under Article 25. The issue of whether a breach is "fundamental" under Article 25 may also be influenced by the seller's ability to cure the breach under Article 48. Finally, Articles 47 and 49(1)(b) provide a unique mechanism for clarifying whether a buyer is entitled to avoid the parties' agreement based on seller's failure to deliver goods by the time contractually required.

APPLYING THE RULES

Problem 1: Builder contracted with Owner to perform remodeling work on Owner's home for a price of $6,000. Owner agreed to pay Builder for the work as follows:

$1,000 for the first 10 days of work;

$1,000 more for the second 10 days of work;

$1,000 more for the third 10 days of work;

$1,000 more upon completion; and, finally,

$2,000 upon issuance of a completion certificate by the project architect.

Owner made the first payment after 10 days, as well as the second after 20 total days of work, but suspended payment after the third 10 days due to Builder's poor quality work. Builder worked another 10 days, but failed to cure the substandard work issues. Owner then terminated the contract with Builder, alleging that the substandard work amounted to a material breach. You may, in fact, assume that Builder's work from day 21 through day 40 was substandard work amounting to a material breach of the contract. The total work performed by was reasonably valued at $3,500. Owner was able to complete the remodeling work, including the repair of Builder's substandard work by paying another contractor $2,500.

Builder sues, seeking an additional payment of $1,500. Owner counter-claims, seeking a return of the $2,000 paid to Builder. Owner further argues that, even if not entitled to a return of the $2,000 paid to Builder, Owner should not be obligated to pay anything further. Upon what legal theories might each party be basing its position(s)? Which argument should prevail here?

The facts of this problem are loosely based on the issues raised in the case of *Kirkland v. Archbold*, 113 N.E.2d 496 (Ohio App. 1953).

Problem 2: K&G, as the general contractor on a housing subdivision project, contracted with Harris to do excavation and earthmoving. The contract between K&G and Harris provided for monthly payments to Harris (on 10th of month), based on submissions by Harris (on 25th of month) for specific work done the prior calendar month. The contract also included the following three provisions:

(1) Harris, as a subcontractor, was required to carry insurance against property damage and provide proof to K&G;

(2) Harris was required to perform all work in a workmanlike manner, subject to best industry practices; and

(3) Harris was not entitled to receive any monthly payments until and unless it had fully complied with the insurance requirement (para 1 above).

On July 25, Harris properly submitted an invoice for $1,200 for work performed in June. Under the terms of the contract, payment by K&G on this invoice was due August 10. On August 9, a bulldozer driven by a Harris employee ran into and largely demolished the K&G construction office, causing $3,400 worth of damage. That same day, K&G contacted the provider of the insurance carried by Harris under para 1, above. Both Harris and the insurer denied any liability for the damage. At this point, there were no other issues with the work provided by Harris.

On August 10, K&G would like to withhold payment of the $1,200. Can it do so without breaching its contract with Harris? Explain your analysis, as well as the nature of any decision to withhold the payment.

Whatever your advice above, you may assume that K&G withheld the August 10 payment, but did not terminate the contract. Harris continued to work and submitted an invoice on August 25 for another $1,300 (separate and apart from the earlier invoice for $1,200) for work performed in July. On September 10, the "bulldozer incident" remained unresolved, and K&G again withheld payment—this time of the August 25 submission (the July 25 submission also remained unpaid). Harris promptly ceased work, notifying K&G that it was "suspending" further work until it was paid the $2,500 for the two outstanding invoices, but would return promptly if paid. K&G demanded that Harris return and complete the work without payment of the outstanding invoices. When Harris refused, K&G terminated the contract with Harris and completed the project with another subcontractor.

Litigation ensued, with each party asserting claims against the other. In the claim involving the "bulldozer incident," a jury found Harris negligent, and K&G prevailed, recovering $3,400. Assuming this "fact" is established for all other purposes, did K&G at any point breach its contract with Harris? You may want to consider multiple theories.

The facts of this problem are loosely based on the issues raised in the case of *K & G Construction Co. v. Harris*, 223 Md. 305, 164 A.2d 451 (1960).

Problem 3: Review and repeat the questions in Problem 2 in the last lesson and be prepared to address hypothetical variations on those questions.

Write out in your own words a brief summary of the rules applicable to a buyer of goods wishing to refuse to take and pay for goods tendered by seller. You should address both UCC Article 2 and the CISG.

Lesson 37: Prospective Nonperformance & Anticipatory Repudiation

Objectives and Expected Learning Outcomes

In this lesson, you will learn of how to analyze "prospective" nonperformance or "anticipatory repudiation." Our coverage to date has addressed past or present "breaches" of contract. In this and the next Lesson, our coverage shifts to future breaches. In this Lesson, we will address the circumstances under which a future breach may give the likely to be aggrieved party a current right to act prospectively in response to that future breach.

In the preceding materials, we addressed the effect of an actual breach on the aggrieved party's right to cease its own performance obligations and bring an immediate action claiming damages for total breach. We now move on to the somewhat more challenging issue involving circumstances in which a breach is likely, or even certain, to occur, but has not yet occurred in fact, because the date by which performance is due has not yet arrived.

One could easily imagine a rule simply ignoring such circumstances and requiring the disadvantaged party to wait until a breach actually takes place before exercising any remedy (in fact, this was the early common law approach). Or, in contrast, one could imagine a rule that treats any uncertainty caused by the promisor as itself a breach giving rise to all of the same remedial options as a breach at the time performance is due. As we will discover, either of the foregoing approaches may lead, in some circumstances, to a number of undesirable consequences. Moreover, neither addresses circumstances in which very real and significant concerns arise regarding the likelihood of a party's performance, through absolutely no fault of either party. Thus, a more nuanced approach is required. This issue of prospective nonperformance raises a number of competing concerns, and a basic understanding of these concerns will enliven a fuller understanding of the rules that follow.

On one hand, if an obligor is going to breach a basic obligation under the contract, the principle of mitigation mandates that the obligee should be allowed to take steps to mitigate or reduce the damages as soon as possible—early mitigation often being far more effective than later mitigation. In order to encourage mitigation, the obligee must of course be allowed to exit the current contract so as to make alternative arrangements to reduce its losses.

On the other hand, early contracting difficulties may often later be overcome, and a recalcitrant party will often have a change of heart and later decide to perform. Keeping the contract together will in either case likely lead to its successful completion; whereas, allowing for earlier termination would likely have precluded such success. The legal regime addressing these issues attempts to balance these two competing concerns.

Prospective nonperformance may be reasonably divided into two basic sets of circumstances. The first presents circumstances involving a *relatively high degree of certainty* that one of the parties *will commit a very significant breach* of its obligations (lesson 37). The second presents circumstances in which the likelihood of performance or nonperformance is less certain, and this very *uncertainty with respect to performance* raises a unique set of issues (lesson 38).

What is "Repudiation"?

Repudiation typically arises from statements or conduct of one of the contracting parties. Repudiation necessarily arises after the formation of the contract, or there would be nothing to repudiate. The repudiation also necessarily occurs prior to the time when performance is due, or it would be an actual breach. Thus, repudiation is an indication of nonperformance that occurs after contracting, but prior to performance. Under certain circumstances, repudiation by one party will excuse the performance of the other, though the aggrieved party will likely have a variety of potential options available in response to the repudiation. The repudiating party may, however, if timely, change its mind and retract its earlier repudiation, as long as it provides any necessary assurances that it will, in fact, perform the obligation in question. A series of problems follows.

Under the common law, repudiation requires a clear and unequivocal statement by the obligor that he or she will not perform the obligation at issue, or an act or omission by the obligor apparently precluding performance of the obligation. UCC Article 2 largely mirrors the common law, as reflected in the comments to UCC 2-610, while the CISG employs a somewhat different approach.

Repudiation under the Common Law

Restatement (Second) of Contracts § 250 states the basic common law rule. A repudiation requires either (1) a statement, including nonverbal conduct, clearly and unequivocally indicating "that the obligor will commit a breach" giving rise to a claim for total breach; or (2) a "voluntary affirmative act," including voluntary omissions, rendering the obligor, by all appearances, "unable to perform" without such a breach. Note that each directly implicates the obligor. A statement, action, or omission by a third party or parties will not give rise to repudiation under the common law.

Any "statement" or conduct by the obligor must be unequivocal. Statements such as, "I am concerned about my ability to perform," or "I may be unable to perform," or "can you give me additional time to perform" (even if time is "essential") are not sufficient to constitute repudiation. In contrast, an obligor's statement that "I am ceasing work today and will not complete the project" is "clear and unequivocal" and likely amounts to a repudiation. Moreover, an unequivocal statement of intent not to perform, except on conditions beyond those agreed upon under the contract, also constitutes repudiation. For example, an obligor stating "I will only complete the excavation if you pay me 125% of the contract price before I continue any further work" has likely repudiated the contract, because the obligor has refused to perform under the original contract terms.

A voluntary action sufficient to amount to repudiation is one that makes performance at least appear impossible. For example, a seller of land who sells the land at issue to a third party intending to develop the land (and not to resell it to the buyer in question), has likely repudiated its contract, because the seller can no longer sell the land to the original buyer. In contrast, a contractor that fires its workforce prior to completing the project might yet be able to complete the project using subcontractors, absent some contractual provision precluding this. A voluntary "omission" or "inaction" may also arguably support repudiation under some circumstances, provided it is actually a "voluntary" omission rather than a simple inability to act. For example, a manufacturer's failure to make any effort to procure essential raw materials from a sole source supplier, who has now exhausted its supply of the material and has absolutely no additional supply available, might well amount to repudiation.

Finally, in either event, the repudiation must be such that the actual breach of the repudiated obligation would be a material breach giving rise to a right to terminate the contract. A statement that the obligor will be a day late (unless time is "of the essence") will rarely amount to a repudiation, nor will any other statement or conduct indicating a minor breach that does not in any way preclude substantial performance of the contract.

Summary of Basic Rule: common law "repudiation"

- Repudiation requires a clear and unequivocal indication of non-performance by the obligor, in the form of either:

  ○ A statement or conduct clearly and unequivocally indicating that the obligor will commit a breach; *or*

  ○ A voluntary act or omission that renders the obligor apparently unable to perform its obligations;

AND

- The repudiated obligation must be such that, if actually breached, it would amount to a "material breach" of the contract.

Repudiation under UCC Article 2

UCC Article 2 addresses repudiation in section 2-610. **STOP NOW and READ the first paragraph of UCC 2-610 below.**

UCC § 2-610 (first paragraph)

When either party repudiates the contract with respect to a performance not yet due the loss of which will substantially impair the value of the contract to the other, the aggrieved party may . . . [await performance or pursue remedies for breach]

The statutory language does not directly explain what it means to "repudiate" an obligation, so the common law definition serves as a useful supplementation. Comment 1 to § 2-610 further confirms the applicability of the basic common law approach to defining repudiation. The statute does, however, expressly address the extent of the repudiated obligation necessary to trigger its provisions—a performance, the loss of which will "substantially impair" the value of the contract to the aggrieved party. This latter aspect of UCC 2-610 raises at least one noteworthy issue.

You will recall that, in a single delivery contract, the buyer may "reject" seller's tender of the goods under UCC 2-601 and "cancel" the contract for anything less than a "perfect tender," and the "substantial impairment" standard applies only to buyer's subsequent attempt to "revoke" its previous "acceptance" of the goods. Thus, one might reasonably expect that, if the seller unequivocally stated that the goods would be a day late, a few items short, or would otherwise fail to conform to the contract, even in a relatively minor way, the buyer could reject the goods in advance and cancel the contract—in exactly the same manner it would be entitled to do so upon actual tender. However, that is not what the statute provides. If the repudiated duty will give rise to a substantial impairment, the buyer may indeed treat it as an anticipatory repudiation and take advantage of its options on repudiation addressed below. However, if the anticipated breach is relatively minor, the buyer must simply wait for the date of performance, absent reaching some sort of contrary agreement with the seller.

You will likely recall the point made earlier that the "rule" requiring "perfect tender" under UCC 2-601 is, in fact, very much an exception. Under UCC 2-610, the perfect tender "rule" is isolated in that it is limited in its application to the actual decision to accept or reject the tender (and not anticipatory repudiation) of goods under a single delivery contract. Why might Article 2 employ different standards under UCC 2-601 and 2-610? Consider the practical commercial considerations of each circumstance, as well as general principles underlying the legal rules governing anticipatory repudiation.

Summary of Basic Rule: "repudiation" under UCC 2-610

- Repudiation requires a clear and unequivocal indication of non-performance by the obligor, in the form of either:

  ○ A statement or conduct clearly and unequivocally indicating that the obligor will commit a breach; *or*

  ○ A voluntary act or omission that renders the obligor apparently unable to perform its obligations;

  AND

  ○ The repudiated obligation must be such that, if actually breached, it would "substantially impair" the value of the contract to the aggrieved party.

Repudiation under the CISG

The CISG does not use the term "repudiation," but provides a rule addressing a set of analogous circumstances in Article 72. **STOP NOW and READ CISG Article 72**.

CISG ARTICLE 72

(1) If prior to the date for performance of the contract it is clear that one of the parties will commit a fundamental breach of contract, the other party may declare the contract avoided.

(2) If time allows, the party intending to declare the contract avoided must give reasonable notice to the other party in order to permit him to provide adequate assurance of his performance.

(3) The requirements of the preceding paragraph do not apply if the other party has declared that he will not perform his obligations.

In reading the statute, consider subsections (1) and (2), together, and then consider subsection (3) as an alternative rule to that provided by subsections (1) and (2). Remember, the CISG must be read, interpreted, and applied, in a manner that is fully autonomous and independent of our notions of domestic law. However, a comparison of UCC Article 2 and analogous CISG provisions will often assist in a greater understanding of both.

Unlike the common law, you will note that Article 72(1) is not limited to statements or voluntary acts or omissions by the obligor. The provision may be triggered by any circumstances, including circumstances entirely unrelated to the contracting parties, as long as such circumstances make it "clear" that a party will commit the breach at issue. For example, a government war effort might result in the unavailability of steel for private civilian construction projects. While such circumstances would not necessarily involve a statement or voluntary conduct by the seller, they might nevertheless make "clear" that the seller would not be able to deliver the steel, as agreed. In contrast, these circumstances would not give rise to repudiation under the common law.

As to the nature of the anticipated breach by an obligor required to invoke the provision, Article 72(1) takes a similar approach to the common law and UCC 2-610, requiring a "fundamental breach" as a pre-requisite to avoidance of the contract (compare the "material breach" and "substantial impairment" requirements, respectively). Uniquely, however, a party wishing to take advantage of Article 72(1) must, if time allows, provide reasonable notice under Article 72(2). If the obligor then provides adequate assurances that it will perform, then it would presumably no longer be "clear" that the obligor would commit a fundamental breach, and the obligee would no longer be entitled to avoid the contract.

CISG Article 72(3), however, functions a bit more like repudiation under the common law or Article 2. If the obligor actually "declares" it will not perform, then notice and opportunity to provide assurances is both logically and legally unnecessary. Note, however, that Article 72(3) seemingly applies only to statements—not to conduct.

Summary of Basic Rule: a CISG rule generally analogous to "repudiation"

- An aggrieved party may declare contract avoided if either:

    ○ Circumstances make it "clear" that counter- party "will commit" a "fundamental breach" of contract; and

    ○ If time allows, aggrieved party intending to avoid gives reasonable notice to counter-party whose performance is in doubt;

        ▪ Party whose performance is in doubt may provide adequate assurance of performance, thereby precluding avoidance

    OR

    ○ Its counter-party has "declared" that it will not perform its obligations.

When Does a Repudiation Excuse Performance by the Other Party and/or Give Rise to a Right to Bring an Action for Total Breach?

Assuming repudiation can be established, under what circumstances does the obligor's repudiation (1) excuse performance by the obligee; and/or (2) provide the obligee with a right to bring an immediate action for total breach? The question itself provides at least part of the common law answer, as reflected in Restatement (Second) of Contracts § 253. The issue is well illustrated by the facts of the classic English case below.

Example 37-1: *Hochster v. De La Tour*

In April, De La Tour contracted with Hochster. Hochster promised to act as a courier for De La Tour for three months, beginning June 1, in exchange for De La Tour's promised payment of 10£ per month. On May 11, De La Tour notified Hochster that he had changed his mind and no longer intended to use or pay for Hochster's services. On May 22, Hochster brought suit against De La Tour for breach of contract. A few days later, and before June 1, Hochster agreed, on similar terms, to serve as a courier for Ashburton, beginning on July 4.

De La Tour asserted that Hochster could not recover because Hochster had, himself, breached his contract with De La Tour when he subsequently contracted with Ashburton. Having done so, Hochster could not prove that he was ready, willing, and able to perform his contract with De La Tour on June 1, as originally promised. However, the court disagreed, explaining that De La Tour's clear and unequivocal declaration of his intent not to perform his obligations under the contract effectively released Hochster from his own obligations. The court also rejected an alternative argument by De La Tour that Hochster should be precluded from bringing any claim until the time for performance has passed, based on the difficulty of calculating damages prior to that time.

Thus, the court ultimately held in favor of Hochster's right to terminate his contract with De La Tour, mitigate his damages by seeking alternative employment, and bring an immediate action for total breach, based solely on De La Tour's anticipatory repudiation, and prior to the date performance was due by either party under the contract.[28]

---

[28] Hochster v. De La Tour, 2 E. & B. 678, 118 Eng. Rep. 922 (Q.B. 1853).

The facts of the actual case present an excellent example of anticipatory repudiation and raise two distinct issues: (1) can Hochster terminate his agreement with De La Tour; and (2) can Hochster bring an immediate action for total breach? These two issues are often conflated (as they seemingly were in *Hochster*), but each is distinct, and the Restatement (Second) of Contracts distinguishes between them in § 253.

In addressing the first issue, we can easily see that Hochster must be allowed to terminate his contract with De La Tour immediately, upon learning of the repudiation, if we expect him to mitigate by seeking alternative employment. In this case, Hochster succeeded in mitigating his losses by arranging for substitute employment for over half of the period in question, thereby reducing De La Tour's liability for damages. Thus, the rule appears to be a sound one.

In the actual case, there is no indication as to when payment was due to Hochster, so, under the normal default rule, we would presume payment as due when Hochster's service was complete—at the end of August. However, suppose the parties had agreed that payment was not due until December 1, and further suppose that, on September 1, after Hochster had fully performed all of his promised services, De La Tour declared that he had no intention of paying Hochster. There is now of course nothing left to mitigate through alternative employment, as Hochster has already performed all of his obligations for De La Tour, himself. Moreover, Hochster has no reason to terminate the contract, because he has no remaining obligations from which to be excused. In effect, the circumstances themselves either logically preclude or render irrelevant Hochster's right to terminate his contract obligations, because he has already fully performed. However, the second issue—whether Hochster can sue for total breach of an obligation not yet due—presents a more difficult question.

The resolution of this second issue does not necessarily follow from the first. Even if all would likely agree that Hochster ought to be excused from his promised service to De La Tour so that Hochster can mitigate his losses, it does not necessarily follow that he should be able to bring an immediate action for total breach. Such an action arguably has no effect on his ability to mitigate. Moreover, it arguably entitles him to claim money not yet due, and might very well make proof of "yet-to-occur" damages far more speculative and difficult to prove. In *Hochster*, the court seemingly conflated these two issues and justified early resort to court based on the same principles supporting Hochster's right to be excused from his own obligations. These two issues largely remain conflated by the law today, as long as the party in Hochster's position has not yet performed. However, where the obligee has already fully performed, as in the variation above in which De La Tour repudiated on September 1 (three months prior to the date payment was due), the obligee may not bring an action for total breach until the date for performance has passed, and an actual breach has occurred. *See* Restatement (Second) of Contracts § 253(1).

One might reasonably debate the logic of this distinction between repudiations before and after the repudiating party has received performance, as it affects a party's right to bring a legal action prior to breach. However, the rule is well established and is also reflected in Restatement (Second) of Contracts § 243(3), which addresses installment payments of money. The latter is particularly important when drafting contracts involving payment of money over time. Absent an express contract provision, the breach of one payment—even if coupled with a clear repudiation regarding future payments—will not give rise to a claim for total breach. The party entitled to payment will have to wait until the due date of each payment before bringing an action to recover it. Thus, from the obligee's perspective, an express "acceleration" clause is essential in a contract involving payments over time, inasmuch as it allows the creditor to bring a single action for the full amount due against the debtor who has misses a single payment, without waiting for the due date of each individual future payment.

Summary of Basic Rule: repudiation as excusing performance

- If one party repudiates the contract, the aggrieved party may terminate the contract and is excused from further performance of its own obligations.

  - *See also* UCC 2-610(b), addressed more fully below.

Summary of Basic Rule: repudiation as giving rise to immediate claim for total breach

- If one party repudiates before the other party has fully performed, the aggrieved party may bring an immediate action for total breach.

  - If, however, the aggrieved party has already fully performed, then it must await actual non-performance before bringing its claim.

    - A failure to make a single payment of an installment due for prior performance does not give rise to a claim for future payments, even if accompanied by a repudiation.

      - *Reminder – This rule is simply a default, and parties may—and often do—contract for a contrary result.*

An Aggrieved Party's Other Options in Response to Repudiation

When a party repudiates, its aggrieved counter-party has a variety of options. It may end the contractual relationship (whether legally characterized as termination, cancellation, or avoidance), or it may choose to wait in hopes that the repudiating party may change its mind. If the aggrieved party takes this latter course, it nevertheless retains the right to terminate later, any time up to and including the time of the actual breach (i.e., when performance comes due)—even if the aggrieved party has urged the repudiating party to retract its repudiation. While the foregoing is an accurate statement of the common law, this same approach is reflected in UCC 2-610, which lays out the relevant rule very clearly. **STOP NOW and READ the rest of UCC 2-610 in full below.**

UCC § 2-610

When either party repudiates the contract with respect to a performance not yet due the loss of which will substantially impair the value of the contract to the other, the aggrieved party may

(a) for a commercially reasonable time await performance by the repudiating party; or

(b) resort to any remedy for breach (Section 2-703 or Section 2-711), even though he has notified the repudiating party that he would await the latter's performance and has urged retraction; and

(c) in either case suspend his own performance or proceed in accordance with the provisions of this Article on the seller's right to identify goods to the contract notwithstanding breach or to salvage unfinished goods.

Under UCC 2-610, the aggrieved party may, initially, await performance for a commercially reasonable time. The aggrieved party may not wait indefinitely or simply wait and watch the market price, in hopes of a windfall at the repudiating party's risk. However, the aggrieved party is afforded a reasonable time to investigate a potential substitute transaction. When such time expires, the aggrieved party does not lose the right to repudiate, but is simply precluded from relying on a subsequent substitute transaction in claiming damages.[29] Consider the following hypothetical below.

---

[29] *See, e.g.*, UCC 2-712 (1) (limiting "cover" by buyer to a substitute purchase made without "unreasonable delay).

Example 37-2: (S)eller and (B)uyer contracted for cocoa beans, a commodity subject to considerable price volatility, depending on global cocoa crop yields. The contract called for S to deliver 1 ton of beans to B on June 1, for $1,500. On March 1, S repudiated. The market price on March 1 was $1,500 per ton, and rose constantly over the next 90 days, eventually reaching $2,200 per ton on May 31. On that day, B purchased a ton of beans for $2,200. B then sought to recover $700 from S under UCC 2-712. B was actually hoping the price would fall, which would have allowed B to go into the market, buy beans below its contract price, and reap a windfall without any need to sue S. However, B is trying to use its right to claim damages from S as, essentially, a "hedge" against the price going up, as it did. Inasmuch as the price went up, B would only get the benefit of its bargain ($1,500 per ton) if allowed to recover the $700, but it might have done much better if the price had gone the other way, and S has essentially covered the "downside" of B's bet on the market price.

UCC 2-610(a) precludes such a course of action by B, inasmuch as waiting 90 days in a volatile market is very likely unreasonable. Moreover, B's purported substitute purchase came only after "unreasonable delay," which precludes its use as "cover" under UCC 2-712. However, B retains a right to recover for S's ultimate breach (whether anticipatory or actual), and we must, therefore, consider how to measure damages in these circumstances under UCC 2-713. This issue is addressed below in lesson 42.

Alternatively, the aggrieved party may resort to any remedy for breach, including cancellation and an action for damages—even if it has previously urged retraction. Finally, the aggrieved party may—in any event—suspend its own performance (as well as other specific steps provided by the statute) prior to any ultimate decision to cancel the contract.

> **Summary of Basic Rule: aggrieved party's options in response to a repudiation**
>
> - In the case of a common law repudiation, the aggrieved party may:
>   - Wait for a potential retraction until the time for performance is due
>   - Though waiting beyond a reasonable time may affect the aggrieved party's right to damages;
>
>   OR
>
>   - Terminate the contract
>
>   AND, IN ANY EVENT
>
>   - Suspend its own performance
> - In the case of Article 2, UCC 2-610 provides the best clear statement of the rule

Retraction by the Repudiating Party

The repudiating party may, however, retract its repudiation prior to any termination (or cancellation or avoidance) or reliance by the aggrieved party. If the repudiation is retracted, then the repudiating party will reinstate its right to perform. Again, this framework is best exemplified by Article 2. **STOP NOW and READ UCC 2-611 below.**

UCC § 2-611

(1) Until the repudiating party's next performance is due he can retract his repudiation unless the aggrieved party has since the repudiation cancelled or materially changed his position or otherwise indicated that he considers the repudiation final.

(2) Retraction may be by any method which clearly indicates to the aggrieved party that the repudiating party intends to perform, but must include any assurance justifiably demanded under the provisions of this Article (Section 2-609).

(3) Retraction reinstates the repudiating party's rights under the contract with due excuse and allowance to the aggrieved party for any delay occasioned by the repudiation.

The repudiation, itself, will not necessarily harm the aggrieved party or affect its expectation interest. Thus, until and unless the aggrieved party acts on it or the date for performance passes, the repudiation generally remains subject to retraction. Retraction is, however, precluded by four events or actions: (1) the passing of the time for performance—the breach is then an actual one; (2) cancellation (or termination under the common law); (3) a material change in position (i.e., detrimental reliance); or (4) any other indication by the aggrieved party that it considers the repudiation final (it is unclear whether this "catch all" would extend to the common law).

The repudiating party may convey its retraction in any reasonable manner, but must provide any reasonably demanded assurances to the aggrieved party. Such assurances are addressed more fully in the next Lesson, but are intended to reassure the aggrieved party whose faith in performance by its contracting partner may have been shaken by the original repudiation. Finally, an effective retraction will reinstate the repudiating party's original contract rights, with due excuse and allowance to the aggrieved party.

Summary of Basic Rule: retraction of a repudiation

- In the case of a common law repudiation, the repudiating party may retract, unless;

  - The time for performance has passed;

  - The aggrieved party has already exercised its right to terminate the contract; or

  - The aggrieved party has detrimentally relied on the repudiation.

- The retraction may be in any reasonable form—including any necessary assurances of performance—and it will reinstate the repudiating party's contract rights.

- In the case of Article 2, UCC 2-611 provides the best clear statement of the rule.

APPLYING THE RULES

Problem 1: McCloskey, a general contractor (GC) contracted with Min-weld Steel (SC) to perform the "steel work" on a construction project. The contract provided that any failure by SC to meet the contract deadlines, as reasonably determined by GC, would give GC a right to terminate the contract with SC. In May, GC provided the project specs for the steel to SC. On June 8, GC sent a letter to SC asking "when will the steel work be completed?" On June 13, SC responded that it would begin delivery of the steel on September 1 and would complete erection of all of the steel work by November 15. GC did not immediately respond. On June 24 (1950), the Korean War began, and the U.S. government immediately took effective control of the U.S. steel market in support of the U.S. war effort. Procurement of steel for civilian projects immediately became extremely difficult. On July 20, GC demanded unqualified assurances from SC that it had acquired a contractual right to delivery of all of the project steel no later than the end of July. On July 24, SC indicated that obtaining the steel was becoming difficult and asked GC if it might be able to assist in doing so. On July 26, GC notified SC that, based on SC's repudiation of its obligation to deliver and erect the steel in a timely manner, GC was terminating the contract. GC later sued for breach and damages and SC counter-claimed for the same. The facts are essentially based on *McCloskey & Co. v. Minweld Steel Co.*, 220 F.2d 101 (3d Cir. 1955) and driven by events surrounding the Korean War and its impact on U.S. steel availability. However, you should apply current law to these facts.

Is this contract governed by Article 2? In this case, does it matter? What if the contract was predominantly one for the sale of steel, the SC was a New York business, and the GC and construction project were located in Montreal, Canada?

Problem 2: Seacoast Gas (SG) contracted with the U.S. Government (US) to sell natural gas for a government housing project, beginning on April 15 and continuing until the middle of the following year. On October 7, SG notified US that it "intended to cancel the contract as of November 15." SG believed that it was entitled to cancel the contract based on its belief that the US had earlier breached the contract. However, SG was wrong in this belief and had no right to cancel. The US replied later in October, explaining that SG had no right to cancel, and demanded that SC retract its repudiation, or the US would seek an alternative gas supplier and sue SC for damages. On November 6, the US notified SG that it then had a bid from an alternative supplier, and SG had only 3 days to retract, or the US would contract with the alternative supplier. On November 10, SC expressly refused to retract its cancellation. The same day, November 10, the US accepted the alternative bid by telephone. On November 13, SC notified the US that it was retracting its repudiation and fully intended to perform its obligations for the remainder of the contract period. On November 17, the US executed the formal signed agreement with its alternative gas supplier (based on the earlier agreement by telephone on November 10). A law suit ensued. The facts are essentially based on *United States v. Seacoast Gas Co.*, 204 F.2d 709 (5th Cir. 1953). However, you should apply current law to these facts.

Did SG successfully retract its repudiation?

Problem 3: Maddox (GC) had a contract to replace a loading facility in a coal mine. Maddox subcontracted the work to Coalfield Services (SC). The subcontract was concluded orally in mid-March. It called for SC to complete the work within three weeks, beginning March 20, and for GC to pay $230,000 for the work, with bi-weekly progress payments based on the percentage of work completed. GC also promised to sign the written memorialization of the parties' agreement (it was prepared on March 19). On March 20, SC began work. However, the work progressed more slowly than expected. During this same time period, SC repeatedly requested that GC sign the written agreement, but GC had not done so. On April 8, SC stopped work and came to the surface of the mine (SC had been working far underground, and going to and from the underground job site was a very burdensome and lengthy process). That same day, April 8, the parties exchanged the following communications:

- SC to GC – no more work unless you (1) sign the contract; and (2) pay $103,500, as a progress payment for 45% of the work done thus far;

- GC to SC – will pay amount requested, but only if you sign a modification providing that you get one extra week to complete the project, but agree to liquidated damages of $1,000 per day for any days beyond that it takes to complete the work;

- SC to GC – no more work unless you pay $103,500 and sign the original March 19 written agreement, and extend the date of completion—if you agree, SC will resume work on April 16;

- GC to SC – resume work on April 9, or will terminate for breach

No further work was performed by SC for GC, and a lawsuit ensued. The facts are essentially based on *CL Maddox v. Coalfield Services*, 51 F.3d 76 (7th Cir. 1995).

Who wins—SC or GC?

Lesson 38: Dealing with Uncertainty in the Absence of a Clear Repudiation

Objectives and Expected Learning Outcomes

In this lesson, you learn how a party may sometimes resolve uncertainty as to its contracting partner's future performance. This is particularly important in circumstances in which the likely aggrieved party does not yet have a legal right to exit the contract. This lesson addresses the means by which a party with legitimate concerns regarding future nonperformance can either obtain assurances of future performance, thereby relieving such concerns, or turn its concerns into a legal basis to exit the contract prospectively, as in the prior Lesson.

Absent repudiation, an insecure common law obligee could historically do little but wait for the date of performance. Article 2, however, provides a novel solution to this issue of insecurity and, under certain circumstances, allows an insecure party to demand adequate assurance of due performance under UCC 2-609. Courts have been somewhat inconsistent in their willingness to adopt the approach reflected in UCC 2-609 as part of the common law. CISG Article 71 provides a loose analog to UCC 2-609, and a comparison of the two helps to emphasize certain aspects of each. Installment contracts raise a unique context for insecurity and demands for adequate assurance. A series of problems follows.

UCC 2-609

Historically, the common law provided relief to an insecure obligee only in the case of the insolvency of its obligor.[30] Otherwise, the insecure obligee simply had to await the date of performance before taking any legally effective action in response to that insecurity. Thus, UCC 2-609 provided a novel approach novel approach to the issue in that it expressly recognized "an obligation on each party that the other's expectation of receiving due performance will not be impaired" and provides a means of resolving either party's "reasonable grounds for uncertainty" as to the performance of its contracting partner. **STOP NOW and READ UCC 2-609 below.**

UCC § 2-609

(1) A contract for sale imposes an obligation on each party that the other's expectation of receiving due performance will not be impaired. When reasonable grounds for insecurity arise with respect to the performance of either party the other may in writing demand adequate assurance of due performance and until he receives such assurance may if commercially reasonable suspend any performance for which he has not already received the agreed return.

(2) Between merchants the reasonableness of grounds for insecurity and the adequacy of any assurance offered shall be determined according to commercial standards.

(3) Acceptance of any improper delivery or payment does not prejudice the aggrieved party's right to demand adequate assurance of future performance.

(4) After receipt of a justified demand failure to provide within a reasonable time not exceeding thirty days such assurance of due performance as is adequate under the circumstances of the particular case is a repudiation of the contract.

Recall the rule regarding "repudiation" in last Lesson. Anything less than a clear and unequivocal statement or conduct by the obligor effectively precluding performance will not suffice in establishing repudiation. However, statements or conduct by the obligor that falls short of this relatively high standard may very well give rise to a reasonable person in the position of the obligee of that performance. Moreover, external circumstances having

---

[30] *See* Restatement of Contracts (Second) § 252.

nothing directly to do with the parties may provide reasonable grounds for insecurity. UCC 2-609 addresses each of these circumstances.

When either party has "reasonable grounds" for insecurity as to its contracting partner's willingness or ability to perform, the insecure party may "in writing demand adequate assurance of due performance" by its contracting partner. Moreover, the insecure party may suspend its own performance, with two caveats. First, the suspending party must not have yet received the agreed exchange for the performance to be suspended, and the suspension must be commercially reasonable. Second, the reasonableness of any purported grounds for insecurity between merchants shall be determined according to commercial standards, as shall the adequacy of any assurances.

In making such a demand, the obligee is hoping to achieve one or two possible objectives. On one hand, the obligor may provide the adequate assurances sought, and the parties can move forward with their respective obligations with full confidence in receiving the performance promised by each other. On the other, the obligor may fail to provide such assurances within a reasonable time not exceeding thirty days. In this event, the obligor is deemed to have repudiated the contract, such that the obligee may then invoke the provisions of UCC 2-610. Either way, the insecure party's uncertainty is resolved, and the party can move forward with its business planning—either in contemplation of full performance, or in an effort to address the breach, including any effort to mitigate damages.

Of course, the actual communications of the parties are not always so clear cut as to provide a certain answer with respect to any reply to a demand for assurance. What sort of demand is appropriate? What sort of assurance is adequate? The obligor may also challenge whether the obligee's grounds for insecurity were reasonable in the first instance. All of these are fact intensive issues to be resolved on a case-by-case basis. However, two observations are useful here. First, commercially reasonable behavior is the touchstone of Article 2, generally, and UCC 2-609, specifically. Second, if time allows, an incremental request may be useful. If the initial reply by the obligor is arguably inadequate or, itself, raises additional concerns, then a second demand may be appropriate before attempting to determine whether obligor's failure to assuage obligee's concerns amount to a repudiation under UCC 2-609(4).

> ### Summary of Basic Rule: demands for adequate assurances under UCC 2-609
>
> - If a party has reasonable grounds for insecurity,
>   - ○ It may demand assurances of performance.
>   - ▪ Demand must be in writing
>   - ▪ Demanding party may suspend its own performance,
>   - ▪ If reasonable; and
>   - ▪ If it has not received the agreed exchange for the performance suspended.
>   - ▪ Between merchants, commercial standards govern issues.
>   - ○ If no adequate assurances are provided within reasonable time (not greater than 30 days), the party failing to provide such assurances is deemed to have repudiated.

Adopting UCC 2-609 as Common Law (or not)

Restatement of Contracts (Second) § 251 provides for a common law rule comparable to UCC 2-609. The drafters of the second restatement in fact modeled this provision after UCC 2-609, as an aspirational suggestion for state court adoption as part of the common law. State courts, however, have been inconsistent in their willingness to do so, as exemplified by the following case.

Example 38-1: *Norcon Power Partners v. Niagra Mohawk Power Corp.*

In a case involving the sale of electrical power, one of the parties sought assurances of performance based on allegedly reasonable grounds for insecurity. Electricity is not a "good," so Article 2 did not directly govern the contract. The New York Court of Appeals expressly declined to adopt Restatement of Contracts (Second) § 251, as part of the common law of New York. Instead, the court suggested this issue should be framed as whether UCC 2-609 should be applied "by analogy" on a case-by-case basis, depending on the circumstances of the individual case. In *Norcon*, the Court of Appeals held that the application of UCC 2-609, by analogy, to a contract to purchase and sell electricity was appropriate.[31]

---

[31] *Norcon Power Partners v. Niagra Mohawk Power Corp.*, 92 N.Y.2d 458, 705 N.E.2d 656 (1998).

Inasmuch as natural gas is a good, the application of Article 2, by analogy, to the sale of electricity seems reasonable. One might take note, however, of CISG Article 2(f), which expressly excludes "electricity" from its scope.

CISG Article 71

The CISG does not speak expressly of reasonable grounds for insecurity or demands for adequate assurances, but provides a rule addressing a set of analogous circumstances in Article 71. **STOP NOW and READ CISG Article 71 below**.

CISG ARTICLE 71

(1) A party may suspend the performance of his obligations if, after the conclusion of the contract, it becomes apparent that the other party will not perform a substantial part of his obligations as a result of:

    (a) a serious deficiency in his ability to perform or in his creditworthiness; or

    (b) his conduct in preparing to perform or in performing the contract.

(2) If the seller has already dispatched the goods before the grounds described in the preceding paragraph become evident, he may prevent the handing over of the goods to the buyer even though the buyer holds a document which entitles him to obtain them. The present paragraph relates only to the rights in the goods as between the buyer and the seller.

(3) A party suspending performance, whether before or after dispatch of the goods, must immediately give notice of the suspension to the other party and must continue with performance if the other party provides adequate assurance of his performance.

In reading the statute, consider the following. How do the standards for invoking its provisions differ from Article 72? If a party invokes the provisions of Article 71, suspends performance, and demands adequate assurance of due performance, what happens if such assurance is not forthcoming? Try your hand at constructing your own summary of the basic rule of CISG Article 71, along with its inter-connection, if any, to Article 72.

Insecurity, Demands for Assurances, and Installment Contracts

The breach of an installment contract for the sale of goods raises two issues addressed earlier: (1) under what circumstances will a breach of an obligation regarding an individual installment allow the aggrieved party to cancel or avoid its own obligations regarding the individual installment; and (2) under what circumstances will the same breach allow the aggrieved party to cancel or avoid its own obligations with respect to the entire remaining contract. In addressing the latter question, we looked to UCC 2-612(3) and CISG 73(3), each of which focus on the relationship between the single installment and the sum of all installments. If the latter are significantly impacted based on an interdependent relationship with the former, then the aggrieved party may be entitled to cancel or avoid the whole. However, a breach of an individual installment may also raise a separate issue. Does the breach of one installment suggest the likelihood of similar future breaches? **STOP NOW and READ UCC 2-612(3) and the excerpt from comment 6, along with CISG Article 73(2) and (3), all below.**

UCC § 2-612(3)

. . .

(3) Whenever non-conformity or default with respect to one or more installments substantially impairs the value of the whole contract there is a breach of the whole. But the aggrieved party reinstates the contract if he accepts a non-conforming installment without seasonably notifying of cancellation or if he brings an action with respect only to past installments or demands performance as to future installments.

OFFICIAL COMMENT (UCC § 2-612)

6. . . . Whether the non-conformity in any given installment justifies cancellation at to the future depends, not on whether such non-conformity indicates an intent or likelihood that the future deliveries will also be defective, but whether the non-conformity substantially impairs the value of the whole contract. If only the seller's security in regard to future installments is impaired, he has the right to demand adequate assurances of proper future performance but has not an immediate right to cancel the entire contract. . . .

CISG ARTICLE 73(2) and (3)

. . .

(2) If one party's failure to perform any of his obligations in respect of any instalment gives the other party good grounds to conclude that a fundamental breach of contract will occur with respect to future instalments, he may declare the contract avoided for the future, provided that he does so within a reasonable time.

(3) A buyer who declares the contract avoided in respect of any delivery may, at the same time, declare it avoided in respect of deliveries already made or of future deliveries if, by reason of their interdependence, those deliveries could not be used for the purpose contemplated by the parties at the time of the conclusion of the contract.

Comment 6 to UCC 2-612 specifically distinguishes between issues arising from the interdependency of installments and the fear of future similar breaches, and clearly indicates that the latter are to be addressed, if at all, as issues of insecurity under UCC 2-609. In contrast, CISG Article 73 directly addresses the issue in subsection (2) and provides a party with "good grounds to conclude that a fundamental breach . . . will occur" in the future a direct right to avoid the contract, without any demand for assurances.

APPLYING THE RULES

Problem 1: Return to the facts of Problem 1 in the last Lesson. What should the GC have done, and when? What if the GC took your advice and the SC did not provide a timely reply?

Problem 2: Pittsburgh-Des Moines Steel Co. (PDM) contracted to build a water tower for Brookhaven Manor Water Co. (BMW). In negotiating the contract, PDM initially sought progress payments, but ultimately agreed to a single payment by BMW of $175,000 after the water tower had been completed. Soon after concluding the contract, BMW sought bank financing for the project. PDM asserted that it did not know at the time of contracting that BMW needed a loan for the project, while BMW asserted that PDM was aware of the need for financing from the beginning. In either event, the bank denied the loan request by BMW. Upon learning of this, PDM wrote a letter to the President of Brookhaven in which it demanded either (1) a personal guarantee of BMW's payment obligation by the President, individually; or (2) the immediate placement of $175,000 in an escrow account. BMW declined to do either. PDM asserted that BMW had repudiated, canceled the contract, and sued BMW for damages. The facts are essentially based on *Pittsburgh-Des Moines Steel Co. v. Brookhaven Manor Water Co.*, 532 F.2d 572 (7th Cir. 1976).

Was PDM legally entitled to consider BMW's refusal of its written demand as a repudiation? If not, was there anything PDM might have done differently that might have led to a more favorable outcome? If so, what?

Problem 3: Return to the facts of Problem 3 in the last Lesson. Might the SC have framed its initial communication of April 8 somewhat differently? What would you have advised as to the content of that initial communication?

Problem 4: A Virginia seller and a German buyer entered into a contract for the sale of chemicals to be delivered in installments over a period of 24 months. The chemicals delivered in each of the first three installments failed to conform to the contract description in a manner that fully precluded buyer's use of the chemicals, and the seller should have reasonably expected such a result. In each case, the buyer promptly inspected the chemicals, notified the seller of the nonconformity, and further notified the seller that it would not take or pay for the chemicals. The seller did nothing to cure any of these three nonconforming deliveries, but indicated that it intended to continue to make the remaining deliveries under the contract. The buyer's intended use of the chemicals delivered in each installment is fully independent of its use of chemicals delivered in other installments. However, the buyer is very worried that seller's future deliveries will exhibit the same problems as the first three deliveries. The facts are loosely based on excerpts from an Arbitral Award in ICC Case 9887 at: http://www.unilex.info/case.cfm?pid=1&do=case&id=469&step=Abstract

Does the buyer have the right to avoid its obligations under the remainder of the contract?

What if the buyer was a North Carolina business instead of a German business?

8

Remedies for Breach

Key Concepts

- When is a Party Entitled to Actual Performance?
- How are Damages Calculated as a Substitute for Performance? When Might a Damages Remedy be Limited or Contractually Determined in Advance?
- Specific Performance, Damages, and Limitations

Lesson 39: Specific Performance

Objectives and Expected Learning Outcomes

In this lesson, you will begin to explore the expectation remedy in detail, and you will learn, in particular, about the remedy of specific performance. You will be reminded (from Lesson 3) that money damages is the normal form of the expectation remedy, but will learn under which circumstances the extraordinary remedy of specific performance may be appropriate. You will further learn to evaluate the availability of performance based remedies under the common law, UCC Article 2, and the CISG.

In the first seven chapters, we have addressed the basic requirements for a binding and enforceable contract, the means by which the content of the parties' rights and obligations is determined, and the circumstances in which such rights and obligations may come due or be excused. In addressing the latter, we focused to a large degree on the potential effect of a breach of contract in excusing the performance obligations of the aggrieved party. In doing so, the additional right to damages was frequently noted. In the current chapter, we will examine the right to damages in detail. However, we will begin in this lesson with an overview of remedies, following by a more detailed consideration of the circumstances in which a party may be entitled to demand the actual performance of the promised obligation.

A Brief Overview of Remedies for Breach of Contract

Simply put, "remedies" are legal "rights" arising from the legal "wrongs" of another. We are focused, primarily, on "remedies" arising from the "breach" of a "contract" and actually began our exploration of "remedies" in the last chapter. The rule of "constructive conditions" is itself a remedial rule inasmuch as it arises from a breach by one of the parties. Thus, the right to "terminate," or "cancel," or "avoid" a contract is simply one of a variety of potential "remedies" for certain breaches. In fact, certain breaches of contract may present the aggrieved party with a very clear choice between exiting the contract and asserting a right to require performance.

Common sense ought to tell us that a party cannot simultaneously demand that its own performance obligations must be excused, while the other party's must be enforced. Consider the following example.

> **Example 39-1:** A seller and buyer contract for the sale of widgets. On the day of delivery, the seller informs the buyer it will not deliver the promised widgets. In view of seller's refusal to perform, we know that the buyer has the right to exit the contract ("cancel" or "avoid," depending on governing law). Alternatively, the buyer may have a right to demand that the seller perform its promise and deliver the goods (we will explore this possibility further below). However, the buyer cannot "have it both ways"— demanding that the seller deliver the goods, while simultaneously refusing to take and pay for those goods.

While excusing performance and requiring performance are clearly alternative remedies, neither precludes the right to damages. A decision to seek an early exit or to require performance may affect the quantum of such damages, but will not generally affect the right to claim them. In short:

- All breaches give rise to claims for damages by the aggrieved party, if proven (Lessons 40 through 45);

- Some breaches may also give rise to a right of the aggrieved party to exit the contract (Lessons 33 through 38); and

- Some breaches may also give rise to a right of the aggrieved party to require performance by the breaching party (this Lesson); however,

- An aggrieved party is not entitled to exit and enforce dependent contract obligations at the same time.

Of course, in some cases of breach, the breaching party may wish to continue performing, and the aggrieved party may wish to accept that performance, simply retaining the right to sue for any damages. In that instance, the aggrieved party has no interest in exiting the contract and no need for specific enforcement.

In the current chapter, our focus now moves to enforcement of the "expectation" interest, initially introduced in Lesson 3. When a promisor breaches its contractual promise, the aggrieved promisee is normally entitled to be placed in as good a position as if the contract had been fully performed. As a "rule," this remedy is achieved by requiring the breaching promisor to pay damages. Traditionally, the remedy of specific performance has been considered "exceptional," and dependent upon the equitable discretion of the court. Our earlier summary of the basic expectation interest is reproduced below for ease of reference.

Summary of Rule (from Lesson 3): remedy based on "expectation interest"

- An aggrieved promisee is entitled to recover his or her "expectation interest" in the event of breach by the promisor;

  - This "expectation" remedy entitles the promisee to be placed in as good a position as if the contract had been fully performed,

    - But not in a better position than full performance, and

    - The aggrieved party is not entitled to punitive damages in a simple breach of contract case, even if the breach was willful

  - This "expectation" remedy is normally achieved by awarding a sum of money equal to the difference in value between promised performance and actual performance

    - However, in exceptional cases, such as a sale of real property, a party may be entitled to specific performance of the promise at issue

While "damages" remain the common law "rule," and "performance" the common law "exception," we will see a somewhat more "liberalized" approach to specific performance under UCC Article 2, and a very different approach to the issue under the CISG.

Specific Performance under the Common Law

The only "legal" form of an expectation remedy for a common breach of contract is "damages." However, courts of equity have long recognized exceptions in certain cases in which damages seemingly failed to protect the aggrieved party's reasonably expected interest under the contract. The classic example is land—the idea being than each piece of real property is sufficiently unique that money alone cannot reasonably serve as a substitute for a given unique parcel of land. In addition, the "performance" of a promise to convey land involves a relatively simple act. Thus, it is relatively easy to "enforce" directly. The same cannot generally be said for contracts for services.

As a general matter, a court is far more hesitant to require a party to perform services than to convey property. An order compelling the performance of services presents a series of challenges, including (1) the difficulty in measuring the quality of performance; (2) the moral hazard of involuntary servitude; and (3) any burden of continuing supervision of such performance. However, a court may have other equitable tools available to achieve a similar result. The following classic example is illustrative.

> ### Example 39-2: *Lumley v. Wagner*
>
> Lumley contracted with Wagner to sing exclusively at Lumley's opera house for three months. Wagner subsequently contracted to sing at a different opera house for more money. Lumley sought to enjoin Wagner from singing at any opera house other than Lumley's for the period in question.
>
> In deciding the issue, the court initially noted that it clearly "had no power to compel [Wagner] to perform at [Lumley's opera house]," or otherwise "[compel] her to sing." However, the Lord Chancellor further observed that

Wagner should have "no cause of complaint if I compel her to abstain from the commission of an act which she has bound herself not to do, and thus possibly cause her to fulfil her engagement."[1]

In the foregoing case, Wagner had clearly made two distinct promises—a positive one to perform for Lumley and a negative one not to perform elsewhere during the same time period. Thus, the court had no problem distinguishing between a request for specific performance of the positive promise (generally unavailable in a contract for services) and an injunction to enforce a negative promise (generally available, as appropriate). In other cases, the distinction may be less clear. For example, a request to enforce a positive promise might be reframed as a request to enjoin a breach. In close cases, this sort of framing may make a difference.

The general rule with respect to service contracts may also, on occasion, be subject to exception. For example, a construction contract requiring a business entity to complete a near-finished project in which the required performance is relatively clear might be subject to an order of specific performance—especially if the project provides for construction on real property owned by the aggrieved party. Under these circumstances, the earlier described general concerns about ordering performance would be minimized, and might therefore be outweighed by the general rule providing for performance of contracts involving real property. Such exceptions are, however, relatively rare.

Inasmuch as specific performance is an equitable remedy under the common law, it is further limited my traditional principles of equity. For example, in *McKinnon v. Benedict* (Lesson 20), McKinnon sought "equitable" relief in the form of an injunction (note the "framing" of what might alternatively be viewed as a request for specific performance by the Benedicts of their contract promises). However, the court denied McKinnon's request based on what it considered a bargain too "sharp" to be enforced as a matter of equity (even though the court would have likely given effect to a legal claim for damages). In *Campbell Soup Co. v. Wentz*, in Example 23-4, the court determined that the form contract drafted by Campbell contained numerous provisions not only favoring Campbell, but operating in a man-

---

[1] Lumley v. Wagner, 42 Eng. Rep. 687 (Ch. 1852).

ner going far beyond that which a reasonable person would expect. While declining to grant specific performance, the court made clear that it would have reached a different result on a legal claim for damages.

Finally, a court will often decline to award specific performance in cases in which the aggrieved party has an adequate remedy at law. In effect, if an ordinary remedy of money damages will provide and aggrieved party with the value of its expectation interest, then an extraordinary award of actual contract performance may be more difficult to justify. Moreover, an equitable award of specific or injunctive relief may, in some cases, actually provide a better means of quantifying the value of the expectation interest than any attempt to quantify damages otherwise.

Consider the following example from an opinion by Judge Richard Posner.

Example 39-3: *Walgreen Co. v. Sara Creek Property Co.*

Sara Creek leased a shopping center space to Walgreens. The lease prohibited Sara Creek from leasing to any other pharmacy. When Sara Creek subsequently sought to lease space to Phar-Mor (a discount pharmacy), Walgreens sought an injunction barring Sara Creek from doing so. Sara Creek argued that an injunction was inappropriate, because the damages to Walgreens based on lost sales were easily quantifiable (and presumably less than the additional profit to Sara Creek in leasing to Phar-Mor in breach of its lease contract with Walgreens). In contrast, Walgreens argued that its damages arising from the loss of goodwill and other intangibles were not reasonably quantifiable.

The court sought to weigh competing interests in deciding whether injunctive relief was appropriate. On one hand, the court agreed with Walgreens that a complete quantification of all damages would be difficult and further noted that granting an injunction might be the best means to determine damages. If the lease to Phar-Mor was worth more to Sara Creek than the loss to Walgreens, then presumably Sara Creek would negotiate an appropriate payment Walgreens to forego its right to enforce the injunction—thus quantifying damages in the process.

On the other, the court considered the cost of such an injunction. Any negotiation would be necessarily limited to Sara Creek and Walgreens, thereby inhibiting normal "market" based negotiations. Moreover, and injunction could have public costs (no discount pharmacy in the neighborhood) and might require continuing court supervision. In this case, the court nevertheless deemed the difficulty of quantifying damages and the benefits of an injunction outweighed its costs. Thus, the court determined injunctive relief to be appropriate.[2]

The foregoing example represents a classic case of "efficient" breach, and it reflects one of the basic challenges presented—who gets the windfall or "profit" arising from the breach?

Suppose the damages to Walgreens were fully quantifiable at $1 million, and further suppose that Sara Creek would reap to $2 million profit in leasing to Phar-Mor. Clearly, the Phar-Mor lease will result in an overall gain, but who should be entitled to that gain? If Walgreens receives $1 million in damages, then Sara Creek will keep the entire additional $1 million gain. In contrast, if Walgreens receives an injunction, then presumably, Walgreens will agree to forego enforcement for some price between $1 million and $2 million (e.g., at a price of $1.5 million, each party is $500,000 ahead as a result of the lease to Phar-Mor). The problem, as noted by the court, is that any negotiation is limited to these two parties (sometimes called a "bilateral monopoly"), which can easily lead to a stalemate if each party holds out for a greater share of the windfall, thereby potentially imposing costs on the public interest in having a local discount pharmacy.

On balance, the court in the foregoing case found the benefits of the injunction outweighed its potential costs. However, the court's analysis is also useful in further understanding the question of "efficient breach," as well as further understanding the relationship performance-based remedies and money damages.

---

[2] Walgreen Co. v. Sara Creek Property Co., 966 F.2d 273 (7th Cir. 1992).

Specific Performance under UCC Article 2

UCC Article 2 addresses specific performance in a manner consistent with the common law approach, but further liberalizes or expands the circumstances in which it may be appropriate. **STOP NOW and READ UCC § 2-716(1) below.**

UCC § 2-716(1)

(1) Specific performance may be decreed where the goods are unique or in other proper circumstances.

The Comments to § 2-716 make clear the intent of the statute to liberalize the circumstances under which specific performance is available, which retaining its essentially discretionary nature based on its equitable roots. Comment 2 further explains both "uniqueness" and "other proper circumstances."

OFFICIAL COMMENT 2 (UCC § 2-716)

2. . . . The test of uniqueness under this section must be made in terms of the total situation which characterizes the contract. Output and requirements contracts involving a particular or peculiarly available source or market present today the typical commercial specific performance situation, as contrasted with contracts for the sale of heirlooms or priceless works of art which were usually involved in the older cases. . . . [R]elief may also be granted "in other proper circumstances" and inability to cover is strong evidence of "other proper circumstances".

"Unique" goods might of course be analogized to real property. However, statute adds "other proper circumstances," and the comments clarify the intent to go beyond some traditional common law boundaries—especially in circumstances in which the aggrieved party is unable to arrange for a substitute ("cover") transaction in lieu of the breached performance obligation.

Consider the following examples.

Example 39-4: In Lesson 9, Problem 3, and Example 19-1, we earlier encountered Dr. Oswald, who was seeking to purchase the collection of original Swiss art held by Ms. Allen. In this example, we assume that they have concluded a contract and both live in the U.S. When the time comes to deliver the collection, Ms. Allen declines to perform, and Dr. Oswald seeks specific performance of their agreement.

The art represents goods, so the transaction is governed by UCC Article 2, and Dr. Oswald's request for specific performance is governed by UCC § 2-716(1). Inasmuch as a piece of original art is "unique" (much like land), Dr. Oswald will very likely be entitled to specific performance (absent any other countervailing equitable concerns), and Ms. Allen will be ordered to deliver the art in exchange for the agreement upon payment.

The foregoing is an "easy" case because an original work of art is, by definition, unique—and a collection of unique individual works arguably even more unique. Other circumstances may just as clearly fail to support specific relief.

Example 39-6: In this example, we again encounter our seller and buyer of cocoa beans from Example 37-2—in this case, a Texas seller and California buyer. If the Texas seller refuses to deliver cocoa beans, as promised, the buyer will not likely have a right to specific performance. As a "commodity," cocoa beans are not typically unique, and the disappointed buyer ought to be able to purchase beans from another seller in substitution for those promised by the Texas seller. We will see in Lesson 42 that the buyer will be entitled to recover for any difference between the contract price and the substitute purchase price, as damages.

However, even the sale of a basic commodity may justify an award of specific relief under certain circumstances.

Example 39-7: As in example 39-6, a Texas seller contracts to deliver cocoa beans to a California buyer, but subsequently refuses to perform. In this example, however, there is a global shortage of cocoa beans due to extraordinary weather events in multiple cocoa growing regions, and the California buyer is unable to cover.

Under these facts, a court is likely to grant the buyer's request under UCC § 2-716(1) based on "other proper circumstances," as indicated by the buyer's inability to cover. Of course, one might reasonably ask "what if the seller cannot itself perform because of this global shortage of cocoa beans caused by the weather? We will address that question in Chapter 9.

One might suggest that an inability to cover indicates that the circumstances are "unique," even if the goods are not. Other circumstances making cover difficult might include those involving output or requirements contracts or other long term supply contracts. A "spot" purchase or individual substitute purchase of goods—especially commodities if generally reasonably easy—it is simply a question of price. However, an aggrieved party may have a far more difficult time finding a substitute for a long term contract on which its business depends.

Performance Remedies under the CISG

The CISG provides broad access to performance based remedies, as a matter of legal right—and not simply judicial discretion based on equity. **STOP NOW and READ CISG Article 46 below.**

CISG ARTICLE 46

(1) The buyer may require performance by the seller of his obligations unless the buyer has resorted to a remedy which is inconsistent with this requirement.

(2) If the goods do not conform with the contract, the buyer may require delivery of substitute goods only if the lack of conformity constitutes a fundamental breach of contract and a request for substitute goods is made either in conjunction with notice given under article 39 or within a reasonable time thereafter.

(3) If the goods do not conform with the contract, the buyer may require the seller to remedy the lack of conformity by repair, unless this is unreasonable having regard to all the circumstances. A request for repair must be made either in conjunction with notice given under article 39 or within a reasonable time thereafter.

Article 46(1) provides a buyer with a near absolute right to performance by a non-performing seller, unless of course the buyer avoids the contract (avoidance being inconsistent with requiring performance). The issue of practical impossibility will be addressed later in Chapter 9. However, if performance is possible, then a buyer has a right to demand it under Article 46(1), without satisfying any further requirement.

Article 46(2) goes even further in allowing a buyer to demand delivery of substitute goods if the seller's initial delivery amounts to a fundamental breach. Alternatively, article 46(3) allows a buyer to require a seller to repair non-conforming goods, unless such repair is unreasonable under the circumstances ("repair" of course looks a great deal like "services," and such an order would be very unlikely under the common law).

While going much further in allowing performance than the common law or UCC Article 2, CISG Article 46 is actually very similar to the civil law upon which it is largely based. Predictably, common law countries were not entirely amenable to this distinctly "civilian" approach, so the drafters of the CISG reached a compromise. That compromise is reflected in Article 28. **STOP NOW and READ CISG Article 28 below.**

CISG ARTICLE 28

If, in accordance with the provisions of this Convention, one party is entitled to require performance of any obligation by the other party, a court is not bound to enter a judgment for specific performance unless the court would do so under its own law in respect of similar contracts of sale not governed by this Convention.

To some degree, Article 28 provides parties from common law countries with the "best of both worlds—the civil law approach of Article 46, as a buyer, and the common law approach under Article 28, as a seller. Consider the following two-part example.

> **Example 39-8:** We can take the basic cocoa contract in Example 39-6 and change the locations of the parties. First, we consider a Brazilian seller and a Florida buyer. If the seller does not deliver, the buyer is entitled to require performance of seller under Article 46(1). Such an order would likely be enforced in Brazil (where the seller is located), and Article 28 would not likely limit any such enforcement in Brazil's legal system based on civil law.
>
> In contrast, suppose the roles were reversed, with a Florida seller and a Brazilian buyer. If the seller failed to deliver, the buyer might again seek performance under Article 46(1). However, the buyer would likely have to enforce that order in Florida (the seller's location), and Florida courts would not likely enforce the order. Under UCC § 2-716(1), the buyer would not likely be entitled to specific performance. Thus, Article 28 of the CISG relieves the Florida court of any obligation to enforce the order issued under Article 46 of the CISG.

For a U.S. party buying and selling goods across national borders, the combination of Articles 46 and 28 may be legally advantageous. At the very least, such a party might want to consider the issue in making any choice of applicable law.

APPLYING THE RULES

Problem 1: In Lesson 25, and Problem 2, we addressed covenants not to compete. At the time, we focused on issues of enforceability, in any form. However, the form of enforcement—specific performance or damages will also often be at issue.

Judy has worked for Emma for three years, learning Emma's business methods and becoming well acquainted with her customers along the way. Judy's agreement for employment with Emma includes a promise not to compete for three years after termination. You may assume that the agreement is satisfactory with respect to any public policy concerns. Emma seeks an injunction barring Judy from opening her own business in competition with Emma. Judy argues that the public will benefit from greater competition, and Emma's lost sales are easily calculable. Emma, predictably, disagrees. What should you do as the judge considering the case?

Problem 2: Morris owned a cattle ranch and also raised horses. Sparrow was a cowboy experienced in training horses. The two contracted for Sparrow to perform specified work for Morris in exchange for $400 plus an unbroken brown horse named "Keno." While working on the ranch for Morris, Sparrow personally broke and trained Keno, turning him into a "first class roping horse." When Sparrow completed the job, Morris refused to turn over the horse, and Sparrow sought specific performance. The court found in favor of Sparrow on the basic contractual dispute (finding Morris in breach), thus squarely facing the question of an appropriate remedy. Morris argued that Sparrow was, at most, entitled to the value of a "first class roping house" (as a general matter, you may assume that such value was undisputed), while Sparrow argued that he was entitled to an order requiring Morris to deliver Keno. Who is right and why?

The facts of this problem are loosely based on the issues raised in the case of *Morris v. Sparrow*, 225 Ark. 1019, 287 S.W.2d 583 (1956)

Problem 3: Amoco and Laclede concluded a long term contract under which Amoco was to supply at an agreed price all propane requited by Laclede, which Laclede would in turn supply to homeowners. The homeowners needed the propane on an interim basis until such time as a natural gas supply was made available. As such, the contract was terminable by Laclede, but not by Amoco (until natural gas was available to all homes).

After a period of time, Amoco sought to terminate the contract, asserting that it lacked "mutuality." What issues of a purported lack of "mutuality" might Amoco have raised? Was Amoco right?

Whatever your answer above, assume Amoco's argument failed. Laclede then sought to preserve its supply of propane from Amoco. How should Laclede frame its request? Should a court grant the request? Why or why not? The following facts were stipulated. Propane is generally available, but price varies significantly over time in the relevant market. Natural gas is not yet available to the homes in question, and there is no clear timetable for such availability.

The facts of this problem are loosely based on the issues raised in the case of *Laclede Gas Co. v. Amoco Oil Co.*, 522 F.2d 33 (8th Cir. 1975).

Problem 4: Tamales, Inc. (TI) operates a chain of restaurants in Texas specializing in Tamales. TI buys all of its corn husks (the "wrap" for tamales) from Max, a Mexican supplier of food products. Max is well known in Texas for superior food products—especially corn husks for tamales—and TI notes this on its menus. In fact, Ted, a Texas food supplier sells exactly the same corn husks as Max (they come from exactly the same source—no difference).

Max fails to make an agreed delivery of corn husks to TI. Ted has plenty of corn husks available at the same price, but TI seeks an order in an appropriate Mexican court requiring Max to deliver. Is TI likely entitled to such an order?

Lesson 40: Seller's Damages—Common Law

Objectives and Expected Learning Outcomes

In this lesson, you will begin to learn the details of the basic rule for quantifying the "expectation" interest in terms of money damages. This lesson will focus on quantifying seller's damages for buyer's breach of a contract governed by the common law. You will also begin, in this lesson, to explore the details of an aggrieved party's obligation to minimize or reasonably "mitigate" "avoidable" damages, as well as the effect of a failure to do so. Finally, you will encounter a special application of restitution as a possible preferable alternative to expectation in certain unique circumstances.

Seller's Damages under the Common Law

The basic common law rule for quantifying "expectation" is clearly articulated in Restatement (Second) of Contracts § 347. The aggrieved or injured party is entitled to recover money damages measured by:

(a) the "loss in value" to him caused by the breach; AND

(b) any "other loss," including "incidental" and "consequential" loss, caused by the breach; BUT REDUCED BY

(c) any "cost avoided" or "loss avoided" by not having to perform.

The restatement articulation was sometimes expressed as formulae by the late E. Allan Farnsworth. The following reflect slight variations on two of the formulas he employed in addressing a seller's damages for a buyer's breach of a contract governed by the common law.[3]

(A) damages = loss in value – cost avoided + other loss – loss avoided

(B) damages = profit + actual cost incurred + other loss – loss avoided

---

[3] *See, e.g.,* E. Allan Farnsworth, Contracts, §§ 12.9, 12.10, at 768-770 (4th ed. 2004).

Formula A might be characterized as a "top down" approach, starting with the total contract price due, as reduced by unspent costs, while Formula B might be characterized as a "bottom up" approach, starting with seller's expected profit and adding any out-of-pocket expenses. Consider the following hypothetical requiring a very basic calculation of seller's damages.

The Basic Calculation

A contractor agrees to build a structure for 100 (percent, dollars, Euro, or whatever—it's a nice round number). The project owner changes her mind while the project is under construction, and the contractor ceases all work at her request. At that time, the contractor has actually incurred 50 in direct costs. By ceasing further work, the contractor has saved 30 in anticipated costs. The contractor had reasonably anticipated making 20 in profits (including overhead recovery) had the project been completed. These amounts are graphically illustrated below.

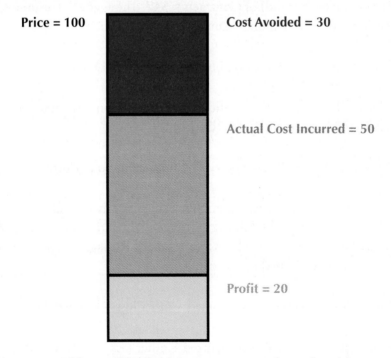

Price = 100   Cost Avoided = 30

Actual Cost Incurred = 50

Profit = 20

We can quickly see that the three amounts on the right add up to the total price or "value" of 100 promised to the contractor. In this hypothetical, we have no "other losses" or "losses avoided," which each apply in the same manner under Formula A or B. Thus, we can focus on the differences in these two formulas. Using Formula A, we begin with the loss in value (the price, at 100) and subtract the cost avoided (30), giving us a damage calculation of 70. Using Formula B, we begin with the expected profit (20) and add the actual costs incurred in performing (50), again giving us a total of 70.

In some cases, the use of Formula A or B may be dictated by available data. However, as illustrated by the foregoing diagram, the necessary data points for each can typically be calculated from the other. Ideally, one should use both as a means of verifying the result. If the results don't match, then there is necessarily an error in one or both of the calculations. While our initial focus is limited to loss in value, cost avoided, profit, and actual cost incurred (as used in Formulas A and B, respectively), we will also address "other loss" and "loss avoided" in the materials below. These latter two elements apply to both Formula A and B in exactly the same manner.

One further distinction is crucial to the above calculation—the difference between "fixed" "overhead" and "variable" costs or expenses. Certain costs are "fixed" in that they do not vary depending on the volume of work performed. For example, building rent is often "fixed," irrespective of the volume or work or revenue generated, as are many "administrative" salaries. The "fixed" costs are typically treated as "overhead" and allocated on some sort of basis to all sources of revenue. Thus, the more revenue generated, the lower the fixed cost per revenue source. In contrast, variable costs are just that—they vary directly with revenue produced because they arise specifically in relation to producing a particular source of revenue. These might include materials or labor needed to perform a service or construct a building.

When we speak of "profit" in the context of damages, we mean actual net profit (after all expenses), including reasonable overhead recovery. In effect, both profit and overhead recovery (or contribution) are essential elements of the seller's expectation. Thus, reasonable overhead recovery is included in Formula B in that it is treated as a part of "profit" (profit, including reasonable overhead recovery). We get the same result when addressing the issue under Formula A. We start with the loss in value (the full price, unless part of that price has already been paid), which of course includes an expected overhead recovery. From this loss in value, we subtract costs avoided, which include variable costs or expenses, but not overhead. Overhead is not subtracted from the loss in value precisely because it is fixed and not avoided as a result of ceasing work on any particular project. Thus, the recovery of reasonable overhead, included in lost value, and not subtracted as cost avoided, remains included in total damages.

The following example illustrates the basic application of Formulas A and B, as well as the distinction between fixed overhead and variable expenses.

> **Example 40-1:** Acme provides window tinting treatments for office buildings. Zenith contracts with Acme to tint all of the windows on a 20 story office building at a total price of $20,000. In preparation, Acme purchases tinting materials and hires the necessary workers (Acme uses "at-will" employees, as needed). In pricing the project, Acme reasonably expected to make a $3,000 net profit and to cover $1,000 of its business overhead (admin salaries, rent, etc.) reasonably allocated to this project.
>
> After Acme began working, Zenith decided to sell the building to a party intending to tear it down and redevelop the area. Acme was, therefore, instructed to cease working immediately. At that time, Acme had incurred actual labor costs of $5,000 and material costs of $2,000 in performing the window tinting work. Zenith has breached the contract, and Acme's damages may be calculated as follows:
>
> Formula B: Profit (3,000+1,000) + Actual Cost Incurred (5,000 + 2,000) = 4,000 + 7,000 = 11,000
>
> Formula A: Loss in Value (20,000) – Cost Avoided (?)
>
> The cost avoided is not provided above, but can be calculated by taking the project price (20,000) and subtracting the expected profit, including overhead (3,000 + 1,000), as well as the actual variable costs incurred (5,000 + 2,000), as follows: 20,000 – 4,000 – 7,000 = 9,000. Thus, we can return to Formula A.
>
> Loss in Value (20,000) – Cost Avoided (9,000) = 11,000

The data provided in the example made the calculation in Formula B somewhat easier here. However, the data for Formula A could also be calculated, and both calculations give us the same result. To be clear, the actual determination of the above referenced variables can often be quite challenging and will frequently require accounting experts. However, the basic principles are reasonably mastered by lawyers and allow for the proper use of expert accounting calculations.

One variation is worth noting, as it can otherwise be confusing, but can easily be mastered if properly understood. The earlier example assumed that the work preceded any payment. In fact, this is the normal default presumption, as addressed earlier in Chapter 7. However, many contracts for services will include provisions for advance or progress payments. Any such payment made prior to a breach will necessarily affect the calculations under Formulas A and B.

Under Formula A, any payment must be subtracted from the loss in value. In effect, any portion of the original price that has been paid prior to breach is not "lost" as a result of the breach. Under Formula B, any payment must be subtracted from the actual cost incurred. In effect, the actual cost incurred is a "net" amount—out-of-pocket variable expenses, less any amount received to date. Net actual costs incurred are thus properly reduced by any payment received. The following variation on Example 40-1 illustrates the issue.

> **Example 40-2:** Assume all of the same facts from Example 40-1, except that Zenith had made $6,000 in progress payments prior to the breach. Acme's damages may now be calculated as follows:
>
> Formula A: Loss in Value (20,000 – 6,000) – Cost Avoided (9,000) = 14,000 – 9,000 = 5,000
>
> Formula B: Profit (4,000) + Actual Cost Incurred (7,000 – 6,000) = 4,000 + 1,000 = 5,000

In Example 40-2, Acme's damages are $6,000 less than in Example 40-1, which makes perfect sense in view of the fact that Acme had already been paid $6,000 at the time of the breach.

Mitigation of Avoidable Damages

In each of the foregoing examples, the aggrieved party stopped working when instructed to do so by the breaching party, thereby reducing damages by the "cost avoided." However, one might reasonably ask whether this is required. In Example 40-1, Zenith contracted with Acme to do the entire job, so why should Acme not be allowed to complete the contract and receive the full price? The reason has to do with the idea of minimizing damages, while simultaneously protecting the aggrieved party's expectation interest. This principle of minimizing damages generally requires reasonable "mitigation" of "avoidable" damages and precludes any award for damages that were reasonably avoidable.[4] Perhaps the simplest and clearest example is the "passive" obligation to avoid running up damages unnecessarily, as illustrated by the following example.

Example 40-3: *Rockingham County v. Luten Bridge Co.*

Rockingham County (the "County") contracted with Luten Bridge Company ("Luten") to build a bridge for $18,000. Luten began building the bridge, but the County repudiated the contract after Luten had spent $2,000 on constructing the partially completed bridge. Luten ignored the County's communication and completed the bridge, suing for the agreed price of $18,000.

The appellate court declined, however, to award the full amount to Luten, pointing out that County had decided not to complete the road the bridge was to connect, thus leaving a "bridge to nowhere" in the middle of a forest. By completing the useless bridge, Luten has simply run up the damages unnecessarily.

If, for example, Luten had reasonably expected a profit of $3,000, then it should have simply stopped working and made a claim for $5,000 (you should be able to reach this amount yourself using Formula A or B). Inasmuch as its additional cost of $13,000 in completing the bridge could have (and should have) reasonably been avoided, its claim

---

[4] Restatement (Second) of Contracts § 350.

for the full price of $18,000 would have been reduced by that $13,000 amount to the proper measure of $5,000.[5]

Luten was precluded from recovering the additional damages that it could have reasonably avoided by simply stopping work. Note, however, that the obligation to mitigate avoidable damages is not a true "duty" that a party might breach. A failure to mitigate is not a breach of contract, itself subject to a counterclaim for damages by the original breaching party. Instead, it is an obligation that is required of a party seeking to preserve its right to recover its full expectation interest. While one often hears the term "duty to mitigate," this is not a true "duty" in the normal contractual sense.

Of course, in some circumstances, damages may actually be reduced or "mitigated" by completing the work. For example, where the market value of the completed project is increased by more than the additional cost of completing it, damages will actually be reduced by completing the contract—even in the face of a clear repudiation by the buyer. We will encounter an example of this in the context of a sale of goods under UCC § 2-704(2), addressed in Lesson 43.

You will note that the discussion of mitigation in the last paragraph involved a form of "active" mitigation (completing the project), as compared to "passive" mitigation (stopping work). In fact, mitigation may even require going beyond any actions required by the contract. We can return to Acme and Zenith for an example.

Example 40-4: When Zenith repudiated the contract, Acme had $1,200 worth of unused window treatment materials, which were included in the material costs Acme had incurred. Acme could reasonably sell those materials by paying a broker a commission of $200, thus reducing its overall loss. With this information at hand, we can now return to our original damages calculations from Example 40-1. Acme's damages may now be calculated as follows:

Formula B: Profit (4,000) + Actual Cost Incurred (7,000) + Other Loss (200 paid in commission) − Loss Avoided

---

[5] Rockingham County v. Luten Bridge Co., 35 F.2d 301 (4th Cir. 1929).

(1,200 from sale of unused materials) = 4,000 + 7,000 + 200 – 1,200 = 10,000

Formula A: Loss in Value (20,000) – Cost Avoided (9,000) = 11,000 + Other Loss (200) – Loss Avoided (1,200) = 10,000

As explained earlier in this lesson, any "other loss" or "loss avoided" is treated exactly the same under either Formula A or B. A "loss avoided" generally arises from a reduction in damages based on reasonable "active" mitigation (generally an act beyond what is required under the contract itself), as compared to a "cost avoided" through "passive" mitigation (generally declining to do something originally required under the contract because it is no longer beneficial). You may recall from the beginning of this lesson that Restatement (Second) of Contracts § 347(c) addresses both costs avoided and losses avoided.

An "other loss" may include either (or both) "incidental" or "consequential" damages. Restatement (Second) of Contracts § 347(b) addresses both. "Incidental" damages are those costs incurred incidental to dealing with the breach—and often involving mitigation of the effects of the breach. In Example 40-4, Acme incurred an incidental loss of the $200 commission as a direct result of its efforts to mitigate its damages by selling off $1,200 of unused materials it had purchased for the project. We will address "consequential" damages in the next Lesson, inasmuch as such damages are far more often suffered by buyers than sellers.

A seller may also be required to seek other work in mitigation of work lost as a breach by the buyer. For example, a contractor may be required to seek other work to replace that lost as a result of a project owner's breach. However, it may not always be easy to tell whether such work reflects "mitigation" of the losses incurred as a result of the breach or additional work the contractor would have done anyway. Consider the following example loosely based on a variation of a case encountered in Chapter 3.

Example 40-5: Drennan, a general contractor, subcontracted with Star for the paving work on a parking lot, but then repudiated the contract with Star (hiring someone who bid less for the work). Soon after Drennan repudiated the contract, Star got another contract to do some very similar paving work at a different school, but at exactly the same price as the original job with Drennan. Star sought to recover its lost profit on the job with Drennan. However, Drennan asserted that Star had no loss, because it obtained another identical paving job after Drennan breached, thereby mitigating its loss to zero.

Star's claim against Drennan will likely turn on whether Star would have and could have obtained the second job irrespective of Drennan's breach. In other words, was the second job truly a "replacement" for the first, or would Star have likely done the second job irrespective of Drennan's breach. Absent further facts, Star is likely to prevail, inasmuch as a contractor is generally presumed to be able to take on additional work by hiring additional labor and purchasing additional raw materials.

We will again encounter this same "lost volume" issue in the context of a sale of goods in Lesson 43. If a seller could have done both jobs at issue, then it cannot be said that the second job was in "mitigation" of the loss of the first. Instead, the seller lost one of two possible jobs and is entitled to recover the expected profit on the job lost. However, the same cannot generally be said for employees.

Example 40-6: Joe is employed by Kay as an accountant under a contract of employment for one year. After 6 months, Kay fires Joe in breach of the contract. Joe immediately finds another job at the same salary he had been paid by Kay. Unlike Star, in the prior example, Joe cannot likely recover from Kay, because the second job will likely be considered to be a replacement for the first—in effect, mitigating Joe's loss arising from Kay's breach.

In effect, the law generally assumes that an employee works one job (admittedly, an increasingly suspect assumption today); whereas, a business is generally presumed to have the ability to do additional work by simply expanding its capacity. As such, an employee's efforts to seek additional work after being wrongfully terminated are generally seen as required efforts at "mitigation." Of course, an employee need not necessarily take any job as a "replacement" for the one lost. As with mitigation generally, an aggrieved employee need only make "reasonable" efforts to mitigate his or her damages.

Restitution as an Alternative to Expectation?

Sometimes a seller of services, such as a building contractor, will enter into a "losing contract"—one in which it will lose money instead of making a profit. The reasons for this are multifold, but include everything from simple mistakes in bidding a project, to intentionally proposing to do work at a loss (as sometimes less injurious to a business than no work at all), to a change in circumstances affecting the cost of the job after contract formation. In many instances involving a losing contract, the aggrieved party may be better off seeking restitution than contract damages. Should the aggrieved party be allowed to choose the more favorable remedy? Consider the following example.

> **Example 40-7:** Let us return, one final time, to Acme and Zenith, in Example 40-1, but with one significant change. The project price remains $20,000, and at the time Zenith repudiated the contract, Acme had incurred actual costs of $7,000. However, in this variation on the example, Acme would have to spend another $15,000 to complete the project. We can immediately see that, if Acme completed the project, it would spend $22,000 in costs and would, therefore, lose $2,000 on the contract. This result is borne out by our Formulae, as follows:
>
> Formula A: Loss in Value (20,000) – Cost Avoided (15,000) = 5,000
>
> Formula B: Profit (-2,000) + Actual Cost Incurred (7,000) = 5,000
>
> In each case, Acme recovers $5,000, but has incurred $7,000 in out-of-pocket costs, thus ending up with its "expected" $2,000 loss.

Suppose, however, that the reasonable value of the work done by Acme at the time of breach was, in fact, $7,000 (exactly what it cost Acme to do the work). If so, Acme might seek restitutionary damages in the amount of $7,000 (instead of the $5,000 expectation damages), thereby at least "breaking even" on the project and avoiding its "expected" loss.

In effect, the availability of a restitutionary remedy, as an alternative to expectation damages, may provide a sort of "insurance policy" to an aggrieved seller in the event of a breach. Predictably, courts have sometimes struggled with this issue. The general rule allows the aggrieved seller to choose restitution if more favorable, unless the seller has fully performed (or nearly so).[6] To some degree, the rationale is that the amount of any expected profit under the contract may be difficult to ascertain if the breach occurs early in the project. In contrast, the actual expectation interest may be far more certain when the contract has been fully performed. Moreover, in the latter case, the equity of turning the breaching party into an insurer against the contractor's loss becomes more questionable. As with any equitable issue, the outcome may well turn on the specific circumstances of the individual case.

APPLYING THE RULES

Problem 1: Honest Abe's Use Cars contracts with Mary's Paint Shop to paint 25 of Abe's used cars for a total price of $5,000. Abe gets arrested for rolling back odometers (Mary knew nothing about this) and calls Mary, telling her to stop all work and return the cars in their current state—whatever that may be. Mary has expended $1,800 worth of labor and materials so far in painting the cars, and reasonably expected to make $2,000 (including profit and fixed overhead recovery) on the job. Mary was able to return $250 of the paint she had purchased to her supplier, but had to pay a $50 restocking charge when she did so. What are Mary's damages? Does the court need to know how much of the $2,000 was profit and how much was overhead? How, if at all, would Mary's damages change if Abe had paid $1,000 of the purchase price in advance?

---

[6] Restatement (Second) of Contracts § 373.

Problem 2: What if Mary got a call from Pam's Perfect Used Cars right after the above repudiation by Abe, and Mary and Pam contracted for Mary's Paint Shop to paint 10 used cars for Pam at a total price of $2,000, at an expected profit and overhead recovery to Mary of $800. Does the contract between Mary and Pam have any bearing on Mary's damages claim against Abe? What additional facts would you need to know?

Problem 3: Jane, the President of Acme Co., fires her secretary, Bob, in the middle of a two-year contract for employment at $40,000 per year. Bob immediately begins looking for employment and, 6 months later takes the first job offer he receives as a secretary at Zenith for $24,000 per year, for which Bob is required to pay a $300 fee to an employment agency. A year after taking the Zenith job, Bob is still working there and comes to you seeking advice on a breach of contracts suit against Acme. Assuming he can prove a contract and breach, what are Bob's damages?

Problem 4: Algernon Blair, Inc. (Blair) had a contract with the U.S. Government to construct a hospital, and Blair had contracted with Coastal Steel Erectors, Inc. (Coastal) to perform steel erection and to supply certain equipment in doing so. During the project, a dispute arose between Blair and Coastal over Blair's obligation to pay for certain equipment. After Blair refused to pay, Coastal refused to perform further, and Blair completed the job with another contractor. A court subsequently found that Blair was obligated to pay for the equipment and its refusal to do so was a material breach of its contract with Coastal, thereby justifying Coastal's subsequent termination of the contract.

The original contract price was $60,000. At the time the contract was terminated, Blair had paid Coastal $25,000 in progress payments. Coastal had actually spent $40,000 on the project to date, and reasonably expected to spend another $50,000 to complete the project. Assuming that the work done by Coastal was performed in a reasonable, cost-effective manner and was fully worth the amount actually expended by Coastal, how much is Coastal entitled to recover as damages as a result of Blair's breach?

The facts of this problem are loosely based on the issues raised in the case of United States v. Algernon Blair, Inc., 479 F.2d 638 (4th Cir. 1973).

Lesson 41: Buyer's Damages—Common Law

Objectives and Expected Learning Outcomes

In this lesson, you will focus on quantifying buyer's damages for seller's breach of a contract governed by the common law. You will learn a variety of means by which a buyer's "loss in value" may be quantified, and you will also learn to identify and quantify any "consequential" damages suffered by a buyer. Finally, you will learn about certain limits on a buyer's right to recover consequential damages and any actions required of a buyer to preserve its right to recover such damages.

Buyer's Damages under the Common Law

In addressing a buyer's damages under the common law, we begin with the same basic rule applied to seller's damages in the last Lesson. The Restatement (Second) of Contracts § 347 initially provides that the aggrieved buyer (like the aggrieved seller) is entitled to recover money damages measured by:

(a) the "loss in value" to him caused by the breach; AND

(b) any "other loss," including "incidental" and "consequential" loss, caused by the breach; BUT REDUCED BY

(c) any "cost avoided" or "loss avoided" by not having to perform.

The challenge, however, is that it is sometimes far more difficult to ascertain the buyer's "loss in value" than that of the seller.

A seller almost always loses money, which in most instances is relatively easy to quantify (even if accounting experts may be required in some cases). In contrast, a buyer loses the value of one or more elements of performance by the seller—for example, a service, a building project, or a parcel of land. Moreover, the buyer's loss is measured "subjectively." While extraordinarily individualized sentimental value may not be recognized, the measure of the loss generally focuses on the value to the individual aggrieved buyer—and not on a purely objective standard. While individual subjective value is typically irrelevant in measuring a seller's damages (money pretty much has the same value to all), the subjective value of any given performance by a seller can vary dramatically from one buyer to another.

There is another important difference between the damages typically incurred by a commercial buyer and seller. The seller generally makes its commercial "profit" on the transaction at issue—the difference between its selling price to the buyer and its cost of production or procurement. In contrast, the buyer generally makes its commercial "profit" on a subsequent transaction or transactions—utilizing the services (or goods) provided by the seller in the buyer's own business for production of services (or goods), or for resale of the purchased services (or goods) to another. When a buyer breaches its promise to pay, the seller's loss of profits is typically "direct," as it arises directly from the breached transaction. When a seller breaches its promise to provide services (or goods), the buyer's loss of profits is typically "indirect," as it arises from the loss of a separate subsequent transactional profit. Thus, the buyer's lost profits resulting from a seller's breach are generally characterized as "consequential" damages.

In addressing the foregoing challenges and others, the law provides a buyer with a variety of alternatives in measuring damages. The most significant of these alternatives are provided below.

The Basic Loss in Value

In some instances, an aggrieved buyer may simply be able to prove the loss in value—especially where that value can be determined objectively and the buyer's individual subjective value does not vary from the objective measure. Consider the following example.

> **Example 41-1:** Ms. Allen, our art dealer encountered in various earlier lessons, contracted with ArtRestore for the restoration of a painting Ms. Allen held in her inventory of art for resale. The painting was reasonably valued at $40,000 prior to restoration. Ms. Allen agreed to pay $25,000 upon successful completion of the restoration, and reasonably expected that the restored painting would sell for $100,000. During the restoration process, the painting was destroyed.

Ms. Allen is entitled to recover damages resulting from the breach based on her "expectation" interest in the value of the painting, as if fully restored. Her direct "loss in value" is $60,000—the difference between the original and restored value. She also suffered "consequential" damages of $40,000 as a result of the destruction of the original, but avoided the $25,000 cost of paying for the restoration. Thus, her damages would be $75,000.

We will focus on "consequential" damages in far more detail later in the lesson. However, this example illustrates a very simple and straightforward calculation of loss in value to a buyer (in this case, of art restoration services).

The calculation can become somewhat more challenging when the buyer's individual subjective value differs from an objective market valuation.

Example 41-2: Zoe contracted with ArtRestore for the restoration of a painting that was part of her personal collection of French impressionist art. She had been assembling the collection for much of her life, and this painting was her personal favorite—the centerpiece of the collection. The painting was destroyed during the restoration process. Whereas, Ms. Allen in Example 41-1 solely held the painting for resale, the value of the restoration service for which Zoe contracted was based on her own subjective perspective. Assuming that Zoe can establish that value with reasonable certainty, she will likely be entitled to recover based on her subjective valuation—even if greater than an objective market value of the same painting. The calculation of damages would otherwise be the same as in the prior example.

Of course, a buyer's right to recover for a subjective loss in value has its limits, and courts typically do not allow for recovery of losses based on purely sentimental value. For example, if Zoe had placed an extraordinarily high subjective value on the painting at issue because it had been painted by her great, great, great grandfather, it is doubtful that she could recover based on that value.

The Cost of Replacement

In the last section, the destruction of the original art work precluded simply hiring another person to restore the painting. However, when a seller fails to perform at all, an aggrieved buyer will often be able to contract for someone else to perform the desired promises.

> **Example 41-3:** Beth contracts with Able to remodel her living room. They agree on a specific set of plans and materials, as well as a price of $20,000. Before beginning the work, Able decides he bid it too low and tells Beth is in unwilling to do the work. Beth seeks an alternative contractor to do the work promised by Able, and concludes an agreement with Anne. The contract between Beth and Anne is identical to the earlier one, but the price is $30,000—a reasonable price for the work to be done.
>
> Beth's damages for Able's breach can easily be calculated based on her "loss in value," as determined by reference to Anne's price to do the same work, as reduced by the $20,000 originally promised to Able (Beth's "cost avoided" by not having to perform her obligation to pay Able).

Of course, the cost of a replacement performance is only a fair measure of an aggrieved party's loss in value if it is reasonable. An aggrieved party paying an unreasonably high price for a replacement service will have failed its obligation to mitigate its damages. And of course an unreasonably high price for a given service cannot be said to represent fairly the reasonable value of the service.

In the foregoing example, Beth's replacement contract with Anne serves as an easy means of determining her loss in value as a result of Able's breach. If Beth, instead, had to quantify the monetary value to her of the remodeling work, this might be very difficult. We can reasonably assume it was worth at least the $20,000 she agreed to pay Able, or she would not have concluded the original contract. However, it may be worth a great deal more. The difficulty comes in proving such a value with reasonable certainty (we will address this requirement of certainty in greater detail in Lesson 44). Of course, Beth may be able to do so in some circumstances. However, she avoids the issue entirely by contracting with Anne.

In this case, Beth receives the remodeling services she wanted in the first place (i.e., receiving something much like specific performance of the contract from an alternative source) and easily quantifies her damages resulting from Able's breach, so it is clearly in her interest to conclude the second contract with Anne. In some circumstances, however, Beth may actually be required to seek a replacement contract, as a means of mitigating her damages. We will explore this issue further below when we address consequential damages in greater detail.

The Cost of Completion or Repair

The cost of a reasonable substitute for a wholly unperformed promise will generally serve as a sound basis for quantifying the loss in value to an aggrieved buyer. However, the issue of replacement services often becomes more challenging in the case of "defective" work or work that has been begun, but not completed. The cost of remedying defective work may be significantly greater than its value, and changing circumstances may in some cases call into question the value of completing work left unfinished.

In such cases, the law seeks to balance the aggrieved buyer's right to complete performance or repair any defects with the economic value of doing so. The "framing" of the rule can be a bit tricky and is worth laying out in a series of detailed steps.

Summary of Basic Rule: Buyer's damages for a defective or unfinished project

- Buyer may recover the "loss in value" to the buyer (a largely subjective measure), if proven with reasonable certainty;[7]

    o If the buyer is unable to prove the "loss in value" with reasonable certainty, then the buyer may, instead, recover based on one of two alternative theories:[8]

        ▪ In any case, the buyer may recover any reduction in market value of the property caused by the unaddressed breach; or

        ▪ The buyer may alternatively recover the reasonable cost of completing performance or remedying any defects

---

[7] Restatement (Second) of Contracts § 347(a).
[8] Restatement (Second) of Contracts § 348(2).

> ▪ Unless the cost of doing so is clearly disproportionate to the probable loss in value to the buyer (necessarily an approximation or the buyer would have succeeded in proving the loss in value in the very first step)

To be clear, the relevant comparison in determining whether a buyer is entitled to complete or repair is not reduced market value versus the cost to complete or repair. It is the approximate (but insufficiently certain) loss to this particular buyer versus the cost to complete or repair. The market value reduction simply takes priority when the buyer's actual loss in value fails to bear any reasonable relationship to the cost of realizing that value.

The case of *Jacob & Youngs v. Kent*, first encountered in Lesson 33, is exemplary.

Example 41-4: *Jacob & Youngs v. Kent (redux)*

Jacob & Youngs breached its construction contract with Kent by using Cohoes instead of Reading pipe. Whatever the value of Reading pipe to Kent (presumably even any strong subjective preference for Reading over Cohoes pipe), the cost of tearing out the Reading pipe and replacing it with Cohoes pipe was clearly disproportionate to any loss in value suffered by Kent as a result of the breach.

Thus, the court declined to award the cost of replacing the pipe, instead limiting Kent's recovery to any loss in the market value of his home and explaining "[i]n the circumstances of this case, we think the measure of the allowance is not the cost of replacement, which would be great, but the difference in value, which would be either nominal or nothing."[9]

Of course, the difference in project market value will often be more than "nominal." However, a buyer will be limited to such difference whenever the cost to remedy the problem is clearly disproportionate to the buyer's actual loss.

---

[9] Jacob & Youngs v. Kent, 230 N.Y. 239, 129 N.E. 889 (1921).

Consequential Damages

"Consequential" damages come in a variety of forms. As the name implies, such damages arise as a natural "consequence" of the breach. One might think of dominoes in which the toppling of one pushes over the next, and so on. In describing common law damages, however, the term is generally limited to effects beyond the actual contract at issue. One classic example involves personal injuries caused by defective performance.

> **Example 41-5:** We can return to Beth and Anne in Example 41-3, and their contract for remodeling (which happened to be a replacement for Beth's contract with Able, but is also of course itself a separate contract). Anne performed all of the work, and Beth paid the agreed $30,000. However, about a week later, a defective piece of the new ceiling installed by Anne fell on Beth injuring her.
>
> The defective work by Anne is undoubtedly a breach, and Beth will very likely be able to recover the cost of repairing the ceiling (assuming of course it is not clearly disproportionate to the value of a proper ceiling to Beth). This recovery of the cost of repair—as a surrogate for "loss in value"—involves what are often called "direct" damages. Anne promised a properly remodeled ceiling, and Beth did not receive one.
>
> While Anne did not likely promise Beth that she would not be injured by Anne's remodeling work, Beth's injury certainly arose as a natural "consequence" of Anne's defective work. Thus, Beth will also be entitled to recover for her personal injuries as "consequential" damages.

These sorts of consequential damages—external to the contract breach, but fully a consequence of that breach—will often involve injury to person or property. In Example 41-1, we saw an illustration of injury to a painting, as property.

As indicated at the outset of this lesson, "consequential" damages are also common in commercial transactions in which a buyer is often purchasing something for use in a subsequent transaction, series of transactions, or broader enterprise. If the seller fails to perform, the most significant financial loss to the buyer will often involve the peripheral financial effects, occurring as a natural consequence of the breach.

> **Example 41-6:** In this example, Beth contracts with Arthur to remodel her factory production floor, installing a new fully robotic assembly line. She explains that it is absolutely essential that Arthur complete the work by May 1, because she has a contract to deliver a very large order for the products to be produced on this new assembly line. If Arthur is late in completing the work, it will very quickly cost her more in lost profits than the entire price of the contract with Arthur. All of this is clearly spelled out in the contract, and Arthur is fully aware of the potential consequential damages at issue.
>
> If Arthur fails to perform by May 1, and Beth loses sales as a result, then Arthur will very likely be liable for Beth's loss of profits on the sales at issue, as well as any other associated damages arising as a "consequence" of Arthur's breach.

As noted earlier, the seller's loss of "profits" generally arises directly from the contract at issue, while the buyer's loss of "profits" will generally involve other, peripheral transactions. The foregoing example also raises a number of additional issues. Inasmuch as consequential damages are external to the contract actually breached, they can often be far greater in amount than the value of the contract at issue. Recall Example 23-2, in which we encountered a very common limitation of liability on the back of a coat check stub. Predictably, someone checking your coat for a couple of dollars does not want to be liable for the loss of a $1,000 garment.

In fact, limitations on consequential damages are quite common in many contexts because of the relatively "open ended" nature of such damages. In Lesson 44, we will address the effectiveness of express limitations on damages, generally. In the next section, we will also address a default limitation provided by law. First, however, we must address the issue of mitigation of consequential damages.

Suppose, in Example 41-6 that Arthur's work runs into extraordinary difficulties and is likely to run significantly beyond the May 1 completion date. Should Beth be required to consider alternative substitute sources of production in the interim? Predictably, the answer is yes, if reasonable under the circumstances. Assuming that Beth is able to arrange for alternate production, she would of course be entitled to recover any additional costs, including the cost of arranging for such an alternative. As you should recall from the last lesson, the costs associated with active efforts to mitigate damages are recoverable as "incidental" damages. In effect, such costs are often incurred "incidental" to proactive efforts by the aggrieved party to mitigate losses.

Thus, we can see that, while "consequential" and "incidental" damages are each recoverable under the common law as "other losses," they are actually quite different in nature. Consequential damages are typically those losses external to the contract at issue that naturally occur as a result of the breach, while incidental damages include those costs incurred in mitigation of the aggrieved party's damages—including (though certainly not limited to) consequential damages. We will further explore the requirement of mitigation, as related to consequential damages, in the next lesson. For now, we will move on to the limit on consequently damages based on foreseeability.

Foreseeability as a Limit on Consequential Damages

The following classic case beautifully illustrates the potential perils of consequential damages and a limitation designed to encourage parties to communicate unexpected risks.

FROM THE COURT

Hadley v. Baxendale

Court of Exchequer (1854)
9 Exch. 341, 156 Eng. Rep. 145

[Hadley operated a mill in Gloucester. When the crankshaft on a steam engine at the mill broke, the broken shaft had to be sent to Greenwich as a model for a new one. Until the new shaft arrived, however, the mill was fully inoperative. Hadley sent one of the employees of the mill to arrange with Baxendale (d/b/a Pickford & Co.) for carriage of the shaft to Greenwich at a price of £ 2 and 4 shillings. However, Baxendale failed to deliver the shaft by the agreed upon date, and the mill was shut down for several additional days, losing additional profits many times greater than the cost of the carriage. Hadley sued for its losses caused by carrier's breach, including consequential damages based on the profits lost as a result of the additional days the mill was shut down. A jury granted Hadley's claim, and Baxendale appealed.]

[The court began by noting the basic remedy of expectation, explaining that] "there is a clear rule, that the amount which would have been received if the contract had been kept, is the measure of damages if the contract is broken."

Now we think the proper rule in such a case as the present is this: Where two parties have made a contract which one of them has broken, the damages which the other party ought to receive in respect of such breach of contract should be such as may fairly and reasonably be considered either arising naturally, *i.e.*, according to the usual course of things, from such breach of contract itself, or such as may reasonably be supposed to have been in the contemplation of both parties, at the time they made the contract, as the probable result of the breach of it. Now, if the special circumstances under which the contract was actually made were communicated by the plaintiffs to the defendants, and thus known to both parties, the damages resulting from the breach of such a contract, which they would reasonably contemplate, would be the amount of injury which would ordinarily follow from a breach of contract under these special circumstances so known and communicated. But, on the other hand, if these special circumstances were wholly unknown to the party breaking the contract, he, at the most, could only be supposed to have had in his contemplation the amount of injury which would arise generally, and in the great multitude of cases not affected by any special circumstances, from such a breach of contract. For, had the special circumstances been known, the parties might have specially provided for the breach of contract by special terms as to the damages in that case; and of this advantage it would be very unjust to deprive them. Now the above principles are those by which we think the jury ought to be guided in estimating the damages arising out of any breach of contract. . .

Now, in the present case, if we are to apply the principles above laid down, we find that the only circumstances here communicated by the plaintiffs to the defendants at the time of the contract was made, were, that the article to be carried was the broken shaft of a mill, and that the plaintiffs were the millers of the mill. But how do these circumstances shew reasonably that the profits of the mill must be stopped by an unreasonable delay in the delivery of the broken shaft by the carrier to the third person? Suppose the plaintiffs had another shaft in their possession put up or putting up at the time, and that they only wished to send back the broken shaft to the engineer who made it; it is clear that this would be quite consistent with the above circumstances, and yet the unreasonable delay in the delivery would have no effect upon the intermediate profits of the mill. Or, again, suppose that, at the time of the delivery to the carrier, the machinery of the mill had been in other respects defective, then, also, the same results would follow. Here it is true that the shaft was actually sent back to serve as a model for the new one, and that the want of a new one was the only cause of the stoppage of the mill, and that the loss of profits really arose from not sending down the new shaft in proper time, and that this arose from the delay in delivering the broken one to serve as a model. But it is obvious that, in the great multitude of cases of millers sending off broken shafts to third persons by a carrier under ordinary circumstances, such consequences would not, in all probability, have occurred; and these special circumstances were here never communicated by the plaintiffs to the defendants.

It follows therefore, that the loss of profits here cannot reasonably be considered such a consequence of the breach of contract as could have been fairly and reasonably contemplated by both the parties when they made this contract. For such loss would neither have flowed naturally from the breach of this contract in the great multitude of such cases occurring under ordinary circumstances, nor were the special circumstances, which, perhaps, would have made it a reasonable and natural consequence of such breach of contract, communicated to or known by the defendants. The Judge ought, therefore, to have told the jury that upon the facts then before them they ought not to take the loss of profits into consideration at all in estimating the damages. There must therefore be a new trial in this case.

CASE QUESTIONS

(1) Why does the court provide for an exception to the general rule of expectation in the case of consequential damages? It was clear that if the carrier had performed the contract, as promised, the mill would not have lost the profits at issue.

(2) What is the nature of the precise rule announced in this case?

    a. Is the carrier liable if a broken shaft would in the majority of circumstances, generally, shut down a mill pending the return of a new one?

    b. Is the carrier liable if the mill actually told the carrier specifically what was at stake here and why?

    c. Is the carrier liable if it neither (a) nor (b) is satisfied?

    d. Why are these limitations on recovery of consequential damages important? What is the objective of the rule of this case?

The rule of Hadley is often referred to as a "penalty" default, as compared to the more typical "majoritarian" default rule. The idea of the rule, as a penalty, is to encourage the buyer to share with the seller any information indicating the potential for unusual or unique consequential damages, thereby allowing the seller to consider such a possibility in the contracting process.

We can thus summarize the basic rules regarding consequential damages.

Summary of Basic Rule: the buyer's right to consequential damages

- "Consequential" damages are losses involving events and circumstances external to the contract at issue, but occurring as a natural consequence of the breach;

- Such damages are recoverable, as an element of the aggrieved party's expectation interest, except where:

  ○ The resulting losses were not foreseeable as a probable consequence of the breach based on either

    ▪ The ordinary course of events surrounding the contract and its breach, or

    ▪ Special circumstances of which the breaching party had reason to know.[10]

  ○ Or where the losses could have avoided by reasonable efforts at mitigation (most typically a replacement transaction).[11]

APPLYING THE RULES

Problem 1: Willie and Lucille Peevyhouse owned 60 acres of farmland containing coal deposits and leased the farmland to Garland Coal for 5 years for the purpose of strip-mining coal. Garland was entitled to perform surface mining of the coal in exchange for lease payments to the Peevyhouses. The lease contract also included a promise by Garland to perform restorative and remedial work to return the farm, largely, to its original condition, prior to the mining operation. The Peevyhouses also owned another 100 acres adjacent to the leased land, on which they had built a house and pastured livestock. They insisted on the restoration and remediation provision in negotiating the contract with Garland and indicated that they would not agree to lease the 60 acres in question without it.

---

[10] Restatement (Second) of Contracts § 351
[11] Restatement (Second) of Contracts § 350.

Both parties fully performed all of their obligations under the lease, except for one. Garland refused to perform the promised restorative and remedial work. The cost of the work was $29,000, and the effect of failing to perform the work was to reduce the market value of the 60 acres by $300 (the entire 60 acre parcel was worth less than $1,000 after the mining operation had been completed—it had been worth $3,600 prior to the mining operation). However, the land was left with open mining scars and the water upstream of the other 100 acre parcel owned by the Peevyhouses had been polluted.

The Peevyhouses sued for breach. How would you argue the damages issue on behalf of Garland? How would you argue on behalf of Peevyhouse? What sort of testimony would you seek to elicit from the Peevyhouses? Who should prevail?

The facts of this problem are loosely based on the issues raised in the case of *Peevyhouse v. Garland Coal & Mining Co.*, 382 P.2d 109 (Okla. 1963).

Problem 2: Groves and John Wunder Co. (Wunder) each owned and operated sand and gravel pits. In 1927, Groves leased a parcel of undeveloped land to Wunder for 7 years for the purpose of removing sand and gravel. Wunder agreed to pay Groves $105,000 over the term of the lease, and further promised to leave the property at a uniform grade at road level, using fill as necessary. Both parties fully performed all of their obligations under the lease, except for one. Wunder refused to perform the promised grading. The cost of the work was $60,000, and the effect of failing to perform the work was to reduce the market value of the parcel by $12,000. During this same 7 year period, the overall market value of the parcel had fallen dramatically (the "Great Depression" took place during this time period).

Groves sued for breach. How would you argue the damages issue on behalf of Wunder? How would you argue on behalf of Groves? Who should win?

Should it matter whether Groves would use any damages award to perform the actual grading? If so, how might a court give appropriate weight to this issue in fashioning a remedy for the breach? Think back to Lesson 39.

The facts of this problem are loosely based on the issues raised in the case of Groves v. John Wunder Co., 205 Minn. 163, 286 N.W. 235 (1939).

Problem 3: Beach City operated a small College (BCC) that partially offset is operating costs (thereby reducing student tuition) by hosting professional conferences (e.g., doctors, lawyers, bankers, government leaders, etc.) on weekends. Beach City was a very popular destination for tourism, so the conferences were very financially lucrative. Each of these conferences used the BCC auditorium for large presentations, and BCC had equipped it with the latest in multimedia presentation technology. While spectacularly effective when it worked, this presentation system was very expensive to fix when it did not—especially on short notice. BCC therefore concluded an annual service contract with FastFix, a regional presentation technology repair service in Center City. BCC paid FastFix $1,800 per year for the service, and FastFix guaranteed in the contract that any service request would be satisfactorily completed within 24 hours of receipt.

On Friday morning, at 7 AM, BCC notified FastFix that its presentation system was not working and requested immediate repair service pursuant to the contract. FastFix indicated that its technical staff had been hit unusually hard by a flu bug, and it had also just received three earlier requests that morning—all involving major extended repair projects. As a result, there was simply no way that FastFix could respond to BCC's request until Sunday morning.

BCC has a conference scheduled on Saturday and Sunday that will generate $30,000 in revenue, but absolutely requires the use of the currently broken multimedia presentation technology. If the conference cannot be held as planned, BCC will not only lose the revenue, but will likely be sued for breach of contract by the conference organizers. BCC might be able to find someone else to repair the system in time, but it would likely cost $3,000 to $5,000 on such short notice, and it may not be possible at all within the needed time frame. At 7:15 AM, the BCC President calls you for legal advice (as a dedicated lawyer, you gave her your cell phone number). First, she wants to know what to do. She really does not want to spend up to $5,000, when she contracted for an entire year worth of service at $1,800. Second, she is worried about the potential cancellation of the conference and wants to know if she will be able to sue FastFix for any losses. The contract contains no other relevant provisions.

What is your advice?

Problem 4: Big is a manufacturer of widgets, while Sally is an individual. Each contracts with Coding Corp. for custom software—Big to run its production process and Sally to automate everything in her home to be fully responsive to her voice and only her voice. Coding Corp. begins both jobs, but fails to complete either. What sorts of legal issues might you expect to arise in each case? How would they likely differ? How would they likely be similar?

Lesson 42: Buyer's Damages—Sales of Goods

Objectives and Expected Learning Outcomes

In this lesson, you will learn to quantify the buyer's damages for seller's breach of a contract for the sale of goods. In doing so, you will learn to distinguish between circumstances in which the buyer retains the goods and those in which buyer does not. You will also learn more about distinguishing between incidental and consequential damages, as well as limitations on the latter based on the requirement of mitigation. At the end of the lesson, you will have an opportunity to apply the various statutory rules in calculating a buyer's damages under various factual scenarios.

Introduction to Buyer's Damages under UCC Article 2

The remedial provisions of Article 2 addressing damages are largely consistent with the common law principles addressed in the last two lessons. In fact, the statute confirms, in Article 1, that it is firmly grounded upon the basic expectation interest. **STOP NOW and READ UCC § 1-305(a) below.**

UCC § 1-305(a)

(a) The remedies provided by [the Uniform Commercial Code] must be liberally administered to the end that the aggrieved party may be put in as good a position as if the other party had fully performed but neither consequential or special damages nor penal damages may be had except as specifically provided in [the Uniform Commercial Code] or by other rule of law.

However, the statutory provisions are predictably more highly structured and contain greater detail in addressing the right to recover damages for breach of a contract for the sale of goods. Before exploring the buyer's right to damages under Article 2 in detail, it is useful to step back and look broadly at the buyer's options in response to a seller's breach.

If the seller fails to perform at all, the buyer may, in some cases, seek specific performance, as addressed earlier in Lesson 39. Even if specific relief is granted, however, the buyer may nevertheless suffer damages, such as losses arising from any delay in delivery of the goods. These losses are recoverable under provisions addressing circumstances in which the buyer ends up retaining the goods. If the buyer, instead, decides to cancel the contract, then the buyer's damages will be recoverable under provisions addressing circumstances in which the buyer does not retain the goods.

If the seller attempts to perform, but makes a non-conforming tender, the buyer may, depending on the circumstances, retain the goods or decline to do so (either rejecting them or revoking an earlier acceptance). Again, the provisions governing the buyer's right to damages will depend on whether or not the buyer has retained the goods. Thus, our initial analysis of buyer's damages is broken down into two basic categories—those in which the buyer retains the goods and those in which the buyer does not retain the goods. We begin with the latter.

Buyer's Damages When the Buyer Does Not Retain the Goods

In many, though not all, instances of a breach by seller, the buyer will be entitled to refuse to retain or pay for the goods and cancel the contract. Lesson 34, along with subsequent lessons in Chapter 7, addressed the buyer's right to cancel the contract. The same statutory provision also addresses the cancelling buyer's damages. **STOP NOW and READ UCC § 2-711(1) below.**

UCC § 2-711(1)

(1) Where the seller fails to make delivery or repudiates or the buyer rightfully rejects or justifiably revokes acceptance then with respect to any goods involved, and with respect to the whole if the breach goes to the whole contract (Section 2-612), the buyer may cancel and whether or not he has done so may in addition to recovering so much of the price as has been paid

(a) "cover" and have damages under the next section [§ 2-712] as to all the goods affected whether or not they have been identified to the contract; or

(b) recover damages for non-delivery as provided in this Article (Section 2-713).

Thus, the canceling buyer has two alternative bases for claiming damages. The buyer can arrange for a substitute or "cover" purchase, and claim the price difference as damages, or the buyer can simply claim the difference between market and contract price. The latter might in some respects be viewed as a "hypothetical" cover transaction at market price. However, there are significant differences with respect to the two approaches as affecting the right to consequential damages.

Buyer's Damages Based on a "Cover" Transaction

A "cover" purchase is a purchase in substitution of the buyer's original contract with the seller. **STOP NOW and READ UCC § 2-712 below.**

UCC § 2-712

(1) After a breach within the preceding section the buyer may "cover" by making in good faith and without unreasonable delay any reasonable purchase of or contract to purchase goods in substitution for those due from the seller.

(2) The buyer may recover from the seller as damages the difference between the cost of cover and the contract price together with any incidental or consequential damages as hereinafter defined (Section 2-715), but less expenses saved in consequence of the seller's breach.

(3) Failure of the buyer to effect cover within this Section does not bar him from any other remedy.

Comment 2 to § 2-712 describes the liberal approach encouraging cover under UCC Article 2.

OFFICIAL COMMENT 2 (UCC § 2-712)

2. The definition of "cover" under subsection (1) envisages a series of contracts or sales, as well as a single contract or sale; goods not identical with those involved but commercially usable as reasonable substitutes under the circumstances of the particular case; and contracts on credit or delivery terms differing from the contract in breach, but again reasonable under the circumstances. The test of proper cover is whether at the time and place the buyer acted in good faith and in a reasonable manner, and it is immaterial that hindsight may later prove that the method of cover used was not the cheapest or most effective.

. . .

This liberal approach to the issue of cover is fully consistent with the general principle encouraging reasonable efforts to mitigate damages. The basic test is one of reasonableness rather than perfection.

As often typical with mitigation, generally, the buyer will frequently incur "incidental" costs related to arranging for a cover transaction. As indicated in § 2-712(2), such incidental damages are recoverable under § 2-715. **STOP NOW and READ UCC § 2-715(1) below.**

UCC § 2-715(1)

(1) Incidental damages resulting from the seller's breach include expenses reasonably incurred in inspection, receipt, transportation and care and custody of goods rightfully rejected, any commercially reasonable charges, expenses or commissions in connection with effecting cover and any other reasonable expense incident to the delay or other breach.

As indicated in earlier lessons, incidental damages are not in any way limit to efforts to mitigate and may arise in a variety of other contexts in which the buyer incurs unexpected costs in responding to the seller's breach. However, the process of cover is certainly one of the more contexts for such damages.

Finally, the buyer's damages are of course reduced by any expenses saved in consequence of the seller's breach. The following example illustrates the basic operation of "cover" and the resulting calculation of damages, including incidental damages, but less any expenses saved as a result of the breach.

> **Example 42-1:** A Wyoming wholesale fruit distributor contracted with a Florida grower to purchase 20 metric tons of oranges at $1,000 per metric ton. The Florida harvest was less abundant that projected, and the seller failed to deliver. The buyer then arranged for a replacement transaction with a California grower (the California harvest had been much better) at a price of $1,050 per metric ton. The buyer was required to pay a brokerage commission of $500 to arrange for the California transaction, but the transportation costs were $300 less than from Florida.
>
> The buyer is entitle to recover $1,000 as the difference between the cover purchase price and the original contract price (20 x 50), plus incidental damages of $500 based on the brokerage commission, but less the $300 saved on transportation. Thus, the buyer is entitled to $1,200 (1,000 + 500 – 300).

While Florida and California orange growers would likely say that their oranges are not the same, California oranges would certainly seem to be a commercially reasonable substitute for Florida oranges—especially where the latter were in short supply due to a lower than expected harvest. In contrast, common sense would tell us that Florida grapefruits would not likely be deemed a commercially reasonable substitute for Florida oranges. While both are "citrus," they are distinctly different products. As indicated by the statutory language and comment, the test is one of commercial reasonableness under the circumstances.

A reasonable cover transaction will almost always provide the buyer with an easy means of proving damages and will often preserve the buyer's other commercial relationships dependent on the failed transaction at issue. We will also see below that a failure to arrange for a reasonably available cover transaction may bar the buyer from recovering consequential damages in some cases. However, the failure to arrange for cover will not—as a general matter—bar other remedies. Specifically, a buyer that chooses not to cover will always be able to seek damages based on market price, as explained in the next section below.

Buyer's Damages Based on Market Price

If the buyer decides not to arrange a "cover" transaction, the buyer may nevertheless claim damages based on the difference between market price (i.e., a "hypothetical" cover price) and the contract price. **STOP NOW and READ UCC § 2-713 below.**

UCC § 2-713

(1) Subject to the provisions of this Article with respect to proof of market price (Section 2-723), the measure of damages for non-delivery or repudiation by the seller is the difference between the market price at the time when the buyer learned of the breach and the contract price together with any incidental and consequential damages provided in this Article (Section 2-715), but less expenses saved in consequence of the seller's breach.

(2) Market price is to be determined as of the place for tender or, in cases of rejection after arrival or revocation of acceptance, as of the place of arrival.

In the case of cover, the buyer recovers based on the difference between the cover price and the market price. Without actual cover, the market price serves as a surrogate reflecting the buyer's legal right to cover and, therefore, compensates the buyer for the difference between market and contract price.

The following example illustrates a basic calculation in the absence of cover.

Example 42-2: A Wyoming wholesale fruit distributor contracted with a Florida grower to purchase 20 metric tons of oranges at $1,000 per metric ton, all costs and risk of delivery to be borne by seller. The seller delivered oranges that were rotten when they reached the buyer (and bore the risk of spoilage in transit—a subject we will explore further in Chapter 9). The buyer rightfully rejected the non-conforming oranges under § 2-601, but declined to arrange for a cover transaction (as it turned out, the buyer had plenty of oranges to meet is sales obligations at the time). However, the market price of Florida oranges was $1,100 at the time of delivery (having risen since contract formation).

The buyer is entitled to recover $2,000 as the difference between the current market price and the original contract price. In this case, there are no other damages, and buyer saved nothing as a result of the breach.

Of course, the buyer's damages would be reduced by any savings resulting from the breach (e.g., if buyer had been obligated to pay for transportation in the foregoing example), and the buyer would be entitled to recover incidental and consequential damages, subject to the limitations discussed later in this lesson.

At the beginning of Lesson 41, we drew a distinction between commercial sellers and buyers, noting that the former typically expected profits in any given contract at issue, while the buyer typically expected to make money in ancillary or subsequent transactions. In a sale of goods, the seller sells the goods to the buyer for more than they cost the seller (either the cost of acquisition or manufacture), thus making a profit, while the buyer makes any profit by either reselling the goods to another buyer (for more than it paid the seller) or using the goods in some sort or manufacturing or services business transaction with the expectation of making a profit therefrom. As such, it is important to distinguish a buyer's expectation in the breached contract at issue, as separate and distinct from any expectation based on associated contracts (e.g., contract for resale, etc.).

Buyer's expectation in purchasing from seller is to gain a financial advantage by owning certain goods at a specific agreed price. The buyer may or may not choose to use the goods in some particular manner after acquiring them. However, assuming the seller performs as agreed, seller has no interest or right in defining how the buyer uses the goods (absent some other contractual or intellectual property restriction). If the seller breaches, then the buyer has a right to a remedy that approximates that financial advantage as closely as possible. In the absence of cover, an award based on the difference between market and contract price is reasonably reflective of the buyer's expected financial advantage, as reflected in the parties' contract terms.

The following example brings out an issue that has challenged some lawyers and courts that have failed to recognize this important distinction.

> **Example 42-3:** Wes, our Wyoming orange purchaser, has a contract with Flo, our Florida grower, to purchase oranges, priced at $1,000 per metric ton, delivered to Wes in Wyoming. Wes then contracts to resell the oranges to Walt at $1,010 per metric ton. As it happens, Wes is trying to build his business relationship with Walt, and he is willing to take a very "thin" profit on the deal. However, Flo fails to deliver the oranges as agreed, and the market price at the time is $1,050 per metric ton. It turns out that Walt does not need the oranges (and Wes has no interest in suing Walt and is happy to terminate their contract by mutual agreement), so Wes declines to cover.
>
> Wes asserts a damages claim of $50 per metric ton against Flo under § 2-713. However, Flo argues that can recover no more than his expected profit of $10 per metric ton (on the contract with Walt), as provided by § 1-305(a). After all, if Flo, Wes, and Walt had all fully performed, Wes would have ended up with only $10 in "profits" at the end of the day. Who is right?

The above question has generated considerable discussion and confusion. However, the author's view is that Wes is clearly right, and one need only recognize the distinction between the two transactions to see this. The question is who gets the windfall benefit of the $50 appreciation on the price of oranges since the contract was concluded.

When a buyer and seller make a forward contact for sale, it is a form of a "bet" (as earlier pointed out in Example 25-1), in which the buyer bets the market price will rise or at least remain constant, and the seller bets the market price will fall or at least remain constant. In this case, Wes won his bet and is entitled to recover the price increase based on his expectation under the contract that Flo breached. The contract between Wes and Walt has no bearing on the contract between Wes and Flo, unless Wes asserts a right to consequently damages. In fact, Wes has fully waived his profit under the contract with Walt by declining to enforce it. However, he has in no way waived his right to recover against Flo.

You will have the chance to try your own hand at a case addressing the foregoing issue (and you can compare your analysis with that of the reviewing court) in the Problems that follow this lesson. For now, however, we will turn our attention to the issue of consequential damages.

Buyer's Right to Consequential Damages

In the last section, we ended with a focus on the nature of a commercial buyer's typical uses for purchased goods. Most often, the buyer will intend to use the goods in some sort of ancillary transaction. The buyer may resell the goods or may use them in some sort of manufacturing process (either as production line equipment or raw materials) or in providing some sort of a service.

In many cases, the seller's breach will cause by far the greatest losses to the buyer in these ancillary transactions. Thus, the right to recover "consequential" damages may be very important to the buyer. We will often see in Lesson 44 that the seller will often seek to limit or eliminate such damages, by contract. **STOP NOW and READ UCC § 2-715(2) below.**

UCC § 2-715(2)

(2) Consequential damages resulting from the seller's breach include

    (a) any loss resulting from general or particular requirements and needs of which the seller at the time of contracting had reason to know and which could not reasonably be prevented by cover or otherwise; and

    (b) injury to person or property proximately resulting from any breach of warranty.

Subsection (2)(b) is of course the clearest and simplest part of the provision. The seller is liable for consequential injuries to person or property, without limitation. All other losses, however, are limited in two significant ways—very much akin to the limits on consequential damages we encountered in the last lesson.

First, we see a limit based on foreseeability—much like the common law rule of *Hadley v. Baxendale*. Second, we see a limit based on the principle of mitigation. The buyer is precluded from recovering for consequential damages that could have reasonably been prevented by cover (or otherwise). Of course, the most typical issue of mitigation will arise in circumstances in which the buyer does not cover and sues for its loss of profits on a subsequent transaction.

> **Example 42-4:** Zenith Computers contracts to buy a new "state-of-the-art" chip from Alpha Electronics. Zenith has contracted with many of its own customers to sell a new computer using the new Alpha chip. Unfortunately, Alpha runs into production problems and fails to deliver. Beta has also introduced a new chip that is similar, but not identical to the Alpha chip. The Beta chip was available for immediate delivery at the time of Alpha's breach, albeit at a 20% price premium.
>
> Zenith might be in a bit of a quandary. On one hand, if Zenith purchases Beta chips, as cover, then Alpha might argue that the differences in the chip are such that a Beta chip is not a reasonable commercial substitute for an Alpha chip under § 2-712. On the other hand, if Zenith does not purchase Beta chips, as cover, then Alpha will likely argue that Zenith failed to mitigate, thereby seeking to avoid liability for the substantial consequential damages based on Zenith's resale contracts.
>
> Thus, Zenith's best option may be to contact Alpha at the time of the breach and ask Alpha whether it agrees that a cover transaction using Beta chips is reasonable.

In most instances, the issue of cover should be reasonably straightforward. A higher price will rarely be deemed to precluded cover, as it is recoverable as damages (unless of course the price is so high as to be commercially unreasonable). If a commercially reasonable substitute is available, then the buyer should generally cover.

Thus, we can again see the desirability of cover, where reasonably possible. If substitute goods are reasonably available, then the buyer should make the necessary arrangements for cover and sue for damages under § 2-712. If substitute goods are not available, then the buyer may sue for damages under § 2-713, including consequential damages under § 2-715(2)(a).

The foreseeability requirement under § 2-715(2)(a) encourages disclosure, in much the same manner as the common law. The seller will generally be liable for any damages reasonably expected as a probable result of the breach based on the general circumstances of the transaction, and the buyer is charged with notifying the seller of any special circumstances unique to the buyer.

Thus, we can reasonably summarize the buyer's most typical claims for damages as follows when buyer does not retain the goods. The buyer is strongly encouraged to engage in a cover transaction and is entitled to damages for any cost differential, as well as any incidental damages. Where cover is not reasonably possible, the buyer is entitled to recover the difference between market price and contract price, plus any consequential damages. Finally, where consequential damages are not at issue, a buyer will always have a right to recover the difference in market and contract price, irrespective of the availability of cover. We now move to the buyer's right to damages when the buyer retains the goods.

Buyer's Damages When Buyer Retains the Goods

As indicated at the outset of this lesson, the buyer may end up with the goods either because the buyer has demanded performance of an initially resistant seller or because the buyer has elected to retain the goods notwithstanding a non-conformity in their tender or character. In either circumstance, the buyer retains a right to damages. **STOP NOW and READ UCC § 2-714 below.**

UCC § 2-714

(1) Where the buyer has accepted goods and given notification (subsection (3) of Section 2-607) he may recover as damages for any non-conformity of tender the loss resulting in the ordinary course of events from the seller's breach as determined in any manner which is reasonable.

(2) The measure of damages for breach of warranty is the difference at the time and place of acceptance between the value of the goods accepted and the value they would have had if they had been as warranted, unless special circumstances show proximate damages of a different amount.

(3) In a proper case any incidental and consequential damages under the next section may also be recovered.

In many instances, a buyer who has retained the goods may not have yet paid the full purchase price. Having retained the goods, the buyer's obligation to pay will not be excused (as in the case of cancellation). However, the buyer will likely wish to reduce any payment obligation by any right to damages. **STOP NOW and READ UCC § 2-717 below.**

UCC § 2-717

The buyer on notifying the seller of his intention to do so may deduct all or any part of the damages resulting from any breach of the contract from any part of the price still due under the same contract.

Thus, a buyer who retains non-conforming goods (or goods for which the seller's tender was otherwise non-conforming) will typically remain obligated to pay the contract price for the goods, less any right to damages.

The following example illustrates an example of the operation of § 2-714, including buyer's right to recover for incidental and consequential damages under § 2-715, as well as buyer's right to deduct the resulting damages from the purchase price under § 2-717,

Example 42-5: Zenith Computers contracts to buy a new "state-of-the-art" chip from Alpha Electronics, with deliveries to be made in installments. Zenith has contracted with many of its own customers to sell a new computer using the new Alpha chip. Alpha delivers the promised chips, but their performance is only 90% of the promised chip speed. While Zenith is not happy about the diminished chip speed, it nevertheless represents an improvement over existing technology (and does not therefore "substantially impair" the value of the chip). Thus, Zenith decides to retain and use the chips.

The contract price for the chips was $300, and the parties stipulated that the value of the chips, as delivered, was 10% less than the value of the chips, as promised. The parties further stipulated that Zenith would realize an average reduced selling price on the computers containing the chip of $100 per computer (including the reduced value of the chip itself; the reduction in Zenith's profits on the computer; and the reduced value of other associated computer components as a direct result of slower chip speed). Finally, Zenith was required to spend $15 per computer in modifications to accommodate the slower chip speed.

Zenith will be entitled to claim the following as damages:

$30 per chip (10% of 300) as reduced value under § 2-714(2);

$70 per computer (100 minus the 30 already claimed above) as consequential damages under § 2-715(2)(a); and

$15 per computer as incidental damages under § 2-715(1).

Thus, Zenith will recover a total of $115 per computer in damages based on Alpha's breach in failing to deliver chips that conformed to the parties' contract (specifically, the chips failed to conform to the expressly warranted chip speed). Assuming that Zenith has not yet paid Alpha for the chips, Zenith may, upon notice to Alpha, reduce its payment from $300 to $185 per chip (300 − 115) under § 2-717.

The most significant challenge in this sort of case will often be proving the precise loss caused by a late delivery or reduced value of non-conforming goods. However, with these amounts in hand, the actual damages calculations are relatively straightforward.

Buyer's Damages under the CISG

In contrast to the detailed multiple detailed provisions of UCC Article 2, virtually any claim for damages under the CISG may be supported by reference to two brief provisions. **STOP NOW and READ CISG Articles 74 and 77 below.**

CISG Article 74

Damages for breach of contract by one party consist of a sum equal to the loss, including loss of profit, suffered by the other party as a consequence of the breach. Such damages may not exceed the loss which the party in breach foresaw or ought to have foreseen at the time of the conclusion of the contract, in the light of the facts and matters of which he then knew or ought to have known, as a possible consequence of the breach of contract.

CISG Article 77

A party who relies on a breach of contract must take such measures as are reasonable in the circumstances to mitigate the loss, including loss of profit, resulting from the breach. If he fails to take such measures, the party in breach may claim a reduction in the damages in the amount by which the loss should have been mitigated.

Article 74 states the basic rule of "expectation" and, in most instances, will result in damage calculations much like those calculated under the common law or the more detailed provisions of UCC Article 2. Article 77 also provides a mitigation requirement quite similar to the common law or UCC Article 2. However, two provisions of Article 74 are worthy of note here, as both can be easily misunderstood by anyone whose understanding of damages is grounded in the common law tradition.

First, Article 74 applies a foreseeability requirement to all damages (subject to an exception addressed by Articles 75 and 76 below)—not just those damages deemed "consequential" under the common law or UCC Article 2. The phrase "as a consequence of the breach" in Article 74 merely requires basic causation—a breaching party is liable only for damages caused by the breach—and is not intended to limit in any way the broad application of Article 74. This broader foreseeability requirement can also be quite important in the context of cross-border trade—much like the foreseeability requirement of Article 25 encountered earlier.

The phrasing and meaning of Article 74 also provides an excellent example of the potential challenges of what are sometimes called "*faux ami*" or false friends—words that appear familiar, but in fact mean something quite different from the meaning with which we are familiar. In Article 74, the term "consequence" has a very broad use, including common law "consequential" damages, but in no way limited to such a narrow use of the term. The requirement of "foreseeability" therefore has a much broader reach than it does under the common law, potentially limiting any claim for damages—not just those the common law would characterize as "consequential."

The second important difference is found in the requirement of foreseeability itself. While the common law (and UCC Article 2) requires that damages must be foreseeable as a "probable" result of the breach, CISG Article 74 only requires proof of foreseeability as a "possible" consequence of the breach. At first glance, this difference may seem insignificant. However, a probability almost certainly requires that an event be "more likely than not," while a mere possibility would seem to require significantly less.

This difference between standards can easily be seen by reference to the application of law to facts in *Hadley v. Baxendale* itself. Return to the case in the last lesson and reread the penultimate paragraph, beginning with "Now, in the present case . . . ." Do you think one could reasonably say based on the court's speculations that it was "possible" that the mill would have been shut down pending the return of the new shaft—even if it was not "probable"?

Again, the calculation of damages under the CISG is, generally, quite similar to the common law or UCC Article 2. However, the foregoing distinctions are intended as a reminder of the admonition first encountered in Lesson 2. The CISG must be addressed on its own terms—and not through an interpretive lens based on the common law or Article 2.

As a final note regarding the CISG, Articles 75 and 76 provide special rules for calculating damages in the cases in which the contract has been avoided—by either the buyer or the seller. Article 75 addresses cases in which the buyer or seller has arranged for a substitute transaction (much like buyer's "cover" under UCC Article 2 above), awarding the difference between the cost of the substitute and the contract price. Article 76 addresses cases in which no substitute transaction has been arranged, instead awarding the difference between market and contract price. While either type of damages might also be recoverable under Article 74, Articles 75 and 76 do not require any proof of foreseeability. In effect, in the event of avoidance of the contract (a requirement of both Articles 75 and 75), foreseeability of the sorts of damages recoverable under Articles 75 and 76 is presumed.

APPLYING THE RULES

Problem 1: H&H Meat Products, a meat processing plant, contracted to sell its output of cow hides to Laredo Hides, a buyer for resale to various hide tanneries. A dispute arose over payment, and H&H refused to deliver, asserting the refusal was justified by Laredo's failure to make timely payment. However, a court ultimately ruled that the refusal by H&H to perform was not justified, and therefore amounted to repudiation of the contract, entitling Laredo to cancel and sue for total breach.

The contract price was $30 per hide, and the market price at the time of delivery was $36. Laredo had contracts to resell the hides to tanneries at $48 per hide. At the point when H&H refused to perform, what where Laredo's options, broadly, in terms of remedies? What if similar hides were not in fact available, at any price—how would this affect Laredo's options? What if similar hides were available to Laredo, at market price—how would this affect Laredo's options? Based on the available facts, what is Laredo entitled to recover as damages under each option?

If Laredo arranges for a substitute purchase, it will incur a cost of $1 per hide in doing so. How, if at all, would this affect any of your above calculations?

The facts of this problem are loosely based on the issues raised in the case of Laredo Hides Co., Inc. v. H & H Meat Products Co., Inc., 513 S.W. 2d 210 (Tex. Civ. App. 1974).

Problem 2: Assume the basic facts of the preceding Problem, but instead assuming that H&H delivered the hides. Unfortunately, H&H had not properly cared for the hides prior to delivery. As a result, the hides were worth only half of their expected value under the contract at the time of delivery. Laredo nevertheless accepted the hides, knowing of the problem. Laredo then reasonably discounted the price of the hides to its own buyers by 50%, reflecting the reduced value of the hides. How much is Laredo entitled to recover from H&H (refer to Problem 1 for relevant pricing information)?

Problem 3: (S)eller and (B)uyer contracted for cocoa beans, a commodity subject to considerable price volatility, depending on global cocoa crop yields. The contract called for S to deliver 1 ton of beans to B on June 1, for $1,500. On March 1, S repudiated. The market price on March 1 was $1,500 per ton, and rose constantly over the next 90 days (approximately $55 per week), eventually reaching $2,200 per ton on May 31. On that day, B purchased a ton of beans for $2,200. How much is B entitled to recover as damages? This is a good opportunity to revisit anticipatory breach, addressed earlier in Chapter 7. When did B "learn of the breach"? In answering the question, you may want to consider both UCC §§ 2-712 and 2-713, as well as UCC § 2-610. The same basic issue was addressed in *Cosden Oil & Chemical Co. v. Karl O. Helm Aktiengesellshcaft*, 736 F.2d 1064 (5th Cir. 1984).

Problem 4: Farmer Tongish contracted to sell seeds to the Decatur Coop Association (the "Coop," a cooperative entity that purchased, handled, store, and resold farm products) at $12 per hundred-weight. The Coop contracted to resell the seeds to Bambino at $13 per hundred-weight. Between the time of the contract and the delivery date, the market price of the seed charged by the farmers rose from $12 to $20. Tongish failed to deliver the promised seed to the Coop, instead selling it to Thomas at $20 per hundred-weight. The Coop chose not to cover, even though seed was available in the market at the $20 price. The Coop did, however, bring an action against Tongish for breach.

How much is the Coop entitled to recover? Explain your statutory authority, as well as the arguments likely to be made by both Tongish and the Coop, along with your own conclusion and reasoning.

Is the Coop entitled to bring a claim for the profits it lost in the transaction with Bambino as a result of the breach by Tongish?

The facts of this problem are loosely based on the issues raised in the case of *Tongish v. Thomas*, 251 Kan. 728, 840 P.2d 471 (1992).

Lesson 43: Seller's Damages—Sales of Goods

Objectives and Expected Learning Outcomes

In this lesson, you will learn to quantify the seller's damages for buyer's breach of a contract for the sale of goods. In doing so, you will learn to distinguish between a variety of remedies available to seller under different circumstances. You will also discover that Article 2 does not provide seller with a right to consequential damages (and you will learn why that might be a reasonable choice). You will also learn about mitigation in the context of a breach by the buyer. At the end of the lesson, you will have an opportunity to apply these statutory rules in calculating a buyer's damages under various factual scenarios.

Seller's Damages under UCC Article 2

We begin by examining the question addressed at the outset of the last lesson. If a buyer has wrongfully refused the goods, should not the seller have the same range of options as the buyer—seeking either to require performance (at least in certain circumstances) or to cancel the contract? In fact, a seller of goods in a transaction governed by the CISG has an unequivocal right under Article 62 to compel the buyer to accept and pay for the goods, unless the seller has avoided the contract (subject of course to the enforceability limits of CISG Article 28 discussed in the last lesson). In contrast, UCC Article 2 provides no right to compel a buyer to accept goods the buyer does not want, and seller's right to demand payment of the price is narrowly limited by the principle of mitigation.

As common sense would dictate, the seller is always entitled to recover from buyer the price of any goods accepted by the buyer (and not properly revoked). This is the easy part. However, "[w]here the buyer wrongfully rejects or revokes acceptance of goods or fails to make a payment due on or before delivery or repudiates," then the seller is generally entitled under **UCC § 2-703 (d-f)** to:

- resell the goods and recover damages under § 2-706; or

- recover damages for non-acceptance under § 2-708; or

- in a proper case, recover the price under § 2-709; and

- cancel the contract

Seller's Right to Recover the Price

We begin with seller's right to bring an action against buyer for the price of the goods, the operation of which will depend on whether the goods are accepted or not. **STOP NOW and READ UCC § 2-709(1) below.**

UCC § 2-709(1)

(1) When the buyer fails to pay the price as it becomes due the seller may recover, together with any incidental damages under the next section, the price

    (a) of goods accepted or of conforming goods lost or damaged within a commercially reasonable time after risk of their loss has passed to the buyer; and

    (b) of goods identified to the contract if the seller is unable after reasonable effort to resell them at a reasonable price or the circumstances reasonably indicate that such effort will be unavailing.

Again, the seller is entitled to recover the price of accepted goods (as well as those legally deemed to belong to the buyer at the time of any loss of or damage to the goods). However, in all other circumstances (articulated above from § 2-703), the seller must make reasonable efforts "to resell them at a reasonable price," absent circumstances indicating that such efforts would be wasted. Only after making such efforts and failing, is the seller otherwise entitled to recover the full price of the goods from the buyer. In short, the seller's right to recover the price for goods refused by the buyer is subject to reasonable efforts by the seller to mitigate its losses by reselling the goods.

> **Identified Goods and Risk of Loss**
> "Identified" goods are the specific goods intended for buyer. "Risk of loss" rules determine whether buyer or seller bears the risk of damage or loss to the goods while in transit. The risk of loss is initially borne by seller. After it passes to buyer, then the buyer generally bears any risk of loss or damage and must pay for the goods, even if lost or damaged.

The following example illustrates the distinction between accepted goods and goods that are wrongfully refused (in this case, rejected).

> **Example 43-1:** Seller contracts to sell 100 widgets to buyer for $10,000. Buyer accepts the widgets, but refuses to pay for them. Absent further facts (such as a non-conformity justifying revocation of buyer's acceptance), the seller has an absolute right to recover the price under § 2-709(1)(a).
>
> If, instead, buyer had rejected the goods, but lacked any right to do so (thereby breaching the buyer's obligation to take the goods), the rejection is said to be wrongful, and the seller is entitled to recover damages. However, the seller is not entitled to recover the price under § 2-709(1)(b), absent making any reasonable efforts to do so without success.

While the details of § 2-709(1) differ from our common law analysis of seller's damages, the principle is quite similar. The seller is only entitled to recover the full price (i.e., the seller's "loss in value") to the extent the seller cannot reasonably reduce its loss through mitigation.

Seller's Right to Damages in the Event of Resale

Of course, the seller who successfully resells the goods will often incur damages nevertheless, including the cost of arranging for the loss-mitigating resale. Seller's right to recover such damages is addressed by § 2-706. **STOP NOW and READ UCC § 2-706(1) below.**

UCC § 2-706(1)

(1) Under the conditions stated in Section 2-703 on seller's remedies, the seller may resell the goods concerned or the undelivered balance thereof. Where the resale is made in good faith and in a commercially reasonable manner the seller may recover the difference between the resale price and the contract price together with any incidental damages allowed under the provisions of this Article (Section 2-710), but less expenses saved in consequence of the buyer's breach.

In § 2-706, we see a provision quite similar to § 2-712, addressing the buyer's right to cover. Each addresses the calculation of the aggrieved party's damages in the event of a substitute sale or purchase transaction, respectively. In the instant case, seller is entitled to recover the different between the price for which it contracted and the price it received in a reasonable resale transaction. Of course, the seller is also entitled to incidental damages.

Note that § 2-710 solely addresses seller's right to incidental damages (in contrast to § 2-715, which provides a buyer with rights to both incidental and consequential damages—this issue is discussed further below). **STOP NOW and READ UCC § 2-710 below.**

UCC § 2-710

Incidental damages to an aggrieved seller include any commercially reasonable charges, expenses or commissions incurred in stopping delivery, in the transportation, care and custody of goods after the buyer's breach, in connection with return or resale of the goods or otherwise resulting from the breach.

As explained earlier in connection with buyer's damages, incidental damages reflect those costs incurred in dealing responsively with the breach, and often involve the cost of efforts to mitigate damages.

The following example illustrates the basic application of § 2-706(1), in connection with § 2-710.

Example 43-2: We can return to the second variation in Example 43-1, in which buyer had wrongfully rejected the goods. In this example the seller successfully completed a commercially reasonable resale of the widgets at a total price of $9,500, and reasonably paid a brokerage commission of $300 and additional transportation costs of $200 in doing so.

The seller is entitled to recover $500, based on the difference between the resale price ($9,500) and the contract price ($10,000), plus $500 as incidental damages, for a total of $1,000.

As with buyer's cover, a commercially reasonable resale by the seller provides a relatively straightforward calculation of damages and also fully satisfies the seller's obligation to mitigate. The key, of course, is that the resale be made in good faith and in a commercially reasonable manner.

In some cases, a seller will not be entitled to recover the full amount of the price absent reasonable and unsuccessful efforts to resell, but may nevertheless choose not to resell (or it may simply be difficult to prove a specific resale transaction in some cases). In such a case, the seller may nevertheless recover damages under § 2-708.

Seller's Right to Recover Damages in the Absence of either Resale or a Right to the Recover the Price

We can again refer back to the buyer's alternative means of calculating damages under § 2-713. In fact, § 2-708(1) operates in a manner very similar to § 2-713. However, § 2-708 also contains a second alternative—subsection (2), which is quite different from any statutory remedies available to buyer. Subsection (2) is, however, very similar to the seller's common law right to recover its profits lost as a result of the breach (including reasonable overhead). We will consider each subsection independently, in turn. **STOP NOW and READ UCC § 2-708(1) below.**

UCC § 2-708(1)

(1) Subject to subsection (2) [below] and to the provisions of this Article with respect to proof of market price (Section 2-723), the measure of damages for non-acceptance or repudiation by the buyer is the difference between the market price at the time and place for tender and the unpaid contract price together with any incidental damages provided in this Article (Section 2-710), but less expenses saved in consequence of the buyer's breach.

The seller is entitled to recover from buyer the difference between the seller's "expected" selling price and that actually obtainable from a hypothetical buyer at market price at the time and place of delivery. Where a seller is responsible for paying the cost of delivery or carriage, the seller's damages will typically be reduced by that amount if the seller does not engage in any actual substitute transaction.

The following example is illustrative of both the computation of seller's loss, as well as seller's savings on carriage in the absence of a substitute transaction.

Example 43-3: Seth contracts to sell 500 bushels of apples to Beth for $20 per bushel, or $10,000, delivered to Beth's produce market. At the time and place of delivery, the market price for apples was $18 per bushel, or $9,000. The price of carriage (transportation) from Sam's place of business to Beth's produce market was $400. Beth repudiated the contract before Seth delivered the apples. Seth neither engaged in a substitute transaction, nor incurred the cost of carriage.

Under § 2-708(1), Seth can recover $1,000, as the difference between the contract price and market price, less the $400 cost of carriage saved as a result of the breach, or a total of $600 in damages.

Another conceptual way to visualize the above transaction is that the seller had a right to deliver 100 widgets at a specific time and place for a net return (price minus cost of delivery) for $9,600. If the seller could hypothetically go into the market and buy those 100 widgets for $9,000, for immediate resale, then the seller's financial loss is $600.

We can vary the foregoing example to illustrate the operation of § 2-708(1) in the case of a wrongful rejection of the goods by the buyer.

Example 43-4: Seth contracts to sell 500 bushels of apples to Beth for $20 per bushel, or $10,000, delivered to Beth's produce market. At the time and place of delivery, the market price for apples was $18 per bushel, or $9,000. The price of carriage (transportation) from Sam's place of business to Beth's produce market was $400. Beth wrongfully rejected the apples (she asserted they did not conform to the contract when in fact they did). Seth arranged with the carrier to bring the apples back to his warehouse (where Seth simply returned them to his general inventory for sale to other buyers) at an additional cost of $200. Seth did not arrange for any specific substitute resale transaction (Beth's apples likely went to many customers).

Under § 2-708(1), Seth can recover $1,000, as the difference between the contract price and market price, plus his incidental damages of $200 in returning the apples to his warehouse inventory, or a total of $1,200 in damages.

In comparing Examples 43-3 and 43-4, we see that Seth recovered an additional $600 in the latter Example based on the cost of transportation both ways. He failed to save the expected cost of $400 and he incurred an unexpected cost of $200. Thus, Beth would be well advised to repudiate early if that is her intent, rather than waiting to receive and reject the apples. Such is result is also of course fully consistent with the principle of mitigation.

While § 2-708(1) often works quite well in the context of goods for which the market price fluctuates over time, it is much less likely to compensate a seller for its lost expectation interest in goods for which the price is relatively constant, or fixed. Instead, the sale of goods at a fixed price (and at a reasonably expected profit) is addressed by the next subsection. **STOP NOW and READ UCC § 2-708(2) below.**

UCC § 2-708(2)

(2) If the measure of damages provided in subsection (1) [above] is inadequate to put the seller in as good a position as performance would have done then the measure of damages is the profit (including reasonable overhead) which the seller would have made from full performance by the buyer, together with any incidental damages provided in this Article (Section 2-710), due allowance for costs reasonably incurred and due credit for payments or proceeds of resale.

Comment 2 helps to explain further the relationship between §§ 2-709, 2-708(1), and 2-708(2). A seller is generally precluded under § 2-709 from recovering the full price for resalable goods that have been wrongfully refused by the buyer, and the seller is also unlikely to recover under § 2-708(1) where the price is relatively constant (the contract and market price will rarely differ). However, the seller may have lost its expected profit on the transaction with the breaching buyer, thus justifying resort to § 2-708(2).

OFFICIAL COMMENT 2 (UCC § 2-708(2))

2. The provision of this section permitting recovery of expected profit including reasonable overhead where the standard measure of damages is inadequate, together with the new requirement that price actions may be sustained only where resale is impractical, are designed to eliminate the unfair and economically wasteful results arising under the older law when fixed price articles were involved. This section permits the recovery of lost profits in all appropriate cases, which would include all standard priced goods. The normal measure there would be list price less cost to the dealer or list price less manufacturing cost to the manufacturer. . . .

As further explained by the foregoing Comment, the seller's profit may be calculated by reference to its cost of purchase (for resale) or its cost of manufacture (for sale). Either calculation will also of course include reasonable overhead (just like seller's profits under the common law).

The real challenge in determining whether a seller is entitled to recover under § 2-708(2) comes in determining whether seller, in fact, lost its profits. The statute allows seller to recover "[i]f the measure of damages provided in [§ 2-708(1)] is inadequate to put the seller in as good a position as performance would have done." It is not enough that the seller merely deems the measure of subsection (1) "inadequate." Seller must affirmatively establish the loss of profits that seller would have earned had the contract been fully performed, but lost as a result of the buyer's breach. This may arise in two typical circumstances, each described in turn.

If a seller is manufacturing goods specifically for the buyer, and the buyer repudiates, the seller will typically cease work on the goods, except to the extent any continued work will reduce overall damages by increasing the net value (price, less cost) for which the goods may be sold. In this instance, a seller's damages will be calculated under § 2-708(2) in a manner very much like the common law. The seller will receive its lost profit (including reasonable overhead), plus its actual manufacturing costs reasonably incurred, plus and incidental damages, but less any loss avoided through resale of the incomplete product or any elements thereof. This should be very reminiscent of Formula B introduced earlier in Lesson 40. In fact, a seller's damages when a buyer repudiates in mid-manufacture of goods are very much like a seller's damages when a buyer repudiates in the middle of a construction project.

The following example illustrates this first circumstance.

> **Example 43-5:** Seller contracts to manufacture a unique SuperWidget, specifically designed for buyer, at a price of $5,000. Seller reasonably expects to make a profit (including reasonable overhead recovery) of $1,000 on the sale. After the seller begins work, the buyer repudiates. The seller reasonably ceases work on the SuperWidget after incurring $1,200 in manufacturing costs. Seller is able to resell the unfinished parts for $600, but incurs costs of $100 in doing so.
>
> Under § 2-708(2), seller is entitled to recover $1,000 in lost profits, plus $1,200 in manufacturing costs reasonably incurred, plus $100 in incidental damages, less $600 in losses avoided through resale, for a total of $1,700.

While not expressly limited to custom goods, the above-described circumstance most often arises in that context. In contrast, the second circumstance, addressed next, will most often arise with respect to standard model fixed price goods produced in quantity.

A typical manufacturer/seller of goods will produce certain specified items in quantity, generally selling these goods at a listed price (perhaps varying by quantity or customer, but generally constant over time, absent inflation). The seller will typically seek to sell as many of any given item as it can, assuming that each additional sale results in additional profit. If a buyer breaches by refusing to take the goods for which it contracted, those goods will likely go to another buyer. However, the seller lost one "sale" (and more importantly, the profits on one sale)—if and only if the seller would have made both sales irrespective of the breach.

To recover lost profits under § 2-708(2), the seller must establish that it "could" have made both sales (i.e., had the production or purchasing capacity to do so) and "would" have made both sales (i.e., was engaged in soliciting additional sales volume)—irrespective of buyer's breach. The following example illustrates the possible variations, only one of which allows for recovery by seller.

Example 43-6: Seller contracts with Buyer One to sell 100 OmniWidgets, at $100 each, or $10,000. Buyer One repudiates, and Seller sells the same widgets to Buyer Two at exactly the same price.

If Seller can establish that it had the capacity to sell 200 OmniWidgets during the relevant time period and was actively engaged in sales efforts to do so, irrespective of the breach by Buyer One, then Seller will be entitled to recover its expected profits on the sale to Buyer One.

If, however, Seller lacked the capacity to sell 200 OmniWidgets, or had not been engaged in seeking to sell to Buyer Two prior to the repudiation by Buyer One, then Seller will not be entitled to recover under § 2-708(2) because Seller will not have lost any profits. In effect, the second transaction with Buyer Two would be more accurately characterized as a substitute for that with Buyer One in mitigation of the breach by Buyer One. Inasmuch as Seller never would have sold 200 OmniWidgets, it did not lose any sales volume or any associated profits.

In the latter variation, the seller could of course recover any incidental damages (e.g., a second selling commission), but would not otherwise have suffered any loss. Only in the first variation can the seller be said to have actually lost profits. This sort of seller is sometimes called a "lost volume seller" in that it loses volume (and the associated profit) when a buyer breaches a purchase obligation.

What of Seller's Consequential Damages?

We can now turn briefly to the omission from Article 2 of any reference to seller's consequential damages. In understanding the potential rationale behind the omission, it helps to step back and compare the basic expectations of the buyer and seller (much as we did in the last lesson when focusing on the buyer's lost profits as consequential damages).

The buyer's basic expectation is to receive goods, which a commercial buyer will typically plan to use in some manner (e.g., resale, provision of a service, or use as raw materials or equipment for manufacturing) to make a profit on a subsequent transaction or transactions. Thus, the commercial buyer's consequential damages most typically reflect a loss of profits to be made in some manner from the use or resale of the goods. As reasonably limited by the principles of mitigation and foreseeability, we have a serviceable rule providing the buyer with a right to recover consequential damages, consistent with principles of minimizing losses and information sharing (as promoted by the foreseeability rule).

In contrast, the seller's basic expectation is money. What sort of associated "consequences" might arise from the buyer's failure to pay the seller? Presumably, the seller would lose the benefit of the cash flow expected from the transaction. As a result, the seller might not have adequate financial resources to pay its own bills. Presumably, such a seller could simply borrow money (i.e., "cover" for the money expected from buyer in much the same manner the buyer "covers" for goods expected from seller) and recover the interest costs as incidental damages. In fact, such interest costs are typically awarded pursuant to statute, and we rarely, if ever, think of a seller's borrowing as "cover" for an unpaid obligation of a buyer. However, this raises the question of what sort of consequential damages might arise if an unpaid seller was unable to borrow. Should a buyer be liable for the failure of seller's business as a consequence of buyer's failure to pay? Is foreseeability sufficient to limit such recovery? Would a rational buyer deal with a seller without knowing its financial stability?

These questions of course would raise some troubling challenges in allowing sellers a general right to recover consequential damages from buyers. While the logic of the omission from Article 2 of consequential damages has sometimes been questioned, the foregoing analysis is meant to provide at least one possible rationale for that omission. It is also intended to emphasize further the unique differences between the expectations of a typical seller and those of a typical buyer, and the extent to which these differences drive a few of the unique remedies available to each.

APPLYING THE RULES

Problem 1:

(A) Diasonics contracted to sell a specified item of medical diagnostic equipment (the "Equipment") to Davis, who intended to resell it to a medical facility. Davis agreed to pay Diasonics $1 million for the Equipment—$300,000 in advance and the balance due 10 days after receipt of the equipment. Davis paid the advance deposit, as agreed, but subsequently repudiated the contract when Davis's own buyer changed its mind about the purchase. A short time later, Diasonics sold the Equipment (the same equipment originally intended for Davis) to Jones for $1 million. Diasonics paid a $25,000 sales commission on both the sales to Davis and the sale to Jones (and remained legally obligated to pay both). At a selling price of $1 million, Diasonics reasonably expected to make $150,000 in profits (including reasonable overhead recovery).

Diasonics sued Davis for breach, which Davis did not contest, but the parties disputed the quantum of damages recoverable by Diasonics. As a threshold matter, is Davis entitled to a return of its $300,000 advance down payment? Read closely UCC § 2-718(2) before answering the question. We will further explore "liquidated" damages in the next lesson. § 2-718(3) further provides that any right to return of the down payment is of course offset by any right of Diasonics to recover damages. We can now return to the main question. Under which statutory provision will Davis likely seek to quantify damages recoverable by Diasonics? Under which statutory provision will Diasonics seek to recover? What must Diasonics prove in order to do so?

(B) For purposes of this question, assume that the Equipment was to be specially manufactured, based on specific instructions provided by Davis. The entire $1 million price was to be paid at the time of delivery. At the time Davis repudiated, Diasonics had incurred $300,000 in costs. At this stage of the production process, the partially manufactured equipment was worthless in terms of resale. However, Diasonics incurred another $100,000 in manufacturing costs, and, as a direct result, was able to resell the partially completed Equipment to Smith at a salvage price of $150,000. Diasonics reasonably incurred $10,000 in additional sales and transportation costs related to the salvage sale. All other facts from Part A remain the same. Diasoncis brings an action against Davis for breach. Which provision of Article 2 governs the damages claim and how much is Diasonics entitled to recover?

The facts of this problem, are very loosely based on the issues raised (and a variation thereon) in the case of *R.E. Davis Chemical Corp. v. Diasonics, Inc.*, 826 F. 2d 678 (7th Cir. 1987).

Problem 2: We return to our generic buyer and seller of cocoa beans from the last lesson (Problem 3), but turn the tables in terms of breach. The contract again called for S to deliver 1 ton of beans to B on June 1, for $1,500. In order to be able to meet its obligation to B, S had entered into its own "forward" contract to purchase beans from its supplier, for delivery directly to B on June 1. However, B repudiated the contract on March 1. The market price on March 1 was $1,500 per ton, but it fell constantly over the next 90 days, eventually reaching $1,200 per ton on May 31. On that day, S resold to C the cocoa beans originally intended for B, at $1,225 per ton, for delivery the next day. S was required to pay its supplier an additional delivery cost of $50 per ton for deliver to C instead of B.

How much is S entitled to recover in damages for B's breach, and upon what statutory provision will S likely rely?

Suppose that S would prefer not to identify any specific resale transaction (S is often in the market buying and selling cocoa beans at wildly varying prices). Upon which statutory provision will S likely wish to rely, and how much will S recover in damages under that provision?

Lesson 44: Certainty, Liquidated Damages and Express Limitations on Remedies

Objectives and Expected Learning Outcomes

In this lesson, you will learn the degree of certainty required of a party seeking to prove damages. You will also learn how parties may sometimes agree in advance or "liquidate" the amount of damages for a specified breach. In doing so, you will learn to distinguish between an enforceable liquidated damages provision and an unenforceable "penalty." Finally, you will learn the extent to which the parties may agree to limit the remedies available to the aggrieved party in the event of a breach.

In this final lesson on damages, we will address two issues that may arise in a broad variety of contexts, some of which have already been encountered briefly in earlier material. The first is the requirement of certainty. While any breach of contract will give rise to a claim for damages caused by the breach, such damages must be proven to a reasonable degree of certainty. One or both of the parties may sometimes recognize in advance the likely difficulty of quantifying damages in the event of a breach and may, therefore, include a provision for "liquidated" damages—in effect, specifying in advance the damages associated with a particular breach and thereby avoiding any lack of certainty in proving the actual amount of damages.

The second issue addressed in this lesson involves the parties' contractual right to limit or exclude remedies, including damages. As indicated in Lessons 41 and 42, the rule of foreseeability, as applied to consequential damages is intended to encourage a buyer to share information with the seller regarding any unique risks. Once such risks are known, the seller may seek to limit them contractually. We will explore the extent to which the law allows for such limits on these and other potential remedies of an aggrieved party.

The Requirement of Certainty

Damages must be proven and quantified with reasonable certainty.[12] Claims for damages based on mere speculation or conjecture are not sustainable. While reasonable certainty is required, perfect mathematical precision

---

[12] Restatement (Second) of Contracts § 352.

is not. This distinction between "reasonable" and "absolute" certainty is nicely illustrated by a claim for lost future profits.

> **Example 44-1:** Able concludes a 5 year lease with Baker for commercial retail space. However, Baker fails to deliver the space as agreed. Able had intended to operate a retail business from the space, and Baker's breach caused Able to lose that opportunity. The problem of course is that it will be impossible to determine the precise amount of profits Able would have made over the duration of the 5 year lease.
>
> In the case of an established business, Able may be able to prove expected profits to a reasonably high degree of certainty based solidly on historical data. Of course, even with an established business, the level of certainty with respect to future profits will diminish over time (e.g., in year 5, as compared to year 1 above).
>
> If Able's business is a new one, proof of future profits will typically be even more challenging. Historically, some courts categorically rejected such claims. However, the modern trend is to allow such claims, subject to a reasonable basis for the quantification (e.g., other comparable businesses)—beyond mere speculation or conjecture.

In some cases, the reason for the difficulty of proof may have an affect on the level of certainty required in proving damages. For example, if the difficulty arises largely from the fact of the breach, a somewhat lesser degree of certainty may be required; whereas a difficulty arising from the claimant's acts or omissions may result in a more strictly applied standard.

The requirement of certainty required in a sale of goods transaction is even more liberalized. Comment 1 to UCC § 1-305(a), provided earlier at the beginning of lesson 42, explains that subsection (a) "reject[s] any doctrine that damages must be calculable with mathematical accuracy. Compensatory damages are often at best approximate: they have to be proved with whatever definiteness and accuracy the facts permit, but no more." The comment further references § 2- 204(3), which requires only a "reasonably certain" basis for providing an appropriate remedy. **STOP NOW and READ UCC § 2-204(3) below.**

UCC § 2-204(3)

(3) Even though one or more terms are left open a contract for sale does not fail for indefiniteness if the parties have intended to make a contract and there is a reasonably certain basis for giving an appropriate remedy.

This liberalized approach is fully consistent with Article 2's general focus on reasonableness, as applied to the specific circumstances of any given transaction. Of course, even under Article 2, an aggrieved party is unlikely to succeed in establishing damages based on pure speculation.

Liquidated Damages

Parties to a contract may sometimes recognize, in advance, the potential uncertainty reflected in quantifying a particular form of damages. If so, they may decide in advance that a breaching party must pay a specified amount of damages in the event of a specified associated breach. This concept is illustrated by the following example.

> **Example 44-2:** Able concludes a 5 year lease with Baker for commercial retail space. Able intends to operate a new business out of the space, and he is concerned that, in the event of any breach of the lease agreement, he may have a difficult time proving damages in the form of lost future profits. Able therefore succeeds in negotiating a provision requiring Baker to pay $10,000 per year (prorated for any partial year) in liquidated damages for Able's loss of profits in the event of a breach of the lease by Baker precluding Able's use of the leased premises.
>
> If Baker fails entirely to deliver the premises to Able, as promised, then Baker will be required to pay $50,000 in liquidated damages based on a breach of the lease with 5 years remaining. This $50,000 is intended to compensate Able for the loss of expected profits, irrespective of whether Able would otherwise be able to prove those lost profits to a reasonable degree of certainty.

A liquidated damages provision may be broad, addressing any and all possible damages for breach of the contract at issue, or it may be very specific, addressing only certain specified breaches. In the case of a narrow and specific liquidated damages provision, any other breach remains subject to traditional proof of damages arising from the breach. However, the liquidated damages clause will represent the exclusive damages remedy for breach of the provision to which the clause relates.

The vast majority of liquidated damages clauses relate to a narrowly specified breach, rather than breaches of the contract broadly. This makes common sense when we consider that the purpose of such a clause is to provide a reasonable estimate of actual damages that might otherwise be difficult to prove with sufficient certainty. Such an estimate is often reasonable with respect to a specific identified breach, but typically impossible if one is trying to estimate the loss arising from any possible breach that might occur.

The foregoing example might have also led the reader to question "why would the lessor ever agree?" In fact, a liquidated damages provision, like any provision involving dispute resolution, often presents special negotiating difficulties in that parties do not typically want to contemplate breach at the time of contract formation. However, in many contracting situations, both parties may value a predetermination of damages for a breach they each acknowledge may occur, as each will likely save the time and expense of litigating damages. In other cases, a party wishing to include a liquidated damages clause will simply give way on another point desired by its contracting partner, as a matter of bargaining.

As explained above, a true "liquidated damages" provision represents a good faith estimation of damages likely to be caused by the specified breach. However, a contract may instead include a term intended to "coerce" performance by requiring, in the event of non-performance, the payment of a fixed sum that exceeds any reasonable estimate of actual damages. The latter such provision is often called a "penalty" clause, because its effect, as damages, is punitive.

A "penalty" clause goes beyond compensating the aggrieved party for its expectation interest and is intended to deter breach and compel performance. This is known as the "*in terrorem*" effect of a penalty clause. This deterrent effect is inconsistent with the fundamental remedial approach of the common law focus on redressing breach through damages—but not generally compelling performance. Common law damages are intended to be, in effect, neutral as between performance and payment of damages for non-performance. A liquidated damages provision is intended to achieve that balance, while a penalty clause is intended to tilt the balance in favor of performance.

Thus, the law enforces good faith efforts to "liquidate" damages, but does not enforce efforts to "penalize" a party for breach. In distinguishing between the two, courts generally presume a provision fixing damages is valid, absent proof that it is a penalty. Moreover, the party seeking to enforce the provision may justify it as a good faith estimate with respect to either of two time frames—the time when the contract is concluded, or the time when the breach occurs. And, finally, a court will generally grant the enforcing party greater latitude in justifying the amount in circumstances in which quantifying the resulting damages will be the most difficult to determine with reasonable certainty.

Summary of Basic Rule: enforceability of a provision "liquidating" damages[13]

- A provision liquidating damages in advance for a specified breach will be enforceable, provided that it reflects a reasonable effort to estimate damages, by reference to either:

    ○ damages reasonably anticipated at the time the contract was concluded; or

    ○ damages actually incurred as a result of the breach.

- The difficulty of determining the precise quantum of damages from the specified breach shall also be considered in determining the reasonableness of the liquidated amount

- A term fixing unreasonably large payment of damages in the event of a breach is unenforceable as a penalty

The basic rule governing liquidated damages in a sale of goods transaction is virtually identical to the common law rule. **STOP NOW and READ UCC § 2-718(1) below.**

---

[13] This basic rule is reflected in Restatement (Second) of Contracts § 356(1).

UCC § 2-718(1)

(1) Damages for breach by either party may be liquidated in the agreement but only at an amount which is reasonable in the light of the anticipated or actual harm caused by the breach, the difficulties of proof of loss, and the inconvenience or nonfeasibility of otherwise obtaining an adequate remedy. A term fixing unreasonably large liquidated damages is void as a penalty.

While both the common law and UCC Article 2 render a penalty void, neither the common law nor Article 2 address an unreasonably small provision, essentially serving as more of a limitation on damages than a good faith estimate. Such a "limitation" is generally effective, subject to limits discussed more fully in the section that follows on contractual limitations on remedies.

The following example illustrates the operation and evaluation of two provisions fixing damages in a contract for the sale of goods. However, the analysis would be very much the same under the common law.

Example 44-3: Delta contracts to deliver 1,000 widgets to Echo on June 1, for which Echo promises to pay $100 each on July 15. Echo intends to use the widgets to manufacture a brand new product it has never sold, and any failure of Delta to provide the promised widgets will very likely prevent Echo from bringing the product to market in a timely manner (Echo would not be able to obtain the widgets elsewhere in time). Echo reasonably estimates that it would lose between $200,000 and $300,000 if it failed to bring the product to market in time. The June 1 delivery date is 30 days earlier than Echo absolutely needs the widgets (on July 1), but Echo prefers the earlier delivery date, as this will save Echo $5,000 in manufacturing costs to be able to begin work early.

The contract between Delta and Echo includes two other provisions: (1) in the event Delta fails to deliver the widgets by June 1, Delta shall pay $2,000 per day as damages for late delivery; (2) in the event Delta fails to deliver the widgets by July 1, Delta shall pay as damages for non-delivery the sum of $275,000.

Provision 1 is not likely enforceable, as the $2,000 per day amount (perhaps as much as $60,000 if 30 days late) is far greater than Echo's likely $5,000 actual loss. Provision 2, however, is likely enforceable, as it appears to represent a good faith estimate of Echo's loss in the event of non-delivery (even though it is slightly on the high side of the estimated range). Neither provision would affect Echo's right to recover damages for any other breach. For example, if Delta delivered non-conforming widgets, but Echo accepted and used the widgets in its manufacturing process, then Echo would be able to recover its actual damages for the accepted widgets under § 2-714.

Of course, Delta would likely have to think long and hard about entering into the above contract, in which it could be liable for liquidated damages for non-delivery of almost three times the contract price. In this respect, a discussion of liquidated damages may actually assist the parties in assessing and allocating the risks associated with the contract and pricing their respective performance obligations accordingly.

In any discussion of unenforceable "penalty" clauses, it is also important to note a few variations, which look in some ways like penalties, but are distinguishable in a way that generally makes them enforceable. The first variation involves "take or pay" contracts, which are often found in the energy industry. A natural gas provider will contract to supply a certain volume of natural gas over a certain period at a specified price. In a "take or pay" contract, the buyer must pay for the specified amount of gas, even if the buyer takes none during the relevant period, and even if the seller is able to sell it to other buyers. At first blush, this seems like a penalty inasmuch as the seller has arguably suffered no loss (assuming it has a finite supply of natural gas to sell each month). However, these contracts are characterized such that the buyer is paying for the availability of the gas—whether taken or not—and may then take the gas, as needed, or not—at the buyer's option. Under these terms, the buyer's failure to take the gas does not amount to a breach at all. The buyer is simply choosing between alternative forms of performance.

A second involves discounts and bonuses. A seller will often offer a buyer a "cash discount" for early payment—sometimes quite significant (e.g., a 2% discount for paying 15 days earlier than required). No one would suggest that such a "discount" amounts to a "penalty," even though the buyer who fails to take advantage of the discount ends up paying 2% more when paying only 15 days later (i.e., an interest rate of 48% per year, which appears quite "penal"). In a similar vein, a buyer may offer to pay a seller a "bonus" for early completion—perhaps a significant one. Again, no one would seriously suggest that an early completion bonus amounts to a "penalty," even though a seller failing to complete performance in time to earn the bonus might suffer what looks very much like a "penalty" in failing to do so.

To some degree, the enforceability of "take or pay" contracts or contracts involving conditional "discounts" or "bonuses" may seem to elevate form over substance. However, the differing treatment may also be attributed to the differing context. A "take or pay" contract involves the parties' respective rights and obligations under the contract—as fully performed in accord with their respective promises. Likewise, a conditional "bonus" or "discount" affects the amount payable as performance under the contract rather than as damages for breach. In contrast, a "penalty" provision triggered only by a "breach" involves a remedy, over which courts tend to exercise far more control than the substance of the parties actual performance obligations (remember, a court does not generally "weigh" consideration). Of course, each of the above theories has its limits in avoiding treatment as a "penalty," and a particularly egregious substantive penalty will likely be treated as such—irrespective of form.

Contractual Limitations on Remedies

The common law generally provides for enforcement of limitations on remedies, as a simple matter of contract, subject only to the doctrine of unconscionability addressed earlier in Chapter 5. UCC Article 2, however, provides somewhat more guidance as an element of its overall remedial provisions. **STOP NOW and READ UCC § 2-719 below.**

UCC § 2-719

(1) Subject to the provisions of subsections (2) and (3) of this section and of the preceding section on liquidation and limitation of damages,

(a) the agreement may provide for remedies in addition to or in substitution for those provided in this Article and may limit or alter the measure of damages recoverable under this Article, as by limiting the buyer's remedies to return of the goods and repayment of the price or to repair and replacement of nonconforming goods or parts; and

(b) resort to a remedy as provided is optional unless the remedy is expressly agreed to be exclusive, in which case it is the sole remedy.

(2) Where circumstances cause an exclusive or limited remedy to fail of its essential purpose, remedy may be had as provided in this Act.

(3) Consequential damages may be limited or excluded unless the limitation or exclusion is unconscionable. Limitation of consequential damages for injury to the person in the case of consumer goods is prima facie unconscionable but limitation of damages where the loss is commercial is not.

Two of the above provisions are worthy of particular note. The first involves the effects of any limitations, as undermining the basic purpose of the remedy at issue. While § 2-719(1) grants a seller considerable latitude in defining and limiting remedies, § 2-719(2) prevents those definitions or limitations from operating to deprive the buyer of the essential purpose of the remedy. The operation of subsection (2) is somewhat similar to that of § 2-316(1), addressed earlier in Lesson 30. In the same way that § 2-316 precludes a seller from making an express warranty and then disclaiming it, § 2-719(2) prevents a seller from providing a remedy and then rendering it ineffective.

The second significant provision is found in subsection (3). While a seller is generally free to disclaim any liability for consequential damages (and most do so—by now you can likely understand why), the statute expressly notes that the right to do so is subject to the doctrine of unconscionability. The statute then goes on to define any limitation involving consequential damages for injury to person involving consumer goods as unconscionable (thus providing a bright line limit on this specific issue).

Liquidated Damages and Limitations under the CISG

Both liquidated damages provisions and contractual limitations on damages will often raise issues of "validity," which Article 4 excludes from the scope of the CISG. The question of "penalties" is one on which common and civil law differ, with the former generally invalidating and the latter generally enforcing penal fixed sums (though even the civil law limits such provisions where excessive—even as penalties). Thus, the domestic law governing the transaction will generally determine the effectiveness of a penalty in a cross-border transaction.

APPLYING THE RULES

Problem 1: We can now return to Problem 1, Lesson 41, and our story of Willie and Lucille Peevyhouse and their lease to Garland Coal (you may want to refer back to the original problem to refresh your recollection of some of the broader facts). Both parties performed their obligations under the lease, except that Garland refused to perform the promised restorative and remedial work. The cost of the work was $29,000, and the effect of failing to perform the work was to reduce the market value of the 60 acres by $300 (the entire 60 acre parcel was worth less than $1,000 after the mining operation had been completed—it had been worth $3,600 prior to the mining operation). However, the land was left with open mining scars and the water upstream of the other 100 acre parcel owned by the Peevyhouses had been polluted. For the following questions, you should further assume that Garland paid $20,000 per year to lease the land for 5 years for purposes of extracting the coal.

Suppose that Willie and Lucille testify under oath that the loss in value to them as a result of Garland's breach is in the range of $15,000 to $30,000, based on the combination of their likely lost income on their farm, as well as the loss in their own quality of life on that farm. Is that testimony sufficient, if believed, to allow them to recover damages without reference to the actual cost of remediation? Assuming that they believed the foregoing range to reflect their likely loss at the time of contracting, what, if anything, might they have done at that time?

Suppose that, at the time of contracting, Willie and Lucille expected a loss of no more than $5,000, but included a contract provision requiring payment by Garland of $30,000 in the event Garland failed to remediate. As above, at the time of the breach, Willie and Lucille testify under oath that the loss in value to them as a result of Garland's breach is in the range of $15,000 to $30,000, based on the combination of their likely lost income on their farm, as well as the loss in their own quality of life on that farm. Is that testimony sufficient, if believed, to allow them to enforce the provision requiring Garland to pay $30,000 as a result of the breach?

Suppose Willie simply disliked coal mining companies because he believed they often left the land scarred without performing restorative or remedial work. If he inserted a contract clause requiring Garland to pay $50,000 if it failed to perform the work, would that clause be enforceable? Might Willie accomplish the same thing a bit differently?

Problem 2: Returning to our parties from Example 44-3, Delta again contracts to deliver 1,000 widgets to Echo on June 1, for which Echo promises to pay $100 each on July 15. Echo again intends to use the widgets in its manufacturing process. However, Delta is not willing to agree to any sort of fixed sum payable in the event of breach. Instead, the parties' ultimate agreement includes the following provision:

(15) In the event that any widget fails in any way to conform to the contract, including any warranty, express or implied, Echo's sold remedy shall be replacement by Delta of the widget or widgets at issue. Echo shall not be entitled, in any event, to damages for any breach.

(16) In addition to the limitations contained in the prior paragraph—and irrespective of any limits on enforcement of the prior paragraph—Echo is expressly precluded from recovering any consequential damages, whether arising from injury to person, or property, or any economic or financial loss of any kind.

Delta delivered the widgets as promised. However, as soon as Echo started using them, they caught fire during normal use, in many instances causing injury to Echo's production employees. When Delta replaced the widgets, the same thing happened with the new ones (though, by this time, Echo was testing them before anyone was injured in trying to use them).

Echo sued Delta for breach and sought damages for all of its losses. The injured Echo employees also sued for their personal injuries. In each action, Delta asserted that that it was not liable for any damages in any amount, pointing to paragraphs 15 and 16 above. Is Delta liable for Echo's losses, assuming Echo can establish them with reasonable certainty? Might Delta be liable for the injuries of Echo's employees? This latter question raises the additional challenge that Delta did not contract directly with the employees. We will address that issue in Chapter 10. In this question, however, you should focus solely on the effectiveness of paragraph 16 in limiting Delta's liability for such injuries.

9

Rescission and Excuse Based on Mistaken or Unexpected Circumstances

Key Concepts

- When is a Party Entitled to Rescission or Excused Performance Based on Mistaken or Unexpected Circumstances?

- Risk, Mistake, Impossibility (or Nearly So), and Frustration of Purpose

Lesson 45: Basic Contract Risks and the Doctrine of Mistake

Objectives and Expected Learning Outcomes

In this lesson, you will begin to learn about issues involving contract risks arising from mistaken or unexpected circumstances. In particular, you will learn in this lesson when a mistake by one or both of the parties may render the contract voidable and subject to rescission by the party whose basic contract expectations are materially and adversely affected.

In the first eight chapters, we have addressed the basic requirements for a binding and enforceable contract, the means by which the content of the parties' rights and obligations is determined, the circumstances in which such rights and obligations may come due or be excused based on express or constructive conditions of exchange, and a full panoply of remedies for breach. In the current chapter, we focus on the basic issue of "risk" in contracting. A contract "risk" typically involves either a lack of complete and accurate factual information at the time of contracting or a lack of clairvoyance as to the course of subsequent events affecting the performance of the contract or the value of such performance to the contracting parties. When one or both of the parties act on mistaken information in concluding the contract or encounter an unexpected subsequent event, some or all of the expected benefits of the bargain may be lost.

The risks we address in this chapter are largely those for which neither party bears any responsibility for the loss. When a loss is caused by the act or omission of one of the parties, it will typically involve a breach, subject to one or more of the remedies addressed in the last chapter. However, when a loss occurs without fault of either party, we must look to other rules to allocate that loss.

Risk of such losses may be addressed expressly by the parties' agreement, or a loss may simply fall and remain on one party or another by virtue of general default legal rules. Alternatively, certain exceptional legal rules may have the effect of shifting the loss to the other party in narrowly specified circumstances, absent an express agreement to the contrary. In essence, any loss of an expected benefit must necessarily fall on one or both of the parties to the contract. This chapter explores a variety of rules for deciding where the loss arising from any particular risk shall ultimately fall.

A Brief Overview of Basic Contract Risks

In thinking about the nature of contract risks, it is useful to step back and consider the difference between the typical obligations of a seller and buyer—much as we did in the last chapter in addressing damages. A seller generally expects money from the buyer, while a buyer generally expects goods or services from the seller. These differing expectations of seller and buyer drive the basic nature of the risks to each.

As long as the buyer pays, the seller's risk of receiving the expected contract value is largely limited to the effect of inflation (the effect of which is to reduce the value of a fixed sum of currency). This risk may be very real in a long term contract (and is often addressed by a price adjustment mechanism). However, it does not typically present a significant risk in most contracts. In contrast, the buyer's expected value of the promised goods or services may be very much dependent on a set of basic assumptions as to either current facts or subsequent events. Thus, the buyer generally bears a greater risk in terms of the value of the agreed exchange.

The seller, however, typically bears the greatest risks related to performance obligations. A buyer's ability to pay is not likely to be affected by external circumstances (other than deflation or currency restrictions—each of which is very rare). In contrast, the difficulty, cost, or market value of a seller's performance obligation may be very much dependent on a set of basic assumptions as to either current facts or subsequent events. We can see of course that certain "value" assumptions may affect both seller and buyer, and we will explore this issue further in the current lesson. However, we must first address the baseline "rule" governing contract risks.

Our starting point is grounded in the Latin maxim *pacta sunt servanda*. In effect, contract promises must be kept. If not, the party failing to do so will be liable for damages for breach—irrespective of the reason for failing to do so. While unanticipated hardship may affect "equitable" remedies (as we have seen in a variety of contexts), as a rule, it has no bearing on a legal claim for damages caused by a breach. Thus, the seller bears the risk of unanticipated challenges in performance, the buyer bears the risk of unanticipated events affecting the value of performance, and each party bears the risk of acting upon mistaken information in concluding the contract.

Of course, this is not the end of the story, or we would have nothing to talk about in the next three lessons. The "exceptions" to the general rule stated above fall into three basic categories: (1) mistaken facts at the time of contracting; (2) unanticipated circumstances making performance by the seller far more challenging; and (3) unanticipated circumstances making performance far less valuable to the buyer. We will address each of these in turn. In doing so, we will also address briefly the circumstances in which a risk initially borne by one party will naturally pass to the other party pursuant to the contract.

Mutual Mistake

Factual "mistakes" come in two basic forms—"mutual" and "unilateral." We begin with mutual mistakes, shared by both parties, which were traditionally more likely to provide exceptional relief by excusing performance. We then conclude with a discussion of the circumstances in which a party's unilateral mistake may excuse performance.

We can begin with the obvious—a "mutual" mistaken belief must be shared by both of the parties. A "mistake" is merely "a belief that is not in accord with the facts."[1] Thus, a mutual mistake is a belief that is shared by

---

[1] Restatement (Second) of Contracts § 151

both parties, but is not in accord with the facts. However, not all mutual mistakes will form a basis for relief. A mutual mistake will only render a contract voidable and subject to rescission by an adversely affected party where:

- At the time of the contract,

- Both parties shared the same mistaken belief,

- As to a basic assumption on which the contract was made,

- That had a material effect on the agreed bargain.[2]

The first two elements are reasonably straightforward in their application in most instances, and we have already seen the concept of "materiality" in other contexts. The key to understanding the doctrine of mistake is its limitation to a "basic assumption on which the contract was made," in combination with the "materiality" of the effect on the parties' bargain. A "basic assumption" must go to the very essence of the bargain and a "material" effect at least practically deprives the affected party of that essential element of the bargain.

The following example is illustrative.

> **Example 45-1:** A timber company contracted to purchase a tract of land for the express purpose of cutting timber. Both seller and buyer fully believed that the land was densely forested. In fact, a forest fire had fully consumed most of the timber the prior summer, without the knowledge of either party.
>
> The presence of timber was a basic assumption upon which the land was sold, and the assumption was shared by both parties at the time the contract was made. While a few trees might remain, the destruction of most of the timber had a material effect on the bargain, depriving the buyer of the essence of the bargain. Thus, the contract is voidable and subject to rescission by the buyer.

---

[2] Restatement (Second) of Contracts § 152.

Of course, not every "assumption" is a basic one. Nor does every mistaken belief materially affect the bargain so as to justify rescission of the contract. Consider the following variation on the first example.

> **Example 45-2:** A timber company contracted to purchase a tract of land for the express purpose of cutting timber. Both seller and buyer fully believe that the land was densely forested with high quality timber. In fact, both the quality and density of the timber were somewhat less than either party had expected.
>
> While the buyer certainly has reason to be disappointed, the land has timber on it that can be harvested by the buyer. Where seller has fully performed as agreed, the buyer's mere disappointment in the quantity or quality of the resulting benefits will not typically provide a basis for rescission based on mistake.

Another way to view the foregoing result is that the buyer effectively "assumes the risk" of common or typical variations in the factual circumstances of the transaction, and is only entitled to rescission based on extraordinary variations going to the very essence of the bargain.

The rule allowing for rescission based on "mutual mistake" is merely a default rule, applied in cases in which neither party bore the risk in question. This rule does not apply to the extent that the risk of the mistake at issue was already assigned to the adversely affected party:

- By agreement;

- Through assumption of the risk by knowingly acting on incomplete information; or

- By other circumstances suggesting this party bore the risk.[3]

---

[3] Restatement (Second) of Contracts § 154.

Consider the following variations on Example 45-1.

> **Example 45-3:** A timber company contracted to purchase a tract of land for the express purpose of cutting timber. Both seller and buyer fully believed that the land was densely forested. While the buyer was aware of a major forest fire in the general area the prior summer, she believed that it probably had not reached the tract of land in question. The information regarding the actual extent of the fire was available, but the buyer did not investigate further before concluding the contract. In fact, the forest fire in question had fully consumed most of the timber on the land, without the actual knowledge of either party.
>
> The presence of timber was a basic assumption upon which the land was sold, shared by both parties at the time of contract, and the absence of timber materially affected the bargain. However, the buyer likely assumed that risk when she concluded the contract while aware of the possibility she might be wrong and failed to investigate further.

As a rule, a party is far more likely to be deemed to have assumed a risk as a result of acting on incomplete information when that information is easily available to the party. In many instances, the seller is more likely to be deemed to bear the risk of mistaken value of goods, inasmuch as the seller typically has a greater opportunity to correct any mistaken understanding prior to concluding the transaction.

Like contracts for the sale of land, contracts for the sale of goods provide fertile ground for mistaken factual beliefs. UCC Article 2 does not address the issue of "mistake," so it is supplemented by the common law, as expressly provided by UCC § 1-103(b) (expressly noting the common law doctrine of mistake). Consider the following example of a mistaken sale of valuable art.

Example 45-4: *Estate of Nelson v. Rice*

The executor of an estate had hired an appraiser to value the personal property of the estate for subsequent sale. The appraiser indicated at the time that she lacked any expertise in fine art, but the executor simply asked to be notified by the appraiser of any fine art she encountered so that an expert appraisal could be arranged. The appraiser provided no such notice, so the executor assumed the estate contained no fine art.

The estate then sold a pair of oil paintings, believing them to be mere copies of the originals, and selling the two paintings for $60. In fact, both paintings were originals, worth more than $1 million. The buyer also believed the paintings to be copies based on the price, but purchased them solely because he liked the frames and subject matter.

When the parties both later learned of the originality and value of the paintings, the estate sought rescission based on mutual mistake. The court agreed that the parties had shared a mutual mistake at the time of contracting in their basic assumption that the paintings were copies, and the mistake certainly had a material effect on the price of the paintings. However, the court denied the relief, explaining that the estate bore the risk of the mistake, citing Restatement (Second) of Contracts § 154(b) and noting that the estate knew it had limited knowledge of the authenticity of the paintings, but treated that knowledge as sufficient (even though it had every opportunity to learn of the mistaken assumption before concluding the sale).[4]

Even without the sort of blatant "conscious ignorance" (relying on another who expressly disclaimed any relevant expertise) noted by the court in the foregoing case, a buyer's claim of mutual mistake may be treated more sympathetically than that of a seller.

---

[4] Nelson v. Rice, 198 Ariz. 563, 12 P.3d 238 (Ct. App. 2000).

Consider the following two examples—one directly from the restatement and one from a case decided by the same court as the foregoing example.

Example 45-5: *Renner v. Kehl and § 154, comment a.*

Kehl sold land leases to Renner, who intended to grow crops on the land. Both seller and buyer assumed that adequate water could be accessed by drilling wells on the land. In fact, such water was not available by drilling wells or otherwise. The court granted rescission to the buyer based on the parties' mutual mistake as to the basic assumption that water was available and resulting material effect that buyer could not grow crops.[5]

However, suppose the above seller and buyer made exactly the same transaction, but the buyer not only found the expected water when it drilled, but also unexpectedly found oil. The restatement explains that it is "commonly understood" that such a seller of farm land would not be entitled to rescission under such circumstances, "even though the price was negotiated on the basic assumption that the land was suitable only for farming and the effect on the agreed exchange of performances is material."[6]

As suggested above, one way to understand this distinction is based on the idea that this sort of risk is more appropriately assigned to a seller, who has a greater opportunity to correct any mistaken assumption. However, there is another way one might distinguish the two cases in Example 45-5, based on the nature of the "basic assumptions" (or lack thereof) made by the parties.

In the first transaction, the parties made an affirmative assumption with respect to the availability of water, and that assumption went to the very essence of their reason for concluding the contract. In contrast, the parties to the second contract made no assumption at all with respect to the availability of oil beneath the surface of the farm land. Of course, they did not assume there was oil there, but they did not assume a lot of things about the land that might have made it more valuable (e.g., gold deposits, proximity to a major city, etc.). In effect, it may be easier to rescind a con-

---

[5] Renner v. Kehl, 150 Ariz. 94, 722 P.2d 262 (1986).

[6] Restatement (Second) of Contracts § 154, comment a.

tract based on a mutual mistake about an affirmative assumption than later proves false than based on the lack of an assumption that later proves true. Allowing rescission based on the latter might well expand this exceptional doctrine far more than intended.

Restitution in Cases of Rescission Based on Mistake

As in other cases involving contract rescission, each party will generally be entitled to restitution for any benefit conferred.[7] In extraordinary circumstances, a party may also be entitled to recover losses arising from its reasonable reliance on the contract at issue prior to discovery of the parties' mistake.[8]

Unilateral Mistake

Unilateral mistake traditionally provided far narrower grounds for relief than the doctrine of mutual mistake. A unilateral mistake only provided grounds for rescission where the other party had reason to know of the mistake or caused the mistake. Each of these grounds is easily supported based on previously discussed principles. An offeree who should recognize the mistake cannot reasonably believe that an obviously erroneous offer is subject to acceptance, and a party who has caused the mistake might be said to be estopped from enforcing the resulting contract. Each of these traditional grounds for rescission based on unilateral mistake can be found in Restatement (Second) of Contracts § 153(b). However, this strict traditional approach was expanded in the Restatement (Second) of Contracts to provide for rescission on grounds virtually identical to those of mutual mistake, with a single additional element—that enforcement of the mistaken contract would be unconscionable.[9]

This liberalized approach is well illustrated in the decision of the California Supreme Court addressing a case we first encountered in Chapter 3 on the question of whether an advertisement might, in some circumstances, constitute an offer. In the opinion below, the California Supreme Court left undisturbed the Court of Appeals determination that RRL Corporation had made an "offer," but reached its own conclusion on the question of unilateral mistake.

---

[7] Restatement (Second) of Contracts § 158(1).
[8] Restatement (Second) of Contracts § 158(2).
[9] Restatement (Second) of Contracts § 153(a).

FROM THE COURT

Donovan v. RRL Corporation

Supreme Court California (2001)
26 Cal. 4th 261, 27 P.3d 702, 109 Cal. Rptr. 2d 807

George, C.J.

[Donovan sought to buy a specific used Jaguar advertised by RRL, which the dealer had mistakenly advertised at $12,000 less than the intended price. There was no indication that Donovan was aware the price was a mistake at the time he sought to purchase the car. The court first addressed and affirmed the decision of the Court of Appeals that the dealer's advertisement of the specific car amounted to an effective offer, subject to acceptance by Donovan. *All statutory and case citations in the text that follows are omitted in order to focus on the basic common law analysis.*]

IV

Having concluded that defendant's advertisement for the sale of the Jaguar auto-mobile constituted an offer that was accepted by plaintiff's tender of the advertised price, and that the resulting contract satisfied the statute of frauds, we next consider whether defendant can avoid enforcement of the contract on the ground of mistake.

A party may rescind a contract if his or her consent was given by mistake. A factual mistake by one party to a contract, or unilateral mistake, affords a ground for rescission in some circumstances. Mistake of fact is a mistake, not caused by the neglect of a legal duty on the part of the person making the mistake, and consisting of [a]n unconscious ignorance or forgetfulness of a fact past or present, material to the contract. . . . Defendant's mistake in the present case . . . resulted from an unconscious ignorance that the Daily Pilot advertisement set forth an incorrect price for the automobile. . . . [and] constituted a mistake of fact . . .

Plaintiff [argues] that rescission is unavailable to defendant, because plaintiff was unaware of the mistaken price in defendant's advertisement when he accepted the offer. [However, this Court has] rejected a strict application of the foregoing [traditional] rule regarding unilateral mistake of fact. We have previously stated: "Rescission may be had for mistake of fact if the mistake is material to the contract and was not the result of neglect of a legal duty, if enforcement of the contract as made would be unconscionable, and if the other party can be placed in status quo." . . .

Thus, California law does not adhere to the [traditional] requirements for rescission based upon unilateral mistake of fact—i.e., only in circumstances where the other party knew of the mistake or caused the mistake. Consistent with [our own] decisions . . . . , the Restatement (Second) of Contracts authorizes rescission for a unilateral mistake of fact where "the effect of the mistake is such that enforcement of the contract would be unconscionable." (§ 153 (a)) . . .

Because the [Restatement rule] is consistent with our previous decisions, we adopt the rule as California law. . . . We reject plaintiff's contention and the Court of Appeal's conclusion that, because plaintiff was unaware of defendant's unilateral mistake, the mistake does not provide a ground to avoid enforcement of the contract.

Having concluded that a contract properly may be rescinded on the ground of unilateral mistake of fact as set forth in section 153, subdivision (a), of the Restatement (Second) of Contracts, we next consider whether the requirements of that provision . . . are satisfied in the present case. Where the plaintiff has no reason to know of and does not cause the defendant's unilateral mistake of fact, the defendant must establish the following facts to obtain rescission of the contract: (1) the defendant made a mistake regarding a basic assumption upon which the defendant made the contract; (2) the mistake has a material effect upon the agreed exchange of performances that is adverse to the defendant; (3) the defendant does not bear the risk of the mistake; and (4) the effect of the mistake is such that enforcement of the contract would be unconscionable. We shall consider each of these requirements below.

A significant error in the price term of a contract constitutes a mistake regarding a basic assumption upon which the contract is made, and such a mistake ordinarily has a material effect adverse to the mistaken party. In establishing a material mistake regarding a basic assumption of the contract, the defendant must show that the resulting imbalance in the agreed exchange is so severe that it would be unfair to require the defendant to perform. Ordinarily, a defendant can satisfy this requirement by showing that the exchange not only is less desirable for the defendant, but also is more advantageous to the other party.

Measured against this standard, defendant's mistake in the contract for the sale of the Jaguar automobile constitutes a material mistake regarding a basic assumption upon which it made the contract. Enforcing the contract with the mistaken price of $25,995 would require defendant to sell the vehicle to plaintiff for $12,000 less than the intended advertised price of $37,995—an error amounting to 32 percent of the price defendant intended. The exchange of performances would be substantially less desirable for defendant and more desirable for plaintiff. Plaintiff implicitly concedes that defendant's mistake was material.

The parties and amici curiae vigorously dispute, however, whether defendant should bear the risk of its mistake. Section 154 of the Restatement (Second) of Contracts states: "A party bears the risk of a mistake when (a) the risk is allocated to him by agreement of the parties, or (b) he is aware, at the time the contract is made, that he has only limited knowledge with respect to the facts to which the mistake relates but treats his limited knowledge as sufficient, or (c) the risk is allocated to him by the court on the ground that it is reasonable in the circumstances to do so." Neither of the first two factors applies here. Thus, we must determine whether it is reasonable under the circumstances to allocate to defendant the risk of the mistake in the advertisement.

[The] neglect of a legal duty is described in section 157 of the Restatement (Second) of Contracts, which addresses situations in which a party's fault precludes relief for mistake. Only where the mistake results from "a failure to act in good faith and in accordance with reasonable standards of fair dealing" is rescission unavailable. (§ 157.) This section . . . provides that a mistaken party's failure to exercise due care does not necessarily bar rescission under the rule set forth in section 153.

"The mere fact that a mistaken party could have avoided the mistake by the exercise of reasonable care does not preclude ... avoidance ... [on the ground of mistake]. Indeed, since a party can often avoid a mistake by the exercise of such care, the availability of relief would be severely circumscribed if he were to be barred by his negligence. Nevertheless, in extreme cases the mistaken party's fault is a proper ground for denying him relief for a mistake that he otherwise could have avoided. . . . [T]he rule is stated in terms of good faith and fair dealing. . . . [A] failure to act in good faith and in accordance with reasonable standards of fair dealing during pre-contractual negotiations does not amount to a breach. Nevertheless, under the rule stated in this Section, the failure bars a mistaken party from relief based on a mistake that otherwise would not have been made. During the negotiation stage each party is held to a degree of responsibility appropriate to the justifiable expectations of the other. . . ." (§ 157, com. a) . . .

Plaintiff contends that [California law] imposes a legal duty upon licensed automobile dealers to ensure that their advertisements containing sale prices are accurate. [The applicable statute] provides that it is a violation of the Vehicle Code for a dealer to "[f]ail to sell a vehicle to any person at the advertised total price . . . while the vehicle remains unsold, unless the advertisement states the advertised total price is good only for a specified time and the time has elapsed." Plaintiff also [points to the legal requirement that a] licensed dealer shall not "[m]ake or disseminate . . . in any newspaper . . . any statement which is untrue or misleading and which is known, or which by the exercise of reasonable care should be known, to be untrue or misleading . . ." According to plaintiff, defendant's alleged violation of the duties arising from these statutes also constitutes the neglect of a legal duty . . .

Even if we were to conclude that the foregoing statutes impose a duty of care upon automobile dealers to ensure that prices in an advertisement are accurate, a violation of such a duty would not necessarily preclude the availability of equitable relief. Our prior decisions instruct that the circumstance that a statute imposes a duty of care does not establish that the violation of such a duty constitutes "the neglect of a legal duty" that would preclude rescission for a unilateral mistake of fact. . . .

[I]f we were to accept plaintiff's position that [California law], by requiring a dealer to sell a vehicle at the advertised price, necessarily precludes relief for mistake, and that the dealer always must be held to the strict terms of a contract arising from an advertisement, we would be holding that the dealer intended to assume the risk of all typographical errors in advertisements, no matter how serious the error and regardless of the circumstances in which the error was made. For example, if an automobile dealer proofread an advertisement but, through carelessness, failed to detect a typographical error listing a $75,000 automobile for sale at $75, the defense of mistake would be unavailable to the dealer. . . .

[Such a result], however, "is contrary to common sense and ordinary business understanding and would result in the loss of heretofore well-established equitable rights to relief from certain types of mistake." [The

Court further found no evidence of legislative intent that the statute should impose such a result] . . . Therefore, absent evidence of bad faith, the violation of any obligation imposed by this statute does not constitute the neglect of a legal duty that precludes rescission for unilateral mistake of fact.

[The Court noted the lower court's factual finding that the dealer's mistake had been an honest one, which no intent to deceive. The error was one of simple negligence on the part of the dealer in failing to proofread the ad. There was no indication that the dealer was aware of the error until Donovan sought to purchase the car at the advertised price.]

Defendant's fault consisted of failing to review a proof sheet reflecting the change made on Thursday, April 24, 1997, and/or the actual advertisement appearing in the April 26 edition of the Daily Pilot—choosing instead to rely upon the Daily Pilot's advertising staff to proofread the revised version. Although, as the Court of Appeal found, such an omission might constitute negligence, it does not involve a breach of defendant's duty of good faith and fair dealing that should preclude equitable relief for mistake. In these circumstances, it would not be reasonable for this court to allocate the risk of the mistake to defendant.

As indicated above, the Restatement (Second) of Contracts provides that during the negotiation stage of a contract "each party is held to a degree of responsibility appropriate to the justifiable expectations of the other." (§ 157, com. a.) No consumer reasonably can expect 100 percent accuracy in each and every price appearing in countless automobile advertisements listing numerous vehicles for sale. The degree of responsibility plaintiff asks this court to impose upon automobile dealers would amount to strict contract liability for any typographical error in the price of an advertised automobile, no matter how serious the error or how blameless the dealer. We are unaware of any other situation in which an individual or business is held to such a standard under the law of contracts. Defendant's good faith, isolated mistake does not constitute the type of extreme case in which its fault constitutes the neglect of a legal duty that bars equitable relief. . . .

The final factor defendant must establish before obtaining rescission based upon mistake is that enforcement of the contract for the sale of the 1995 Jaguar XJ6 Vanden Plas at $25,995 would be unconscionable. . . .

. . . In ascertaining whether rescission is warranted for a unilateral mistake of fact, substantive unconscionability often will constitute the determinative factor, because the oppression and surprise ordinarily results from the mistake—not from inequality in bargaining power. Accordingly, even though defendant is not the weaker party to the contract and its mistake did not result from unequal bargaining power, defendant was surprised by the mistake, and in these circumstances overly harsh or one-sided results are sufficient to establish unconscionability entitling defendant to rescission. . . .

In the present case, enforcing the contract with the mistaken price of $25,995 would require defendant to sell the vehicle to plaintiff for $12,000 less than the intended advertised price of $37,995—an error amounting to 32 percent of the price defendant intended. Defendant subsequently sold the automobile for slightly more than the intended advertised price, suggesting that that price reflected its actual market value. Defendant had paid $35,000 for the 1995 Jaguar and incurred costs in advertising, preparing, displaying, and attempting to sell the vehicle. Therefore, defendant would lose more than $9,000 of its original investment in the automobile. Plaintiff, on the other hand, would obtain a $12,000 windfall if the contract were enforced, simply because he traveled to the dealership and stated that he was prepared to pay the advertised price.

. . . Defendant entered into the contract because of its mistake regarding a basic assumption, the price. The $12,000 loss that would result from enforcement of the contract has a material effect upon the agreed exchange of performances that is adverse to defendant. Furthermore, defendant did not neglect any legal duty [under California law] or breach any duty of good faith and fair dealing in the steps leading to the formation of the contract. Plaintiff refused defendant's offer to compensate him for his actual losses in responding to the advertisement. . . . In this situation, it would not be reasonable for this court to allocate the risk of the mistake to defendant.

Having determined that defendant satisfied the requirements for rescission of the contract on the ground of unilateral mistake of fact, we conclude that the municipal court correctly entered judgment in defendant's favor.

CASE QUESTIONS

(1) The dealer made a unilateral clerical error in publishing a price 32% below its intended price. Do you agree that this was a mistake as to a basic assumption on which the offer was made?

(2) The doctrine of "unilateral" mistake adds an element of "unconscionability," which is not required for rescission based on mutual mistake. To what degree is this "unconscionability" element useful in narrowing the application of the same doctrine without the element?

(3) In multiple passages, the court states that it would "not be reasonable" to "allocate the risk of the mistake to the defendant."

   a. What is the nature of the loss caused by the mistake?

   b. Where did the loss caused by the mistake naturally fall?

   c. Does the court purport to shift this loss to Donovan? What sort of element does the California court add to the analysis to avoid such an effect?

   d. Do you agree that Donovan can be returned to the "status quo"? Under what sort of circumstances would rescission for unilateral mistake be precluded based on this requirement?

   e. Early in the opinion, the court states that Restatement (Second) of Contracts § 154(b) is inapplicable to these facts. Do you agree? Is the result in the above case consistent with the result in Example 45-4?

The court's analysis of the effect of simple negligence, as affecting assumption of risk, may also be relevant to the same issue in a case of mutual mistake. If one adopts the approach of the California court above, what is left of the basic rule of *pacta sunt servanda*? Is this an appropriate result?

APPLYING THE RULES

Problem 1: Walker, a cattle breeder, agreed to sell to Sherwood, a banker, one "Rose 2nd of Aberlone," a cow of distinguished lineage. Under normal circumstances, Rose would have fetched $750 to $1,000. However, both parties reasonably believed Rose to be "barren" or sterile. As a result, Rose was sold for $80, her basic value as "beef on the hoof." When the parties subsequently discovered Rose to be "with calf," Walker sought rescission of the contract. What result?

The facts of this problem are loosely based on the issues raised in the case of *Sherwood v. Walker*, 33 N.W. 919 (Mich. 1887).

Problem 2: Wood found a pretty stone about the size and shape of a canary egg and, thinking it might be topaz, took it to Boynton, a jeweler, to inquire of its nature and value. When Wood suggested she thought it might be topaz, the jeweler nodded and said it might indeed be topaz, though he really wasn't sure. Boynton said he had never seen anything quite like it before. When Wood asked whether Boynton might be interested in purchasing the stone, he stated that he would be willing to pay her $1 for it and would keep it as a specimen. Wood decided not to sell the stone at the time, but later came back when she needed money. Consistent with his earlier offer, Boynton purchase the stone for $1. Later, of course, both discovered that the stone was in fact a rough diamond worth about $700. Neither Wood nor Boynton knew any more at the time of the transaction than is described above. While Boynton sold finished diamonds, he had never seen a rough diamond or one this size. Wood sought rescission of the contract. What result?

The facts of this problem are loosely based on the issues raised in the case of *Wood v. Boynton*, 25 N.W. 42 (Wis. 1885).

Problem 3: Ann, a contractor, was preparing a bid for a construction project at the request of Ben, the project owner. Ann was in a bit of a time crunch when Al, her bookkeeper, handed her the final cost data, and she really did not have time to check it. She also knew that Al virtually never made mistakes, so she used his cost calculations in making her bid without any further review. When Ann presented the proposal to Ben, he immediately accepted it. While the price of the proposal was very attractive, it certainly wasn't so far out of the ordinary as to suspect any inaccuracy in its calculation. Ben also knew that contractors often bid projects very cheaply when they need the work to avoid demobilizing their construction crews. The very next day, Ann decided she ought to check Al's work and discovered a major error—amounting to one third of the entire bid price. Ann seeks to rescind her agreement with Ben. Can she do so?

Suppose that Ben was not the project owner, but was a general contractor, and Ann had been bidding to do work as a subcontractor. Further suppose that right after accepting Ann's bid (and relying on it in calculating his own), Ben had made his own bid to Cass, the project owner, and Cass had accepted Ben's bid for the overall project. Again, Ann subsequently discovers the error and seeks to rescind her contract with Ben. Do the above changes in the facts affect your earlier analysis?

Lesson 46: Impossibility of Performance (or Nearly So)

Objectives and Expected Learning Outcomes

In this lesson, you will receive a brief introduction to "risk of loss" rules used to determine who bears the risk of casualty to the subject of the parties' bargain. You will then learn when a party's performance obligation may be excused as a result of unexpected events or circumstances affecting the basic nature of the parties' bargain.

In this lesson, we move from mistaken facts to unexpected events—most typically arising after contract formation. The timing of such events, occurring after contract formation, may also raise additional questions of whether a risk borne by one party has passed to the other party prior to the unexpected event at issue. Thus, we will begin with a very brief overview of "passage of risk."

The "Risk of Loss" and Passage Thereof

Under traditional common law analysis, the owner of anything subject to loss generally bore the risk of such a loss based on property law concepts of "title." When title passed, so did the risk of loss. Predictably, this proved unworkable when selling goods from one state to another with different property laws regarding passage of title. Perhaps most significantly, it provided challenges in insuring goods against any risk of loss, when it was unclear whose loss was being insured at any point in time. UCC Article 2 therefore abandoned the use of title for purposes of passage of risk, instead substituting a relatively clear set of uniform default rules addressing the issue.

The basic default risk of loss rules in UCC Article 2 are found in §§ 2-509 and 2-510. While a detailed examination is beyond the scope of this text, we can look at a simple example to see how the rules work.

> **Example 46-1:** Seller contracts to deliver wheat to buyer, and the contract further provides that the wheat shall be transported by rail from seller's location to buyer's location. The seller delivers the wheat to the rail carrier, as per the contract. However, en route, the rail car carrying the wheat

is struck by lightning and destroyed. The question of course is "whose wheat was destroyed—buyer's or seller's?"

§ 2-509(1)(a) provides in this instance that the risk of loss passes from seller to buyer when the seller hands the goods over to the carrier. Thus, the lightning destroyed the buyer's wheat. Before, however, we shed any tears for the buyer, we should remember that (1) the parties can always contract for different rules regarding risk, and (2) buyer will almost certainly have insured the risk. The key is having a clear rule so that everyone understands where the risk lies at any given point in time.

Later in this lesson, we will briefly return to this issue in addressing excused performance based on commercial impracticability. For now, it is enough to understand the basic concept of rules for determining who bears the risk of loss and when that risk passes from one party to the other.

The CISG provides the same sort of rules for the same reason. Article 4(2) makes clear that the CISG does not purport to govern the passage of property rights in the goods (i.e., "title" to the goods), but instead relies on a series of rules governing the passage of risk. For example, in a contract involving carriage of goods, the CISG provides a default rule in Article 67(1) that, absent contrary agreement or countervailing facts, the risk of loss passes from seller to buyer then the seller hands over the goods to the first carrier, as required by the contract. As with UCC Article 2, the purpose of these rules is to provide reasonable certainty with respect to the risk of loss in transactions between parties who may come from jurisdictions with very different property rules governing passage of title.

With this very basic understanding of "risk of loss" rules, we now move on to discuss the effect of unexpected events affecting the performance of the contract. Most often, such events will affect a seller's ability to perform as promised. The question is whether the loss based on the inability to perform shall remain with seller, who cannot perform as promised, or be shifted to buyer, who fails to receive the promised performance.

The Common Law Doctrine of Impossibility

As with the doctrine of "mistake" addressed in the last lesson, we start with the basic rule that contract promises must be kept. The discussion that follows throughout the remainder of this lesson will address the potential exceptions to this basic rule based on unexpected events making performance considerably more difficult, or even impossible. The common law doctrine of impossibility was originally grounded in the idea that where the subject of the contract had been destroyed, the substance of the contract also lost its continuing vitality.

> ### Example 46-2: *Taylor v. Caldwell*
>
> Caldwell and Bishop owned and rented to Taylor the Surrey Gardens & Music Hall for a series of concerts and related events. After the conclusion of the rental contract, but before any of the planned events, the Hall and Gardens were destroyed by fire. Neither party bore any fault for the fire. Taylor sued, and Caldwell and Bishop sought to be excused from liability based on the unexpected fire for which they bore no fault.
>
> The contract included no express assignment of risk or condition, excusing performance in the event the premises were destroyed, but the court implied such a condition by analogy to the death of a party in a personal services contract. The death of such a party naturally excuses the performance of the deceased, and this doctrine had previously been expanded to include the death of a horse, as subject to contract for sale. Thus, in the instant case, the court deemed the performance obligation of Caldwell and Bishop impliedly conditional upon the continuing existence of the Hall and Gardens and fully excused by their untimely demise by fire.[10]

The foregoing case is generally regarded as having established the basic common law doctrine of impossibility. As such, it is unsurprising that the

---

[10] Taylor v. Caldwell, 122 Eng. Rep. 309 (King's Bench 1863).

original doctrine generally required actual "impossibility" for its application, as compared to any sort of lesser challenge that might simply render
performance considerably more difficult or burdensome. Modern doctrine
has, however, evolved beyond these strictly limited roots.

The duty of a promisor to render performance is discharged where that duty:

- is rendered impracticable,

- without fault of either party,

- by an event or circumstance occurring after conclusion of the
  contract,

- and the non-occurrence of that event or circumstance was a basic assumption (expressly or impliedly) on which the contract
  was made,

- unless the contract language or circumstances indicate otherwise.[11]

We can easily restate the result in Example 46-2 based on this rule. The
duty of the owner to make the hall and gardens available was rendered impracticable, without fault of either party, by the fire that destroyed the hall
and gardens, and non-occurrence of such destruction was a basic (albeit
implied) assumption on which the contract was made.

As with the doctrine of mistake, the difficulty comes in application of the
key elemental standards. What is required to render performance "impracticable"? When is the non-occurrence of any given event or circumstances
a "basic" assumption upon which the contract was made? What is required
to establish that the promisor assumed an obligation to perform notwithstanding the occurrence of such an event or circumstance (i.e., assuming
that risk)?

The basic assumption must address an essential element of performance,
and not simply its cost or ease of completion. Moreover, performance is not
rendered impracticable simply because it has been made far more costly or

---

[11] Restatement (Second) of Contracts § 261.

burdensome. While not always dispositive, a promisor will more often be deemed to have assumed the risk of foreseeable events than unforeseeable ones. When an event or circumstance is foreseeable, the promisor's failure to address it in the parties' contract might well suggest that the risk has been impliedly assumed.

Consider the following example.

> **Example 46-3:** Carrier contracts to deliver goods by sea to a port on the north shore of Alaska during the month of June—a time when the port is always accessible by sea. Unprecedented late season cold weather results in the port remaining locked in ice and inaccessible by sea in June. The only means of delivering the goods to the port is by air, which is far more expensive and extraordinarily difficult to arrange due to the unexpected late season closure of the port.
>
> While carrier's delivery of the goods remains theoretically possible, it has likely been rendered impracticable, without fault of either party, by an unusually late closure of the port by ice. Access to the port by sea was a basic assumption on which the contract was made. Thus, the carrier's performance is likely excused, absent contrary agreement or circumstances. Delivery by air would not merely be more expensive, but would likely fundamentally change the nature of the parties' contract for carriage. Moreover, the unprecedented nature of the weather event suggests that it was not reasonably foreseeable by the parties.

Note that, while the foregoing contract involves goods, it is a contract for carriage of goods—not a contract for the sale of goods. Much of the current common law doctrine of impracticability, as reflected in the Restatement (Second) of Contracts, is actually rooted in UCC Article 2, which is more thoroughly addressed below. However, one final "common law" question is worthy of note.

As indicated at the outset of this section, the doctrines of impossibility or impracticability generally involve supervening events or circumstances arising after the conclusion of the contract. However, the Restatement (Second) of Contracts and at least one rather notable case suggest that impracticability may also be grounded in an "existing fact."[12] The Official Comments seem to make clear that the treatment of "impracticability" in Article 2 is limited to "supervening" events or circumstances, rather than unknown existing facts at the time of contract. One might also reasonably ask whether any lack of awareness by the parties with respect to existing facts is better addressed by reference to the doctrine of mistake. This issue is explored further in one of the problems at the end of this lesson.

Restitution When Performance is Excused Based on Impracticability

In a manner similar to restitution involving cases of rescission for mutual mistake, each party will generally be entitled to restitution for any benefit conferred in exchange for the performance that is excused.[13] In extraordinary circumstances, a party may also be entitled to recover losses arising from its reasonable reliance on the contract provision that was excused.[14]

Commercial Impracticability under UCC Article 2

We began this lesson with a brief discussion of risk of loss rules and now return to this issue in addressing the issue of excuse in a very specific context of casualty to identified goods. **STOP NOW and READ UCC § 2-613(a) below.**

UCC § 2-613(a)

Where the contract requires for its performance goods identified when the contract is made, and the goods suffer casualty without fault of either party before the risk of loss passes to the buyer, . . . then (a) if the loss is total the contract is avoided . . .

Where specific goods identified as those to be delivered to the buyer are destroyed, while their risk of loss remains on the seller, the seller is relieved of its obligation to deliver the goods, and neither party has any further obligations (except of course restitution of any benefit previously conferred).

---

[12] Restatement (Second) of Contracts § 266 and the case addressed by illustration 5.
[13] Restatement (Second) of Contracts § 272(1).
[14] Restatement (Second) of Contracts § 153(a).

In some respects, this particular provision might reasonably be analogized to the destruction of the music hall and gardens in Example 46-1. The seller suffers the loss of the goods (for which the buyer does not have to pay), but would presumably have insured against that loss.

In contrast, if the risk of loss had already passed to the buyer when the goods were destroyed, the buyer would be fully obligated to pay for them under § 2-709(1)(a). Again, however, the buyer would presumably have insured against such a loss.

The foregoing rule provided by § 2-613 is a very narrow and specific one. The more general rule of "impracticability" is found in § 2-615. **STOP NOW and READ UCC § 2-615 below.**

UCC § 2-615

Except so far as a seller may have assumed a greater obligation and subject to the preceding section on substituted performance:

(a) Delay in delivery or non-delivery in whole or in part by a seller who complies with paragraphs (b) and (c) is not a breach of his duty under a contract for sale if performance as agreed has been made impracticable by the occurrence of a contingency the non-occurrence of which was a basic assumption on which the contract was made or by compliance in good faith with any applicable foreign or domestic governmental regulation or order whether or not it later proves to be invalid.

(b) Where the causes mentioned in paragraph (a) affect only a part of the seller's capacity to perform, he must allocate production and deliveries among his customers but may at his option include regular customers not then under contract as well as his own requirements for further manufacture. He may so allocate in any manner which is fair and reasonable. (c) The seller must notify the buyer seasonably that there will be delay or non-delivery and, when allocation is required under paragraph (b), of the estimated quota thus made available for the buyer.

The basic rule breaks down much like the common law. The seller's duty to deliver goods is excused (subject to certain provisions when only part of seller's inventory is affected and notice) where the seller's ability to perform:

- "has been made impracticable,"

- "by the occurrence of a contingency,"

- "the non-occurrence of which was a basic assumption on which the contract was made,"

- "except so far as a seller may have assumed a greater obligation."

This provision of the statute carves out certain issues involving "substituted performance," which are addressed in § 2-614 and are beyond the scope of this text.

While the statute does not expressly discuss the issue of foreseeability, Comment 1 expressly provides that the statute excuses the seller "where performance has become commercially impracticable because of *unforeseeable supervening circumstances* not within the contemplation of the parties at the time of contracting" (emphasis added). Presumably, the parties to a contract are capable of addressing foreseeable circumstances in their agreement. Thus, a lack of foreseeability would seem to strengthen the seller's argument that the "non-occurrence" of the contingency at issue was indeed a "basic assumption" of the parties' contract and one that had not been assumed by the seller.

Comment 4 clarifies that "increased cost alone does not excuse performance" unless "due to some unforeseen contingency which alters the essential nature of the performance." We again see reference to the issue of foreseeability, and, here, we also see an emphasis on the fundamental nature of the contingency in altering the essential nature of the parties' performance.

The comments to § 2-615 also provide an extensive and useful narrative addressing a common problem faced by sellers. What happens when the seller's supplier fails to perform, thereby causing the seller to breach its own contract with its buyer? If the seller and buyer have contracted for generic goods available elsewhere, then the seller will presumably engage in a "cover" transaction, as addressed in Chapter 8. As such, the seller will be able to deliver to buyer, as promised, and can recover any additional costs associated with the cover transaction in a claim against seller's own supplier under § 2-712. However, if seller and buyer agree on a specific source of supply, then the seller will presumably have no opportunity to cover in the event that supply fails. In such a circumstance, a seller might reasonably seek to be excused.

Comment 5 specifically addresses circumstances in which an agreed source of supply fails through no fault of either seller or buyer.

OFFICIAL COMMENT 5 (UCC § 2-615)

5. Where a particular source of supply [as established by the parties' agreement or the circumstances] is exclusive under the agreement, and fails though casualty, [§2-615] applies rather than [§ 2-613]. . . . There is no excuse under this section, however, unless the seller has employed all due measures to assure himself that this source will not fail. . . .

    In the case of failure of production by an agreed source for causes beyond the seller's control, the seller should, if possible, be excused since production by an agreed source is without more a basic assumption of the contract. Such excuse should not result in relieving the defaulting supplier from liability nor in dropping into the seller's lap an unearned bonus of damages. . . . A condition of [the seller's] making good the claim of excuse is the turning over to the buyer of [seller's] rights against the defaulting source of supply to the extent of the buyer's contract in relation to which the excuse is being claimed.

In effect, where an agreed source of "supply" to seller fails, the seller who has contracted with the supplier in an effort to secure that source is excused, provided the seller turns over to the buyer any right of action against the supplier. In this way, the defaulting supplier is held liable, and the buyer is provided a direct right of action to enforce the claim.

A seller who is aware that it is relying on a sole source of supply will, of course, be well advised to do two things: (1) identify that source as an agreed source of supply under the parties' contract, and (2) take all reasonable steps to ensure the performance of that source, including a contract binding the supplier in a manner allowing the seller to deliver to its own buyer. It is worth noting, however, that such an agreement on a source of supply will effectively transfer the risk of the supplier's non-performance to the buyer. While the buyer will have a direct claim against the supplier, any inability of supplier to pay will result in the buyer bearing the ultimate loss arising from the supplier's non-performance. Such a result is likely reasonable in the common circumstance in which the buyer has either directly or indirectly chosen a supplier by reference to a specified product.

Of course, the parties may also allocate risks directly, as a matter of contract, and often do so through the use of "force majeure" clauses. Such clauses are frequently used in contracts governed by either the common law or UCC Article 2 to address the proverbial "act of God" or any other contingencies beyond the control of the parties. Any given risk can be assigned to either party in such a provision. However, the most common use is to excuse the seller's performance in any of the listed circumstances. In this respect, at least a portion of the seller's loss is effectively shifted to the buyer, who will no longer be entitled to performance.

Impediment under the CISG

The CISG uses the term "impediment" to describe an event or circumstances that may excuse a party's performance. While not expressly limited to sellers, the nature of seller's performance obligations is such that the relief provided by the statute will far more often be sought by sellers than buyers. **STOP NOW and READ CISG Article 79(1) below.**

CISG ARTICLE 79(1)

(1) A party is not liable for a failure to perform any of his obligations if he proves that the failure was due to an impediment beyond his control and that he could not reasonably be expected to have taken the impediment into account at the time of the conclusion of the contract or to have avoided or overcome it or its consequences. . . .

A detailed examination of the statute and its subsections (omitted above) is beyond the scope of this text. However, its basic elements are worthy of note by way of comparison to UCC § 2-615. In order to establish a defense to liability for breach based on "impediment," a party must prove that its failure was:

- due to an impediment beyond the party's control,

- that the party could not have reasonably been expected to take into account at the time of contracting, and

- that the party could neither have been expected to have:

  o avoided, or

  o overcome.

As a whole, the requirements of Article 79 have often been applied quite strictly, such that a successful defense of "impediment" is likely more difficult than a successful defense based on "impracticability" under UCC § 2-615.

APPLYING THE RULES

Problem 1: Acme contracts to sell widgets to Zenith, and the contract provides that the widgets are to be shipped via Transcon Rail Service (TRS). Acme plans to use its own truck to deliver the widgets to TRS, which will then transport and deliver them to Zenith, as provided under the contract, much like the facts of Example 46-1. Consider the following two different hypothetical examples:

(A) The Acme truck crashes in route to deliver the widgets to TRS (the other vehicle is at fault—not Acme), and all of the widgets are destroyed;

(B) The TRS train derails while carrying the widgets to Zenith, and all of the widgets are destroyed.

For each variation, answer the following questions, with citation to appropriate statutory authority. Is Acme liable for breach of contract? Is Zenith obligated to pay for the widgets? If so, how much?

Problem 2: Transatlantic Finance Company (TFC) contracted with the U.S. government to transport wheat from Texas to Iran. Soon after the ship carrying the wheat had sailed from Texas, war broke out in the Middle East, and the Suez Canal was closed. Ocean freight carriers virtually always used the Suez Canal when transporting goods between the two locations in question. While it was also possible to travel around the Cape of Good Hope, this route was considerably longer in duration and more expensive. At the time of contracting, political tensions had been high in the Middle East, but not particularly more so than on many other occasions in which neither war not closure of the Canal had ensued.

When TFC learned of the Canal closing, it immediately contacted the U.S. and stated that it would require additional time and more money for the delivery around the Cape of Good Hope. Is TFC excused from its original performance terms by the closure of the Suez Canal?

The facts of this problem are loosely based on the issues raised in the case of *Transatlantic Financing Corporation v. United States*, 363 F.2d 312 (D.C. Cir. 1966).

Problem 3: Canadian Industrial Alcohol (CIA) (which you should initially assume to be a Vermont business despite its name) contracted to purchase molasses from Dunbar, for delivery in installments, with the goods described as "approximately 1,500,000 wine gallons Refined Blackstrap Molasses of the usual run from the National Sugar Refinery, Yonkers, N.Y." During the contract period, the production of National Sugar Refinery was far less than anticipated, and many of its customers, including Dunbar, received far less molasses than requested. Consider each of the two following factual variations:

(A) Dunbar had never had a problem getting molasses from National Sugar Refinery in the past, so it did not bother to contract in advance for the molasses necessary to satisfy its contract with CIA; and

(B) Dunbar contracted with National Sugar Refinery for molasses sufficient to satisfy its contract with CIA, but National Sugar breached the contract.

Fully describe the rights and obligations of the parties in each of the two foregoing variations.

How, if at all, would your answer to the second variation change if another customer of the National Sugar Refinery had an excess of the same molasses available at the relevant time period and was willing to sell it at a price equal to 125% of the contract price between Dunbar and CIA?

The facts of this problem are loosely based on the issues raised in the case of *Canadian Industrial Alcohol Co. v. Dunbar Molasses Co*, 258 N.Y. 194, 179 N.E. 383 (1932).

Problem 4: Howard was building a bridge and contracted to take all of the sand and gravel Howard needed for the bridge from Mineral Park Land, paying a specified price for each 1,000 cubic feet needed. Both parties assumed that sufficient sand and gravel was reasonably available to complete the job.

Howard used a total of 100,000 cubic feet of sand and gravel in completing the bridge, but took only half of it from Mineral Park Land. As it turned out, only 50,000 cubic feet of sand and gravel was available above water level, and removing additional sand and gravel located below water level required a very different extraction process, costing 10 times the amount of extraction above water level.

Howard sought to be excused from the half of obligation relating to sand and gravel below the water line—result? What theory should Howard rely upon?

The facts of this problem are loosely based on the issues raised in the case of *Mineral Park Land Co. v. Howard*, 172 Cal. 289, 156 P. 458 (1916).

Lesson 47: Frustration of Purpose

Objectives and Expected Learning Outcomes

In this lesson, you will learn when the parties' performance is excused because the intended purpose of the recipient of the promised performance has been frustrated. You will learn the difference between impossibility (or impracticability) and frustration of purpose, as well as a variety of limits on the application of the latter.

The Common Law Doctrine of Frustration of Purpose

In the last lesson, we focused on unexpected events making performance considerably more difficult, if not impossible. In this lesson, we shift our focus from events affecting the difficulty of performance to unexpected events affecting the utility of that performance to its recipient. Typically, the recipient of a promised performance obligation need only accept and pay for the performance, and payment obligations are rarely affected by unexpected external events (a party's financial ability to pay is of course entirely another matter). However, when the promised performance unexpectedly loses its utility to the recipient, that recipient will no longer wish to complete the transaction. This brings us to the common law doctrine of "frustration of purpose."

As with other issues addressed in this chapter, our baseline "rule" is that promises must be kept—including the promise to accept and pay for the other party's promised performance. In fact, it ought to be immediately obvious that any "exception" to this general rule has the potential to undermine our entire theory of contract. Surely a buyer cannot decide after concluding a contract that it no longer wants what it earlier bargained for—simply because its purpose in making the contract has been undermined in some unexpected manner. The materials that follow will address both the common law rule and the means by which its effect is constrained.

The Basic Rule

The basic rule of "frustration of purpose" is nicely illustrated by the following classic English case. As with many English cases, the basic oral arguments of counsel are included and followed by the decision of the court.

Krell v. Henry

Court of Appeal 1903
2 KB 740

The plaintiff, Paul Krell, sued the defendant, C. S. Henry, for 50l., being the balance of a sum of 75l., for which the defendant had agreed to hire a flat at 56A, Pall Mall on the days of June 26 and 27, for the purpose of viewing the processions to be held in connection with the coronation of His Majesty. The defendant denied his liability, and counter-claimed for the return of the sum of 25l., which had been paid as a deposit, on the ground that, the processions not having taken place owing to the serious illness of the King, there had been a total failure of consideration for the contract entered into by him.

The facts, which were not disputed, were as follows. The plaintiff on leaving the country in March, 1902, left instructions with his solicitor to let his suite of chambers at 56A, Pall Mall on such terms and for such period (not exceeding six months) as he thought proper. On June 17, 1902, the defendant noticed an announcement in the windows of the plaintiff's flat to the effect that windows to view the coronation processions were to be let. The defendant interviewed the housekeeper on the subject, when it was pointed out to him what a good view of the processions could be obtained from the premises, and he eventually agreed with the housekeeper to take the suite for the two days in question for a sum of 75l. On June 20 the defendant wrote the following letter to the plaintiff's solicitor:

"I am in receipt of yours of the 18th instant, inclosing form of agreement for the suite of chambers on the third floor at 56A, Pall Mall, which I have agreed to take for the two days, the 26th and 27th instant, for the sum of 75l. . . . I inclose herewith cheque for 25l. as deposit, and will thank you to confirm to me that I shall have the entire use of these rooms during the days (not the nights) of the 26th and 27th instant. You may rely that every care will be taken of the premises and their contents. On the 24th inst. I will pay the balance, viz., 50l., to complete the 75l. agreed upon."

On the same day the defendant received the following reply from the plaintiff's solicitor:

"I am in receipt of your letter of today's date inclosing cheque for 25l. deposit on your agreeing to take Mr. Krell's chambers on the third floor at 56A, Pall Mall for the two days, the 26th and 27th June, and I confirm the agreement that you are to have the entire use of these rooms during the days (but not the nights), the balance, 50l., to be paid to me on Tuesday next the 24th instant."

The processions not having taken place on the days originally appointed, namely, June 26 and 27, the defendant declined to pay the balance of 50l. alleged to be due from him under the contract in writing of June 20 constituted by the above two letters. Hence the present action.

[The lower court] held, upon the authority of Taylor v. Caldwell [referenced earlier in Example 46-1], that there was an implied condition in the contract that the procession should take place, and gave judgment for the defendant on the claim and counter-claim.

The plaintiff appealed.

[The colloquy that follows reflects the arguments of counsel for the parties, along with injections by the appellate judges hearing the argument. **Counsel for Plaintiff, Krell**, the owner of the flat, began.]

In the contract nothing is said about the coronation procession, but it is admitted that both parties expected that there would be a procession, and that the price to be paid for the rooms was fixed with reference to the expected procession. [The lower court] held that both the claim and the counter-claim were governed by Taylor v. Caldwell, and that there was an implied term in the contract that the procession should take place. It is submitted that the learned judge was wrong. If he was right, the result will be that in every case of this kind an unremunerated promisor will be in effect an insurer of the hopes and expectations of the promisee.

[Counsel began by seeking to distinguish the present case from Taylor v. Caldwell.] In the present case there has been no default on the part of the defendant. But there has been no physical extinction of the subject-matter, and the performance of the contract was quite possible. [Thus, the rule of Taylor v. Caldwell does not excuse the obligation of Henry in this case.] . . .

The real question is, what was the position of the parties on June 20, and what was the contract then entered into between them? The right possessed by the plaintiff on that day was the right of looking out of the window of the room, with the opportunity of seeing the procession from that window; the only sale to the defendant was of such right as the plaintiff had, and that was all that the plaintiff was parting with by the contract.

There was, of course, the risk that the procession, the anticipation of which gave the room a marketable value, might, from some cause or other, never take place; but that risk passed to the defendant by the contract. On entering into the contract with the defendant the plaintiff put it out of his power to let the room to anyone else: he passed the right and the risk at the same time. No implied condition can be imported into the contract that the object of it shall be attained. There can be no implied condition that the defendant shall be placed in the actual position of seeing the procession. [Counsel then recounted numerous cases in which an apparently good bargain had gone bad due to changed circumstances, but the court had held the parties to their original bargain.] The rule is that the Court will not imply any condition in a contract except in case of absolute necessity. . . . No doubt, under the Sale of Goods Act, 1893, where the specific goods, the subject of the contract, perish, the contract is gone; but this is not a case of that kind. . . .

In conclusion it is submitted that the Court cannot imply an express condition that the procession should pass. Nothing should be implied beyond what was necessary to give to the contract that efficacy which the parties intended at the time. There is no such necessity here; in fact, the inference is the other way, for [all of the money was to be paid] before the days specified; which shews that the passing of the procession did not really constitute the basis of the contract, except in a popular sense. The truth is that each party had an expectation, no doubt; but the position is simply this: one says, "Will you take the room?" and the other says, "Yes." That is all. The contract did nothing more than give the defendant the opportunity of seeing whatever might be going on upon the days mentioned.

[**Counsel for Defendant, Henry**, the party contracting for use of the flat, then responded.] The question is, what was the bargain? The defendant contends that it was a bargain with an implied condition that the premises taken were premises in front of which a certain act of

State would take place by Royal Proclamation. A particular character was thus impressed upon the premises; and when that character ceased to be impressed upon them the contract was at an end. It is through nobody's fault, but through an unforeseen misfortune that the premises lose that character. The price agreed to be paid must be regarded: it is equivalent to many thousands a year. What explanation can be given of that, except that it was agreed to be paid for the purpose of enabling the defendant to see the procession? It was the absolute assumption of both parties when entering into the contract that the procession would pass.

The principle of Taylor v. Caldwell—namely, that a contract for the sale of a particular thing must not be construed as a positive contract, but as subject to an implied condition that, when the time comes for fulfilment, the specified thing continues to exist—exactly applies. The certainty of the coronation and consequent procession taking place was the basis of this contract. Both parties bargained upon the happening of a certain event the occurrence of which gave the premises a special character with a corresponding value to the defendant; but as the condition failed the premises lost their adventitious value. There has been such a change in the character of the premises which the plaintiff agreed the defendant should occupy as to deprive them of their value. When the premises become unfit for the purpose for which they were taken the bargain is off: Taylor v. Caldwell, . . . What was in contemplation here was not that the defendant should merely go and sit in the room, but that he should see a procession which both parties regarded as an inevitable event. There was an implied warranty or condition founded on the presumed intention of the parties, and upon reason . . . No doubt the observations of the Court in that case were addressed to a totally different subject-matter, but the principle laid down was exactly as stated in Taylor v. Caldwell . . .

To sum up, the basis of the contract is that there would be a procession—that is to say, it is a contract based upon a certain thing coming into existence: there is a condition precedent that there shall be a procession. But for the mutual expectation of a procession upon the days mentioned there would have been no contract whatever. The basis of the contract was also the continuance of a thing in a certain condition; for on June 20 the rooms were capable of being described as a place from which to view a procession on two particular days; whereas when those days arrived the rooms were no longer capable of being so described.

[A month later, Judge Williams read the following written judgment.]
The real question in this case is the extent of the application in English
law of the principle of the Roman law which has been adopted and
acted on in many English decisions, and notably in the case of Taylor v.
Caldwell. That case at least makes it clear that "where, from the nature
of the contract, it appears that the parties must from the beginning
have known that it could not be fulfilled unless, when the time for
the fulfilment of the contract arrived, some particular specified thing
continued to exist, so that when entering into the contract they must
have contemplated such continued existence as the foundation of what
was to be done; there, in the absence of any express or implied warranty
that the thing shall exist, the contract is not to be considered a positive
contract, but as subject to an implied condition that the parties shall be
excused in case, before breach, performance becomes impossible from
the perishing of the thing without default of the contractor." . . . It is
said, on the one side, that the specified thing, state of things, or condition the continued existence of which is necessary for the fulfilment of
the contract, so that the parties entering into the contract must have
contemplated the continued existence of that thing, condition, or state
of things as the foundation of what was to be done under the contract,
is limited to things which are either the subject-matter of the contract or
a condition or state of things, present or anticipated, which is expressly
mentioned in the contract. But, on the other side, it is said that the
condition or state of things need not be expressly specified, but that it is
sufficient if that condition or state of things clearly appears by extrinsic
evidence to have been assumed by the parties to be the foundation or
basis of the contract, and the event which causes the impossibility is
of such a character that it cannot reasonably be supposed to have been
in the contemplation of the contracting parties when the contract was
made. In such a case the contracting parties will not be held bound
by the general words which, though large enough to include, were not
used with reference to a possibility of a particular event rendering performance of the contract impossible. I do not think that the principle
of the civil law as introduced into the English law is limited to cases in
which the event causing the impossibility of performance is the destruction or non-existence of some thing which is the subject-matter of the
contract or of some condition or state of things expressly specified as
a condition of it. I think that you first have to ascertain, not necessarily from the terms of the contract, but, if required, from necessary

inferences, drawn from surrounding circumstances recognised by both contracting parties, what is the substance of the contract, and then to ask the question whether that substantial contract needs for its foundation the assumption of the existence of a particular state of things. If it does, this will limit the operation of the general words, and in such case, if the contract becomes impossible of performance by reason of the non-existence of the state of things assumed by both contracting parties as the foundation of the contract, there will be no breach of the contract thus limited.

Now what are the facts of the present case? The contract is contained in two letters of June 20 which passed between the defendant and the plaintiff's agent, Mr. Cecil Bisgood. These letters do not mention the coronation, but speak merely of the taking of Mr. Krell's chambers, or, rather, of the use of them, in the daytime of June 26 and 27, for the sum of 75l., 25l. then paid, balance 50l. to be paid on the 24th. But the affidavits, which by agreement between the parties are to be taken as stating the facts of the case, shew that the plaintiff exhibited on his premises, third floor, 56A, Pall Mall, an announcement to the effect that windows to view the Royal coronation procession were to be let, and that the defendant was induced by that announcement to apply to the housekeeper on the premises, who said that the owner was willing to let the suite of rooms for the purpose of seeing the Royal procession for both days, but not nights, of June 26 and 27. In my judgment the use of the rooms was let and taken for the purpose of seeing the Royal procession. It was not a demise of the rooms, or even an agreement to let and take the rooms. It is a licence to use rooms for a particular purpose and none other. And in my judgment the taking place of those processions on the days proclaimed along the proclaimed route, which passed 56A, Pall Mall, was regarded by both contracting parties as the foundation of the contract; and I think that it cannot reasonably be supposed to have been in the contemplation of the contracting parties, when the contract was made, that the coronation would not be held on the proclaimed days, or the processions not take place on those days along the proclaimed route; and I think that the words imposing on the defendant the obligation to accept and pay for the use of the rooms for the named days, although general and unconditional, were not used with reference to the possibility of the particular contingency which afterwards occurred.

It was suggested in the course of the argument that if the occurrence, on the proclaimed days, of the coronation and the procession in this case were the foundation of the contract, and if the general words are thereby limited or qualified, so that in the event of the non-occurrence of the coronation and procession along the proclaimed route they would discharge both parties from further performance of the contract, it would follow that if a cabman was engaged to take someone to Epsom on Derby Day at a suitable enhanced price for such a journey, say 10l., both parties to the contract would be discharged in the contingency of the race at Epsom for some reason becoming impossible; but I do not think this follows, for I do not think that in the cab case the happening of the race would be the foundation of the contract.

No doubt the purpose of the engager would be to go to see the Derby, and the price would be proportionately high; but the cab had no special qualifications for the purpose which led to the selection of the cab for this particular occasion. Any other cab would have done as well. Moreover, I think that, under the cab contract, the hirer, even if the race went off, could have said, "Drive me to Epsom; I will pay you the agreed sum; you have nothing to do with the purpose for which I hired the cab," and that if the cabman refused he would have been guilty of a breach of contract, there being nothing to qualify his promise to drive the hirer to Epsom on a particular day. Whereas in the case of the coronation, there is not merely the purpose of the hirer to see the coronation procession, but it is the coronation procession and the relative position of the rooms which is the basis of the contract as much for the lessor as the hirer; and I think that if the King, before the coronation day and after the contract, had died, the hirer could not have insisted on having the rooms on the days named. It could not in the cab case be reasonably said that seeing the Derby race was the foundation of the contract, as it was of the licence in this case. Whereas in the present case, where the rooms were offered and taken, by reason of their peculiar suitability from the position of the rooms for a view of the coronation procession, surely the view of the coronation procession was the foundation of the contract, which is a very different thing from the purpose of the man who engaged the cab—namely, to see the race—being held to be the foundation of the contract.

Each case must be judged by its own circumstances. In each case one must ask oneself, first, what, having regard to all the circumstances, was the foundation of the contract? Secondly, was the performance of the contract prevented? Thirdly, was the event which prevented the performance of the contract of such a character that it cannot reasonably be said to have been in the contemplation of the parties at the date of the contract? If all these questions are answered in the affirmative (as I think they should be in this case), I think both parties are discharged from further performance of the contract. I think that the coronation procession was the foundation of this contract, and that the non-happening of it prevented the performance of the contract; and, secondly, I think that the non-happening of the procession . . . was an event "of such a character that it cannot reasonably be supposed to have been in the contemplation of the contracting parties when the contract was made, and that they are not to be held bound by general words which, though large enough to include, were not used with reference to the possibility of the particular contingency which afterwards happened." The test seems to be whether the event which causes the impossibility was or might have been anticipated and guarded against. It seems difficult to say, in a case where both parties anticipate the happening of an event, which anticipation is the foundation of the contract, that either party must be taken to have anticipated, and ought to have guarded against, the event which prevented the performance of the contract. . . I myself am clearly of opinion that in this case, where we have to ask ourselves whether the object of the contract was frustrated by the non-happening of the coronation and its procession on the days proclaimed, parol evidence is admissible to shew that the subject of the contract was rooms to view the coronation procession, and was so to the knowledge of both parties. When once this is established, I see no difficulty whatever in the case. It is not essential to the application of the principle of Taylor v. Caldwell that the direct subject of the contract should perish or fail to be in existence at the date of performance of the contract. It is sufficient if a state of things or condition expressed in the contract and essential to its performance perishes or fails to be in existence at that time. In the present case the condition which fails and prevents the achievement of that which was, in the contemplation of both parties, the foundation of the contract, is not expressly mentioned either as a condition of the contract or the purpose of it; but I think for the reasons which I have given that the principle of Taylor v. Caldwell ought to be applied.

CASE QUESTIONS

(1) Consider first the arguments of counsel for Krell that Henry's promise to pay for the flat should not be excused. At the most basic level, what is Krell arguing? Who, if anyone, do you think assumed the risk of the cancellation of the coronation procession?

   a. Counsel for Krell argues that, if the decision of the lower court is affirmed, "the result will be that in every case of this kind an unremunerated promisor will be in effect an insurer of the hopes and expectations of the promisee." Do you agree? If not, where does the court propose to draw a line precluding such a result?

   b. Counsel for Krell distinguishes the present case from one involving casualty to goods under the English Sales Act. Which provision of UCC Article 2 addresses casualty to goods? Do you see why that sort of casualty is distinguishable from the present case?

   c. How did Counsel for Krell ask the court to limit excuse based on unexpected events or circumstances?

(2) How did Counsel for Henry argue that the court should expand the rule of Taylor v. Caldwell so as to excuse Henry's performance in this case?

(3) How does the court choose between the parties' positions?

   a. How, if at all, did the court limit the application of the rule of this case to avoid the concerns expressed by Counsel for Krell in Question (1)a. above.

   b. What is the significance of the court's characterization of the contract as a "license," rather than the rental of a room?

   c. What, if any, relevance does the court afford to the question of whether the cancellation of the procession was foreseeable?

The court concludes by distinguishing the instant case from one involving a contract to hire a cab for transportation to the English Derby on Derby Day. The court's distinction can be taken one step further by contrasting the contract for a cab with the purchase of a ticket for the English Derby, itself.

> **Example 47-1:** While more frequent than the coronation procession for a new monarch, the Derby at Epsom Downs is unquestionably a major event each year. One who was interested in attending the Derby might therefore contract in advance for (1) a seat in the grandstands to watch the derby (i.e., a "ticket" to the Derby); and (2) a cab to be transported to Epsom Downs (the demand for such cabs on the day itself being quite high and availability therefore limited). If, as hypothesized by the court in the foregoing case, the unthinkable happened and the Derby was not run, then both the seat in the grandstands and the seat in the cab would have little value to the party who had contracted for each. However, the party's contract obligation to pay for the thing purchased would be excused only in the former case—and not in the latter.

Much like Henry's contract for the flat on Pall Mall from which he could watch the coronation procession, a ticket to the Derby is more in the nature of a "license" to watch the event from a specific location than the rental of a particular seating fixture. The very nature of the agreement is a contract to watch the event—not a contract to occupy a space for whatever purpose might be available at the time. If the Derby is not held, there is simply nothing to watch. Indeed, we would be quite surprised to purchase a ticket for an event and then to be denied a refund of the ticket price if the event were cancelled. While Krell did not cancel the coronation procession in the foregoing case, the effect is largely the same.

In contrast, an advance contract to hire a cab is a contract for transportation. While the purpose of the transportation is undeniably related solely to the attendance of the Derby, the substance of the contract—transportation to Epsom Downs can nevertheless be performed and received (whether desired or not). In effect, the party contracting in advance for transportation to the Derby has, indeed, assumed the risk that the Derby might not be held (as well as the risk of failing to acquire a ticket to the Derby), as argued by Counsel for Krell in the foregoing case.

Of course, it is not always easy to draw the sort of line described in the example above. The doctrine of frustration of purpose is generally stated as follows.

The duty of a party to render performance is discharged where:

- after the contract is concluded,

- the party's principal purpose is substantially frustrated,

- without the party's own fault,

- by the occurrence of an event the non-occurrence of which was a basic assumption on which the contract is made,

- unless the contract language or circumstances indicate otherwise.[15]

While important, the first three elements might be established in the majority of cases in which a contracting party no longer wants that for which it contracted, and the last element is necessarily somewhat vague in its reference to general circumstances. Thus, any defense seeking to excuse performance based on frustration of purpose will often come down to one question—was the non-occurrence of the event in question a "basic assumption" on which the contract was made.

Consider the following variation on the last example.

---

[15] Restatement (Second) of Contracts § 265.

Example 47-2: Smith owns a small storefront just outside the gates of Derby Downs. Jones wishes to sell various Derby souvenirs (hats, t-shorts, pins, etc.) and rents the storefront from Smith solely for use for 8 hours during Derby Day. The Derby is canceled, and Jones seeks rescission of the contract based on "frustration of purpose."

In some respects, the rental of the storefront by Jones looks very much like the rental of the room overlooking Pall Mall by Henry. However, Jones is not renting space to watch or attend the Derby, but to sell souvenirs relating to the Derby. Jones can still do so. The fact that no one will likely buy such souvenirs is analogous to the uselessness of a cab ride to Epsom Downs without a Derby to attend. This was essentially a risk Jones took in leasing the space useable only in the event the Derby was held. The contract between Smith and Jones was purely a contract for the rental of space—not a contract granting Jones the specific right to sell Derby souvenirs. Thus, Jones is bound to pay Smith for the space, as agreed.

Finally, consider one more variation on the court's Derby Day example.

Example 47-3: Baker wishes to make a video of the running of the Derby and sell it. To that end, she contracts with the organization running the Derby for the right to do so. The Derby is canceled, and Baker seeks rescission of the contract based on "frustration of purpose."

In this case, the essence of Baker's contract was to record the Derby. Without the running of the Derby, there is simply nothing to record. Thus, Baker can reasonably establish that the non-occurrence of the "cancellation" (i.e., the occurrence of the Derby) was a "basic assumption" on which the contract is made. Baker is therefore likely excused from her contract obligation to pay for the video recording rights.

Both Smith and Baker contracted for the right to engage in a business opportunity in hopes of making a commercial profit off of the running of the Derby. In each case, the cancellation of the Derby defeated their plans, and each lost their intended profits. However, Smith also lost the cost of renting the space from Jones; whereas, Baker was able to recover the cost of the recording rights based on "frustration of purpose." You will have further opportunities to try to draw such distinctions in the problems that follow.

Language or Circumstances Indicating a Party has Assumed the Risk

In some instances, the language or circumstances of the contract may indicate that one of the parties has assumed the risk of the event in question—even though its non-occurrence was a basic assumption of the agreement. This might arise directly from the contract language, or it might be implied from the surrounding circumstances.

Restitution When Performance is Excused Based on Frustration of Purpose

In a manner similar to restitution involving cases of impossibility or commercial impracticability, each party will generally be entitled to restitution for any benefit conferred in exchange for the performance that is excused.[16] In extraordinary circumstances, a party may also be entitled to recover losses arising from its reasonable reliance on the contract provision that was excused.[17]

We can return to the case of *Krell v. Henry* for an example of restitution.

> **Example 47-4:** Henry prepaid Krell 25l., as a deposit on the room. This issue was waived by Henry in the original case. However, having excused the parties' performance, a court would also likely require Krell to return the 25l. as a matter of restitution.

---

[16] Restatement (Second) of Contracts § 272(1).
[17] Restatement (Second) of Contracts § 272(2).

We might also change the facts of the actual case to illustrate a claim for reliance where performance has been excused.

> **Example 47-5:** Suppose, at Henry's request, and as part of the parties' agreement, Krell installed a special telescope on the balcony of the room so as to enhance Henry's viewing of the expected procession. If Henry's obligation to pay the overall price of the room (presumably reflecting the increased cost associated with the installation of the telescope) was excused, he would nevertheless likely be liable to Krell for the cost of the telescope as a matter of reliance.

Frustration of the Buyer's Purpose for Purchased Goods

UCC Article 2 does not address frustration of purpose, as it focuses almost entirely on the performance of the seller. The only provisions that might affect the buyer are those in §2-614 involving facilities related to transport or delivery, or buyer's payment obligation, and those each relate to difficulties in performance, and not the utility of any such performance. Thus, any issue involving frustration of purpose in relation to a sale of goods would be governed by the common law, as supplementing UCC Article 2.

While CISG Article 79 is not expressly limited to sellers, its language clearly focuses on "impediments" to performance, rather than any effects on the utility of that performance. The question of whether CISG Article 79 precludes resort to domestic law or other international principles excusing performance in unexpected circumstances is subject to some debate and beyond our scope here. However, Article 79 is the only exemption for unexpected events or circumstances provided by the text of the CISG.

APPLYING THE RULES

Problem 1: Ann owns a hotel, and Ben owns a spa next door. Ann would like for her hotel guests to be able to use the spa. She enters into a signed, written 5 year contract with Ben, in which she pays $3,000 per month in exchange for Ben providing Ann's hotel guests with unlimited use of the spa. At the end of year 4, a tornado levels Ann's hotel, and it will take more than 1 year to rebuild it. Ann seeks to avoid the monthly payments to Ben during the final year of the contract. Can she do so without breaching the contract?

Problem 2: On June 1, Alpha contracted to sell to Beta specified quantities of Wonderdrug, a new pharmaceutical recently approved by the USFDA. Alpha is the manufacturer of the drug, and Beta is an online seller of drugs, solely selling FDA approved drugs for human use. The contract calls for delivery on August 1. Consider the following hypothetical variations. In each case, explain how the stated facts might affect the parties' obligations (i.e., who might want to be excused from the contract and under what theory)?

(A) On July 1, the FDA revokes its approval of the drug for human consumption. The drug is not formally banned, but may only be used as plant food (another well-known use of the drug).

(B) On July 1, Alpha and Beta each realized that they had misread the FDA approval letter, which was limited Wonderdrug's use in animals—not humans.

(C) On July 1, the FDA banned the sale of Wonderdrug for any purpose.

Problem 3: Paonessa contracted to perform specified road work for the State of Massachusetts. Part of that road work required Paonessa to provide precast concrete median barriers. Paoness subcontracted with Chase to supply these barriers. The contract between the State and Paonessa expressly provided the State with the right to eliminate any of the barriers it found unnecessary, while the contract between Paonessa and Chase contained no such provision. Otherwise, each contract provided for the same number of barriers, and Chase was familiar with terms of the contract Paonessa had with the State.

The installation of concrete median barriers (replacing previous strips of grass) drew substantial protests by local citizens, and the State decided to cancel any further barrier installations. The State simply exercised its contract right with Paonessa to eliminate the remainder of the uninstalled barriers, as "unnecessary." Each of the original contracts had provided for 25,000 linear feet of barriers. The state eliminated 10,000 of those 25,000 linear feet. At that time, Chase had delivered 15,000 feet of barriers (all of which Paonessa had installed) and had produced another 3,000 feet of barriers ready for delivery, leaving a final 7,000 feet to be produced.

Is Paonessa excused from its obligation to purchase the remaining barriers from Chase? If so, to what extent? How would you go about calculating damages, assuming Paonessa bore at least some liability for breach of its contract with Chase?

The facts of this problem are loosely based on the issues raised in the case of *Chase Precast Corp. v. John J. Paonessa Co.*, 409 Mass. 371, 566 N.E.2d 603 (1991).

10

Rights and Obligations of Third Parties to the Original Contract

Lesson 48: Third-Party Beneficiaries of Contract Promises

Objectives and Expected Learning Outcomes

In this lesson, you will learn when the beneficiary of a contract promise may enforce that promise—even though not a party to the contract. You will learn that only an "intended" beneficiary may enforce such a promise and will further learn to distinguish between "intended" and "incidental" beneficiaries. You will also learn when the actual parties to a contract may be precluded by an intended beneficiary from modifying their agreement. Finally, you will learn rules allowing certain non-parties to enforce express or implied warranties involving goods.

Having now fully addressed the rights and obligations of the original parties to a contract, we move to consider the rights and obligations of certain non-parties to that original agreement. The original parties bargained for the specified rights, so their claims to enforce them naturally follow. However, others may sometimes have colorable claims to enforcement, which will raise a variety of additional issues—most obviously a lack of "privity." One who is not a party to a contract is generally said to lack the privity necessary to enforce that contract.

In this final chapter, we will primarily focus on three distinct questions.

- Under what circumstances may a third-party who stands to benefit from the contract of another enforce a promise made pursuant to that contract?

- Under what circumstances may a party delegate a contract to another, and what is the legal effect of such a delegation?

- Under what circumstances may a party assign contract rights to another, and what is the legal effect of such an assignment?

We will address each of these questions in turn and begin with the rights of third-party beneficiaries.

Intended and Incidental Third-Party Beneficiaries

We began our exploration of contract law by observing that the law enforces bargains in which each party generally gets something it wants. While we noted the lack of any formal requirement of an actual "benefit," most bargains do entail some sort of benefit to each party, whether clearly and purely financial or somewhat more amorphous in nature. However, such bargains may also benefit others—perhaps by design or perhaps by pure chance. If so, to what extent, if at all, should such third-party beneficiaries be allowed to enforce the contract? The answer it turns out is quite simple—though its application is often considerably more challenging.

Simply put, an "intended" beneficiary of a contractual promise has a right to enforce that promise, while an "incidental" beneficiary does not. Perhaps the most clear and obvious example of an "intended" beneficiary is the beneficiary of a life insurance policy.

> **Example 48-1:** Pam purchases a life insurance policy from Insurer, naming Nate as the beneficiary of the policy. Nate is not a party to the contract of insurance, and may not even know about it at the time. Upon Pam's death, Nate will be entitled to enforce Insurer's promise to pay the policy amount to Nate (assuming he then knows of it)—even though that promise was made to Pam, and not to Nate.

Another traditional example of an intended beneficiary involves a "trust," in which a grantor contracts with a "trustee" to manage the assets of the trust for the benefit of an intended "beneficiary." The details of such "trusts" are left to other courses. However, the beneficiary will almost certainly be entitled to enforce any promise made by the trustee to the grantor for the benefit of the beneficiary—even though the beneficiary was not a party to the contract between the grantor and the trustee.

Of course, many claims by third-party beneficiaries will be far less clear and obvious than those made to the benefits of a life insurance policy or trust. In most such cases, the challenge comes in determining whether the third-party is an "intended" or "incidental" beneficiary of the promise at issue. We begin our examination of these challenges with an example based on another classic case—this one from the New York Court of Appeals.

Example 48-2: *Lawrence v. Fox*

Holly loaned Fox $300 in exchange for Fox's promise to repay $300 to Lawrence the next day. In bargaining for Fox's promise to pay the $300 to Lawrence the next day, Holly sought to perform a pre-existing obligation to pay $300 to Lawrence. While Fox's performance of his promise was to run directly to Lawrence, his promise was made solely to Holly. Thus, Lawrence was not an actual party to the bargain at issue.

Lawrence might, under proper circumstances, have sought to recover from Fox by arguing that Holly had conveyed the $300 to Fox to be held "in trust" for Lawrence, as "beneficiary." If so, the case would have been an easy one, as explained above. However, the nature of the bargain was clear that Fox intended and was entitled to use the $300 for his own benefit prior to paying the same amount to Lawrence the next day. This sort of self-interested use of the $300 would have been fully inconsistent with the "fiduciary" duty of a "trustee" to use the money "held in trust" solely for the benefit of the beneficiary.

The court nevertheless allowed Lawrence to enforce Fox's promise directly, as Fox's promise to pay Lawrence had clearly been sought and intended by Holly to satisfy Holly's pre-existing debt to Lawrence. Thus, Lawrence was entitled, as an intended third-party beneficiary of Fox's promise to Holly, to enforce against Fox outside of the context of a traditional trust.[1]

---

[1] Lawrence v. Fox, 20 N.Y. 268 (1859).

In considering third-party contract issues, diagrams are often helpful. The diagram below is intended specifically for use in analyzing third-party beneficiary questions. In the foregoing Example, Fox was of course the "Promisor," Holly the "Promisee," and Lawrence the "Third-Party Beneficiary" of the promise "at issue"—the promise to pay Lawrence $300.

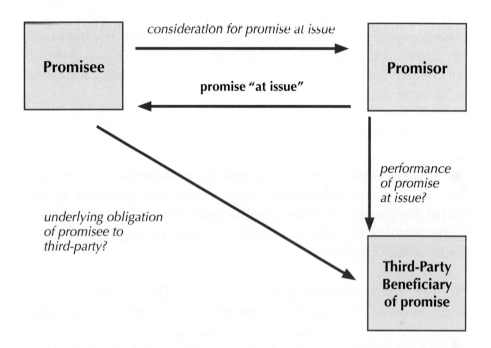

In *Lawrence v. Fox*, the underlying debt obligation of Holly to Lawrence was clear; however, the nature any such obligation may be less clear in other cases. The performance of Fox's promise also ran directly to Lawrence; however, this will not necessarily be true in all cases involving third-party beneficiaries. Each of these issues are addressed below and may be relevant in analyzing any third-party beneficiary claim.

It is also important in this sort of transaction potentially implicating the interests of multiple parties to determine to whom the promise at issue was actually made. In *Lawrence v. Fox*, the court distinguished the instant case from one in which one party (in the position of Holly) provided consideration to another (in the position of Fox) in exchange for a promise made directly to another (a promise by one in the position of Fox directly to one in the position of Lawrence). In effect, such a transaction would simply involve three parties to the contract and would not require a non-party analysis at all. There is simply no issue of "privity."

The "backstory" to this particular case is presumed to have been a colorful one, involving gambling winnings (by Lawrence) and losses (by Holly, to Lawrence, and later, by Fox, who subsequently declined to pay Lawrence), which was likely the reason for the circuitous transaction and action by Lawrence against Fox, instead of Holly. However, the principle is now solidly enshrined in the common law and often important in cases in which the promisee (the person in the position of Holly in this case) is insolvent or otherwise not subject to collection.

The Easy Case—Satisfaction of an Obligation to Pay Money

The basic rule of *Lawrence v. Fox*, as reflected in the restatement, provides that, absent contrary agreement, the beneficiary of a promise is an "intended" beneficiary to the extent that the promise was sought and intended by the promisee to satisfy an existing obligation of the promisee to pay money to the beneficiary.[2]

This basic rule is obviously quite a narrow one. However, the definition of an "intended" beneficiary has, over time, been expanded considerably beyond the narrow circumstances in which it was initially applied.

The More Challenging Cases—Other Circumstances Indicating Intent

The beneficiary of a promise may also be an "intended" beneficiary—even in the absence of any obligation of the promisee to pay money to the beneficiary—to the extent that the overall circumstances indicate that the parties (at lease the promisee) intended to provide the beneficiary with the benefit of the promised performance.[3] The restatement speaks of both effectuating the intention of the "parities" (presumably, both parties) and circumstances indicating that the "promisee" intends the benefit of the promise to flow to the beneficiary. In many cases, the intent of the promisor will be far less clear than the promisee.

---

[2] Restatement (Second) of Contracts § 302((1)(a).
[3] Restatement (Second) of Contracts § 302(1)(b).

Example 48-3: *Seaver v. Ransom*

Ms. Beman, in ill health and soon expecting to die, sought to complete her last will and testament. Her husband, Judge Beman, was assisting her. When she read the will, she thought it was perfect—with one exception. The will left her home to Judge Beman "for life" (you will learn more about the nature of a "life estate" in property law), with the remainder interest (after the Judge's death) to a charity. However, she wanted instead for her favorite niece, Ms. Seaver, to receive this remainder. Fearing that her health might fail before the will could be changed (this sort of thing took much longer 100 years ago), Ms. Beman promised to sign the will, as drafted, in exchange for Judge Beman's promise to make a bequest to Ms. Seaver in his own will equal to the value of the house. Ms. Beman signed the will. However, Judge Beman failed to provide for Ms. Seaver in his own will, as promised. Upon Judge Beman's death (which followed that of Ms. Beman), Ms. Seaver sought to recover from the estate of Judge Beman the value of the promise he made to Ms. Beman.

Unlike the prior Example, Ms. Beman owed neither a debt nor any other legal obligation to Ms. Seaver. However, the nature of their close familial relationship was such that the circumstances reasonably established Ms. Beman's clear intent to benefit Ms. Seaver in bargaining for Judge Beman's promise to make the bequest at issue to Ms. Seaver. Thus, the court allowed Ms. Seaver to enforce the promise directly against Judge Beman's estate, even though Ms. Seaver had not been a party to the agreement between the Bemans.[4]

Ms. Beman clearly intended to benefit Ms. Seaver. The intent of Judge Beman to benefit Ms. Seaver is far less clear (his intent seemingly more focused on relieving any anxiety of his wife with respect to her will). However, effectuating the intent of the bargain sought by Ms. Beman and agreed

---

[4] Seaver v. Ransom, 224 N.Y. 233, 120 N.E. 639 (1918).

upon by both parties required that Ms. Seaver be treated as an intended third-party beneficiary and, therefore, allowed her to enforce the promise Judge Beman made to Ms. Beman.

In the foregoing example, Judge Beman's promise obviously ran directly to Ms. Beman. However, his *performance* of that promise ran directly to Ms. Seaver, the beneficiary, in a manner much like Fox's promise to pay $300 to Lawrence. In some cases, however, the performance of the promise will not run directly to the beneficiary. The next example again includes a will, but the third-party beneficiary is seeking to enforce a very different sort of "promise,"

> **Example 48-4:** *Lucas v. Hamm*
>
> Emmick engaged Hamm, as counsel, to draft a will leaving certain property to Lucas (and others). Due to a mistake by Hamm, the will failed to achieve the purpose sought by Emmick and promised by Hamm. Lucas sought to bring a claim against Hamm for legal malpractice, though he was not a party to the contract for legal services.
>
> As in the case of *Seaver v. Ransom*, the intent of Emmick in seeking to benefit Lucas was clear. However, the performance of Hamm's promise ran directly to Emmick, inasmuch as Hamm was drafting a will for Emmick—not Lucas. Nevertheless, the court deemed Lucas an "intended" third-party beneficiary allowed to enforce Emmick's contract with Hamm for legal services (though the claim failed for other reasons).[5]

As in the foregoing example, the lack of any performance running directly from the promisor to the third-party beneficiary is not necessarily a bar to recovery, as long as the beneficiary can otherwise establish he or she (or, for that matter, "it") is an "intended" beneficiary of the promise at issue. However, the nature of the performance and the party to whom that performance runs may, in many cases, be factors in determining whether a beneficiary was "intended" or "incidental."

---

[5] Lucas v. Hamm, 56 Cal.2d 583 (1961).

Example 48-5: Kay contracts with Lee to perform certain landscaping work on her property, including the removal of a row of pine trees along the border of her property and that owned by Meg, her next door neighbor. Unbeknownst to Kay, Meg is very allergic to pines and has been taking medication for some time to counter the effect of the pines on Kay's property. Meg was ecstatic when she learned that the pines were to be removed (but said nothing). Lee became ill while doing the landscaping work and finished everything but the tree removal. While Kay never formally released Lee from the obligation to remove the trees, she felt sorry for him and did not bother to enforce it (she also paid him in full).

Meg might wish to enforce Lee's promise to Kay to remove the trees, as she was certainly a "beneficiary" of the promise. However, Lee's promise did not run directly to Meg. Moreover, there is no indication that Kay in any way intended to benefit Meg by removing the trees. Thus, Meg is merely an "incidental" beneficiary of Lee's promise to Kay and is not entitled to enforce that promise.

In the foregoing example, Kay never actually agreed to relieve Lee of his obligation to remove the trees. However, the possibility that she might have done so raises two different issues. First, to what extent should the failure of the promisee to bring an enforcement action against the promisor preclude a third-party beneficiary from doing so? In Examples 48-3 and 48-4, the promisee was deceased, so this may have been less of an issue. However, a conscious decision by the promisee not to enforce the promise might very well call into question the intent of the promisee that the third-party receive the benefit.

The second question is the extent to which the promisee and promisor may alter an agreement so as to change or eliminate a promise that is otherwise enforceable by an intended third-party. This issue was recognized as potentially problematic by the court in *Lawrence v. Fox*, but was left unanswered, as it was not raised by the facts of that case.

Vesting of Third Party Rights

The parties to an agreement including a promise subject to enforcement by an intended third-party beneficiary may generally modify or discharge their agreement, unless the rights of the third-party beneficiary have "vested." Such vesting may occur if the beneficiary:

- materially and justifiably relies or brings suit on the promise before receiving notice of the modification or discharge; or

- manifests assent to the performance of the promise by the promisor at the request of either the promisee or promisor.

Vesting by virtue of reasonable and justifiable reliance is based on a straight-forward application of general contract principles of estoppel. However, one might reasonably ask why the promisee or promisor would ever request that the beneficiary assent to receive the promised performance from the promisor? This issue involves the legal effect of delegation of duties and is addressed in the next lesson.

Contracts for Public Services

In many instances, a governmental entity will contract for services intended to benefit the public. For instance, a municipality may contract with a private entity for snow removal. If the contractor responsible for the snow removal fails to plow some of the agreed streets, should an individual whose street was not plowed be entitled to bring a direct claim against the snow removal contractor for breach?

In this sort of case, the municipality may or may not have a legal obligation to its citizens to provide the service at issue. Moreover, the performance of the service may or may not run directly to the citizenry, thus further complicating the question of whether any particular citizen is an intended beneficiary of the promise at issue. Nevertheless, third-party beneficiary claimants have sometimes succeeded in establishing their status as intended beneficiaries based on the circumstances of the specific case. One of the potential challenges in such a case is the significant potential for consequential damages.

Example 48-6: *H.R. Moch Co. v. Rensselaer Water Co.*

The Water Company contracted to provide water to the City of Rensselaer for various municipal purposes. Due to an alleged lack of adequate water pressure, a fire spread and consumed the Plaintiff's business. The Plaintiff sought to bring a claim for breach by the Water Company of its contract with the City. The court declined to find the Plaintiff an "intended" beneficiary, explaining that it would be unreasonable to assume that the Water Company would have ever intended to take on such a risk in contracting with the City.[6]

As with any contract claim potentially involving multiple parties, one should step back and ask if a beneficiary of any given promise might actually be a party to the contract. For example, a Water Company customer might very well have a right to sue the Water Company for failing to provide clean, potable water based on an actual contract between the customer and the Water Company.

Example 48-7: *Kornblut v. Chevron Oil Co.*

Chevron contracted with the New York State Thruway Authority to provide service to motorists whose cars became disable on the thruway. When Kornblut's car became disabled, he contacted Chevron for assistance and was told that he would receive prompt assistance. While Chevron had promised assistance within 30 minutes in its contract with the Thruway Authority, it took more than 3 hours to reach Kornblut. The court distinguished this case from that in the prior Example by noting that Kornblut had actually contracted directly with Chevron when he made the phone call, and Chevron agreed to provide the requested service. Thus, Kornblut had a direct right of action against Chevron.[7]

---

[6] H.R. Moch Co. v. Rensselaer Water Co., 247 N.Y. 160, 159 N.E. 896 (1928).
[7] Kornblut v. Chevron Oil Co., 48 N.Y.2d 853, 400 N.E.2d 368 (1979) (Judge Fuchsberg dissenting on other grounds involving the foreseeability of the resulting death of Kornblut when he suffered a heart attack as a result of the delay).

Additional Problems with Large Classes of Potential Beneficiaries

There is another fundamental challenge in allowing third-party claims when there are multiple beneficiaries with potentially divergent interests. These claims may occur in the context of contracts with public entities or in purely private contexts.

> **Example 48-8:** The government contracts with an entity charged with operating a dam and reservoir for the benefit of the public. As a result of the decisions made by the operator with respect to the timing and quantity of water releases, certain downstream farmers seek to bring an action against the dam operator. The farmers assert that they are intended third-party beneficiaries of the operator's promise to the government to operate the dam and reservoir for the benefit of the public.
>
> Claimants such as these farmers will almost invariably be deemed incidental beneficiaries based, at least in part, on the fact that the interest of the farmers is only one such interest, and it will often conflict with other "public" interests. For example, different farmers (raising different crops needing water at different times), fisherman, recreational boaters on both the reservoir and the downstream river, and any municipalities served by the reservoir will likely have very different interests in the timing and quantity of water releases from the reservoir. Thus, none can individually claim status as "intended" beneficiaries.

> **Example 48-9:** Your torts professor likely has a contract with the institution you attend, but you are not likely a party to that contract. If you are not happy with your professor (this would of course never happen with your contracts professor), you might seek to bring an action against the professor as a third-party beneficiary of the professor's contract with the institution. However, you are almost certainly only an "incidental" beneficiary.

Much like the different beneficiaries of the dam and reservoir in the prior example, law students will often have very different interests. One may wish for more thorough and rigorous coverage, while another may wish for less. One may wish for more examinations, while another may wish for less. One may wish for a more interactive class, while another may wish to be left alone. Thus, no single student can likely be said to be an "intended" beneficiary of the professor's contract with the law school.

Third-Party Beneficiaries of Contracts for the Sale of Goods

A seller of goods will often provide express or implied warranties under UCC Article 2. However, the breach of such warranties will often affect persons or business entities other than the buyer from the seller making the warranty. Thus, a party suffering injury caused by seller's breach might be precluded from bringing a claim against the seller based on a lack of privity. UCC Article 2 addresses the issue directly in § 2-318. However, it provides three possible options from which states may choose. **STOP NOW and READ each of the three variations of UCC § 2-318 below.**

UCC § 2-318

Alternative A

A seller's warranty whether express or implied extends to any natural person who is in the family or household of his buyer or who is a guest in his home if it is reasonable to expect that such person may use, consume or be affected by the goods and who is injured in person by breach of the warranty. A seller may not exclude or limit the operation of this section.

Alternative B

A seller's warranty whether express or implied extends to any natural person who may reasonably be expected to use, consume or be affected by the goods and who is injured in person by breach of the warranty. A seller may not exclude or limit the operation of this section.

Alternative C

A seller's warranty whether express or implied extends to any person who may reasonably be expected to use, consume or be affected by the goods and who is injured by breach of the warranty. A seller may not exclude or limit the operation of this section with respect to injury to the person of an individual to whom the warranty extends.

The three alternatives provide an excellent exercise in class statutory reading. Which provides the broadest available protection to non-parties?

In what manner does Alternative B expand beyond Alternative A the range of non-parties who may enforce a seller's warranty? In what manner does Alternative C expand beyond Alternative B the range of non-parties who may enforce a seller's warranty? Can you think of specific examples of each? These differences are further highlighted by the final problems at the end of the lesson.

Comments 2 and 3 clarify that the statute is solely intended to remove certain limitations to warranty enforcement based on a lack of privity. It is not intended to displace any existing common law right an intended third-party beneficiary may have to enforce a promise made in contract for the sale of goods.

Third-Party Issues under the CISG

CISG Article 4 clarifies that the CISG "governs only the formation of the contract of sale and the rights and obligations of the seller and buyer arising from such a contract." Thus, the CISG does not govern third-party issues, even if it does govern the relationship between the seller and buyer. Any third-party issues must be resolved under otherwise governing contract law, typically by reference to the domestic law selected based on applicable conflict of laws rules. Thus, we will not see any further reference to the CISG in this final chapter.

APPLYING THE RULES

Problem 1: Abe owes $5000 to Bev for some building materials Abe had purchased earlier. Zoe contracts with Abe to perform remodeling work for her for $3000. Under their agreement, Zoe is to pay the $3000 to Bev—not Abe. Bev is not aware of the agreement between Abe and Zoe at the time, but later learns of it when Zoe fails to pay as agreed. Abe has no money. Can Bev directly sue Zoe? If Bev prevails, how much of the $5000 owed by Abe can Bev recover from Zoe?

Problem 2: Lang contracted to sell a parcel of real estate to Grigerik. Under the contract, Lang was obligated to obtain approval by the Town to build on the lot. The Town sanitary official told Lang he had to arrange for certain drainage engineering work to be done in connection with the planned septic system, and Lang contracted with Sharpe for that purpose. However, the Town rejected the application by Lang for the building permit based on flaws in the plans provided by Sharpe. Grigerik sought to bring a direct action against Sharpe for breach of his contract with Lang. Can he do so?

The facts of this problem are loosely based on the issues raised in the case of *Grigerik v. Sharpe*, 247 Conn. 293, 721 A.2d 526 (1998).

Problem 3: Splendid Nature Park is operated for the express benefit of the general public by the Park Service under contract with the state. A group of longtime regular park users is very unhappy over plans to increase the number of roads within the park, as this will undoubtedly add traffic, noise, people, and pollution, thereby spoiling much of the current "wild" feeling of the park. This group of users seeks to bring an action against the Park Service based on its contract with the state. Can they do so?

Problem 4: Seller contracts to sell widgets to buyer, providing both express and implied warranties with respect to the widgets. Buyer resells the widgets to Buyer2, but makes no express warranties and effectively disclaims any and all implied warranties. When Buyer2 attempts to use the widgets in its manufacturing process, they do not work, and the entire production line is shut down for days, causing Buyer2 $25,000 in lost profits. Under which, if any, of the available alternative versions of UCC § 2-318 can Buyer2 bring an action against Seller (you need not consider whether Buyer2 will prevail, but simply whether it is legally entitled to bring the claim)?

Lesson 49: Delegation of Duties

Objectives and Expected Learning Outcomes

In this lesson, you will learn about delegation of contract duties. You will learn under what circumstances a duty may be delegated, as well as the legal effect of such a delegation. You will also learn how a "delegation" may sometimes implicate potential claims by a "third-party beneficiary."

Delegation of Contract Duties

When two parties conclude a contract, each party bargains for consideration and provides consideration sought by the other party. We know from Chapter 2 that consideration may take a variety of different forms. However, more often than not, consideration will be found in a promise by each party to perform an affirmative act. In some circumstances, the personal performance of the party making the promise will be essential. However, in many others it will not. Where personal performance of the original contracting party is not essential, the duty of performance is typically subject to delegation.

We can return to Example 48-2 for our first example of delegation.

> **Example 49-1:** Holly owed money to Lawrence under one contract. Holly then entered into a second contract with Fox in which Holly "delegated" to Fox his obligation to pay Lawrence under the earlier contract.
>
> If Fox had paid Lawrence, as he had promised Holly, then Holly's promise to pay Lawrence would have been fully discharged by the performance of Fox. Thus, we can say that Holly's promise to pay Lawrence was fully subject to "delegation" or "delegable."

As with third-party beneficiaries, a diagram is often useful in thinking about issues involving delegation. The diagram below is intended specifically for use in analyzing questions involving delegation. In the foregoing Example, Holly was the original "Obligor" to Lawrence, the "Obligee" on Holly's original promise to pay $300. Holly, as "Delegor," then delegated the payment obligation to Fox, the "Delegee."

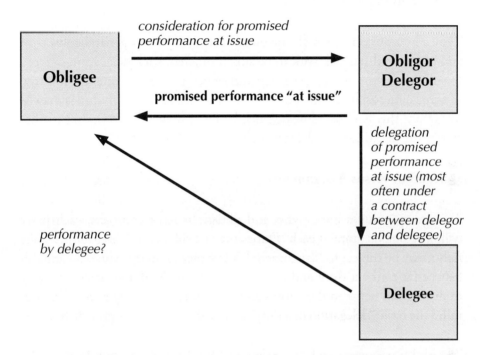

Of course, if one rotates the above diagram counter-clockwise by 90 degrees, it will look very much like the diagram of the same transaction, but with a focus on recovery by the third-party beneficiary, as compared to the current focus on the delegation of the payment obligation. Not all transactions involving third-party beneficiaries will involve delegation. For example, there was no prior contract or underlying legal obligation to "delegate" in *Seaver v. Ransom*, Example 48-3. However, when a claim by a third-party beneficiary does involve a delegated duty, it is helpful to understand the connection between the two issues.

We will further define and address a few potential issues presented by the delegation of a duty below. However, another example may be useful. Throughout this text, we have seen examples of delegation involving general contractors and subcontractors.

Example 49-2: General contracts with Owner to construct a building on Owner's land. General then contracts with Sub to do all of the electrical work in constructing the building. General has "delegated" its obligation to do the electrical work to Sub in exchange for its promise to pay Sub to perform the work.

Typically, a project in which the owner contracts with a general contractor and expects substantial work to be subcontracted, such delegation of work to subcontractors will be expressly authorized in the agreement. However, in some circumstances, the obligor's right to delegate certain duties may be less clear. This issue is addressed below. First, however, we should further clarify the definition of "delegation."

Delegation versus Assignment

A contract includes both rights and duties. In most contracts, each party will have one or more of each. Duties may be subject to "delegation," while rights may be subject to "assignment." It is typically pretty easy to distinguish between a contract duty and a contract right, so it should be equally easy to distinguish between delegation and assignment—as long as one keeps in mind the basic "delegation of a duty" and "assignment of a right" dichotomy.

The problem comes in when a party transfers both rights and duties under a contract, as such a transfer is also called an "assignment" of the contract—even though it includes both rights and duties. Thus, any "delegation" necessarily involves a "duty," while an assignment may involve only "rights," or may include both "rights" and "duties." However, duties—by themselves—are never "assigned." They are always "delegated."

Example 49-3: Pam contracts with Dan to provide lawn and gardening service to Dan for $150 per month. If Pam hires Peg to do the lawn and garden service, she has "delegated" her "duty" to Peg to perform the service for Dan. If Pam instead conveys to the Bank her right to receive $150 per month, she has "assigned" her "right" to payment to the Bank. Finally, if Pam transfers the entire contract (both rights and obligations) with Dan to another lawn service, she has "assigned" the "contract."

With this terminology in hand, we can move forward to examine a variety of issues involving delegation and assignment in this lesson and the next.

The Effect of Delegation and the Original Performance Obligation

An obligor of a contract duty is generally entitled to delegate that duty, as illustrated by the examples above, unless such delegation is expressly precluded or the nature of the duty is such that the obligee has a substantial interest in personal performance by the obligor.[8] Any contractual bar on delegation is simply a matter of contract interpretation. However, the question of whether the obligee has a substantial interest in performance by the obligor will generally require examination of the nature of the promised performance.

> **Example 49-4:** Pam's obligation in Example 49-3 to provide lawn and gardening service is likely delegable, as—absent additional facts—there is no indication that Dan has any substantial interest in Pam actually performing the service. Thus, Pam's obligation would be delegable, unless precluded by the contract terms.
>
> In contrast, if Dan hired Pam to perform as a singer in his night club, Pam would likely be precluded from delegating her singing engagement to Peg. The nature of a singing performance is such that the obligee, in this case Dan, would typically have a substantial interest in personal performance by the obligor.

This sort of "personalized" obligation is akin to the one we encountered in Example 46-2, when analogizing the destruction of the music hall to the death of an obligor who was personally expected to perform the contract obligation at issue. Of course, it is sometimes unclear whether a particular obligee has a substantial interest in personal performance by the obligor, and the inquiry is largely fact specific.

---

[8] Restatement (Second) of Contracts § 318(1) and (2).

When a duty is effectively "delegated," then full performance by the delegee (the party to whom the duty has been delegated) will satisfy or discharge the contractual obligation of the original obligor, as long as the performance complies with the contract requirements. However, the mere "delegation" of the duty has no effect on the liability of the original obligor to the contract obligee.[9] Thus, the new obligation of the delegee only augments the obligation of the original obligor, who remains liable to the original obligee, unless otherwise agreed by the obligee.

The "delegation" of a duty—yet to be performed—will only discharge the obligation and liability of the original obligor in the event of a "novation." We first encountered the concept of a "novation" in Chapter 4, in distinguishing between a novation and a promise of surety. As noted at that time, a "novation" has the effect of substituting or replacing one promise with another. Thus, if the obligee agrees to accept a new promise from the delegee, in substitution of (not "in addition to") the original promise by the obligor, then the new obligation amounts to a "novation," and the original obligor is relieved of liability.

The following example illustrates the difference.

> **Example 49-5:** In Example 49-3, Pam's delegation to Peg of her duty to provide lawn and gardening services will not relieve her of liability to Dan if Peg fails to perform the services, as agreed.
>
> In contrast, if Dan agrees to accept the agreed services from Peg, instead of Pam, in effect substituting Peg for Pam and relieving Pam of any liability, then the subsequent agreement between will be considered a "novation" of the first.

We can now bring these issues together, along with third-party rights and the "vesting" issue we talked about in the last lesson, to see how this might all play out in a classic fact pattern addressed much earlier. For this example, we return to the basic fact pattern of the contract between Wood and Lucy, Lady Duff-Gordon, in Lesson 6.

---

[9] Restatement (Second) of Contracts § 318(3).

Example 49-6: Duff-Gordon contracted with Wood to market her designs, granting him the exclusive right to do so. As factually implied by the court, Wood was required to use his best efforts to market the designs. During the contract period, Wood wished to assign his contract with Duff-Gordon to Sears (contrary to the facts of the actual case in which Duff-Gordon contracted with Sears in breach of her contract with Wood). However, his lawyers explained that they could not assure him of his right to do so. While the agreement said nothing about assigning rights or delegating duties, the lawyer was concerned that Duff-Gordon might assert that she had a "substantial interest" in the personal performance by Wood of the obligation to use "best efforts" in the marketing of her designs on an exclusive basis.

In hopes of resolving the issue, Wood contacted Duff-Gordon and sought her agreement in allowing Wood to assign the contract to Sears (for which Sears would of course pay Wood). Duff-Gordon's lawyer indicated that assenting to the delegation might be useful, as it would "vest" any rights she might have as an intended third-party beneficiary of the promise made to Wood by Sears to assume the obligation of marketing Duff-Gordon's fashions. Her acceptance of performance by Sears would amount to a manifestation of assent to the performance by Sears of Wood's promise at the request of Wood (see discussion of vesting in last lesson).

Her lawyer further pointed out, however, that her right to performance by Sears would be far clearer if she had a contract directly with Sears. Thus, Duff-Gordon explained to Wood that she would be happy to accept performance by Sears, but would require a modification of the overall contract to add Sears as a party directly obligated to her. Wood, sensing an opportunity, said he was quite certain that Sears would agree, but that he would only agree to such a modification if Duff-Gordon released Wood from any and all liability under the original contract. Assuming Duff-Gordon agreed to this final proposal, the ultimate agreement between Sears and Duff-Gordon would amount to a "novation" of the contract between Wood and Duff-Gordon.

You should use the diagrams in this lesson and the last to be sure you understand the delegation and third-party beneficiary issues raised in this example.

Delegation of Duties in Contracts for the Sale of Goods

While contracts for services often involve promises of performance of a personalized nature, a contract for the sale of goods typically focuses far more on the goods themselves than on the person providing them. UCC § 2-210 addresses delegation of duties, assignment of rights, and assignment of a contract. We will focus more on issues of assignment of rights in the next lesson. However, the statute is best introduced as a coherent whole. **STOP NOW and READ the excerpts from UCC § 2-210 below.**

UCC § 2-210

(1) A party may perform his duty through a delegate unless otherwise agreed or unless the other party has a substantial interest in having his original promisor perform or control the acts required by the contract. No delegation of performance relieves the party delegating of any duty to perform or any liability for breach.

(2) Except as otherwise provided in Section 9-406, unless otherwise agreed, all rights of either seller or buyer can be assigned except where the assignment would materially change the duty of the other party, or increase materially the burden or risk imposed on him by his contract, or impair materially his chance of obtaining return performance. A right to damages for breach of the whole contract or a right arising out of the assignor's due performance of his entire obligation can be assigned despite agreement otherwise.

. . .

(4) Unless the circumstances indicate the contrary a prohibition of assignment of "the contract" is to be construed as barring only the delegation to the assignee of the assignor's performance.

(5) An assignment of "the contract" or of "all my rights under the contract" or an assignment in similar general terms is an assignment of rights and unless the language or the circumstances (as in an assignment for security) indicate the contrary, it is a delegation of performance of the duties of the assignor and its acceptance by the assignee constitutes a promise by him to perform those duties. This promise is enforceable by either the assignor or the other party to the original contract.

(6) The other party may treat any assignment which delegates performance as creating reasonable grounds for insecurity and may without prejudice to his rights against the assignor demand assurances from the assignee (Section 2-609).

Comment 1 to § 2-210 notes that this section generally "recognizes both delegation of performance and assignability as normal and permissible incidents of a contract for the sale of goods." Much like the common law, Comment 2 goes on to note that delegation of performance is presumed to be allowed, absent contract terms to the contrary, "where no substantial reason can be shown as to why the delegated performance will not be as satisfactory as personal performance."

In most transactions involving goods, the personal identity or characteristics of the performing party will have little bearing on the value of performance, as long as the buyer receives the promised goods and the seller receives the promised money. Another question might also reasonably be raised here, though it might apply equally in a transaction governed by the common law. Can a party have a special interest in performance by a fictional "person" in the form of a business entity? You will recall from the last lesson that different versions of § 2-318 distinguished between "natural" persons (i.e., humans) and the broader concept of personage (including both natural persons and fictional "persons" based on legally recognized organizational structures). There is no single answer to this question, though the nature of the "person" with whom one is dealing may certainly be a factor in determining whether a duty is delegable.

The nature of the transaction may also affect the question of whether a duty is delegable. For example, one party is far more likely to have an interest in performance by a specific contracting partner in a long term contract in which the prospects for continuing performance are at least as important as the current conformity of goods or promptness of payment. A party is also more likely to have an interest in performance by a specific contracting party in a contract in which good faith or implied best efforts are important in measuring contract performance.

Example 49-7: Alpha contracted to supply Beta with a new processor chip developed by Alpha for a period of 3 years. During the contract period, Beta promised to use the chip exclusively in its new SuperSmartPhone, and Alpha promised not to sell the chip to anyone other than Beta.

Thus, Beta had promised to purchase its "requirements" from Alpha "as may occur in good faith," as provided by § 2-306(1), and Alpha has granted Beta an "exclusive" right to purchase the chip, thus imposing on Beta a duty of best efforts to promote the sale of its SuperSmartPhone making use of the chip, as provided by § 2-306(2). As such, either Alpha or Beta might have a "substantial interest" in performance by the other original contracting party—even though the transaction simply involves chips and money, and neither party is a "natural" person.

Where it is unclear whether a delegation is allowable under § 2-210(1), subsection (6) provides a possible mechanism for resolving uncertainty by reference to § 2-609. Subsection (6) statutorily provides that any delegation of a duty of performance provides reasonable grounds for insecurity.

APPLYING THE RULES

Problem 1: Kay contracted with Hal to paint the exterior of her house. Kay's friend, Ike had enthusiastically recommended Hal for the job based on the excellent job he had done in painting Ike's home. Kay was primarily interested in the price (Hal's price had been quite low) and the paint to be used (Kay had specified a particular brand, and Hal had agreed), but it was also very nice to know that Ike had been happy with Hal's work. About a week later, Kay received a call from Jan, who said Hal had contracted with her to paint Kay's house and she wanted to set up dates to perform the work.

Does Kay have to accept performance by Jan under her contract with Hal?

Suppose Kay expresses reservations about Jan doing the work, and Jan provides references regarding her work in hopes that Kay will agree to allow Jan to perform the work under Kay's contract with Hal. Kay checks the references—all glowing—and subsequently notifies Jan that she is welcome to do the work on specified dates discussed earlier. The next day, Kay learns that Jan and Hal mutually terminated their delegation agreement, and Hal has left the country (apparently leaving numerous unpaid bills behind). Jan now refuses to perform the paint job at the agreed price, stating that she will only do it for double the price earlier agreed upon by Hal. Does Kay have any legal claim against Jan?

Instead, suppose that Kay had not expressed any reservations about Jan doing the work and had simply set up dates for performance. Jan did the work, but did a very poor job (the paint blistered). Against whom will Kay have a right to bring claims for the defective performance? Is there any way that Hal could have avoided this result?

Problem 2: Nexxus Products contracted with Best Barber & Beauty Supply for Best to distribute Nexxus hair care and beauty products exclusively in the state of Texas. The contract could be terminated by Nexxus only at certain specified times, and upon specified notice and repurchase of any Best inventory of Nexxus products. After the contract had been concluded and performance begun, Best was merged into Sally Beauty, a wholly-owned subsidiary of Alberto-Culver, a major competitor of Nexxus in the manufacture and sale of hair care and beauty products. Nexxus immediately notified Sally Beauty that it was ending the distribution arrangement, stating "we have great reservations about allowing our Nexxus products to be distributed by a company which is, in essence, a direct competitor." Sally Beauty subsequently sued Nexxus for breach of contract.

Was Nexxus required to continue perform with Sally Beauty the contract it originally concluded with Best?

To the extent that Nexxus was uncertain of its legal rights when it learned of the merger of Best and Sally Beauty, is there any other reasonable course of action that Nexxus might have taken?

The facts of this problem are loosely based on the issues raised in the case of Sally Beauty Co. v. Nexxus Products Co., 801 F.2d 1001 (7th Cir. 1986).

Lesson 50: Assignment of Rights

Objectives and Expected Learning Outcomes

In this lesson, you will learn about the assignment of contract rights, as well as the notice required to give full effect to an assignment. You will learn when rights are assignable and when and how assignment may be precluded by contract. You will also learn about certain defenses that may affect the rights of an assignee.

Assignment of Contract Rights

As explained in the last lesson, contracting parties may sometimes delegate duties or assign rights to others not parties to the original agreement. Such duties may be delegated or rights assigned in isolation, often as part of a broader agreement, or duties may be delegated and rights assigned together through the assignment of an entire contract (or at least whatever rights and obligations remain undischarged and enforceable at the time). In this lesson, we will begin by focusing on issues unique to the assignment of specific rights (most typically the right of a party to payment of money), and then we will conclude by examining some of the issues that may arise in the context of assignment of a complete contract.

One of the clearest and simplest rules governing assignment is that involving the assignment of a right to payment of money. A right to payment of money is generally assignable (subject only to a variety of narrow statutory exceptions), and any contractual attempt to bar or otherwise restrict such assignment is ineffective.

> **Example 50-1:** Under the basic facts of Example 49-3, Pam is entitled to assign her right to payment of $150 per month by Dan. She might, for example, assign this right to a bank as part of a loan transaction or might simply sell her right to future payments for cash now (albeit, typically at a substantial discount to reflect both the time value of money and any risk of non-payment by Dan).

Pam's ability to assign her right to payment is absolute, even if her agreement with Dan expressly precludes such assignment. Any such contractual preclusion is simply ineffective.

The diagram below is intended specifically for use in analyzing questions involving assignment. In the foregoing example, Dan was the Obligor to Pam, the Obligee on Dan's promise to pay her $150 per month. Pam, as "Assignor," then assigned the right to payment to an "Assignee."

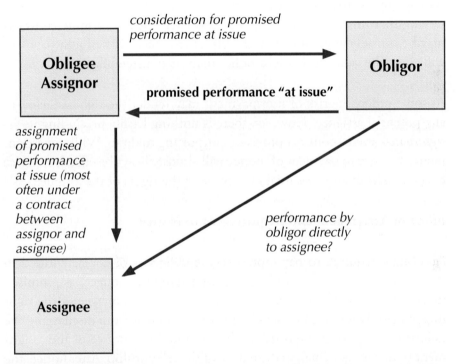

This is the same diagram used in the last lesson for delegation, except that the transfer takes place on the left side of the transaction with the assignment of the obligee's right to performance, in contrast to the transfer on the right side of the transaction of the obligor's duty (the author's choice of "right" and "left" here is purely illustrative and could just as easily be reversed).

The statutory preclusion of restrictions on assignment addressed in Example 50-1 is found in UCC § 9-406(d), which governs secured transactions generally. While the subject of security interests is beyond the scope of this course, this particular issue is addressed in UCC Article 9, because it applies equally to assignments of an actual right to payment (our focus here) or assignment of only a security interest (e.g., as collateral for a loan). In some instances, it may be difficult to distinguish between an assignment of an absolute right to payment and an assignment solely as security, so the same rule is applied to both.

The policy underlying the foregoing rule relates to the nature of a right to payment of money. In effect, such a right functions in many ways like money itself. A right to payment may often function much like a financial instrument, so the ease with which it may be transferred is essential in serving that function. While the right to payment under some contracts may be considerably less certain than in others, such risks of non-payment will affect the value of the right rather than its transferability.

At some point, the risk of non-payment may render the right valueless to any potential assignee. However, there is nothing legally precluding its assignment—even a contract provision purporting to do so. While an assignment of a right to payment of money will almost always be effective, notice of such assignment is essential in preserving the rights of the assignee.

Effect of Assignment and Requirement of Notice

An obligor required to pay money to the obligee is of course entitled to discharge (i.e., satisfy) that obligation by paying the obligee, as promised in the contract between them. An assignment by the obligee of the right to payment does not—by itself—prevent the obligor from discharging the obligation by paying the original obligee. However, notice of the assignment to the obligor changes the nature of the relationship. After notice, the obligor may only discharge its contract obligation to the original obligee by paying the assignee, as indicated in the notice of assignment.

Discharge and notice of assignment involving assignments of payment rights are governed by UCC Article 9. **STOP NOW and READ the excerpts from UCC § 9-406(a) below.**

UCC § 9-406(a)

(a) . . . [A]n account debtor . . . may discharge its obligation by paying the assignor until, but not after, the account debtor receives a notification, authenticated by the assignor or the assignee, that the amount due or to become due has been assigned and that payment is to be made to the assignee. After receipt of the notification, the account debtor may discharge its obligation by paying the assignee and may not discharge the obligation by paying the assignor.

The same rule is broadly applied to the assignment of any right (not just the right to payment of money) under the common law.[10] The purpose of the rule should be obvious. The burden should be on the parties to the assignment to notify the obligor on the original contract obligation, who may otherwise be entirely unaware of the assignment. In particular, it is in the interest of the assignee to notify the obligor in order to receive payment directly.

If, prior to notice of the assignment, the obligor pays the original contract obligee, the obligor has fully discharged the payment obligation. The assignee will of course have a right to recover the assigned payment from the assignor. However, if the assignor does not (or cannot) pay, the assignee will have no further recourse against the obligor. In contrast, if the assignee has provided prompt notice, but the obligor nevertheless pays the original obligee after such notice, then the assignee is entitled to recover from the obligor, even if the obligor has to pay twice. The obligor can of course seek to recover from the obligee/assignor, but has no further recourse if the obligee/assignor does not (or cannot) pay.

We can return to Pam and Dan in Example 50-1 for an illustrative example.

Example 50-2: Pam assigned to Owen her right to payment of $150 per month by Dan. However, neither Pam nor Owen mentioned anything about the assignment to Dan for 60 days, and Dan made two additional payments to Pam—after the assignment. When Owen finally contacted Dan, demanding the two late payments, Dan explained that he paid Pam. When Owen then contacted Pam, he learned, predictably, that she had no money. Owen

---

[10] Restatement (Second) of Contracts § 338(1).

has no right to recover the two missed payments from Dan, because Dan discharged his obligation by paying Pam. Dan will, however, be required to make all future payments to Owen now that he has received notice of the assignment (other issues as to future payments may, however, arise in Example 50-5 below).

If Owen had, instead, immediately notified Dan of the assignment (including proper documentation thereof), and Dan had nevertheless continued to make the two payments to Pam, then Owen would be entitled to recover the payments from Dan (again assuming that Pam has no money, and the loss will necessarily fall on Dan or Owen for the payments erroneously made to Pam). Dan will be obligated to pay Owen even though he already paid Pam.

As indicated earlier, most rights to payment of money are assignable, notwithstanding contrary contract language. However, other rights may not be subject to assignment, based either (1) on the nature of the assignment or (2) on contract provisions restricting or precluding assignment. These two potential limitations are addressed in the next two sections below.

Implied or Inherent Limitations on a Specific Assignment

General contract rights may be freely assigned, unless the substitution of the assignee for the assignor would material change the nature of the obligor's bargain. Such changes might arise from an increase in the burden of the obligor's performance or adverse effects on the value of the contract or any associated return performance (typically arising from the assignment of any entire contract).[11]

Perhaps the most common circumstance of an increased burden on the obligor is the assignment of a "requirements" contract. Assignments of sales of goods are addressed further at the end of this lesson, but a classic sale of goods case (decided under the common law before the drafting of UCC Article 2) is exemplary.

---

[11] Restatement (Second) of Contracts § 317(2)(a).

Example 50-3: *Crane Ice Cream v. Terminal Freezing & Heating*

Frederick, a local Baltimore maker of ice cream, entered into a long term contract with Terminal to supply Frederick's requirements of ice for use in the making of ice cream. The contract said nothing about assignment. With more than 2 years remaining on the contract, Frederick assigned the agreement, including the right to the delivery of ice and the duty to pay for that ice, to Crane, a much larger regional maker of ice cream (the assignment was made a part of the sale by Frederick of his business assets to Crane).

While there were no facts to suggest any increased risk of payment or performance by Crane, as compared to Frederick, it seemed clear that Crane's "requirements" in running Frederick's former business would almost certainly exceed those reasonably anticipated by Terminal when it contracted with Frederick. Thus, the court deemed the assignment precluded by the circumstances without the consent of Frederick.[12]

In the foregoing case, the court also discussed the personal nature of the relationship between Frederick and Terminal, which might be less of an issue today. However, the issue of a potential increased burden in the assignment of a requirements contract remains an issue under current law, just as it was then. The other common problem arises when a right to performance (such as the delivery of ice) is assigned, along with the corresponding duty to pay for such performance. While not an issue in the foregoing case, any significantly increased risk of non-payment by the assignee would likely preclude the assignment, absent consent of the original contracting partner.

Express Limitations on Assignment

Assuming the assignment is not precluded by its basic nature, it may nevertheless be restricted or fully barred by the parties' agreement (assuming

---

[12] Crane Ice Cream Co. v. Terminal Freezing & Heating Co., 147 Md. 588 (1925).

724 • Learning Contracts •

of course it is not simply an assignment of a right to payment of money).[13]
However, the presumption in favor of assignability of most rights is sufficiently strong that any prohibition on assignment must be quite clear to
be effective.

First, any bar on the assignment of the "contract" bars only the delegation of duties to a contract assignee.[14] Any bar on the assignment of rights
must be much more specific.[15] Second, even a contract provision expressly
barring assignment of a specified right will not render such an assignment
ineffective, but will only provide the obligor with the right to bring a claim
for damages for breach of the bar on assignment.[16] To actually preclude and
render ineffective any attempted assignment, the provision must actually
state that such an attempted assignment is null and void.

> **Example 50-4:** Alpha leases office space from Beta. The
> lease includes a provision barring assignment of Alpha's
> right to occupy the premises. If Alpha subleases the prem-
> ises to Delta, Beta will have a claim for breach against Alpha
> for doing so (assuming it can establish damages). However,
> the assignment of the lease to Delta is likely effective, as
> there is no provision expressly stating that such an assign-
> ment in null and void or otherwise rendered fully ineffec-
> tive.

In short, most assignments may be contractually limited (e.g., requiring
consent of the other contracting party) or even barred. However, the language must generally be quite specific to be effective.

Defenses against an Assignee

In considering implied or inherent limitations on assignment above, one
of the potential limitations involved additional risks to the obligor whose
contract rights may be affected by any impairment in the performance
of its newly assigned contracting partner. However, an assignee may also
incur risks in contracting for an assignment of rights previously held by the
assignor.

---

[13] Restatement (Second) of Contracts § 317(2)(c).
[14] Restatement (Second) of Contracts § 322(1).
[15] Restatement (Second) of Contracts § 322(2).
[16] Restatement (Second) of Contracts § 322(2)(b).

As a general rule, an assignee takes the assigned rights, subject to any defenses arising from the transaction out of which the rights arise, as well as any defenses the obligor may have against the assignor—whatever the nature of those defenses—as of the time of notice of the assignment. The assignee is also of course subject to any defense arising from assignee's own conduct.[17]

This same rule applies to assignments of a right to payment of money. **STOP NOW and READ the excerpts from UCC § 9-404(a) below.**

UCC § 9-404(a)

(a) Unless an account debtor has made an enforceable agreement not to assert defenses or claims . . . the rights of an assignee are subject to:

(1) all terms of the agreement between the account debtor and assignor and any defense or claim in recoupment arising from the transaction that gave rise to the contract; and

(2) any other defense or claim of the account debtor against the assignor which accrues before the account debtor receives a notification of the assignment authenticated by the assignor or the assignee.

The key issue often involves distinguishing between "recoupment" and "setoff." A claim in recoupment is one by the obligor against the assignor arising from the same transaction giving rise to the right assigned to the assignee. In contrast, a claim based on setoff generally arises from any other obligation of the assignor to the obligor—except one based on recoupment. An example may be helpful.

Example 50-5: We now return to Pam, Dan, and Owen, from Example 50-2. Pam assigned to Owen the right to receive $150 per month from Dan. Pam and Owen each provided Dan with notice on July 1, and payment for lawn and gardening service is due on the last day of each month for the service provided that month. Dan correctly pays Pam the full $150 on June 30 and intends to pay Owen on July 31.

---

[17] Restatement (Second) of Contracts § 336.

Pam purchases two paintings from Dan, and payment is due on June 15 and July 15, respectively. Pam also failed to perform 20% of the work required by the lawn and gardening contract in both June and July (Dan reasonably became aware of both breaches in July). Assuming that each of the paintings is worth $30, and each of the breaches resulted in $30 in damages (20% of the monthly contract price). Dan will want to deduct appropriate amounts when he pays Owen on July 31. These deductions are based on Dan's "defenses" against Pam, as assignor, but they are applied to Dan's obligation to pay Owen, which was assigned by Pam. Dan is entitled to assert against Owen each of the defenses based on Pam's breach of the lawn and gardening contract, because these are claims in the nature of "recoupment." However, Dan is only entitled to assert against Owen a defense related to one of the paintings—the one for which payment was due at the time of notice of assignment. In effect, Owen takes the assignment from Pam, subject to all then existing defenses, including setoff and recoupment. However, his right to payment is subject only to future defenses based on recoupment.

The foregoing example should clearly illustrate the fact that an assignee should carefully consider whether any right to be assigned may be subject to any potential defenses.

Assignment of Rights in Contracts for the Sale of Goods

We first encountered this provision in the last lesson, but then focused primarily on the delegation of performance duties. **STOP NOW and re-READ the excerpts from UCC § 2-210 below—focusing specifically on subsections (2), (4), and (5).**

UCC § 2-210

(1) A party may perform his duty through a delegate unless otherwise agreed or unless the other party has a substantial interest in having his original promisor perform or control the acts required by the contract. No delegation of performance relieves the party delegating of any duty to perform or any liability for breach.

(2) Except as otherwise provided in Section 9-406, unless otherwise agreed, all rights of either seller or buyer can be assigned except where the assignment would materially change the duty of the other party, or increase materially the burden or risk imposed on him by his contract, or impair materially his chance of obtaining return performance. A right to damages for breach of the whole contract or a right arising out of the assignor's due performance of his entire obligation can be assigned despite agreement otherwise.

. . .

(4) Unless the circumstances indicate the contrary a prohibition of assignment of "the contract" is to be construed as barring only the delegation to the assignee of the assignor's performance.

(5) An assignment of "the contract" or of "all my rights under the contract" or an assignment in similar general terms is an assignment of rights and unless the language or the circumstances (as in an assignment for security) indicate the contrary, it is a delegation of performance of the duties of the assignor and its acceptance by the assignee constitutes a promise by him to perform those duties. This promise is enforceable by either the assignor or the other party to the original contract.

(6) The other party may treat any assignment which delegates performance as creating reasonable grounds for insecurity and may without prejudice to his rights against the assignor demand assurances from the assignee (Section 2-609).

Most of these provisions should now be familiar, based on their encounter in the last lesson, their similarity to the treatment of the issue under the common law, or both. Note, as well, subsection (5), presuming an assignment of the "contract" to include all remaining rights and duties, unless the language or circumstances indicate otherwise.

APPLYING THE RULES

Problem 1: FastAir contracts with FuelCo to supply all of the jet fuel it needs at certain specified airports, at a specified price (complete with a reasonable price adjustment mechanism), for 5 years. The specified airports are all FastAir hubs, so FastAir's requirements at the specified airports are substantial. The contract says nothing about assignment. 2 years into the contract, FastAir is in need of additional operating capital and assigns its contract with FuelCo to BigAir for cash. While BigAir is comparable in size to FastAir, overall, the airports subject to the assigned contract are not Bi-gAir hubs. Thus, BigAir will likely have considerably lower "requirements" than FastAir did at these locations. Is the contract assignable?

Whatever your answer above, assume that FuelCo consented to the assignment, and received notice on June 1. Under the contract, FuelCo is entitled to cease fuel deliveries for any claim for breach of any contract between FuelCo and FastAir involving damages of $100,000 or more, until such claim is resolved. Which of the following would give FuelCo the right to cease fuel deliveries to BigAir—assuming that each involves more than $100,000? Consider each independently of the others.

(A) Fast Air failed to pay for April deliveries of fuel under this contract (payment was due May 15);

(B) Fast Air failed to pay for April deliveries of fuel under another contract (for other airports—payment also due May 15);

(C) Fast Air failed to pay for May deliveries of fuel under this contract (payment was due June 15);

(D) Fast Air failed to pay for May deliveries of fuel under another contract (for other airports—payment also due June 15).

What, if anything, should BigAir have done about the above issue in negotiating the assignment?

Problem 2: Bel-Ray developed lubricants, using a secret formula that it closely protected. Bel-Ray contracted with Chemrite to produce (using the Bel-Ray secret formula under license rights granted by Bel-Ray) and sell

Bel-Ray lubricants in California in exchange for payment of royalties on those sales by Chemrite to Bel-Ray. The contract between Bel-Ray and Chemrite contained a provision stating that "assignment of any contract rights by either party is expressly prohibited, without written consent of the other." Consider each of the two following questions independently.

If Bel-Ray wishes to assign to BigBank its right to receive royalties from Chemrite, does such an assignment require Chemrite's consent? If Bel-Ray makes the assignment, what should BigBank do?

If Chemrite enters into a contract with Lubritene, assigning its entire contract with Bel-Ray to Lubritene in exchange for $1,000,000, what is the legal effect of the transaction between Chemrite and Lubritene?

The facts of this problem are loosely based on the issues raised in the case of *Bel-Ray Co. v. Chemrite Ltd.*, 181 F.3d 435 (3d Cir. 1999).

Problem 3: Metro Steel brought an action against Presbyterian Hospital for payment of obligations owed to Metro, a subcontractor, by Walsh, the general contractor, on a construction project for the Hospital. Under the contract between Walsh and Metro Steel, Walsh was solely responsible for payments to Metro. The Hospital terminated the contract with Walsh in "mid-project" for poor performance. Under the contract between the Hospital and Walsh, such a termination entitled the Hospital to an assignment of all of the Walsh's contracts, including that with Metro Steel. The stated purpose of this provision was to allow the Hospital to complete the project in the event the general contractor failed to perform as agreed. Consistent with its obligation to the Hospital, Walsh made the required assignment. At the time of the assignment to the Hospital by Walsh of its contract with Metro Steel, Walsh owed Metro Steel $50,000 for worked previously performed (before the assignment). Prior to the assignment, the Hospital had no obligation to pay any amount to Metro Steel.

Is Metro Steel entitled to recover the $50,000 owed by Walsh pursuant to the assignment of Walsh's contract with Metro Steel to the Hospital?

The facts of this problem are loosely based on the issues raised in the case of *A.C. Associates v. American Bridge Div. of the U.S. Steel Corp.*, 1989 WL 1111034 (S.D.N.Y. 1989).